ESSENTIALS OF MODERN MARKETING

Marketing Management for the 21ˢᵗ Century and Beyond

TÜRKİYE EDITION

By Kotler-i & Partners, Elif Akagun Ergin

ELIF AKAGUN ERGIN
OSTIM Technical University

DENIZ AKGUL
Altınbaş University

RAUL AMIGO
CEO & President of UMUNTU SAS, Colombia

SIRIN ATAKAN DUMAN
Cyprus International University

BARIS BATUHAN GECIT
University of Doha for Science and Technology

GABRIELE CARBONI
Co-founder of Weevo, Italy

ELIF HASRET KUMCU
Aksaray University

SERAY KAGITCI CANDAN
OSTIM Technical University

SADIA KIBRIA
Founder of Socialpreneurship, CEO of WMS Group & Kotler Impact

PHILIP KOTLER
Father of Modern Marketing & Founder of WMS

MARC OLIVER OPRESNIK
CRO of Kotler Impact, Germany

HANDAN OZDEMIR
OSTIM Technical University

OZNUR OZKAN TEKTAS
Hacettepe University

BULENT OZSACMACI
Çankaya University

DENIS ROTHMAN
Expert on Artificial intelligence, France

HASEEB SHABBIR
University of Huddersfield, U.K.

MANOJ SINGH
CEO of RUBIKA, India

Publisher's Note

Every possible effort has been made to ensure that the information contained in this book is accurate at the time of going to press, and the publisher and authors cannot accept responsibility for any errors or omissions, however caused. No responsibility for loss or damage occasioned to any person acting, or refraining from action, as a result of the material in this publication can be accepted by the editor, the publisher or any of the authors.

TABLE OF CONTENTS

INDEX

HONORARY PARTNER
OF THE BOOK LAUNCH CEREMONY

ŞİŞECAM

PRIMARY STRATEGIC MEDIA PARTNER

Marketing Türkiye

INTRODUCTION TO THE TÜRKİYE EDITION

Books on marketing can inevitably be called into question as there are so many works on the subject. However, many of them are either too difficult to understand, too lengthy or not related to practical decision making. Against this background, the aim of this book is to deal with modern marketing in such a way that covers as few pages and is as accessible as possible, while communicating the fundamental, most important theoretical aspects and facilitating the transfer of this knowledge to real-life decision situations. It concentrates on the essential marketing know-how for both, practitioners, and students worldwide. The **TÜRKİYE Edition** edition is packed with 25 market-specific success stories and examples.

TARGET AUDIENCE

This book is aimed at students, MBA/graduate students and advanced undergraduates who wish to go into business. It will provide the information, perspectives, and tools necessary to get the job done. Our aim is to enable them to make better marketing decisions.

A second audience for this book is the large group of practitioners who want to build on the existing skills and knowledge already possessed.

A final target audience is the large group of students of marketing who want to effectively prepare for an examination and pass a test or the final exam.

READING AND LEARNING OUTCOMES

Having read this book:

- Unique feature of this book You will have a basic understanding of modern marketing and the process of marketing management.

- You will know the most important marketing tools and how they interact.

- You can develop your own marketing strategy.

Most introductory texts deal solely with the operational aspect of marketing or the strategic part. This modern marketing text not only integrates all relevant aspects of marketing but also structures them in such a way, that both practitioners and students acquire a comprehensive and holistic overview, how it all fits together. This is achieved by the structure of the book which follows the marketing planning and decision-making process inside the company. Consequently, the book has a clear structure according to the marketing planning process of the firm (Figure 1).

The marketing planning process

Chapter 1:Fundamentals of Marketing and Marketing Management
- Definition, Tasks and Scope of Marketing
- Company Orientation towards the Marketplace
- The Role of Marketing in the Company
- Fundamentals of Marketing Planning
- The Main Stages in Developing a Marketing Plan

Phase 1 Analysis

Chapter 2: situational analysis in the marketing planning process
- Assessing the internal and external marketing situation
- Analyzing the buying behavior in B2B and B2C markets
- Comparing B2B and B2C markets
- SWOT Analysis

Where are we and which value are we offering?

Phase 2 Strategy formulation

Chapter 3: Strategy formulation in the marketing planning process
- Strategic Marketing Planning
- Market Segmentation, targeting, and positioning

Which customers should we serve?

Phase 3 Tactical decisions

Chapter 4: Marketing Mix in the marketing planning process
- Product and service decisions
- Pricing decisions
- Distribution decisions
- Communication decisions

How should we offer our value to these customers?

Phase 4 Implementation and control

Chapter 5: Implementation and controlling the marketing planning process
- Organizing and implementing the marketing plan
- Budgeting and control

How are we implementing and controlling that we are on course?

Key questions

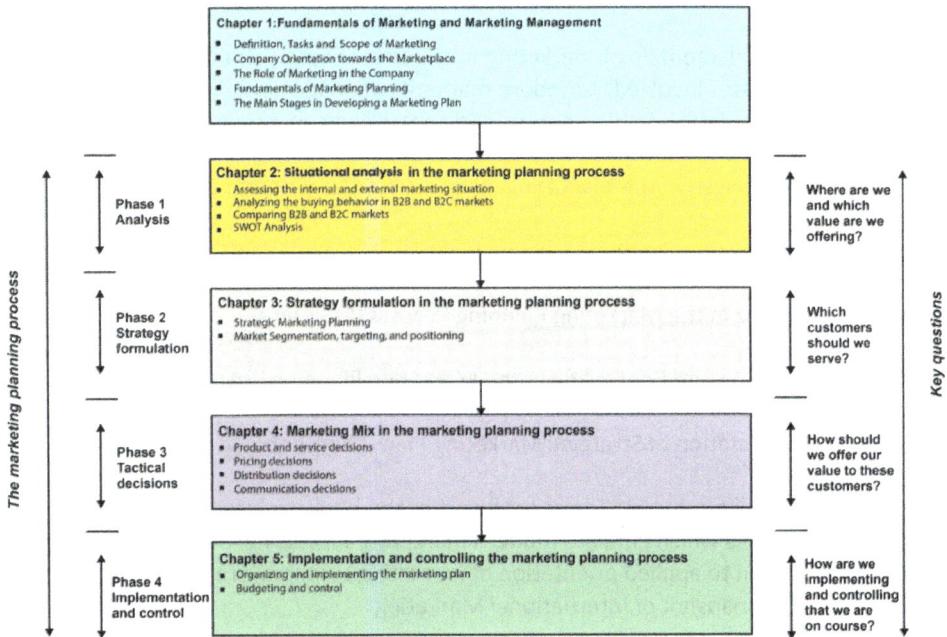

Figure 1: Structure of the Book According to the Marketing Planning Process.

In addition, this book touches base on very specific business-related topics such as AI Marketing, Disruptive Digital Marketing and Research in Marketing, all being covered in one this comprehensive modern marketing guide.

Outline

After outlining the fundamentals of marketing in the first chapter, the first part of the book is based on the main phases involved in modern marketing management, i.e., the decision-making process regarding formulating, implementing, and controlling a marketing plan:

Phase 1: Situational analysis in the Marketing Planning Process (Chapter 2)

Phase 2: Strategy formulation in the Marketing Planning Process (Chapter 3)

Phase 3: Marketing Mix in the Marketing Planning Process (Chapter 4)

Phase 4: Implementation and Controlling in the Marketing Planning Process (Chapter 5)

Phase 5: External Orientation of Strategic Marketing Plan (Chapter 6)

Modern marketing is all around us. The second part of the book explores the innovative & intuitive marketing strategies which entail to modern marketing success i.e. metamorphosis of digital marketing, introduction to applied orientation of marketing research, creating value through design, a contemporary snapshot of International Marketing:

Phase 6: Disruptive Digital Marketing Strategies (Chapter 7)

Phase 7: The Rise of AI-Driven Metahumans (Chapter 8)

Phase 8: Leading by Innovation & Design; Strategies & Value Creation (Chapter 9)

Phase 9: Designing Value (Chapter 10)

Phase 10: Remodeling the Marketing Research (Chapter 11)

Phase 11: Better World Through Socialpreneurship (Chapter 12)

Phase 12: Adaptive Public Policy & Marketing During Covid-19 (Chapter 13)

Phase 13: Marketers without borders (Chapter 14)

Phase 14: The New Marketing Normal: Digitized, Disrupted, and Ready for Upskilling & Upscaling (Chapter 15)

PREFACE BY PHILIP KOTLER

My warm greetings to everyone reading "Essentials of Modern Marketing." This book presents an up-to-date and insightful account of the working of modern marketing in today's turbulent times.

This book is not only about marketing and selling a product or service. It is about finding and building a future using the new tools of modern marketing. I hope this book will be read by managers and employees at all levels as well as professors teaching management and marketing. It can produce a generation of students who care about humanity, innovation, society, and a better world through marketing.

This book can lead your company to discover new talents, capabilities, and opportunities. It deals with modern marketing in such a way that covers as few pages and is as accessible as possible, while communicating the fundamental, most important theoretical aspects and facilitating the transfer of this knowledge to real-life decision situations. It concentrates on the essential marketing know-how for both, practitioners, and students worldwide.

Most marketing textbooks deal exclusively with the operational aspect of marketing or the strategic part. This modern marketing book not only integrates all relevant aspects of marketing but also structures them in such a way, that both practitioners and students acquire a comprehensive and holistic overview, how it all fits together. This is achieved by the structure of the book which follows the marketing planning and decision-making process inside the enterprise.

Due to COVID-19 and other uncertainties, all industries and businesses are challenged. In addition, organizations and companies alike are having to deal with constant change and mega trends such as digitization and disruption which calls for continuous innovation and change and tough decisions on staffing, procurement, finance, and marketing. You need to think ahead on how to find new markets, create new marketing strategies, innovate new products, and build new partnerships.

Against this background, another unique feature of this book is that it touches base on very specific business-related topics such as Health Marketing, Disruptive Marketing, Negotiation in Marketing to provide a more holistic and comprehensive perspective on marketing management.

In this connection, the World Marketing Summit (WMS) is expanding to address the concerns of businesses all over the world with a new initiative, eWMS and our online version of our regular city located WMSs. We hope to educate, train, and stimulate marketing and business professionals around the world. WMS enjoys the support of its global and local partners.

Remember Peter Drucker's emphasis on marketing and innovation as the fundamental crafts of a winning company. "When you're disrupted, don't give up. Never Stop!"

Philip Kotler

S. C. Johnson & Son Distinguished Professor of International Marketing at North-western University's Kellogg School of Management Founder of WMS.

A FEW WORDS ABOUT TÜRKİYE EDITION BY ELIF AKAGUN ERGIN

In a world marked by uncertainty, where wars and crises loom large, writing new books and building partnerships with companies present a significant challenge. Yet, as we hold this book today, we can proudly declare that we have risen above these obstacles. This work emerged under extraordinary circumstances, during a time when global unrest seemed unrelenting—the war in Israel, the conflict in Ukraine, the energy crisis, and renewed tensions in the Middle East. Each of these events has undeniably shaped our perspective, influencing the way we see and understand the world.

That is why we are deeply grateful to everyone who recognized the potential of the TÜRKİYE edition of *The Essentials of Modern Marketing* and to all who answered the call from Philip Kotler and us, contributing to the creation of this remarkable publication. Your support and collaboration have made this project truly special.

A special thanks goes to the companies that contributed to this project by creating their own case studies. We also extend our gratitude to their directors, marketing managers, and everyone we had the pleasure of collaborating with throughout the creation of this book. Your case studies serve not only as valuable sources of knowledge and inspiration but also as shining examples of how to navigate modern marketing in a world where customer behavior is constantly evolving.

We would also like to express our gratitude to Handan Ozdemir, Seray Kagitci Candan, and Sirin Atakan Duman from OSTIM Technical University for their substantive contribution. Thank you for your support and passion for learning and business.

We would also like to thank our media partners, with special appreciation for *Marketing Türkiye*. A heartfelt thanks to Günseli Özen, Editor-in-Chief at *Marketing Türkiye*, and Duygu Su Ocakoglu, whose efforts helped share the news of this book with a wider audience. Your support has been instrumental in bringing this project to life.

Particular recognition goes to Şişecam company, the Honorary Partner of the Book Launch Ceremony for making it possible to organize the launch on the 31st of October 2024 in Istanbul.

At Kotler Impact, We Never Stop.

We wish you an enjoyable and insightful reading experience!

Elif Akagun Ergin

1. ESSENTIALS OF MODERN MARKETING MANAGEMENT

1.1 DEFINITIONS, TASKS AND SCOPE OF MARKETING

Peter Drucker, an Austrian-born American management consultant, educator, and author, whose writings contributed to the philosophical and practical foundations of the modern business corporation once stated: 'A business has two, and only two, basic functions: marketing and innovation. Marketing and innovation produce results; all the rest are costs. 'In the future, marketing will play an increasingly important role for companies to achieve a sustainable competitive advantage and sustainable business growth (Hollensen and Opresnik, 2020).

But what is marketing? Many people think of marketing as only sales and advertising! Every day we are bombarded with TV commercials, flyers, catalogues, sales calls, and commercial e-mail. However, selling and advertising are only one element of marketing. Today, marketing must be understood not in the old sense of making a sale but in a contemporary and holistic sense of satisfying customer needs. Marketing guru Philip Kotler defines marketing as societal and managerial process by which individuals and organizations obtain what they need and want through creating and exchanging value with others (Hollensen and Opresnik, 2020).

To put in into a nutshell, Marketing is the achievement of corporate goals through meeting and exceeding customer needs and expectations better than the competition.

To apply this concept, three conditions must be met (Ellis-Chadwick and Jobber, 2016):

- First, company activities should be focused on providing customer satisfaction.

- Second, the achievement of customer satisfaction relies on an integrated effort.

In the framework of a holistic and integrative approach to marketing today's marketers must work closely with a variety of marketing partners when it comes to creating customer lifetime value and building strong customer relationships. The responsibility for the implementation of the concept lies not just within the marketing department. As the late David Packard of Hewlett-Packard observed: 'Marketing is too important to leave it to the marketing organization.' Consequently, the belief that customer needs are instrumental to the operation of an enterprise should be internalized right through production, finance, research and development, engineering, and all other departments. It is paramount to emphasize that marketing must affect every aspect of the customer experience. Every employee has an impact on the customer and must regard the customer as the source of the company's success and sustainable development. This concept of marketing implies it to be not just a function in the organization but a business philosophy which affects the entire company.

- Finally, management must be convinced that corporate goals can be achieved through satisfied customers.

Marketing has to be considered as a process by which companies create value for customers and build sustainable relationships in order to capture value from customers in return. Thus, marketing is the central driver of corporate profit and growth. The marketer 's role is to choose target markets, to build superior customer value and a sustainable competitive advantage by integrating all the activities in the company that affect the value offered to the customer.

A marketer is someone who seeks a response (attention, a purchase, a vote, a donation) from another party, called the prospect. If two parties are seeking to sell something to each other, they are both called marketers. Marketers are skilled at stimulating demand for their products, but that is merely a very limited view of what they do. Just as production and logistics professionals are responsible for supply management, marketers are responsible for demand management. They seek to influence the level, timing, and composition of demand to meet the organization's objectives. Depending on a company's specific situation, there are different states of demand, which confront the marketer with challenges.

Against the background of a holistic marketing philosophy, you can identify a specific set of tasks that make up successful marketing management (Kotler, Keller and Opresnik, 2017):

- Developing marketing strategies and plans: A key task is to identify potential opportunities and core competencies. You must develop concrete marketing plans that specify the marketing strategy and tactics going forward.

- Capturing marketing insights: You need a reliable marketing information system to monitor their marketing environment so they can continually assess market potential and forecast demand. To transform strategy into programs, marketers must make basic decisions about their expenditures, activities, and budget allocations.

- Connecting with customers: As a marketer you have the task to consider how to best create value for its chosen target markets and develop strong, profitable, long-term relationships with customers. To accomplish these tasks, companies need to understand consumer markets as well as organizational buying behavior: Who buys which products, and why? What features and prices is the customer looking for, and where do they shop? In this respect, companies need a sales force well trained in presenting product benefits. They must divide the market into major market segments, evaluate each one, and target those it can serve best.

- Building strong brands: You must understand the strengths and weaknesses of their brands as perceived by customers. They have to decide how to position them and must also pay attention to competitors, anticipating their strategies and knowing how to react adequately.

- Shaping the market offerings: The product is at the hearts of the marketing program and includes the product quality, design, features, and packaging. A critical marketing decision relates to the price. Marketers must decide on wholesale and retail prices, discounts, allowances, and credit terms.

- Delivering value: You must also determine how to deliver to the target market the value embodied in its products and services. Channel activities include those the company undertakes to make the product accessible and available to target customers. Marketers have to understand the various types of retailers, wholesalers, and physical-distribution firms and how they make their decisions.

- Communicating value: You must also communicate to the target market the value of their products and services. They need and integrated marketing communication program consisting of advertising, sales promotion, events, public relations, and personal communications. Companies also need to hire, train, and motivate salespeople.

- Creating successful long-term growth: Based on its product positioning, you must initiate new-product development, testing, and launching. Furthermore, they must build a marketing organization capable of implementing the marketing plan. Finally, a company needs feedback and control to understand the efficiency and effectiveness of its marketing activities.

While marketing originally concentrated on physical goods (especially consumer goods), today many more types of 'goods 'are marketed. Marketers market 10 main types of entities (Kotler, Keller and Opresnik, 2017):

- **Goods:** Physical goods constitute the bulk of most countries' production and marketing efforts. Companies market diverse goods such as food products, cars, refrigerators, machines, televisions, and other articles.

- **Services:** As economies advance, there is more focus on the production of services. Services include the work of hotels, car rental companies, barbers, maintenance and repair people, accountants, software programmers, management consultants and other market offerings. Many merchandises mix goods and services, such as a fast-food meal.

- **Events:** Marketers also promote events, such as trade shows, artistic performances, company anniversaries and global sporting events such as the Olympics and the World Cup.

- **Experiences:** By combining several services and goods, a company can create, stage, and market experiences. Examples includes parks like Disney World or Sea World.

- **Persons:** Artists like Madonna, musicians like the Rolling Stones, sport stars like David Beckham and other professionals get support from celebrity marketers.

- **Places:** Place marketers include economic development specialists, real estate agents, commercial banks, local business associations, and advertising and public relations agencies. In this respect, cities, states, regions, and whole nations compete to attract tourists, residents, factories, and company headquarters and consequently are marketed.

- **Properties:** Properties are intangible rights of ownership to either real property or financial property. They are bought and sold, and these exchanges require marketing. Examples include real estate agents marketing houses, or investment companies marketing securities to both institutional and individual investors.

- **Organizations:** Organizations work to build a strong, favorable, and unique image in the minds of their target groups. Companies, museums, universities, and non-profits all use marketing to enhance their public images and compete for audiences and funds.

- **Information:** The production, packaging, and distribution of information are major industries. Information is ultimately what books, schools and universities produce, market, and distribute at a price to their customers.

- **Ideas:** Every market offering includes some basic idea. Products and services are platforms for delivering ideas or benefits.

1.2 COMPANY ORIENTATION TOWARDS THE MARKETPLACE

A company has to decide which philosophy should guide their marketing efforts. There is no guarantee that all companies will adopt a holistic marketing orientation. In fact, there are five alternative concepts (Kotler, Keller and Opresnik, 2017):

- **The production concept:** It is one of the oldest concepts in business and holds that customers prefer products that are widely available and inexpensive. Managers of production-oriented businesses focus on achieving high production efficiency, low costs, and mass distribution. It believes that the central focus of the job is to attain economies of scale by producing a limited range of products in a form that minimizes production costs.

  This concept is still an applicable philosophy in some situations. For example, computer manufacturer Lenovo dominates the highly competitive, price-sensitive Chinese PC market through low labour costs, high production efficiency, and mass distribution. Possessing the lowest cost is seen as the major source of competitive advantage. The danger is that, in rapidly changing markets, an internal focus on production can lead to so-called marketing myopia in which implies that companies make the mistake of paying more attention to the specific products they offer than to the benefits and experiences produced by these products. Companies adopting this orientation run a major risk of focusing too narrowly on their own operations and losing sight of the real objective - satisfying customer needs and building customer relationships.

- **The product concept: This** philosophy holds that customers will favor products that offer the most in quality, performance, and innovative features. Under this concept, marketing strategy focuses on making continuous product improvements. Product quality and continuous improvement are important parts of most marketing strategies. However, focusing predominantly on the company's products can also lead to marketing myopia. A new or improved product will not necessarily be successful unless it is being priced, distributed, advertised, and sold adequately.

- **The selling concept:** Production-orientated businesses often make the transition to a sales orientation. Many companies actually follow the selling concept, which states that customers will not buy enough of the firm's products unless it undertakes a large-scale selling and promotion effort. This philosophy is typically practiced with unsought goods and companies regard aggressive selling, advertising and sales promotion as means to penetrate the market. But selling is not marketing – in fact it can be just the opposite. As Theodore Levitt put in his famous 'Marketing myopia' article: ,Selling tries to get the customer to want what the company has, marketing on the other hand, tries to get the company to produce what the customer wants.' Aggressive selling focuses on creating sales transactions rather than on building long-term, profitable customer relationships. This concept assumes customers coaxed into buying a product not only will not return or bad-mouth it or complain to consumer organizations but might even buy again which, in fact, are usually poor assumptions.

- **The marketing concept:** This philosophy holds that achieving organizational goals depends on knowing the needs and wants of target markets and delivering the desired satisfactions better than the competition do. Figure 1.1 contrasts the selling concept and the marketing concept.

  The selling concept takes and inside-out perspective. It starts with the existing products of the company and calls for aggressive selling and promotion to obtain profitable sales. It focuses predominantly on getting short-term sales with little concern about who buys or why.

  In contrast, the marketing concept takes an outside-in perspective. It focuses on customer needs and wants and integrates all the marketing activities that affect customers. In turn, it yields profits by creating lasting customer satisfaction.

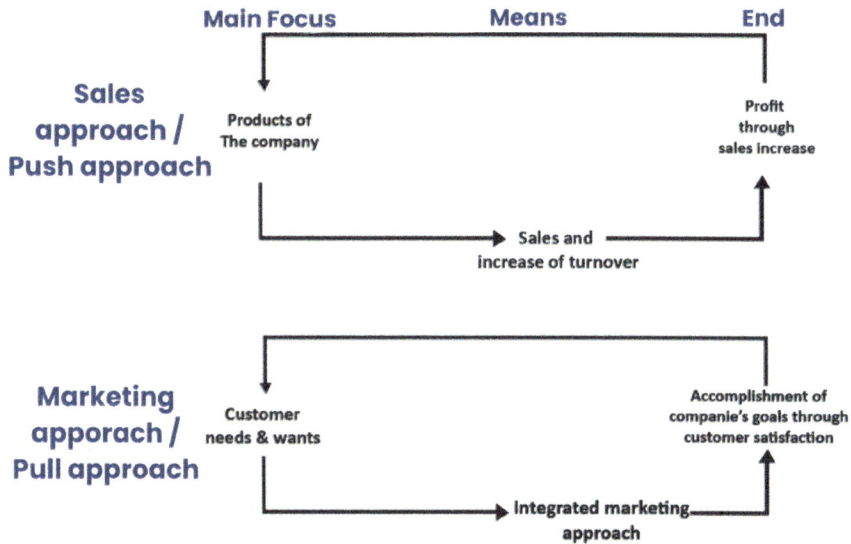

Figure 1.1 Selling and Marketing Concepts Contrasted.

- **Relationship marketing concept:** In recent years, marketing has been undergoing extensive self-examination and internal debate. The overriding emphasis in the 'traditional' marketing approach is on acquiring as many customers as possible. Evidence is mounting, however, that traditional marketing is becoming too expensive and is less effective given changes in the micro-and macro environments of firms. Many leading marketing academics and practitioners have concluded that many of the long-standing practices and operating modes in marketing need to be re-modelled, and we need to move towards an integrated relationship approach that is based on repeated market transactions and mutual sustainable gain for buyers and sellers. Relationship marketing reflects a strategy and process that integrate customers, suppliers, and other partners into the company's design, development, manufacturing, and sales processes. In the framework of this integrated and holistic concept, marketing exists to efficiently meet the satisfaction of customer needs, as well as those of the marketing organization. Marketing exchange seeks to achieve satisfaction for the consumer and the marketing organization (or company). In this latter group we include employees, shareholders, and managers. Other stakeholders like competitors, financial and governmental institutions are also important. While recognizing that customer acquisition is, and will still remain, part of marketer's responsibilities this viewpoint emphasizes that a relationship view of marketing implies that maintenance and development are of equal or perhaps even greater importance to the company in the long run than customer acquisition. By differentiating between customer types, the concept further suggests, that not all customers or potential customers should be treated in the same way. Relationship marketing, in contrast, sees the need to communicate in different ways dependent on customer's status and value.

This view of marketing also implies that suppliers were not alone in creating or benefiting from the value created by the corporation. Rather this philosophy can be seen as an on-going process of identifying and creating new value with individual consumers and then sharing the value benefits with them over the lifetime of the association.

This is due the *lifetime value* concept which concludes that a higher customer value will raise customer satisfaction; thereby customer loyalty will be instilling, which, in turn, creates higher profit due to increased volume resulting from positive word-of-mouth and repeat purchases.

Consequently, an enterprise should restrict taking a short-term view but rather should consider the income derived from that company's lifetime association with the consumer (see Figure 1.2).

In the framework of an integrative customer retention strategy a company should consequently project the value of individual customers over time rather than focus on customer numbers only. Thus, the overall objective of the relationship marketing concept is to facilitate and maintain long-term customer relationships, which leads to changed focal points and modifications of the marketing management process. The familiar superior objectives of all strategies are enduring unique relationships with customers, which cannot be imitated by competitors and therefore provide sustainable competitive advantages (Hollensen and Opresnik, 2020).

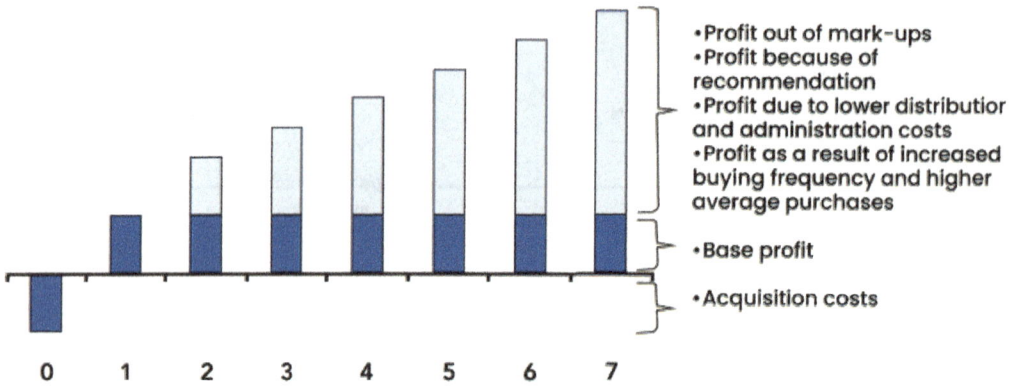

• Profit out of mark-ups
• Profit because of recommendation
• Profit due to lower distribution and administration costs
• Profit as a result of increased buying frequency and higher average purchases

• Base profit

• Acquisition costs

Figure 1.2: Profit Growth over Time.
Source: Adapted from Hollensen and Opresnik, 2020, modified.

1.3 THE ROLE OF MARKETING IN THE COMPANY

As outlined already, it is paramount that marketing must not be a function in the organization but moreover a business philosophy. Marketing must affect every aspect of the customer experience. Consequently, every employee has an impact on the customer and must regard the customer as the source of the company's success.

Against this background, the **concept of internal marketing** is of key importance: It originates primarily from service organizations where it was first practiced as a strategy for making all employees aware of the need for customer satisfaction. In general, internal marketing refers to the managerial actions necessary to make all members of the organization understand and accept their individual roles in implementing marketing strategy. This means that all employees, from the chief executive officer to frontline marketing personnel, must realize how each individual job assists in implementing the marketing strategy. Under this approach, every employee has two sets of customers: external and internal. Ultimately, successful marketing implementation results from an accumulation of individual actions where all employees are responsible for implementing the marketing strategy. Ensuring that all staff, whatever their status, deliver a service of the highest quality to both internal and external customers is a key issue for all organizations. Essentially, this is what an integrative marketing management really implies, namely, to direct each and every activity towards the customer, making formerly product-focused companies fully customer-centric. In this framework, the holistic and integrated relationship marketing approach can help imbue companies to rethink marketing and develop a more inclusive approach directing all departments, functions, and staff towards the customer.

Although this requires organizational transformation and a change in mindset, we suggest it to be an inevitable way to focus on customers need and wants and ensure a sustainable growth of companies (Hollensen and Opresnik, 2020).

1.4 FUNDAMENTALS OF MARKETING PLANNING

Marketing is the organization function charged with defining customer targets and the best way to satisfy their needs and wants competitively and profitably. Because consumers and business buyers face an abundance of suppliers seeking to satisfy their every need, companies and not-for-profit organizations cannot survive today by simply doing a good job. They must do an excellent job if they are to remain in the increasingly competitive global marketplace. Many studies have demonstrated that the key to profitable performance is knowing and satisfying target customers with competitively superior offers. This process takes place today in an increasingly global, technical, and competitive environment.

The importance of competition and competitor analysis in contemporary strategic marketing cannot be overemphasized. Indeed, because of this we shall be looking at this aspect in more depth in later chapters. This importance is now widely accepted amongst both marketing academics and practitioners. Successful marketing in a competitive economy is about competitive success and that in addition to a customer focus a true marketing orientation also combines competitive positioning.

The Marketing concept holds that the key to achieving organizational goals lies in determining the needs and wants of target markets and delivering the desired ˙satisfaction ˙more effectively and resourcefully than competitors.

Marketing planning is an approach adopted by many successful, market-focused companies. While it is by no means a new tool, the degree of objectivity and thoroughness with which it is applied varies significantly.

Marketing planning can be defined as the structured process of researching and analyzing the marketing situations, developing, and documenting marketing objectives, strategies, and programs, and implementing, evaluating, and controlling activities to achieve the goals. This systematic process of marketing planning involves analyzing the environment and the company˙s capabilities and deciding on courses of action and ways to implement those decisions. As the marketing environment is so changeable that paths to new opportunities can open in an instant, even as others become obscured or completely blocked, marketing planning must be approached as an adaptable, ongoing process rather than a rigid, static annual event.

The outcome of this structured process is the marketing plan, a document that summarizes what the marketer has learned about the marketplace and outlines how the firm plans to reach its marketing objectives. In addition, the marketing plan not only documents the organization˙s marketing strategies and displays the activities that employees will implement to reach the marketing objectives, but it entails the mechanisms that will measure progress toward the objectives and allows for adjustments if actual results take the organization off course.

Marketing plans generally cover a 1-year-period, although some may project activities and financial performance further into the future. Marketers must start the marketing planning process at least several months before the marketing plan is scheduled to go into operation; this allows sufficient time for thorough research and analysis, management review and revision, and coordination of resources among functions and business units.

Marketing planning inevitably involves change. It is a process that includes deciding currently what to do in the future with a full appreciation of the resource position; the need to set clear, communicable, measurable objectives; the development of alternative courses of action; and a means of assessing the best route towards the achievement of specified objectives. Marketing planning is designed to assist the process of marketing decision making under prevailing conditions of risk and uncertainty.

Plans must be specific to the organization and its current situation. There is not one system of planning but many systems, and a planning process must be tailor-made for a particular firm in a specific set of conditions.

Marketing planning as a functional activity has to be set in a corporate planning framework. There is an underlying obligation for any organization adopting marketing planning systems to set a clearly defined business mission as the basis from which the organizational direction can develop.

Without marketing planning, it is more difficult to guide research and development (R&D) and new product development (NPD); set required standards for suppliers; guide the sales force in terms of what to emphasize, set realistic, achievable targets and avoid competitor actions or changes in the marketplace. Above all, businesses which fail to incorporate marketing planning into their marketing activities may therefore not be in a position to develop a sustainable competitive advantage in their markets (Hollensen, 2006).

1.5 THE MAIN STAGES IN DEVELOPING A MARKETING PLAN

Marketing planning is a methodical process involving assessing marketing opportunities and resources, determining marketing objectives, and developing a plan for implementation and control.

Marketing planning is an ongoing analysis/planning/control process or cycle (see Figure 1.3). Many organizations update their marketing plans annually as new information becomes accessible.

Once built-in, the key recommendations can then be presented to key stakeholders within the organization. The final task of marketing planning is to summarize the relevant findings from the marketing analysis, the strategic recommendations, and the required marketing programs in a report: the written marketing plan. This document needs to be concise, yet complete in terms of presenting a summary of the marketplace and the business's position, explaining thoroughly the recommended strategy, and containing the detail of marketing mix activities. The plan should be informative, to the point, while mapping out a clear set of marketing activities designed to satisfactorily implement the desired target market strategy (Hollensen, 2006).

Figure 1.3 illustrates the several stages that have to be gone through in order to arrive at a marketing plan. Each of the stages illustrated here will be discussed in more detail later in this chapter and in later sections of the book.

As illustrated in Figure 1.3 the development of a marketing plan is a process, and each step in the process has a structure that enables the marketing plan to evolve from abstract information and ideas into a tangible document that can easily be understood, evaluated, and implemented. The following section is devoted to an in-depth discussion of each step in this process (Gilmore et al., 2001; Day, 2002).

Step 1: Mission, Corporate Goals and Objectives

An organisation's **mission** can be described as a broadly defined, enduring statement of purpose that distinguishes a company from others of its type. It is enduring and specific to the individual organization and tells what the organization hopes to accomplish and how it plans to achieve this goal. This expression of purpose provides management with a clear sense of direction.

The corporate **mission statement** needs comprehensive considerations by top management to establish the business, which the company is really in and to relate this consideration to future business intentions. It is a general statement that provides an integrating function for the business, from which a clear sense of business definition and direction can be derived.

This stage is often overlooked in marketing planning, and yet without it the plan will lack a sense of contribution to the development of the entire enterprise. By deriving a clear mission statement, boundaries for the `corporate entity `can be conceived in the context of environmental trends that influence the company (Hollensen, 2006).

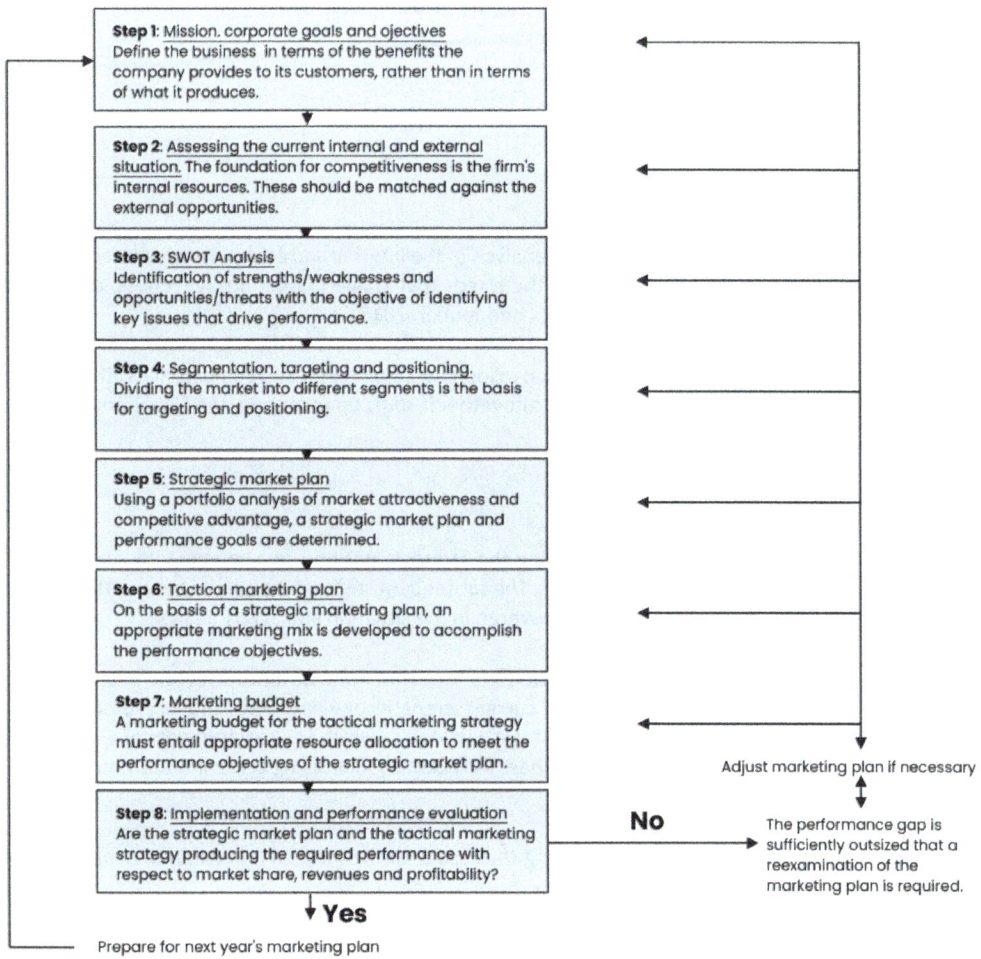

Step 1: Mission. corporate goals and ojectives
Define the business in terms of the benefits the company provides to its customers, rather than in terms of what it produces.

Step 2: Assessing the current internal and external situation. The foundation for competitiveness is the firm's internal resources. These should be matched against the external opportunities.

Step 3: SWOT Analysis
Identification of strengths/weaknesses and opportunities/threats with the objective of identifying key issues that drive performance.

Step 4: Segmentation. targeting and positioning. Dividing the market into different segments is the basis for targeting and positioning.

Step 5: Strategic market plan
Using a portfolio analysis of market attractiveness and competitive advantage, a strategic market plan and performance goals are determined.

Step 6: Tactical marketing plan
On the basis of a strategic marketing plan, an appropriate marketing mix is developed to accomplish the performance objectives.

Step 7: Marketing budget
A marketing budget for the tactical marketing strategy must entail appropriate resource allocation to meet the performance objectives of the strategic market plan.

Step 8: Implementation and performance evaluation
Are the strategic market plan and the tactical marketing strategy producing the required performance with respect to market share, revenues and profitability?

No

Adjust marketing plan if necessary

The performance gap is sufficiently outsized that a reexamination of the marketing plan is required.

Yes

Prepare for next year's marketing plan

Figure 1.3: The Stages of Building a Marketing Plan.
Source: Adapted from Hollensen and Opresnik, 2020, modified.

It is useful to establish the distinctive competences of the organization and to focus upon what customers are buying rather than upon what the company is selling. This will assist in the development of a marketing-oriented mission statement. A clear mission statement should include the customer groups to be served the consumer needs to be served and the technologies to be utilized.

The general purpose expressed in the organization's mission statement must be translated into more specific guidelines as to how these general intentions will operate. Organizations and the people who manage them tend to be more productive when they have established standards to motivate them, specific directions to guide them, and stated achievements levels against which to assess their performance.

Step 2: Assessing the Current Internal and External Situation

The situation analysis attempts to provide answers to the following questions:

- 'Where are we now?'

- 'How did we get here?'

- 'Where are we heading?'

Answers to these key questions depend upon an analysis of the internal and external environment of a business. Thus, the situation analysis encompasses the forces that shape market attractiveness, competitive position, and present performance (Ellis-Chadwick and Jobber, 2016).

The basis for competitiveness is the firm's internal resources, capabilities, and competences. These should be matched with the external opportunities, and altogether it sums up to step 3 – the SWOT analysis.

Step 3: SWOT analysis

A SWOT analysis is a structured tool to evaluating the strategic position of a company by identifying its strengths, weaknesses, opportunities, and threats. The subsequent steps will be only as good as the situation analysis and key performance issues that are uncovered in the situation and SWOT analysis.

In assessing current situations, SWOT analysis attempts to identify one or more strategic relationships or matchups between strategic business units (SBU) current strengths or weaknesses and its present or future opportunities and threats. Corporations face strategic windows in which key requirements of a market and the particular competencies of the organization best fit together. Identifying these limited time periods is a rationale for employing a SWOT analysis.

The tool provides a simple method of synthesizing the results of the internal and external analysis undertaken in step 2.

Strengths are the bases for building company competences and finally competitiveness. An internal organizational check attempts to ascertain the type and degree of each SBU's strengths and weaknesses. By recognizing their special capabilities and limitations, firms are better able to adjust to the external environmental conditions of the marketplace. In this respect, it is of key importance to always question the strengths identified for their impact on customer satisfaction.

'Know yourself and your competence 'is the basic tenet that guides this assessment of the abilities and deficiencies of the organization's internal operations. It is also the basic tenet in the so-called Resource Based View (RBV), which will be further discussed in Chapter 2.

All businesses do have weaknesses. Successful businesses try to minimize their shortcomings. A weakness can be any business function or operation that is not able to resist external forces or withstand attack. A weak business function or operation is one that is deficient or inferior in its ability to reap the benefits presented by an external opportunity. Weaknesses are most viewed in comparative terms; a company has a weakness when it is unable to perform a business function or conduct a business operation as effectively and efficiently as its competitors (Hollensen, 2006).

The internal factors that may be viewed as strengths or weaknesses depending upon their impact on the organization's positions (they may represent a strength for one organization but a weakness, in relative terms, for another), may include all of the four elements of the marketing mix, as well as other functions such as personnel, finance etc.

The second part of a SWOT analysis involves the organization's external environments. This environmental scanning process involves the opportunities and threats that are part of a SWOT analysis. The external factors, which again may be threats to one organization whereas they offer opportunities to another, may include factors such as technological change, legislation, and socio-cultural changes, as well as changes in the marketplace or competitive position.

Opportunities are unsatisfied customer needs that the organization has a good chance of meeting successfully. For an environmental occurrence to be considered an opportunity by a particular business, a favorable juncture of circumstances must exist. A unique business strength must fit an attractive environmental need in order to create a high probability of a successful match, as when a low-cost producer identifies an unserved market of low-income consumers. Good opportunities are needs that the company can satisfy in a more complete fashion than can existing competitors. In this context it has to emphasized that these opportunities are indeed external factors which are not controllable by the company such as demographic change, the fitness trend etc.

Threats are finally aspects of the external environment that create challenges posed by an unfavorable trend or development that would lead, in the absence of defensive marketing action, to lower sales or profit.

Once a SWOT analysis has been completed management has to evaluate how to turn weaknesses into strengths and threats into opportunities. For example, a perceived weakness in customer focus might suggest the need for extensive staff training to create a new strength. Because these activities are designed to convert weaknesses into strengths and threats into opportunities, they are called conversion strategies.

Another option provided is to match strengths with opportunities. An example of a company that successfully matched strengths with opportunities in the UK clothing retailer Next, which identified an opportunity in the growing demand for telemarketing services. One of the company's strengths was the fact that it had run its own call centers for more than a decade to service its own home shopping operation. As a result, Next has created a profitable business running call centers for other organizations (Ellis-Chadwick and Jobber, 2016). These activities are called matching strategies.

The SWOT-analysis is just one tool to assess the current situation. It has its own weaknesses in that it tends to persuade companies to compile lists rather than to think about what is really important to their business. It also presents the resulting lists without clear prioritization, so that, for example, weak opportunities may appear to balance strong threats.

The aim of any SWOT analysis should be to identify potential ˙strategic windows˙ and isolate what will be important to the future of the organization and that subsequent marketing planning will address.

Step 4: Segmentation, Targeting and Positioning

In addition to analyzing the environment, marketers need to analyze their markets and their customers, whether consumers or businesses. This means looking closely at market trends, changing customer behavior, product demand and future projections, buying habits, needs and wants, customer attitudes, and customer satisfaction.

Marketers have to apply their knowledge of the market and customers – acquired through research – to determine which parts of the market, known as segments, should be targeted for marketing activities as marketing is not about chasing any customer at any price. A decision has to be made regarding those groups of customers respectively segments that are attractive to the business (Ellis-Chadwick and Jobber, 2016). This implies dividing the overall market into separate groupings of customers, based on characteristics such as age, gender, geography, needs, behavior, or other variables.

The purpose of segmentation is to group customers with similar needs, wants, behavior, or other characteristics that affect their demand for or usage of the good or service being marketed.

Once the market has been segmented, the next set of decisions focuses on targeting, including whether to market to one segment, to several segments, or to the entire market, and how to cover these segments. The company also needs to formulate a suitable positioning, which means using marketing to create a competitively distinctive place (position) for the brand or product in the mind of targeted customers. This positioning must effectively set the product apart from competing products in a way that is meaningful to customers.

Step 5: Strategic Market Plan (Marketing Strategy)

At this point in the marketing planning process, the company has examined its current situation, looked at markets and consumers, set objectives, and identified segments to be targeted and an appropriate positioning. Now management can create the marketing strategies, effectively combining the basic marketing mix tools of product, place, price, and promotion, enhanced by service strategies to build stronger customer relationships.

Marketing strategies must be consistent with the organisation's overall corporate goals and objectives. As marketing objectives are essentially about the match between products and markets, they must be based on realistic customer behavior in those markets.

To be most effective, objectives must be measurable. The measurement may be in terms of sales volume, turnover volume, market share, or percentage penetration of distribution outlets. As it is measured, it can, within limits, be unequivocally monitored and corrective action taken as appropriate. Usually marketing objectives must be based, above all, on the organisation's financial objectives; financial measurements are converted into the related marketing measurements. An example of a measurable marketing objective might be 'to enter market X with product Y and capture 15 percent of the market by value within the first three years.'

In principle, the strategic market plan describes how the firm's marketing objectives will be achieved. It is essentially a pattern or plan that integrates an organisation's major goals, policies, and action sequences into a cohesive whole.

Marketing strategies are generally concerned with the 4Ps:

1. **Product strategies**

- Developing new products, repositioning or re-launching existing ones, and scrapping old ones.
- Adding new features and benefits.
- Balancing product portfolios.
- Changing the design or packaging.

2. Pricing strategies

- Setting the price to skim or to penetrate.
- Pricing for different market segments.
- Deciding how to meet competitive pricing.
- Promotional strategies.

3. Specifying the advertising platform and media

- Deciding the public relations brief.
- Organizing the sales force to cover new products and services or markets.
- Place distribution strategies.
- Choosing the channels.
- Deciding levels of customer service.

One often-overlooked aspect of the marketing strategy is timing. Choosing the best time for each element of the strategy is often vital. Sometimes, taking the right action at the wrong time can be almost as bad as taking the wrong action at the right time.

Timing is, therefore, an essential part of any plan and should normally appear as a schedule of planned activities (Hollensen, 2006).

Step 6: Tactical Marketing Plan

The next step in the marketing planning process is the development of a tactical marketing plan to put the strategic market plan into operation. Although the overall marketing strategy to protect, grow, harvest, enter, or exit a market position is set by the strategic market plan, more-specific tactical marketing strategies need to be developed. Marketing managers have at their disposal four marketing tools with which they can match their products and services to customer's requirements. These marketing mix decisions consist of evaluations about price levels, the blend of promotional techniques, the distribution channels, and the types of products to manufacture (Ellis-Chadwick and Jobber, 2016).

Therefore, the firm's overall marketing strategies need to be developed into detailed plans and programs. Although these detailed plans may cover each of the 4Ps, the focus will vary, depending on your organisation's specific strategies. A product-oriented company will focus its plans for the 4Ps around each of its products. A market or geographically oriented company will concentrate on each market or geographical area. Each will base its plans on the detailed needs of its customers and on the strategies chosen to satisfy these needs.

The most important element is the detailed plans, which spell out exactly what programs and individual activities will take place over the period of the plan (usually over the next year). Without these specified – and preferably quantified – activities the plan cannot be monitored, even in terms of success in meeting its objectives.

Step 7: Marketing Budget

The traditional quantification of a marketing plan appears in the form of budgets. The purpose of a marketing budget is to pull all the revenues and costs involved in marketing together into one comprehensive file. It is a managerial tool that balances what is needed to be spent against what can be afforded and helps make choices about priorities. It is then used in tracking the performance in practice.

Resources need to be allocated in a marketing budget based on the strategic and operational marketing plan. Without adequate resources, the tactical marketing strategies cannot succeed, and, as a consequence, performance objectives cannot be achieved.

Specifying a marketing budget is perhaps the most difficult part of the market planning process. Although specifying the budget is not a clear-cut process, there must be a logical connection between the strategy and performance objectives and the marketing budget.

Each area of marketing activity should be allocated to centres of responsibility. Indeed, as a key functional area of business the marketing budget is one of the key budgets to concentrate towards the total budgetary control system of the organisation.

In many organisations, budgeting is the transitional step between planning and implementation, because the budget, and allocated centres within it, will project the cost of each activity over the specified period of time, and also act as a guide for implementation and control (Hollensen, 2006).

Step 8: Implementation and Performance Evaluation

The best marketing plan is useless unless it 'degenerates into work '(Drucker, 1993, p. 128). Consequently, the business must design an organisation that has the capability of implementing the strategy and the tactical plan. Once strategies and plans are implemented, the company needs to plan for ways to determine effectiveness by identifying mechanisms and metrics to be used to measure progress toward objectives. Most companies use sales forecasts, schedules, and other tools, to set and record standards against which progress can be assessed. By comparing actual results against daily, weekly, monthly, quarterly, and yearly projections, management can see where the firm is ahead, where it is behind, and where it needs to adjust to get back on the right path.

In the course of reviewing progress, marketers also should look at what competitors are doing and what the markets are doing so they can put their own outcomes into context.

To control implementation, marketers should start with the objectives they have set, establish standards for measuring progress toward those targets, measure the performance of the marketing programs, diagnose the results, and then take corrective action if results fail to measure up. This is the marketing control process. The control process is iterative; managers should expect to retrace their steps as they systematically implement strategies, assess the results, and act to bring performance in line with expectations. Companies use this control process to analyze their marketing implementation on the basis of such measures as market share, sales, profitability, and productivity.

There are three main marketing planning approaches, in terms of involvement of the organisation as a whole. They are:

- **Top-down planning:** Here top management sets both the goals and the plan for lower-level management. While decision making may be immediate at the top level, implementation of the plans may not be as swift because it takes time for various units (division, groups, and departments) to learn about the plans and to reorganize their tasks accordingly to accomplish the new goals.

- **Bottom-up planning:** In this approach, the various units of the organisation create their own goals and plans, which are then approved (or not) by higher management. This can lead to more creative approaches, but it can also pose problems for coordination. More pragmatically, strategy all too frequently emerges from a consolidation of tactics.

- **Goals-down-plans-up-planning:** This is the most common approach, at least among the organisations that invest in such sophisticated planning processes. Top management set the goals, but the various units create their own plans to meet these goals. These plans are then typically approved as part of the annual planning and budgetary process.

BIG CHEFS

CASE STUDY
BIG CHEFS

A WOMAN, A DREAM, A SUCCESSFUL BRAND

Written by: Derya Önel (Personal Assistant to Gamze Cizreli), Aylin Gürlek (Marketing Director)

Introduction

At just 24 years old, Gamze Cizreli embarked on her entrepreneurial journey in Ankara, driven by her inner ambition and boundless dreams.

With a forward-thinking vision and creativity ahead of the industry, Cizreli opened her first all-day, full-service, casual dining BigChefs restaurant where the service ranged from breakfast in the morning to weekend meetups, from coffee breaks during the day to the most elegant dinners in the evening, welcoming guests at any hour of the day. In addition to its modern interpretations of Turkish cuisine, the menu, featuring a selection of popular dishes from around the world, has garnered significant attention.

This new venture of Cizreli was entirely financed through a 100% bank loan, without any equity capital. Combining her passion for gastronomy with an entrepreneurial spirit as a young woman and a single mother in a male-dominated sector, BigChefs quickly achieved great success, expanding both across Türkiye and internationally.

Despite the challenges of being a woman in the demanding industry, Cizreli remained undeterred and persevered with determination, ultimately establishing the greater group of BigChefs, which now encompasses over 130 locations in Türkiye and abroad. This impressive growth reaching a colossal structure, uniting four leading brands BigChefs, NumNum, NumNum by Streetfood, and Buselik, reached the pinnacle of the sector through Gamze Cizreli's unwavering resolve and innovative approach. She has in a sense, single-handedly shattered the glass ceiling in an industry that traditionally places women in a secondary role.

Under Cizreli's vision and innovative strategies, BigChefs became a leading brand in its sector, achieving a significant milestone in 2022: According to the results of the "Türkiye Food Service Market Report" prepared by Deloitte, a multinational professional services network, it was declared the leader in the full-service restaurant category in Türkiye, in terms of the number of domestic and international branches. In 2023, Cizreli accomplished the long-awaited IPO process for her brand with great success.

Gamze Cizreli stands out as a prominent business figure not only in Türkiye but also globally. She was listed among the "50 Over 50: EMEA" in 2023 by Forbes, which accolades fifty successful women entrepreneurs, leaders, and scientists who have made significant impact in their fields. As the most awarded female entrepreneur in Türkiye, she continues to inspire, encouraging women worldwide to pursue their dreams. Through her courage, story, and vision, Cizreli creates an ever-expanding circle of influence.

With Cizreli's "Prosperity Thinking" approach, BigChefs has embedded the mission of benefiting the nature and the world into its DNA, thus prioritizing projects where women create added value. Placing social impact at its center, the brand adopts an ecosystem-sensitive vision with its environmentally friendly practices. BigChefs serves water in glass bottles, carefully manages energy and water consumption, and uses recyclable paper towels and napkins. It reduces plastic waste by opting for biodegradable straws instead of plastic ones and prevents food waste by using bulk sugar. In 2023, BigChefs took another significant step towards environmental sustainability with its Solar Power Plant (SPP) Agreement, investing in a solar power plant to create a new vision for an environmentally friendly future.

BigChefs embraces a holistic approach in its sustainability efforts, ensuring that no flavor in the kitchen goes to waste. As part of its zero-waste commitment, BigChefs partnered with Michelin-starred Chef Tommaso Arrigoni, founder of Innocenti Evasioni, to create the "Kitchen of Tomorrow" menu based on the zero-waste kitchen principle. This menu, which ensures that ingredients not utilized in one dish are made use of in another, serves as an inspiration for a zero-waste kitchen throughout the industry. Furthermore, Arrigoni and BigChefs chefs designed a zero-waste kitchen training to contribute to the sector, sharing this with all restaurant chefs who are members of the country's leading association in the food and hospitality sector, TURYID, Tourism Restaurant Investors and Gastronomy Enterprises Association.

Challenge

31 Years in a Male-Dominant Food & Beverage Sector

Gamze Cizreli, as a pioneering woman entrepreneur, has created significant economic value in the male-dominated food and beverage industry. Not only did she transform the BigChefs Group, with its BigChefs, Buselik, NumNum, and NumNum by Street Food brands, into a group with over 130 branches today, but she further successfully completed the IPO process to share the brand's values with small and corporate investors who have been guests for years. For 31 years, Cizreli has continued to create brands, inspire the food and beverage industry, society, and women.

Incorporating Social and Regional Culture into the Brand's DNA

Drawing strength from the culture and family values she was raised with, Gamze Cizreli built the foundations of her brand on the principle of preserving Türkiye's cultural heritage and history. She prioritized establishing a societal cultural connection with her guests in every region and city where her restaurants are located. An example of this is the free offering of "ashure," a traditional ritual sweet dish made from a bounty of ingredients that symbolize abundance and prosperity, to BigChefs guests at the relevant festive month of the year, highlighting that the brand is founded on cultural values of society.

Transforming Turkish Hospitality into an Unforgettable Experience with "Perfect Serve"

A principle that Gamze Cizreli emphasized in creating the brand was making guests feel at home with a "Perfect Service" approach that reflected the hospitality of welcoming guests as if they were in one's home. This philosophy was first applied to a restaurant chain. BigChefs' presentation of Turkish tea was also a first in the industry, conducted with a specially designed serving tray and traditional "akide" candy, the symbol of reconciliation.

The First "Bistronomique" Restaurant Chain in the Country: BigChefs

Gamze Cizreli established cultural and social ties with different regions, incorporating products from local women producers into BigChefs' menus. This initiative was the first in Turkish gastronomy where an all-day service chain localized its menus. Not stopping there, Cizreli included the beloved flavors of cities considered the gastronomic capitals of the country in the menus, reflecting their culinary culture. Iconic dishes from gastronomic cities under UNESCO protection, such as Gaziantep and Hatay, continue to be served in all BigChefs restaurants through a special menu created with this localization approach. This concept elevated the idea of a "casual dining menu" and redefined BigChefs restaurants as "bistronomique," introducing this term to the industry in Türkiye for the first time.

First to Include Women Producers in the Supply Chain

Gamze Cizreli, who has achieved great successes that inspire women, launched the "From the Women of Land to Dining Tables" initiative, a project supporting women farmers within the framework of the United Nations' "Gender Equality" and "Responsible Production and Consumption" principles. By involving BigChefs restaurants in this project and purchasing products from women producers, BigChefs enabled women's co-operatives and farmers to reach hundreds of thousands of people. This project marked the first inclusion of products grown by women producers in a restaurant supply chain in the sector, thus had a great impact in empowering women. Being a single mother of two young boys, she has been a role model for women to follow their aspirations.

The First Brand to Support Small Businesses in the Sector

In 2023, Gamze Cizreli launched a significant project called "Neighborhood Flavors." As a supporter of this project, BigChefs purchases products from small local businesses producing traditional street flavors and includes these flavors in its menu. This initiative contributes to the preservation of signature flavors of local neighborhoods and the continuation of cultural culinary heritage. Moreover, BigChefs became the first brand to feature and recommend these businesses and their products on its communication channels to its guests.

Promoting Gastronomic Experience and Supporting Social Life in Anatolia

Gamze Cizreli brought a new perspective to the food and beverage sector with BigChefs, becoming the first brand to implement a branching strategy in the full-service category in Anatolia. BigChefs created an environment that would change social habits in the Anatolian cities where its restaurants are located. In these cities, BigChefs, serving all day and at any hour, transformed breakfast and lunch, traditionally enjoyed at home, into a dining-out experience, offering a safe and comfortable social environment. Restaurants were created where women in many Anatolian cities could socialize more freely. By raising the gastronomic bar in every city where it operates, BigChefs contributed to the development of the region's food and beverage sector. BigChefs, which plays a significant role in shaping the social life of the city, continues to inspire the sector and investors as it progresses on its path.

From Guest to Partner

Sharing the opportunities in the all-day service restaurant category, which is expected to grow 39% more from its current state in the future according to Deloitte's report, BigChefs made a significant contribution to the country's food and beverage sector by going public in 2023. Today, alongside all its investors, BigChefs continues to grow as a Turkish brand both domestically and internationally. BigChefs keeps expanding its flavors and culture to wider audiences.

Conclusion

BigChefs is a unique success story created by a woman founder in a male-led industry. What sets Gamze Cizreli apart the most is her ability to inspire not just within her field but across her sector, creating a ripple effect of influence with zero initial capital. The mission to share and contribute to her country, which is at the core of Cizreli's culture, has led BigChefs to develop a business model that serves the economy of goodness.

Drawing inspiration from Cizreli every day, BigChefs keeps expanding its flavors and culture to wider audiences, reinforcing its success both in Türkiye and abroad. Integrating BigChefs into the social responsibility projects she personally leads, Cizreli aims to ensure that the contribution she provides to society serves as an example across all sectors. Cizreli carries on developing BigChefs as a brand with sustainable and global achievements that transcend geographical boundaries.

Questions to stimulate conversation on the case

1.   What was the biggest challenge faced while introducing different service definitions to the sector?

BigChefs, being the leader in Türkiye in terms of the number of branches in the full-service category, allocates extra time in its business planning for the development of its marketing, operations, and service teams and to provide impeccable service to its guests. As a result of this "Teach and Develop" model it has adopted in many areas, the return of this extra time management brings extra costs for BigChefs.

For example:

Within the scope of sustainability efforts, BigChefs not only prioritizes the singular success of its own teams and brand but also aims to contribute to the food and beverage sector. It supports sector development by sharing all the training outcomes conducted with global education partners with the industry or providing similar training to the F&B sector.

BigChefs continues to contribute to the quality standards and sustainability of business models of the producers it supports. Particularly focusing on vocational training, BigChefs allocates budget and time to enhance the technical knowledge of local producers to support product development and proper R&D activities.

In 2022, BigChefs launched the "One Touch is Enough" project in collaboration with MEMEDER, an organization dedicated to raise awareness in breast cancer and support women's health. The project, personally supported by Gamze Cizreli, began in October, recognized as Breast Cancer Awareness Month. Within the scope of this project, breast self-examination training was provided to female employees of BigChefs through MEMEDER.

BigChefs continued to provide breast self-examination training to many women, especially those involved in the "From the Women of Land to Dining Tables" initiative, including women living in rural areas. Just like in the project's initial training provided to members of the Soma Women's Cooperative, in order to support the women in the Soma district of Manisa, where the biggest mining disaster of Türkiye took place on May 13, 2014, BigChefs and Gamze Cizreli continue to allocate time and budget for NGO collaborations to sustain and expand social responsibility initiatives.

2.   What challenges were faced as the only growing all-day service brand in Anatolian cities?

One significant challenge BigChefs faced was finding human resources in the sector, especially kitchen and service personnel that met the company's quality standards in terms of operations. In certain areas where the master-apprentice relationship is key, the younger generation (Gen Z) showed a lack of interest in these jobs. This, coupled with the food and beverage sector being among the hardest hit during the pandemic due to closures, led to a growing shortage of qualified personnel in the sector. To contribute to the sector and provide employment, BigChefs established BigChefs Academy, designed to train skilled personnel aligned with its quality standards and values. The academy was founded to address the critical issue of qualified human resources, kitchen, and service personnel not only for BigChefs but for the entire food and beverage sector by offering training to young individuals whose financial situations may not allow for formal culinary education.

Over time, another issue that transformed into an opportunity was the inclusion of dozens of international flavors such as nachos, buns, and schnitzels, which guests had not previously experienced on the menu. This presented a great opportunity for the brand. Guests had the chance to experience dishes from international cuisines for the first time, paired with the quality and taste of BigChefs, and they ingrained these experiences in their memories with the BigChefs standard.

Another challenge to consider was the importance of opening restaurants in the right locations in Anatolia, which BigChefs confirmed through research and R&D studies. The company often had to wait long periods for the construction of locations deemed the best fit for their restaurants.

3. What commercial opportunities arose from partnering with NGOs on projects that align with your brand's philosophy?

Brands that are considered successful globally and resonate with their communities have invariably developed business models that contribute to societal benefit. Gamze Cizreli identified the mission of creating mutual benefit in society as a personal value and established it as one of BigChefs' key principles. With this principle and in line with the requirements of a stakeholder economy, the brand formulated a strategy and business model that allowed for long-term progress by creating value for all stakeholders while also ensuring its own growth.

Through these strategies, BigChefs gives scheduled orders to its small producers, thereby increasing the producers' profitability and preventing food loss that begins at the field within its ecosystem. This not only ensures cost standardization but also minimizes the impact of economic fluctuations and price increases on the company itself.

By investing in training for its employees, BigChefs raises its service and quality standards while contributing to the personal development of the teams that host its guests. Beyond her personal involvement in all significant projects in the sector, Gamze Cizreli supports all initiatives and projects she believes are beneficial for the sector under the BigChefs brand, helping to expand the circle of influence. With a sustainable approach and a business model that serves the common good, BigChefs continues to contribute to the sector and society.

Case Highlights

A Female Leader Taking Her Brand from a Male-Dominant Sector to a Global Scale

Gamze Cizreli has achieved extraordinary success as a woman founder in the conservative and challenging food and beverage sector dominated by men. By creating a brand that leads the industry in its category, she has rapidly expanded in both domestic and international markets and carries on doing so.

From the First Restaurant Established with a Bank Loan to a Publicly Listed Chain Restaurant Brand: BigChefs

Starting out without any equity, and no personal capital, initiated entirely by a bank loan, BigChefs was established with Gamze Cizreli's principles of societal benefit, being a social brand, and preserving culinary culture and socio-cultural values for the future. Its entry into the Istanbul Stock Exchange with high demand and receiving requests exceeding its IPO size by five times is another success story in this field.

The "Bistronomique" Concept Introduced by Differentiating Menus Through Localization

BigChefs elevated the gastronomic standard by blending Turkish culinary culture and hospitality with local values and flavors, developing them in its menus. Thus, with its unique menu and the unforgettable experiences it offers guests, BigChefs became the first brand to introduce the concept of "Bistronomique" to the industry in Türkiye.

A Social Brand That Inspires Its Sector

By succeeding once again in creating a brand that is both a commercial and social entity, Gamze Cizreli pioneered this area within her sector. Through her own initiatives and with the support of BigChefs, she purchased products from local small businesses and tradespeople in the neighborhoods where her restaurants are located and incorporated local produce them in her menus. BigChefs was the first brand to initiate and provide support to earthquake-affected areas. The company offered training support in every area it believed would contribute to the development of both it and its stakeholders. To preserve the country's culinary heritage for the future, BigChefs included dishes reflecting the iconic flavors of gastronomic capitals in its menus. Under Gamze Cizreli's leadership, BigChefs continues to create economic value and societal benefits as the first and only chain restaurant brand in the country that supports hundreds of inspiring projects and provides direct support to numerous social benefit initiatives.

2. SITUATIONAL ANALYSIS IN THE MARKETING PLANNING PROCESS

2.1 MARKETING RESEARCH

2.1.1 DEFINITION OF MARKETING RESEARCH

As discussed in chapter one, the marketing concept is a business philosophy that puts the customer and customer satisfaction at the center of things. Marketing research is an organizational activity that plays an important role in implementing this marketing philosophy. It helps in improving management decision making by providing relevant, accurate, and timely information. Every decision pose unique need for information, and relevant strategies can be developed based on the information gathered through marketing research in action.

To find out a) if there is a market, b) how big the market is and c) what the competition is doing, a systematic and scientifically valid approach is required. This approach is called market research. Sometimes the term 'Marketing research 'is used as well. When this distinction is made, 'market research 'is defined more narrowly as the research of markets (excluding e. g. competitors and customers). 'Marketing research 'goes beyond 'market research 'and includes competitor and customer research as well as other sources of information like internal records and software-based marketing decision support systems. Thus, marketing research can be defined as the systematic collection, analysis, and interpretation of data about markets, customers, and competitors. It has to provide a reliable basis for marketing decision-making. However, marketing research is no guarantee for business success e.g., studies put the failure rate of new consumer products at 95 per cent in the United States and at 90 per cent in Europe. Especially in high-tech marketing, e. g. in telecommunications, computers, consumer electronics and biotech, failure risks are particularly high. The reasons are:

* High market uncertainty.
* Highly competitive volatility.
* High investment cost.
* Short product life cycles.

Nevertheless, there are also marketing success stories, which involve little or no market research at all e. g. the 'Sony Walkman 'was based on the 'gut feeling 'and vision of Sony's chairman, who allegedly pushed his idea through against the fierce resistance of his managers. In that case, Sony was 'market-driving', not 'market-driven'. It created a new market by launching a product that no consumer could even imagine!

Marketing research not only looks at the market in general, but that it also seeks to obtain sophisticated and detailed information about customers, market segments and the competition. In addition, if a company wants to assess the market position, it has to look inside the organisation in order to identify those parameters that determine its competitive strengths, e. g. the cost structure or innovation power.

Looking at approaches to conducting marketing research, the two main forms of market research are **ad-hoc research** and **continuous research**. Ad-hoc research focuses on a specific problem and can take the form of custom designed surveys or omnibus studies. Continuous research involves interviewing the same sample of people repeatedly. Continuous research methods include consumer panels, retail audits and television viewership panels. Marketing databases and website analysis are also means of collecting data on customers on an on-going basis. Regardless of which form of research is chosen the company must decide whether it should carry out the research using internal company resources or employ a market research agency.

This decision is likely to depend on the company resources: time, money, skills, and experience available.

2.1.2 CATEGORIES OF RESEARCH

The researcher can gather two types of data collection, secondary data, and primary data:

- **Primary data:** These can be defined as information that is collected first-hand, generated by original research tailor-made to answer specific current research questions.

- The major advantage of primary data is that the information is specific ('fine grained'), relevant and up to date.

- The disadvantages of primary data are, however, the high costs and amount of time associated with its collection.

- **Secondary data:** These can be defined as information that has already been collected for other purposes and is thus readily available.

- The major disadvantage is that the data are often more general and 'coarse grained 'in nature.

The advantages of secondary data are the low costs and amount of time associated with its collection. For those who are unclear on the terminology, secondary research is frequently referred to as 'desk research'.

The two basic forms of research (primary and secondary research) are roughly characterized in Figure 2.1.

2.1.3 SECONDARY RESEARCH

With many international markets to consider, it is essential that firms begin their market research by seeking and utilising secondary data.

2.1.3.1 Advantages of Secondary Research

Secondary research conducted from the home base is less expensive and less time consuming than research conducted abroad. No contacts have to be made outside the home country, thus keeping commitment to possible future projects at a low level. Research undertaken in the home country about the foreign environment also has the benefit of objectivity. The researcher is not constrained by overseas customs. As a preliminary stage of a market-screening process, secondary research can quickly generate background information to eliminate many countries from the scope of enquiries.

Data sources

Primary data sources → Data collection with a specific purpose in mind - typical personal interviews

Internal data sources:
- Sales reports
- Market share reports
- Marketing activities
- Cost information
- Sales force feedback
- Sales reps' reports
- Customers
- End user feedback
- Etc.

Secondary data sources

External data sources

Published data - offered for all companies

Internal (electronic):
- Private market research firms (e.g. Statista Euromonitor, Frost & Sullivan)
- Government Web databases
- Trade Magazines / journals
- Article databases (e.g. Springer EBSCO)
- Websites of competitors
- Firms' annual reports
- Newspaper
- Books
- Industry Associations

Printed

Standardized sources of data - offered for companies in specific industries:
- Consumer purchase panels (GFK)
- Store audits (Store checks)
- Nielsen's Television Index
- Multimedia services
- Web - traffic (monitoring traffic on web-sites)

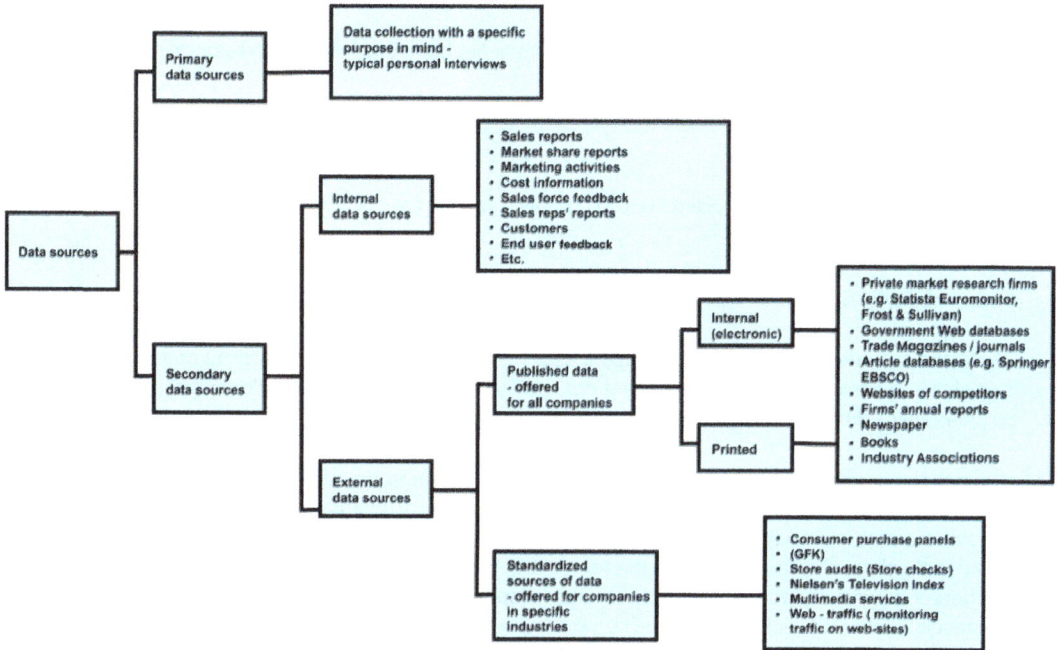

Figure 2.1: Primary and Secondary Data Sources.
Source: Adapted from Hollensen and Opresnik, 2020, modified

2.1.3.2 Disadvantages of Secondary Research

Problems with secondary research are as follows.

Non-availability of data

In many developing countries, secondary data are very scarce. Weak economies have poor statistical ser-vices – many do not even carry out a population census. Information on retail and wholesale trade is especially difficult to obtain. In such cases, primary data collection becomes vital.

Reliability of data

Sometimes political considerations may affect the reliability of data. In some developing countries, govern-ments may enhance the information to paint a rosy picture of the economic life in the country. In addition, due to the data collection procedures used, or the personnel who gathered the data, many data lack statis-tical accuracy.

As a practical matter, the following questions should be asked to judge the reliability of data sources (Cateora, 1993, p. 346):

- Who collected the data? Would there be any reason for purposely misrepresenting the facts?
- For what purpose was the data collected?

- How was the data collected (methodology)?
- Are the data internally consistent and logical in the light of known data sources or market factors?

Data classification

In many countries, the data reported are too broadly classified for use at the micro level.

Comparability of data

International marketers often like to compare data from different countries. Unfortunately, the secondary data obtainable from different countries are not readily comparable because national definitions of statistical phenomena differ from one country to another.

Although the possibility of obtaining secondary data has increased dramatically, the international community has grown increasingly sensitive to the issue of data privacy. Readily accessible large-scale databases contain information valuable to marketers, but they are considered sensitive by the individuals who have provided the data. The international marketer must therefore also pay careful attention to the privacy laws in different nations and to the possible consumer response to using such data. Neglecting these concerns may result in research backfiring and the corporate position being weakened.

In doing secondary research or building a decision support system, there are many information sources available. Generally, these secondary data sources can be divided into internal and external sources (Figure 2.1). The latter can be classified as either international/global or regional/country-based sources.

2.1.4 PRIMARY RESEARCH

2.1.4.1 Qualitative and Quantitative Research

If a marketer's research questions are not adequately answered by secondary research, it may be necessary to search for additional information in primary data. These data can be collected by quantitative research and qualitative research. Quantitative and qualitative techniques can be distinguished by the fact that quantitative techniques involve getting data from a large, representative group of respondents (Hollensen and Opresnik, 2020):

- Quantitative research: Data analysis based on questionnaires from a large group of respondents.

- Qualitative research: Provides a holistic view of a research problem by integrating a larger number of variables but asking only a few respondents. The objective of qualitative research techniques is to give a holistic view of the research problem, and therefore these techniques must have many variables and few respondents. Choosing between quantitative and qualitative techniques is a question of trading off breadth and depth in the results of the analysis.

- Data retrieval and analysis of qualitative data, however, are characterised by a high degree of flexibility and adaptation to the individual respondent and his or her special background. Another considerable difference between qualitative and quantitative surveys is the source of data (Hollensen and Opresnik, 2020):

- Quantitative techniques are characterised by a certain degree of distance as the construction of the questionnaire, data retrieval and data analysis take place in separate phases. Data retrieval is often done by people who have not had anything to do with the construction of the questionnaire. Here the measuring instrument (the questionnaire) is the critical element in the research process.

- Qualitative techniques are characterised by proximity to the source of data, where data retrieval and analysis are done by the same person, namely, the interviewer. Data retrieval is characterised by inter-action between the interviewer and the respondent, where each new question is to a certain degree dependent on the previous question. Here it is the interviewer and his or her competence (or lack of the same) which is the critical element in the research process.

2.1.4.2 Research Design

Figure 2.2 shows that designing research for primary data collection calls for a number of decisions on re-search approaches, contact methods, sampling plan and research instruments. The following pages will look at the various elements of Figure 2.2 in further detail (Hollensen and Opresnik, 2020).

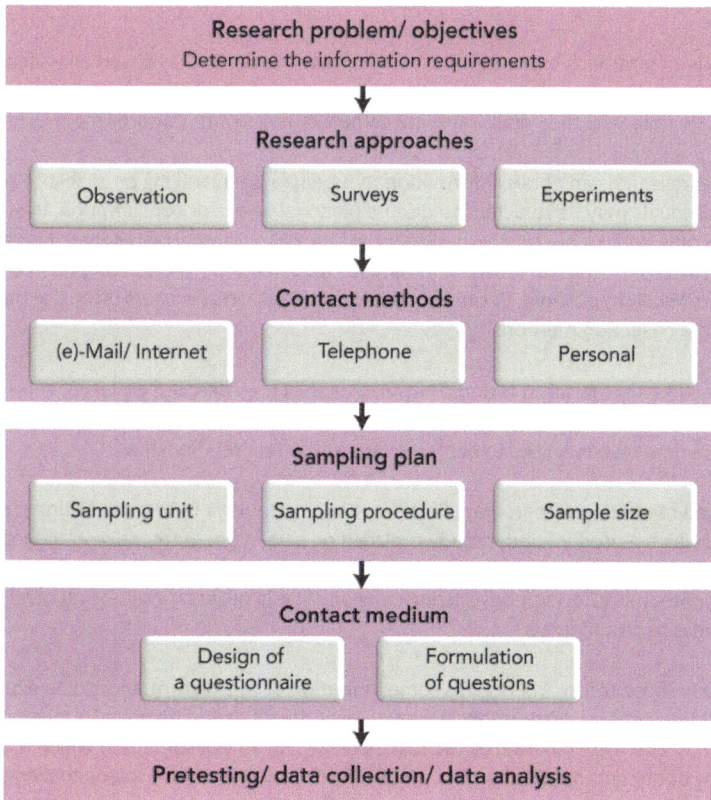

Figure 2.2: Research Design within Primary Data Collection.
Source: Adapted from Hollensen and Opresnik, 2020, modified.

2.1.4.2.1 Research Problem and Objectives

Companies are increasingly recognizing the need for primary international research. As the extent of a firm's international involvement increases, so does the importance and complexity of its international research. The primary research process should begin with a definition of the research problem and the establishment of specific objectives. The major difficulty here is translating the business problem into a research problem with a set of specific researchable objectives. In this initial stage researchers often embark on the research process with only a vague grasp of the total problem. Symptoms are often mistaken for causes, and action determined by symptoms may be oriented in the wrong direction.

Research objectives may include obtaining detailed information for better penetrating the market, for designing and fine-tuning the marketing mix, or for monitoring the political climate of a country so that the firm can expand its operations successfully. The better defined the research objective is, the better the researcher will be able to determine the information requirement.

2.1.4.2.2 Research Approaches

In Figure 2.2 three possible research approaches are indicated: observation, surveys, and experiments (Hollensen and Opresnik, 2020):

- **Observation** is an approach to the generation of primary data which is based on watching and sometimes recording market-related behavior. Observational techniques are more suited to investigating what people do than why they do it. Here are some examples of this approach:

  Observational research can obtain information that people are unwilling or unable to provide. In some country's individuals may be reluctant to discuss personal habits or consumption. In such cases observation is the only way to obtain the necessary information. In contrast, some things are simply not observable, such as feelings, attitudes and motives, or private behavior. Long-term or infrequent behavior is also difficult to observe. Because of these limitations, researchers often use observation along with other data collection methods.

- **Experiments** gather casual information. They involve selecting matched groups of subjects, giving them different treatments, controlling unrelated factors and checking for differences in group responses. Thus, experimental research tries to explain cause-and-effect relationships.

  The most used marketing research application of experiments is in test marketing. This is a research technique in which a product under study is placed on sale in one or more selected localities or areas, and its reception by consumers and the trade is observed, recorded, and analyzed. In order to isolate, for example, the sales effects of advertising campaigns, it is necessary to use relatively self-contained marketing areas as test markets.

  Performance in these test markets gives some indication of the performance to be expected when the product goes into general distribution. However, experiments are difficult to implement in global marketing research. The researcher faces the task of designing an experiment in which most variables are held constant or are comparable across cultures. To do so represents a major challenge. For example, an experiment that intends to determine a casual effect within the distribution system of one country may be difficult to transfer to another country where the distribution system is different. As a result, experiments are used only rarely, even though their potential value to the international market researcher is recognised.

- **Surveys** are based on the questioning of respondents and represents, both in volume and in value terms, perhaps the most important method of collecting data. Typically, the questioning is structured:

a formal questionnaire is prepared and the questions are asked in a prearranged order. The questions may be asked verbally, in writing or via a computer.

2.1.4.2.3 Contact Methods

The method of contact chosen is usually a balance between speed, degree of accuracy and costs.

In principle, there are four possibilities when choosing a contact method: mail, internet/e-mail, telephone interviews and personal (face-to-face) interviews (Hollensen and Opresnik, 2020):

- Mail surveys are among the least expensive. The questionnaire can include pictures – something that is not possible over the phone. Mail surveys allow the respondent to answer at their leisure, rather than at the often-inconvenient moment they are contacted for a phone or personal interview. For this reason, they are not considered as intrusive as other kinds of interviews. However, mail surveys take longer than other kinds. You will need to wait several weeks after mailing out questionnaires before you can be sure that you have obtained most of the responses. In countries of lower educational and literacy levels, response rates to mail surveys are often too small to be useful.

- Internet/e-mail surveys can collect a large amount of data that can be quantified and coded into a computer. A low research budget combined with a widely dispersed population may mean that there is no alternative to the mail/Internet survey. E-mail surveys are both very economical and very fast. It is possible to attach pictures and sound files. However, many people dislike unsolicited e-mail even more than unsolicited regular mail. Furthermore, it is difficult to generalise findings from an e-mail survey to the whole population. People who have e-mail are different from those who do not, even when matched on demographic characteristics, such as age and gender. In section 7 the online research method will be further discussed.

- Telephone interviews are somewhere between personal and mail surveys. They generally have a response rate higher than mail questionnaires but lower than face-to-face interviews, their cost is usually less than with personal interviews, and they allow a degree of flexibility when interviewing. However, the use of visual aids is not possible and there are limits to the number of questions that can be asked before respondents either terminate the interview or give quick (invalid) answers to speed up the process. With computer-aided telephone interviewing (CATI), centrally located interviewers read questions from a computer monitor and input answers via the keyboard. Routing through the questionnaire is computer controlled, helping the process of interviewing. Some research firms set up terminals in shopping centres, where respondents sit down at a terminal, read questions from a screen, and type their answers into the computer.

- Personal interviews take two forms – individual and group interviewing. Individual interviewing involves talking with people in their homes or offices, in the street or in shopping arcades. The interviewer must gain the cooperation of the respondents. Group interviewing (focus-group interviewing) consists of inviting six to ten people to gather for a few hours with a trained moderator to talk about a product, service, or organisation. The moderator needs objectivity, knowledge of the subject and industry, and some understanding of group and consumer behavior. The participants are normally paid a small sum for attending. Personal interviewing is quite flexible and can collect large amounts of information. Trained interviewers can hold a respondent's attention for a long time and can explain difficult questions. They can guide interviews, explore issues and probe as the situation requires. Interviewers can show subjects actual products, advertisements, or packages, and observe reactions and behavior. The main drawbacks of personal interviewing are the high costs and sampling problems. Group interview studies usually employ small sample sizes to keep time and costs down, but it may be hard to generalise from the results. Because interviewers have more freedom in personal interviews the problem of interviewer bias is greater.

- There is no 'best 'contact method – it all depends on the situation. Sometimes it may even be appropriate to combine the methods.

2.1.4.2.4 Sampling Plan

A sampling plan is a scheme outlining the group (or groups) to be surveyed in a marketing research study, how many individuals are to be chosen for the survey, and on what basis this choice is made.

Sampling unit: Except in very restricted markets, it is both impractical and too expensive for a researcher to contact all the people who could have some relevance to the research problem. This total number is known statistically as the 'universe 'or 'population'. In marketing terms, it comprises the total number of actual and potential users/customers of a particular product or service.

The population can also be defined in terms of elements and sampling units. Suppose that a lipstick manufacturer has a **sampling plan** to assess consumer response to a new line of lipsticks and wants to sample females over 15 years of age. It may be possible to sample females of this age directly, in which case a sampling unit would be the same as an element. Alternatively, households might be sampled and all females over 15 in each selected household interviewed. Here the sampling unit is the household, and the element is a female over 15 years old.

What is usually done in practice is to contact a selected group of consumers/customers to be representative of the entire population. The total number of consumers who could be interviewed is known as the 'sample frame', while the number of people who are actually interviewed is known as the 'sample '(Hollensen and Opresnik, 2020).

Sampling procedure: There are several kinds of sampling procedure, with probability and non-probability sampling being the two major categories:

- **Probability sampling:** here it is possible to specify in advance the chance that each element in the population will have of being included in a sample, although there is not necessarily an equal probability for each element. Examples are simple random sampling, systematic sampling, stratified sampling, and cluster sampling.

- **Non-probability sampling:** here it is not possible to determine the above-mentioned probability or to estimate the sampling error. These procedures rely on the personal judgement of the researcher. Examples are convenience sampling, quota sampling and snowball sampling.

Sample size: Once we have chosen the sampling procedure the next step is to determine the appropriate sample size. Determining the sample size is a complex decision and involves financial, statistical, and managerial considerations. Other things being equal the larger the sample, the less the sampling error. However, larger samples cost more money, and the resources (money and time) available for a particular research project are always limited.

In addition, the cost of larger samples tends to increase on a linear basis, whereas the level of sampling error decreases at a rate only equal to the square root of the relative increase in sample size. For example, if sample size is quadrupled data collection costs will be quadrupled too, but the level of sampling error will be reduced by only one-half. Among the methods for determining the sample size are the following:

- Traditional statistical techniques (assuming the standard normal distribution).

- Budget available: although seemingly unscientific this is a fact of life in a business environment, based on the budgeting of financial resources. This approach forces the researcher to carefully consider the value of information in relation to its cost.

- Rules of thumb: the justification for a specified sample size may boil down to a 'gut feeling' that this is an appropriate sample size, or it may be a result of common practice in the industry.

- Number of subgroups to be analyzed: generally speaking, the more subgroups that need to be analyzed, the larger the required total sample size.

- In transnational market research, sampling procedures become a rather complicated matter. Ideally a researcher wants to use the same sampling method for all countries to maintain consistency. Sampling desirability, however, often gives way to practicality and flexibility. Sampling procedures may have to vary across countries to ensure reasonable comparability of national groups. Thus, the relevance of a sampling method depends on whether it will yield a sample that is representative of a target group in a certain country, and on whether comparable samples can be obtained from similar groups in different countries (Hollensen and Opresnik, 2020).

2.1.4.2.5 Contact Medium

Designing the questionnaire: A good questionnaire cannot be designed until the precise information requirements are known. It is the vehicle whereby the research objectives are translated into specific questions. The types of information sought, and the types of respondents to be researched, will have a bearing upon the contact method to be used, and this in turn will influence whether the questionnaire is relatively unstructured (with open-ended questions), aimed at depth interviewing, or relatively structured (with closed-ended questions) for 'on the street 'interviews (Hollensen and Opresnik, 2020).

Formulation (wording) of questions: Once the researcher has decided on specific types of questions the next task is the actual writing of the questions. Four general guidelines are useful to bear in mind during the wording and sequencing of each question:

- The wording must be clear: for example, try to avoid two questions in one.

- Select words so as to avoid biasing the respondent: for example, try to avoid leading questions.

- Consider the ability of the respondent to answer the question: for example, asking respondents about a brand or store that they have never encountered creates a problem. Since respondents may be forgetful, time periods should be relatively short. For example: 'Did you purchase one or more cola(s) within the last week?'

- Consider the willingness of the respondent to answer the question: 'embarrassing' topics that deal with things such as borrowing money, sexual activities and criminal records must be dealt with carefully. One technique is to ask the question in the third person or to state that the behavior or attitude is not unusual prior to asking the question. For example: 'Millions of people suffer from haemorrhoids. Do you or does any member of your family suffer from this problem?' It is also a feasible solution to ask about 'embarrassing' topics at the end of the interview.

When finally evaluating the questionnaire, the following items should be considered:

- Is a certain question necessary? The phrase 'It would be nice to know' is often heard, but each question should either serve a purpose or be omitted.

- Is the questionnaire too long?

- Will the questions achieve the survey objectives?

2.1.4.2.6 Pretesting, Data Collection and Analysis

Pretesting: No matter how comfortable and experienced the researcher is in international research activities, an instrument should always be pretested. Ideally such a pre-test is carried out with a subset of the population under study, but a pre-test should at least be conducted with knowledgeable experts and/or individuals. The pre-test should also be conducted in the same mode as the final interview. If the study is to be 'on the street 'or in the shopping arcade, then the pre-test should be the same. Even though a pre-test may mean time delays and additional cost the risks of poor research are simply too great for this process to be omitted.

Data collection: The global marketing researcher must check that the data are gathered correctly, efficiently and at a reasonable cost. The market researcher has to establish the parameters under which the research is conducted. Without clear instructions, the interviews may be conducted in different ways by different interviewers. Therefore, the interviewers have to be instructed about the nature of the study, start and completion time, and sampling methodology. Sometimes a sample interview is included with detailed information on probing and quotas. Spot checks on these administration procedures are vital to ensure reasonable data quality.

Data analysis and interpretation: Once data have been collected the final steps are the analysis and interpretation of findings in the light of the stated problem. Analyzing data from cross-country studies calls for substantial creativity as well as skepticism. Not only are data often limited, but frequently results are significantly influenced by cultural differences. This suggests that there is a need for properly trained local personnel to function as supervisors and interviewers; alternatively, international market researchers require substantial advice from knowledgeable local research firms that can also take care of the actual collection of data. Although data in cross-country analyzes are often of a qualitative nature the researcher should, of course, use the best and most appropriate tools available for analysis. On the other hand, international researchers should be cautioned against using overly sophisticated tools for unsophisticated data. Even the best of tools will not improve data quality. The quality of data must be matched with the quality of the research tools (Hollensen and Opresnik, 2020).

2.1.4.3 Problems with Using Primary Research

Most problems in collecting primary data in international marketing research stem from cultural differences among countries and range from the inability of respondents to communicate their opinions to inadequacies in questionnaire translation (Cateora et al., 2000).

Sampling in field surveys

The greatest problem of sampling stems from the lack of adequate demographic data and available lists from which to draw meaningful samples. For example, in many South American and Asian cities street maps are unavailable, and streets are neither identified nor houses numbered. In Saudi Arabia, the difficulties with probability sampling are so acute that non-probabilistic sampling becomes a necessary evil. Some of the problems in drawing a random sample include:

- no officially recognised census of population;

- incomplete and out-of-date telephone directories;

- no accurate maps of population centres, therefore no area samples can be made.

Non-response

Non-response is the inability to reach selected elements in the sample frame. As a result, opinions of some sample elements are not obtained or properly represented. A good sampling method can only identify elements that should be selected; there is no guarantee that such elements will ever be included.

Language barriers

This problem area includes the difficulty of exact translation that creates problems in eliciting the specific information desired and in interpreting the respondents 'answers. In some developing countries with low literacy rates written questionnaires are completely useless. Within some countries, the problem of dialects and different languages can make a national questionnaire survey impractical – this is the case in India, which has 25 official languages. The obvious solution of having questionnaires prepared or reviewed by someone fluent in the language of the country is frequently overlooked. In order to find possible translation errors marketers can use the technique of back translation, where the questionnaire is translated from one language to another, and then back again into the original language (Douglas and Craig, 2007). For example, if a questionnaire survey is going to be made in France, the English version is translated into French and then translated back to English by a different translator. The two English versions are then compared and, where there are differences, the translation is checked thoroughly.

Measurement

The best research design is useless without proper measurements. A measurement method that works satisfactorily in one culture may fail to achieve the intended purpose in another country. Special care must therefore be taken to ensure the reliability and validity of the measurement method.

2.2 ASSESSING THE INTERNAL MARKETING SITUATION

The foundation of any marketing plan is the firm's **mission and vision statement,** which answers the question, 'What business are we in and where should we go? 'Business mission definition profoundly affects the firm's long-run resource allocation, profitability, and survival. The mission statement is a statement of the organisation's purpose—what it wants to accomplish in the larger macro environment. A clear mission statement acts as an 'invisible hand 'that guides people in the enterprise (Hollensen and Opresnik, 2020). When examining internal strengths and weaknesses, the marketing manager should focus on organisational resources, company or brand image, employee capabilities and available technology.

When examining external opportunities and threats, the marketing managers must analyze aspects of the marketing environment. This process is called **environmental scanning** – the collection and interpretation of information about forces, events and relationships in the external environment that may affect the future of the organisation or the implementation of the marketing plan. Environmental scanning helps identify market opportunities and threats and provides guidelines for the design of marketing strategy. The six macro-environmental forces studied most often are social, demographic, economic, technological, political, and legal, and competitive.

The matching of the internal strengths and weaknesses with external opportunities and threats automatically leads us to the two important views we will discuss in this chapter (Hollensen and Opresnik, 2020):

- Market Orientation View (MOV) – outside-in perspective

- Resource Based View (RBV) – inside-out perspective

2.2.1 MARKET ORIENTATION VIEW (MOV)

The term market (or marketing) orientation generally refers to the implementation of the marketing concept. A market orientation entails (1) one or more departments engaging in activities geared toward developing an understanding of customers 'current and future needs and the factors affecting them, (2) sharing of this understanding across departments, and (3) the various departments engaging in activities designed to meet select customer needs. In other words, a market orientation refers to the organization-wide generation, dissemination, and responsiveness to market intelligence (Kohli and Jaworski, 1990).

One key is achieving understanding of the market and the customer throughout the company and building the capability for responsiveness to market changes. The real customer focus and responsiveness of the company is the context in which marketing strategy is built and implemented.

Another issue is that the marketing process should be seen as interfunctional and cross-disciplinary, and not simply the responsibility of the marketing department. This is the real value of adopting the process perspective on marketing, which is becoming more widely adopted by large organizations (Hollensen, 2006).

In MOV it is also clear that a deep understanding of the competition in the market from the customer's perspective is critical. Viewing the product or service from the customer's viewpoint is often difficult, but without such a perspective a marketing strategy is highly vulnerable to attack from unsuspected sources of competition.

In essence, market orientation refers to the way a firm implements the marketing concept. In principle, this three-component view of market orientation (generation of, dissemination of and responsiveness to market intelligence) makes it possible to diagnose an organization's level of market orientation, pinpoint specific deficiencies and design interventions tailored to the particular needs of an organization. It should be emphasized that a market orientation is not the exclusive responsibility of a marketing department but, rather, is a company-wide mode of operation.

2.2.2 RESOURCE BASED VIEW (RBV)

The traditional market orientation literature emphasizes the superior performance of companies with high quality, organization-wide generation and sharing of market intelligence leading to responsiveness to market needs; the RBV suggests that high performance strategy is dependent primarily on historically developed resource endowments.

Resource-based marketing essentially seeks a long term fit between the requirements of the market and the abilities of the organization to compete in it.

This does not mean that the resources of the organization are seen as fixed and static. Far from it: market requirements evolve over time and the resource profile of the organization must be continuously developed to enable it to continue to compete and, indeed, to enable it to take advantage of new opportunities. The essential factor, however, is that opportunities are seized where the organization has an existing or potential advantage through its resource base, rather than just pursued ad hoc.

Why do organizations exist? The simple answer for commercial organizations may be to earn returns on their investments for shareholders and owners of those organizations. For non-commercial organizations, such as charities, faith-based organizations, and public services and so on, the answer may lie in the desire to serve specific communities. However, organizations, both commercial and non-profit, are rarely driven by such simple goals. Often there are many demands, sometimes complementary, sometimes competing, that drive decisions.

In the context of commercial organizations, a number of primary stakeholders can be identified. These include shareholders and owners, managers, employees, customers, and suppliers. While the market-oriented culture (MOV) discussed above serves to place customers high in the priority ranking, the reality for most organizations will be a complex blend of considerations of all relevant stakeholders.

The RBV of the firm discussed above implies that the first stage in assessing strengths and weaknesses should be to conduct an audit of the resources available to the company, including both the tangible and intangible (Figure 2.3 bottom).

The types of resources and capabilities listed earlier can be simplified as follows (Hollensen and Opresnik, 2020):

- **Technical resources:** a key resource in many organizations, and one becoming increasingly important in a world of rapidly changing technology, is technical skill. This involves the ability of the organization to develop new processes and products through research and development, which can be utilized in the marketplace.

- **Financial standing**: a second important resource is the organization's financial standing. This will dictate, to a large extent, its scope for action and ability to put its strategies into operation. An organization of sound financial standing can raise capital from outside to finance ventures. In deciding marketing strategy, a major consideration is often what financial resources can or cannot be put into the programme.

- **Managerial skills:** managerial skills in the widest possible sense are a further resource of the organization. The experience of managers and the way in which they discharge their duties and motivate their staff, have a major impact on corporate performance.

- **Organization:** the very structure of the organization can be a valuable asset or resource. Some structures, such as the matrix organization, are designed to facilitate wide use of skills throughout the organization. The system has proved useful in focusing control at the brand level, encouraging a co-ordinated marketing mix, and facilitating a flexible, rapid response to changing circumstances. It is not without its drawbacks, however. The product management system can lead to responsibility without authority, conflicts between product managers within the same organization and the 'galloping midget' syndrome – managers moving on to their next product management job having maximized short-term returns at the expense of longer-term market position.

- **Information systems**: the information and planning systems in operation also provide a valuable resource. For example, those organizations, such as banks dealing in foreign currency speculation, rely heavily on up-to-the minute and accurate information systems. New technological developments, such as electronic point-of-scale scanning, allow data to be collected and processed in a much shorter time than a few years ago. These companies with the systems in place to cope with the massive increases in data that such newer collection procedures are creating will be in a stronger position to take advantage of the opportunities afforded.

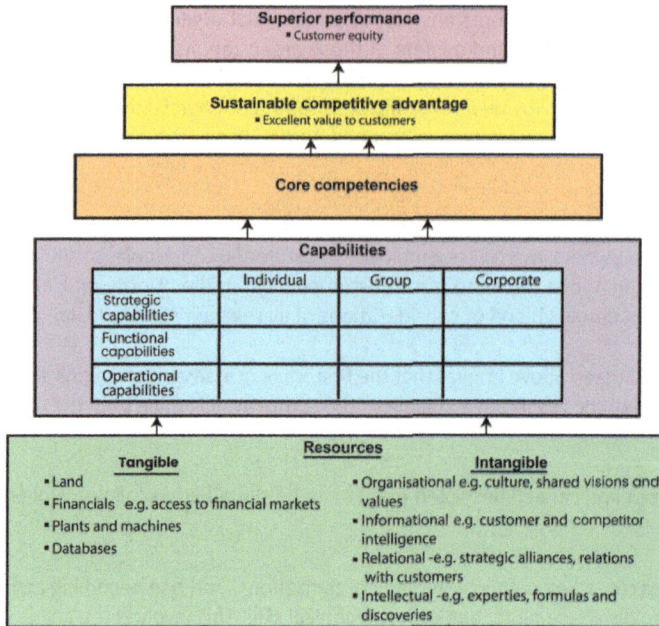

Figure 2.3: The Roots of Competition.
Source: Adapted from Hollensen and Opresnik, 2020, modified.

Resources are broken down into two fundamental categories (Hollensen and Opresnik, 2020):

Tangible resources include those factors containing financial or physical value as measured by the firm's balance sheet. Intangible resources, on the other hand, include those factors that are non-physical (or non-financial) in nature and are rarely, if at all, included in the firm's balance sheet.

Intangible resources essentially fall into two categories: assets and skills (or capabilities). If the intangible resource is something that the firm 'has', it is an asset. If the intangible resource is something that the firm 'does', it is a skill and it is being turned into a capability. However, the distinction between assets and capabilities may not be so easy to make. Intangible assets such as copyrights, patents, registered designs, and trademarks are all afforded legal protection through property rights. Such legal protection can create barriers to competitive duplication. Other forms of intellectual property include held-in-secret technology. Held-in-secret technology – technology specifically developed to fit the firm's unique strategy and particular business model – can lead to unique, socially complex and context specific assets that may be difficult for competitors to understand let alone duplicate. Given their legally enforceable protection or held-in-secret standing, intellectual property assets are argued to be more difficult to duplicate than tangible resources.

Capabilities can be seen as strategic, functional, or operational:

- **Strategic capabilities** underpin the definition of direction for the firm. They include issues such as the dominant logic or orientation guiding management (which will strongly influence strategic direction), the ability of the organization to learn (to acquire, assimilate and act on information) and the ability of senior managers to manage the implementation of strategy.

- **Functional capabilities** lie in the execution of functional tasks. These include marketing capabilities, financial management capabilities and operations management capabilities.

- **Operational capabilities** are concerned with undertaking individual line tasks, such as operating machinery, the application of information systems and completion of order processing.

- Second, capabilities may lie with individuals, with groups, or at the corporate level.

- **Individual competencies** are the skills and abilities of individuals within the organization. They include the ability of the individual to analyze critically and assess a given situation (whether this is a CEO assessing a strategic problem, or the shop-floor worker assessing the impact of a machine failure).

- **Group competencies** are where individual abilities come together in teams or ad hoc, informal, task-related teams. While the abilities of individuals are important, so too is their ability to work together constructively.

- **Corporate-level** competencies relate to the abilities of the firm as a whole to undertake strategic, functional or operational tasks. This could include the ability of the firm to internalize learning, so that critical information is not held just by individuals but is shared throughout the firm.

The need to identify the 'distinctive competence' of a company is underlined by a very influential analysis of successful international businesses by Prahalad and Hamel (1990), who argue that a company is likely to be genuinely world class at perhaps five or six activities, and superior performance will come from focusing on those to the exclusion of others. The late 1990s saw much effort to refocus major organizations on to their core activities. Prahalad and Hamel (1990) define core competencies as the underlying skills, technologies and competencies that can be combined in different ways to create the next generation of products and services.

Three tests are suggested by Prahalad and Hamel for identifying core competencies:

- A core competency should be difficult for competitors to copy. Clearly a competency that can be defended against competitors has greater value than a competency that other companies can share.

- A core competence provides potential access to a wide variety of markets. Competencies in display systems are needed, for example, to enable a company to compete in a number of different markets, including flat-screen TV sets, calculators, laptop or notebook computers, mobile phones, and so on.

- A core competency should make a significant contribution to the benefits the customer derives from using the ultimate product or service. In other words, the competency is important where it is a significant determinant of customer satisfaction and benefit.

These requirements are essentially the same as those emerging from the earlier RBV literature to define resources capable of creating sustainable competitive advantage. Added to these three characteristics a further useful test is whether the competency can be combined with other skills and capabilities to create unique value for customers – the grouping of competencies discussed earlier. It could be, for example, that a company does not fulfil the above criteria, but when combined with other competencies is an essential ingredient in defining the firm's uniqueness. Put another way: what would happen if we did not have that competency?

Prahalad and Hamel (1990) argue that the critical management ability for the future will be to identify, cultivate and exploit the core competencies that make growth possible.

The argument about core competencies is compelling, and it is certainly driving major corporate changes, such as:

- The emergence of a network of strategic alliances, where each partner brings its core competency into play to build a market offering

- The demerger and sale of non-core activities and brands

- Organizational changes away from SBUs to a new 'strategic architecture'.

2.2.3 MAJOR SOURCES OF COMPETITIVE ADVANTAGE

Companies producing offerings with a higher perceived value and/or lower relative costs (compared to competitors) are supposed to have a competitive advantage. The 'high perceived value' advantage can be considered as differentiation, but the elements of this must be evaluated from a customer perspective. The word 'perceived' is used to emphasize the fact that value is a subjective evaluation rather than a direct measure of utility. This involves an element of judgement and is sometimes seen as irrational. It is how customers themselves rate the offering in relation to other competitive products or services that is critical in a purchase decision. The prime consideration of the value of any resource to an organisation lies in the answer to the following question: Does this resource contribute to creating value for customers? Value creation may be direct, such as through the benefits conveyed by superior technology, better service, meaningful brand differentiation and ready accessibility. The resources that contribute to these benefits (technology deployed, skilled and motivated personnel, brand name and reputation, and distribution coverage) create value for consumers as soon as they are employed. Other resources may, however, have an indirect impact on value for customers. Effective cost control systems, for example, are not valuable to customers in and of themselves. They only add value for customers when they translate into lower prices charged, or by the ability of the organisation to offer additional customer benefits through the cost savings achieved (Hollensen and Opresnik, 2020).

The value of a resource in creating customer value must be evaluated relative to the resources of competitors. For example, a strong brand name such as Nike on sportswear may convey more value than a less well-known brand. In other words, for the resource to contribute to sustainable competitive advantage it must serve to distinguish the organisation's offerings from those of competitors.

The 'value' of a product or service should be seen in relation to the customer's cost of obtaining the product/service and the cost of ownership. These costs will include such issues as the buying price of an offering compared to the price of a competitive offering. These elements might be modified by the perceived cost of obtaining and cost of ownership. The way components are assessed and compared could vary from one customer to another. It is often possible to 'delight' customers by exceeding their expectations. The 'perceived value' (compared to price) together with the relative cost is illustrated in Figure 2.4.

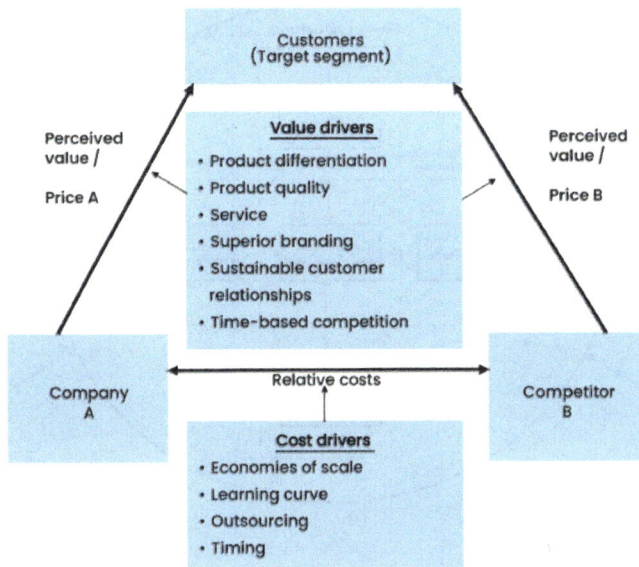

Figure 2.4: The Competitive Triangle.
Source: Adapted from Hollensen and Opresnik, 2020, modified.

2.3 ASSESSING THE EXTERNAL MARKETING SITUATION

A marketing-oriented company continually analyzes the environment in which it operates, adapting to take advantage of emerging opportunities and to minimize eventual threats.

At its simplest, the whole marketing system can be divided into three levels (see Figure 2.5):

- **The focal company**: Understanding and analyzing the internal situation was dealt with already within this chapter.

- **Industry level/value net/micro level**: The focal company's most important actors/stakeholders at this level are suppliers, partners/complementors, competitors and of course the customers.

- **Macro level**: The most important changes taking place in the macro environment can be summarized in the so-called PEST analysis:

P: Political and legal factors

E: Economic factors

S: Social/cultural factors

T: Technological factors

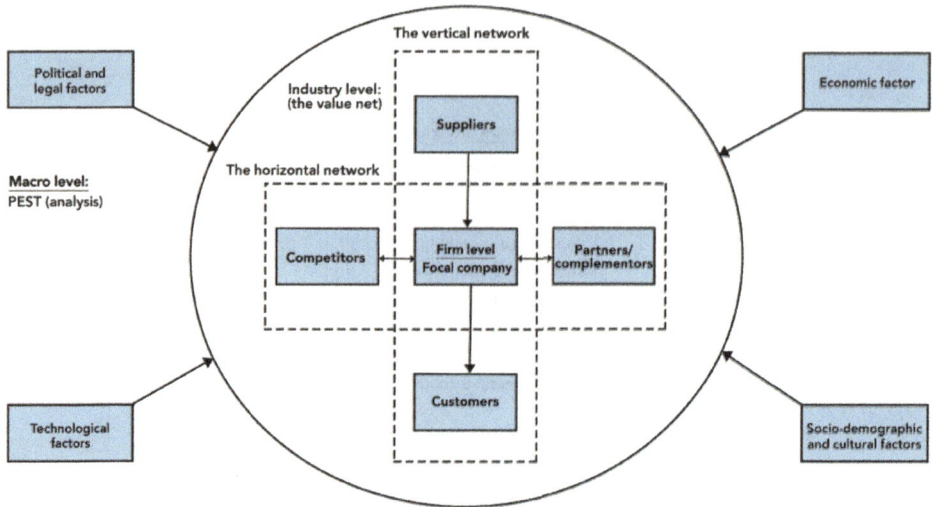

The vertical network

Political and legal factors

Economic factor

Macro level: PEST (analysis)

Industry level: (the value net)

Suppliers

The horizontal network

Competitors

Firm level Focal company

Partners/ complementors

Customers

Technological factors

Socio-demographic and cultural factors

Figure 2.5: The three Levels in the Marketing System/Value Net.
Source: Adapted from Hollensen and Opresnik, 2020, modified.

In the following we will discuss each of the four elements in the PEST analysis. Later in the chapter, the dimensions of the microenvironment will be introduced and examined (Hollensen and Opresnik, 2020).

2.3.1 PEST ANALYSIS

The macro environment consists of a number of broad forces that influence not only the company but also the other stakeholders and actors in the microenvironment. Traditionally, four forces – political/legal, economic, social/cultural, and technological – have been the focus of attention, with the result that the term PEST analysis has been used to describe the macro environmental analysis (Ellis-Chadwick and Jobber, 2016).

Political and Legal Factors: The political environment consists of laws, government agencies, and pressure groups that influence and limit various companies and individuals in each society. Political and legal forces can highly influence marketing decisions by setting the rules by which business can be conducted.

For example, smoking bans in public places do have substantial effects on the demand for cigarettes.

- **Economic Factors:** The economic environment consists of factors that affect consumer buying power and spending patterns. Nations vary vastly in their levels and distribution of income and rates of economic growth.

- **Social/Cultural Factors:** The social and cultural environment is made up of institutions and other forces that affect a society's basic values, perceptions, preferences, behaviors as well as population growth, age distribution and other elements, which in turn can affect marketing decision making.

- **Technological Factors:** The technological environment involves forces that create new technologies, generating new product and market opportunities. It is perhaps the most dramatic force now shaping company's future. The latter part of the twentieth century saw technological change and development impact on virtually every industry.

2.3.2 EXTERNAL RELATIONSHIPS TO STAKEHOLDERS IN THE VALUE NET

The value net or microenvironment consists of the stakeholders in the company's immediate environment that influences its capabilities to operate successfully in its chosen markets. Marketing success requires building relationships with those actors, specifically customers, competitors, distributors, suppliers, and other stakeholders. Since the company has relationships with different types of interdependencies, with different objective for the development of the relationship, etc., it is imperative to differentiate between how different relationships are handled.

In particular, the relationships and interactions are typically established with the following actors (see Figure 2.5):

- Suppliers
- Customers
- Complementors/partners
- Competitors

These relationships will now be introduced and analyzed in more depth (Hollensen and Opresnik, 2020).

2.3.2.1 Relationships with Suppliers

Suppliers form an important link in the company's overall customer value proposition system as they provide the resources needs by the firm to produce its goods and services.

The first strategic issue is to decide what items to procure. This is defined by the range of the operations that are undertaken in-house by the buying organisation. This determines the degree of **vertical integration**, which in purchasing terms has been addressed as the make-or-buy issue. What to produce internally and what to buy from external suppliers has been an issue in manufacturing firms for a very long time, despite the fact that it was actually not identified as a matter of strategic importance until the 1980s. It is obvious that buying firms over time have come to rely more on 'buy 'than 'make'. Consequently, outsourcing to external suppliers has increased noticeably over time. Having suppliers that compete with one another is one way of increasing efficiency in the purchasing operations. A buying company can switch from one supplier to the other and thus influence the vendors towards improving their efforts. The prospect to play off suppliers against each other in terms of price conditions has been a particularly recommended purchasing policy. The core of this strategy is to avoid becoming too integrated with suppliers, because integration leads to dependence. Customer relationships based on this reason are characterized by low involvement from both parties. The tendency in the overall industrial system towards increasing specialization has called for more coordination between the individual companies. Sequentially, this leads to more adaptation between buyer and seller in terms of activities and resources. These adaptations are made because they improve efficiency and effectiveness. They also create interdependencies between consumer and supplier. Such relationships are characterized by a high involvement approach.

Against this background, buyers and suppliers can join forces to improve supply relationship, or even supply network, performance and consequently allow the supply chain to deliver better value to the customer. Lean supply techniques aim to eliminate redundancies in all areas of the business, from the shopfloor to manufacturing processes, and from new product development to supply chain management. Agile supply techniques, on the other hand, are directed towards plummeting the time it takes for a supply chain to deliver a good or service to the end customer and are aimed at supply chains that have to respond to unpredictable demand patterns. Both the 'lean 'and 'agile 'supply schools have provided a great deal of case evidence that demonstrates that collaboration, in the cause of lean or agile goals, can be effective in reducing costs and/or increasing productivity and functionality. For example, the lean school has referred to the Japanese automobile industry, especially the Toyota Motor Corporation, as an excellent example of lean practice. The agile school has pointed to the production of the Smart Car, a car that offers entire customization, backed up by a service that offers responsiveness to customer demands.

There are two basic ways of working in the context of supplier relationship management: arm's length and collaborative. An arm's length way of working involves a low level of contact between the buyer and supplier. By low contact, we mean the absence of initiatives that are aimed at cost reduction or functionality improvement. In arm's length exchanges, the buyer and supplier simply exchange the contractual information that is required for the transaction to occur. For example, information about the placing of the order, the recording of the fulfilment and the settlement of the invoice. Most companies today treat their suppliers as partners in creating and delivering customer value. Walt-Mart goes to large lengths to work with its suppliers. For example, it helps them to test new products in its outlets. In addition, its Supplier Development Department publishes a Supplier Proposal Guide and maintains a supplier Web site, both of which support suppliers to navigate the complex Walmart procurement process. Walmart is aware of the fact, that good partnership relationship management results in success for the company, suppliers, and, ultimately, its customers (Hollensen and Opresnik, 2020).

2.3.2.2 Relationships with Customers

As we have outlined before, customers are at the centre of the marketing philosophy and effort, and it is the task of marketing management to satisfy their needs and wants better than the competition.

In the relationship approach a specific transaction between the focal company and a customer is not a secluded event but takes place within an exchange relationship characterized by mutual dependency and interaction over time between the parties involved. An analysis could not break off at the individual relationship as in the network approach such relationships are seen as interrelated. Thus, the various actors on a market are connected to each other, directly or indirectly. A specific market can then be described and analyzed as one or more networks.

An exchange relationship implies that there is an individual specific dependency between the seller and the consumer. The relationship develops through interaction over time and signifies a joint orientation of the two parties towards each other. In the interaction, the buyer is equally as active as the seller. The interaction consists of social, business and information exchange and an adaptation of products, processes, and routines to better reach the economic objectives of the parties. Consequently, marketing planning should start at the relationship level. Interaction with the buyers and potential buyers is an important aspect of the planning process. The planning should include objectives and activities regarding the development of the relationships. The objectives should not only be formulated for the business exchange, such as sales volume and type of products, but also for social and information exchange, and for adaptation processes for products and processes (Hollensen, 2006).

Although marketing authors acknowledge the benefits of a 'broadened view of marketing 'there is no doubt that 'customer markets 'should remain the most important focus. RM focuses not on what you can do to your customer but on what you can do for your customer and what you can do with your customer, to ensure customer satisfaction. The goal is to treat your customers as valued partners, to establish their needs and develop their loyalty.

2.3.2.3 Relationships with Partners

This kind of relationship is based on cooperation between manufacturers of complimentary functions and or products/services. In such an affiliation, each partner has a strategic resource that the other needs and in this way each partner is motivated to develop some kind of exchange process between supplier and customer.

For example, partners segregate the value chain activities between themselves. One partner develops and produces a good while letting the other partner market it. The focal company, A, may want to enter a foreign market, but lacks local market knowledge and does not know how to get admittance to foreign distribution channels for its products. Therefore, A seeks and find a partner, B, which has its competencies in the downstream functions, but is rather feeble in the upstream function. In this way, A and B can create a coalition where B can help A with distribution and selling in a foreign market, and A can help B with R&D or production.

2.3.2.4 Relationships with Competitors

As the marketing concepts states that to be successful, a company must provide greater customer value than its competitors do, marketers must gain strategic advantages by positioning their offerings strongly against competitor's offerings in the minds of the consumers. Therefore, marketing-oriented companies not only monitor and seek to understand customers but also research competitors and their brands to understand their strengths, weaknesses, strategies, and response patterns.

In analyzing competition, a number of factors need to be well thought-out. These range from the number and size of competitors, their capabilities (strengths and weaknesses), their international marketing strategies, their sales volume and relative market share, to the type of competitor, i.e., multinational versus local and their relative resources. The major international competitors, such as Microsoft or Procter&Gamble, have access to extensive financial and other resources. But local competitors should not be ignored, as they have less administrative overhead, lower operating costs, greater flexibility, and most likely sophisticated local market knowledge. When competitors are involved in resource exchange alliances, competition implies some issues. The dilemma is that in creating an alliance with a competitor, a company is, in fact making them more competitive. Interaction among competitors has been treated traditionally within economic theory and has been explained in terms of the structure of an industry within it operates. It is further argued that intensity in competition is dependent on the degree of symmetry between companies, while the degree of concentration determines whether competitors act in collusion or competition with each other. Based on the motives for interaction and the intensity of the relationship concerned, five types of interaction are distinguished: conflict, competition, co-existence, co-operation, and collusion. Conflict and competition are described as active vis-à-vis competitors, although they differ in terms of the motives for specific interaction. Conflict represents object-oriented competition, geared towards destroying the opposing counterpart. Competition is goal-oriented, directed towards achieving one's own goals even though this may have a negative effect on other competitors. Co-existent competition occurs when actors do not see one another as competitors and therefore act independently of each other. Tacit collusion arises from implicit agreements among the actors to avoid active competition. Finally, in co-operation, the companies involved strive towards the same goals, for example by working together in strategic alliances or projects. The interaction between competitors is variable and can involve both co-operative and competitive interaction (Hollensen, 2006).

2.4 ANALYZING BUYING BEHAVIOR IN THE B2C MARKET

Customer buying behavior refers to the buying behavior of final consumers - individuals and households who buy goods and services for personal consumption. All of these final consumers combine to make up the consumer market. Organizational buying, on the other hand, focuses on the purchase of products and services for use in an organization's activities. Sometimes, it is difficult to classify a product as either a consumer or an organizational good. Cars sell to customers for personal consumption and organizations for use in carrying out their activities e.g., to provide transport for a sales executive.

For both types of buyers, an understanding of customers can be gained by answering the following questions (Ellis-Chadwick and Jobber, 2016):

- Who is important in the buying decision?
- How do they buy?
- What are their choice criteria?
- Where do they buy?
- When do they buy?

Buyer behavior as it relates to customers will now be examined based upon the first three questions as these are often the most intractable aspects of buyer behavior.

Who is important in the buying decision?

Consumers around the world vary vastly in age, income, education level, and tastes. They can also buy an enormous variety of goods and services. How these diverse customers connect with each other and with other elements of their surroundings impacts their choices among products, services, and companies (Hollensen and Opresnik, 2020).

The marketing implications of understanding who buys mainly lie within the areas of marketing communications and segmentation. An identification of the roles played within the buying centre is a prerequisite for targeting effective communications.

The person, who actually uses or consumes the product may not be the most influential member of the buying centre, nor the decision-maker. Even when the user does play the predominant role, communication with other members of the buying centre can be useful when their knowledge may function as persuasive forces during the decision-making process. The second implication is that the changing roles and influences within the family buying centre are providing new opportunities to segment hitherto stable markets.

How do they buy?

The central question for marketers is: How do customers respond to the various marketing efforts of the company? The company actively has a strong role to play in designing and providing appropriate stimulation to the purchase decisions.

The customer buying process is a dynamic interaction between the consumer and the environment. The consumer actively participates in the process by searching for information on alternatives available, by providing evaluations of products and services, and by expressions of risk.

In this process, the company also plays an active role by manipulating the variables under its control. The company modifies the marketing mix to accommodate the demands expressed by consumers. The more successful it is in matching its marketing mix with expressed and latent demands in the market, the greater is the possibility that consumers will patronize the company's products now and in the future. Consumer behavior is determined by a host of variables studied in different disciplines (Hollensen and Opresnik, 2020).

Consumer behavior may be described with the help of the **stimulus-organisms-response model (S-O-R model)** as a relationship between a stimulus of some sort, such as a new product, the way information about the innovation is processed by the consumer, and the response the consumer makes having evaluated the alternatives (Figure 2.6).

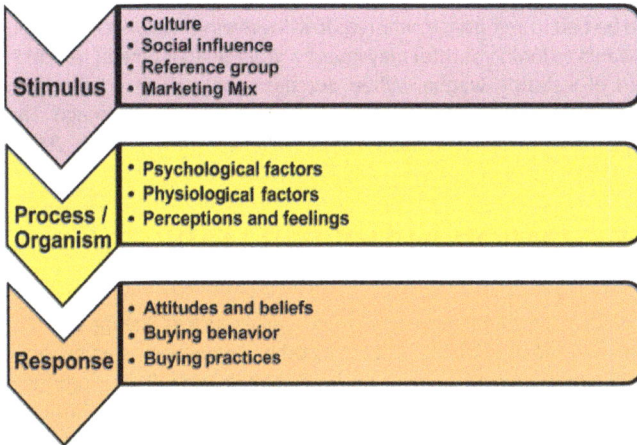

Stimulus
- Culture
- Social influence
- Reference group
- Marketing Mix

Process / Organism
- Psychological factors
- Physiological factors
- Perceptions and feelings

Response
- Attitudes and beliefs
- Buying behavior
- Buying practices

Figure 2.6: The S-O-R Model. Source: Adapted from Hollensen and Opresnik, 2020, modified.

The stimulus is driven by the range of elements in the marketing mix, which the company can manipulate to achieve its corporate objectives. These stimuli derive from the product or service itself, or from the marketing programme developed by the company to support its products and services. A number of symbolic stimuli derive from the use of media such as television. Stimuli also include many of the conditioning variables discussed above. Chief among these are the cultural and social influences on consumer behavior and the role of reference groups. As cultural factors exert a broad and deep influence on consumer behavior marketers need to understand the role played by the buyer's culture, subculture, and social class.

Process refers to the sequence of stages used in the internal process of these influences by the consumer. This sequence highlights the cause-and-effect relationships involved in making decisions. The processes include the perceptual, physiological, and inner feelings and dispositions of consumers towards the product or service being evaluated.

The third component refers to the consumer's response in terms of changes in behavior, awareness and attention, brand comprehension, attitudes, intentions, and actual purchase. This response may indicate a change in the consumer's psychological reaction to the product or service. As a result of some change in a stimulus, the consumer may be better disposed to the product, has formed a better attitude towards it, or believes it can solve a particular consumption-related problem. Alternatively, the response may be in the form of an actual change in purchasing activity. The consumer may switch from one brand to another, or from one product category to another. Consumer responses may also take the form of a change in consumption practices, whereby the pattern of consumer behavior is changed. Supermarkets frequently offer incentives to get people to shop during slack periods of the week, which involves a change in shopping practice.

Generally speaking, a great deal of interest is focused on responses that involve buying or the disposition to buy. Manufacturers spend considerable sums of money in developing and promoting their products, creating brands, and otherwise designing marketing effort to influence consumer behavior in a particular way. At the same time, consumers may be more or less disposed to these efforts. Through the influence of external stimuli and internal processing mechanisms, a convergence may occur between consumer needs and wants, and the products and services provided. On other occasions, no such convergence occurs.

A key determinant of the extent to which consumers evaluate a brand is their **level of involvement**. Different buyers may engage in different types of decision-making processes depending on how highly involved they are with the product. High-involvement products for one buyer may be low-involvement products for another.

The level of involvement with any product depends on its perceived importance to the consumer's self-image. High-involvement products tend to be tied to self-image, whereas low-involvement products are not. A middle-aged consumer who feels (and wants to look) youthful may invest a great deal of time in her decision to buy a sport-utility vehicle instead of a station wagon. When purchasing an ordinary light bulb, however, she buys almost without thinking, because the purchase has nothing to do with self-image. The more visible, risky, or costly the product, the higher the level of involvement (Hollensen and Opresnik, 2020).

2.5 ANALYZING BUYING BEHAVIOR IN THE B2B MARKET

In one way or another, most large enterprises sell to other organizations. Companies such as Boeing, DuPont, IBM, Caterpillar, and countless other firms sell most of their products to other organizations. Even large consumer-products companies, which make products used by final consumers, must first sell their products to other enterprises. The business buying process can be described as the decision process by which business buyers determine which products and services their organizations need to purchase, and then find, evaluate, and choose among alternative suppliers and products. Consumer behavior relates to the buying behavior of individuals (or families) when purchasing products for their own use. Organizations buy to enable them to provide goods and services to the final customer. This has implications for marketing management, as we shall see later. Organizational buying behavior has many similarities to consumer behavior. Both encompass the behavior of human beings, whether individually or in groups. Organizational buyers do not necessarily act in a more rational manner than individual consumers. Organizational buyers are affected by environmental and individual factors, as outlined in the previous section. One of the main differences from consumer buying is that organizational buying usually involves group decision making (known as the `**decision-making unit** `(DMU) and sometimes referred to as the **buying centre**). In such a group, individuals may have different roles in the purchase process.

These can be categorized as (Anderson and Narus, 2004):

- **Initiator**: the person who first suggests making a purchase.

- **Influencers / evaluators**: people who influence the buying decision. They often help define specifications and provide information for evaluating options. Technical personnel are especially important as influencers.

- **Gatekeepers**: group members who regulate the flow of information. Frequently, the purchasing agent views the gatekeeping role as a source of his or her power. A secretary may also act as a gatekeeper by determining which vendors get an appointment with a buyer.

- **Decider**: the person who has the formal or informal power to choose or approve the selection of the supplier or brand. In complex situations, it is often difficult to determine who makes the final decision.

- **Purchaser**: the person who negotiates the purchase. It could be anyone from the president of the company to the purchasing agent, depending on the importance of the decision.

- **Users**: members of the organization who will use the product. Users often initiate the buying process and help define product specifications.

One person may play all the above roles in the purchase decision, or each role may be represented by a number of personnel. The salesperson trying to sell to an organization should be aware of the roles people assume in the buying centre. Another difference in organizational buying is that many products are more complex and require specialist knowledge to purchase. As many products are changed according to the specifications of the buyer there is more communication and negotiation between buyer and sellers. After-sales service is also very important in organizational buying and suppliers are often evaluated quite rigorously after purchase. In general, organizational markets have fewer, larger buyers who are geographically concentrated. Another aspect of organizational buying is the nature of derived demand. That is, demand for organizational (especially industrial) goods is derived from consumer markets. If demand for the end product consumer good falls, then this has an effect along the production line to all the inputs. So, in organizational marketing the end consumers should not be ignored, and trends should be monitored (Hollensen and Opresnik, 2020).

2.6 SWOT ANALYSIS

Successful SWOT analysis is basically a process of finding the optimum fit between the firm's controllable strengths and weaknesses and uncontrollable opportunities and threats of the firm's environment in which it operates; and not just today's environment, but also that of the predictable future. This explains why charting a SWOT profile (strengths, weaknesses, opportunities, and threats) is by one of the most popular marketing planning tools. It provides a means by which all the key internal (company-related) and external (environment-related) issues can be summarized at a glance. A sophisticated SWOT profile facilitates the development of a strategy that capitalizes on a company's strengths, minimises any weaknesses, exploits emerging opportunities and avoids, as far as possible, any threats. By carefully matching environmental trends to the firm's own distinctive competences the strategic market planner is able to develop strategies that build on the company's strengths, whilst at the same time minimising the weaknesses. By doing so, the marketer aims to achieve what is called a `**strategic fit** `(Hollensen, 2006).

The SWOT framework became popular during the 1970s because of its inherent assumption that managers can plan the alignment of a firm's resources with its environment. Subsequently, during the decade of the 1980s, Porter's (1980) introduction of the industrial organisation paradigm with his five forces /diamond models gave dominance to a firm's external environment, overshadowing the popularity of SWOT. In the 1990s, Barney (1991) reinvented SWOT as the foundation framework linking firm resources to sustained competitive advantage (Barney, 1991).

Figure 2.7 illustrates the `roots `back to the beginning of this book's chapter 2, in which there was a comprehensive discussion of roots of the Resource Based View RBC (inside-out) based on the firm's strengths and weaknesses and Market Orientation View MOV (outside-in based on the opportunities and threats in the environment). These roots in Chapter 2 now end up in this section where everything is concluded in form of the SWOT-analysis (Hollensen and Opresnik, 2020).

2.6.1 ELEMENTS OF A SWOT ANALYSIS

When implementing a SWOT analysis to devise a set of strategies, the following guidelines should be taken into account (Hollensen, 2006):

- **Strengths:** Determine your organisation's well-built points, from an internal perspective as well as from the perspective of the external customer. Key questions are as follows: Are there any unique or distinct advantages, which make the organisation stand out in the crowd? What makes the customers choose the organisation over the competition? Are there any products or services which the competition cannot imitate (both now and in the future)?

- **Weaknesses:** Determine the organisation's weaknesses, not only from an internal point of view, but also more importantly, from the external view of the customers. Key questions include: Are there any operations or procedures that can be streamlined? How and why do competitors operate more effective and efficient? Does the competition have a certain market segment occupied?

- **Opportunities:** Another key factor is to determine how the organisation can continue to grow within the marketplace. After all, opportunities are everywhere, such as changes in technology, government policy, social patterns, and so on. The most basic questions are as follows: Where and what are the attractive opportunities within the marketplace? Are there any new emerging trends within the market? What does the organisation predict in the future that may depict new opportunities?

- **Threats:** Threats are external factors and per definition uncontrollable. However, they are instrumental in the design of a sophisticated analysis. It is vital to be prepared and face threats even during unstable situations. Central questions with respect to threats include the following: What is the competition doing that is offsetting the organisational development? Are there any changes in consumer demand, which call for new requirements of products or services? Is the changing technology hurting the organisation's position within the marketplace?

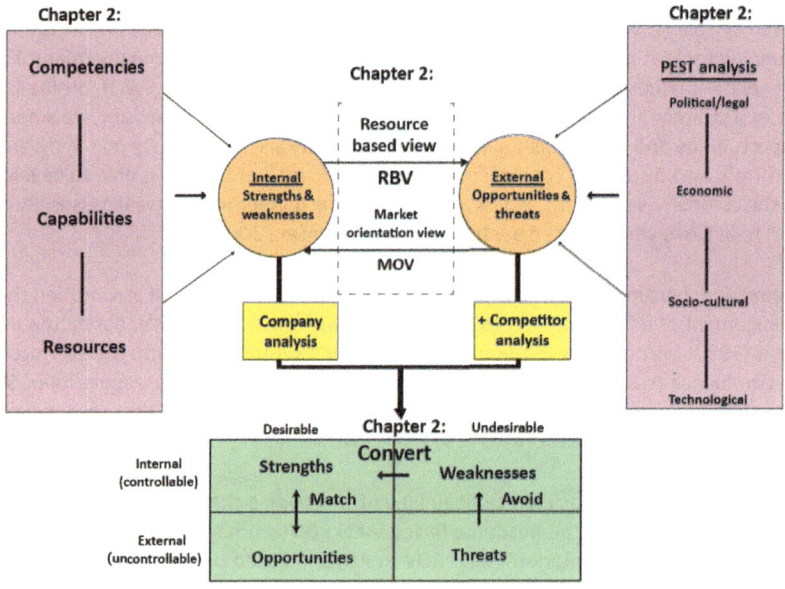

Figure 2.7: SWOT Analysis and the Structure of Chapter 2.
Source: Adapted from Hollensen and Opresnik, 2020, modified.

2.6.2 MATCHING AND CONVERGING IN THE SWOT MATRIX

SWOT analysis should function as a catalyst to facilitate and guide the creation of marketing strategies that will produce the preferred results. The process of organizing information within the SWOT analysis enables the company to discern new opportunities. In many ways, good marketing is the art of finding, developing, and profiting from opportunities. A **marketing opportunity** is an area of customer need and interest in which there is a high probability that a company can profitably satisfy that need (Hollensen and Opresnik, 2020).

To address these opportunities properly, the marketing manager should appraise every strength, weakness, opportunity, and threat to determine its total impact on the firm's marketing efforts. This assessment will also give the manager an idea of the basic strategic options available.

The following actions are those suggested by the SWOT matrix:

1. Make a match between strengths and opportunities
2. Convert weaknesses to strengths
3. Convert threats to opportunities
4. Minimise, if not avoid, weaknesses, and threats

2.6.3 APPLICATION OF THE SWOT ANALYSIS

The application of SWOT analysis is the matching of specific internal and external factors, which creates a strategic matrix. It is essential to emphasize that the internal factors are within the control of the organisation, such as operations, finance, marketing, and in other areas (See Figure 2.8). The external factors are out of the company's control, such as political and economic factors, technology, and competition. The four combinations are called the Maxi-Maxi (Strengths/Opportunities), Maxi-Mini (Strengths/Threats), Mini-Maxi (Weakness/Opportunities), and Mini-Mini (Weaknesses/Threats).

	Strengths (S)	Weaknesses (W)
Opportunities (O)	S / O	W / O
Threats (T)	S / T	W / T

Figure 2.8 The Application of the SWOT-Matrix.
Source: Adapted from Hollensen and Opresnik, 2020, modified.

1. **Maxi-Maxi (S/O):**

   This combination shows the organisation's strengths and opportunities. In essence, an organisation should strive to maximise its strengths to take advantage of new opportunities.

2. **Maxi-Mini (S/T):**

   This combination shows the organisation's strengths in consideration of threats, e.g., from competitors. In essence, an organisation should strive to use its strengths to evade or minimise threats.

3. **Mini-Maxi (W/O):**

This grouping displays the organisation's weaknesses in tandem with opportunities. It is an exertion to conquer the organisation's weaknesses by making the most out of new opportunities and challenges.

4. **Mini-Mini (W/T):**

This combination shows the company's weaknesses by comparison with the existing external threats. This is most definitely a protective strategy, to minimise an organisation's internal weaknesses and avoid external threats.

As mentioned earlier the SWOT analysis is the matching of specific internal and external factors. However, what about the matching items within internal factors and items within external factors. The primary reason this is not applied is that matching these factors will create strategies that do not make sense as strategies must have an external factor as a trigger in order for it to be feasible (Lee et al., 2000).

3. STRATEGY FORMULATION IN THE MARKETING PLANNING PROCESS

The word `strategy `is derived from the Greek term `strategós `and when it appeared in use during the EFU th century, it was seen in its narrow sense as the `art of the general `and `the art of arrangement `of troops. Military strategy deals with the planning and conduct of campaigns, the movement and disposition of forces, and the deception of the enemy. Thus, strategy originally referred to the skills and decision-making process of the general (executive), while `stratagem`, translated as `an operation or act of generalship`, and referred to a specific decision made by the executive (Hollensen and Opresnik, 2020).

3.1 STRATEGIC MARKETING PLANNING

Strategic planning is the process of developing and maintaining a strategic fit between the company`s goals and capabilities and its changing marketing opportunities.

Strategic marketing planning can contribute to the success of marketing in several ways such as the identification of possible opportunities and threats; the development of competitive advantages for the firm.

Planning is a complex process which consists of several inter-related stages. However, with time there is change and hence planning is and should be a continuous process, where each stage needs to be reconsidered for relevancy and in relation to the other stages. The plan is the stages `frozen `in time; the process is a continuous assessment of the relevancy of each of these stages with changes in time.

In planning, we look ahead to decide what to do. The planning process itself is a systematic way of approaching the following questions and they will be used as guidance for the rest of the chapter (Hollensen and Opresnik, 2020):

1. What business are we in? (Vision and Mission statement – section 3.1.1)
2. Where are we today (situation analysis – chapter 2)
3. Where do we want to go (strategic objectives – section 3.1.2)
4. How do we get there?
5. Estimation of planning gap and problem diagnosis (section 3.1.3)
6. The search for strategic alternatives (Ansoff's growth matrix, Porter's three generic strategies, the BCG and GE models – section 3.1.4 – 3.1.8)

NCC | NEWTECH CHEMICAL COMPANY

CASE STUDY
NEWTECH CHEMICAL COMPANY

THE MAGIC WAND OF MARKETING, TECHNICAL SUPPORT

Written by: Ulaş Emre Arslan (Chairman of the Board)

Introduction

NCC – Newtech Chemical Company is a company that operates in the chemical product market and acts with a focus for its growth day by day. NCC, which offers professional technical support and product supply, especially on the water treatment side, continues to be a sought-after address for industrial facilities. NCC has been successfully operating in the Turkish market for nearly 10 years, setting new standards in the country in terms of product diversity and services.

It has adopted the principle of continuous improvement to provide customers with the best technical development experience by helping the integration of modern technology facilities. As a socially responsible company, it supports its customers to lead a sustainable lifestyle by expanding its range of products and services that protect natural resources. Customers appreciate the company's activities, and it is determined as a result of the audits that it has a high value in terms of customer satisfaction in the necessary research.

Marketing Case and Solutions

Only 2 years after its establishment, NCC had to face the fact that it could not grow enough in the market by only selling products. In particular, it has become necessary to carry out a series of studies on which ways it should follow in order to distinguish itself from its competitors that are at least 100 times larger than itself. It felt the need to do thorough research on how the final customer perspectives and attitudes are driven.

What marketing methods should NCC have used to increase sales in the process? The whole story began to be written in response to the question posed here. Upon this question, the following quote from "Abraham LINCOLN" came to mind, and we began to sharpen our axe. "Give me six hours to chop down a tree, I will spend best four hours sharpening my axe."

All of these were serious challenges for a fledgling company. Here the following questions arose basically.

- How can we persuade a customer?
- Are we able to understand the basic needs of customers?
- Is it possible to act according to the basic needs of the customers?
- To what extent were demographic factors an effective parameter in the sale of the product?
- What should have been the form of advertisement spendings?
- What marketing methods should have been used?
- What marketing moves should have been used?

Solution

The company's key answer to these questions was to put the end user at the center and provide them with the best customer experience that no one has ever offered.

However, a top-notch customer experience can only exist if employees take pride in what they do.

That's why NCC first started working on improving the employee experience. It has shown a special focus on valuing his employees, developing, motivating, and empowering employees in a targeted manner, giving them personal advice and everything they need to provide excellent service in order to proudly carry NCC, the brand he serves. Compared to their competitors in the sector, all employees were provided with better opportunities to feel happy. While doing all these, environmental sensitivity was also given up most importance. For example, all vehicles purchased by the company were planned to be at least hybrid.

In this process, NCC rolled up its sleeves to reorganize its supply chain and especially the scope of technical support provided to its customers.

"Since the customer group it works with is predominantly industry, it has been determined how important the speed of technical support is in production processes. It has been determined by researches that today's customer portfolio attaches more importance to this service than the product price. In this context, NCC has earned the title of being the first and only company in its field that guarantees technical support to all its customers within 24 hours. And it maintains its feature of being the only company in Türkiye that provides services with this feature."

NCC's service promises are always fulfilled throughout the supply of all products. The new technical support service allows its customers to develop consciously and trust the company. Thanks to the 24-hour technical support it offers, it has become a company that offers first-class services that go beyond just selling products compared to its competitors.

Despite its B2B business model, NCC has focused its communication on the buyer and user of a product, from the sale of a product to the use of the product. It started to maintain communication with the customer from the moment the products were sent to the receipt of the products and the use of the product. Here, any problem experienced by the customer was seen as a problem of the NCC, eliminating you-us distinction and reinforcing the sense of ownership of the business.

NCC stands out as a company committed to sustainability. The brand sees its commitment to sustainability as both an obligation to contribute to a better future and a business opportunity, continuously strengthening the sustainability of its business operations and providing customers with easy access to a more sustainable lifestyle.

The company increasingly adds energy-efficient and sustainable certified products to its product range, takes certain actions to significantly reduce its own carbon footprint. It is constantly developing and delivering new sustainable services that extend the life of products and conserve resources by adding more products to the circular economy and significantly extending the life cycle of products.

The company has based its ESG (Environmental, Social, Governance) strategy on three pillars that are important to both company operations and actual environmental impact. These are:

1. **People are at the heart of NCC's business.** NCC uses all the necessary tools of technology to ensure that everyone is oriented towards a sustainable future.

2. **NCC offers zero-emission targeted trade.** Continuous improvement of technology and continuous optimization enable the company to set ambitious goals even in such a complex area as climate change prevention and climate adaptation.

3. **NCC constantly motivates employees and business partners.** Acting on the principle of "If we want to change our world, we must first change people", NCC provides knowledge, competence, confidence in their skills and a willingness to share their experiences with others. NCC wants to produce and grow together with its stakeholders.

Although all these have formed the basic building blocks, as a result of the actual details, the final positive results have emerged with the actions taken and stated below.

- **Making monthly visits with CRM integration** – The CRM system has been redesigned to be more efficient and put into use within the company to provide better service to our customers, to follow up the service provided and to follow up internal organizations.

- **KPI measurements and restructuring of internal organizations** – KPI measurements have started to be made for a more detailed evaluation of the performance of employees. Here, customer feedback has also started to play an important role in KPI.

- **Corporate identity design revised** – The company's aging and hard-to-use logo has been revised by the graphic design studio and renewed in the company's corporate image. Here, the company's service area-specific design language and color palette were determined.

- **Revamping the website design** – The company's website has been revised to be mobile-friendly and has blog posts, and a user-friendly design has been introduced.

- **Creating a Blog** – By sharing technical information for users on the company website, technical information was provided to end users, benefiting the awareness of the company.

- **Seo Studies** – Seo studies were carried out to be on the first page and in the top 3 results in search engines in the product groups sold.

- **Web Ads** – Ads were placed until they were organically placed in the top 3 positions in search results in search engines, allowing the company to appear at the top in this process.

- **Swot Analysis** – The Swot Analysis of the company was reviewed, and more detailed and more reliable results were obtained. In this way, Strengths, Weaknesses, Opportunities and Threats were correctly identified, and the right actions were taken.

- **SMART** – Actions to be taken were made sure to follow SMART goals.

- 4P – 4C – 4E –> The transition from 4 – P to 4 – E, which are the basic rules of marketing, was made and the different demands of the customers were studied in detail.

- The marketing policies were reviewed in certain time periods and some strategies were changed out of necessity.

Conclusion

As a result of all these, the NCC brand has become the company that has reached the largest market share in the mining industry and providing the best technical support. Listening to consumer needs and using university-industry collaboration to find solutions to these needs has created a solid foundation of trust in consumers. It has become clear that the company is growing with references resulting from customer experience rather than its own marketing activities. As a result of all these actions, NCC has become the 9th fastest growing company in Türkiye between 2017-2019 and the fastest growing company in the chemical sector. At the same time, it provides the product supply and technical support of the "Büyük Körfez Projesi", which is Türkiye's Largest Environmental Project, on its own.

Questions to stimulate conversation on the case

1. How do marketing and technical support relate?

Both are critical to customer satisfaction and loyalty. Technical support ensures that customers use the product or service smoothly and provides a positive customer experience. Marketing highlights these positive experiences to attract new customers and retain existing ones.

2. How can marketing teams collaborate better with technical support teams?

Regular communication, joint review of customer feedback, setting common goals, and collaborating at all stages of the customer journey are essential.

3. How can technical support be used to market a product?

Customer feedback can be used to highlight product strengths and improve weaknesses. Additionally, the expertise of the technical support team can support marketing efforts by conducting product training and webinars.

Links and media

https://www.ncc.com.tr

Highlights

The marketing plan is as important as the tactical plan of a war.

From a market that was not yet saturated, a saturated market was reached after all strategies. At the end of this period, new marketing strategies are being prepared to protect existing customers and open up to new markets.

With the consensus formed within the team, the fact that "The easiest way for a company to grow is to sell new products to the existing customer" was adopted.

Make all your partners feel special and differentiate from others.

We do scientific studies. (University-Industry Collaborations)

The most important factor that distinguishes us from our competitors is to add value to our customers with university-industry cooperation projects at every point of our business. We are constantly conducting research on technical, scientific, and technological issues.

We really love our jobs.

Perhaps this is the sole reason for our success. Because we know that when you love a job, you work to improve yourself even more and be more successful in that field. Everyone in the NCC team loves their job and strives to improve in their own fields.

We are constantly researching to be better at our job.

We are constantly conducting research on technical, scientific, and technological topics, more than our competitors. We try to keep up with innovative ideas and solutions in these areas and adapt them so that they become usable materials for our customers.

We always turn our face outward.

Unlike our competitors, most of our personnel are people or teams who have signed important projects at home and abroad. By reaching out to these people, we are constantly trying to better understand how our work is done outside. When we do R&D work for a project, we first try to solve our customer's job in the easiest way and with minimum cost.

We produce solutions, not excuses.

We know very well that the work we are trying to do is more difficult than expected. While carrying out important projects of many different companies at the same time, we encounter various problems. But rather than looking for excuses as to why these problems can't be solved, we focus on how to solve them. That's why we produce "solutions", not "excuses", while carrying out these projects.

We work in a disciplined and programmed manner.

Regardless of the sector you serve, no matter how your working conditions are arranged, we believe that if you want to be successful in that field, you must work in a disciplined manner within the framework of certain programs. We organize the workflow for every project we work on, and we take care that all our employees, including the project team, are loyal to this process.

3.1.1 VISION AND MISSION STATEMENT

The **vision and mission** are interlinked but different concepts (Hollensen and Opresnik, 2020):

1. A business mission statement describes 'Who we are and what the overall purpose of our businesses is? It is a company's reason for being and reflects people's idealistic motivations for doing the company's work by capturing the soul of the organization. The core purpose or mission of a company is like a 'guiding star' on the horizon continuously providing direction and inspiring change. It is important to state that mission statements should not only be defined in technology terms (i.e., 'We make and sell furniture') but with respect to the market and in terms of customer needs as products and technologies eventually become outdated, but basic market needs may last forever. For example, the mission of Akbank, one of the leaders of the Turkish banking industry, is not simply to provide banking services, but to "create lasting and high value for all stakeholders through financial solutions and reliability".

2. A **business vision statement** describes 'Where we wish to go,' 'What do we wish to become?' It provides a mental image of the successful accomplishment of the mission. It is typically:

   1. Short
   2. Idealistic, imaginative, and long-term oriented
   3. Inspires enthusiasm.
   4. Ambitious

The rest of this section will primarily be about the mission: Mission reflects unique qualities of the program.

Whether the organisation is a large corporation or a small non-profit agency, its mission statement visibly articulates its strategic scope. The mission statement should answer fundamental questions such as, 'What is our business?', 'Who are our constituencies?', 'What value do we provide customers, employees, suppliers, and other constituent groups? 'and 'What should our business be in the future? 'Senior management in all businesses needs to answer such questions. The responsibility for developing and articulating a mission statement is at the corporate level.

Mission statements should be driven by three factors: heritage, resources, and environment (Hollensen, 2006):

1. The organisation's heritage is about its history – what is the story behind the founding of the firm, where it has been, what it has done well, and what it has done poorly. A superior mission statement cannot ignore previous events and how they shaped the organisation. It also must be sensitive to the organisation's image in the minds of its constituencies. Past successes should be extended, past failures avoided, and the organisation's current image must be addressed realistically.

2. Resources refer to everything the organisation can manage, such as cash reserves, recognized brands, unique technologies, and talented employees. Resources can also include borrowing power, existing relationships with distributors, and excess plant capacity. A good mission statement notes the organisation's resources and sets paths that are compatible with what the organisation has at its disposal. As in the case of heritage, mission statements that are out of touch with organisation's resources elicit scepticism and can do more harm than good. If a minor regional brand were to include 'penetrating Asian markets' in its mission statement, it would be met with substantial scepticism.

3. The environment is everything happening currently that affects the company's ability to achieve objectives or implement strategies, both inside and outside the organisation. Some environmental factors are temporary, such as the floods that devastated parts of the country. Most temporary factors are too short-sighted to be considered in a mission statement. Other factors, however, such as changes in the

political system, rising inflation, terror acts, rise or fall of oil prices may have a longer life and should be considered in the mission statement if they affect the organisation's ability to survive and prosper.

At the corporate level, the mission statement defines the organisation's business and reflects fundamental beliefs about its strengths and weaknesses, as well as its environment.

3.1.2 STRATEGIC OBJECTIVES

Strategic management also requires that firms set strategic objectives-specific and measurable performance standards for strategically important areas. The company's mission needs to be turned into detailed supporting objectives for each level of management. Each manager should have objectives and be responsible for reaching them (Hollensen and Opresnik, 2020).

An organisation cannot set realistic, realizable objectives until it has the requisite information but, on the basis of experience, marketing management will nonetheless have tentative on sales volume, market share or whatever indicators represent progress towards accomplishing the firm's vision. What exactly this tentative will be influenced by subjective estimates of what is considered reasonable at the time in relation to what resources are likely to be available.

For a manager to be able to direct an activity towards the achievement of some objectives it must be possible to imagine the goal in a way that is meaningful for guiding the activity. This is why objectives purely in terms of profit are inadequate; they offer too little direction (Hollensen and Opresnik, 2020).

Strategic objectives can be stated in terms of different criteria, such as sales, market share or return on investment, or they can be stated in absolute or relative terms. To be effective, objectives must be specific in terms of:

1. the performance dimension being measured.
2. the measures most appropriate for the performance dimension
3. the target value for each measure
4. the time by which the target should be achieved.

3.1.3 ESTIMATION OF THE PLANNING GAP AND PROBLEM DIAGNOSIS

What do the 'facts suggest will be the future if the firm takes no action to change current strategies? Such a prediction is known as a 'reference projection'. A reference projection is the future that can be expected in the absence of planned change. The reference projection is compared with some 'target projection 'or the set of tentative goals, which the company sets for itself. The **planning gap (performance gap)** is the difference between the target and the reference projections (see Figure 3.1).

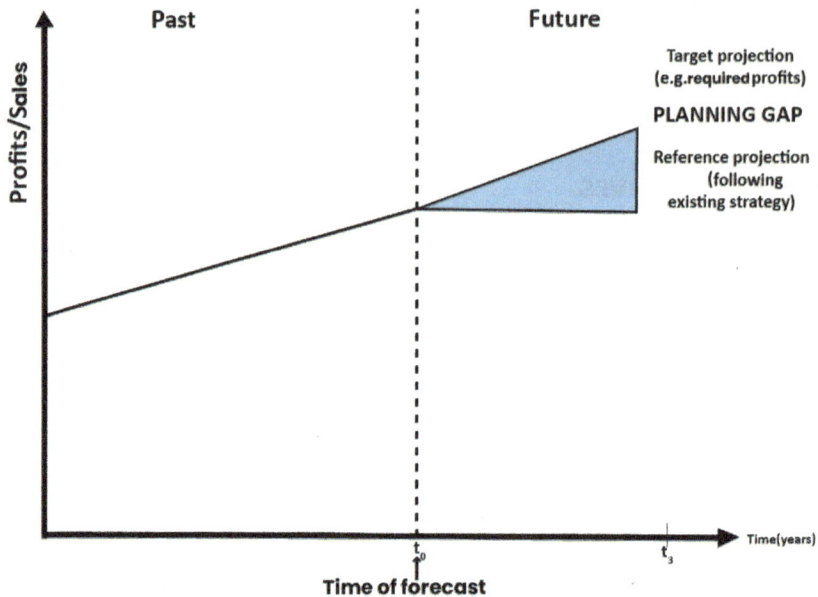

Figure 3.1: Illustration of the planning gap.
Source: Adapted from Hollensen and Opresnik, 2020, modified.

The gap may stem from the difference between future desired profit objectives and a forecast of expected profit based on past performance and following existing strategy.

In the face of such a planning gap, a number of options are available; the intention, however, is to close the gap. For example, the gap could be closed by revising objectives in a downward way. Such a step might be taken where the initial objectives are unrealistic. Alternatively, or in addition, the gap could be closed by actions designed to move the company off the projection curve and towards the desired curve.

The planning gaps identified will depend on which performances are of interest. At the highest level, it could be cash flow projections, economic value added, earnings per share, sales and market share or various financial indices like return on investment (ROI). At the marketing level, it would be in terms of sales, market share, costs, or various behavioral indices like buyer attitudes (Hollensen and Opresnik, 2020).

Problem Diagnosis

If a company has a large planning gap, we speak freely of its being the problem. More accurately, the planning gap is not the problem but the symptom of one. The recognition of a problem situation is not in itself the identification of the actual problem. We do not discover a problem but diagnose one. For example, a drop in monthly sales is a symptom. But there can be many reasons behind the drop in sales. The real cause is the problem itself. Problem diagnosis aims at identifying the type of solution that applies which is the first step on the road to developing an actual solution, just as diagnosing a failure to start the car as being due to some electrical fault, is the first step towards getting the car started again. Unfortunately, different people will make different diagnosis, depending on their experience, professional expertise, and their concerns.

We cannot recognize a problem without understanding what would count as a solution, just as we cannot comprehend an objective without accepting what would count as the achievement of it. The actual problem that is addressed depends somewhat on which individual or group can make the problem, as they see it, count. But all management stakeholders in a company are influenced by believable arguments and so true technical expertise usually succeeds. Hopefully, it must for if the wrong problem is addressed, the wrong decisions are made, and this can be more wasteful of resources than solving the right problem in an inefficient way. Although we hesitate to acknowledge it, the fact is that once we move away from some pure deductive system like mathematics, we are in the realm of persuasion where persuasive rhetoric is crucial so that a dramatic description of what is considered to be the problem can emotionally compel attention and often our assent (Hollensen, 2006).

3.1.4 THE SEARCH FOR STRATEGY ALTERNATIVES FOR CLOSING PLANNING GAP

The strategic options for closing the planning gap should not only fit the challenging situation and take account of trends and competition but should also take advantage of the firm's core competencies and strengths.

The strategy search process should always allow for the possibility of inspiration, which may beat anything arrived at by systematic analysis. It is not uncommon for someone to come up with an idea that is instantly recognizable as being the right answer.

The inspired solution is thus accepted, not because it saves time but because it is perceived to be advanced and effective. This said, the identification of appropriate strategies rests on having the requisite experience and the content of the strategy, not procedure, is all-important. Where the requisite experience is lacking, the search for strategies becomes opaque (Hollensen, 2006).

3.1.5 ANSOFF'S GENERIC STRATEGIES FOR GROWTH

One aspect of strategic management is the development of precise strategies for achieving company objectives. Strategies must respond to the environment and provide specific guidelines for decision-making. Because companies face unique combinations of internal and external factors, the strategies developed by any one organisation are unlikely to be entirely adaptable to any other organisation.

At a more general level, however, it is possible to discern recurring patterns in the strategies adopted by organisations. These recurring patterns are called generic strategies. These strategies are general strategies that the firm takes to grow. So, if we elaborate on the 'planning 'gap in Figure 3.1 we get what is illustrated in Figure 3.2 where the 'gap 'is filled up with **Ansoff's expansion-strategies** (Hollensen and Opresnik, 2020).

	Current products	New products
Current markets	**Market penetration strategies** • Increase market share • Increase product share • Increase frequency of use • Increase quantity used • New applications	**Product development strategies** • Product improvements • Product-line extensions • New products for same market
New markets	**Market development strategies** • Expand markets for existing products • Geographic expansion • Target new segments/customer groups	**Diversification strategies** • Vertical integration • Diversification into related businesses (concentric diversification) • Diversification into unrelated businesses (conglomerate diversification)

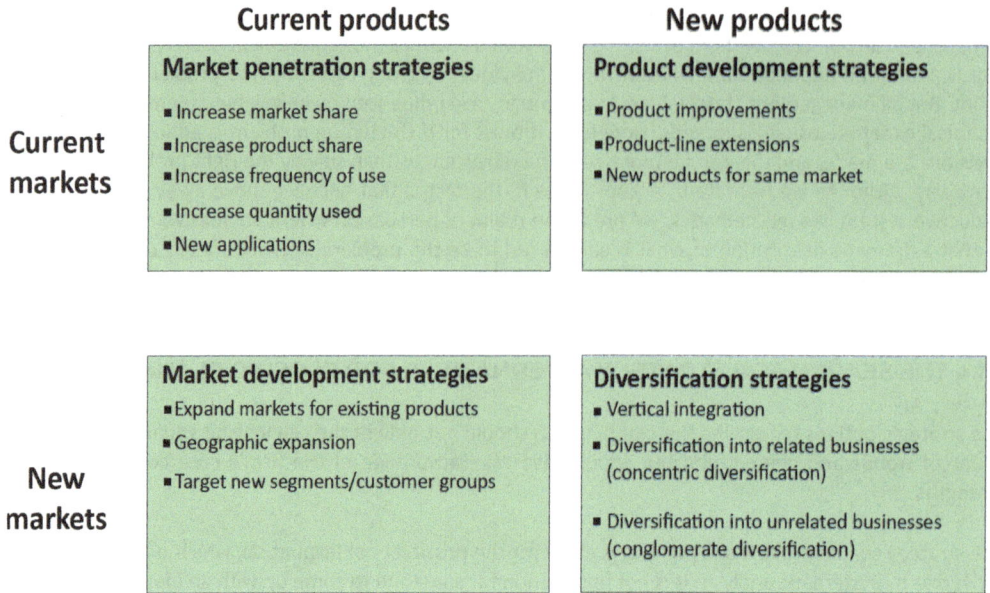

Figure 3.2: Filling the 'planning gap' with Ansoff's strategies.
Source: Adapted from Hollensen and Opresnik, 2020, modified.

Market Penetration

Organisations seeking to grow by gaining a larger market share in their current industry or market follow a penetration strategy. Following alternatives are available:

1. Increase market share on current markets with current products.

2. Increase product share (Increase frequency of use, increase quantity used, new applications).

The most basic method of gaining market penetration in existing markets with current products is by winning competitor's customers. This may be achieved by more effective use of the marketing mix, e.g., by more valuable promotion, distribution, or by cutting prices. For instance, if Kahve Dünyası, a major competitor of Starbucks in the Turkish market, doubles the number of its branches in the market, this is market penetration through distribution channels. If the firm prefers to increase its market share by increasing its communication in the market through an intensive advertising campaign, then it is implementing a market penetration strategy by using a promotion strategy.

Other strategic options in terms of market penetration involve buying competitors and to protect the penetration already gained by discouraging competitive entry. **Market entry barriers (MEB)** can be created by cost advantages (lower labour costs, access to raw materials, economies of scale), high switching costs (the costs of changing from an existing supplier to a new supplier, for example), high marketing expenditures and displaying aggressive tendencies to retaliate (Hollensen and Opresnik, 2020).

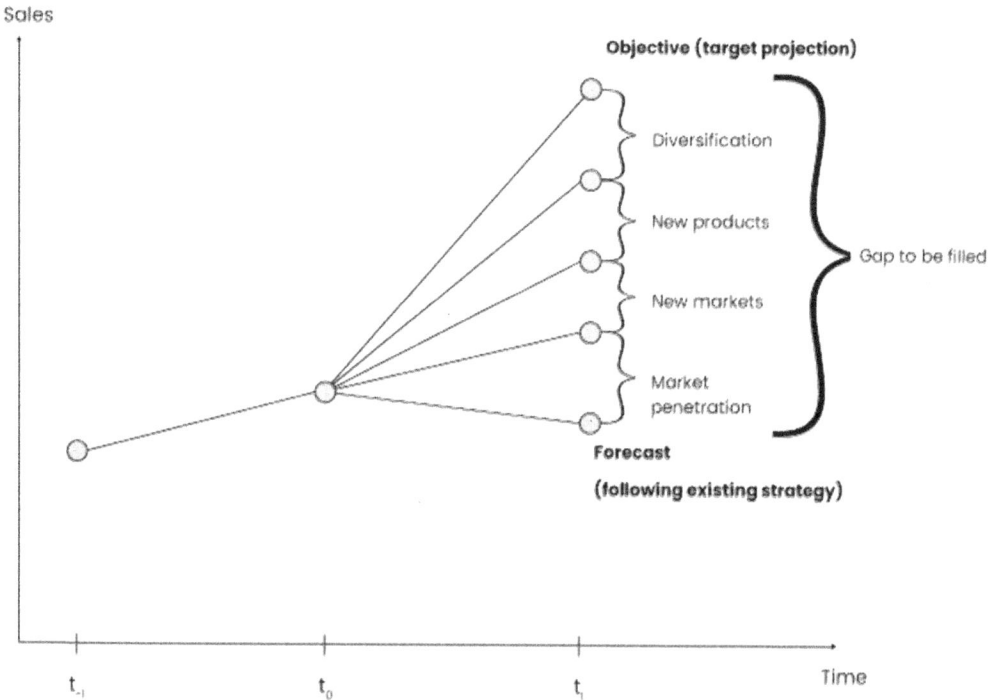

Figure 3.3 Product Market Expansion

Penetration strategies can be very successful when the company has a technological or production advantage that allows it to take market share away from competitors while still operating profitably. However, such strategies can also be very costly if they rely primarily on setting prices below those of competing products.

Market Development Strategies

Market development entails the promotion of new uses of existing products to new customers, or the marketing of existing products and their current uses to new market segments. The strategy involves the following strategic possibilities:

1. Geographic expansion (new countries/regions)
2. New segments/customer groups

For instance, the entry of Mavi Jeans, a Turkish brand that initially started its life as a local brand, into the American and European markets is an example of geographic expansion market development. On the other hand, Mavi Jeans' entry into the children's market and the introduction of jeans and t-shirts for children is an example of new segment market development.

Market development is also feasible through entering new segments by involving the search for overseas opportunities. The growth of markets in China, India, Russia, and Eastern Europe is providing major market development opportunities for all sorts of business (Ellis-Chadwick and Jobber, 2016).

Product Development Strategies

Organisations can also remain within their established industries or markets and seek extension by introducing new products or services in current markets. This is also called a **technology development strategy**.

The strategy may take the following forms (Ellis-Chadwick and Jobber, 2016):

1. In the case of **product-line extensions** customers are given greater choice. For example, the original iPod has been followed by the launches of the iPod nano, shuffle, and touch, giving its target market of young music lovers greater choice in terms of size, price, and capacity. When new features are added trading up may occur, with customers buying the enhanced-value product. However, companies implementing this strategy need to beware of **cannibalization** which can be defined as a new product that reduces the market share of an existing product more than expected. To avoid this, marketers need to adjust their pricing strategies accordingly.

2. **Product replacement strategies** involve the replacement of old brands/products with new ones, often based on technology change. The company thus replaces an old product with an innovation although both may be marketed side by side for a time.

3. **Product development strategies** are in peril if competitors can easily copy the new product being introduced by using lower manufacturing or delivery costs. They can be at the risk of cannibalization if the products are not different enough from existing products to inspire demand.

Diversification Strategies

Pursuing a growth strategy by introducing new products or technologies in new markets or industries is called **diversification**. The following alternatives are available:

1. **Vertical integration** (forward/ backward integration in distribution channel)
2. Diversification into related businesses (**concentric/horizontal diversification**)
3. Diversification into unrelated businesses (**conglomerate/lateral diversification**)

The term 'diversification' is frequently associated with expansion into areas unrelated to the company's current operations in order to offset cyclical downturns in one area with cyclical growth in other areas. Diversification was popular with many large companies in the 1970s and gave rise to legendary conglomerates.

The entry into new markets is the riskiest option, especially when the entry strategy is not based on the core competencies of the business. However, it can also be highly rewarding, as exemplified by Honda's move from motorcycles to cars based on its core competences in engines (Ellis-Chadwick and Jobber, 2016). On the other hand, diversification into related business is the strategy with the least risk but the lowest return. Which diversification strategy a firm chooses depends on its resources and strategic objectives.

3.1.6 PORTER'S GENERIC STRATEGIES

According to Porter (1985), forging successful strategy begins with understanding of what is happening in one's industry and deciding which of the available competitive niches one should attempt to dominate. For example, a company may discover that the largest competitor in an industry is aggressively pursuing cost leadership, that others are trying the differentiation route, and that no one is attempting to focus on some small specialty market. On the basis of this information, the firm might sharpen its efforts to distinguish its product from others or switch to a focus approach. As Porter states, the idea is to position the firm 'so it won't be slugging it out with everybody else in the industry; if it does it right, it won't be directly toe-to-toe with anyone'. The objective is to mark out a defensible competitive position – defensible not just against rival companies but also against the forces driving industry competition.

What it means is that the give-and-take between firms already in the business represents only one such force.

Others are the bargaining power of suppliers, the bargaining power of buyers, the threat of substitute products or services, and the threat of new entrants (**Porter's five-forces model**).

Combining the dimensions of distinctive advantage and business cope (broad versus narrow) in a matrix, results in the strategic typology illustrated in Figure 3.4.: differentiation, cost leadership, differentiation focus, and cost focus.

A **cost leadership strategy** involves the achievement of the lowest cost position in an industry. The company serves segments in the industry and directs great importance to minimising costs on all fronts. For example, Sinbo, a Turkish manufacturer of small household appliances, is a brand that has adopted cost leadership in its industry with its vision of "quality products at affordable prices" as a principle. Walmart is also a cost leader, which allows the company the option of charging lower prices than its competitors to achieve higher sales and yet achieve comparable profit margins, or to match competitor's prices and attain higher profit margins (Ellis-Chadwick and Jobber, 2016). A101, which operates in the same sector in Türkiye, is one of the retailers implementing the cost leadership strategy.

A **differentiation strategy** involves the selection of one or more choice criteria that are used by many customers in an industry. The company aims at uniquely positioning itself to meet these criteria better than the competition. The goal is usually to differentiate in a way that leads to a price premium in excess of the cost of differentiating. Differentiation gives customers a reason to prefer one product or service over another. Nokia, for example, became market leader in mobile phones by being the first to realize that they were fashion items and to design stylish phones to differentiate the brand from its competitors. Hewlett-Packard adopted this strategic orientation when the market for handheld calculators was in the early stages. Hewlett-Packard calculators were more expensive than Texas Instruments products, but their technology and performance were superior. In later years, Texas Instrument matched the performance and technological features of Hewlett- Packard calculators while retaining its cost leadership, forcing Hewlett-Packard to reduce its prices.

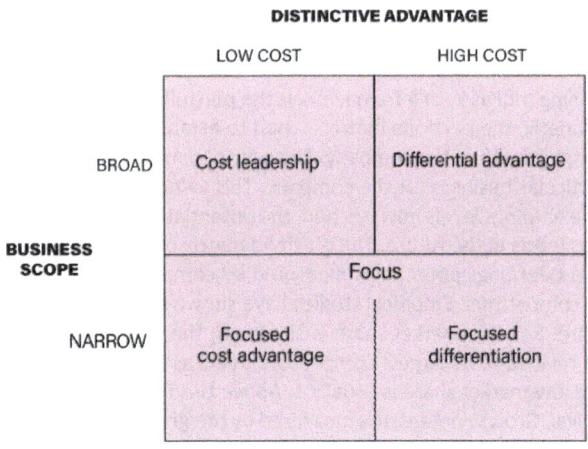

Figure 3.4 Porter's Generic Strategies.
Source: Adapted from Hollensen Opresnik, 2020, modified.

Within the framework of a **cost focus strategy**, a company seeks a cost advantage with one or a small number of target market segments. Examples of cost focusers are easy Jet and Ryanair, who focus on short-haul flights with a basic product trimmed to reduce costs (Ellis-Chadwick and Jobber, 2016).

With the **focused differentiation strategy**, a company aims to differentiate within one or a small number of target segments. The specific needs of the particular segment suggest that there is an opportunity to differentiate the product offering from the competition's, which may be targeting a broader group of customers. For example, Maxx Royal Resorts focuses on a very small percent of corporate and leisure travelers. The company applies a differentiation strategy in the hospitality industry with the promise of offering unique experiences and personalized services to its visitors.

The essence of corporate success, then, is to choose a generic strategy and pursue it consistently. Below-average performance results in a **stuck-in the-middle position**. Sears and Holiday Inn encountered difficult times because they did not stand out as the lowest in cost, highest in perceived value, or best in serving some specific market segment.

3.1.7 THE BCG PORTFOLIO MATRIX MODEL

A major activity in strategic planning is business portfolio analysis, whereby management evaluates the products and business units making up the company. The firm aims at putting strong resources into its more profitable businesses and phase down or drop its weaker ones. The first step within the process is to identify the key strategic business units. A **strategic business unit (SBU)** is a unit of the company that has a separate mission, objectives, budget, and target market and that can be planned independently from other company businesses. An SBU can be a company division, a product line within a division, or a single product, service, or brand (Hollensen and Opresnik, 2020).

The next step in business portfolio analysis is to assess the attractiveness of its various SBUs and decide how much support each one deserves. A good planning system must guide the development of strategic alternatives for each of the company's current businesses and new business possibilities. It must also provide for management's review of these strategic alternatives and for corresponding resource allocation decisions. The result is a set of approved business plans that, taken as a whole, represent the direction of the firm. This process starts with, and its success is largely determined by, the creation of sound strategic alternatives.

The top management of a multi-business firm cannot generate these strategic alternatives. It must rely on the managers of its business ventures and on its corporate development personnel. However, top management can and should establish a conceptual framework within which these alternatives can be developed. The best-known portfolio planning tool as such a framework is the portfolio matrix associated with the **Boston Consulting Group (BCG)**. Briefly, the portfolio matrix is used to establish the best mix of businesses to maximise the long-term earnings growth of the company. The portfolio matrix concept addresses the issue of the potential value of a particular business for the company. This value has two variables: first, the potential for generating attractive earnings levels now; second, the potential for growth or, in other words, for significantly increased earnings levels in the future. The portfolio matrix concept holds that these two variables can be quantified. Current earnings potential is measured by comparing the market position of the business relative to that of its competitors. Empirical studies have shown that profitability is directly determined by **relative market share**. Relative market share is shown on the horizontal axis and refers to the market share of each product relative to its largest competitor. It acts as a proxy for competitive strength. The division between high and low market share is usually 1. Above this figure a product line has a market share greater than its largest rival. Growth potential is measured by the **growth rate of the market** segment in which the business operates. Clearly, if the segment is in the decline stage of its life cycle, the only way the business can increase its market share is by taking volume away from competitors. Within this framework, market growth rate is used as a proxy for market attractiveness (Ellis-Chadwick and Jobber, 2016).

Figure 3.5 shows a matrix with its two sides labelled market growth rate and relative market share. The area of each circle represents sales. The market share position of each circle is determined by its horizontal position. Each circle's product sales growth rate (corrected for inflation) in the market in which it competes is shown by its vertical position.

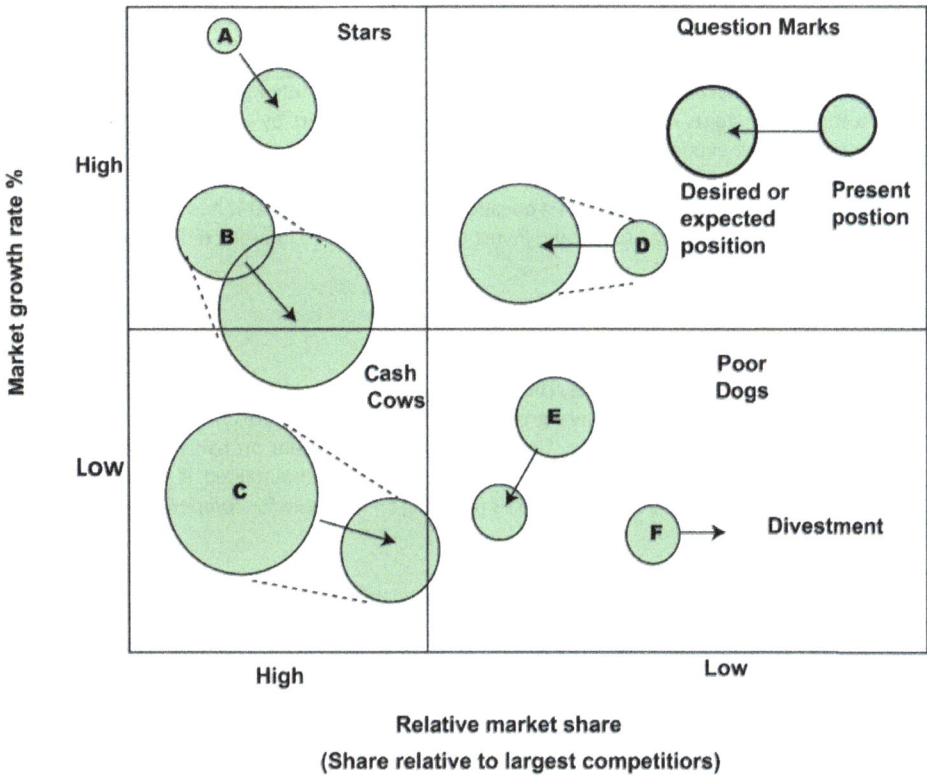

Figure 3.5: The BCG-Model.
Source: Adapted from Hollensen and Opresnik, 2020, modified.

With regard to the two axes of the matrix, relative market share is plotted on a logarithmic scale in order to be consistent with the **experience curve effect**, which implies that profit margin or rate of cash generation differences between two competitors tends to be proportionate to the ratio of their competitive positions. A linear axis is used for growth for which the most generally useful measure is volume growth of the business concerned; in general, rates of cash use should be directly proportional to growth (Hollensen, 2006).

Using the two dimensions discussed here in Figure 3.5, one can classify businesses and products into four basic categories.

Businesses in each category, exhibit different financial characteristics and offer different strategic choices (Ellis-Chadwick and Jobber, 2016):

1. **Question Marks**

Question marks are low-share business units in high-growth markets. Because of growth, these products require more cash than they are able to generate on their own. If nothing is done to increase market share, a question mark will simply absorb large amounts of cash in the short run and later, as the growth slows down, become a – poor – dog. Thus, unless something is done to change its perspective, a question mark remains a cash loser throughout its existence and ultimately becomes a cash trap.

Against this background, the company faces a fundamental choice: to increase investment (**building strategy**) to attempt to turn the question marks into stars. Because the business is growing, it can be funded to dominance. It may then become a star and later, when growth slows down, a cash cow. This strategy is a costly one in the short run. An abundance of cash must be poured into a question mark in order for it to win a major share of the market, but in the long run this strategy is the only way to develop a sound business from the question mark stage. Another strategy is to withdraw support by either **harvesting** (raising price while lowering marketing expenditure) or **divesting** (dropping or selling it). In a few cases it may be viable to find a small market segment (**niche strategy**) where dominance can be achieved. Unilever, for example, identified its specialty chemicals business as a question mark. It realized that it had to invest heavily or exit the market. Unilever's decision was to sell and invest the billions raised in predicted future winners such as personal care and dental products.

2. Stars

High-growth market leaders are called stars. They are likely to be profitable because they are market leaders but require substantial investment to finance growth and to meet competitive challenges. Overall, cash flow is therefore likely to be roughly in balance. Thus, star products represent probably the best profit opportunity available to a company, and their competitive position must be maintained. If a star is allowed to fall because of cutbacks in investment and rising prices (creating an umbrella for competitors) the star will ultimately become a – poor – dog.

The appropriate strategic objective is to build sales and/or market share. Resources should be invested to maintain/increase the leadership position and competitive challenges should be repelled. The ultimate value of any product or service is reflected in the stream of cash it generates net of its own reinvestment. For a star, this stream of cash lies in the future. To obtain real value, the stream of cash must be discounted back to the present at a rate equal to the return on alternative opportunities. It is the future payoff of the star that counts, not the present reported profit. Stars are the cash cows of the future and need to be protected. For example, for Vestel, one of Türkiye's most R&D-invested brands, the television is the star as the locomotive product in which the brand keeps investing.

3. Cash Cows

Cash cows are market leaders in mature (low growth) markets. High market share leads to high profitability and low market growth means that investment – in new production facilities – is minimal. This leads to a large positive cash flow. As a result, these businesses generate cash surpluses that help to pay dividends and interest, provide debt capacity, supply funds for research and development, meet overheads, and make cash available for investment in other products. Consequently, cash cows are the foundation on which everything else depends. These products must be protected. Technically speaking, a cash cow has a return on assets that exceeds its growth rate. Only if this is true will the cash cow generate more cash than it uses. Consequently, the appropriate **strategic objective is to hold** sales and market share. The excess cash that is generated should be used to fund stars, question marks that are being built, and research and development for new products. The products of companies with classic and regular customers are usually in this class. For example, Ülker chocolate wafer is a strategic business unit that has become a classic for the Ülker brand but has maintained its market share for years.

4. Poor Dogs

Products with low market share positioned in low-growth situations are called – poor – dogs. Their insufficient competitive position condemns them to poor profits. Because growth is low, dogs have little potential for gaining sufficient share to achieve viable cost positions. Usually, they are net users of cash. Their earnings are low, and the reinvestment required just to keep the business together consumes cash inflow. The business, therefore, is likely to regularly absorb cash unless further investment is rigorously avoided. For those products that achieve second or third position in the marketplace (cash dogs) a small positive cash flow may result, and for a few others it may be possible to reposition the product into a **defendable niche**. But for the bulk of dogs the appropriate strategic objective is to **harvest** to generate positive cash flow for a time, or to **divest**, which allows resources to be allocated elsewhere. GE's consumer electronics business had been in the dog category, maintaining only a small percentage of the available market in a period of slow growth, when the company decided to unload the business (including the RCA brand acquired in late 1985) to Thomson, France's state-owned, leading electronics manufacturer (Hollensen, 2006).

In summary, the portfolio matrix approach provides for the simultaneous comparison of different products. It also underlines the importance of cash flow as a strategic variable. Thus, when continuous long-term growth in earnings is the objective, it is necessary to identify high-growth product/market segments early, develop businesses, and pre-empt the growth in these segments. If necessary, short-term profitability in these segments may be forgone to ensure achievement of the dominant share. Costs must be managed to meet scale-effect standards. The appropriate point at which to shift from earnings focus to a cash flow focus must be determined and a liquidation plan for cash flow maximisation established. A **cash-balanced mix** of businesses should be maintained (Hollensen, 2006).

3.1.8 THE GE-MATRIX MULTI FACTOR PORTFOLIO MATRIX

The BCG-model discussed above provides a useful approach for reviewing the roles of different products in a company. As stated above, however, the matrix approach leads to many difficulties. Stimulated by this success and some of the weaknesses of the model (particularly the criticism of its over simplicity) McKinsey & Co developed a more wide-ranging Market Attractiveness-Competitive Position (MA-CP) model in conjunction with General Electric (GE) in the USA.

Instead of using market growth rare alone, a range of market attractiveness criteria were used, such as market size, market growth rate, beatable rivals, market entry barriers, social, political, and legal factors. Similarly, instead of using only the relative market share as a measure for competitive strength, a number of factors were used, such as relative market share, reputation, distribution capability, market knowledge, service quality, innovation capability and cost advantages. The framework discussed here may be applied to either a product/market or an SBU. As a matter of fact, it may be equally applicable to a much higher level of aggregation in the organisation, such as a division or a group. Management is permitted to decide which criteria are applicable for their products.

After depicting the criteria, management's next task is to agree upon a weighting system for each set of criteria, with those factors that are most important having a higher weighting, for example ten points to be shared. How much weight to be given to which items may differ according to the industry and the company. Next management assesses the particular market for the product under examination on each of the factors, for example, on a scale from 1-10. By multiplying each weighting by its corresponding rating, and then summing, a total score indicating the overall attractiveness of the market for the product under examination is obtained. The same kind of process is then applied in the framework of the competitive strength assessment. Finally, the market attractiveness and competitive strength scores for the product under appraisal can now be plotted on the MA-CP matrix.

The process is repeated for each product under investigation. Each product position is given by a circle, the size of which is in proportion to its sales (Hollensen and Opresnik, 2020).

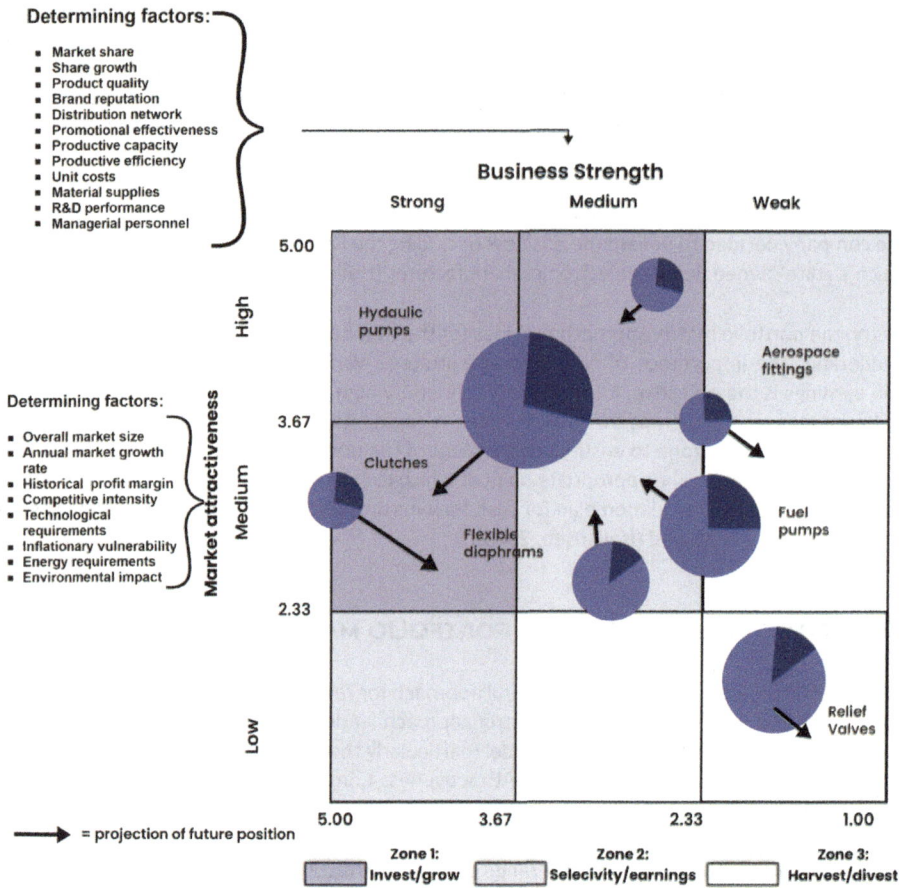

Figure 3.6: The General Electric Market Attractiveness-Competitive Position Model. Source: Adapted from Hollensen and Opresnik, 2020, modified.

Like in the BCG model, for an individual business, the recommendations for setting strategic objectives are dependent on the product's position. Figure 3.6 provides an overview of the appropriate strategies.

Market attractiveness (vertical axis)

	Strong	Medium	Weak
High	**Protect position** • Invest to grow at maximum digestible rate • Concentrate effort on maintaining strength	**Invest to build** • Challenge for leadership • Build selectively on strengths • Reinforce vulnerable areas	**Build selectively** • Specialize around limited strengths • Seek ways to overcome weaknesses • Withdraw if indications of sustainable growth are lacking
Medium	**Build selectively** • Invest heavily in most attractive segments • Build up ability o counter competition • Emphasize profitability by raising productivity	**Selectivity/manage for earnings** • Protect existing program • Concentrate investments in segments where profitability is good and risk is relatively low	**Limited expansion or harvest** • Look for ways to expand without high risk; otherwise, minimize investment and rationalize investment
Low	**Protect & refocus** • Manage for current earnings • Concentrate on attractive strengths • Defend strengths	**Manage for earning** • Protect position in most profitable segments • Upgrade product line • Minimize investment	**Divest** • Sell at time that will maximize cash value • Cut Fixed costs & avoid investment meanwhile

Business strength

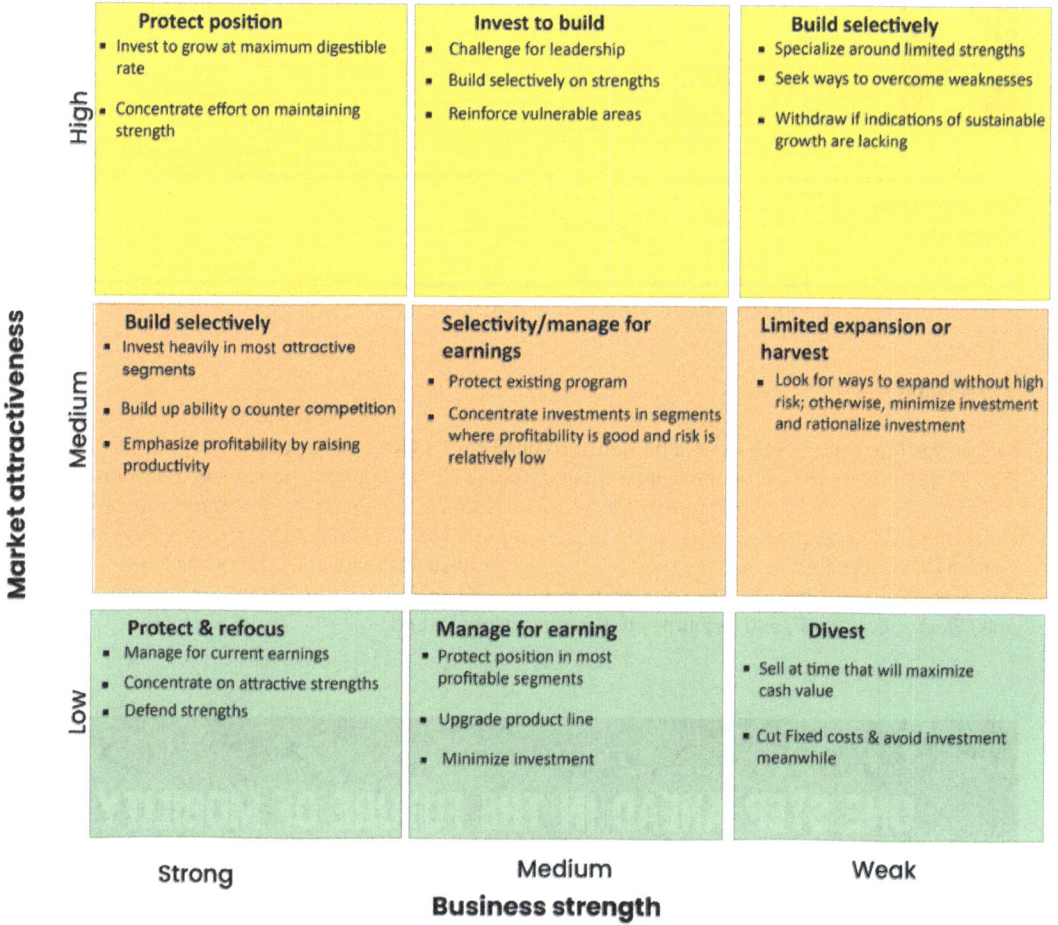

Figure 3.7: The generic strategies of the General Electric Market Attractiveness Competitive Position Model. Source: Adapted from Hollensen and Opresnik, 2020, modified.

KARSAN

Written by: Karsan Automotive Marketing & Communication Team

Introduction

Karsan was founded in 1966 as an automotive company in Türkiye and has been in the industry for more than 58 years. Over the years, the company has assumed a pioneering role in the electrification of public transportation worldwide with its electric vehicles. In 2018, Karsan embarked on a transformation journey to meet not only today's needs but also those of the future. This transformation has repositioned Karsan as a brand that offers electric mobility solutions for public transportation and has propelled Karsan to leadership in the European market. This case study examines Karsan's electric transformation process, which it calls "Electric Evolution", and its journey to become a global brand.

Karsan's Hasanağa plant in Bursa, with its 203,000 square meters of land, has the capacity to produce 20,000 vehicles a year in a single shift, making Karsan an important production center in its region. In 2013, Karsan decided to produce its own branded vehicles, opening a new chapter in the mobility sector as an independent manufacturer. With this decision, the company began its journey to develop innovative and sustainable solutions with a focus on the future.

2018 marked the beginning of an important transformation process for Karsan. The company aimed to become a pioneer in the global mobility sector by switching from internal combustion engine vehicles to electric and autonomous vehicles. This comprehensive transformation has enabled Karsan to focus on producing zero-emission, high-tech and environmentally friendly vehicles with investments in electric vehicle technologies. The transformation initiated by the company was named "Electric Evolution", reflecting its vision of building the cities of the future today. In taking these steps, Karsan aimed both to offer innovative solutions for the future and to be one step ahead in the future of mobility by bringing the technologies of the future into the present.

Challenge

Until 2018, Karsan traditionally produced commercial vehicles. However, increasing environmental concerns worldwide, the rapid growth of urbanization and the need to develop sustainable solutions in public transportation have brought the company to a turning point. Karsan needed to redefine its vision to cope with these dynamics and respond to the mobility needs of the future today.

The company wanted not only to maintain its current market position, but also to become a pioneering brand that is sensitive to the environment and shapes the future. In this process, Karsan also reshaped its marketing strategy. The main objectives were to strengthen the brand's innovative and environmentally friendly image, emphasize the importance of the transition to electric vehicles, and position itself as the pioneer of sustainable mobility solutions in global markets.

Governments and cities around the world have started to develop policies for zero-emission vehicles in line with their carbon emission reduction targets. In this context, the public transportation sector was also undergoing a rapid transformation. If Karsan did not adapt to these changing demands, it would not only lose its competitive edge, but also struggle to survive in the future. The company's sustainability-oriented transformation was not only a matter of environmental responsibility, but also required a radical rethinking of its marketing strategies.

Solution

In 2018, Karsan embarked on a comprehensive transformation process to adapt to the changing dynamics of the global automotive industry and pioneer the mobility solutions of the future. This process aimed to transition the company from traditional internal combustion vehicles to fully electric and autonomous vehicles. This transition required Karsan to make radical changes in its production and engineering infrastructure; significant investments were made in areas such as new generation electric vehicle technologies, procurement and human resources processes, battery management systems and autonomous driving technologies.

As a first step, it launched the e-JEST model in 2018. Developed using the proven BMW electric infrastructure, this model set a new standard in urban public transportation with its high maneuverability, compact dimensions and low operating costs while providing zero emissions. e-JEST quickly became Europe's best-selling electric minibus and demonstrated Karsan's competence in electric vehicle technology.

Launched in 2019, the e-ATAK, an 8-meter midibus, took Karsan's innovative vision even further. Developed with BMW's advanced battery technology and attracting attention with its long range, e-ATAK has set a new bar in the European market in terms of high passenger capacity and environmental sustainability. This vehicle not only offered a zero-emission transportation solution, but also increased efficiency in public transportation.

Introduced in 2021 and revolutionizing urban transportation with its level-4 autonomous technology developed in partnership with ADASTEC, Autonomous e-ATAK achieved a world first by carrying passengers on a 5-kilometer route for 1.5 years on the Michigan State University campus in the USA. In addition, the Autonomous e-ATAK, which has been carrying ticketed passengers in open traffic in Stavanger, Norway, since 2022, expanded its existing route to include a tunnel at the beginning of 2024 and successfully passed another challenging test as the first autonomous vehicle to pass through a tunnel, again achieving a world first. These developments reinforced Karsan's global innovation leadership.

Launched in 2021, the 10m, 12m, 18m models of the born electric e-ATA family were launched, making it the first and only company in Europe to offer the full e-Range from 6 meters to 18 meters.

In 2022, Karsan took its sustainability goals one step further and launched the e-ATA HYDROGEN model. This model, which generates its own electricity with green hydrogen, set new standards in environmentally friendly transportation with its zero emission, high range capacity and fast filling time. This Karsan model continued to make a difference in the sector by utilizing the energy sources of the future.

Karsan, which is the only brand in Europe that can offer all electric, autonomous and hydrogen technologies in public transportation, is expanding its electric park day by day with more than 1100 electric vehicles in 23 countries. The 100% electric e-JEST and e-ATAK models have been the most preferred vehicles in the electric minibus and midibus markets in Europe for the last 4 years without interruption. Karsan, which has a full e-Range from 6 meters to 18 meters, continues to pioneer the transformation of public transportation with these successes crowned with awards. The company reduces its carbon footprint with its zero-emission, naturally electric and autonomous vehicles and offers a quiet, clean, and safe travel experience.

Entering the Canadian market in 2022 and the American market in 2023, Karsan became the first 6m electric "cute bus" in North America with its 6m 100% electric e-JEST vehicle. At the end of 2023, Karsan entered the

Japanese market with its right-hand drive e-JEST model, becoming the first European e-bus brand to enter the Japanese market.

Karsan has defined its transition to electric vehicle production as a journey in which it rebuilds itself with the technologies of the future and leads the evolution of the transportation sector by moving societies forward and has named this journey "Electric Evolution". As a symbol of this, it added the letter "e" in front of the names of the vehicles, permanently symbolizing the electric evolution and bringing it to the sector.

In this transformation process, Karsan emphasized that it is both taking steps towards the future and preparing its public transportation solutions for the future by bringing the technologies of the future into the present. Thus, Karsan has accelerated its steps towards its goal of being one step ahead in the evolution of mobility and building the cities of the future today.

Karsan has adopted a positioning that embraces innovation not only in technology but also in users' experience. While realizing its innovative solutions, Karsan focused on innovation not only in its vehicles but also in all its business processes. The developments carried out at the Experience Innovation Center reflect Karsan's commitment to continuously renewing and improving the experience offered to its target audience at every stage, from production to after-sales services. This approach was indicative not only of Karsan's vision of producing high-tech and environmentally friendly vehicles, but also of a service approach that aims to meet and even exceed customer expectations at every stage.

Karsan's innovative approach is also reflected in its after-sales service approach. With its global technical support network, online help desk, remote diagnostics systems and comprehensive service network that reaches all parts of the world, Karsan has always improved the experience of its customers by offering them fast and effective solutions. This comprehensive service approach reflected Karsan's strategy of providing a constantly renewed experience in line with its goal of increasing customer satisfaction. By innovating in every area, the company reinforced its leadership in the sector and maximized customer experience.

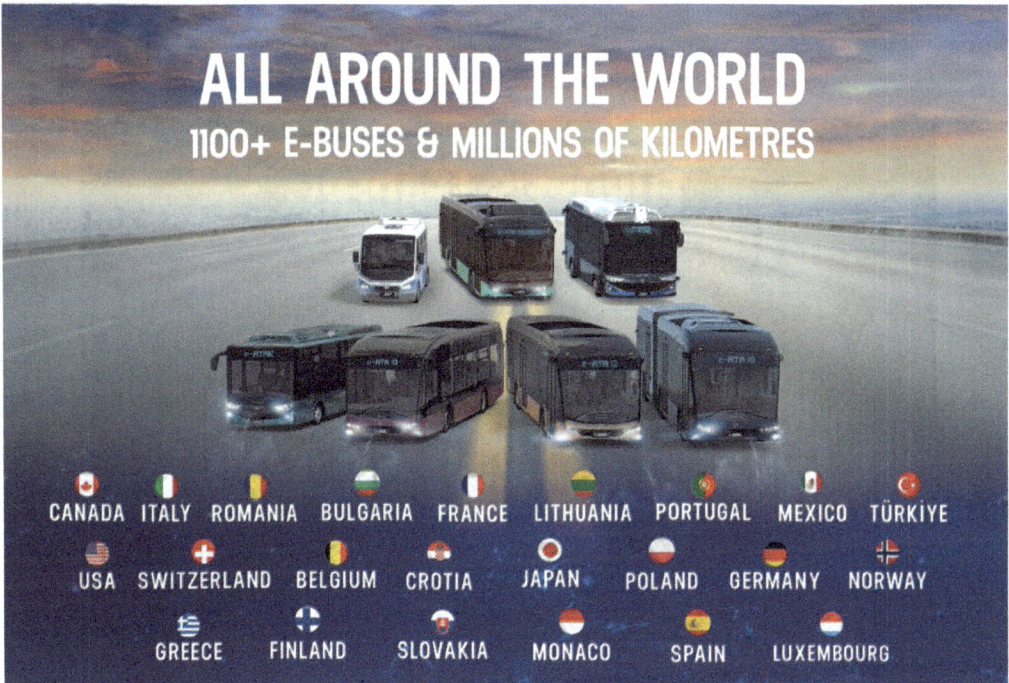

ALL AROUND THE WORLD
1100+ E-BUSES & MILLIONS OF KILOMETRES

CANADA ITALY ROMANIA BULGARIA FRANCE LITHUANIA PORTUGAL MEXICO TÜRKIYE
USA SWITZERLAND BELGIUM CROTIA JAPAN POLAND GERMANY NORWAY
GREECE FINLAND SLOVAKIA MONACO SPAIN LUXEMBOURG

The vehicles it has developed are not only technologically advanced, but also serve the mission of continuously improving the public transportation experience by offering user-oriented solutions. Thanks to both its leadership in experience innovation and its vision for the future, Karsan contributed to the sustainability of cities and continued to make urban transportation more efficient and environmentally friendly. With each new product and service, the company brought a new perspective to the public transportation sector.

Thanks to these innovative steps, Karsan has won dozens of prestigious awards on many global platforms such as Global Business & Finance Magazine, Stevie Awards, Sustainable Bus Awards, Brand Review Magazine, German Design Award, Global Brands Magazine, BusWorld Awards, Sustainablity Awards, Word Business Magazine.

Conclusion

This transformation has made Karsan the first and only brand in the European market to offer full e-Range from 6 meters to 18 meters. With its e-JEST and e-ATAK models, the company has been Europe's market leader for four consecutive years in 2020-2023. Moreover, Karsan's achievements were not limited to Europe; it also entered the North American and Japanese markets, demonstrating its determination to become a global brand. Karsan became the first and only European bus manufacturer to enter the Japanese market by 2023.

In Stavanger, Norway, the Autonomous e-ATAK, which has been experiencing ticketed passengers in open traffic since 2022, successfully passed another challenging test as the first autonomous vehicle to pass through a tunnel by expanding its existing route to include a tunnel in early 2024. Karsan, which has commissioned autonomous projects in many different locations with the Autonomous e-ATAK, which finally started operating in Finland after the USA, Norway, France, Romania, Türkiye, has achieved 90 thousand kilometers of autonomous driving experience and carried over 30 thousand passengers. In addition, Karsan has signed an autonomous airport project in Rotterdam, the Netherlands, and with the two Autonomous e-ATAKs it will deliver at the end of 2024, Karsan will be the first brand in the world to carry out airport transfers with an autonomous vehicle. In 2025, it will become the first autonomous bus in Arbon, Switzerland, carrying ticketed passengers in open traffic. In summary, Otonom e-ATAK is the world's first and only level-4, 8-meter autonomous bus with 10 projects in 8 different parts of the world.

Karsan's innovative approach has helped the company become a globally recognized and appreciated brand. Karsan has also crowned this success with the awards it has received. With its contributions to sustainable mobility, environmentally friendly technologies, and customer-oriented solutions, Karsan has achieved a prestigious position in the international arena.

Today, Karsan's innovative vehicles are in operation in 23 different countries on 3 continents with more than 1100 vehicles. In these 23 countries, Karsan ranks first in searches for "electric bus" on search engines, and as a highly searched brand on digital platforms, Karsan continues its mission to become a leader in global mobility solutions by increasing its contributions to a sustainable future with these achievements. Karsan's journey reflects its determination to offer innovative and sustainable solutions not only for today's cities but also for the cities of the future. With more than 2,600 employees and zero-emission vehicles equipped with environmentally friendly technologies, the company is shaping the public transportation of the future today and continues to be the pioneer of sustainable transportation worldwide.

3.2 MARKET SEGMENTATION, TARGETING AND POSITIONING

Markets consist of buyers, who differ in one or more ways, for example, in their wants, resources, buying attitudes, and locations. The technique that is used by marketers to get grips with the diverse nature of markets is called market segmentation. Through market segmentation, companies divide large, heterogeneous markets into smaller homogenous segments that can be targeted more efficiently and effectively with products and services that match their unique needs and wants. Firms, no matter how big they are, have limited resources and want to use these limited resources more efficiently and effectively for the right target markets. The objective is to identify groups of customers with similar requirements so that they can be served effectively while being of a sufficient size for the product or service to be supplied efficiently. Usually, especially in consumer markets, it is not possible to create a marketing mix that satisfies every individual's specific requirement precisely. Market segmentation, by grouping together customers with similar needs or wants, provides a commercially viable way of serving these consumers (Ellis-Chadwick and Jobber, 2016).

The first step within the process of market segmentation involves the identification of the best ways to segment a market and then pin down the characteristics of each group (this second step is called **profiling**). Next, the company must evaluate the attractiveness of the segments and select the most appropriate target markets (**targeting**). Finally, the business organisation needs to **position** the product or service relative to competitive offerings within the chosen market segments. This is also called STP (**S**egmentation-**T**argeting-**P**ositioning) Strategy.

CHANGING THE GAME: MOLPED'S ROLE IN SHAPING A NEW ERA IN FEMININE CARE

Written by: İlayda Başar (Molped Global Strategy Marketing Manager)

Introduction

Molped is one of the leading brands of Hayat Holding whose foundations were laid in 1937 and is now a global player with its 16 powerful FMCG Trademarks in home care, tissue, baby care and personal hygiene categories. Molped was first introduced to the Türkiye market in 1999 with a challenger positioning against a well-established global feminine care franchise which had become the generic brand as well as the category captain due to over 20 years of monopoly. Molped had to redefine the rules of the game to achieve the impossible i.e. compete with a highly invested global player in a truly stigmatized category and gain sustained leadership.

Challenge

The aforementioned franchise was first-to-market in Türkiye and naturally became the generic brand of the fem-care category during the over 20 years of free ride without competition. In the beginning of 1980's, Türkiye was going through a major socio-political transformation; the liberalization of economy coupled with highly momentous global integration allowed for a prolific playground where consumers accustomed to using local and commoditized products were invited to explore new alternatives and an influx of global brands for the first time. The first fem-care launch came at a time when women used home-made solutions for menstrual care which enabled high-velocity category growth as well as strong brand loyalty for the generic brand part. Despite the liberalization trend in the economy, patriarchal socio-cultural structure and its pressure on women was still at strongly at play which rendering the fem-care category highly stigmatized in terms of communication. At the time, menstrual pads were hidden in black plastic bags and women could not openly discuss their periods to the extent that they were ashamed to ask each other for spare pads. The Category was marked by high shame factor and lacked real innovation, the generic Brand's franchise comprised of a monolithic product portfolio with no product differentiation except that of size and capacity which had become a well-accepted norm among local women. The female target audience had adopted the Brand name as product marker, giving the already monopolized competition the power of being the generic brand of the category.

How could a new and local brand compete with the highly invested Category captain who had enjoyed a long-term monopolized leadership as well as the benefit of being a generic brand?

Solution

Molped, whose building blocks were founded on deep-rooted consumer insight, chose to implement a disruptive brand growth strategy focused on dismantling menstrual stigma via unprecedented communication approach for its initial take-off. From the very first day, Molped stood against all cliches regarding menstruation with a rebellious tone-of-voice thereby offering a refreshing new alternative in the category with an unmatched right-to-win. The launch campaign executed with a high equity national celebrity focused on abolishing the stigma around the category. Young females going around the streets and openly asking" Do you have a spare Molped?" was a real game-changer for the category as well as a major WoM source which served as a trial potential maximization lever in the target audience. The Brand recorded year-on-year turnover and volume growth within the first decade of its launch.

By 2010, the Brand had reached its all-time high SoM (26%) and had become an established player in the market, the introduction of the first-ever pantyliner range was an early testament of the unprecedented innovation approach of Molped which later became the key driver of growth and global expansion. When the calendar hit 2017, the Category had reached medium level of saturation with numerous new players (including private labels) as well as global competition launches which triggered the need for a revamped brand and product strategy. At that time, communication was the sole differentiation point for brands and product solutions were a point of parity. Following extensive consumer research and due diligence efforts, an unmatched growth strategy was formulated to maximize the growth potential of the Brand.

The Winning Growth Formula of Molped

Be the **first-to-market** with **consumer-oriented product innovation** whilst **maximizing profitability** via pioneering production investment, boost Brand affinity by establishing **new consumer communication platforms and touchpoints**.

Thanks to the consumer-oriented innovation strategy the Brand penetrated the market with high resonating product concepts which tripled gross profitability in USD terms whilst EBITDA increased by 9.8-fold within five years. **Achieving growth through real and relevant innovation without cannibalization** was the crux of this strategy; all product ranges were designed to address previously unresolved pain point and each product range was carefully engineered to tackle a different consumer need. The Brand is not only introduced unmatched product solutions but also made sure to differentiate each franchise from one other via clear conceptual product and packaging design elements. The consumer-based innovation approach also enabled significant penetration growth as each range had a distinct target consumer group which allowed for new listings in disparate sales channels bringing trial maximization and thereby new consumers.

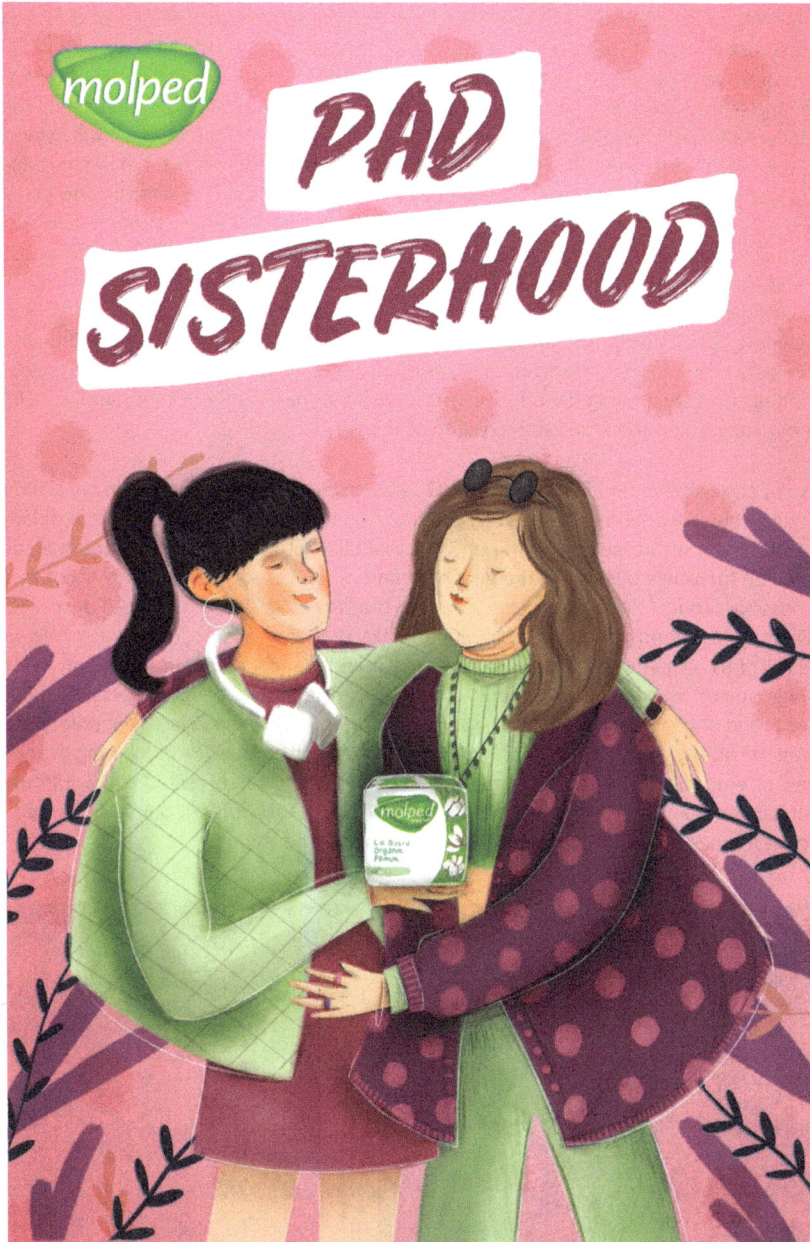

Molped also exerted significant effort into establishing and nurturing unprecedented communication platforms to build engaging dialogues with its target audience. Before Molped paved the way, the communication of the category mainly consisted of unempathetic monologue of Brands', and the key medium was TV. In alignment with the Brand's disruptive growth strategy, Molped set a previously unmatched, sincere but rebellious tone-of-voice by tapping onto the "realities" of menstruation for the first time. Molped became the first brand to start the conversation about periods and constantly took new initiatives to remove the "shame factor" that was downplaying both the Category and young females. The Brand positioned itself as the ultimate BFF and established the "Better Together" platform which in time became the main communication concept for Molped. Fostering sisterhood and removing barriers for young females at every step of the way became the hallmark of Molped; the Brand is not only changed the discourse but shifted the playground by being the first brand to heavily invest in digital. Molped was the first brand in the Category to start a proxy branded Youtube channel "Dünya Tek Biz İkimiz" (Us Against the World) with the aim to build close rapport with target audience via engaging and interactive content pillars. While the "Period Talks" series targeted to shine light on FAQs about menstruation, "The Challenge" videos built together with young influencers allowed young females to actively interact with the Brand through fun. Molped ensured omni-channel SoV consistency and focused heavily on striking the right balance between offline vs digital; all campaigns were built with a 360° approach; while TV medium was used for mass awareness, digital footprint was expanded through medium-fit digital executions and boosted by POSM applications. Another critical pillar to achieve leadership was the Brand's ability to react in real-time; during the global pandemic which triggered the decline of purchasing power of all consumers, Molped initiated the "Pad Sisterhood" campaign to ensure all those in need were provided with sanitary care by donating a pack for each pack sold, solidifying the "BFF" positioning, and building further affinity with target audience. The Brand's secret to success consists of hundreds of executions, tens of campaigns and multiple product ranges that all tie back to a winning strategy, drilling deep for insight to achieve maximum relevancy and remaining true to Molped's unmatched brand character at every step of the way.

The most recent campaign period from 2020 to 2023 was strategically focused on the specialized products by also utilizing a rebellious tone of voice. Each product was catered towards a specific problem, spanning from physiological discomfort, such as irritation, to social discomfort, such as leaks and malodor. Molped wanted to provide the sense of security the generic brand of the category did, however not by claiming to be the best possible product and making everyone feel that they should trust this pad unconditionally, but instead aiming to understand women and striving to make their lives easier. The phrase "We won't fit our pad, our pad will fit us" slogan was created to reflect the Brand's highly emphatic character. Meanwhile, the trend of strong women was increasing its influence in every field, and brands, especially those targeting women, were proud of being associated with women and were breaking patriarchal stereotypes in society. There is a common phrase in Turkish, "a man's promise", that signifies trust. By combining the need for trust and the trend of empowering women, "a man's promise" phrase was reversed to "Girl Promise". Thus, Molped's campaign slogan emerged: "Girl Promise from Molped! We won't fit our pad, our pad will fit us!" This slogan gave Molped the bold stance it needed to dethrone the leader.

Conclusion

Molped's innovative strategy earned the Brand tangible results. From 2019 to 2023, a total of 11-point increase in the top-of-mind-awareness score was achieved, narrowing the gap with the generic brand from 39 to 19 points. In the perception metric "It is the pad I use most frequently," Molped had a 10-point increase within the same time frame, while its global competitors recorded both fluctuating and decreasing trend. Consequently, the gap with the generic brand in this metric decreased from 33 to 14 points. Molped's score also increased in the metric of "feeling close" and "high performance," by total of 23 points and 23 points respectively. There were significant achievements in terms of business results as well. From 2019 to 2023, Molped's volume market share increased by 6.2 points and reached 25.9. Meanwhile, the generic brand lost 7.7 points, declining from 28.8 to 21.1. With these results, Molped became the leader of the sanitary pad category for the first time in 24 years. The leadership was also achieved in value market share in 2023 when Molped's score rose to 28.3, while the generic brand declined to 24.1. When it comes to the volume ratio of Molped's premium products in the total portfolio, which were the focus of communication from 2019 to 2023, a tremendous growth was observed. The proportion of sales from premium products increased by 23.2 points to reach 76.9. Looking at all these measurable results, it is safe to say that Molped completely turned the tides in the fem-care category despite a rival that dominated the category for decades.

Questions to stimulate conversation on the case

1. **What were the main challenges Molped faced when entering the Turkish fem-care market in the late 1990s?**

Molped faced significant challenges when entering the Turkish fem-care market, primarily due to the dominance of a well-established global brand that had become synonymous with the category over more than 20 years. This brand enjoyed strong consumer loyalty, as it had been the first to market during a time when women relied on homemade solutions for menstrual care. The fem-care category was also highly stigmatized, with cultural norms discouraging open discussion about periods. Products were hidden in black plastic bags, and innovation was minimal, with the dominant brand offering only basic variations in size and capacity. This entrenched competition and the socio-cultural barriers made it difficult for new entrants like Molped to establish themselves in the market.

2. **How did Molped address the challenges of menstrual stigma and establish itself in the Turkish fem-care market?**

Molped tackled the challenges of menstrual stigma with a disruptive brand growth strategy centered on challenging traditional taboos through innovative communication. From the outset, Molped adopted a rebellious tone to break away from existing norms, offering a fresh perspective in the fem-care category. The launch campaign featured a high-profile national celebrity and aimed to eliminate stigma by using provocative messaging, such as young females asking, "Do you have a spare Molped?" This approach significantly increased word-of-mouth marketing and trial potential among the target audience. Within the first decade, Molped achieved substantial year-on-year growth, reaching a market share of 26% by 2010. The introduction of a pantyliner range highlighted Molped's commitment to innovation, which fueled further growth and global expansion. By 2017, facing increased market saturation and competition, Molped undertook a comprehensive strategy revamp based on extensive consumer research to sustain its growth and differentiate itself in a crowded market.

3. **How did Molped's consumer-oriented innovation strategy contribute to its market success?**

Molped's consumer-oriented innovation strategy was crucial to its market success by introducing highly resonant product concepts that addressed unresolved pain points and catered to distinct consumer needs. This approach not only led to a significant increase in gross profitability and EBITDA within five years but also enabled the brand to avoid cannibalization. Each product range was carefully designed with unique conceptual and packaging elements, which facilitated significant market penetration and new listings across various sales channels, maximizing trial and attracting new consumers.

4.   In what ways did Molped revolutionize communication in the fem-care category?

Molped revolutionized communication in the fem-care category by moving away from the traditional, un-empathetic monologue typically seen on TV. Instead, Molped adopted a sincere and rebellious tone that addressed the realities of menstruation for the first time. The brand launched innovative communication platforms such as the "Better Together" initiative and a branded YouTube channel, "Dünya Tek Biz İkimiz" (Us Against the World). This strategy involved engaging content like "Period Talks" and "The Challenge" videos, which fostered a strong connection with the target audience and positioned Molped as a supportive and interactive brand.

5.   What was the significance of the "Girl Promise" campaign for Molped?

The "Girl Promise" campaign was significant for Molped as it combined the need for trust with the trend of empowering women. By reversing the traditional Turkish phrase "a man's promise" to "Girl Promise," Molped created a bold and empathetic slogan: "Girl Promise from Molped! We won't fit our pad, our pad will fit us!" This campaign highlighted Molped's commitment to understanding and addressing women's needs, reinforcing its position as a challenger brand capable of dethroning the market leader and differentiating itself with a unique and relatable message.

6.   What were the key outcomes of Molped's innovative strategy between 2019 and 2023?

Between 2019 and 2023, Molped's innovative strategy led to significant gains in both brand perception and market share. The brand achieved an 11-point increase in top-of-mind awareness, narrowing the gap with the generic brand from 39 to 19 points. Molped also saw a 10-point rise in the perception metric "It is the pad I use most frequently," reducing the gap with the generic brand from 33 to 14 points. Additionally, Molped's scores in the "feeling close" and "high performance" metrics each increased by 23 points. In terms of business results, Molped's volume market share grew by 6.2 points to 25.9, overtaking the generic brand, which declined from 28.8 to 21.1, making Molped the category leader for the first time in 24 years. The brand also saw substantial growth in premium product sales, which rose by 23.2 points, accounting for 76.9% of the total portfolio. These results demonstrate that Molped successfully turned the tides in the fem-care category despite facing a long-established rival.

Sources: Molped Marka Sağlığı Araştırması 2023 Konsolide Raporu: Ipsos, 2024; Hane Tüketim Paneli, Ipsos

3.2.1 THE UNDERLYING PREMISES OF MARKET SEGMENTATION

In order to get an overview of segmentation issues it is important to first consider the underlying requirements for market segmentation. To be useful, market segments have to be (Hooley et al., 2004):

1. **Measurable**: The size, purchasing power, and profiles of the segments need to be measured. The operational use of segmentation usually requires that segment targets can be identified by measurable characteristics to enable their potential value as a market target to be estimated and for the segment to be identified. Fundamental to utilizing a segmentation scheme to make better marketing decisions is the ability of the marketing strategist to evaluate segment attractiveness and the current or potential strengths the company has in serving a particular segment. Depending on the level of segmentation analysis, this may require internal company analysis or external market appraisal.

2. **Accessible**: The market segments should be effectively reached and served. A fragrance company, for example, finds that heavy users of its brand are single men and women who stay out late and socialize a lot. Unless this group lives or shops at certain places and is exposed to certain media, its members will be difficult to reach.

3. **Substantial**: The market segments should be large and profitable enough to serve. In this context, a segment could be the largest possible homogenous group worth pursuing with a tailored marketing program.

4. **Differentiable**: The segments should be conceptually distinguishable and respond differently to diverse marketing mix elements and programs. For segmentation to be useful customers must differ from one another in some important respect, which can be used to divide the large heterogeneous market. If they were not different in some significant way, if they were totally homogeneous, then there would be no basis on which to segment the market. However, in reality all customers differ in some respect as already stated above. The key to whether a particular difference is useful for segmentation purposes lies in the extent to which the variations are related to different behavior patterns (e.g. different levels of demand for the product or service, or different use/benefit requirements) or susceptibility to different marketing mix combinations (e.g. different product/service offerings, different media, messages or distribution channels), i.e. whether the differences are important to how we develop a marketing strategy.

5. **Actionable**: Effective programs can be designed for attracting and serving the segments. For example, although a small company might identify multiple target segments, its resources like staff and capital may be insufficient to develop and implement a separate marketing program for each segment.

Some market segmentation criteria that can be used when creating market segments that may have these characteristics are geographic, demographic, psychographic as well as behavioral segmentation. One or more of these criteria can be used separately. However, the more criteria are used simultaneously, the more homogeneous market segments with homogeneous wants and needs can be created. For example, "female consumers between the ages of 25-35, living in big cities, having a middle-income level and doing sports at least three days a week" indicates a much more homogeneous market than "female consumers between the ages of 25-35".

3.2.2 THE SEGMENTATION, TARGETING AND POSITIONING APPROACH

Market segmentation provides a basis for the selection of target markets. A target market is a depicted segment of market that a company has decided to serve. As customers in the target market segment have similar characteristics, a single marketing mix can be developed to match those requirements.

105

The selection of a target market or markets is a three-step process, as shown in Figure 3.8: **Segmentation, Targeting and Positioning (STP)**.

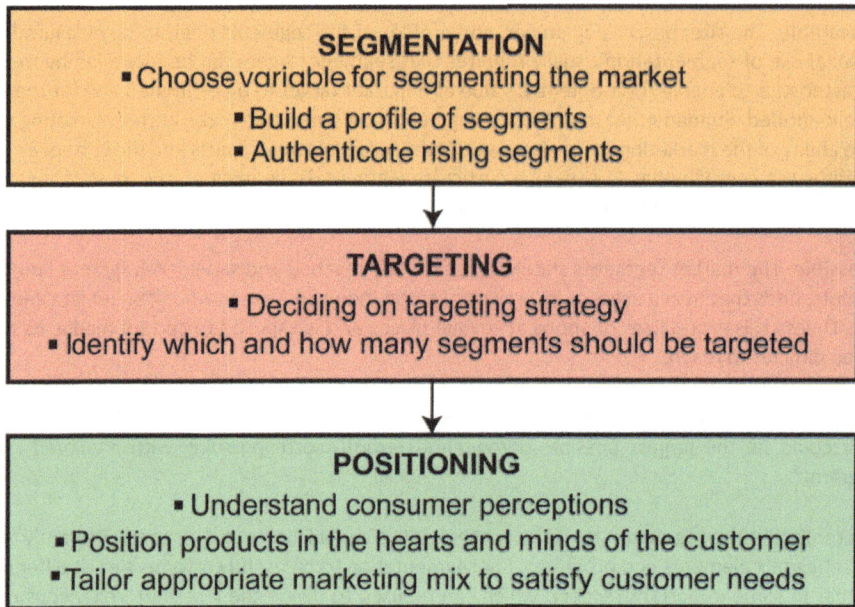

SEGMENTATION
- Choose variable for segmenting the market
- Build a profile of segments
- Authenticate rising segments

TARGETING
- Deciding on targeting strategy
- Identify which and how many segments should be targeted

POSITIONING
- Understand consumer perceptions
- Position products in the hearts and minds of the customer
- Tailor appropriate marketing mix to satisfy customer needs

Figure 3.8: The STP of market segmentation.
Source: Adapted from Hollensen and Opresnik, 2020, modified.

According to this model, the process begins with the aggregation of customers into groups, to maximise homogeneity within, and heterogeneity between the segments (Hollensen and Opresnik, 2020).

The first step is **market segmentation** – dividing a market into smaller groups of buyers with distinct needs, characteristics, or behaviors who might require separate products or marketing mixes. The company identifies different ways to segment the market and develops profiles of the resulting market segments. It is important to state, that a given market can be segmented in various ways depending on the choice criteria at this stage. For example, the market for motor cars could be broken down according to the type of buyer (individual or organisational), by major benefit sought (e.g. functionality or status) or by family size (empty nesters versus family with children). Extremely small groups of customers identified through the segmentation process are called **niche markets**.

The second step is **targeting marketing** – evaluating each market segment's attractiveness and selecting one or more of the market segments to target with an appropriate marketing strategy. The final step is **market positioning** – setting the competitive positioning for the products and services and creating a tailored marketing mix in order to achieve a sustainable competitive advantage and to create a unique spot in customers 'minds (Hollensen and Opresnik, 2020).

The implicit goal of all STP strategy is to improve marketing performance. Thus, an organisation may aim to use STP to increase customer satisfaction, competitive differentiation, and profitability. The STP process offers additional benefits when used accurately. It significantly increases marketers 'ability to develop a thorough understanding of the needs of their well-defined customer segments, and it improves their

106

ability to respond to changing segment needs. Marketing efficiency is improved as resources are targeted at segments that offer the most potential for the organisation. Because the marketing program is better matched with segment requirements, effectiveness of the marketing approach is improved. Specifically, STP analysis aid marketing managers design a product line to meet market demand, determine advertising messages that will have most appeal, select media that will have greatest impact for each segment and time product and advertising launches to capitalize on market responsiveness.

In the following sections, we discuss each of the steps in the STP process, segmenting, targeting, and positioning, in more detail (Hollensen and Opresnik, 2020).

3.2.3 SEGMENTING CONSUMER (B2C) MARKETS

As mentioned already, a market may be segmented in many ways. Segmentation variables are the criteria that are used for dividing a market into segments. When examining criteria, the marketer must try to identify good predictors of differences in buyer behavior. There is an array of options and no single, prescribed way of segmenting a market (Wind, 1978). A marketer has to try different segmentation variables, alone and in combination, to find the best way to view the market structure. In addition, the bases selected must fulfil the criteria outlined earlier for effective segmentation.

The major groups of consumer segmentation criteria are **profile, psychographic and behavioral**.

3.2.3.1 Profile Segmentation

Profile segmentation variables allow customer groups to be classified in such a way that they can be reached by communications media (e.g. advertising, direct mail). Even if behavior and/or psychographic segmentation have successfully separated between consumer preferences there is often an urge to analyze the resulting segments in terms of profile variables such as age and socio-economic group in order to communicate to them. The reason is that readership and viewership profiles of newspapers and television programmes tend to be expressed in that way (Ellis-Chadwick and Jobber, 2016).

We shall now examine a number of the most common **demographic, socio-economic and geographic segmentation variables**.

3.2.3.1.1 Demographic Variables

Demographic variables are the most popular bases for segmenting customer groups. One reason is that customer needs, wants and usage rates often vary closely with these variables. Another is that demographic variables are easier to measure than most other types of variables described hereafter. Even if market segments are first defined using other bases, such as behavior, their demographic characteristics must be known and analyzed in order to assess the size of the target market and to reach it efficiently. We shall look at the demographic variables **age, gender, and life cycle**:

1. **Age** has been used as a basic segmentation variable in many markets. The market for holidays is a classic example, with holiday companies tailoring their products to particular age groups such as 'under 30s' or 'senior citizens'. Another example includes Çilek Furniture, which was founded in 1996 with the mission of "To offer the most functional, safest, highest quality and to be the same everywhere - always", divides and produces furniture for babies, children, and young people according to their age range. Procter & Gamble selling Crest spin brushes featuring favourite children's characters. For adults, it sells more serious models, promising 'a dentist-clean feeling twice a day' (Hollensen and Opresnik,

2020). In these segmentation schemes it is rational that there are significant differences in behavior and product/service requirements between the demographic segments identified.

2. **Gender** segmentation is a basic approach has long been used in clothing, cosmetics, and magazines. Many segmentation schemes use gender as a first step in the segmentation process, but then further refine their targets within the chosen gender category, e.g. by social class. In some markets the most relevant variable is gender preference as marketers have noticed opportunities for targeting women. Citibank, for example, launched Women & Co., a financial program created around the distinct financial needs of women. Another example comes from Elif Şafak, the famous Turkish author, has printed the cover of her book "Love" in pink for women and gray for men (or for those who don't want to walk around with a pink book with the word "love" on it).

3. **Life cycle segmentation** centres on the idea that consumers pass through a series of quite distinct phases in their lives, with each phase being associated with different purchasing patterns and needs. The unmarried person living at home may have very different purchasing patterns from a chronological counterpart who has left home and recently married. It is also recognized that the purchasing pattern of adults often changes as they approach and move into retirement. Modalife, a Turkish furniture manufacturer, creates wedding packages for couples getting married and offers all kinds of furniture that a newlywed couple may need in their home. Producers of baby products, for example, build mailing lists of households with new-born babies on the basis of free gifts given to mothers in maternity hospitals (Hollensen, 2006).

3.2.3.1.2 Socio-Demographic Variables

Socio-demographic variables include social class and income. Here we shall look at **social class** as a predictor of buyer behavior. Like the demographic variables discussed above, social class has the advantage of being fairly easy to measure and is used for media readership and viewership profiles.

In many cases, occupation and social class are linked together because, in numerous developed economies, official socio-economic group (social class) categorizations are based upon occupation. The extent to which social class is a predictor of buyer behavior, however, has been open to question as many people who hold similar occupations have dissimilar lifestyles, values and purchasing patterns. Nevertheless, social class has proved useful in discriminating between owing a dishwasher and having central heating, for example, and therefore should not be discounted as a segmentation variable (O'Brian and Ford, 1988).

3.2.3.1.3 Geographic Variables

Geographic variables facilitate the division of markets into different geographical units such as nations, regions, states, countries, cities, or even neighbourhoods. The geographic segmentation method is useful where there are geographic locational differences in consumption patterns and preferences. For example, since Türkiye is a country with geographically different climates and temperatures, it may be wrong to offer the same goose down coat to a consumer living in the Mediterranean region and a consumer living in the Eastern Anatolia. Geographic segmentation is still widely used, at least as one element in a combination of segmentation bases. Undoubtedly, geographic segmentation is potentially at its most powerful and useful when considering international markets, and therefore is considered in more detail in the framework of segmenting international markets and countries.

The increasing concern regarding the poor predictive power of many of the above stated 'conventional' bases for segmenting consumer markets, coupled with improvements in data collection and analysis methods, has led to the development in recent years of more contemporary and, some would suggest more powerful, bases for segmenting consumer markets like psychographic and behavioral segmentation which shall be discussed in more detail now.

3.2.3.2 Psychographic Segmentation

Psychographic segmentation involves grouping customers according to their **lifestyle and personality characteristics**:

1. **Lifestyle characteristics**: This research attempts to isolate market segments on the basis of the style of life adopted by their members. At one stage these approaches were seen as alternatives to the social class categories discussed above. Lifestyle segmentation is based upon the fact that individuals have characteristic modes and patterns of living, which may influence their motive to purchase selected products and brands. For example, some individuals may prefer a 'homely' lifestyle, whereas others may see themselves as living a 'sophisticated' lifestyle. Lifestyle segmentation is concerned with three main elements: *Activities* (such as leisure activities, sports, hobbies, entertainment, home activities, work activities, professional work, shopping behavior, house work and repairs, travel and miscellaneous activities, daily travel, holidays, charitable work); *interaction with others* (such as self-perception, personality and self-ideal, role perceptions, as mother, wife, husband, father, son, daughter, etc., and social interaction, communication with others, opinion leadership); and *opinions* (on topics such as politics, social and moral issues, economic and business-industry issues and technological and environmental issues).

2. **Personality characteristics** are more difficult to measure than demographics or socioeconomics. They are generally inferred from large sets of questions often involving detailed computational (multivariate) analysis techniques. Although the idea that brand choice may be related to personality is intuitively appealing, the usefulness of personality as a segmentation variable is likely to depend on the product category. Buyer and brand personalities are likely to match where brand choice is a direct manifestation of personal values but for the majority of fast-moving consumer goods (FMCG), such as detergents and tea, the reality is that people buy a repertoire of different brands (Lannon, 1991).

The approaches to consumer market segmentation that have been described so far have all been associative segmentation. That is to say, they are used where differences in purchasing behavior/customer are perceived as being associated with them. If a company uses social class, for example, to segment a market it is assuming that purchasing behavior is a function of social class. Most of the problems with using such associative bases tend to be related to the issue of the extent to which they are in fact associated with, or reflect, actual purchasing behavior.

Because of this, numerous marketers believe that it is more sensible to use direct bases for segmenting markets. Such bases take actual consumer behavior as the starting point for identifying different segments. They are often referred to as **behavioral segmentation bases** and shall be described in more detail now (Hollensen and Opresnik, 2020).

3.2.3.3 Behavioral Segmentation

The key behavioral bases for segmenting consumer markets are benefits sought, purchase occasion, purchase behavior, usage, and perceptions, beliefs, and values. Each will now be discussed.

3.2.3.3.1 Benefits sought

A powerful form of segmentation is to group buyers according to the different benefits that they seek from the product or service. For example, a consumer who is allergic to fragrances may prefer unscented shampoo because of the benefits they will derive from it. Benefit segmentation takes the basis of segmentation right back to the underlying reasons why customers are attracted to various product offerings. As such it is perhaps the closest means yet to identifying segments on bases directly relevant to marketing decisions. Developments in techniques such as conjoint analysis make them particularly suitable for identifying benefit segments. The total market for a product or service is broken down into segments distinguished by the principal benefits sought by each segment. A 'benefits sought 'basis for segmentation can provide useful insights into the nature and extent of competition and the possible existence of gaps in the market.

3.2.3.3.2 Purchase occasion

Customers can be distinguished according to the occasions when they purchase a product. Attitudinal characteristics attempt to draw a causal link between customer characteristics and marketing behavior and occasion segmentation can help companies build up product usage. For example, orange juice is most often consumed at breakfast, but orange growers have promoted drinking orange juice as a cool and refreshing drink at other times during the day. In contrast, Coca-Cola's 'Coke in the Morning 'campaign attempts to increase Coke consumption by promoting the beverage as an early morning pick-me-up. Another example is Carte D'or, which emphasizes the joy of eating ice cream in winter to Turkish consumers who are not used to eating ice cream in winter and produces ice cream with winter fruits such as chestnuts and oranges.

3.2.3.3.3 Purchase behavior

The most direct method of segmenting markets is on the basis of the behavior of the consumers in those markets. Study of purchasing behavior has centered on such issues as the time of purchase (early or late in the product's overall life cycle) and patterns of purchase (the identification of brand-loyal customers). Differences in purchase behavior can be based on the time of purchase relative to the launch of the product. When a product is launched, a key task is to identify the innovator segment which consists of customers who purchase a product when it is still new. Evidently during the launch of new products isolation of innovators as the initial target segment could significantly improve the products or service's chances of acceptance on\the market. However, attempts to seek out generalized innovators have been less successful than looking separately for innovators in a specific field. Generalizations seem most relevant when the fields of study are of similar interest. Opinion leaders can be particularly influential in the early stages of the product life cycle. Recording companies, for example, recognize the influence that disc jockeys have on the record-buying public and attempt to influence them with free records and other inducements to play their records.

3.2.3.3.4 Usage

Customers may also be segmented on the basis of being 'heavy', 'light 'and 'non-users 'of a product or service category. The profiling of heavy users allows this group to receive most marketing focus on the assumption that creating brand loyalty among these people will pay large dividends. Consequently, brands are sometimes developed to target heavy users. Noticeably, the usage segmentation concept is more useful in some markets than in others. For example, many banks operating in the Turkish market considers their customers who shop more with credit cards as a separate market segment and provide them with a number of additional advantages.

3.2.3.3.5 Perceptions, Beliefs and Values

The final behavioral base for segmenting consumer markets is by studying perceptions, beliefs, and values. This is categorized as a behavior variable because perceptions, beliefs and values are often linked to behavior. Customers are grouped by identifying those people who view the products in a market in a similar way (perceptual segmentation) and have similar beliefs (belief segmentation). Car manufacturers use belief segmentation to segment the market and target specific groups. For example, Mazda targets car buyers who believe their car is their friend, with which they can have fun and enjoy new experiences (Bruce, 2005).

3.2.3.4 Combining Segmentation Variables

As stated above, marketers rarely limit their segmentation analysis to only one of a few variables. Rather, they are increasingly using multiple segmentation bases in an effort to identify smaller, yet better defined target groups. For example, Research Services Ltd, a UK marketing research company, has developed 'SAGACITY', a market segmentation scheme based upon a combination of occupation, life cycle and income. 12 distinct customer groupings are formed with different aspirations and behavior patterns (Ellis-Chadwick and Jobber, 2016).

3.2.4 SEGMENTING THE BUSINESS MARKETS (B2B)

The imperative to divide the market into different segments in order to offer products that match differing needs is at the very heart of both B2B and B2C marketing. The strength, width and depth of the segmentation demands will vary from industry to industry and from country to country depending on factors that often change, which will be discussed later in the section. Only if the varying and diverse benefits demanded by different industries and organisations are known can products and services be offered with benefits that will satisfy these many disparate needs.

The basic approach to segmentation, targeting and positioning does not differ greatly between B2C and B2B markets. Although there are not many differences, market segmentation in B2B markets is based on identifying and grouping businesses according to their industry, size, location, product, or service usage and buying behavior. As one might expect, segmenting industrial product markets introduces a number of additional bases for segmentation, whilst precluding some of the more frequently used ones in consumer product markets (Hollensen and Opresnik, 2020).

3.2.5 TARGET MARKETING

Market segmentation reveals the company's market segment opportunities. The firm now has to evaluate the various segments and decide how many and which segments it can serve and apply distinct and appropriate marketing mix strategies. In evaluating different market segments, a company must look at three basic factors: **segment size**, **segment growth**, **segment structural attractiveness**, and **company objectives and resources** (Hollensen and Opresnik, 2020).

The organisation must first collect and analyze data on current segment sales, growth rates, and expected profitability for various segments. In general, large-sized segments are more attractive than small ones since sales potential is greater, and the chance of achieving economies of scale is improved. However, the 'right size and growth 'of segments is a relative matter as the largest, fastest-growing segments are not necessarily the most attractive ones for every company. Smaller companies, as already mentioned above, may lack the skills and resources needed to serve the larger segments or they may find these segments too competitive. Such enterprises may select segments that are smaller and less attractive, in an absolute dimension, but that are potentially more profitable for them (Hollensen and Opresnik, 2020).

The company also needs to examine the structural factors that affect long-term segment attractiveness. Michael **Porter's Five Forces Model** (Porter, 1985) provides a useful tool in this context. For example, a segment is less attractive if it already contains many strong and aggressive **competitors**. The existence of many actual or potential **substitutes** (products or services) may limit prices and the profits that can be gained in a specific segment. In addition, the **threat of new entrants** is another factor to be considered: a segment may seem superficially attractive because of the lack of current competition, but care must be taken to assess the dynamics of the market. A judgement must be made regarding the likelihood of new entrants, possibly with new technology, which might change the rules of the competitive game. The **relative power of buyers** also affects segment attractiveness. Buyers with strong bargaining power relative to sellers will try to force prices down, demand more services, and set competitors against one another – all the expense of seller profitability. Finally, a segment may be less attractive if the **bargaining power of suppliers** is strong as they are in a position to control prices or reduce the quality or quantity of ordered goods and services.

Having evaluated the relative attractiveness of different market segment the company is then in a position to select a **targeting strategy**. A company can select from three generic strategies with respect to targeting.

These three strategies are **undifferentiated target marketing, differentiated target marketing, concentrated target marketing** and **micro marketing**, each of which shall be discussed now (Hollensen and Opresnik, 2020):

1. Using an **undifferentiated marketing** or **mass marketing strategy**, a company decides to ignore market segment differences and go after the whole market with one offer. This strategy focuses on what is common in the needs of consumers rather than on what is different. The company designs a product and a marketing strategy that will appeal to the largest number of potential buyers. This is only feasible, if a market analysis will show now strong differences in customer characteristics that have implications for marketing strategy. Alternatively, the cost in developing a separate marketing mix for separate segments may outweigh the potential gains of meeting customer needs more accurately (Hollensen and Opresnik, 2020).

2. Using a **differentiated marketing** or **segmented marketing strategy**, a company decides to target several market segments and designs distinct offers for each. This is a powerful strategy when market segmentation reveals several potential targets and specific marketing mixes can be developed to appeal to all or some of the segments. For example, airlines design different marketing mixes for first-class and economy passengers, including varying prices, service levels, quality of food, in-cabin comfort and waiting areas at airports (Ellis-Chadwick and Jobber, 2016).

3. A third market-coverage strategy, **concentrated marketing** or **niche marketing** or **focused marketing**, is especially viable when company resources are limited. Instead of going after a small share of a large market, the company goes after a large share of just one or a few segments or niches. Focused marketing allows research and development expenditure to be concentrated on meeting the needs of one set of customers, and managerial activities can be devoted to understanding their specific needs. Large organisations may not be interested in serving the needs of this one segment, or their energies may be so dispatched across the whole market that they pay insufficient attention to their requirements (Ellis-Chadwick and Jobber, 2016). An example of focused marketing in the consumer market is provided by the brand "Milimetric", which sews customized men's shirts according to the customer's specifications and optionally embroider names on the shirt cuffs.

4. **Customized Marketing:** In some markets the requirements of individual customers are unique and their purchasing power sufficient to make designing a separate marketing mix for each customer viable. Segmentation at this disaggregated level leads to the use of **customized marketing** (also labelled **individual marketing, one-to-one marketing, mass customization** and **markets-of-one marketing**). Many service providers, such as advertising and marketing research agencies, architects, and solicitors, vary their offerings on a customer-to-customer basis. Customized marketing is often associated with close

relationships between supplier and buyer because the value of the order justifies large marketing and sales efforts being focused on each customer. The move toward individual marketing mirrors the trend in consumer self-marketing which implies that individual customers are taking more responsibility for determining which products and brands to buy (Hollensen and Opresnik, 2020).

3.2.6 POSITIONING STRATEGY

The final stages of the STP-process involve the development of positioning strategies together with an appropriate marketing mix. In their seminal work in this area, Ries and Trout (1981) suggested that positioning is essentially `a battle for the mind `of the customer. Consequently, successful positioning is often associated with products possessing favourable associations in the minds of customers. These add up to a differential advantage in the minds – and hearts – of the target customers of the company.

A useful tool for determining the position of a brand in the marketplace is the **perceptual map** (also called a **brand map** or **positioning map)**. This is a visual representation of consumer perceptions of the brand and its competitors using attributes (dimensions) that are important to customers. The key steps in developing a perceptual map are as follows (Ellis-Chadwick and Jobber, 2016):

1. Identify a set of competing brands.
2. Identify important attributes or purchase criteria that are important to consumers that consumers use when choosing between brands using qualitative research (e.g. group decisions)
3. Conduct qualitative marketing research where consumers score each brand on all key attributes.
4. Plot brand on a two-dimensional map.

For example, suppose that a company seeks to enter the market for `instant coffee`, in which there are already competitors producing brands A, B, C, D, E, F and G. The company must establish what the customers believe to be the appropriate attributes when choosing between brands in this market and the perceived position of existing competitors with respect to these attributes. If we imagine that the important attributes have been found to be `price `and `flavour`, a possible **positioning map** might be drawn as shown in Figure 3.9.

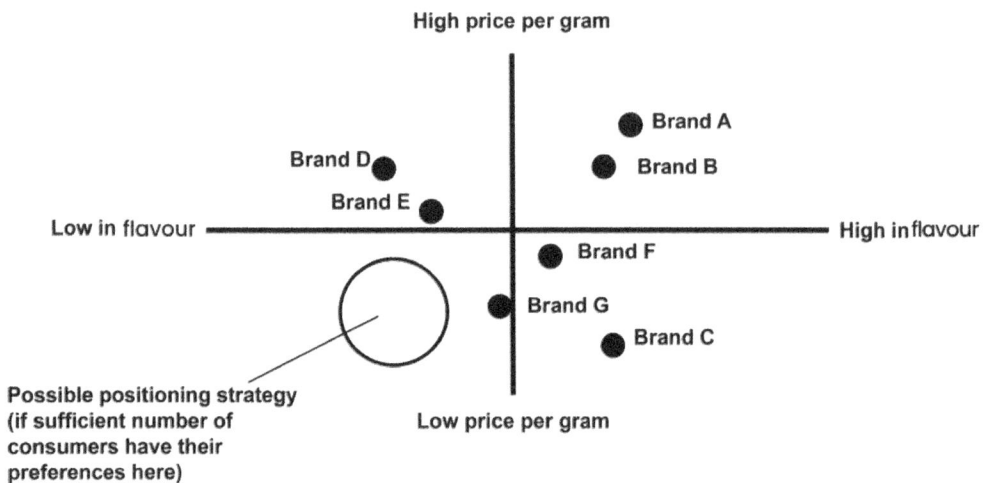

Figure 3.9 Hypothetical Positioning Map: Instant Coffee Market.
Source: Adapted from Hollensen and Opresnik, 2020, modified.

113

With this information, the company must decide where to position its product within this specific market segment. Possibilities are contained within the box, the parameters of which are low to medium price per gram and low to medium in flavour. Perhaps a 'caffeine free 'product could also be taken into consideration? Such a product would give the new brand distinctiveness, as opposed to positioning the brand next to another and fighting 'head on 'for market share.

What is the most appropriate position for the new coffee brand depends on a number of factors? For example, as outlined earlier, we must assess the relative attractiveness of a particular position in a market for the new brand compared to the resources and competences of the company. Obviously, it is also important to consider if the number of customers in the chosen position is large enough to generate sufficient profit. Similarly, and related to this, we must assess the relative strengths of existing competitive brands in the market and whether we want to tackle this competition head on or not. Finally, we must consider what our objectives for the new product are, particularly with regard to brand image.

Once the company has assessed brand positioning in the market and determined where it wants to position its products and brands, the final step in the process of segmentation, targeting and positioning involves the design of marketing programmes, which will support the positional strategy in selected target markets. In the 'instant coffee 'example above the company must therefore determine what price, flavour (product) distribution and promotional strategy will be necessary to achieve the selected position in the market (Hollensen, 2006).

CASE STUDY
NUROL TEKNOLOJI

BUILDING TRUST, DELIVERING EXCELLENCE, ADVANCING TOGETHER

Written by: K. Cihansah Dumlu (Market Specialist, Harvard University)

Introduction

Nurol Teknoloji (NT), headquartered in Türkiye, stands as a global leader in advanced ballistic armor solutions. Leveraging its robust R&D capabilities and extensive experience, Nurol Teknoloji produces personnel, vehicle, and structural protection solutions that are up to 60% lighter than conventional steel protection products. Over its 15-year history and momentum gained after the top management change, this innovative competency has facilitated exports to five continents and 61 countries.

A key differentiator for Nurol Teknoloji is that its solutions are "combat proven." The company has safeguarded the lives of allied forces in numerous peacekeeping missions and conflicts. Notably, in the 2022 Ukraine conflict, Nurol Teknoloji played a critical role by supplying over 250,000 personnel ballistic plates within six months, significantly impacting the war's trajectory.

Nurol Teknoloji continues to set industry standards with its commitment to excellence and innovation, consistently providing superior protection solutions worldwide.

Challenge

As a result of COVID-19 and regional conflicts, the sensitive ballistic protection industry has faced significant challenges. Supply chain bottlenecks emerged, sudden surges in demand disrupted the demand-supply equilibrium, and various projects were canceled. Compared to other global markets, the U.S. market offers more stabilized and systematic purchasing processes, accounting for one-third of the global market. Recognizing this stability, NT initiated a strategy in 2022 to expand into the U.S. market to achieve sustainable growth and increase business volume.

The U.S. market is characterized by high expectations and stringent standards, positioning NT advantageously by its capabilities. However, various macro and micro factors complicate market entry. On a macro scale, the strained relations between Türkiye and the U.S. pose challenges, while on a micro scale, market conservatism, sector concentration, and high entry barriers are significant obstacles. Consequently, NT's market expansion risk coefficient, particularly in B2G transactions with state and federal agencies, remains notably high.

Background

Nurol Teknoloji has established a unique business model through its comprehensive grand strategy. While the sector has focused on expanding its sales channels, NT has prioritized vertical integration. Utilizing both composite materials and advanced technological ceramics in its armor panels and plates, NT distinguishes itself as one of the few companies globally capable of producing ballistic ceramics. The company manufactures its own ceramics, developing proprietary formulations for its armor products.

Nurol Teknoloji's Comprehensive Protection Solutions Portfolio

In 2023, NT further strengthened its capabilities by acquiring Industriekeramik Hochrhein, a leading German ceramic powder manufacturer. This acquisition enabled NT to achieve seamless integration from raw material to final product, enhancing its R&D competence, production speed, capacity, and quality. NT has also developed specialized marketing models to leverage these strengths in the market effectively.

Nurol Technology USA Establishment – Solution Provider

In 2022, it was decided to extend this unique business model and its associated initiatives to the U.S. market—the most challenging yet largest market in the world. In the ballistics industry, 90%+ of companies attempting to enter this market have faced significant failures. By strategically addressing the risk factors associated with expanding into the U.S. market, and capitalizing on its unique competencies, NT has achieved effective and efficient market penetration within 2 years. This demonstrates that NT's competencies and strategies have become its most valuable assets in marketing, enabling it to establish a strong presence in the U.S. market.

In 2022, Nurol Technology USA (NT USA) decided to position itself in the market with a robust and strategic approach. This strategy emphasized a B2B model, positioning NT as a "Solution Provider" leveraging its extensive competencies. In the highly competitive market, this strategy aimed to address all customer challenges, fostering more partnerships than competition. By developing solutions that also benefit competitors, NT created collaborative synergies, not only for today's needs but also for the partners' future needs.

Under its strategic vision, NT established two distinct brands. The NT Armor brand offers finished armor solutions to partners, while the NT Cera brand markets NT's unique ceramic recipes, specifically armor raw materials. NT's mission to integrate its solutions into every armor system in the USA has been well-received by the market. Today, NT USA collaborates with all major players in the U.S. market, developing joint solutions and fostering strong partnerships.

Two Distinct Brands: NT Armor & NT Cera for comprehensive solutions

The "Solution Provider" positioning crafted by NT USA, grounded in NT's core competencies, has made the entire market accessible. This approach offers a comprehensive perspective, enhancing NT's market presence, awareness, and influence rather than limiting its scope.

To enhance the impact and sustainability of this strategic positioning, NT has established specific market practices.

Rule 1: Partnership > buyer-seller (traditional customer) relationship.

Rule 2: Matching the 7C value promises (created by NT USA) with partners in maximum harmony.

Rule 3: Think about your partner's problems and needs from yesterday.

COMPETENCY - 360° Experience and Interaction - Know What is Needed

CONSISTENCY - Full Control Over the Production Process - Ensuring Consistency

COST MANAGEMENT - Effective Cost Management - EBITDA Increase for Partners

CONTROL - Optimal Control Over the Supply Chain - Keeping the Promise

COMPETITIVENESS - Infrastructure to Meet Global and Local Market Needs - Help Partners to Win

CAPABILITY - Double-sided Experience Flow Between Raw Material and End Product - Do More Than What is Needed

CAPACITY - Effective Resource/Efficiency Management - Never Say Never

NT 7C's Model – Roadmap of thinking for customers

By adopting the above approach, NT facilitated a collaborative market entry, which created the opportunity to effectively learn the market and customer dynamics, leading to successful product and brand adaptations. In addition, our market presence was further strengthened through strategic co-branding activities.

As a result, NT has conducted one of the best executed market entries within the industry. This success has not only provided significant access to the U.S. market but has also opened doors to numerous other global markets. NT has effectively leveraged its strengths and strategic capabilities, demonstrating the power of its unique approach.

Conclusion

Nurol Teknoloji's (NT) strategic foray into the U.S. market underscores the company's commitment to leveraging its unique competencies and innovative business model to achieve global success. The decision to expand into the U.S. market—the most challenging yet largest market in the world—was driven by a recognition of the stabilizing effect of systematic purchasing processes in this region, which comprises one-third of the global market. NT's comprehensive approach to addressing the macro and micro challenges inherent in this market, from geopolitical tensions to high entry barriers, highlights its strategic foresight and adaptability.

NT's vertical integration, particularly its capability to produce ballistic ceramics in-house, has positioned the company as a formidable player in the industry. The acquisition of Industriekeramik Hochrhein in 2023 exemplifies NT's dedication to enhancing its R&D, production speed, capacity, and quality. This vertical integration not only sets NT apart from its competitors but also ensures that the company can deliver bespoke, high-quality solutions to its partners efficiently.

The establishment of NT USA and the strategic positioning as a "Solution Provider" have been pivotal in NT's successful market penetration. By fostering partnerships rather than traditional customer relationships, NT has created a collaborative market entry strategy that addresses the needs of its partners both in the present and future. The development of two distinct brands—NT Armor and NT Cera—has further solidified

118

NT's presence in the U.S. market, offering comprehensive solutions that cater to various segments of the ballistic protection industry.

NT's market practices, encapsulated in the 7C's Model, have been instrumental in ensuring the sustainability and impact of its strategic positioning. By prioritizing partnership over a buyer-seller dynamic, aligning value promises with partner needs, and proactively addressing partner problems, NT has established a robust framework for long-term success. This approach has facilitated effective market and customer understanding, leading to successful product and brand adaptations, and strengthening NT's market presence through strategic co-branding activities.

The outcome of NT's meticulous strategy and execution is evident in its enhanced market presence and influence. The success in the U.S. market has not only opened doors to other global markets but has also demonstrated the power of NT's unique approach. By selling its strength and strategy, NT has effectively positioned itself as a global leader in ballistic protection solutions, driving innovation and excellence in the industry. This achievement underscores NT's ability to adapt and thrive in challenging environments, solidifying its reputation as a trusted partner and solution provider worldwide.

Questions to stimulate conversation on the case

1. **How did NT leverage its vertical integration to gain a competitive advantage in the U.S. market?**

NT leveraged its vertical integration by producing its own ballistic ceramics and acquiring Industriekeramik Hochrhein, a leading German ceramic powder manufacturer. This allowed NT to control the entire production process from raw material to final product. As a result, NT enhanced its R&D competence, production speed, capacity, and quality. This comprehensive control over the supply chain enabled NT to offer superior and reliable products. By ensuring high-quality standards and rapid response to market demands, NT distinguished itself from competitors.

2. **What strategic steps did NT take to position itself successfully in the highly competitive U.S. market?**

NT adopted a B2B model, positioning itself as a "Solution Provider" rather than a traditional seller. This strategy focused on addressing all partner challenges, fostering partnerships instead of competition. NT created two distinct brands: NT Armor for finished armor solutions and NT Cera for ceramic materials, catering to specific market needs. The company also developed the 7C's Model to align its value propositions with partner needs. These strategic steps facilitated a collaborative market entry, effectively learning market dynamics and ensuring successful product adaptations.

3. **How did NT's market practices contribute to its successful market entry in the U.S.?**

NT's market practices were designed to enhance the impact and sustainability of its strategic positioning. Rule 1 emphasized partnerships over traditional customer relationships, fostering deeper collaboration. Rule 2 involved matching the 7C value promises with partners to ensure maximum harmony and alignment. Rule 3 focused on anticipating and addressing partners' problems proactively. These practices created a cooperative market environment, enabling NT to learn and adapt quickly. As a result, NT established a strong presence, leveraging strategic co-branding activities to solidify its market position.

Links and media

Nurol Teknoloji Website – https://www.nurolteknoloji.com/
NT Armor Website – https://www.ntarmor.com/
NT Cera Website – https://www.ntcera.com/

Case Highlights

Nurol Teknoloji (NT), headquartered in Türkiye, has emerged as a global leader in advanced ballistic armor solutions, thanks to its robust R&D capabilities and innovative approach. In 2022, NT strategically extended its unique business model to the U.S. market, the world's most challenging yet largest market. This move was driven by a need for stable and systematic purchasing processes amidst global supply chain disruptions and fluctuating demands. The U.S. market, which accounts for one-third of the global market, provided the perfect landscape for NT's sustainable growth ambitions.

NT's vertical integration, bolstered by its in-house production of ballistic ceramics and the acquisition of Industriekeramik Hochrhein in 2023, has enhanced its R&D competence, production speed, capacity, and quality. By positioning itself as a "Solution Provider" and adopting a B2B model, NT has fostered partnerships rather than traditional customer relationships, addressing partner needs comprehensively.

NT's dual-brand strategy—NT Armor for finished armor solutions and NT Cera for ceramic materials—has been well-received in the U.S. market. The company's strategic market practices, encapsulated in the 7C's Model, have ensured a collaborative and effective market entry. This success has not only solidified NT's presence in the U.S. but also opened doors to numerous other global markets, affirming its status as a trusted global leader in ballistic protection solutions.

4. MARKETING MIX IN THE MARKETING PLANNING PROCESS

To this point, we have discussed the analysis, which is essential in the framework of the development of detailed marketing programmes designed to meet corporate and strategic marketing objectives. In this and the following chapters, we will consider strategic decisions concerned with planning and implementing elements of the marketing mix, i.e., product, price, promotion, and place decisions. In this chapter, we will start with the product element of the marketing mix (Hollensen and Opresnik, 2020).

4.1 PRODUCT AND SERVICE DECISIONS

Essentially, a product can be defined as anything that can be offered to a customer for attention, acquisition, use, or consumption and that might satisfy a want or need. Product is a core element in the marketing mix as it provides the functional requirements sought by customers. Careful management of the product offering is essential if your company is to produce the desired responses from customers, but the product is only part of the story. In an age of intense competition where it is of critical importance to differentiate one's offerings from competitors.

In creating an acceptable product offer for international markets, it is necessary to examine first what contributes to the 'total 'product offer. In the product dimensions, we include not just the core physical properties, but also additional elements such as packaging, branding and after-sales service that make up the total package for the purchaser. We can look at three levels of a product (Hollensen and Opresnik, 2020):

- **Core product benefits:** Functional features, performance, perceived value, image and technology.

- **Product attributes:** Brand name, design, packaging, price, size, colour variants, country of origin.

- **Support services:** Delivery, installation, guarantees, after-sales service (repair and maintenance), spare part services.

In this respect, it is much easier to standardize the core product benefits (functional features, performance, etc.) then it is to standardize the support services, which often have to be tailored to the business culture and sometimes to individual customers.

4.1.1 DIFFERENT PRODUCT LEVELS

Product differentiation seeks to increase the value of the product or service. Levitt (1986) has suggested that products and services can be seen on at least four main levels which we shall quickly summarize to add comprehensiveness in the framework of product policy. These levels are the core product, the expected product, the augmented product, and the potential product. Figure 4.1 shows these levels.

Differentiation is possible in all these respects.

At the centre of the model is the core, or generic, product. This is the central product or service offered. The **core benefit** addresses the following question: What is the buyer really buying? When designing products, marketers must first define the core, problem-solving benefits, or services that consumer want.

Beyond the generic product, however, is what customers expect in addition, the **expected product**. When buying petrol, for example, customers expect the possibility of paying by credit card, the availability of screen wash facilities, and so on. Since most petrol forecourts meet these expectations, they do not serve to differentiate one supplier from another.

At the next level, Levitt identifies the **augmented product**. This constitutes all the additional features and services that exceed customer expectations to convey added value and hence serve to differentiate the offer from that of competitors.

Product planners must build an augmented product around the core benefit and expected product by offering additional customer services and benefits. The petrol station where one attendant fills the car with petrol while another cleans the windscreen, headlamps, and mirrors, is going beyond what is expected. Over time, however, these means of distinguishing can become copied, routine, and ultimately merely part of what is expected.

Finally, Levitt describes the **potential product** as all those further additional features and benefits that could be offered. At the petrol station these may include a free car wash with every fifth fill up. While the model shows the potential product bounded, in reality it is only bounded by the imagination and ingenuity of the supplier (Hollensen and Opresnik, 2020).

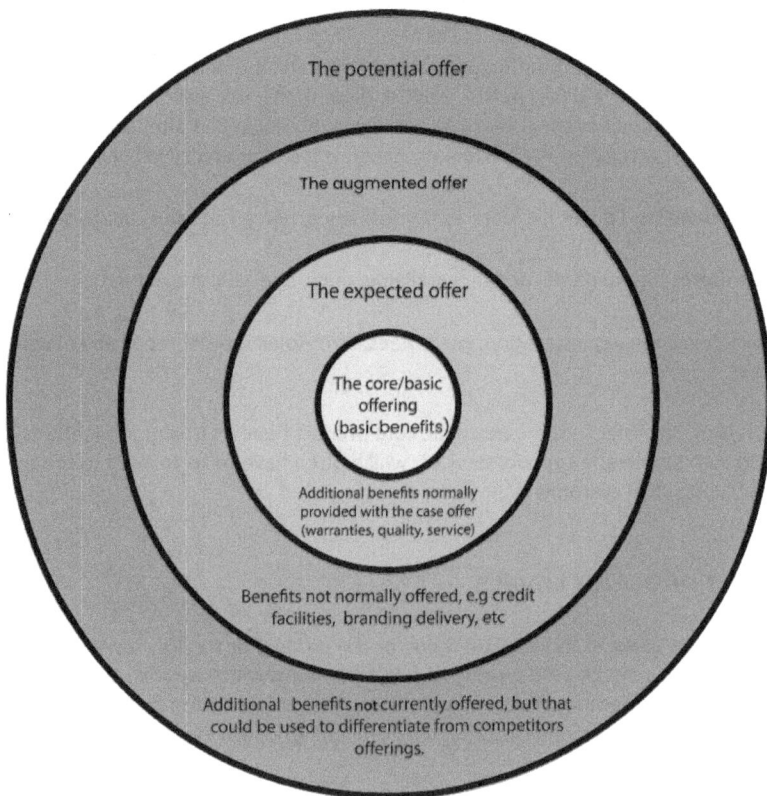

The potential offer

The augmented offer

The expected offer

The core/basic offering (basic benefits)

Additional benefits normally provided with the case offer (warranties, quality, service)

Benefits not normally offered, e.g credit facilities, branding delivery, etc

Additional benefits not currently offered, but that could be used to differentiate from competitors offerings.

Figure 4.1: Different Product Levels.
Source: Adapted from Hollensen and Opresnik, 2020, modified.

In the past, suppliers have concentrated on attempts to differentiate their offerings on the basis of the core and expected product that convergence is occurring at this level in many markets. As quality control, assurance and management methods become more widely understood and practiced, delivering a performing, reliable, durable, conforming offer (a 'quality 'product in the classic sense of the word) will no longer be adequate. In the future, there will be greater emphasis on the augmented and potential product as ways of adding value, creating customer delight and hence creating competitive advantage.

The key decisions in the development and marketing of individual products and services include **product attributes, branding, packaging, labelling** and **product support services**.

4.1.2 PRODUCT LINE DECISIONS

Beyond decisions about individual products and services, product strategy also calls for building a product line. A **product line** is a group of products that are closely related because they function in a similar manner, are sold to the same customer groups, are marketed through the same types of outlets, or fall within given price ranges. For example, Nokia produces several lines of telecommunication products.

The major product line decision involves **product line length** – the number of items in the product line. The line is too short if the manager can enlarge profits by adding items and the line is too long if the marketer can increase profits by dropping items. Product line length is influenced by company objectives and resources. For example, one goal might be allowing for **upselling**. Thus, BMW wants to move customers up from its 3-series models to 5- and 7-series models. Another objective might be to allow **cross-selling**: Hewlett-Packard sells printers as well as cartridges.

A firm can lengthen the product line in two ways: by **line stretching** or by **line filling**. Product line stretching occurs when a company lengthens its product line beyond its current range. The firm can stretch its line downward, upward, or both ways. Mercedes-Benz, for example, stretched its Mercedes line downward because of the following reasons: Facing a slow-growth luxury car market and attacks by Japanese automakers on its high-end positioning, it successfully introduced its Mercedes C-Class cars.

Product line filling involves adding more items within the present range of the line. Reasons for this approach include reaching for extra profits, satisfying dealers, using excess capacity and being the leading full-line company. Sony, for example, filled its Walkman line by adding solar-powered and waterproof Walkmans, ultra-light models for exercises, and the Memory Stick Walkman. Line filling is overdone if it results in cannibalization and customer confusion (Hollensen and Opresnik, 2020).

4.1.3 PRODUCT MIX DECISIONS

An organisation with several product lines has a product mix. A **product mix** (or **product assortment**) consist of all the product lines and items that a particular company market.

A company's product mix has four important dimensions: width, length, depth, and consistency:

- **Product mix width** refers to the number of different product lines the company carries. For example, Procter & Gamble markets a wide product mix consisting of 250 brands organized into five major product lines: personal and beauty, house and home, health and wellness, baby and family, and pet nutrition and care products.

- **Product mix length** refers to the total number of items the firm carries within its product lines. P&G carries many brands within each line. For example, its house and home lines include seven laundry detergents, six hand soaps, five shampoos, and four dishwashing detergents (Hollensen and Opresnik, 2020).

- **Product line depth** refers to the number of versions offered for each product in the line. P&G's Crest toothpaste comes in 16 varieties.

- Finally, **the consistency** of the product mix refers to how closely relate the various product lines are in end use, production requirements, distribution channels, or some other way. P&G's product lines are consistent insofar as they are consumer products that go through the same distribution channels. The lines are less consistent insofar as they perform different functions for customers.

The hypothetical company in Figure 4.2 manufactures and markets three product lines (= product width). Product depth refers to the number of product items in each line – 3, 4 and 2 respectively – with the average being 3. By looking at Figure 4.2 a strategic assessment of a company's product offering can be made. For example, the product width could be extended by adding more product lines. The same could happen to the product depth. The depth of the product line depends upon the pattern of customer requirements, the product depth being offered by competitors, and company resources (Hollensen and Opresnik, 2020).

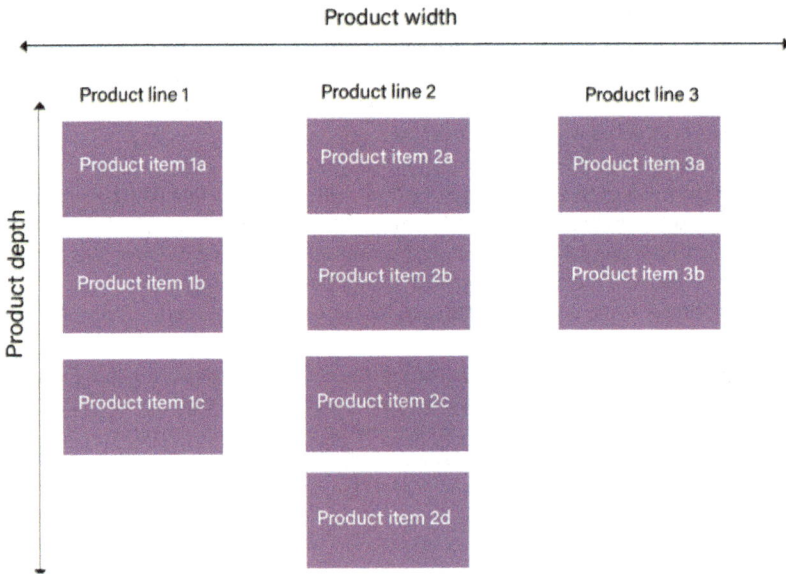

Figure 4.2: The Product Mix for a Hypothetical Company.
Source: Adapted from Hollensen and Opresnik, 2020, modified.

4.1.4 SERVICES MARKETING

Services have grown dramatically in recent years. It is seen from the definition of a product that services often accompany products. Increasingly it is accepted that because buyers are concerned with benefits or satisfactions this is a combination of both tangible 'products', and intangible 'services.

4.1.4.1 Characteristics of Services

Services are characterized by the following features (Hollensen, 2006):

- **Intangibility** means that services cannot be seen, tasted, felt, heard, or smelled before they are bought. For example, as services like air transportation or education cannot be touched or tested, the buyers or services cannot claim ownership or anything tangible in the conventional sense.

Payment is for use or performance. Tangible elements of the service, such as food or drink on airlines, are used as part of the service in order to confirm the benefit provided and to enhance its perceived value.

Against this background, a service marketing strategy consistently tries to `make the intangible tangible ` and send the right signals about the quality. This is called **evidence management**, in which the service organisation presents its customers with organized, honest evidence of its capabilities.

- **Perishability** means that services cannot be stored for future usage – for example, unfilled airline seats are lost once the aircraft takes off. This characteristic causes considerable problems in planning and promotion in order to match supply and demand. To maintain service capacity constantly at levels necessary to satisfy peak demand will be very expensive.

The marketer must therefore attempt to estimate demand levels in order optimise the use of capacity.

- **Heterogeneity** implies that services are rarely the same because they involve interactions between people. Furthermore, there is high customer involvement in the production of services.

This can cause problems of maintaining quality, particularly in international markets where there are quite different attitudes towards customer service. For example, within a given Marriott hotel, one registration-desk employee may be cheerful and highly efficient, whereas another standing just a few feet away may be unpleasant and slow. Even the quality of a single Marriott employee`s service varies according to his or her energy at the time of each customer encounter.

Consequently, the management of staff is of supreme importance in the framework of service marketing.

- **Inseparability** means that services cannot be separated from their providers. The time of production is very close to or even simultaneous with the time of consumption. The service is provided at the point of sale. This means that economies of scale and experience curve benefits are difficult to achieve, and supplying the service to scattered markets can be expensive, particularly in the initial setting-up phase. If a service employee provides the service, then the employee is a part of the service.

Because the customer is also present, **provider-customer-interaction** is a special feature of services marketing and both the provider, and the customer affect the service outcome.

4.1.4.2 Categories of Service

All products, both goods and services, consist of a core element that is surrounded by an array of optional supplementary elements. If we look first at the core service products, we can assign them to one of three broad categories depending on their tangibility and the extent to which customers need to be physically present during service production. These categories are presented in Figure 4.3.

Categories of service	Characteristics	Examples
People processing	Customers become a part of the production process. The service needs to maintain local geographic presence	Education Healthcare Food service Hotel service
Possession processing	The object needs to be involved in the production process, but the owner of the object (the customer) does not. Involve tangible actions to physical objects to improve their value for the customers	Car repair
Information based services	Collecting, interpreting and transmitting data to create value to others. Minimal tangibility. Minimal customer involvement in the production process	Banking internet services

Figure 4.3: Categories of Service.
Source: Adapted from Hollensen and Opresnik, 2020, modified.

4.1.4.3 The 7Ps Model of Service Marketing

In the case of service organisations, the 4Ps marketing mix is felt to be insufficient. Some authors have suggested extending it to the so-called **7Ps approach** which includes people, process, and physical evidence. In services, people often *are* the service itself; the process of how the service is delivered to the customer is usually a key part of the service, and the physical evidence – the design of a shop, for example – is so critical to success that it should be considered as a separate element in the services marketing mix. Figure 4.4 contrasts the 4Ps and the 7Ps approach.

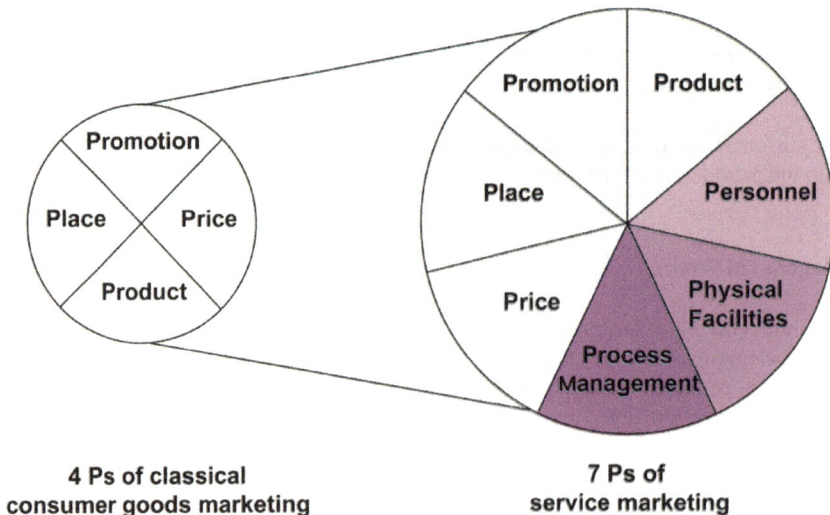

4 Ps of classical consumer goods marketing

7 Ps of service marketing

Because of the specific characteristics described above, managing services enterprises involves specific challenges with the extended marketing mix. Therefore, we shall now briefly describe them:

- **Physical evidence:** Customers look for clues to the likely quality of a service by inspecting the tangible evidence of the service. For example, the ambience of a retail store is highly dependent on décor, and colour plays an important role in establishing mood.

- **People:** Because of the simultaneity of production and consumption in services, the firm's personnel occupy a key position in influencing customer perceptions of product quality. The term service encounter is used to describe an interaction between a service provider and a customer. These encounters may be short and quick such as when a customer picks up a newspaper at a newsstand or long and protracted involving multiple encounters such as receiving a university education.

- **Process:** The service process refers to the procedures, mechanisms, and flow of activities by which a service is acquired. This process usually contains two elements, namely, that which is visible to the customer and where the service encounter takes place and that which is invisible to the customer but is still critical to service delivery. For example, waiting staff in a restaurant are a key part of the service encounter and they need to be well selected and well trained. How they treat customers is a key element of the service experience. But what happens in the kitchen, even though it is invisible to the customer is also critical to the experience. Both parts of the service process need to be carefully managed. Service process decisions usually involve some trade-off between levels of service quality (effectiveness) and service productivity (efficiency). For instance, if more people can be served (output) using the same number of staff (input), productivity per employee has risen. For example, a doctor who reduces consultation time per patient raises productivity at the risk of lowering service quality. Consequently, a balance must be struck between productivity and service quality.

Contrasting the 4Ps and the 7Ps model, there is no reason the – useful – extensions of the latter cannot be integrated within the 4Ps framework. People, process, and physical evidence can be discussed under 'product', for example. The important issue is not to neglect them, whether the 4Ps approach or some other method is used to conceptualise the decision-making areas of marketing.

TURKISH AIRLINES

CROSSING THE ATLANTIC IN TURKISH STYLE

Written by: Mehmet Can Sahin (Customer Experience Specialist)

Introduction

Turkish Airlines is one of the leading airlines in the aviation industry with flying more than 80 million passengers on 400 plus aircrafts in the year 2023. Its expansive network criss-crosses more than 130 countries across 6 continents which makes it the airline flying more countries than any other. Though the airline operates a vast network with thousands of flights per day, it proved that has the ability to respond to any global shocks with prompt and calculated strategies. The way the company gets through Covid-19 by applying operational, marketing, and financial measures is a testament to its agility as an organization. Beyond operational capability, it is the best choice among air travellers in different categories, such as catering, business class service, and economy class offering. Turkish Airlines, together with 8 prominent airlines across the world, was named as a Word Class airline by APEX Passenger Choice Awards in the years of 2022, 2023, and 2024. Turkish Airlines has quite good acquaintance of being crowned as Europe's Best Airline by renowned rating organisation Skytrax. It comes naturally to repeat the success for the ninth time in 2024. Passengers are very much into the onboard meals of the airline, so it was, awarded with 2024 Skytrax prizes for both Best Business Class Catering across the world and Best Economy Onboard Catering in Europe.

As customers are seeking out all-around value out of their transactions with companies, Turkish Airlines keeping up to date with consumers' needs and wants with its service offers from extensive online channels, physical attributes of the service itself and front-end staff to 7/24 customer relationship services. Turkish Airlines always has fingers on the pulses of customers, so it has moved all its operations in 2019 to the grandeur new Istanbul Airport to forestall passenger experience reducing possible congestion at any ground side touch points. Besides, Turkish offers business class and frequent flyer passengers privileged services both on the air and ground with exclusive lounge access, airport reception bay, and exquisite service up in the sky. Unmatched onboard meals with well recognition by awards including unique flying chef experience make Turkish Airlines a top service providing company. Beyond those, for the sake of accommodating customer delight at the augmented level of the brand, it offers exclusive complimentary Stopover accommodation in Istanbul for free of charge to all passengers in any cabin class should they fit the programme terms and conditions. Moreover, Turkish Airlines stops at nothing in the pursuit of finding out the best possible treats for its passengers. If transfer passengers plan to spend less time in Istanbul between their flights, the airline offers them Touristanbul service in which they would take in historical attractions of İstanbul. As a part of Touristanbul, the airline holds 7 different tours for free on all days of the year. Turkish Airlines passengers who have transit time from 6 to 24 hours at Istanbul Airport are eligible to experience the bounties of the programme.

Turkish Airlines already sets its eyes on far more higher peaks in which it aims by 2033 to double up its fleet size well over to 800 aircrafts, flying more than 170 million passengers and with revenue well above 50 billion USD. Besides, by 2028, Turkish Airlines would like to be ranked in the top three airlines worldwide in terms of market share and service quality. Meanwhile, it etched the target of being the most sought-after airline of passengers on the stone, so it will keep continue to press ahead with service offering well above par to its rivals.

The company, in line with its future looking aim, conjures up new offers to influence travellers' behaviors in order to increase its passenger numbers together with its RPM and load factor for both healthy and sound financial and customer lifetime value future.

Thus began, the Stopover programme to move in on the US market more profusely.

Challenge

Though the airline industry is all razzle and dazzle that enchants anyone outside of the fold, it is fraught with horde of pitfalls and unexpected headwinds getting any company off its tracks. Hence, airlines on average recorded around the meagre 2.7% net profit margin in 2023. So, any airline should take a step forward for their good after optimum managerial and financial deliberations.

As the USA market presents itself with promising prospects of well above 300 million population, Turkish Airlines geared up its efforts to solidify its market share in the US market. However, it is not low hanging fruit for any airline no matter what extent the size it has. Challenges for Turkish Airlines to make a big success in the US market could be compiled into 2 dimensions stated below.

1.   Existing Rivalry

There are already plenty of established carriers crisscrossing the Atlantic for the sake of capturing shares of business and leisure traveller markets in both point-to-point and transit means. So, it naturally brings about the pressure on airfare prices. Airlines in the saturated market have a kind of go-to market strategy which is an application of promotional fares to convince would-be passengers to fly with them. However, this kind of practises comes with a catch which eats into the yields and possible bottom lines of the company. Besides, airlines not anymore are out in the market all alone. They have already brought their strength together in the form of alliances, which are namely Star Alliance, One World and Sky Team. Since all these airline pacts have proliferated flights across the pond, travellers opting for one particular loyalty programme offered by any member of a particular alliance must stick to the airline which is a member of that particular alliance. Therefore, leaving the alliance ecosystem for an airline that belongs to other alliances raise the switching cost for travellers. Since it is the case, travellers are wary of drifting to other competitors. The aforementioned reasons (switching cost and pressure on airfare prices) together with applying shotgun marketing activities such as a flurry of mass media coverages, active mass social media presence, agent incentives, a mass web wide marketing display ads make customer acquisition costlier. Customers from all walks of life with different demographic backgrounds and distinct loyalty patterns make the circumstances no easier for airline executives. So, thus comes the second dimension of the challenges.

2.   Shifting Consumer Habits

No matter which generation customers represent, the **value and benefit** they gain drive their behavior, hence airlines as all companies should keep close tabs on the customers' mindsets, feelings, and possible intentions for their next purchases. It appears that customers value **time** the most, but they also do not want to compromise on their overall **comfort**. However, in some cases, price plays a significant factor. Since mainly full-service carriers dominate the overseas Atlantic market, the threat posed by low costs remains negligible. Even though the market predominantly sees the presence of companies in the same business model with some sort of identical cost structure, airlines have meaningful intent to **cut down their price levels**, especially for economy class. Passengers in their decision-making process face up with some **dilemmas**. To state a few, time saving by direct flight options usually comes with one string attached which is higher fares. Lower fares come with downsides such as transfer at a particular airport enroute to his final destination in which the passenger should disembark and all of his registered baggages should be transferred to the next flight. Some worries might buzz across the minds such as whether bags are transferred soundly or whether they will be held up on the first flight causing passenger to miss the latter one, besides those prevalent anxiety factors the length of time spent at the airport is another dilemma for the travellers.

Meanwhile, all previously stated challenges stand where it is, one other is coming very strong. **Social media and fast communication** altered all the build-up in human nature in the last two decades. Thus, travellers' penchant for turning their **journeys into travel itself** to walk off with long-lasting memories, as they catch moments worth to share and keep with their loved ones. With this factor in mind, a trump card for success should not be looked into elsewhere other than experience constructing practices.

One recent phenomenon called **"Bleisure"** among Business globetrotters, especially for those millennials and Generation Z, catches them to the core. This group of customer segments are up for extracting more out of their travels and they basically have inclined to blend their work purpose trip with visits to some attractions at the destination or along the way.

Last but not least, many airlines are well aware that point to point passengers are the most lucrative ones. Thus, each transit passenger going beyond the airline's hub city should be treated as a tourist prospect for the hub destination. Well to put it in other way, customers wholeheartedly choose the airline upon having received effective communication, later on, should witness unmatched experience by the airline service so that they can be translated into possible P2P passengers for their upcoming journeys.

So, then as an airline how did Turkish Airlines leverage its unique selling proposal to offer would be prospects a value driven service in order to stay above the competition and create long term customer value for a sound future?

Solution: Location & Heritage Are the Trump Cards

The company, at the time, had already gotten its head around what customers hold dear in their top of mind and heart. First in first, strategic customer insight research had been set in motion detailing important needs of 21st century US travellers from all walks of the society. Sound balancing of the time spent for the journey, experience, and comfort come to the fore as the best elixir for optimum customer satisfaction. Therefore, the human capital of the company apparatus worked on a strategy that revolves around value-driven customer offers and that underlies a unique selling point for leapfrog its rivals.

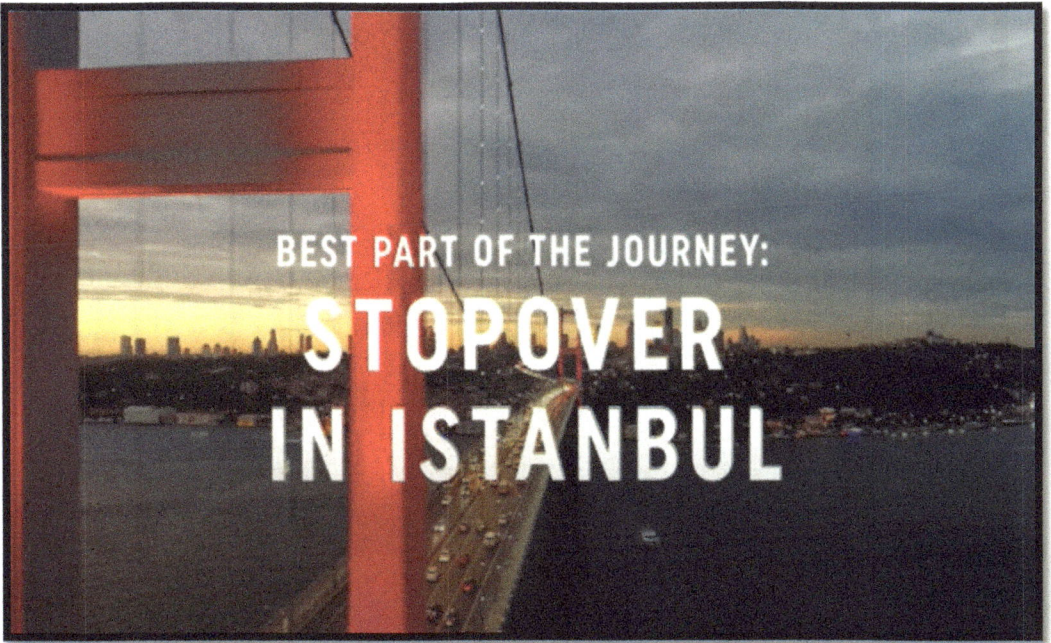

BEST PART OF THE JOURNEY:
STOPOVER IN ISTANBUL

So, the company had an inventory of one valuable gem to use as a unique selling point to one up on its competitors, which is its hub location straddling both Europe and Asia with an unparallel rich history hosting civilizations from the Roman Empire to Ottomans. It is not hard to guess the name of this enchanting metropolis, which goes with the name of Istanbul.

Factors such as customers' active social media post sharing inclination -especially among Gen Z and millennials-, business travel warriors craving for blending business and leisure, and experience chase frenzy among travellers all make Istanbul a great spot to swing by en route to their booked destination.

Thus, the company decided on tapping into its very inimitable asset of Istanbul for using it as a unique selling point. Up next task on hand was to match the most appropriate customer markets with the service in the pipeline, so customer segmentation was applied at the onset of the strategy. The company focused on which sorts of ticketed passengers departing from the USA fit the service by analyzing a couple of factors such as passenger transit time spent at the airport between 2 connecting flights, would-be passengers who might want to break up with traditional travel habits and worked up on demographical definers as well.

Upon figuring out the perfect possible matching customer segment kinds with the service offer, which will be stated below, Turkish Airlines came up with Stopover programme to enable passengers to have a short getaway from the ordinary. Service offer, in essence, is constructed based on 3 experiential dimensions namely functional, emotional, and social ones. To break down those dimensions for the sake of clarity.

As for **Functional Dimension,** service construct of the design aims to provide customers pleasant get away en route to their journey. In view of having 2 million tourists from the USA market, Turkish Airlines extended Stopover nightly stays for the passengers departing from one of the US departure cities. In this construct, economy class passengers **departing from the US enjoying** 2-night in a smart 4-star hotel, as business class passengers savour the solid 3-night stay in exclusive 5-star hotel stay. So, it is like cheery on the cake for passengers wishing to break with the traditional approach of travel. Also, hotels in the programme locates in the right heart of the Istanbul, by which travellers get the most out of their short stay and might treat their senses with glimpse of Istanbul tastes and sights which attract them to book for next travel to Istanbul alone. So, functional dimension of product provides great strength to company at the augmented level.

As for **Emotional Dimension**, passengers are well likely stroke a good affective rapport with company based on the fact of having this kind of favour from the airline. Customers, upon receiving all-round travel ecosystems, produce warm feeling towards the company together with favourable sentiment. Having this level of rapport make for sound and productive customer brand attachment. Other than direct brand customer relation, passengers experiencing Istanbul on route to their destination will feel that they have selected most savvy choice among others, so they will share the presence of the offer with their personal contacts. As a result of it, brand of Turkish Airlines and its Stopover service will make round among immediate or extended circle of the customer.

As for **Behavioral Dimension**, customers experiencing as much comfortable experience as they have in their connecting flight journeys cease to look upon them as cumbersome, they rather treat it as chance to discover hidden gems along the way. One more good note for Turkish Airlines after the customers shifted behaviors in favour of the transit flights is high rate of possibility WOM among target markets. Last but not least, passengers experiencing Istanbul first hand and walk off the city with great memories rebook their next travel directly Istanbul which brings about better yields compared to transit flights.

Apart from programme's design itself, Turkish Airlines marketing team invest their wits to raise awareness for it. Company worked as one team from very top to down in order to drum up support for Stopover programme from corporate travel to leisure travel agencies. Even company's top-level executive Chairman Prof. Ahmet Bolat throw its weight behind the marketing campaigns by joining roadshows in person.

Conclusion: Uplifting Results

Turkish Airlines known by top service quality had already exercised great results in the USA market by its customer value-driven service experience construct. On top of it, the more scrumptious results have trickled not long after the Stopover practices kick started in the USA market back in 2017. Stopover is the icing on

132

the cake for the passengers who had already pampered with great Turkish hospitality. Service offering spiced up with Stopover endow Turkish Airlines with unmatched feature. Aforementioned marketing activities and stopover offering had proved their indispensable nature by improving, to some extent, passenger numbers from the USA to other destinations for the Turkish Airlines. The graphic demonstrates increase in the passenger numbers in the USA market is basically testament to Turkish Airlines experience-based strategy.

USA PASENGER & DESTINATION GROWTH

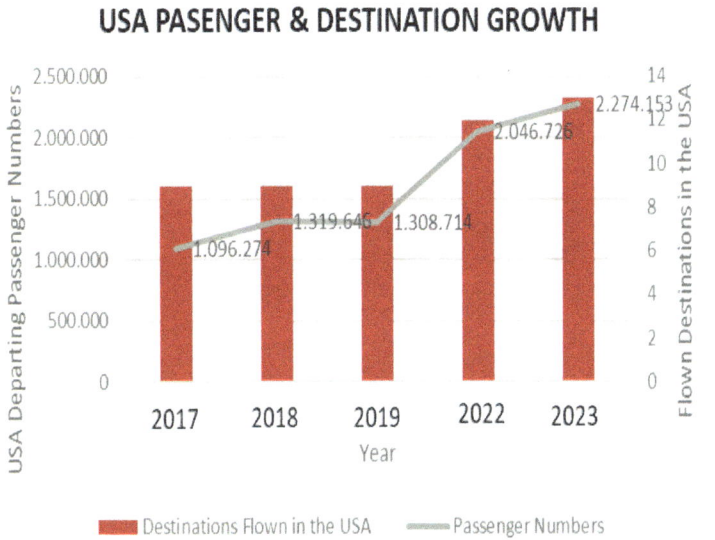

As it is shown in the Figure 1 Turkish Airlines witnessed more than doubled increase in passenger numbers in 6-year period. At the time of writing only first half of the year 2024 outbound passenger numbers from the USA released and which stands at above staggering 1 million. So, by the end of 2024, it is very likely that Turkish Airlines fly more than 2,5 million USA passengers from 14 destinations in the USA. (Table -1-).

Year* (First 6 months)	Destinations Flown in the USA	Passenger Numbers
2024	14	1.115.023

Table 1

Number of passengers using the programme displays exponential growth thanks to its customer value driven offer. As seen in Figure -2- Turkish Airlines has almost seen staggering 20-fold increase on the demand for Stopover just within 6 years, especially between year of 2022 and 2023, though Covid-19 related restrictions forced airline to suspend the programme for almost 2 years. It is the well calculated strategy behind this leap. In which, airline fine-tuned all programme. over again by extending nightly hotel Stopover stays of USA travellers by 1 day regardless of cabin category of passengers preferring Stopover. One more fine dialling in the programme for the USA market was raising the number of destinations eligible for featuring Stopover treat from handful numbers to all network destinations. On top of it, Stopover programme take on new digital capabilities in the year 2024 for streamlining passenger experience. For example, any passenger choosing to use Stopover offer can issue hotel confirmation letters through airline's own mobile app and

133

web page. Thus, outlook for the demand to the programme is very bright with more than 15.000 passengers showed their interest in first five months of the year 2024.

USA PASENGER & DESTINATION GROWTH

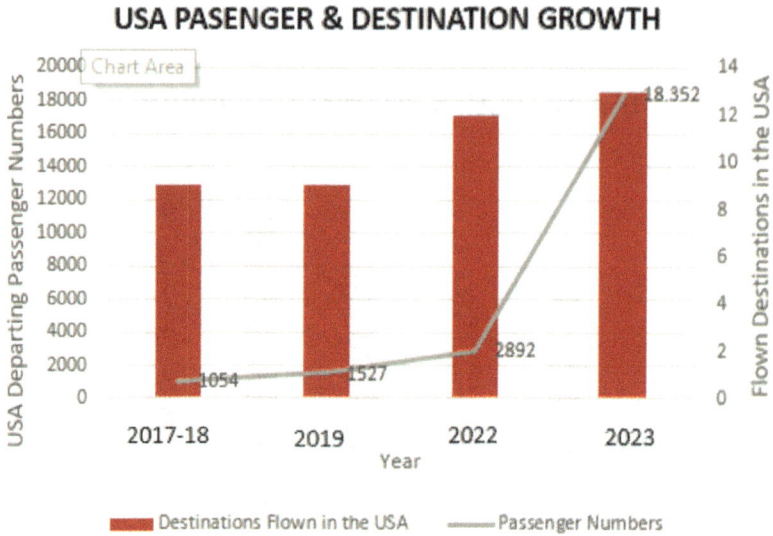

Stopover Demand Growth In

Therefore, given the fact that US market holds very much importance to Turkish Airlines, so company is adamant to not leave anything to chance and its management looking every unturned stone to constantly improve experience level for the passengers.

As a final foot note, Turkish Airlines does not see itself only an institution seeking a profit, it has mission congruent with 21st global public and social needs. Its ambition is far wider than generating value only for its customers, Turkish Airlines is keen supporter of societal development, so it aims to be both carbon natural company by 2050 and the company to generate over 50 billion USD to the global economy.

Questions to stimulate conversation on the case

1. **What are the challenges of airlines in transatlantic flights?**

Given the number of existing rivals, transatlantic flights present heavy competition characteristics. So, market saturation with too many players comes off as one of prime hurdles for airlines to overcome. The competitive nature pressure airlines to reduce the airfares. As an outcome of intense competition, some partnerships formed in the market, so switching cost rises exponentially for passenger invest heavily in one alliance with consistent ticket purchases gifting a certain amount of miles to redeem. As a result, acquisition of new customers from rivals become costlier.

2. **What did Turkish Airlines come up with to edge out its rivals in the market?**

*   Turkish Airlines did quite good research on shifting tendencies of customers. So, the company come up with the product to accommodate newly shaped wants of customers. Outcome of the

134

research flagged up importance of unique strategy. So, Turkish Airlines worked out Stopover Programme in order to tool up itself with unique selling proposal laden with customer focus designs.

- In which programme, eligible US departing passengers could enjoy the bounties of Istanbul regardless of their travel class.

3. What is the make-up of Turkish Airlines Stopover Programme?

Programme constitutes 3 main experience dimensions. All of which takes customers to the centre to give passengers perfect experience sentiment.

As for Functional Dimension, service construct of the design aims to provide customers pleasant get away en route to journey.

As for Emotional Dimension, passengers are well likely stroke a good affective rapport with company based on the fact of having this kind of favour from the airline.

As for Behavioral Dimension, customers experiencing as much comfortable experience as they have in their connecting flight journeys cease to look upon them as cumbersome, they rather treat it as chance to discover hidden gems along the way.

4.1.5 NEW PRODUCT DEVELOPMENT (NPD)

Given the rapid changes in customer tastes, technology and competition, companies must develop a steady stream of new products and services (question marks in the terminology of the BCG matrix). A company can create new products in two ways. One is through acquisition – by buying another company, a patent, or a license to produce someone else's product. The other is through **new product development (NPD)** in the company's own research-and-development (R&D) department.

The traditional new product development models involve the following stages in product development: idea generation, screening, concept development and testing, business analysis, product development and testing, test marketing, commercialization, or launch (Baker and Hart, 1999).

An effective commercialization strategy relies upon marketing management making plain choices regarding the target market, and the development of a marketing strategy that provides a differential advantage.

A useful starting point for choosing a target market is an understanding of the **diffusion of innovation process** which explains how a new product spreads throughout a market over time. Figure 4.5 shows the diffusion of innovation curve which categorizes people or organisations according to how soon they are willing to adopt the innovation (Hollensen and Opresnik, 2020).

The graph shows that those actors (**innovators** and **early adopters**) who are willing to purchase the new product soon after launch are likely to from a minor part of the total number of actors who will eventually be willing to buy it. As the new product is accepted and approved by these customers, and the decision to purchase it becomes less risky, the customers that make up the bulk of the market, comprising the **early** and **late majority**, begin to try the product themselves. Finally, after the product has gained full acceptance, a group describes as the **laggards** adopt the new product.

Figure 4.5:
The diffusion of innovation process.
Source: Adapted from Hollensen and Opresnik, 2020, modified.

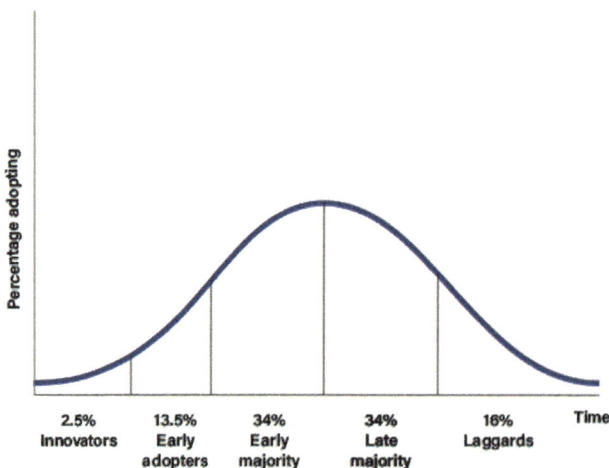

| 2.5% | 13.5% | 34% | 34% | 16% | Time |
| Innovators | Early adopters | Early majority | Late majority | Laggards | |

136

ŞİŞECAM

FROM LOCAL TO GLOBAL: ŞİŞECAM'S JOURNEY OF PROGRESS

Written by: Arzu Özcan (Şişecam Communication Coordinator)

Abstract

Şişecam's evolution from a local Turkish glass producer to a global leader reflects its strategic vision and adaptability. Founded in 1935 by Mustafa Kemal Atatürk, Şişecam steadily expanded its product range while overcoming challenges like high raw material costs and infrastructure limitations. By the 1960s, Şişecam extended its global reach with investments in Eastern Europe, Russia, and India. In the 2010s, the company embraced digital transformation with the "Roots and Wings" program and a focus on sustainability. As Şişecam continues to grow globally, it aims to be among the top three in its core sectors while leading innovation and sustainability.

Introduction

Şişecam is a reputable company that made significant contribution to the industrialization goals of the young Republic of Türkiye under the directives of its founder Mustafa Kemal Atatürk, a great leader respected worldwide. In 1935 the company began its production journey in Paşabahçe Factory in Istanbul with only 400 people with no prior glass production experience. Today, Şişecam has over 24,000 employees worldwide and stands as a global leader in the glass and chemicals industries. The company is the leading global producer of glassware and a top five player in both glass packaging and flat glass industries, while also being the world leader in chromium chemicals. Şişecam strives to be among the top three companies in its core sectors by employing data driven strategies and innovative approaches to sustain its profitable growth and competitive advantage.

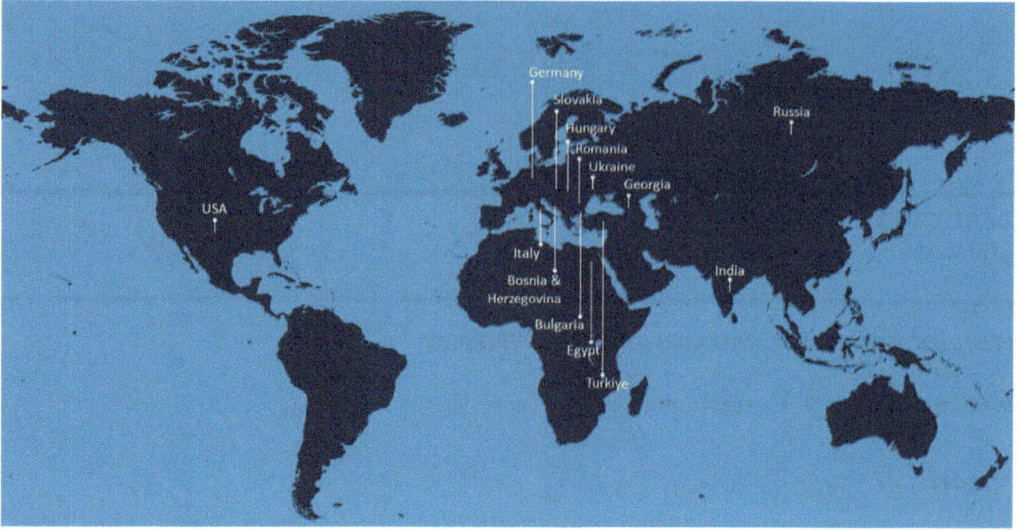

Challenges & Solutions

How did Şişecam overcome the lack of supporting industries and high raw material costs in its early years? (1935-1950)

Şişecam overcame significant challenges in a market that lacks an established glass industry. High raw material costs, absence of supporting industries, and poor infrastructure disrupted supply chains and distribution. Frequent energy interruptions, in an era when electricity was coal-generated, escalated challenges for this energy-dependent sector.

How did Şişecam manage to diversify its product range and ensure a stable supply chain from 1960 to 1990?

Şişecam, Türkiye's first glass producer, has consistently played a pivotal role by expanding its product range across all core areas of glass and structuring its operations to support its robust growth.

From the 1960s to the 1990s, Şişecam broadened its international trade vision starting with the first export to the USA in 1960. A year later, the Çayırova Glass Factory began flat glass production followed by factories for glass tubing and laboratory glassware to further diversify its product portfolio.

To secure supply of raw materials, Şişecam established a soda ash production factory and mining operations as part of its vertical integration efforts in the coming years.

During the 1980s and mid-1990s, Şişecam strategically focused on producing value-added products and launched projects to boost efficiency. Şişecam then established Türkiye's first modern automotive glass factory and introduced new products such as mirrors, tempered glass, and colored glass.

In 1986, Şişecam took a significant step forward and became a publicly traded company in Türkiye.

How did Şişecam expand its global footprint through strategic partnerships and investments from 1990 to 2010?

In the early 1990s, Türkiye's open economic policies and customs union with the EU expanded Şişecam's export and expansion opportunities. Şişecam started employing on-site production strategies in target markets.

In 1998, Şişecam made its first international investment by acquiring the majority stake in the only glass bottle factory of Georgia and became a production JV partner in Bulgaria's soda ash producer, Sodi.

Starting from the mid-2000s, Şişecam embarked on a strategic investment targeting Eastern Europe and emerging countries. In 2002, Şişecam established its first glass packaging production facility in Russia, its first ever greenfield FDI, which helped the company penetrate the local market and secure its position through long-term customer agreements and customized products.

By 2004, Şişecam rapidly expanded by establishing five new factories and initiated its first greenfield investment in Bulgaria. This vertical integration decision played a crucial role in the company's sustainable growth.

In 2005, Şişecam made its first investment in the chromium chemicals sector in Italy with a 50% JV partnership, after expanding into Bosnia and Herzegovina by partnering in a soda production facility. Further investments included factories in Russia, Bulgaria, and a glass packaging factory acquisition in Ukraine.

To support its global expansion strategy, Şişecam established flat glass sales offices in Greece and Romania as a strategic approach to significantly enhance its production footprint and market reach.

How did Şişecam successfully implement technological transformation and digitalization between 2015 and 2025?

Şişecam's success stems from its commitment to transformation and adaptability. Recognizing that continuous development is vital for a global company, Şişecam launched its comprehensive "Roots and Wings" program, covering all its business areas and functions across various countries.

This program, which SAP referred to as one of the most comprehensive digital transformation projects carried out in the world until then, also significantly strengthened Şişecam's ability to manage its business with data and numbers. With the ERP system, planned to be completed in the end of 2024, Şişecam gained the capability to centralize data collection and analysis from 45 different production facilities and a global sales network spanning over 150 countries. This project was awarded the "SAP Digital Transformation Award" in 2022.

Was the transformation in digital infrastructures robust enough to enable Şişecam to effectively manage its extensive operations spread across diverse areas and on a global scale? (2020 and beyond)

Şişecam's transformation highlights its dedication to innovation and excellence. The company restructured itself beyond digital, unifying its business units under "One Şişecam" initiative for greater efficiency and agility. This consolidation clarified its global presence and strategies, enabling effective long-term planning to achieve market leadership.

This initiative marked a key milestone in the company's global growth strategy. Focusing on optimization and synergy, Şişecam invested in diverse production fields across its operating countries. In 2022, it announced its first glass packaging facility in Europe with advanced furnaces in Hungary, to boost production capacity and strengthen its European presence. That same year, Şişecam acquired Refel, a leading Italian refractory manufacturer, to ensure operational stability amid global supply chain disruptions. This acquisition highlights Şişecam's commitment to efficient, resilient operations and reinforces its position as a forward-thinking leader in the glass industry.

Marketing Strategies of Şişecam: Crafting a Global Presence

Şişecam's market entry strategy emphasizes selecting locations based on raw material access, market size, economic stability, and local regulations. This has resulted in production facilities in key markets like Russia, Bulgaria, Italy, and India, expanding its global presence and driving growth.

Strategic Investments and Partnerships:

Şişecam penetrates diverse markets through strategic investments, acquisitions, and partnerships. By adapting to local market dynamics and leveraging its global expertise, the company has transformed its production hubs into "glocal" points, integrating global standards with local preferences to meet ever-changing customer needs.

Strengthening Brand Positioning:

Şişecam's robust brand positioning strategy supports its global expansion. By establishing representative offices in major markets like France, the Netherlands, the UK, and the USA, the company stays closer to its customers, gaining insights into market dynamics and expectations. This enables Şişecam to create tailored products and solutions to different markets and customers.

Evolution and Innovation in Product Lines:

Starting production in 1935 with gas lamps, glassware, and pharmaceutical bottles, Şişecam has become the only global company operating in all core areas of the glass industry. To maintain competitiveness and ensure its offerings to remain relevant and innovative, Şişecam consistently introduces new products, tailors offerings to regional needs, and invests in cutting-edge technologies.

Overcoming Challenges with Strategic Management:

Managing expertise and resources across diverse business units requires careful planning and coordination. Şişecam's strategic portfolio management targets high-growth sectors, aligning investments with existing strengths to drive innovation. The company's focus on talent development and strategic partnerships ensures expertise, access to new markets, and risk mitigation, solidifying its position as a global leader in the glass industry.

Embracing Digital Marketing:

Şişecam has boosted local brand awareness through an intensive digital marketing strategy, using social media, content marketing, and e-commerce while aligning the brand with the digital requirements of the era. By offering glass consultancy services, it enhances customer engagement and satisfaction across the entire value chain.

Through these innovative marketing strategies, Şişecam strengthens its global presence, adapts to market changes, and meets customer needs with agility ensuring its leadership in the global glass industry.

Şişecam's Approach to Sustainability and Innovation

Sustainability has been central to Şişecam's global growth. Under the 2030 CareforNext strategy, the company employs eco-friendly production methods, recycling projects, and energy efficiency initiatives to ensure a greener world for future generations.

Under this strategy, "Protect the Planet" approach emphasizes resource efficiency, waste reduction, environmental management, and sustainable product design. While "Empower Society" approach integrates diversity and inclusion into every aspect of Şişecam's practices. Promoting the use of digital intelligence and encouraging societal progress are key elements of this strategy. Through these efforts, Şişecam aims to drive positive change and to "Transform Life."

Guided by science and reason, Şişecam's Science, Technology, and Design Center, one of the largest R&D centers in Europe, develops cutting-edge solutions, production-efficient technologies, and valuable inventions enhancing both Şişecam's product offerings and leadership in innovation.

Conclusion

Şişecam is now the only global company that is operating in all core areas of the glass and chemicals industries. It's amongst the top 5 players globally and targets top 3 ranking.

Although Şişecam's globalization journey faced challenges throughout its history, Şişecam accomplished successful business results by addressing different customer expectations in various markets through continuous product innovation and adaptation.

Şişecam tailored its products to geographic trends and invested in new technologies. By enhancing its digital infrastructure and operating model it became a data-driven organization, delivering effective solutions globally.

Şişecam's comprehensive approach has accelerated growth and progress for both the company and its ecosystem with initiatives such as ecosystem financing to help stakeholders through tough periods, solidifying its leadership in the glass industry.

Questions to stimulate conversation on the case

1. **Glass is a material that requires energy-intensive production. How will Şişecam achieve its sustainability goals while continuing to grow?**

    *   Glass is one of the most strategic materials in the world's sustainability needs. Şişecam is making significant efforts to make its production processes more sustainable. Şişecam integrates glass production with new technologies and alternative energy sources, leveraging innovation to support industry growth, stakeholders, and the ecosystem.

2. **How did Şişecam leverage data from its production facilities across four continents to align with modern technologies and continuously improve its infrastructure?**

- By becoming a data-driven organization, Şişecam enhances operational efficiency, employs "managing with numbers" practices and provides customer-centric solutions.

- The transformation that turned data into valuable insights gave Şişecam the ability to align with technologies that bring new conveniences to our lives every day. Beyond adopting digital twins, artificial intelligence, and machine learning into its processes, it also developed an infrastructure that continuously evolves with these technological advancements.

3. **How will Şişecam address the evolving regulatory environments and trade policies in its key markets to sustain growth and competitive advantage?**

- As a global company, Şişecam operates as a local player in each market, monitoring regulatory changes and trade policies. It engages with local authorities and industry associations to stay informed and ensure compliance. By staying flexible and responsive, Şişecam aims to sustain profitable growth and maintain its competitive edge.

pluxee

Written by: Sinem Hekimoğlu (Chief Marketing Officer at Pluxee), Ekin Kutevu (Vice President Client Services, the Agency)

Introduction

This campaign showcases the transformation of Sodexo, a well-known brand in Türkiye for 30 years, into the new Pluxee. While Sodexo was recognized primarily for meal cards, its services included gifts, rewards, corporate transportation, and more. Prior to this campaign, Sodexo underwent a major global transformation, changing its corporate identity, name, positioning, and promise. Our goal was to demonstrate that this was more than just rebranding. Pluxee now represents a comprehensive world of employee benefits and engagement, offering a personalized and sustainable experience both at work and beyond.

Pluxee is an innovative solution designed to meet the evolving needs of modern businesses and their employees. The transformation involved creating a new identity that preserved and expanded the brand's values while retaining its existing customer base and market share. Pluxee's vision focuses on providing solutions that keep employees satisfied and engaged with their employers' services.

Challenge

The primary challenge was to ensure a smooth transition from Sodexo to Pluxee within the Turkish market. Given Sodexo's strong 30-year presence in Türkiye and its association with the "meal cards" category, this transition needed careful handling. It was essential to clearly communicate the brand's name and positioning changes, given its deep-rooted involvement in daily life.

Brand Recognition and Trust:

We aimed to leverage Sodexo's established recognition and reliability to introduce the Pluxee brand, ensuring a seamless transition that fostered trust with our core target audiences' consumers/employees, merchants, and clients. It was equally important that our own employees embraced this transformation and understood Pluxee's new positioning. This shift was more than just a name change; it was representation of a new brand with a fresh vision and an innovative approach to business.

- **Transforming Traditional Perception:** Transitioning from Sodexo, a well-established brand in Türkiye, to Pluxee involved convincing the existing customer base to embrace the new identity. While Sodexo was known for meal cards, Pluxee repositions itself as a brand providing solutions for all aspects of life.

Employee Satisfaction and Engagement:

Due to economic and social challenges in Türkiye, compounded by the pandemic and remote working conditions, employee engagement and satisfaction levels have plummeted. In Türkiye, 40% of employees reported feeling unhappy, and 46% expressed anger during their workday. (Gallup, Employee Satisfaction and Engagement Survey, 2022) These figures underscore the low morale and motivation among employees.

Employee Morale and Motivation: In a climate where employees were feeling discontented and frustrated, Pluxee's solutions were crucial in reversing this trend. The brand focuses on enhancing the overall quality of life, delivering "that extra bit of joy that brightens employees' days." By simplifying processes for employers and enriching the employee experience, Pluxee significantly improves engagement, making it an essential contributor to a more positive and fulfilling work environment.

Localization of Global Discourse:

Adapting Pluxee's global messaging for the Turkish market was crucial to ensure clarity and effectiveness. The slogan "A World of Opportunities" might be misinterpreted in Türkiye, as it is commonly associated with debit and credit cards. Thus, it was important to clearly define Pluxee's brand before introducing this slogan to the target audience.

- **Communicating the Right Message:** A global brand must tailor its messages to align with the local market, taking into account cultural and linguistic nuances. In this process, it was crucial to reference the intended meaning behind "A World of Opportunities" and craft a narrative that would resonate more clearly with the target audience.

Solution

Pluxee initiated the transformation of Sodexo, a brand that has long been trusted and recognized in Türkiye. During this transformation, a brand identity was crafted that went beyond being merely a meal card provider, addressing the full spectrum of needs for both employees and employers. In this context, the approach of "A World That Makes Employees Happy" was embraced, offering services designed to boost employee happiness and engagement.

What Did We Aim For?

Pluxee aimed to increase brand awareness, attract new customers, add value for existing ones, and expand merchant partnerships. It also focused on delivering flexible, digital, and innovative solutions to meet the evolving needs of employers and employees, positioning the brand as a competitive choice in the modern business landscape.

In transitioning from Sodexo to Pluxee, the brand's focus expanded beyond meal cards to include wellness programs, training courses, digital innovations, and giftable experiences. This evolution repositioned Pluxee as a provider of a more comprehensive employee experience. Additionally, with a "B2B2C" approach, Pluxee developed a strategy to reach both employees and end-users through their employers.

What Should We Have Adapted To?

Pluxee needed to adapt to changing market dynamics and technological advancements. Innovations were made in digitalization, personalized experiences, and building a strong social media presence. Embracing a B2B2C model, Pluxee effectively connected with target audiences as B2B and B2C approaches increasingly overlapped.

What Is the B2B2C Concept and What Was Our Approach?

B2B2C, or "Business to Business to Consumer," involves a business reaching end consumers through another business. Pluxee adopted this model to offer employees benefits and privileges through their employers. Employers enhance employee satisfaction with Pluxee's solutions, while employees directly enjoy these benefits. Pluxee aimed to build an emotional connection with business decision-makers to boost brand credibility and recognition.

By adapting the strong brand legacy from Sodexo to modern business needs, Pluxee enhanced both employee and employer satisfaction. Pluxee gained a market edge by emphasizing digitalization, personalized services, and innovative solutions. The B2B2C approach continues to boost brand loyalty and customer satisfaction with tailored solutions for employers and employees.

Accordingly, the following 3 steps required further attention:

Brand Positioning and Promotion

Promotional efforts were launched to highlight that Pluxee was a distinct brand with a new vision and approach to business, while leveraging Sodexo's established trust and recognition. This journey involved consumers, merchants, clients, and employees, each with unique needs that required a holistic communication strategy. The goal was to ensure that all target audiences perceived Pluxee as a strong and innovative brand, rather than merely a continuation of Sodexo.

- **Announcing Pluxee to current clients: PR and events have never been that important before.** Our approach involved hosting an exclusive event for current clients to share Pluxee's vision for the future. To position Pluxee as a thought leader in employee engagement, we presented research on employee engagement in Türkiye, enhanced by AI-generated video graphics that visualized the results for a dynamic and informative experience.

- **Educating Our Merchants:** Merchants are vital to Pluxee's sustainability, and it was essential to ensure they fully understood the brand's transformation. To facilitate this, we created and distributed a special **brand kit** to all merchants and conducted field visits to provide in-depth education about Pluxee's new offerings and positioning.

- **Innovative Campaigns:** Pluxee communicated its transformation and new brand positioning to the target audience through innovative communication campaigns and compelling content. These campaigns were disseminated across social media, digital platforms, and traditional media channels. Social media communication, particularly crafted from employee insights, was highly effective in portraying Pluxee as a "brand that understands employees."

- **Strategic Collaborations:** To implement a B2B2C strategy effectively, forming value-driven partnerships was essential. Pluxee boosted brand recognition through strategic collaborations and sponsorships. For example, the "Monday Syndrome" campaign provided free coffee every Monday at a popular coffee shop, increasing engagement. Sponsoring theater events and launching Pluxee Plus campaigns also expanded Pluxee's appeal and improved brand perception.

Employee Experience Improvement Message

Pluxee provides a variety of opportunities and innovative platforms to enhance employee happiness and engagement, including meal programs, shopping perks, fuel benefits, and giftable experiences. These services aim to make employees feel valued and supported, boosting their engagement at work.

- **Human-Centric Approach:** Pluxee's global slogan, "World of Opportunities," was localized to "A World That Makes Employees Happy" to better fit the Turkish market and highlight the brand's industry contributions. This localization emphasized Pluxee's commitment to enhancing employee experiences and engagement at work.

- **Emotional Bonding:** Rather than focusing solely on practical benefits, Pluxee establishes an emotional connection with employees, enriching their workplace experience. This emotional approach was a key factor in increasing employee satisfaction and engagement.

Media and Communication Strategy

Pluxee's communication strategy does not rely on TV or traditional mass media; instead, it maintains a continuous presence in the lives of the target audience. This approach ensured that the brand remained visible through social media activities, sponsorships, collaborations, and events.

- **Use of Digital and Traditional Media:** Pluxee effectively reached a broad audience through a strategic mix of digital and traditional media channels. Social media campaigns, websites, e-mail marketing, and printed materials all played a role in conveying the brand's messages.

- **Sustainable Communication:** Pluxee boosted brand recognition and kept the target audience engaged with ongoing sustainable communication campaigns. These campaigns highlighted the unique opportunities and benefits Pluxee offers, helping the brand resonate more strongly with its audience.

Our work centers on stakeholder satisfaction to ensure success for clients, consumers, merchants, and employees, aiming to be at the heart of a connected ecosystem. Sodexo's B2B strategy shifted from practical benefits to highlighting that "where there are people, there is emotion," aligning with behavioral economics. As consumer influence grows, Pluxee adapted its communication to engage directly with them, supported by localized campaigns like "A World That Makes Employees Happy" and vibrant new brand assets.

Beyond a name change, Pluxee is committed to providing innovative solutions in the Turkish market to enhance employee work experiences and boost their happiness and engagement. This new positioning and communication strategy has been crucial in increasing brand recognition and building trust in Türkiye, making Pluxee a brand stakeholders aspire to associate with.

Conclusion

Pluxee's social media performance during the post-launch communication period from November 2023 to June 2024 provides compelling evidence of the success of the brand's transformation. Significant increases in follower count and engagement rates on Instagram and YouTube underscore the effectiveness of Pluxee's strategic and innovative marketing efforts, which were predominantly driven by digital channels.

Increase in Followers and Reach:

Notable follower growth of 11.3% on Instagram and 16.5% on YouTube between November 2023 and June 2024 demonstrate Pluxee's strengthened brand awareness and market presence. Peak reaches of 73,148 on Instagram in January 2024 and 398,665 in March 2024 highlight the success of strategically published content targeting special occasions and campaigns.

Success in Engagement and Content

The 393,691 views recorded on YouTube in April 2024, along with the strong performance of awards and event-related content, highlight the effectiveness of Pluxee's video content strategy. Additionally, the high engagement rates on Instagram during eids and special campaign periods demonstrate that the brand has successfully connected with users on an emotional level and has effectively steered its social media strategy.

The outcomes during this period highlight the impact and effectiveness of Pluxee's brand transformation strategy. Specifically, the rise in reach and engagement rates reveals the positive influence of social media content and campaigns on the target audience, further solidifying brand loyalty.

Questions to stimulate conversation on the case

1. **What strategy did Pluxee's new brand positioning in the Turkish market follow to reach new audiences while maintaining its existing customer base?**

Pluxee entered the Turkish market with a new identity, leveraging Sodexo's strong brand image. The rebranding expanded from a meal card to a broader life card concept, addressing existing customers' needs and offering a wider range of solutions. Innovative campaigns and strategic digital collaborations engaged current customers and attracted new ones, enhancing brand recognition by showcasing Pluxee's innovative and inclusive nature.

2. **In what ways have Pluxee's strategies to increase employee satisfaction and engagement helped alleviate morale and motivation issues in the workplace?**

Pluxee introduced wellness programs, training courses, and digital innovations to boost employee satisfaction and engagement, including initiatives like giftable experiences. This approach has improved employee happiness and engagement, addressing high turnover and low satisfaction in Türkiye. By emphasizing the slogan "A World That Makes Employees Happy," Pluxee has created a brand image that meets employees' emotional needs beyond practical benefits.

3. **How did localizing Pluxee's global slogan "A World of Opportunities" impact its success in the Turkish market, and what challenges were overcome in this process?**

Pluxee adapted its global slogan "A World of Opportunities" to the Turkish market as "A World That Makes Employees Happy" to better engage employees and highlight the brand's advantages. The challenge in this process was to position the slogan in a way that accurately reflected the diverse range of benefits and life solutions Pluxee offers while distancing it from the common perception of debit and credit cards in Türkiye. Through effective market research and target audience analysis, the brand message was communicated clearly and effectively to Turkish consumers, successfully differentiating Pluxee as a comprehensive life partner.

Case Highlights

Sodexo underwent a major global transformation, changing its corporate identity, name, brand positioning, and overall promise. The challenge was to effectively introduce this transformation to the Turkish market, where Sodexo had a strong 30-year presence and was closely associated with "meal cards." Clear communication of the brand's new name and positioning was crucial due to its deep-rooted presence. Our goal was to show that this was more than a rebranding; Pluxee represents a comprehensive solution that goes beyond food to include various aspects of life, offering a superior alternative to Sodexo.

We approached our strategic roadmap by redefining category dynamics to align with our communication goals. In the B2B segment, Pluxee's communication targeted both employers and employees. Moving beyond practical benefits, the strategy highlighted that "where there are people, there is emotion," in line with behavioral economics. The slogan "A World That Makes Employees Happy" was designed to resonate with both employees and their employers.

CASE STUDY
TURKCELL

---

30 YEARS OF LEADERSHIP

Written by: Mustafa Alcan (Corporate Communication, Media & Brand Management Director), Özlem Arın Kiremit (Brand Management & Communication Associate Director)

Introduction

Throughout its history, Turkcell has positioned itself as the most successful telecommunications company in Türkiye, having established a powerful brand identity. Accordingly, Turkcell has become one of the most well-known and respected brands in its industry and country thanks to its enduring successes, wide network strength, cutting-edge technological products, and services, excellent customer service, and social responsibility initiatives carried out as a brand mindful of social issues in its nation.

Nevertheless, as Turkcell approached its 30th anniversary, the reputation and image of Turkcell, the industry leader, suffered along with the entire industry in the wake of the earthquakes Türkiye suffered, which were considered the "Disaster of the Century."

There are numerous instances worldwide of powerful brands that have been unable to triumph over such significant crises and regain their previous image and reputation before their demise. Although the reputation of brands that demonstrated sensitivity and responsibility in the aftermath of natural disasters improved, the scale of the crisis and the fact that the brand was damaged in the area where it was strongest may have prevented a quick correction of image parameters. In this study, we examine the actions that Turkcell took to return to its situation prior to the crisis, as well as the ways in which it managed to sustain its leadership position as the year of celebration grew closer.

Challenge

The erosion in brand perception was not only played out in the area of attractiveness, where Turkcell is the clear leader, but also in terms of the perception of a "beloved brand." Since Turkcell was the market leader, the loss of points was relatively significant, and the gap between Turkcell and its competitors, which had been wide open for many years, began to show signs of narrowing.

As the thirtieth anniversary turned into a year of celebration, and the teams responsible for brand communication planned to restore the firm emotional connection with their customers, the greatest challenge for the teams in charge of brand communication was to once again raise the image values.

The challenge was not only that the brand perception had fallen below the norm, but that there was also a limited window of opportunity in which to restore the confidence and admiration of customers. This was because the company was getting close to a crucial period in which it would celebrate its thirty-year success story.

Solution

The senior management and brand management of Turkcell underwent a period of transition in this period. During this difficult time, the authorities' top priority was to devise a strategic communication campaign that was meticulously planned to restore Turkcell to its former strength in the minds and hearts of its customers.

With reference to the brand's thirty-year history, the campaign aimed to reassure consumers and convey the company's commitment to investing in the country across the board. Furthermore, it was necessary for it to bring to our attention the robust foundations of a beloved brand.

Big Idea: The idea that Turkcell, as a provider and developer of technology, is present in every aspect of life was the foundation upon which the big idea was built. **"It's Working with Turkcell"** is the name given to this significant concept; one that demonstrates the company's presence in every moment, whether visible or not. Numerous elements have been gathered under the concept of "It's working with Turkcell." These range from greeting machines at work in factories to online shopping and mobile payment systems, secure data storage, and a super content app that also offers TV enjoyment, among many others.

Music: The Turkcell brand makes effective use of the power of music in its marketing and communication efforts. Furthermore, it possesses the most memorable slogan in Türkiye in terms of recognition. Connect to life with Turkcell...

We needed a jingle that would work together with "Connect to life with Turkcell..." which had been discontinued for some time but could also stand on its own. This was necessary for us to realize the big idea. Not only did the unique jingle communicate the concept of "It's working with Turkcell," but it also contributed to concept development through its various iterations.

Everything is working with Turkcell; everyone is working with Turkcell; young people are working with Turkcell; technology is working with Turkcell; and so on.

Collaboration with the Artist: One of the most essential aspects of the campaign was our collaboration with a celebrated artist who enjoys a sizable following in Türkiye and internationally. This artist had active participation in social responsibility projects and an emotional connection with various segments of society, having played an active role in such projects. In addition, the campaign was able to reach a wider audience thanks to the artist's warm and genuine image, as well as their robust use of social media and high level of engagement.

Content Strategy: The campaign that was held to celebrate Turkcell's 30th anniversary highlighted the company's investments made since its founding, the value that it brings to individuals and society, and its leadership in the technology arena. Three consecutive commercials were broadcast during the initial phase of the 360-degree campaign. These commercials included a film about the benefits for the youth segment, a film about the doubling of the GB, and one about the 30th-anniversary image film. In July, the campaign significantly increased the number of packages available to all its subscribers. Additionally, it added value to customers by providing them with hundreds of gifts, which ranged from mobile phones to domestic automobiles, through the 30th Anniversary lottery, held at 1040 stores across Türkiye. At the same time, the company enhanced its communication with customers by transforming its social media accounts into a friendlier and more sincere format through the implementation of the 'talking account' strategy. In addition, the dinner organized with the company's first fifty customers and the letter sent to its thirty-year subscribers during the customer experience week were significant components of this planning strategy.

Turkcell realized the 'Türksel Hareketler' campaign which includes beautiful traditions unique to Turkish people, during the second phase. This is a follow-up communication imbued with powerful insights. Taking this into consideration, the commercials that, through effective communication, explained the sustainability investments made also positively contributed to maintaining the same level of connection with customers as in the past.

Media Strategy: The campaign received extensive coverage across a variety of platforms, including television, social media, radio, outdoor, and digital channels. On each channel, conventional and innovative media production was utilized. An example of this, in the scenes devoted to food in the television series, was the announcement that the food benefit for the GNÇ campaign would be given in the upper rather than the lower band.

GNÇ'NIN EFSANE KAMPANYASI GERİ DÖNDÜ!

HEMEN *İNDİR*

SEÇİLİ UYGULAMA VE RESTORANLARDA

100 TL YEMEK ÇEKİ

Conclusion

The campaign was swiftly picked up by a large number of people and was instrumental in Turkcell's efforts to regain its reputation. In surveys conducted to measure the success of the campaign the perception of Turkcell as the best operator increased by 2.6 points. On the other hand, the results for 'Turkcell as a brand that I like' increased by 4 points. Consumers reestablished their faith in the brand and acknowledged the company's positive social impact. The brand identity reverted to what it had been prior to the catastrophe; thereafter, it began to widen the gap between itself and its rivals.

Enhancement of **Image Indicators:** Through the collaboration of artists, all sectors of society demonstrated an increase in their loyalty to Turkcell. A positive shift occurred in the perception of the brand being criticized.

Strong Connections with the Community: Turkcell was able to reestablish a strong connection with the public because of the campaign. Through this process, Turkcell was able to increase its brand value in the eyes of the public by implementing campaigns that encompassed all its customers. As a result, the brand expanded beyond its traditional role as a provider of telecommunications services.

Questions to stimulate conversation on the case

1. **How would you evaluate the decision of a well-established brand like Turkcell to collaborate with an artist to refresh its image on its 30th anniversary? What are the advantages of implementing this strategy per the brand's long-term objectives?**

    *   The collaboration between Turkcell and this artist aimed to strengthen the brand's image as a young and dynamic company. Because of the artist's widespread popularity and the interaction, he sparked on various social media platforms, Turkcell began to be regarded as more influential and contemporary. Both the awareness of the brand and its preference increased significantly, particularly among younger consumers.

    *   When compared to attempting to accomplish this with an idea alone, working with a well-known artist takes significantly less time. On the other hand, it is of utmost significance to strike a balance between the popularity and appreciation of the artist and the connection that your idea and brand wish to establish.

2. **How does Turkcell intend to take these communication activities to the next level in the future?**

    *   Identifying an idea that is straightforward, fertile, and capable of being replicated is the most important step. And so, 'It's working with Turkcell' is a particularly beneficial idea for us. When it comes to telling stories and even working together with other artists, addressing diverse topics, segments, offers, and technologies are all highly suitable options. And now, with our company having reached its thirtieth anniversary, we will continue to demonstrate our presence in all aspects of life under the concept of "It's working with Turkcell."

Key Points

*   Sincerity: The sincerity and authenticity of the collaboration made it possible to communicate with the targeted audience more effectively.

*   Sustainability: The sustainability of this collaboration over a longer period, as opposed to being a one-time event, was observed to be an important criterion in strengthening the brand image.

154

- Diversity: The collaboration with the artist should not be restricted to advertising campaigns; rather, it should be expanded to include the development of joint projects across a variety of fields. This was a particularly valuable development that helped support the project.

4.1.6 THE PRODUCT LIFE CYCLE

The concept of the **product life cycle (PLC)** provides useful inputs into making product decisions and formulating product strategies. The product life cycle visualizes the course of a product's sales and profits over its lifetime. It involves four distinct stages: introduction, growth, maturity, and decline (see Figure 4.6). Each stage is identified by its sales performance and characterized by different level of profitability, various degrees of competition and distinctive marketing programmes (Hollensen and Opresnik, 2020).

The four stages of the product life cycle can be briefly summarized as follows (Hollensen and Opresnik, 2020):

- **Introduction** is a period of slow sales as the product is introduced in the market. Profits are non-existent in this stage because of the large expenses of product introduction.

- **Growth** is a period of rapid market acceptance and increasing profits. Profits may begin to decline towards the latter stage of growth as new rivals enter the market, attracted by fast sales growth and high profit potential. The end of this stage is often associated with competitive shakeout, whereby weaker suppliers terminate production.

- **Maturity** is a period of slowdown in sales growth because the product has achieved acceptance by most potential buyers. Saturation occurs, hastening competitive shakeout. The remaining companies are engaged in a fierce battle for market share by employing product improvements, advertising and sales promotional offers, and price cutting; the result is strain on profit margins. The need for successful brand building is increasingly recognized as brand leaders are in the strongest position to resist the pressure on profit margins (Doyle, 1989).

- **Decline** is the period when sales and profits fall as new technology or changes in consumer tastes work to reduce demand for the products and services. Suppliers may decide to end production completely or reduce product depth. Advertising may be used to defend against rivals and prevent the sales from falling further.

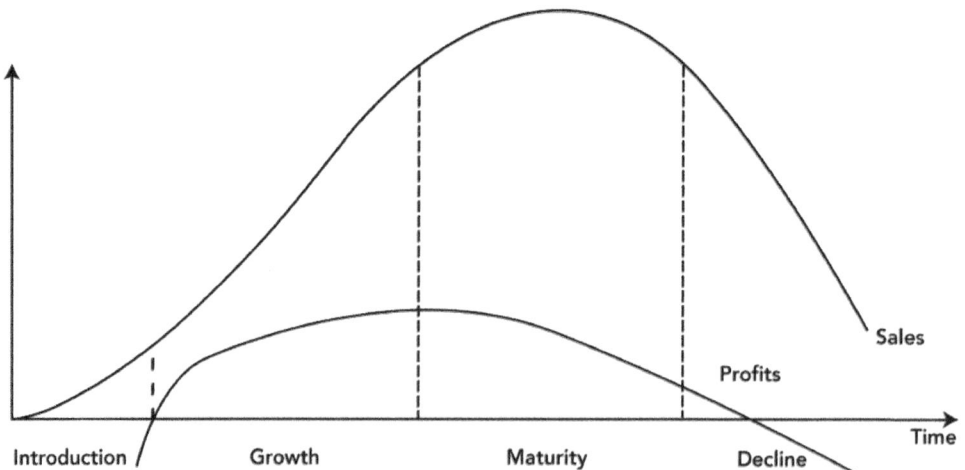

Figure 4.6: The Product Life Cycle.
Source: Adapted from Hollensen and Opresnik, 2020, modified.4.1.7

Branding.

Branding is the process by which companies distinguish their product offerings from the competition. By developing a distinctive name, packaging and design, a brand is produced. However, a brand name is more than a label employed to differentiate among the manufacturers of a product. It is a complex symbol that represents a variety of ideas and attributes. It tells the consumer numerous things by the body of associations it has built up and acquired as a public object over a period of time. The net result is the public image, the character or personality that may be more important for the customers. Essentially, a brand is a collection of perceptions in the eyes of the consumer influenced by values, communication, the marketing mix, and behavior of staff.

The concept of the brand represents an acceptance of the fact that all purchasing decisions for both products and services involve a combination of *rational* and *emotional* criteria. The rational criteria are the physical components or factual elements of the product or service in question. The emotional criteria are the sum of the impressions, ideas, opinions, and random associations that the potential purchaser has stored in their mind about the product or service. Rational and emotional elements combine to form a brand image. The word 'brand 'is used to represent everything that people know about, think about, or feel about anything. There are a number of implications of this definition.

Successful brand management necessitates the company innovating to stay abreast of constantly changing market conditions, ideally anticipating evolving tastes, and telling their brand stories to each new generation of consumers. The notion of **storytelling** is of key importance. Well-managed brands are continually telling stories about themselves and updating these stories to take account of underlying change in society, though their core values usually remain constant. Astute management of brands also involves decisions about the service element that supports a brand and the extent to which a brand should embrace some higher order universal value. Charles Revson of *Revlon* stated early: 'In the factory, we make cosmetics; in the store we sell hope '(Hollensen and Opresnik, 2020).

4.1.6.1 Brand Equity

As stated above, brands represent customer's perceptions about a product and its performance. Finally, brands exist in the minds of consumers. Therefore, the real value of a strong brand is its power to capture consumer preference and loyalty. A powerful brand has high **brand equity**. Although the definition of brand equity is often debated, the term deals with the brand value, beyond the physical assets associated with its manufacture.

Aaker (1991), one of the leading authorities on brand equity, has defined the term as a set of brand assets and liabilities linked to the brand, its name and symbol that add to or subtract from the value provided by a product or service to a firm or to the firm's customers. Aaker has clustered those assets and liabilities into five categories:

- **Brand loyalty.** Encourages customers to buy a particular brand time after time and remain insensitive to competitors' offerings.

- **Brand awareness.** Brand names attract attention and convey images of familiarity. May be translated to: how a big percentage of the customers know the brand name.

- **Perceived quality**. 'Perceived' means that the customers decide upon the level of quality, not the company.

- **Brand associations**. The values and the personality linked to the brand.

- **Other proprietary brand assets**. Include trademarks, patents, and marketing channel relationships.

4.1.6.2 Brand Sponsorship

The basic purposes of branding are the same everywhere in the world. In general, the functions of branding are as follows (Hollensen and Opresnik, 2020):

- To distinguish a company's offering and differentiate one particular product from its competitors.

- To create identification and brand awareness.

- To guarantee a certain level of quality and satisfaction.

- To help with promotion of the product.

All these purposes have the same ultimate goals: to create new sales (market shares taken from competitors) or induce repeat sales (keep customers loyal).

Basically, a manufacturer has four brand sponsorship options (Hollensen and Opresnik, 2020): The product may be launched as a **manufacturer's brand** (or **national brand**), as when IBM sells their output under their own brand names. Or the manufacturer may sell to resellers who give it a **private brand** (also called **store brand** or **distributor brand**). Another option is to market **licensed brands**. Finally, two companies can join forces and pursue a **co-branding** strategy (Hollensen and Opresnik, 2020).

4.1.6.3 Brand Development

Basically, a company has four options when it comes to developing brands (see Figure 4.7).

In the framework of brand development, an organisation can introduce **line extensions**, **brand extensions**, **multibrands**, or **new brands** (Hollensen and Opresnik, 2020):

- **Line extensions** occur when a company introduces additional items in a given product category under the same brand name, such as new forms, sizes and flavours. A company might introduce line extensions as a low-cost, reduced-risk way to introduce 'new' products. Or it might want to meet customer desire for variety, to use excess capacity, or to claim more shelf space from resellers. However, an overextended brand name might potentially lose its specific meaning, or strongly extended brands can cause customer confusion. Another risk which has to be taken into account is that sales of an extension may come at the expense of other items in the line and increase cannibalisation.

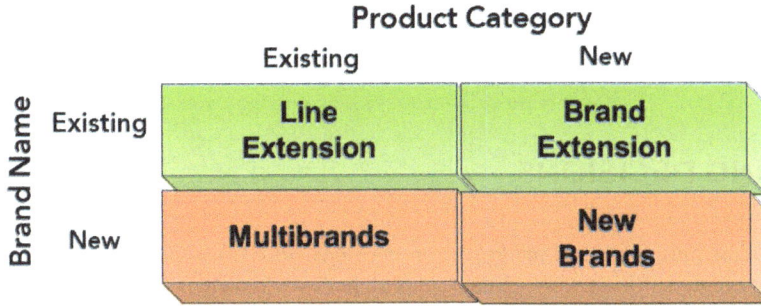

Product Category

	Existing	New
Brand Name — Existing	**Line Extension**	**Brand Extension**
Brand Name — New	**Multibrands**	**New Brands**

Figure 4.7: Brand Development Strategies.
Source: Adapted from Hollensen and Opresnik, 2020, modified.

- A **brand extension** strategy involves the use of a successful brand name to launch new or modified products in a new category. For example, Mattel has extended its enduring Barbie Doll brand into new categories ranging from Barbie home furnishings, Barbie cosmetics, and Barbie electronics to Barbie books and Barbie sporting goods. A brand extension is also referred to as brand stretching and can give a new product immediate recognition and quicker acceptance. It may also save the high advertising costs usually required to build a new brand name. On the other hand, brand extensions may confuse the image of the main brand as line extensions. And if brand extension fails, it may harm customer attitudes toward the other products carrying the same brand name. A major test of any brand extension opportunity is to ask if the new brand concept is compatible with the values inherent in the core brand to ensure a 'fluent fit' between them. An example is the failure to extend the Levi's brand name to suits in the USA partly as a result of customers refusing to accept the casual, denim image of Levi's as being suitable for smart, exclusive clothing. Consequently, brand extensions are not viable when a new brand is being developed for a target group that holds different values and aspirations from those in the original market segment. When this occurs, the use of the brand extension strategy would detract from the new brand. The answer is to develop a separate brand name, as did Toyota with the Lexus, and Seiko with its Pulsar brand name developed for the lower-priced mass market for watches. Finally, management needs to guard against the loss of credibility if a brand name is extended too far, which can be called **brand overstretching**. The use of the Pierre Cardin name for such diverse products as clothing, toiletries and cosmetics has tarnished the brand name's credibility (Aaker, 1990).

- In the case of **multibrands**, new brand names are introduced in the same product category. A **single brand** or **family brand** (for a number of products) may be helpful in convincing consumers that each product is of the same quality or meets certain standards. In other words, when a single brand on a single market is marketed by the manufacturer, the brand is assured of receiving full attention for maximum impact. Conversely, the company may also choose to market several brands on a single market. This is based on the assumption that the market is heterogeneous and consists of several segments. For example, Procter & Gamble markets many different brands in each of its product categories.

- Within the framework of this brand development strategy a company might believe that the power of its existing brand name is waning, and a **new brand** name is required. Alternatively, a company may create a new brand name when it enters a new product category for which none of the company's current brand names is appropriate. For example, Japan's Matsushita uses separate brand names for its different families of products: Technics, Panasonic National, and Quasar. As with multibranding, offering too many new brands can result in a company spreading its resources too thin. And in some industries, such as consumer packaged goods, customers and retailers have become concerned that there are already too many brands, with too few differences. Against this background, Procter &

Gamble, Unilever, and other large consumer-product marketers are pursuing megabrand strategies – weeding out weaker brands and focusing their marketing spending primarily on brands that can achieve the number one or two market share positions in their categories.

4.2 PRICING DECISIONS

Pricing is one of the most important marketing mix decisions, price being the only marketing mix variable that generates revenues. Pricing is not a single concept, but a multi-dimensional one with different meanings and implications for the manufacturer, the middleman, and the end-customer. Pricing strategy is of great importance because it affects both revenue and buyer behavior. The whole pricing environment is therefore considered, first from the point of view of the company and its strategies and then from the aspect of the consumer (Hollensen and Opresnik, 2020).

4.2.1 A PRICING FRAMEWORK

A company's pricing decisions are affected by both internal company factors and external environmental factors. It is important that firms recognize that the cost structures of product are very significant, but they should not be regarded as sole determinants when setting prices.

Figure 4.8 presents a general framework for pricing decisions. According to this model, factors affecting pricing can be broken down into two main groups (internal and external factors) which consist of various factors.

We shall now consider the most important elements in more detail.

4.2.1.1 Internal Factors Affecting Pricing Decisions

Internal factors affecting pricing include the firm's marketing objectives, marketing mix strategy, costs, and organisational considerations (Nagle and Holden, 2001):

- **Marketing objectives:** Before determining the price, the company must decide on its strategy for the product. If the company has selected its target market and positioning, its marketing mix strategy will be straightforward. Pricing strategy is largely determined by decisions on market positioning. In addition, a company may seek other general or specific objectives. General objectives include survival, profit maximisation, market share leadership, and product quality leadership. At a specific level, a company may set prices low to prevent competition from entering the market. Thus, pricing plays an important role in helping to accomplish the company's objectives at many levels.

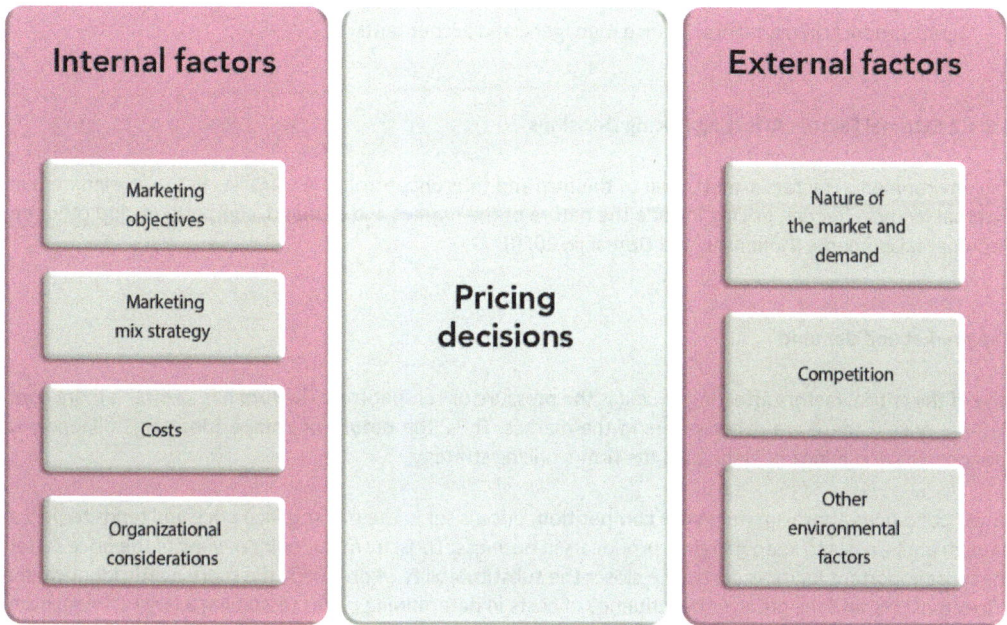

Figure 4.8: Factors Affecting Price Decisions
Source: Adapted from Hollensen and Opresnik, 2020, modified.

- **Marketing mix strategy:** As price is only one element of the marketing mix price decisions must be coordinated with product design, distribution, and promotion decisions to form a coherent and effective marketing mix strategy. Decisions made for other marketing mix variables affect pricing decisions. For example, a decision to position the product on high-performance quality will suggest that the seller must charge a higher price to cover higher costs. Marketers must consider the complete marketing mix when setting prices. If the product is positioned on on-price factors, then decisions about quality, promotion, and distribution will largely affect price. If price is a crucial positioning factor, then price will strongly affect decisions made about the other marketing mix elements.

- **Costs:** Costs set the baseline for the price that the company can charge. The firm wants to charge a price that both covers all its costs for producing, distributing, and selling the product and delivers a fair rate of return. A company's costs are an important element in its pricing strategy. However, the company must consider costs alongside all of the other factors rather than in isolation. A company's costs take two forms, fixed and variable. Fixed costs (also known as overhead) are costs that do not vary with production or sales level. Examples include rent, interest, and executive salaries. Variable costs vary directly with the level of production. Each PC produced by Hewlett Packard, for example, involves a cost of computer chips, wires, packaging, and other inputs. Finally, total costs are the sum of the fixed and the variable costs for any given level of production. Management wants to charge a price that will at least cover the total production costs at a given level of production.

- **Organisational considerations:** Management must decide who within the organisation should set prices. In small enterprises, prices are often set by top management rather than by the marketing or sales department. In large companies, pricing is typically handled by divisional or product line managers. In industries in which pricing is a key factor such as aerospace and oil, companies often have

161

a pricing department to set the best prices. Others who have an influence on pricing include sales managers, production managers, finance managers, and accountants.

4.2.1.2 External Factors Affecting Pricing Decisions

The environmental factors are external to the firm and thus uncontrollable variables in the foreign market. External factors affecting pricing include the nature of the market and demand, competition, and other environmental elements (Hollensen and Opresnik, 2020).

The market and demand

One of the critical factors affecting pricing is the pressure of competitors. The firm has to offer a more competitive price if there are other sellers in the market. Thus, the **nature of competition** (e.g., oligopoly or monopoly) can significantly influence the firm's pricing strategy.

Under conditions approximating **pure competition**, price is set in the marketplace price and tends to be just enough above costs to keep marginal producers in business. Thus, from the point of view of the price setter, the most important factor is costs. The closer the substitutability of products, the more nearly identical the prices must be, and the greater the influence of costs in determining prices (assuming a large enough number of buyers and sellers).

Under conditions of **monopolistic or imperfect competition**, the seller has some discretion to vary the product quality, promotional efforts, and channel politics in order to adapt the price of the total product to serve pre-selected market segments. Nevertheless, the freedom to set prices is still limited by what competitors charge, and any price differentials from competitors must be justified in the minds of customers on the basis of differential utility: that is, perceived value.

Whereas costs set the lower limit of prices, the market and demand set the upper limit. Both customers and industrial buyers balance the price of a product or service against the benefits of owning it. Thus, before setting prices, the marketer must comprehend the relationship between the price and demand for its product. Each price the company might charge will lead to a different level of demand. The relationship between the price charged and the resulting demand level is shown in the **price demand curve** in Figure 4.9.

The demand curve shows the number of units the market will buy in a given time period at different prices that might be charged. In the normal case, demand and price are inversely related; that it, the higher the price, the lower the demand and vice versa. Thus, the company would sell more if it lowered its price from P1 to P2. In the case of prestige goods, the demand curve sometimes sloes upward. Customers think that higher prices imply more quality. Marketers also need to know **price elasticity** – how responsive demand will be to a change in price. Consider the demand curve in Figure 4.9. The price decrease from P1 to P2 leads to a relatively small increase in demand from X1 to X2. If demand hardly changes with a small change in price, the demand is categorized as being **inelastic**. If demand changes greatly, the demand is **elastic**.

What determines the price elasticity of demand? Buyers are like to be less price sensitive when the product they are buying is unique or when it is high in quality, prestige, or exclusiveness. Consumers are also less price sensitive when substitute products are difficult to find or when they cannot easily compare the quality of substitute. Finally, buyers are less sensitive to price changes when the total expenditure for a product is low relative to their income or when the cost is shared by another party (Nagle and Holden, 2001).

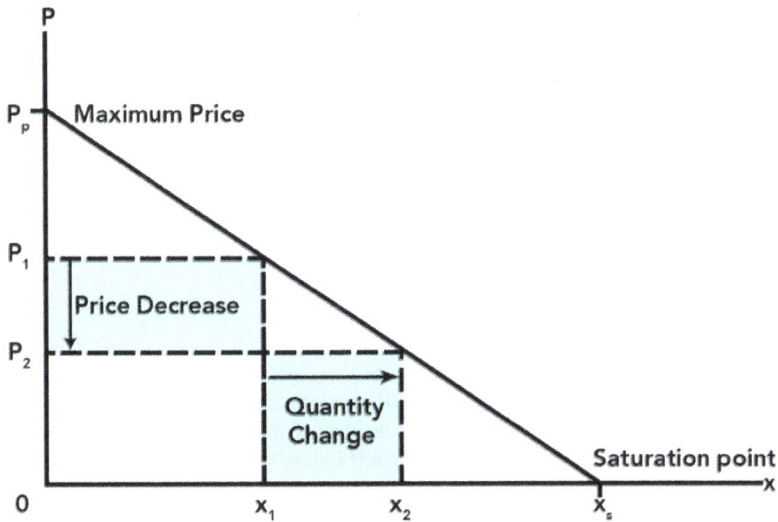

Figure 4.9: The Price Demand Curve.
Source: Adapted from Hollensen and Opresnik, 2020, modified.

Competition

In setting its prices, the company must carefully consider competitors' costs and prices and possible reactions to the company's own pricing moves. A consumer who is considering the purchase of a Sony digital camera, for example, will evaluate Sony's price and values against the prices and values of comparable products made by Canon, Olympus, and others.

If a business lowers prices to gain share, and competitors follow, there is likely to be very little real share gain. And at reduced margins, with a limited increase in volume, total contribution is likely to go down. On the other hand, if a business raises prices to improve margins and competitors do not follow, the business could lose share and lower total contribution, even with higher margins (Hollensen and Opresnik, 2020).

Other external factors

When setting prices, the company also must consider a number of other factors in its external environment. **Economic conditions** can have a strong impact on the company's pricing strategies. Economic factors such as boom or recession, inflation, and interest rates affect pricing decisions because they affect both the costs of producing a product and customer perceptions of the product's price and value. The enterprise must also think about what impact its prices will have on other parties in its environment (e.g. resellers).

The **government** is another important external stakeholder in the framework of pricing decisions. For example, import controls are designed to limit imports in order to protect domestic producers or reduce the outflow of foreign exchange. Direct restrictions commonly take the form of tariffs, quotas, and various non-tariff barriers. Tariffs directly increase the price of imports unless the exporter or importer is willing to absorb the tax and accept lower profit margins. Quotas have an indirect impact on prices. They restrict supply, thus causing the price of the import to increase. Since tariff levels vary from country to country, there is an incentive for exporters to vary the price somewhat from country to country (Hollensen, 2003).

163

In the following sections, we shall discuss the different available pricing strategies (Hollensen and Opresnik, 2020).

4.2.2 GENERAL PRICING APPROACHES

Companies set prices by selecting a general pricing approach. We will examine the following approaches in detail: the **cost-based approach** (**cost-plus pricing** and **break-even analysis**), the **value-based pricing**, and the **competition-based pricing** (**going-rate pricing** and **sealed bid pricing**).

4.2.2.1 Cost-Based Pricing and Break-Even-Pricing

Companies often use **cost-oriented methods** when setting prices. The simplest pricing method is **cost-plus pricing** – adding a standard mark-up to the cost of the product. Construction companies, for example, submit project bids by estimating the total cost and adding a standard mar-up for profit.

Cost-plus pricing can be best explained by using a simple example: suppose a watch manufacturer had the following costs and expected sales (Hollensen and Opresnik, 2020):

- Variable cost   EUR 10

- Fixed costs   EUR 300.000

- Expected unit sales   50.000

Then the manufacturer's cost per watch/unit is given by:

- Unit Cost = Variable Cost + (Fixed Costs/Unit Sales) = 10 + (300.000/50.000) = EUR 16

Now, we shall suppose the manufacturer wants to earn a 20 per cent mark-up on sales. The manufacturer's mark-up price is given by:

- Mark-up Price = Unit Cost/(1-Desired Return on Sales) = 16/(1-0,2) = EUR 0,20

Consequently, the manufacturer would charge resellers EUR 20 a watch and make a profit of 20 per cent or EUR 4 per unit. The dealers, in turn, will mark up the watch. If resellers, for example want to earn 50 per cent on sales price, they will mark up the watch to EUR 40 (EUR 20 + 50 % of EUR 40). This number is equivalent to a mark-up on cost of 100 per cent (EUR 20/EUR 20).

The problem with this pricing approach is that it ignores demand and competitor prices and all other internal and external factors discussed above. In addition, the procedure is illogical because a sales estimate is made *before* a price is set. Furthermore, it focuses on internal costs rather than the customer's willingness to pay. Finally, there may be a technical problem in allocating overheads in multi-product companies (Christopher, 1982). Still, mark-up pricing remains popular for many reasons. First, manufacturers are more certain about costs than about demand. By tying the price to cost, sellers simplify pricing – they do not have to make regular adjustments as demand changes. Furthermore, this approach does give an indication of the minimum price necessary to make a profit. Another reason is that many stakeholders feel that cost-plus pricing is fairer to both buyers and sellers (Hollensen and Opresnik, 2020).

Another cost-oriented pricing approach is **breaking even pricing.** This approach involves setting the price to break even on the costs of making and marketing a product; or setting the price to make a target profit.

Break-even analysis is generally viewed as an accounting concept, but it is extremely useful in evaluation the profit potential and risk associated with a pricing strategy, or any marketing strategy. This section is to examine, from a marketing viewpoint, the usefulness of break-even volume. For a given price strategy and marketing effort, it is useful to determine the number of units that need to be sold in order to break even (produce a net profit equal to zero). The **break-even point** is normally represented as that level of output where the total revenue from sales of a product or service matches exactly the total costs of its production and marketing (break-even quantity). Such an analysis of cost-revenue relationships can be very useful to the pricing decision-maker.

One use of break-even analysis is to compare the break-even volumes associated with different prices for a product. Break-even volume is the volume needed to cover the fixed cost on the basis of a particular contribution per unit. It can be estimated graphically using a break-even-chart, which shows the total cost and total revenue expected at different sales volume levels. Figure 4.10 shows a break-even chart for the watch manufacturer discussed above. Fixed costs are EUR 300.000 regardless of sales. Variable costs are added to fixed costs to form the total cost's function, which rise with volume. The total revenue curve starts at zero and rises with each unit sold. The slope of the total revenue curve reflects the price of EUR 20 per unit. The total revenue and total cost curves cross at 30.000 units. This is the break-even volume. At EUR 20, the company must sell at least 30.000 units to break even; that is, for total revenue to cover total cost.

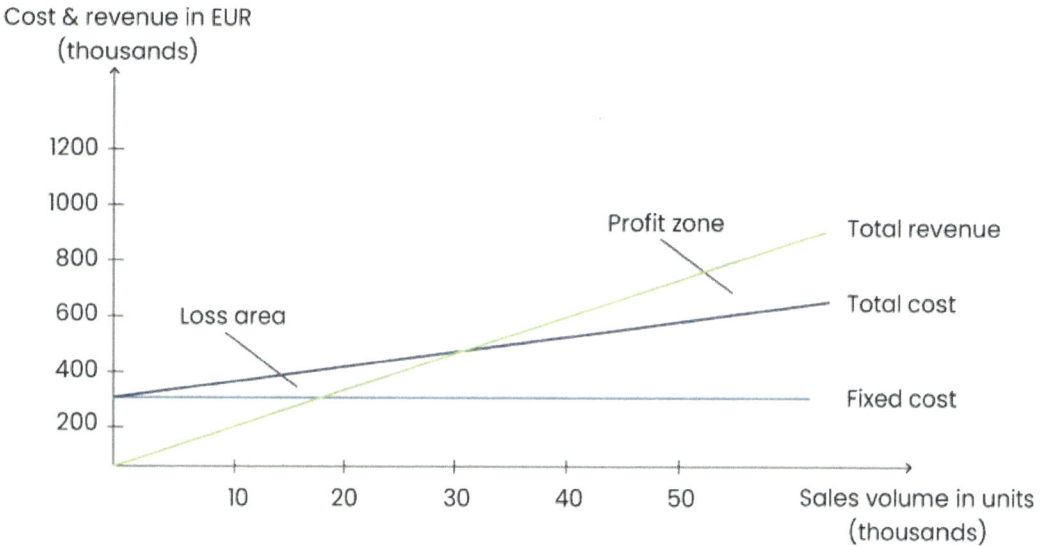

Figure 4.10: Break-Even Chart.
Source: Adapted from Hollensen and Opresnik, 2020, modified.

Break-even volume can be computed using the following procedure:

- Contribution per Unit = Selling Price − Variable Cost per Unit

- Break-Even-Volume = Fixed Cost/(Price − Variable Costs) = 300.000/(20-10) = 30.000

If the enterprise wants to make a target profit, it must sell more than 30.000 units at EUR 20 each.

165

In summary, neither the cost-plus pricing model nor the break-even analysis is in itself a sufficient basis on which to determine prices. Nevertheless, taken together, they do point to a clear-cut and universal presumption for delineating pricing decisions which can be incorporated into a more realistic and marketing-oriented approach to pricing. This more market-oriented approach to pricing will be discussed in the following sections.

4.2.2.2 Value-Based Pricing

An increasing number of companies are basing their prices on the product's perceived value. Value-based pricing uses buyers 'perceptions of value, not the seller's total costs, as the key to pricing. Value-based pricing implies that the marketer cannot design a product and marketing program and then set the price. Price in this context is considered along with the other marketing mix variables and other factors *before* the marketing program is determined.

Figure 4.11 compares cost-based pricing with value-based pricing. Cost-based pricing is product driven. The company designs what it considers to be a good product, totals the cost of making the product, and sets a price that covers costs plus a target profit. Once the price was set, the marketer's job was to convince customers that the product was worth it. If the marketer was not successful, then the price was lowered. If demand turned out to be higher than anticipated, then the price was raised.

An important point is that the customer was the last person to be considered in this chain of events (Hollensen and Opresnik, 2020).

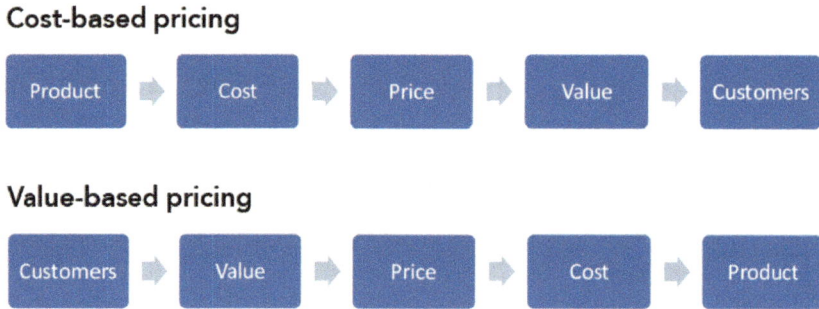

Figure 4.11: Cost-Based versus Value-Based Pricing.
Source: Adapted from Hollensen and Opresnik, 2020, modified.

Value-based pricing reverses this process and begins by understanding customers and the competitive marketplace. The first step is to look at the value customers perceive in owning the product and to examine their options for acquiring similar products and brands. The targeted value and price then drive decisions about product design and what costs can be incurred.

Although cost-based pricing is easier, it ignores the customer and the competition as already noted above. Marketers recognize that it is impossible to predict demand or competitors 'actions simply by looking at their own costs. Consequently, cost-based pricing is becoming less popular (Hollensen and Opresnik, 2020).

4.2.2.3 Competition-Based Pricing

Consumers will base their judgements of a product's value on the prices that competitors charge for similar products. One form of competition-based pricing is **going-rate pricing**, in which a company bases its price largely on competitors 'prices. Less attention is paid to its own costs or to demand. The enterprise might charge the same as, more than, or less than its competitors.

Competition-based pricing is also used when firms bid for jobs. Using **sealed-bid pricing**, a company bases its price on how it believes competitors will price rather than on its own costs or on the demand. The organisation wants to win a contract, and winning the contract requires piecing less than competitors. Yet the company cannot set its price below a certain level. It cannot price below cost without harming its competitive position (Hollensen and Opresnik, 2020).

4.2.3 PRICING NEW PRODUCTS

Pricing strategies usually change as the product passes through its life cycle. The introductory stage is especially challenging. Companies bringing out a new product face the challenge of setting prices for the first time. They can choose between two generic strategies: **market-skimming pricing and market-penetration pricing** (Hollensen and Opresnik, 2020).

Market-Skimming Pricing

Numerous companies that invent new products set high initial prices to 'skim 'revenues layer by layer from the market. Market-skimming pricing involves setting a high price for a new product to skim maximum revenues from the segments willing to pay the high price. A skimming approach, appropriate for a distinctly new product, provides the firm with an opportunity to profitably reach market segments that are not sensitive to the high initial price. As a product ages, as competitors enter the market, and as organisational buyers become accustomed to evaluating and purchasing the product, demand becomes more price elastic.

Market skimming is appropriate under certain conditions. First, the product's quality and image must support its higher price, and a reasonable number of buyers must want the product at that price. Second, the costs of producing smaller volume cannot be so high that they cancel the advantage of charging more. Finally, competitors should not be able to enter the market quickly and easily and undercut the high price (Hollensen and Opresnik, 2020).

Problems with skimming are as follows:

- Having a small market share makes the firm vulnerable to aggressive local competition.

- Maintenance of a high-quality product requires a lot of resource (promotion, after-sales service) and a visible local presence, which may be difficult in distant markets.

- If the product is sold more cheaply at home or in another country, grey marketing (parallel importing) is possible.

Market-Penetration Pricing

Rather than setting a high initial price to skim off small but profitable market segments, companies might use market-penetration pricing. They set a low initial price in order to penetrate the market quickly and deeply – to attract a large number of buyers rapidly and win a large market share. The high-sales volume results in falling costs, allowing the company to cut its price even further.

A penetration policy is appropriate when there is (1) high price elasticity of demand, (2) strong threat of imminent competition, and (3) opportunity for a substantial reduction in production costs as volume expands. Drawing upon the experience effect, a firm that can quickly gain substantial market share and experience can gain a strategic advantage over competitors. The viability of this strategy increases with the potential size of the future market. By taking a large share of new sales, experience can be gained when there is a large market growth rate. Of course, the value of additional market share differs between industries and often among products, markets, and competitors within a particular industry. Factors to be assessed in determining the value of additional market share include the investment requirements, potential benefits of experience, expected market trends, likely competitive reaction, and short- and long-term profit implications (Hollensen and Opresnik, 2020).

4.2.4 PRICE BUNDLING

Products can be bundled or unbundled for pricing purposes. Using **product bundling**, sellers often combine several of their products and offer the bundle at a reduced price. Many physical goods and services unite a care product with variety of supplementary products at a set price. This has become a popular marketing strategy. Food and beverage suppliers bundle ready-to-serve meals while computer vendors bundle a central processing unit, a monitor, a printer, and software at a single price. Manufacturers of industrial goods, such as machine tools, electronic components, and chemical substances, frequently offer their products at a system price in conjunction with an assortment of services. In the service sector, travel companies bundle flights, rent-a-cars, accommodations, and events into a one-price vacation package. Strategically this bundling activity is designed to benefit the consumer by reducing administration cost and consequently transaction costs.

Bundled prices offer a service firm a guaranteed revenue from each customer, while giving the latter a clear idea in advance of how much the bill will be. Unbundled pricing provides customers with flexibility in what they choose to acquire and pay for but may also cause problems. For instance, customers may be put off by discovering that the ultimate price of what they want, is substantially higher than the advertised base price that attracted them in the first place (Hollensen, 2003).

4.3 DISTRIBUTION DECISIONS

A product must be made accessible to the target market at an affordable price. Distribution decisions deal with the problems of moving products from points of origin to points of consumption. Often referred to as the **place element** in the marketing mix, distribution decisions are directed at ensuring that the right product is in the right place at the right time and in the right quantities. The creation of place, time, and possession utility for a select group of customers located in a specific geographic location provides the focus of the logistics manager's efforts. The distribution network is referred to as a **marketing channel** – a set of interdependent marketing institutions involved in the process of making a product or service available for use or consumption by the customer. Producers need to consider not only the needs of their ultimate customer but also the requirement of **channel intermediaries**, those organizations that facilitate the distribution of products to customers.

Using an intermediary as opposed to selling direct to the customer can provide producers with a number of benefits. Channel intermediaries fill several valuable functions: reconciling the needs of producers and consumers by breaking bulk; improving distribution efficiency by reducing the number of transactions and creating bulk for transportation; improving accessibility between producer and consumer by reducing the location and time gap; and providing specialist services such as selling, servicing and installation to customers (Hollensen and Opresnik, 2020).

4.3.1 TYPES OF DISTRIBUTION CHANNEL

Companies can design their distribution channels to make their products available to consumers in different ways. Each layer of marketing intermediaries that performs work in bringing the product closer to the final buyer is a **channel level**. The number of intermediary levels indicates the length of a channel.

Figure 4.12 shows several consumer distributions channels of various lengths.

The first channel at the top of the figure is called a **direct marketing channel** as it has no intermediary levels. In this case, the company sells directly to the customer. For example, Avon and Amway sell their products directly to their consumers. Cutting out distributor profit margin make this option attractive.

The elimination of a layer of intermediaries from a distribution channel is called **disintermediation**. For example, iTunes is displacing record shops in the distribution of music (Mills and Camek, 2004).

The remaining channels in Figure 4.12 are **indirect marketing channels**, containing one or more intermediaries.

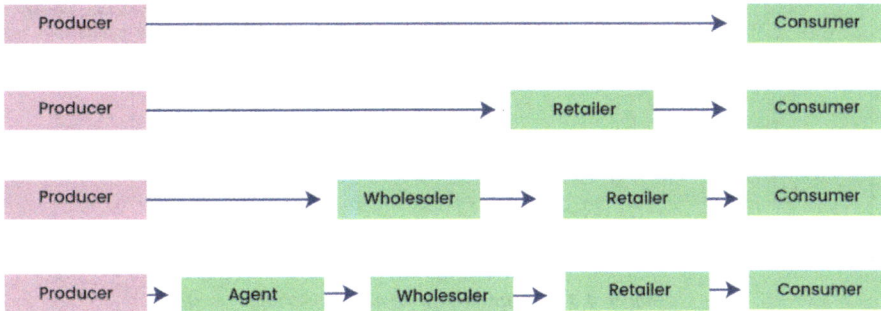

Figure 4.12: Distribution Channels.
Source: Adapted from Hollensen and Opresnik, 2020, modified.

4.3.2 STRATEGIES FOR MARKET COVERAGE

The amount of market coverage that a channel member provides is important. Coverage is a bendable term. It can refer to geographical areas of a country (such as cities and major towns) or the number of retail outlets (as a percentage of all retail outlets). Regardless of the market coverage measure(s) used, the company has to create a distribution network (dealers, distributors, and retailers) to meet its coverage goals (Hollensen and Opresnik, 2020).

As shown in Figure 4.13, three different approaches are available (Hollensen and Opresnik, 2020):

169

- **Intensive distribution.** This calls for distributing the product through the largest number of different types of intermediary and the largest number of individual intermediaries of each type. For example, many mass-market products, such as cigarettes, foods, toiletries, beer and newspapers, and other similar items are sold in millions of outlets to provide maximum brand exposure and consumer convenience.

- **Selective distribution.** This entails using more than one, but fewer than all, of the intermediaries who are willing to sell a company's products. Thus, a producer uses a limited number of outlets in a geographical area to sell its products. The advantages to the manufacturer are the opportunity to select only the best outlets to focus its effort to build close relationships and to train distributor staff on fewer outlets than with intensive distribution, and, if selling and distribution is direct, to reduce costs. Upmarket brands are often sold in carefully selected outlets. Retail outlets and industrial distributors like this arrangement since it reduces competition. Products such as audio and video equipment, cameras, personal computers, and cosmetics are distributed in this manner. Selective distribution gives producers good market coverage with more control and less cost than does intensive distribution.

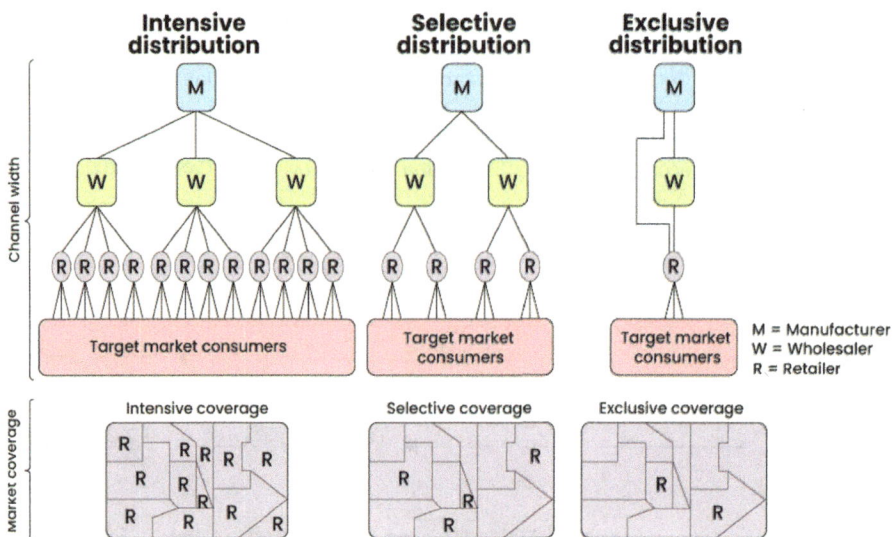

Figure 4.13: Strategies for Market Coverage.
Source: Adapted from Hollensen and Opresnik, 2020, modified.

- **Exclusive distribution.** This is an extreme form of selective distribution in which only one wholesaler, retailer or industrial distributor is used in a geographic area. Exclusive distribution is often found in the distribution of luxury automobiles. For example, Bentley dealers are few and far between – even large cities may only have one dealer. This reduces a purchaser's power to negotiate prices for the same product between dealers. It also allows very close cooperation between producer and retailer over servicing, pricing, and promotion. Initially, Apple's iPhone was also subject to exclusive distribution in the UK through the mobile phone operator O2 and retailer the Carphone Warehouse. The right to exclusive distribution may be requested by distributors as a condition for stocking a manufacturer's product line (Ritson, 2008).

- **Channel coverage** (width) can be identified along a continuum ranging from wide channels (intensive distribution) to narrow channels (exclusive distribution).

170

Regarding the types of intermediaries to be used at each level in the channel structure, this can vary quite extensively depending upon the industry in question.

4.3.3 VERTICAL INTEGRATION IN THE DISTRIBUTION CHANNEL

Channel integration is the process of incorporating all channel members into one channel system and uniting them under one leadership and one set of goals. Channel integration is relevant for the manufacturer to consider when high transaction costs occur between manufacturer and distributor, as a result channel conflicts and/or bad cooperation climate. There are two different types of integration (Hollensen and Opresnik, 2020):

- **Vertical integration**: seeking control of channel members at different levels of the channel.

- **Horizontal integration**: seeking control of channel members at the same level of the channel (i.e., competitors).

Integration is achieved either through acquisitions (ownership) or through tight cooperative relationships. Getting channel members to work together for their own mutual benefit can be a difficult task. However, today cooperative relationships are essential for efficient and effective channel operation.

Historically, conventional distribution channels have lacked such relationships and leadership, often resulting in damaging conflict and poor performance. One of the biggest channel developments over the years has been the emergence of **vertical marketing systems** (VMS) that provide channel leadership. Figure 4.13 contrasts conventional distribution channels and a vertical marketing system.

A **conventional distribution channel** consists of one or more independent producers, wholesaler, and retailers. Each is a separate stakeholder seeking to maximise its own profits, even at the expense of the system as a whole. No channel member has much control over the other members, and no formal means exists for assigning roles and resolving channel conflict.

In contrast, a **vertical marketing system (VMS)** consists of producers, wholesalers, and retailers acting as a unified system. One channel member owns the others, has contracts with them, or wields so much power that they must all cooperate. Vertical integration offers the promise of potential efficiencies gained from a reduction in management overhead, integration information systems, reduction, or elimination of selling costs within the integrated channel, and better management and control of marketing campaigns and physical distribution logistics. It is sometimes the only way to introduce new technological advances into a channel. Integration enables unilateral decisions on who is going to do what and the more direct rewarding of key personnel down the channel for responding to the changes. It also gives the integrating firm more control over training and management succession. However, competitive market forces often make the use of independent channel agents more efficient, and vertical integration should be employed only when the market fails – when gross inefficiencies result from working with independent channel participants (Hollensen and Opresnik, 2020).

Figure 4.14 shows an example of vertical integration. The starting point is the conventional marketing channels (CMCs), where the channel composition consists of isolated and autonomous participating channel members. Channel coordination is here achieved through arm's-length bargaining. At this point, the vertical integration can take two forms: forward and backward (Hollensen and Opresnik, 2020):

- The manufacturer can make **forward integration**, when it seeks control of businesses of the wholesale and retail levels of the channel.

- The retailer can make **backward integration**, seeking control of businesses at wholesale and manufacturer levels of the channel.

- The wholesaler has two possibilities: both forward and backward integration.

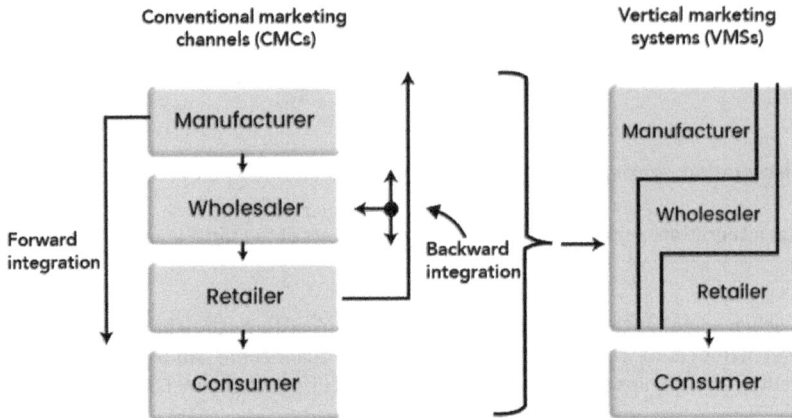

Figure 4.14: Vertical Integration.
Source: Adapted from Hollensen and Opresnik, 2020, modified.

The result of these manoeuvres is the vertical marketing system. Here the channel composition consists of integrated participating members, where channel stability is high due to assured member loyalty and long-term commitments.

4.3.4 MULTICHANNEL DISTRIBUTION SYSTEMS

Distribution channels can be seen as sets of interdependent organisations involved in the process of making a product or service available for consumption or use. When making channel choices, companies can choose from a wide variety of alternatives. In the past, many companies used a single channel to sell to a single market or market segment. Today, more and more companies have adopted **multichannel distribution systems** – often called **hybrid marketing channels**. A multichannel distribution system (or hybrid marketing channel) occurs when a single company sets up two or more marketing channels to reach one or more customer segments.

The increasing popularity of this strategy results from the potential advantages provided: extended market coverage and increased sales volume; lower absolute or relative costs; better accommodation of customers 'evolving needs; and more and better information. This strategy, however, can also produce potentially disruptive problems: consumer confusion; conflicts with intermediaries and/or internal distribution units; increased costs; loss of distinctiveness; and, eventually, an increased organisational complexity (Hollensen and Opresnik, 2020).

4.3.5 MARKETING LOGISTICS AND SUPPLY CHAIN MANAGEMENT

Marketing logistics – also called **physical distribution** – involves planning, implementing, and controlling the physical flow of goods, services, and related information from points of origin to points of consumption. In summary, it involves getting the right product to the right customer in the right place at the right time.

It is important to state that logistics is also a critical component of the firm's marketing capability. The right product, price and promotional mix are ineffective without dependable and timely product availability (place). Timely availability creates value by allowing customers to purchase products or services where desired and if appropriate arrange delivery when and where desired. For a customer, availability or timely availability is equally as important as price and assortment. Consequently, physical distribution and logistics effectiveness has a major impact on both customer satisfaction and company cost structures (Hollensen and Opresnik, 2020).

While the role of logistics has not always been visible and well defined in commercial enterprises, transportation, inventory storage and customer service have always been performed. However, top management did not always fully appreciate the strategic importance and competitive impact of integrated logistics. Wide acceptance of enterprise operating philosophies such as just-in-time, total quality management, customer satisfaction and customer responsiveness served to enhance the role of logistics in achieving competitive advantage. A well-planned and executed logistics effort can achieve timely shipment arrival, undamaged product, and satisfied customers at the lowest attainable total cost.

Logistics plays a major role in achieving customer expectations. The participants involved in logistical process management include wholesalers, distributors, retailers, and third-party service providers necessary to provide warehousing, transportation and a wide range of other value-added services. The transportation service decision includes selection of transport modes and providers. The managerial aspect of logistics includes scheduling and execution of activities to respond to customers and facilitate shipments. Management or execution activities include order processing, selection, and shipment. Measurement includes monitoring activities to ensure performance both satisfies customers and deploys firm resources effectively. Typical measures include customer service level, cost, productivity, asset utilization and quality (Hollensen, 2006).

4.3.6 LOGISTICS VALUE CHAIN

Marketing logistics involves not solely **outbound distribution** (moving products from the factory to resellers and ultimately to customers) but also **inbound distribution** (moving products and materials from suppliers to the factory of the manufacturer) and **reverse distribution** (moving broken, unwanted, or excess products returned by consumers or resellers). Consequently, marketing logistics entails entire **supply chain management** – managing upstream and downstream flows of materials, final goods, and relating information among the stakeholders involved (Hollensen and Opresnik, 2020).

The logistics value chain links all activities required to support profitable transactions as a single process linking business with customers. In some situations, the value chain is owned by a vertically integrated firm which controls all activities from raw material procurement to retail sales. Such vertical integration is found, for example, in the petroleum industry where firms control product value added from the drill to retail sales (Hollensen, 2006).

4.4 COMMUNICATION DECISIONS

Communication is the remaining decision about the marketing programme. The role of communication is to communicate with customers and to provide information which buyers need to make purchasing decisions. Although the communication mix carries information of interest to the customer, in the end it is designed to persuade the customer to purchase a product. Communication involves sharing points of view and is at the heart of forming relationships. A company simply cannot connect with customers unless it – directly or indirectly – communicates with them.

Promotion is the process whereby marketers inform, educate, persuade, remind, and reinforce consumers through communication. It is designed to influence buyers and other stakeholders. Although most marketing communications are aimed at consumers, a significant number also address shareholders, employees, channel members, suppliers, and society. In addition, effective communication is a two-way road: Receiving messages is often as important as sending them.

Integrated marketing communication (IMC) is the coordination of advertising, sales promotion, personal selling, public relations, and sponsorships to reach consumers with a powerful unified effect. These five elements should not be considered separate entities. In fact, each element of the communication plan often has a multiplier effect on the other. For example, it implies that website visuals are consistent with the images portrayed in advertising and that the messages conveyed in a direct marketing campaign are in line with those developed by the public relations department (Hollensen and Opresnik, 2020).

4.4.1 KEY OPINION LEADER MANAGEMENT

Marketing communications reach customers directly and indirectly. In **one-step communication**, all members of the target audience are simultaneously exposed to the same message. **Multiple-step communication** uses influential members of the target audience, known as **opinion leaders**, to filter a message before it reaches other group members, modifying its effect positively or negatively for the rest of the group. Because of their important role, opinion leaders have often been called **gatekeepers** to indicate the control they have over ideas flowing into the group. Marketers interested in maximising communication effectiveness nearly always attempt to identify opinion leaders. This is called **Key Opinion Leader (KOL) Management**. Opinion leaders are open to communication from all sources and more inclined to be aware of information regarding a broad range of subjects. They read a lot, talk to salespeople and other people who have information about products. Opinion leaders can have a sort of **multiplier effect**, intensifying the strength of the message if they respond positively and pass it on to others, especially if it is going on through the mass media. Consequently, the resources used to gain support from opinion leaders are eventually well spent (Hollensen and Opresnik, 2020).

4.4.2 THE PROMOTIONAL MIX

To communicate with and influence customers, several tools are available. Advertising is usually the most visible component of the **promotional mix** and to many people advertising epitomizes marketing: it is what they believe marketing to be. Evidently, this is a restricted view as marketing concerns much broader issues than simply how to advertise. Nevertheless, advertising is an important element in the promotional mix. The entire range of techniques available to the marketer is the promotional mix and comprises seven key elements (Hollensen and Opresnik, 2020):

- **Advertising**: any paid form of non-personal communication of products in the prime media, i.e., television, the press, outdoor, cinema, and radio.

- **Sales promotion**: incentives to customers or the trade that are designed to stimulate purchase.

- **Public relations**: the communication of a product or business by placing information about it in the media.

174

- **Sponsorship**: the association of the company or its products with an individual, event or organisation.

- **Internet promotion**: the promotion of products to customers and businesses through internet technologies.

- **Direct marketing**: the distribution of products, information, and promotional benefits to target customers through interactive communication in a way that allows response to be measured.

- **Personal selling**: oral communication with potential purchasers with the intention of making a sale.

In addition to these key tools, the marketer can also use other techniques, such as exhibitions, and product placement in movies, songs or video games. It is of paramount importance to stress that promotional mix decisions should not be made in isolation as all aspects of the marketing mix need to be consistently blended in order to achieve a sustainable competitive advantage. Consequently, the promotional mix must be aligned with the decisions made regarding product, pricing and distribution, in order to effectively communicate benefits to target customers.

In the following sections, we will now describe each of the tools in more detail (Hollensen and Opresnik, 2020).

4.4.3 ADVERTISING

Advertising is one of the most visible forms of communication. Because of its wide use and its limitations as a one-way method of communication, advertising in international markets is subject to a number of difficulties. Advertising is often the most important part of the communications mix for consumer goods, where there are a large number of small-volume customers who can be reached through mass media. For most business-to-business markets, advertising is less important than the personal selling function. Of all the elements of the marketing mix, decisions involving advertising are those most often affected by cultural differences among country markets. Consumers respond in terms of their culture, style, feelings, value systems, attitudes, beliefs, and perceptions.

Because advertising`s function is to interpret or translate the qualities of products and services in terms of consumer needs, wants, desires, and aspirations, the emotional appeals, symbols, persuasive approaches, and other characteristics of an advertisement must coincide with cultural norms if the ad is to be effective.

We shall revert to international communication strategies and its affecting factors later in this chapter (Hollensen and Opresnik, 2020).

4.4.3.1 Theories of How Advertising Works

For many years, there has been substantial debate about how advertising works. Researchers agree that there can be no single all-embracing theory that explains how all advertising works because it has varied tasks.

The basic competing views on how advertising works have been phrased the **strong theory of advertising** and the **weak theory of advertising** (Jones, 1991).

The strong theory is shown on the left-hand side of Figure 4.15. A person passes through the stages or awareness, interest, desire and action (**AIDA model**). According to this theory, advertising is powerful enough to increase people's knowledge and change their attitudes, and as a consequence is capable of persuading people who had not previously bought a product to buy it.

It is therefore a conversion theory of advertising: non-buyers are converted to become buyers. Advertising is assumed to have a powerful influence on consumers (Hollensen and Opresnik, 2020).

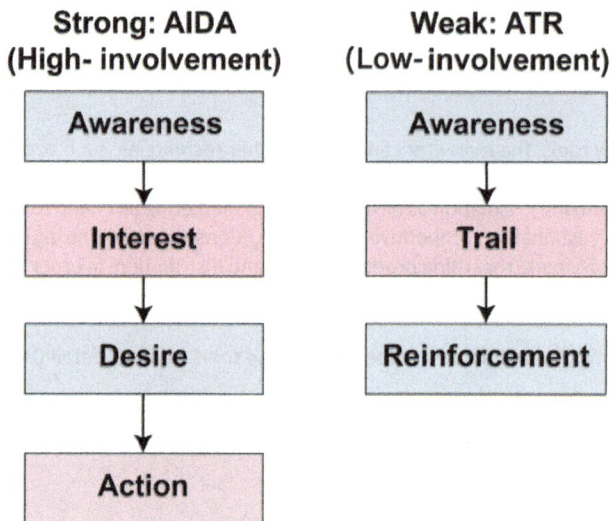

Strong: AIDA (High- involvement)	Weak: ATR (Low- involvement)
Awareness	Awareness
Interest	Trail
Desire	Reinforcement
Action	

Figure 4.15: Strong and Weak Theories of How Advertising Works.
Source: Adapted from Hollensen and Opresnik, 2020, modified.

This model has been criticized substantially as for many types of products there is little evidence that customers experience a strong desire before buying the brand. For example, in rather inexpensive product fields a brand may be bought on a trial basis without any strong conviction that it is superior to competing brands. Furthermore, the theory is criticized because it is limited to the conversion of a non-buyer to a buyer and ignores what happens after action (Ehrenberg, 1992).

The major opposing model is shown on the right-hand side of Figure 4.15. The stages in this model are awareness, trial, and reinforcement (**ATR model**). The ATR model suggests that advertising has a much less powerful influence than the AIDA model would suggest. Ultimately, the target is existing buyers who presumably are well disposed to the brand, and advertising is designed to reinforce these favourable perceptions, so they continue to buy it.

As already mentioned in earlier chapters, level of involvement plays a critical part in determining how people make purchasing decisions. Jones (1991) suggests that involvement may explain when the strong and weak theories apply. For high-involvement decisions such as the purchase of expensive consumer durables, the decision-making process is studied with many alternatives evaluated and an extensive information search undertaken. Therefore, advertising is more likely to follow the strong theory. However, for low-involvement purchase decisions such as low-cost packaged goods people are less likely to consider a wide range of brands thoroughly before purchase. Consequently, the weak theory of advertising is more probable to apply. Advertising is mainly intended to keep customers doing what they already do by providing reassurance and reinforcement (Hollensen and Opresnik, 2020).

4.4.3.2 Developing an Advertising Strategy

We now examine the different steps in developing an effective advertising strategy. The basic framework and concepts of international advertising are essentially the same wherever used.

Figure 4.16 shows the different steps and decisions, which are involved. It is worthwhile to state that each of the stages identified in Figure 4.16 is appropriate irrespective of whether the company is conducting an advertising campaign, a direct marketing or sales promotion campaign, all that changes is the detail involved.

In the following we examine some specific advertising issues (Hollensen and Opresnik, 2020).

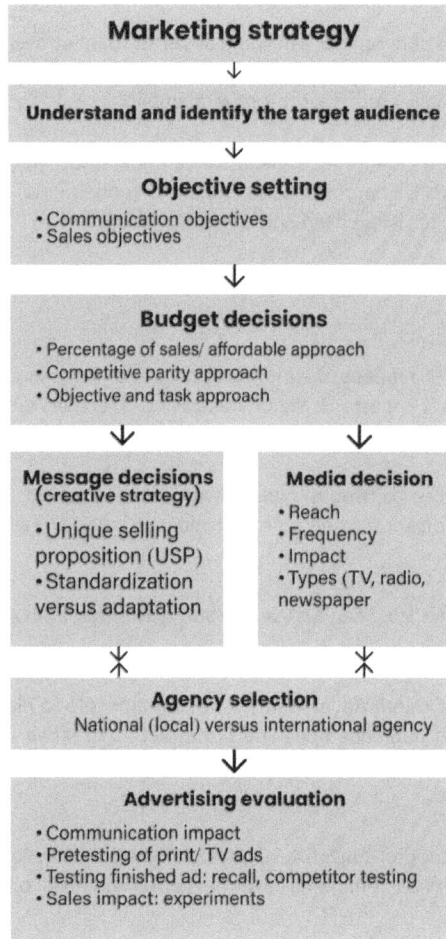

Marketing strategy
↓
Understand and identify the target audience
↓
Objective setting
- Communication objectives
- Sales objectives

↓

Budget decisions
- Percentage of sales/ affordable approach
- Competitive parity approach
- Objective and task approach

↓ ↓

Message decisions (creative strategy)
- Unique selling proposition (USP)
- Standardization versus adaptation

Media decision
- Reach
- Frequency
- Impact
- Types (TV, radio, newspaper)

↓ ↓

Agency selection
National (local) versus international agency

↓

Advertising evaluation
- Communication impact
- Pretesting of print/ TV ads
- Testing finished ad: recall, competitor testing
- Sales impact: experiments

Figure 4.16: Developing an Advertising Strategy.
Source: Adapted from Hollensen and Opresnik, 2020, modified.

Marketing Strategy

The foundation for developing an advertising strategy is a clear definition of the marketing strategy as advertising is only one element of the marketing mix and decisions should not be taken in isolation. The following questions are of central importance in this respect: what is the product's competitive position? What is the target market and what differential advantage doing the product possess? Target market definition allows the target audience to be identified in rough terms and identification of the product's differential advantage points to the features and benefits of the product that should be highlighted in its advertising (Hollensen and Opresnik, 2020).

Identify and Understand the Target Audience

The target audience is the group of people at which the advertisement strategy is aimed. The audience may be potential buyers or current users, those who make the buying decision or those who strongly influence it. The audience may be individuals, groups, or the general public.

Once the target audience has been identified, it needs to be understood. Buyer motives and choice criteria need to be thoroughly analyzed. This process is vital as it has fundamental implications for message and media decisions and all later stages (Hollensen and Opresnik, 2020).

Objective Setting

Although ultimately advertising is a means of stimulating sales and increasing profits, a clear understanding of its communication objectives is important. Major advertising objectives (and means) might include some of the following (Ellis-Chadwick and Jobber, 2016):

Create awareness: Advertising can be used to create awareness of a brand, or a particular service. Awareness creation is of critical importance when a new product is being launched or when the company is entering a new market.

Stimulate trial: In addition, advertising can be used to stimulate trial, such as car advertising encouraging motorists to take a test drive.

Position products in customers' mind: Advertisement has a major role to play in positioning brands in the 'hearts and minds' of the target audience (Ries and Trout, 2001). Creative positioning involves the development or reinforcement of an image or set of associations for a brand, such as L'Oréal's repeated use of the slogan 'Because I'm worth it'.

- **Correct misconceptions:** Another objective of advertising might include the correction of misconceptions about a product or service, reminding customers of sales, special offer and specific benefits of the product.

- **Remind and reinforce:** Once a clear collection of perceptions in the minds of the target audience has been established, the objective of advertising might be to remind consumers of the product's existence, and to reinforce image. This strategic objective is especially appropriate for leading brands in mature markets, such as Coca-Cola and Nivea cosmetics. The goal of those companies is to maintain top-of-mind awareness and positive associations. Given their rather strong market position, a major advertising task is to defend against competitive products trying to gain market share.

Budget Decisions

The amount that is spent on advertising governs the achievement of communication objectives. Controversial aspects of advertising include determining a proper method for deciding the size of the promotional budget, and its allocation across markets and over time.

In general, there are four methods of setting advertising budgets (Lane et al., 2005):

- **Percentage-of-sales method**

  This approach bases advertising on a specific percentage of current or expected sales revenue. Alternatively, the company may budget a percentage of the unit sales price. This method is easy to apply and makes management think about the relationships between promotion spending, selling price, and profit per unit. However, this approach fosters a decline in advertising expenditure when sales decline, a move that may encourage a further downward spiral of sales. In addition, it ignores market opportunities, which may suggest the need to spend more (or less) on advertising. Finally, the method fails to provide a means of determining the correct percentage to use.

- **Affordable method**

  This approach bases advertising expenditure on what level management regards as an amount that can be afforded. SMEs often use this method, reasoning that the company cannot spend more on advertising that it actually has. Problematically, this approach of setting budgets completely ignores the effects of promotion on sales. Its use as the sole criterion for budget neglects the communication objectives that are highly relevant for a firm's products and the market opportunities that may exist to grow sales and profits.

- **Competitive-parity method**

  Some firms use the competitive-parity method, setting their promotion budgets based upon matching expenditure to, or using a similar percentage of sales figure as their major competitors. However, matching expenditure assumes that the competition has arrived at the 'correct' level of budget, and ignores market opportunities and communication objectives. Using a similar percentage of sales ratio likewise lacks strategic vision and might only be justified if it can be shown to prevent costly advertising wars. Furthermore, the method does not recognize that the firm is in different situations in different markets. If the firm is new to a market, its relationships with customers are different from those of existing domestic companies. This should also be reflected in its promotion budget.

- **Objective-and-task method**

  The weaknesses of the above approaches have led some firms to follow this approach, which develops the promotion budget by defining specific objectives, determining the tasks that must be performed to achieve those objectives, and estimating the costs of performing these tasks. The sum of these costs is the proposed promotion budget. The advantage of this approach is that it stimulates management to think about objectives, media exposure levels and the resulting costs. However, it is also the most difficult method to apply. Often, it is extremely complicated to figure out, which specific tasks will achieve a stated objective.

Message Decisions (creative strategy)

This step concerns decisions about what **unique selling proposition (USP)** needs to be communicated, and what the communication is intended to achieve in terms of consumer behavior in the country concerned.

These decisions have important implications for the choice of advertising medium, since certain media can better accommodate specific creative requirements (use of colour, written description, high definition, demonstration of the product, etc.) than others.

Before a message can be decided, a sound understanding of the advertising platform should be acquired. The advertising platform is the foundation on which advertising messages are built. The platform should be important to the target audience and communicate competitive advantages. This is why an understanding of the motives and choice criteria of the target audience is essential for effective advertising.

The advertising message translates the platform into words, symbols and illustrations that are attractive and meaningful to the target audience. As we shall see below, the choice of media available to the advertiser is vast, therefore one of the central challenges of message formulation is to keep the message succinct and adaptable across various media.

Most of those who look at a press advertisement read the headline but not the body copy. Because of this, some advertisers suggest that the company or brand name should appear in the headline otherwise the reader may not know the source of the advertisement. A variety of creative treatments can be used, from lifestyle, to humour, to shock advertising (Hollensen and Opresnik, 2020).

Media Decisions

The selection of the media to be used for advertising campaigns needs to be done simultaneously with the development of the message theme. A key question in media selection is whether to use a mass or target approach. The mass media (television, radio and newsprint) are effective when a significant percentage of the general public are potential customers. This percentage varies considerably by country for most products, depending on, for example, the distribution of incomes in different countries.

The selection of the media to be used in a particular campaign typically starts with some idea of the target market's demographic and psychological characteristics, regional strengths of the product, seasonality of sales, and so on. The media selected should be the result of a careful fit of local advertising objectives, media attributes and target market characteristics. Furthermore, media selection can be based on the following criteria (Hollensen and Opresnik, 2020):

- **Reach**. This is the total number of people in a target market exposed to at least one advertisement in a given time period ('opportunity to see', or OTS).

- **Frequency**. This is the average number of times within a given time period that each potential customer is exposed to the same advertisement.

- **Impact**. This depends on compatibility between the medium used and the message.

High reach is necessary when the firm enters a new market or introduces a new product so that information about, for example, a new product's availability is spread to the widest possible audience. A high level of frequency is appropriate when brand awareness already exists, and the message is about informing the consumer that a campaign is under way. Sometimes a campaign should have both a high frequency and extensive reach, but limits on the advertising budget often create the need to trade off frequency against reach.

A media's **gross rating points (GRPs)** are the result of multiplying its reach by the frequency with which an advertisement appears within the media over a certain period. Hence it contains duplicated exposure but indicates the critical mass of a media effort. GRPs may be estimated for individual vehicles, for entire classes of media or for a total campaign.

The cost of running a media campaign also has to be taken into consideration. Traditionally, media planning is based on a single measure, such as 'cost per thousand GRPs'.

The media planner faces the choice of using television, press, cinema, posters, radio or a combination of median classes. Each medium possesses its own set of creative qualities and restrictions. We shall now take a closer look at the main media types (Hollensen and Opresnik, 2020):

- **Television** is an expensive but commonly used medium in attempting to reach broad national markets. It can be used to demonstrate the product in action, or to use colour and sound to build an atmosphere around the product, thus enhancing its image. Although TV was traditionally one of the most powerful advertising mediums, concerns about fragmentation of the audience have led many advertisers to move away from it or reduce their spending accordingly. In addition, research has again questioned whether viewers actually watch ads when they are on, finding that people may spend as little as 23 per cent of the time the ads are on watching them, with the remainder spent talking, reading, surfing between channels or doing tasks such as cleaning, ironing of office work. However, television is still the largest advertising medium, and it continues to play a significant role in brand building.

- **Newspaper** and press advertising is useful for providing factual information and offers an opportunity for consumers to re-examine the advertisement at a larger stage. In virtually all urban areas of the world, the population has access to daily newspapers. In fact, the problem for the advertiser is not having too few newspapers but too many. Most countries have one or more newspapers that can be said to have a truly national circulation. However, in many countries' newspapers tend to be predominantly local or regional and, as such, serve as the primary medium for local advertisers. Attempting to use a series of local papers to reach a national market is considerably more complex and costly.

- **Magazines** have a narrower readership than newspapers and can be used to target particular markets. One growing sector is customer magazines, whereby leading brand such as Audi and Mercedes-Benz produce colour magazines of pictures and editorial about their products. For technical and industrial products, magazines can be quite effective. Technical business publications tend to be international in their coverage. These publications range from individual businesses (e.g., beverages, construction, textiles) to world-wide industrial magazines covering many industries. Marketers of international products have the option of using international magazines that have regional editions (e.g. Newsweek, Time, and Business Week).

- **Radio** is limited to the use of sound and it therefore more likely to be useful in communicating information rather than building brand image. Radio is a lower-cost broadcasting activity than television. Commercial radio started several decades before commercial television in many countries. Radio is often transmitted on a local basis and therefore national campaigns have to be built up on an area-by-area basis.

- **Cinema** benefits from colour, movement, and sound, as well as the presence of a captive audience. In countries where it is common to subsidize the cost of showing movies by running advertising commercials prior to the feature film, cinema advertising has become an important medium. India, for example, has a relatively high level of cinema attendance per capita (few have television at home). Therefore, cinema advertisements play a much greater role in India than in, for example, the United States. Cinema is a particularly good but expensive medium for brands trying to reach young audiences.

- **Outdoor advertising** includes posters/billboards, shop signs and transit advertising. This medium shows the creative way in which space can be sold to customers. In the case of transit advertising, for example, a bus can be sold as an advertising medium. Outdoor posters/billboards can be used to develop the visual impact of advertising. In some countries, legal restrictions limit the poster space available. Outdoor advertising is believed to be effective for reminder advertising. Technology is helping outdoor advertising gain a bigger share of advertising in the prime media as backlit and scrolling sites are gradually replacing more traditionally glued posters.

- **Internet Advertising and Social Media Marketing** allow global reach to be achieved at relatively low cost. The number of website visits, clicks on advertisements and products purchased can be measured and interactivity between supplier and consumer is enabled. Google is market leader in so-called 'paid search' or 'pay-per-click' advertising. The disadvantages of Internet advertising are that it is impersonal and requires consumers to visit a website. This may require high expenditure in traditional media or the placing of sponsored links on search engines. Because of the growing significance of this tool, it is further dealt with in a separate section.

Agency Selection

Confronted with the many complex problems that international advertising involves, many businesses instinctively turn to an advertising agency for advice and practical assistance. Agencies employ or have instant access to expert copywriters, translators, photographers, film makers, package designers and media planners who are skilled and experienced in the international field. Only large multinational enterprises can afford to carry such people in-house.

Advertising Evaluation

Advertising evaluation and testing is the final stage in the advertising decision process. The key questions in advertising research are what, when and how to evaluate. What should be measured depends on whatever the advertising is trying to achieve. Measurement can take place before, during and after campaign execution. **Pre-testing** takes place before the campaign is executed and is part of the creative process. This is typically done with a focus group, which is shown various alternative commercials, and the members are asked to discuss their likes, dislikes and understanding of each other. **Post-testing** can be used to assess a campaign's effectiveness once it has run in order to provide necessary information to plan future campaigns. The major measures used in post-test television advertising research are image/attitude change, actual sales, and usage, though other financial measures such as cash flow, shareholder value and return on investment are increasingly being used (Ellis-Chadwick and Jobber, 2016).

4.4.4 SALES PROMOTION

Sales promotions are marketing activities that stimulate consumer purchases and improve retailer or middlemen effectiveness and relationship. Sales promotion communicates via an array of promotions not encompassed by any of the definitions above, each aiming for exposure to a target audience and some furthermore offering an incentive to respond actively. Examples include money off and free gifts (**consumer promotions**), price discounts (**trade promotions**) and sales force competitions (**business promotions**).

Sales promotions are short-term efforts directed to the customer or retailer to achieve such specific objectives as consumer-product trial or immediate purchase, consumer introduction to the store, gaining retail point-of-purchase displays, encouraging stores to stock the product, and supporting and augmenting advertising and personal sales efforts. In this sense, sales promotion may be regarded as a short-term tactical device. A typical sale pattern initially involves sales boost during the promotion period because of the incentive effect. This is followed by a fall in sales to below normal level because some consumers will have stocked up on the product during the promotion. The long-term sales effect of the promotion could be positive, neutral, or negative. If the promotion has attracted new buyers, who find that they like the brand, repeat purchases from them may give rise to a positive long-term effect. Alternatively, if the promotion has devaluated the brand in the eyes of customers, the effect may be negative (Rothschild and Gaidis, 1981).

A vast amount of money is spent on sales promotion and many companies are engaging in joint promotions. Some of the key reasons for the growth in sales promotion include the following (Peattie and Peattie, 1983):

- **Increased impulse purchasing:** the rise in impulse purchasing favours promotions that take place at the point of purchase.

- **The rising cost of advertising and advertising clutter:** these factors erode advertising's cost-effectiveness.

- **Shortening time horizons:** the attraction of the fast sales boost of a sales promotion is raised by greater competition and shortening product life cycles.

- **Competitor activities:** in some markets, sales promotions are used so often that all competitors are simply forced to follow suit.

- **Measurability**: measuring the sales impact of sales promotions is relatively easy compared to advertising since its effect is more direct and, usually, short term.

4.4.4.1 Major Sales Promotion Tools

Sales promotion can be directed at the customer, the trade or the business. We shall now discuss the main consumer, trade, and business promotion tools (Hollensen and Opresnik, 2020).

4.4.4.1.1 Consumer Promotion Tools

Consumer promotion tools include premiums, money off, free samples, coupons, prize promotions, bonus packs, and loyalty cards (Hollensen and Opresnik, 2020):

Premiums are any merchandise offered free or at very low cost as an incentive to purchase a product. They can come in three forms: free in- or on-pack gifts, free in-the-mail offers and self-liquidating offers, where customers are asked to pay a sum of money to cover the costs of the merchandise. The key objective of premiums is in encouraging bulk purchasing and maintaining share.

Money off promotions provide direct value to customer, and consequently an unambiguous incentive to purchase. Although they have proven track record of stimulating short-term sales increases, they can easily be matched by competitors and if used frequently, can devalue brand image.

Free samples of a brand may be delivered to the home or given out in a store and are used to stimulate trial. For new brands or brand extensions (for example, a new shampoo) this is an effective, if sometimes expensive, way of generating trial. There are a variety of methods of delivering samples including direct mail, inserts within publications or packages, or sampling points inside stores.

Coupons are certificates that give buyers a saving when they purchase specified products. They can promote early trial of a new brand or stimulate sales of a mature brand. Coupons can be delivered by direct mail, in stores, as inserts in publications or on packages. The traditional disadvantages of couponing are in the logistical effort of the redemption handling process, and consumer resistance to the need to physically clip and carry coupons. New technology may overcome all of these problems with innovations such as barcode scanning for coupons, and 'smart cards' for consumers, which store information about coupon entitlements.

Prize promotions can be competitions, draws and games. These are often used to attract attention or stimulate interest in a brand. Competitions require participants to exercise a certain degree of skill and judgement and entry is usually dependent or purchase at least. Draws make no demands on skill or judgement and the result depends on chance. A classic example of draw is when direct mail recipients are asked to return a card on which there is a set of numbers. These are then compared against a set of winning numbers. An example of game promotion is where a newspaper encloses a series of bingo cards and customers are told that, over a specified period of time, sets of bingo numbers will be published. If these numbers form a line or full house on a bingo card a prize is won. Such a game fosters repeat purchase of the newspaper.

Bonus packs give added value by giving customers extra quantity at no additional cost and are often used in the drinks, confectionary and detergent markets. The promotion might be along the lines of 'Buy 10 and get 2 extra free'. Because the price is not lowered, this form of promotion is less risky concerning the devaluation of the brand image.

Loyalty cards are becoming increasingly popular in retailing. Points are then gained every time money is spent at an outlet. Other loyalty schemes might involve the accrual of points that can be swapped for money-off vouchers to be used against purchases at the store or for bargain offers on other purchases such as theatre tickets. The goal is to attract customers back to the outlet. In addition, some schemes collect information on the customer including his or her name and address and, when it is swiped through the checkout machine detailed information on purchases is recorded. This implies that the purchasing behavior of individual customers is better known to the retailer, which can then use this information to target tailored direct mail promotions at those who are likely to be responsive. Despite their growth, loyalty schemes have attracted their critics. Schemes may simply raise the cost of doing business and, if competitors respond with me-too offerings, the final outcome may be no more than a minor tactical advantage (Dowling and Uncles, 1997).

4.4.4.1.2 Trade Promotion Tools

The trade may be offered or may demand discounts in return for purchase, which may be part of a joint promotion whereby the retailer agrees to devote extra shelf space, buy larger quantities, engage in a joint competition and/or allow demonstrations in the outlet. Manufacturers may use several trade promotion tools. Many of the tools used for consumer promotions such as prize promotions and premiums can also be used as trade promotions. Major trade promotion tools include price discounts, free goods, and allowances (Hollensen and Opresnik, 2020):

- **Price discounts:** The trade may be offered a straight reduction in price on purchases during a stated period of time. The concentration of buying power into fewer trade outlets has placed increasing power with these institutions and this influence is often translated into discounts from manufacturers. Volume discounts are given to retailers that hit sales targets (Quilter, 2005).

- **Free goods:** An alternative to a price discount is to offer more merchandise at the same price.

- **Allowances:** A manufacturer may offer an allowance in return for retailers providing promotional facilities in store. For example, allowances would be needed to stimulate a supermarket to display cards on its shelves indicating that a brand was being sold at a special price.

4.4.4.1.3 Business Promotion Tools

Companies spend a vast amount of money every year on promotion to industrial customers. These business promotion tools are used to generate business leads, stimulate purchase, reward customers, and motivate salespeople. Business promotion includes many of the same tools used for consumer or trade promotions.

Here, we focus on two additional major tools; conventions and trade shows, and sales contests (Hollensen and Opresnik, 2020):

Conventions and trade shows: Many enterprises and trade associations organize conventions and trade shows to promote their products and services. Companies selling to the industry show their products at the trade show. Vendors receive many benefits, such as opportunities to find new sales leads, contact customers, introduce innovative products, and inform customers with publications.

Sales contests: A sales contest is a contest for salespeople or dealers to motivate them to increase their sales efforts and ultimately performance over a given period. These contests motivate and recognize good company performers, who may receive trips, cash prizes, or other incentives.

4.4.4.2 Developing the Sales Promotion Program

The marketer must make several other decisions in order to define the complete sales promotion program. First, the marketer has to decide on the size of the incentive and set conditions for participation. Incentive might be offered to everyone or merely to specific groups. Hereafter, the marketer must decide how to promote and distribute the promotion program. In this respect, marketers are increasingly blending several media coherent campaign concept. Furthermore, the length of the promotion is also an important issue (Hollensen and Opresnik, 2020). The final stage in a sales promotion program involves testing the promotion. As with advertising, both pre-testing and post-testing methods are available. The major pre-testing techniques include group discussions (testing ideas on groups of potential targets), hall tests (bringing a sample of customers to a room where alternative promotions are tested) and experimentation (where, for example, two groups of stores are selected, and alternative promotions run in each). After the sales promotion has been implemented the results have to be monitored carefully. The company should thoroughly analyze sales before, during and after the promotion (Hollensen and Opresnik, 2020).

4.4.5 PUBLIC RELATIONS

A company is dependent on many groups if it wishes to succeed. The marketing concept focuses on customers and distributors, but the needs and interests of other stakeholders (such as employees, shareholders, the local community, the media, government, and pressure groups) are also of central importance and public relations is concerned with all of these groups. **Public relations** can be defined as building good relations with the company's various publics by obtaining favourable publicity, building a positive corporate image, and handling or heading off unfavourable rumours, stories, and events (Hollensen and Opresnik, 2020).

Public relations can accomplish many objectives, as outlined below (Lesly, 1998):

- **Prestige and reputation**: It can foster prestige and reputation, which can help companies to sell products, attract and keep good employees, and promote favourable community and government relations.

- **Promotion of products**: the desire to buy a product can be supported by the unobtrusive things that people read and see in the press, radio and TV. Awareness and interest in products and companies can be stimulated.

- **Dealing with issues and opportunities**: the ability to handle social and environmental issues to the mutual benefit of all stakeholders involved.

- **Goodwill of customers**: ensuring that customers are presented with useful information, are treated with respect, and have their complaints dealt with fairly and speedily.

185

- **Goodwill of employees**: promoting the sense of identification and satisfaction of employees with their company. Activities such as internal newsletters, recreation activities, and awards for service and achievement can be used.

- **Overcoming misconceptions**: managing misconceptions about a company and its products so that unfounded opinions do not severely damage its operations.

- **Goodwill of suppliers and distributors**: building a reputation as a good customer and a reliably supplier.

- **Goodwill of government**: influencing the opinions of public officials and politicians so that they feel the company operates in the public interest.

- **Dealing with unfavourable publicity**: responding rapidly, accurately and effectively to negative publicity.

Public relations firms 'billings in the international arena have been growing at double digit rates for some years. Handling such international PR problems as global workplace standards is big business for companies serving corporate clients such as Mattel Toys, McDonald's, and Nike. Fast growth is also being fuelled by the expanding international communications industry. New companies need public relations consultation for 'building an international profile'.

Three major reasons for the growth in public relations are a recognition of the power and value of public relations, increased advertising costs leading to an exploration of more cost-effective communication routes, and improved understanding of the embracing role of public relations (Hollensen and Opresnik, 2020).

4.4.6 SPONSORSHIP

Sponsorship can be defined as a business relationship between a provider of funds, resources or services and an individual, event or enterprise which offers in return some rights and association that may be used for commercial advantage (Sleight, 1989).

Companies have a wide range of entities and activities from which to choose, including sports, arts, community activities, teams, tournaments, music festivals, individual personalities or events, competitions, fairs and shows. Sport sponsorship is by far the most popular sponsorship medium as it usually offers high visibility through extensive television coverage, the ability to attract a broad cross-section of the community and to service specific niches (Ellis-Chadwick and Jobber, 2016).

4.4.6.1 Principal Sponsorship Objectives

Organisations should be clear about their reasons for spending money on sponsorship. The five principal objectives of sponsorship are to gain publicity, create entertainment opportunities, foster favourable brand, and company associations, improve community relations, and create promotional opportunities (Hollensen and Opresnik, 2020):

- **Gaining publicity:** Sponsorship provides multiple opportunities to create publicity in the media. With the advent of global media the possibilities for global sponsorships are opening up. Sponsoring soccer World Cup or the Olympic Games by plastering the brand name on the bleachers has helped global companies to establish a strong identity in the global marketplace.

- **Creating entertainment opportunities:** Another major objective of sponsorship is to create entertainment opportunities for customers and the trade. Sponsorship of music, the performing arts and sports events can be particularly effective.

- **Fostering favourable brand and company associations:** A further objective of sponsoring is to create favourable associations for a brand and company. For example, Red Bull's sponsorship of events such as 'Flugtag', at which amateur pilots launch handmade flying machines off a ramp, reinforces its 'weird' image and its energy associations (Clark, 2005).

- **Improving community relations:** Sponsorship of schools – for example, by providing low-cost personal computers – and supporting community programmes can foster a socially responsible, caring reputation for an organisation.

- **Creating promotional opportunities:** Sponsored events provide a perfect opportunity to promote company brands. Sweatshirts, bags, pens, etc., carrying the company logo and the name of the event can be sold to a captive audience.

4.4.6.2 Components of Assessing a Sponsorship Property

Selection of an event, programme or celebrity to sponsor should be undertaken by assessing the following components (Hollensen and Opresnik, 2020):

- **Cost of initial sponsorship outlay**

- **Budget needed for supporting marketing or public relations activity**

- Time & resource implications for firm's staff: the number of staff and the quantity of resources that are needed, so as the sponsorship opportunity can be fully leveraged.

- Duration of relationship: the benefits of a positive sponsorship association can take time to develop. Sponsors frequently seek out options to extend the contracts of their sponsorship relationship. If a sponsor can only avail of a short-term contract, with no options for a contract extension then the sponsorship property, will prove unattractive for investment.

- Targeted groups: a variety of different stakeholders can be targeted by sponsorship campaigns. A firm must ensure there is a match between the audience of the sponsored property and their selected target market. The sponsor can associate itself with a certain lifestyle or consumer segment. The stronger the association between a sponsor's target audience and the sponsorship properties target audience, the better the strategic 'fit'.

- **Geographic scope:** how far reaching is the sponsorship property? Will it have an impact in foreign markets? For example, certain sports sponsorship properties have a far greater reach in global geographic markets (e.g., F1 car racing). Sponsorship properties that have good geographic reach are expensive and scarce in supply.

- **Strategic fit between sponsor and sponsorship property:** compatibility is needed between the two entities. Marketers can use the sponsorship association with a property to give a clear message about their product and what their company stands for.

- **Uniqueness to break through clutter:** companies strive for sponsorship opportunities that break through the sponsorship clutter that exists, gaining sufficient media coverage, and helps form positive brand associations. Specsavers, an optician chain, exploited a unique sponsorship opportunity by sponsoring referees for football games, creating a distinctive and powerful message – 'That referee needs glasses!'

- **Image of sponsored property:** a sponsor has to assess whether the sponsored property is seen in a positive or negative light. Likeability of the sponsored property can transfer through to likeability of the sponsor.

- **Estimated number of viewers, listeners, or attendees to the sponsored property:** the attendance at a sponsored event is a basic evaluation metric used. Similarly viewing or listener figures are used for broadcast sponsorship activities.

- **Estimated media coverage:** the sponsored property needs to acquire the right amount and right type of media coverage. The company should assess the newsworthiness of a sponsorship property.

- **Corporate hospitality potential:** some events are highly sought after for their potential to entertain clients. Sponsoring sports or entertainment events allow firms the opportunity to build and enhance relations with channel members and corporate accounts (e.g., Heineken sponsors European Club Rugby Championship, which provides Heineken the opportunity to provide corporate hospitality to publicans).

- **Leverage potential:** *H*ere the firm evaluates if there are any marketing, sales or sales promotion spin offs that may accrue from the sponsorship. In order for any sponsorship to work effectively to its full potential, it must be supported by other marketing communications activities. The sponsors must communicate the association between themselves and the sponsorship property.

- **Exclusivity on sponsorship property:** some sponsorship properties offer sponsors different tiers of sponsorship association, having multiple sponsors. This in turn may confuse the intended target as to who is sponsoring a particular property. If a sponsor has complete exclusivity over a sponsorship property, then they can leverage the relationship more effectively. For example, Coca-Cola and Pepsi used Beckham in campaigns causing confusion.

- **Legacy effects:** sponsors must assess whether past historical linkages with an incumbent sponsor may be broken. Otherwise, sponsorship confusion may arise. Typically, firms who have strong past relationships with a sponsorship property, that may be have been built over numerous years, have stronger sponsorship legacy effects.

- **Potential for negative exposure:** firms should make risk assessment on whether a potential sponsorship may backfire in a blaze of negative publicity. For example, the Festina, watch brand was decimated when during the Tour de France, the cycling team they sponsored where found to be drug cheats. Similar examples include: Roy Keane & 7Up during the infamous Saipan World Cup incident, Michelle.

4.4.6.3 Sponsorship Evaluation

Despite the phenomenal growth of sponsorship over the last decade, there still remains much ambiguity about sponsorship evaluation. There is no definitive framework for evaluating a sponsorship programme. Yet companies spend millions on sponsorships annually. To evaluate any sponsorship effectively they must first set measurable goals. Firms must utilize both quantitative and qualitative evaluation techniques to accurately measure the effects of sponsorship. We shall describe possible evaluation techniques in more detail now (Hollensen and Opresnik, 2020):

- **Exposure obtained**: an organisation could view the number of people who attended an event as an easy key performance indicator to use in the evaluation process. The amount of media exposure and quality of media coverage could be qualitatively assessed such as radio airplay or editorial space. For example, a media clippings book could be generated, with all the media stories related to the event, documented for assessment. Media audits analyzing the quantity and quality of coverage can be undertaken.

- **Communications results**: the firm could track recall levels amongst target audiences, to gauge any communications impact, from the sponsorship.

- **Increasing sales or market share**: companies could use bottom-line metrics as an indication of the success of a sponsorship programme. However, this would be a naive metric to use in isolation, as sales may have been impacted due to an exogenous variable within the marketing environment, and may not be attributable directly to a sponsorship programme. Competitor activity, changing trends or changing economic conditions, may be the cause of sales changes, not sponsorship activity.

- **Feedback gained from participating groups**: a firm could gauge the reactions of stakeholders to the sponsored property. A firm could undertake surveys or in-depth interviews to gauge stakeholder reactions to these sponsorships.

4.4.7 DIGITAL AND SOCIAL MEDIA MARKETING

4.4.7.1 Evolution

There is no doubt that the Internet has changed the way people communicate. For many, e-mail has virtually replaced traditional letters and even telephone calls as the choice for correspondence. Every day, billions of e-mail messages are sent out. This has also influenced the way of doing business. Against this background, media planning is undergoing a dramatic change from traditional ATL communication tools such as newspapers and magazines to non-traditional BTL tools such as mobile and Internet marketing.

Figure 4.17 displays the respective advertising market shares by medium in the years 2014 to 2019 (compared to the previous year) using the example of Germany. This is not a purely German development, but similar worldwide: since its beginnings in the mid-1990s, Internet advertising (both desktop and mobile advertising) has grown primarily at the expense of newspapers. From 2012 to 2019, global Internet advertising has risen from 18% to 39% in 2019 (Hollensen, Kotler and Opresnik, 2020).

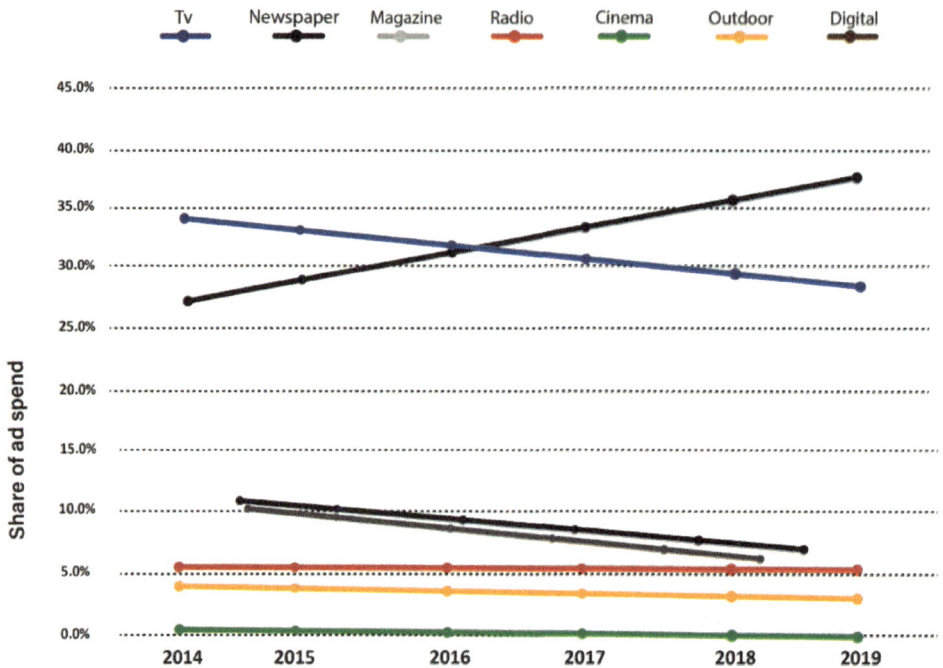

Figure 4.17: Advertising market shares of the individual media in Germany in the years 2014 to 2019 (compared to the previous year).
Source: www.statista.com; accessed 4th May 2020.

This development is due to the advantages of **digital marketing**. For example, a great advantage of "**Direct E-Mail Marketing**" is that it qualifies so-called **leads**. Appropriate software allows the firm to track who is reading and responding along with the types of responses. This enables the firm to segment the audience, accordingly, targeting future communications based on recipients ˙self-reported priorities.

A checklist for launching a successful e-mail marketing campaign includes the following aspects (Linkon, 2004):

- **Solid planning**. Companies are required to have clear and measurable objectives, and they must carefully plan their campaign.

- **Excellent content**. Standards are higher with e-mail, so firms have to make sure they are offering genuine value to the subscriber.

- **Appropriate and real 'from 'field**. This is the first thing recipients look at when they are deciding whether to open an e-mail.

- **Strong 'subject 'field**. The next place recipients look before deciding whether to open an e-mail is the subject field. Therefore, it needs to be compelling.

- **Right frequency and timing**. Organizations must not overwhelm their audience. They are not supposed to send e-mail Friday through Monday or outside of normal business hours.

- **Appropriate use of graphics**. Businesses should not get carried away. If graphics add real value and aren't too big, they could be used.

- **Lead with company's strength**. Companies should not bury the best content or offer. They need to ensure it is at the top or at the e-mail equivalent of 'above the fold'.

- **Shorter is better**. Nobody reads a lot these days, and they read less in e-mail than anywhere else.

- **Personalize**. Marketers should use just three or four elements of personalization, and response rates can potentially improve by 60 per cent. They should try to go beyond just the first name and learn about the subscribers.

- **Link to company's Web site**. This is where the richness of content and interactivity can really reside. Marketers should tease readers with the e-mail so they will link to the Web site. Advertising can also be incorporated, serving the same role as the initial e-mail: to create a desire in the audience for more information. The Web site catch page is crucial to this tactic and is often where many people falter when integrating traditional advertising with online promotions.

- **Measure and improve**. The ability to measure basics such as open and click-through rates is one of the main advantages of e-mail marketing, but companies should not stop there. They should also track sales or other conversions and learn from what works and make necessary adjustments.

Web 2.0 websites allow you to do more than just retrieve information, as this was mainly the case with Web 1.0. Web 2.0 transforms broadcast media monologues (one-to-many = Web 1.0) into social media dialogues (many-to-many). The term Web 2.0 was first used in 2004 to describe a new way software developers and end-users started to utilize the internet to create content and applications that were no longer created and published by individuals, but instead continuously modified by all users in a participatory and collaborative fashion. The popularity of the term Web 2.0, along with the increasing use of blogs, wikis, and social networking technologies, has led many in academia and business to work with these 'new 'phenomena. For marketers, Web 2.0 offers an opportunity to engage consumers. A growing number of marketers are using Web 2.0 tools to collaborate with consumers on product development, service enhancement and promotion. Companies can use Web 2.0 tools to improve collaboration with both its business partners and consumers. Among other things, company employees have created wikis, which are Web sites that allow users to add, delete and edit content, and to list answers to frequently asked questions about each product, and consumers have added significant contributions. Another Web 2.0 marketing feature is to make sure consumers can use the online community to network among themselves on content that they choose themselves. Besides generating content, the Web 2.0 Internet user tends to proactively bring in a whole new perspective on established processes and approaches, so that the users create innovative ideas for the future development of companies (Hollensen and Opresnik, 2020).

With the creation of the World Wide Web and Web browsers in 1990s, the Internet was transformed from a mere communication platform into a certifiably revolutionary technology. For consumers, digital technologies have not only provided the means to search for and buy products while saving time and money, but also to socialize and be entertained. The emergence of social networking sites such as MySpace and Facebook has enabled consumers to spend time socializing, and the development of video streaming and music downloads means that they can be entertained as well. A major challenge for marketers is to tap into the huge audiences using the net.

The Internet is a global channel of communication, but the advertising messages are often perceived in the local context by the potential customer. Herein lays the dilemma that often causes the results from internet promotion to be less than anticipated.

Traditional media have two capabilities – building brands and direct marketing. In general, most promotional forms are useful for one or the other. The internet, however, has the characteristics of both broadcast mass media and direct response advertising.

In the conventional model of communications in the marketplace, there are clear distinctions between the sender, the message and the recipient, and control of the message is with the sender. In 'market space', control of the message is shared between sender and receiver because of the interactivity of the medium, its ability to carry a message back in reply to that sent, and the impact of the information technology on time, space, and communication. The above stated impacts on the feedback loop are built into the Internet and on the aspects of interference. In general, interference is more likely to be from internet clutter and less from external sources.

The web represents a change away from a **push strategy** in international promotion, where a producer focuses on compelling an intermediate to represent the products or services or a distributor to stock its goods, towards a **pull strategy** in which the producer communicates directly with the customer. In this transition process, promotional costs and other transaction costs are reduced. The differentiating feature of the Internet from other promotional vehicles is that of interactivity. This results in the special feature that Internet combines the attributes of both selling and advertising. Interactivity facilitates a completely innovative approach to reaching potential customers. Unlike television, for example, where the consumer passively observes, with the web there is an active intent to go onto the Internet and more attention to content as a result. In the Internet, the potential customer has a high involvement approach to advertising. A continual stream of decisions is demanded from the user. Each click represents a decision and therefore the web is a very high involvement medium. In addition, unlike traditional media, the web is a medium by which the user can click through and obtain more information or purchase the product. Web advertisements can and are often targeted to a user profile that in turn affects the way the message will be received. Increasingly, the ads displayed on the web are specific to user interests and appear as these interests are revealed while the user navigates the web (Hollensen and Opresnik, 2020).

4.4.7.2 Definition of Social Media Marketing

Social media are Internet-based technologies that facilitate online conversations and encompass a wide range of online, word-of-mouth forums including social networking websites, blogs, company sponsored discussion boards and chat rooms, consumer-to-consumer e-mail, consumer product or service ratings websites and forums, Internet discussion boards and forums, and sites containing digital audio, images, movies, or photographs, to name a few. Since 2009, the official company and brand web sites have typically been losing audience. This decline is believed to be due to the emergence of social media marketing by the brands themselves, an increasingly pervasive marketing practice. For social media usage and development, the diversity of languages is creating communication challenges on a global basis. Facebook has 1,100 million weekly users, with more than 70% outside the United States. To effectively communicate with non-English users, Facebook has 70 translations available on its site made possible by a vast network of 300,000 volunteers and translators. Facebook and Twitter are mostly interactive social media on an intimate level. As such, these platforms offer direct selling companies means of communicating with key stakeholders (customers and distributors) in the industry. Figure 4.18 lists the ten most popular social networking sites per March 2020.

Social Media	Country	Comments	Active users per month
1. Facebook	US	In 2018 Facebook came under attack for allowing 3rd parties to access millions of users' personal data	1,600 million
2. WhatsApp	US	Acquired by Facebook in 2014. Give users ability to communicate and share instantly with individuals and groups	1,000 million
3. QQ	China	Tencent owned. Instant messaging (chat-based). It became international, after it was launched in China	860 million
4. WeChat	China	Tencent owned. All-in-one communication app, plus gaming. Growing fast	700 million
5. QZone	China	Tencent owned. Enabling share of photos, watch videos, listen to songs, write blogs, maintain diaries etc.	650 million
6. Tumblr	US	Owned by Yahoo since 2013. A micro blogging platform where users can post anything including multimedia	550 million
7. TikTok	China	Owned by ByteDance. Initially launched as Douyin in September 2016. The app allows the user to create short music video. Especially popular among teenagers.	500 million
8. Instagram	US	Owned by Facebook. Based on sharing photos and videos	450 million
9. Twitter	US	Enabling posts of short text messages (called tweets), containing limited number of characters (up to 280)	330 million
10. Baidu Tieba	China	Owned by Baidu, a search engine. Allow users to create a social network group for a specific topic	300 million

Figure 4.18: Social Media, World Top 10 per March 2020.
Source: Based on www.makeawebsitehub.com/social-media-sites/ and Statista.com

The Chinese social media sites such as QZone and Weibo Tieba are mainly active in their home country. In the West, it is possible to get away with a two-way platform strategy consisting of Facebook and Google. However, in China, there are not only social media platforms that do not exist elsewhere in the world, but there are also multiple overlapping platforms and ecosystems that are in constant movement. For example, WeChat is the go-to platform not only for chatting and e-commerce transactions, but also for P2P transfer, bill payment and even mutual fund investment. For an outsider, an environment like this requires persistent monitoring to understand, plan and execute for maximum impact of the Chinese customers.

One of the 'shooting stars' during the last years is LinkedIn, which is a social networking website for people in professional occupations. Launched in 2003, it is mainly used for professional networking. While Facebook, YouTube, and Twitter continue to dominate social media in the US and Europe some other countries, the global scene tells a different story. In Germany, Russia, China (see above) and Japan, the most visited social networking site is not Facebook but home-grown rivals.

4.4.7.3 Extended Model of Social Media Marketing Communication

Integrated marketing communications (IMC) have traditionally been considered to be largely one-way in nature ('Bowling – 'see below Figure 4.19). In the old paradigm, the organization and its agents developed the message and transmitted it to potential consumers, who may or may not have been willing participants

193

in the communication process. The control over the dissemination of information was in the hands of the firm's marketing organization. The traditional elements of the promotion mix (advertising, personal selling, public relations and publicity, direct marketing, and sales promotion) were the tools through which control was asserted.

The twenty-first century is witnessing an explosion of Internet-based messages transmitted through these media. They have become a major factor in influencing various aspects of consumer behavior including awareness, information acquisition, opinions, attitudes, purchase behavior and post-purchase communication and evaluation. Unfortunately, the popular business press and academic literature offers marketing managers very little guidance for incorporating social media into their IMC strategies (Hollensen and Opresnik, 2020).

Social networking as communication tools has two interrelated promotional roles:

- **Social networking should be consistent with the use of traditional IMC tools.** That is, companies should use social media to talk to their customers through such platforms as blogs, as well as Facebook and Twitter groups. These media may either be company-sponsored or sponsored by other individuals or organizations.

- **Social networking is enabling customers to talk to one another.** This is an extension of traditional word-of-mouth communication. While companies cannot directly control such consumer-to-consumer (C2C) messages, they do can influence the conversations that consumers have with one another. However, consumers 'ability to communicate with one another limits the amount of control companies have over the content and dissemination of information. Consumers are in control; they have greater access to information and greater command over media consumption than ever before.

Marketing managers are seeking ways to incorporate social media into their IMC strategies. The traditional communications paradigm, which relied on the classic promotional mix to craft IMC strategies, must give way to a new paradigm that includes all forms of social media as potential tools in designing and implementing IMC strategies. Contemporary marketers cannot ignore the phenomenon of social media, where available market information is based on the experiences of individual consumers and is channelled through the traditional promotion mix. However, various social media platforms, many of which are completely independent of the producing/sponsoring organization or its agents, enhance consumers 'ability to communicate with one another.

Although a little oversimplified, marketing in the pre-social media era was comparable to 'Bowling '(see Figure 4.19). A game of bowling shows how you may have traditionally communicated with your consumers, with the firm and the brand (the bowler) rolling a ball (the brand communication message) towards the pins (our target customers). Clearly this is a very direct one-way communication approach. This is the old traditional push model. Marketers targeted certain customer groups and sent out their advertising messages like precisely bowled bowling balls. They used traditional media to hit as many bowling pins as possible. One key characteristic of this bowling marketing game was the large amount of control the company retained over marketing communication because consumers were given only limited freedom of action.

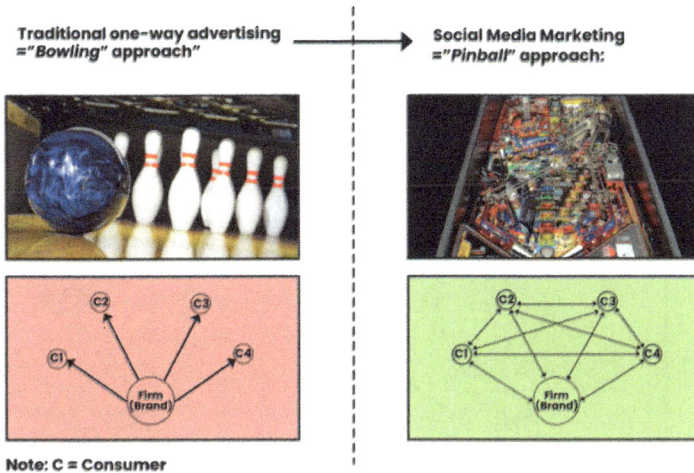

Figure 4.19: The Bowling to Pinball model: Transition of market communication from 'Bowling' to 'Pinball'. Source: Adapted from Hollensen and Opresnik (2015), modified.

For many bigger companies a large TV-budget has been the ball that marketers rolled down the lane, trying to hit as many the pins as possible. Marketers were in control, happily counting how many 'pins 'they had hit, and how often. Success in this game was clear-cut, and the metrics clear (Hennig-Thurau et. al., 2013).

In a social media marketing world, the bowling metaphor does not fit anymore. On this arena, marketing can be better described as playing 'Pinball': Companies serve up a 'marketing ball '(brands and brand-building messages) into a dynamic and chaotic market environment. The 'marketing ball 'is then diverted and often accelerated by social media 'bumpers', which change the ball's course in chaotic ways. After the marketing ball is in play, marketing managers may continue to guide it with agile use of the 'flippers but the ball does not always go where it is intended to.

Consequently, in the 'pinball 'world, you cannot know outcomes in advance. Instead, marketers have to be prepared to respond in real time to the spin put on the ball by consumers. When mastered well, the pinball game can deliver big point multipliers, and if the company is very good, even more balls can be shot into the game. A reason for this may be that today consumers have a large audience to bring up new topics on the communication agenda. In the ideal situation, you are reaching networked influencers, advocates, and other high-value consumers, who may sustain and spread positive conversations about the brand across multiple channels.

Occasionally, the marketing ball will come back to the company. At this point, the firm (brand) has to use the flippers to interact and throw it back into the social media sphere. If the company or the brand do not feed the social marketing media sphere by flipping communications back, the ball will finally drop through the flippers and on longer term, the two-way relationship between consumers and the firm (brand) will die (Hollensen and Opresnik, 2020).

The 'Bowling to Pinball 'model can be further elaborated into an extended model of interactive market communication (Hollensen and Opresnik, 2020).

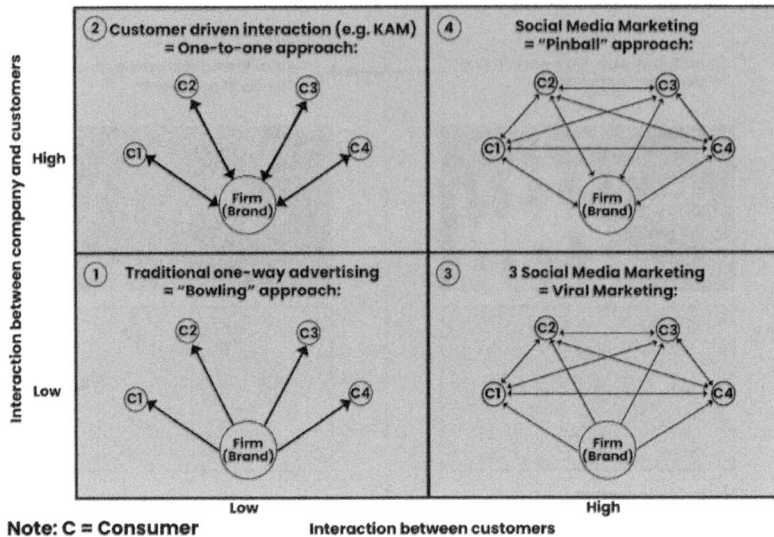

Figure 4.20: The extended interactive market communication model'.
Source: Adapted from Hollensen and Opresnik (2015), modified.

The four different communication styles, represented in Figure 4.20 are (Hollensen and Opresnik, 2020):

- **The Traditional one-way advertising** (mass media advertising like television advertising, newspaper / magazine advertising etc.) represents the 'Bowling 'approach where the firm attempts to 'hit 'as many customers with 'shotgun 'mass media methods. Normally this approach is a one-way communication type.

- **Customer-driven interaction** represents a higher degree of interaction between the company and its different key customers. Often the company finds some Key Account managers, who have the responsibility of taking care of the one-to-one interaction between the firm and its key accounts (customers).

- **Viral Marketing** is representing the version 1.0 of Social Media Marketing, where the company e.g. uses an untraditional YouTube video to get attention and awareness about its brand. The interaction between the potential 'customers 'is quite high (blogging sites etc.), but the feed-back to the company is relatively low (no double arrows back to the company).

- **Social Media Marketing** is representing the version 2.0 of Social Media Marketing, where there is also an extensive feed-back to the company itself (double arrows back to the company). Here the company proactively has chosen to be a co-player in the discussion and blogging on the different relevant social media sites (Facebook, Twitter etc.). This also means that the company here tries to strengthen the interaction with the customers in a positive direction, in order to influence the customer behavior. To do so, the company needs a back-up team of social media employees who can interact and communicate on-line with potential and actual customers. Consequently, this strategy is also very resource demanding.

196

4.4.7.4 The 6C Model of Social Media Marketing

The social media (e.g., Facebook or Twitter) are essentially vehicles for carrying content. This content – in form of words, text, pictures, and videos – is generated by millions of potential customers around the world, and from your perspective (= company's perspective) this can indeed be an inspiration to create further value for these customers.

The following model of Hollensen and Opresnik (2015) mainly represents alternative 4 in Figure 4.20. If there had been no feed-back to the company in the model, it would have been more like alternative 3. Figure 4.21 defines six distinct, interrelated elements (Cs) that explain the creation and retention of consumer engagement, seen from a company perspective; however, the user-generated contents still play an important role in the model (Hollensen and Opresnik, 2020):

- **Company and contents:** The 6C model begins with the company and the content it creates. Basically, the Internet remains a 'pull 'medium, in the way that firms seek to pull viewers to its content, and finally to the company itself. However, before any 'pull 'can happen, the content has to be pushed (seeded) forward in the chain. Content can take the form of e.g., a Facebook product or brand page, and/or a YouTube video pushed out to viewers. Consequently, content pushed into the social media sphere by a company acts as a catalyst for our model of engagement or participation.

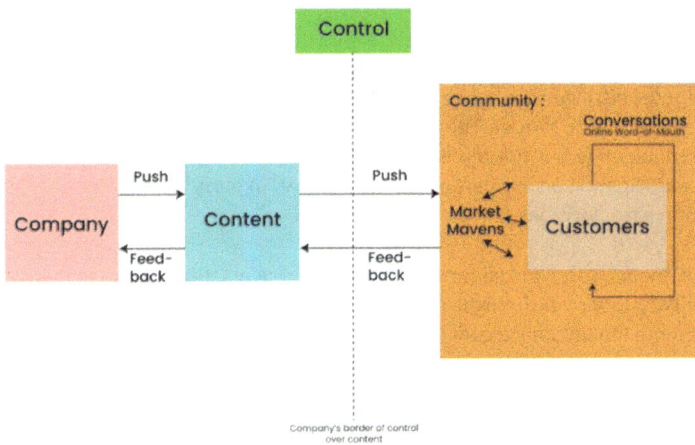

Figure.4.21: The 6C model
(Company, Contents, Control, Community, Consumers, Conversation).
Source: Adapted from Hollensen and Opresnik (2015), modified.

- **Control:** The dashed line denoting control in the 6C model (Figure 4.21) is intended to represent a wall beyond which the company let over control of its brand to the online community and the customers. To accelerate the viral uptake of its brand messaging, the company sometimes gives up the digital rights and blocks in order to encourage online community members to copy, modify, re-post, and forward the content. The content is intended to be copied and/or embedded into people's websites, blogs, and on Facebook walls. The key point to this stage in the process is that the company (the content creator) must be willing, and even embrace, the fact that they no longer have full control over the content: it is free to be taken, modified, commented on, and otherwise appropriated by the community of interest.

197

This may challenge the conventional 'brand management 'wisdom stating that managers must keep control of brand image and messaging.

- **Community:** The Company creates content and pushes it over the symbolic border of control to the other side, where a community of interested consumers now takes it up. At this point, communication becomes bidirectional. The use of arrows in Figure 4.21 for push and pull, attempts to reflect the 'give-and-take 'that goes on between a community and the company, represented by the content creators. In its simplest form, it is reflected in the art of commenting: posting reactions, on Facebook or YouTube, to the content. In some cases, the company can even lean about 'customer behavior 'in the market by following these online community discussions. In an ideal world, a series of reflexive conversations take place in the community, independent of any action by the company, which will often have a passive role as an observer.

- When transferring the 'content 'into the online community, the company and the content providers often try to target the 'Market Mavens', which are defined as individuals who have access to a large amount of marketplace information, and proactively engage in discussions with other online community members and customers to diffuse and spread this content. Market mavens are typically the first to receive the message and transmit it to their immediate social networks. They function as connectors or bridges between different subcultures and their network of social hubs can facilitate immediate transmission of the content to thousands of online community members.

- **Customers and conversations:** The ultimate expression of engagement occurs when a multitude of online conversations circle around the phenomenon and content, as illustrated above and in Figure 4.21. The 6C model distinguishes between the online community and potential customers, as the latter are usually a subset of the former. The online community may also include people who have heard of the Web-based initiative but not directly participated in it. In general, there seems to be a growing escalation in participation on the part of customers; a willingness to engage with a brand that extends beyond just purchase decisions at the point of sale.

According to the 6C model, social media further extend the conversations between marketers and consumers through a feedback loop, which might happen after some on-line conversation (blogging etc.) in the community. After some time of online conversation, the company may have chats with the online community in hopes of influencing purchase decisions. Moreover, social media initiatives provide marketers a glimpse into the world of customer-to-customer communication, which represents a significant extension of the more traditional advertising and word-of-mouth communication.

Furthermore, social media provide insights into the behavior of non-customers. Most social media marketers try to trigger buzz among prospective customers. This has led to social sharing whereby online community member broadcast their thoughts and activities to strangers all over the world. This social sharing has opened the lives of individual consumers that companies can then exploit to tailor their offerings to better match preferences (Hollensen and Opresnik, 2020).

4.4.7.5 Social Media Funnel

Social Media marketing is about using social networks and tools to guide prospect (potential) customers through a series of steps – a **funnel** – to get them to take the desired action, e.g., becoming a new customer and buying the company's product and services, with the end-goal of turning new customers into loyal customers with a high lifetime value.

As shown in Figure 4.22 (the four categories of social media) there are a lot of media tools. With all these Social Media marketing tools at the disposal, how should the company decide which ones fit to optimally to the social media funnel, and in which order they should be used? To answer this question, the company has to know who the potential customers are and how they can be reached most effectively. The social media marketer also has to know about the company's objectives, how it should measure these objectives (i.e., the metrics that should be analyzed) and what numbers should be set for those metrics. Figure 4.22 provides a generic illustration of the social media funnel and the key metrics connected to the three stages of a typical customer buying process: Awareness, Engagement and Action.

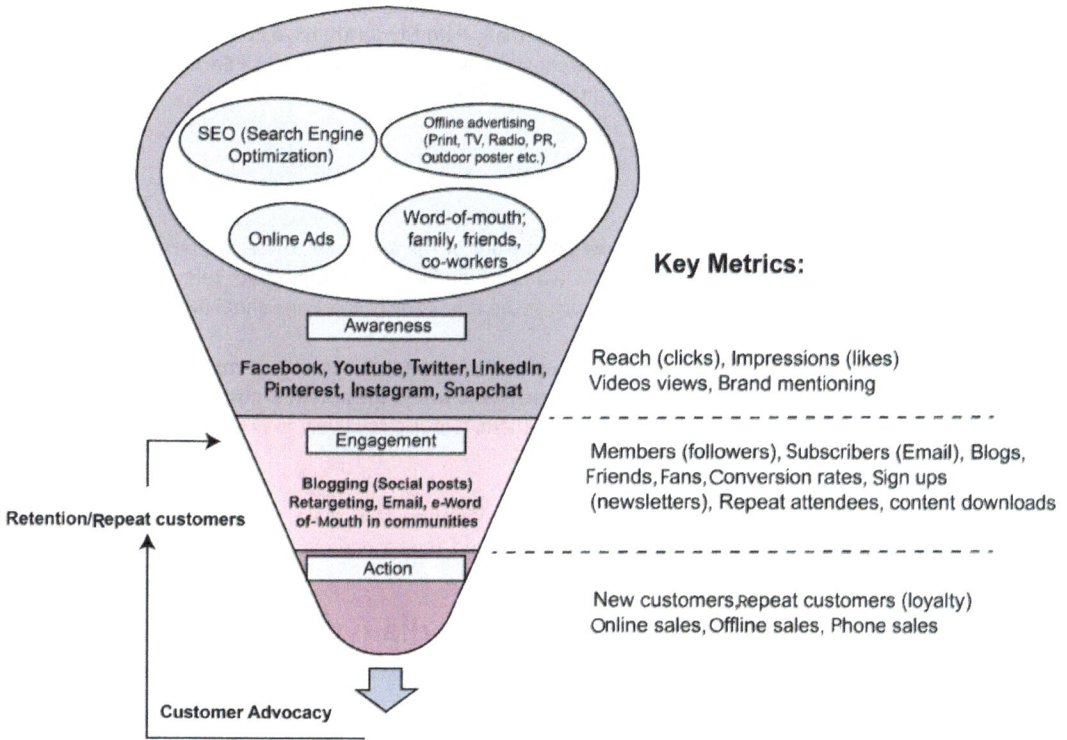

Figure 4.22: The Social Media Funnel. Source: Hollensen, Kotler and Opresnik, 2020.

As illustrated in Figure 4.22, the following tools can act as vehicles to move and drive new potential customers into the funnel:

- SEO (Search Engine Optimization)
- Offline advertising
- Online advertising
- Word-of-Mouth conversation with family members, friends, and co-workers

Any bottlenecks in the social media funnel will slow the momentum of turning prospects into actual customers or stop the process completely. Depending on where the bottleneck happens, the company could miss out on brand awareness opportunities, or conversions into actual sales.

With the key metrics in place, the company should look at each tactic in each part of the funnel and it should try and set industry benchmark standards. These benchmark standards should be used to compare the company with its competitors and the industry in general.

4.4.7.6 POE Media – Paid, Owned and Earned Media

Figure 2.2 shows how the three different digital media (paid, owned, and earned media) can be combined in order to develop an effective digital marketing strategy. The figure shows the interaction and overlap between the three media types in further detail. Normally **Paid Media** are used at the top of the Marketing Funnel (see Figure 2.1.) in order to create awareness whereas **Owned Media** and **Earned Media** are used further down in the Marketing Funnel (Sciarrino et al., 2019).

Paid Media

Here the marketer pays for activities to show up in front of the audience. These are types of media that marketers can buy to create brand awareness (consider online advertising, radio, television, and print.). Therefore, these media are especially good to use at the top of the Marketing Funnel (Montague, 2019).

Paid media is a great way to get an immediate return on investment. It helps the company to generate leads quickly, and it directs the audience back to the owned media where the potential customers can be nurtured and – eventually – the marketer can make a sale on them. It is also relatively easy to measure the effectiveness of the paid media, by using analytics.

The limitations to all this are that the media budget decides how fast 'scale 'can be established, and conversion rates on paid media are generally lower than owned and earned media.

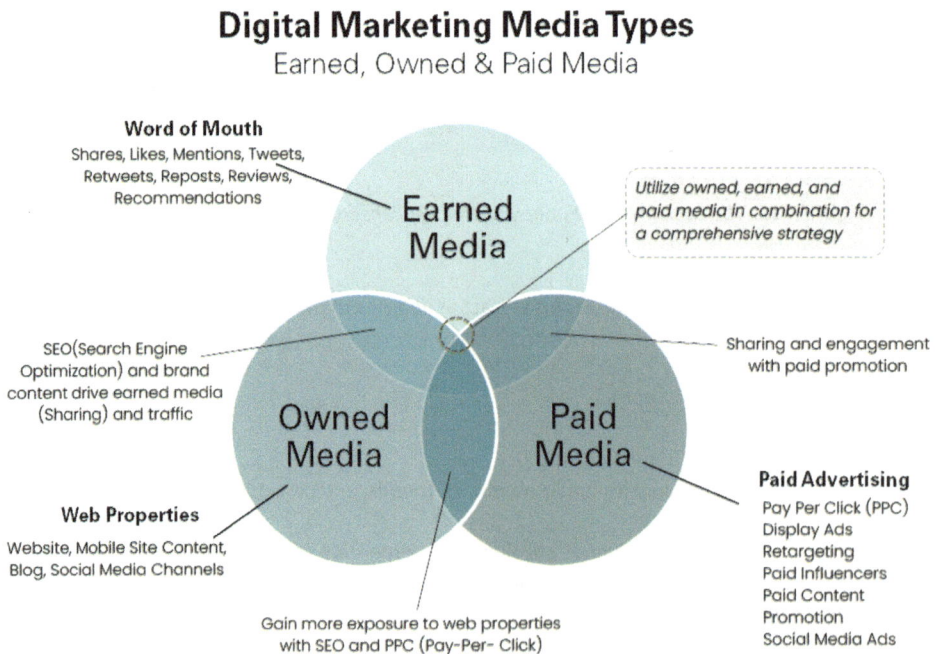

Digital Marketing Media Types
Earned, Owned & Paid Media

Word of Mouth
Shares, Likes, Mentions, Tweets, Retweets, Reposts, Reviews, Recommendations

Utilize owned, earned, and paid media in combination for a comprehensive strategy

Earned Media

SEO(Search Engine Optimization) and brand content drive earned media (Sharing) and traffic

Sharing and engagement with paid promotion

Owned Media

Paid Media

Web Properties
Website, Mobile Site Content, Blog, Social Media Channels

Paid Advertising
Pay Per Click (PPC)
Display Ads
Retargeting
Paid Influencers
Paid Content Promotion
Social Media Ads

Gain more exposure to web properties with SEO and PPC (Pay-Per- Click)

Owned Media

These are types of media that are readily available to marketers themselves and in those they can autonomously decide on the content (for instance websites, apps, email, newsletter etc.).

With owned media, the company owns everything: the websites, blogs, and the social media accounts. The marketer is not paying for this content to show up in front of your audience, but he/she has control over all of it.

Owned media is a smart investment in any marketing strategy because it has staying power. It is possible to start a website and blogs on day one of a business and maintain it all the way until the end.

Creating owned media takes time – both in developing the content and getting it in front of the audience. It is an organic process, but it could grow and gain momentum over time.

The owned media is critical to the marketing mix because it helps the marketer building long-term relationships and earn media too.

Earned Media

These are all types of media that a brand ‘earns ‘thanks to customers, journalists, or bloggers writing about your brand, on social media for instance, or because other organizations refer to your brand on their website. This can be anything from a press release about your business to someone talking about your products on social media.

The big benefit of earned media as part of the marketing strategy is that it is like free advertising. The business shows up in front of the audience at no cost to the marketer.

The downside to this is that the marketer does not own or control what is being put out there – which also means, that there is always a chance it can be negative PR.

How do paid, owned, and earned media work together?

Now that there is an understanding of the differences of each digital media, it is important to see how to they can be combines.

The easiest way to do that is with a good example:

Let us say you have a special deal you want to publish to the social media. Instead of just pushing it organically, you pay for it to show up as an ad on that platform (Paid Media). The ad catches the attention of social media influencers, and they promote it on their account, which shows up in front of even more people (Earned Media). Some of those people may then go to the company's own landing page (website) to buy the product or service. This is a perfect way to combine paid, owned and earned media for a big impact.

4.4.7.7 Customer Journey Mapping

In order to design and produce online products and services that result in a good customer experience, the entire '**customer journey** 'must be viewed from the perspective of the customer. With the help of '**customer journey mapping**', the customer journey and resulting customer experience can be understood, evaluated, and improved.

Customer journey mapping is a technique for optimizing customer processes and developing innovative management concepts. It identifies exactly where improvements to the customer contact processes are possible in order to achieve an optimal customer experience across all channels. It also clarifies how and what can be organized more efficiently and with greater synchronicity to give a more joined-up (seamless) customer experience. The customer journey mapping is, when used properly, an easy and effective tool for improving customer experiences across channels as well as ensuring more efficiency in customer processes.

The **customer journey map** is an indispensable tool in the designing processes of effective websites and apps. Customer journey mapping (CJM) is also a method for visualizing the purchase process or service from the customer's decision perspective (see Figure 4.24). It describes the customer's experience during the 'journey 'a customer makes during the process of orientation, purchasing and eventual use of a product or service - at all points of contact and every 'touchpoint'. The customer's processing through the 'outer circle 'represents the first-time buying process regarding the brand. Importantly, the conceptual model depicts a 'loyalty loop 'by which customers who show post-purchase satisfaction develop brand loyalty. This would lead to future brand purchases in the 'inner circle 'which would bypass some of the stages in the 'outer circle'. This provides opportunities for improvement across all channels and processes.

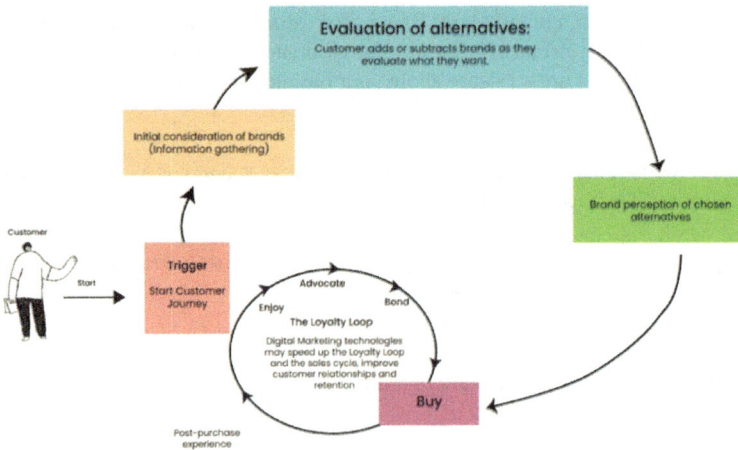

Figure 4.24: The Customer Journey Mapping Model.
Source: Based on Edelman and Singer (2015) and Sciarrino et al. (2019), modified.

Advances in marketing technologies including marketing automation would make it possible (in Figure 2.3) for subsequent purchase journeys to accelerate, speeding up the sales cycle, improving customer retention and strengthening the customer relationship (Edelman and Singer, 2015).

Effective customer journey mapping starts from the same place as the customer starts until the point what that decision-maker considers a successful outcome.

It is important to realize that different customer segments are likely to have different customer journeys. Thus, the holiday maker's journey will look very different from the business traveller's customer journey. Someone who is actively shopping (with a deadline) may have a different journey from someone who is 'just browsing'.

4.4.7.8 Customer Touchpoint Management

Touchpoints are the individual interactions people have with brands before, during and after purchase. Marketers care about touchpoints because they represent opportunities for customers and prospects to learn, have a positive brand experience, and form attitudes and associations about the brand that could lead to future purchases, brand loyalty, and positive word-of-mouth communication.

Based on the visualization of the Customer Journey Mapping (CJM), **offline touchpoints** and **online touch-points** can be recorded, the places where the target group and the organization meet each other (see Figure 4.25). Based on this overview, the marketer can assess whether the most cost-effective solution has been and what adjustments are needed to realize or improve the product or service.

Figure 4.25: Online and Offline Touchpoints along the Customer Journey.
Source: Hollensen, Kotler and Opresnik, 2020.

The stages and the touchpoints in the customer journey can be realized or supported via online communication media, such as websites and apps. A major advantage of online customer contact is that it allows the marketer to monitor customer behavior and with the use of advanced algorithms, elicit the most desirable response from the customer. It is possible to deliver bespoke and personalized customer experiences based on customer profiles. This allows an organization to design and provide products that enhance customer satisfaction, bind the customer to the organization and increase customer loyalty and of course **Customer Lifetime Value (CLV)**.

Customer journey mapping including touchpoints can be applied at several different stages and for a variety of purposes (Thomke, 2019):

- Identification of market and growth opportunities from the customer's perspective
- For the organization and its employees to be able to view Digital Marketing from the perspective of the customer
- Evaluation and improvement of the realized products
- Providing direction for and keeping a handle on the process of measuring customer experiences
- Development of ideas for products and services that provide the desired customer experience.
- Helping to identify those organizational changes are needed to facilitate product realization.
- Development of innovative operating concepts and new services
- Gaining insight into synergy between channels

Without insight into the customer and their close involvement with the different touchpoints, a reliable customer journey analysis is not possible. An important part of this is the determination of the scope.

It is wise to determine in advance which customer segment will be investigated and what products, services, customer processes and channels are relevant.

4.4.7.9 Effective Online Advertising Strategy

Marketers can use online advertising to build their brands or to attract visitors to their Web sites. Online advertising can be described as advertising that appears while customers are surfing the Web, including banner and ticker ads, interstitials, skyscrapers, and other forms (Hollensen and Opresnik, 2020).

An effective advertising strategy for online advertising aims at targeting the right advertisement message to the right person at the right time (Kumar and Shah, 2004).

4.4.7.9.1 Who to Advertise to?

Is online advertising for everyone? Knowledgeable marketers will state that advertisement design depends on the type of product or service being sold and the desired target segment. In this respect, it is instrumental to divide the desired target segment according to first-time visitors to the company's Web site, registered users, and general information seekers. There is bound to be some overlap across these segments. However, this form of segmentation can provide useful insights while designing online advertising. Based on the user segment, the Web site can be programmed to respond appropriately. For example, every first-time visitor to a Web site can be made to see the same advertisement. Visitors identified as information seekers may be shown useful content instead of products and services directly, and registered users may see a customized advertisement message based on their profiles. Technologically, it is feasible to identify the type of user by studying their browsing behavior through clickstream data and by using `cookie `files (Hollensen and Opresnik, 2020).

4.4.7.9.2 How to Advertise?

After identifying the user or the Web site visitor, the next step is determining how to advertise or what format to use for advertising. There are several different formats of Internet advertisements: **banner ads** (which move across the screen), **skyscrapers** (tall, skinny ads at the side of a Web page) and **interstitials** (ads that pop up between changes on a Web site).

Content sponsorships are another form of Internet promotion. Many companies achieve name exposure on the Internet by sponsoring special content on various Web sites, such as news or financial information. These sponsorships are best placed in carefully targeted sites where they can offer relevant information or service to the audience.

The type of advertisement chosen should be directed toward not only ˙pushing ˙the message across but also ˙pulling ˙the customer to click deeper into the Web site by designing ads that contribute to the overall Web site experience. For example, a Web site with too many pop-up ads on the first page runs the risk of driving the user away (Hollensen and Opresnik, 2020).

4.4.7.9.3 What to Advertise?

People use the Internet to seek information as well as products and services. Marketers can be creative and design advertisements that could just give out helpful information to the user. For example, a user browsing for a digital camera may be offered useful tips and pointers on how to get the best results from digital photography. Non-commercial advertising like this may not have a short-term financial gain but may contribute to superior browsing experience leading to customer loyalty and repeat visits from the user. If customer profile or history of purchase is known, it is possible to predict future purchase behavior and companies can program buying information in the Web site code. The next time the company's Web site detects a particular user returning to the Web site, there will be an advertisement ready with an appropriate and tailored content. If deployed properly, this approach can help marketer's cross-selling products through combinations of online advertisement messaging (Hollensen and Opresnik, 2020).

4.4.7.9.4 When to Advertise?

The first three dimensions of the advertising strategy discussed so far would be rendered ineffective if the timing is not right. In the case of offline media, one can proactively call up the customer or send him/her a direct mailer at a specific time with a customized advertising message. However, these rules do not apply online. In the case of the Internet, users may decide to go online and visit the Web site during work, in the middle of the night, or whenever they want to. Therefore, timing in the Internet context would refer to the time from the instance a user is detected online.

The question is when to activate the advertisement. As soon as the user comes online, after he/she has browsed for a while, or at the time of the first purchase? Studies conducted with Internet ad timings have indicated that generally response (click-through) to pop-ups is greater when the ad appears immediately after the user enters the site. However, the results could vary greatly depending on the user segment and the user's information-seeking purposes.

Amazon.com employs a subtle form of advertisement in real time. Basically, while performing a search for a particular book, the search also throws up a list on the side or bottom of the page of relevant books that may complement the book the user was originally considering purchasing. Amazon.com was first to use ˙collaborative filtering ˙technology, which sifts through each customer's past purchases and the purchasing patterns of customers with similar profiles to come up with personalized site content. Furthermore, the site's ˙Your Recommendations ˙feature prepares personalized product recommendations, and its ˙New for You ˙feature links customers through to their own personalized home pages. In perfecting the art of online selling, Amazon.com has become one of the best-known names on the Web (Hollensen and Opresnik, 2020).

4.4.7.9.5 Where to Advertise?

It is crucial to make Internet ads visible at vantage points to maximize their hit-rate with the intended target segment. Unlike other forms of media, where one can pick a well-defined spot within a finite set of possibilities, cyberspace offers an infinite number of possibilities across thousands of portals, search engines, and online publishers, as well as multiple possibilities within the vendor's Web site. Finding the perfect spot may seem like finding a needle in a haystack.

There are two ways to tackle this. The first is the easy way out. Follow intuition and place advertisements at obvious locations, such as frequently visited portals and search engines. However, this is not a cost-effective solution. A more refined approach involves analyzing the browsing pattern of an Internet user on a company's Web site using the Web site's log files. Analysis of the log files can help model the browsing behavior of a random visitor to the Web site. Based on this information, Internet ad displays may be placed at appropriate locations. Marketing managers can also leverage this model to sell complementary products to potential users. For example, a department store such as Marks & Spencer may advertise cosmetics on the page where a user is buying fragrances online. An electronics store like Best Buy may advertise the latest CD releases on the page listing different audio systems.

However, this form of analysis is limited to advertising within the company's Web site. A more advanced research approach involves modelling browsing behavior at multiple Web sites using clickstream data. Information analyzed in this manner renders a total view of a customer's online habits before purchase consideration. Such information is invaluable to marketers who would be interested in knowing when and where they're most likely to find their potential customers and, based on that information, how they should place the Internet advertisements to pull the relevant customers to their site (Hollensen and Opresnik, 2020).

4.4.7.10 Online Performance Tracking

Having designed an online advertising strategy, the next critical step is to track its performance. Traditional offline media (radio, television, and print advertisements) have well-defined and well-researched metrics in place that can accurately measure ad effectiveness.

Some of the most commonly used measures include (Hollensen and Opresnik, 2020):

- **click-through** the number of times that users click on an advertisement

- **cost per click:** the amount spent by the advertiser to generate one click-through.

- **cost per action/lead (CPA/L):** the amount spent by the advertiser to generate one lead, one desired action, or simply information on one likely user. The advertiser pays an amount based upon the number of users who fulfil the desired action.

- **cost per sale (CPS):** the amount spent by the advertiser to generate one sale. Here, the advertiser pays an amount based upon how many users actually purchase something.

Increasingly, many marketers claim to be optimizing their online campaigns using the 'cost per sale 'metric, but it is clear that they are looking at sales (through online advertisements) as strictly margin transactions. The problem with this approach is that, while each individual transaction may look profitable to start with, it may not necessarily hold true over the lifetime duration of the customer. Similarly, initial returns that seem to be unprofitable may translate into very profitable transactions when measured over the lifetime value of the customer.

Therefore, **Customer Lifetime Value (CLV)**, which may be defined as the measure of expected value of profit to a business derived from customer relationships from the current time to some future point, is maybe the most relevant of all metrics. It provides a direct linkage on a customer-by-customer basis to what is most important for any company-profits. Marketing spends and outcome of advertisements guided by lifetime value measures would yield the most superior decision support system for a marketer. As companies become increasingly customer-centric, a switch to a customer lifetime value metric and building of buyer loyalty will become inevitable (Hollensen, 2006).

4.4.7.11 Building Buyer Loyalty

Using the web as a vehicle for building loyalty on the part of international buyers involves several different stages (Fletcher et al., 2004):

- **Attract:** attracting clients to visit the web site. They do so on a voluntary basis and will not come simply because a site has been created. To create awareness of the site, it is necessary to use banner ads and links to other sites.

- Engage: engaging visitor's attention. This is necessary to get the visitor to the site to participate and encourage interaction. Most sites fail as promotional mediums because they are boring and have poorly presented material. In this connection, the content of the site is most important.

- **Retain:** retain the visitor's interest in your site. This is important to ensure repeat visits to the site and the creation of a 'one-to-one 'relationship between the firm and its potential overseas customer. One way of achieving this is by persuading the customer to provide information on their requirements so that the firm can customize its offering and thereby increase switching costs.

- **Learn:** learn about the client and their preferences. This is enabled by providing on the site a facility for easy feedback and comment. The use of cookies can assist.

- **Relate:** adopt a deliberate policy of building relationships with site visitors. This is achieved by providing value added content, by tailoring the product/service to the needs of each customer and promising customized delivery.

4.4.7.12 Smartphone Marketing

Smartphone marketing, mobile marketing or **M-marketing** should be considered within the context of m-business and m-commerce. Emerging from recent developments in communications technology, m-business represents 'mobile 'business and 'refers to the new communications and information delivery model created when telecommunications and the Internet converge'.

Together with the widespread adoption of 3G and 4G smartphones among consumers, mobile marketing has increasingly become an important tool in brands 'international advertising and promotional efforts.

The next generation of the internet standard in mobile marketing (m-marketing) will allow programs to run through a web browser rather than a specific operating system. That means consumers will be able to access the same programs and cloud-based content from any device – personal computer, laptop, smartphone, or tablet – because the browser is the common platform. This ability to work seamlessly anytime, anywhere, on any device could change consumer behavior and shift the balance of power in the distribution systems towards the end of the distribution system – the end-buyer, who has cheaper and cheaper access to the new mobile devices. It will create opportunities for marketers to distribute goods and services more directly to the end-buyers and it will present increasing challenges for the intermediaries between the manufacturers and the end-buyers.

Rapidly emerging innovations have also delivered the possibility of smartphones able to use product bar codes to access product-related information and phones able to act as e-wallets, as either a prepaid card for small purchases or a fully functioning credit/debit card unit.

However, the mobile industry will also see a lot more enforcement on the mobile security and privacy in the coming years, as many questions have been raised regarding mobile payments, coupons and applications. Mobile commerce is on the rise, which means people are more comfortable with the idea of paying with their phones. However, there is still a critical view throughout the mobilized world regarding the safety of this kind of payment system (Hollensen and Opresnik, 2020).

4.4.7.13 App Marketing

In January 2020, 2.57 million Android apps and 1.84 million Apple apps were available. On average, smartphone users have around 40 apps on their mobile phones and regularly use around 15.

As free apps become increasingly prevalent, paid app downloads are expected to decline, and advertising and in-app purchases are likely to become the main revenue streams in the coming years. With the rise in smartphones and tablets across the globe, the mobile app industry has been rapidly growing. Mobile advertising has seen triple-digit percentage growth each year since 2010.

Mobile apps can be classified into **mobile commerce** and **mobile value-added services (MVAS)**:

- **Mobile commerce**: Here the app mostly has the purpose of selling a product or a service. For example, the Domino's Pizza app is designed to generate sales and promote special deals to customers.

- **Mobile value-added services (MVAS):** Here the app offers services that are not directly tied to sales but are designed to help customers solve problems or make decisions. Such an app enriches the total customer experience of a product / service offering.

An example of an MVAS is an airline app that can be used to generate a mobile boarding pass (QR code) in a co-production process between the airline and the customer. Conceptually, the core service (the flight) and the MVAS (mobile boarding pass) need to be interrelated constructs building the final customer experience - flight from A to B.

On the spectrum from mobile commerce to mobile services (MVAS), many apps offer on-the-go services paired with location-based technology. Companies employ technology for both geocoding (based on location latitude and longitude) and reverse geocoding (translating coordinates into a street address) to deliver accurate locations. One example of a location-based app is the **Tinder** dating app, which is a social discovery application that facilitates communication between mutually interested users. The Tinder ‘matchmaking ’ app is based on criteria like geographical location, number of mutual friends, and common interests. Based on these criteria the app then makes a list of geographical near-by potential candidates. The app then allows the user to anonymously like another user by swiping right or pass by swiping left on them. If two users like each other it then results in a ‘match ’and they are then able to chat within the app (Hollensen, Kotler and Opresnik, 2017).

Summing up, developing an effective mobile marketing program is much more challenging than developing a traditional program aimed at laptop and desktop users. The mobile program needs to be planned, implemented, and tested for multiple devices (smartphones, tablets, laptops, and desktops) and different operating systems, and should adjust for the limitations of mobile devices in terms of screen and traditional keyboard size. In addition, the immediacy, location, and personalization attributes of mobile devices increase the need to develop a portfolio of messages to reflect such attributes as weather conditions (immediacy), distance to a store (location), and a consumer's preferences and past purchase behavior (personalization).

4.4.7.14 Influencer Marketing

When transferring the 'content 'into the online community, the company and the content providers often try to target the influencers (or opinion leaders), which are typically some of the first to receive the message and transmit it to their immediate social networks. They function as connectors or bridges between different subcultures, and their network of social hubs can facilitate immediate transmission of the content to thousands of online community members.

The broad group of influencers can be characterized into the following groups (ANA, 2018):

Micro-Influencers: 50 – 25,000 followers

Macro-Influencers: 25,001 – 100,000 followers

Mega-Influencers   100,001 – 500,000 followers

Celebrity-Influencers   Over 500,000 followers

The purpose with 'Influencer Marketing 'is to win customer trust, especially when compared to traditional online ads. Influencer Marketing is less intrusive and more flexible than traditional online ads. An **influencer** is an individual who proactively engage in discussions with other online community members and customers to diffuse and spread this content. It can be a teenage girl posting about her favourite local ice-cream bar to make a few bucks, or it can be a celebrity-influencer like Kim Kardashian posting about a clothing line to make $200,000.

For SMEs it is absolutely relevant to work with **micro-influencers**, who are individuals who work in their special category and are truly knowledgeable, passionate and authentic. They are seen as a trusted source when it comes to recommendations for what to buy. Micro-influencers are affecting a much smaller social circle (segments) around them, but they can do it much more effective than mega- or celebrity influencers. Haenlein and Libai (2018) showed that micro-influencers not only have over 20 times more conversations with their social group than an average consumer, but they also found that 80% of potential customers are very likely to follow their recommendations. Marketers therefore do not have to turn to celebrities to enhance their social media campaigns.

4.4.8 DIRECT MARKETING

Many of the marketing and promotion tools that we have discussed so far in previous sections were developed in the context of mass marketing: targeting broad markets with standardized messages and offers distributed through intermediaries. Today, however, with the trend toward more specifically targeted or one-to-one marketing, many companies are adopting **direct marketing**, either as a primary marketing approach or as an important supplement to other strategies.

Direct marketing consists of direct connections with thoroughly selected individual consumers to both obtain an immediate response and cultivate enduring customer relationships. Direct marketers communicate directly with customers, often on a one-to-one, interactive basis. Making use of detailed databases, they tailor their marketing offers and communications to the specific needs of narrowly defined segments or even individual buyers. Beyond brand image building, direct marketers typically seek a direct, immediate, and measurable consumer response (Hollensen and Opresnik, 2020). Direct marketing is a more encompassing concept than direct sales, which simply refers to sales from the producer directly to the ultimate consumer, bypassing the channel middlemen. This approach is not so much a promotional tool as a new distribution channel, but it grew out of direct mail, which is a traditional advertising medium. The traditional direct mail promotions of various products often offered 'direct response 'options, including requests for more information, redeemable cents-off coupons, and participation in contests and lottery drawings. It was only a small step to a completed sale, and especially since credit cards became common, direct mail has become an important promotion *and* sales channel (Hollensen, 2006).

4.4.8.1 Benefits of Direct Marketing

For customers, direct marketing is convenient, easy to use, and private. From the comfort of their homes or offices, they can browse mail catalogues or company Web sites at any time. Direct marketing gives clients immediate access to a variety of products and information 'at their fingertips'. In addition, direct marketing is immediate and interactive as buyers can interact with sellers by phone or on the seller's Web site to create the configuration of information, products, and services they desire, and then order them instantly.

For Sellers, direct marketing is a powerful tool for building customer relationships. With the use of databases, marketers can target narrow groups or individual consumers, tailor their offers to the specific needs and wants, and promote these offers through personalised communications. Direct marketing can also be timed to reach prospects at just the right moment. Furthermore, this tool enables seller's access to buyers that they could eventually not reach through other channels. Finally, direct marketing can offer sellers a low-cost, efficient alternative for reaching their markets (Hollensen and Opresnik, 2020).

4.4.8.2 Major Direct Marketing Tools

The major forms of direct marketing include personal selling, telephone marketing, direct mail marketing, catalogue marketing, direct-response advertising, and online marketing. We shall look at personal selling later in this chapter and examined online marketing already above. Here, we examine some other tools within the framework of online marketing as well as the other direct marketing forms (Hollensen and Opresnik, 2020).

4.4.8.2.1 Direct Mail Marketing

Direct mail marketing involves sending an offer, announcement, reminder, or other material to a person at a particular address with the purpose of promoting a product and/or maintaining an ongoing relationship. Direct mail at its best allows close targeting of individual customers in a way not feasible using mass advertising media. Direct mail is well suited to direct, one-to-one communication. It permits high target market selectivity, can be personalised, is flexible, and allows easy tracking of results. Clearly, the effectiveness of direct mail relies heavily on the quality of the target customer data.

In summary, direct mail can be very cost-effective at targeting specific segments of the market, with easily measurable results. However, critics point to low response rates, the existence of junk mail, the fact that personal information can be sold to mailers without the knowledge of the subject, and the fact that some firms persist in sending mail even when they have been asked to stop. In addition, direct mail may work out more expensive than e-mail campaigns, which are becoming more attractive as access to broadband expands rapidly (Benady, 2005).

4.4.8.2.2 Telemarketing

Telephone marketing (also called telemarketing) involves using the telephone to sell directly to consumers and business customers. There are a number of reasons why telemarketing has grown substantially in recent years. First, it has lower costs per contact than a face-to-face salesperson visit. Second, it is less time consuming than personal visits. Third, the growth in telephone ownership has increased access to households, and the use of toll-free lines has reduced the cost of responding by phone. Finally, despite the reduced costs compared to a personal visit, the telephone retains the advantage of two-way communication.

However, telephone marketing suffers from a number of disadvantages. First, it lacks the visual impact of a personal visit and it is not possible to assess the mood or reactions of the buyer through observation of the body language. It is easier for a consumer to react negatively over the telephone and the number of rejections can be quite high as telephone selling can be considered intrusive. Finally, although cost per contact is less expensive than a personal sales call, it is more expensive than direct mail, media advertising or the Internet (Ellis-Chadwick and Jobber, 2016).

4.4.8.2.3 Catalogue Marketing

Catalogue marketing is the sale of products through catalogues distributed to agents and consumers, usually by mail or at stores. In addition, most print catalogues have added Web-based catalogues to their marketing offer, and a variety of new Web-only cataloguers have emerged.

When used effectively, catalogue marketing to customers provides a convenient way of selecting products at home that allow in-depth discussion and evaluation with family members in a relaxed atmosphere away from crowded shops. Especially for remote rural locations it provides a valuable service, preventing the necessity to travel long distances to town shopping areas. For catalogue marketers, the expense of high-street locations is removed and there is the opportunity to display a wider range of products than in a shop. Nevertheless, catalogues are quite expensive to produce and they require regular updating, particularly when selling fashion items. In addition, they do not allow goods to be tested (e.g., shaver) or tried on (e.g., clothing) before purchase (Ellis-Chadwick and Jobber, 2016).

4.4.8.2.4 Direct Response Advertising

Direct response advertising appears in the prime media, such as television, newspapers and magazines, but differs from standard advertising as it is designed to elicit a direct response such as an order, enquiry or request for a visit of a salesperson. Typically, a free contact number is included in the advertisement and a website address. This tool combines the ability of broadcast media to reach large sections of the population with direct marketing techniques that allow a rapid response.

Direct response television (DRTV) generally entails telephone numbers to let viewers call for purchases. The advantage is that marketer can get direct response to a mass-market advertisement, but whether viewers will interrupt their programme viewing to surf the Internet for a listed Web site or calling a particular contact number is questionable (Murphy, 2001).

4.4.8.2.5 Online Marketing

For many, e-mail has virtually replaced traditional letters and even telephone calls as the choice for correspondence. Every day, billions of e-mail messages are sent out. This has also influenced the way of doing business. Prepared well, **e-mail marketing** can be one of the most cost-effective communications tools. It is fast, inexpensive, and effective, and its response rates are many times that of direct mail. However, the e-mail marketing landscape is beleaguered with examples of marketers getting labelled as spammers, annoying customers, violators of privacy laws and worse.

A major strength of direct e-mail is its ability to qualify leads. Appropriate software allows the firm to track who is reading and responding along with the types of responses. This enables the firm to segment the audience, accordingly, targeting future communications based on recipients 'self-reported priorities (Hollensen and Opresnik, 2020).

4.4.9 PERSONAL SELLING

The final major element of the promotional mix is **personal selling**. This involves face-to-face contact with a consumer and, unlike advertising, promotion and other forms of non-personal communication, personal selling allows a direct interaction between buyer and seller. This process implies that the seller can identify the specific needs and wants of the buyer and tailor the sales approach and presentation accordingly. However, such flexibility is expensive as the cost of a car, travel expenses and sales office overheads can mean that the total annual investment for a salesperson is often twice the level of a salary (Hollensen and Opresnik, 2020).

4.4.9.1 Sales Management

Establishing the company's own sales force requires sophisticated planning and considerable resources. Sales force management can be defined as the analysis, planning, implementation, and control of sales force activities. The following steps are involved in structuring and managing a sales force (Cateora and Graham, 2004):

- Designing Sales Force Strategy and Structure: Based on analyzes of current and potential customers, the selling environment, competition, and the firm's resources and capabilities, marketing managers face two critical design decisions. They need to determine the sales force size and organize the sales force. The most practical method for deciding the number of salespeople required is the 'workload approach'. It is based on the calculation of the total annual calls required per year divided by the average calls per year that can be expected from one salesperson. A company can divide up sales responsibilities along any of several lines. There are three alternative approaches to organizing the sales force: Territorial, product, and customer sales force structure (Talley, 1961).

- Recruiting Salespeople: At the heart of any successful sales force operation is the recruitment and selection of high-calibre salespeople as the performance difference between an average salesperson and a top salesperson can be quite substantial.

- Selecting Salespeople: To select personnel for marketing positions effectively, management must define precisely what is expected of its people. A formal job description can aid management in expressing long-range needs as well as current needs. In addition to descriptions for each marketing position, the criteria should include special requirements indigenous to various countries (Hollensen, 2006).

- Training Salespeople: New and experienced salespeople may spend anywhere from a few weeks or months to a year or more in training. Many companies send their new sales representatives into the field almost immediately upon hiring them, after only a cursory training program. The rationale is that time is best spent prospecting and meeting with customers, rather than sitting in a training centre (Crittenden and Crittenden, 2004). It is factual that detailed training can be costly and may result in lost opportunities when a seller is not in the field. Yet effective long-term sellers must not only have appropriate personal characteristics, but they must also know and identify with the company and its products, understand customer buying motives, and be prepared to make an effective sales presentation, counter initial resistance, and dose the sale. Moreover, to be successful, the seller has to know how to develop and maintain the records necessary to process orders, service customers, and cultivate repeat sales.

- **Motivating Salespeople:** Effective motivation is based on a deep understanding of salespeople as individuals, their personalities and value systems. According to Luthans (1997) the basic motivation process involves needs (deprivations) which set drives in motion (deprivations with direction) to accomplish goals (anything which alleviates a need and reduces a drive).

- **Designing Compensation Systems:** To attract good salespeople, a company must have an appealing compensation plan. Compensation is made up of several elements – a fixed amount, a variable amount, expenses, and fringe benefits. Developing an equitable and functional compensation plan that combines balance, consistent motivation, and flexibility is extremely challenging in international operations. Besides rewarding an individual's contribution to the firm, a compensation program can be used effectively to recruit, develop, motivate, or retain personnel.

- **Evaluating and Controlling Salespeople:** Sales force evaluation provides the information necessary to check if targets are being achieved and provides the raw information to steer training and motivation. In evaluation and control of salespeople, emphasis is often placed on individual performance, which can easily be measured by sales revenues generated (often compared with past performance, forecasts, or quotas).

4.4.9.2 The Personal Selling Process

The actual selling process consists of several steps that the salesperson must master. These stages focus on the goal of getting new customers and receiving orders from them. However, most salespeople spend a great deal of their time maintaining existing accounts and building long-term customer relationships. The selling process consists of seven steps (Hollensen and Opresnik, 2020):

- **Prospecting and Qualifying:** The first step in the selling process is prospecting – identifying qualified potential consumers. Usually, the salesperson must often approach many prospects to get just a few sales. Although the company supplies some guidance, salespeople require skill in finding their own. They can ask current customers for referrals. They can cultivate referral sources, such as suppliers, dealers, and bankers. Or they can search for prospects in directories or on the Web and track down leads using the telephone and direct mail.

- **Pre-Approach:** The pre-approach is the step in the selling process in which the salesperson learns as much as possible about a prospective customer before making a sales call or visit. The preparation carried out prior to a sales visit can reap dividends by enhancing confidence and performance when the salesperson is face-to-face with the customer. Salespeople will benefit from gaining knowledge of their own and competitor's products, by understanding buyer behavior and by having clear sales call objectives and by having planned their sales representation. This is because the success of the sales interview is customer-dependant.

- **Approach:** During the approach step, the salesperson should know how to create a favourable initial impression with customers as this can often affect later perceptions. This step involves the salesperson's appearance, opening lines, and the follow-up remarks. Positive impressions can be gained by adopting a business-like approach, being friendly but not overly familiar, being attentive to detail, and observing common courtesies. As in all stages of the selling process, listening to the customer is crucial.

- **Presentation and Demonstration:** The presentation step of the selling process offers the opportunity for the salesperson to convince customers that they can supply the solution to their problem.

Consequently, it should focus on customer benefits rather than product features. The salesperson should continue to ask questions during the presentation to ensure that the customer has understood what he or she has said, and to check that what the salesperson has talked about really is of importance to the consumer.

- **Handling Objections:** Customers almost always have abjections during the presentation or when asked to place an order. The problem can be either logical or psychological, and objections are often unspoken. Although objections can cause problems, they should not be regarded negatively per se since they highlight issues that are important to the customer. It is of paramount importance in handling objectives to touch both substantive and emotional aspects. Salespeople have to listen to the objection without interruption and should employ an 'agree and counter' technique, where they agree with the buyer but then put forward an alternative point of view with respect to the problem of the consumer.

- **Closing:** After handling the prospect's objections, the salesperson tries to close the sale. Salespeople should know how to recognize closing signals from the buyer, including physical actions, comments, and questions. They can use several closing techniques: they can simply ask for the order, review points of agreement and offer to help write up the order. In this context, the salesperson may offer the buyer special reasons to close, such as a lower price or an extra quantity at no charge.

- **Follow-Up:** Follow-up is the last step in the selling process. Right after closing, the salesperson should complete any details on delivery time, purchase conditions, and other subjects. The salesperson then should schedule a follow-up call when the initial order is received, to ensure there is proper installation, instruction, and servicing. This visit would eventually reveal any problems, assure the buyer of the salesperson's interest, and reduce any buyer concerns that might have arisen since the sale.

4.4.10 PRODUCT PLACEMENT

Product placement is the deliberate placing or products and/or their logos in movies and television, usually in return for money. While it has been giant business in some countries, like the United States, for some time, restrictions preventing product placement have only recently been relaxed in Europe. For example, Steven Spielberg's science-fiction film 'Minority Report 'featured more than 15 major brands, including Gap, Nokia, Pepsi, Guinness, Lexus, and Amex, with their logos appearing on video billboards throughout the film. These product placements earned DreamWorks and 20th Century Fox $ 25 million, which went some way towards reducing the $ 102 million production costs for the film (Ellis-Chadwick and Jobber, 2016).

Product placement has grown substantially in recent years for the following reasons (Hollensen and Opresnik, 2020):

- **Mass-market reach:** media fragmentation implies that it is increasingly difficult to reach mass markets; Movies can reach hundreds of millions of consumers world-wide, creating instant brand awareness.

- **Positive associations:** brands can benefit from positive images in a film or television programme. For example, James Bond to be seen driving an Aston Martin, imparts the Bond association of sophistication, masculinity, and style to the car.

- **Credibility:** many consumers do not realize that brands have been product-placed. The brands are perceived being used rather than appearing in a paid-for advertisement. This can substantially add to the credibility of the associations sought.

- **Message repetition:** movies are often repeated on television and bought on video or DVD, creating opportunities for brand message repetition.

- **Avoidance of advertising bans:** with bans on advertising certain products, such as alcohol and cigarettes, in particular media, product placement is an opportunity to reach large audiences.

- **Targeting:** by choosing an appropriate film or television programme, specific market segments can be reached.

- **Branding opportunities:** new brands can be launched linked to the movie.

- **Promotional opportunities:** placements in films can provide promotional opportunities by creating related Web sites.

CASE STUDY
OPET

THE MOST LOVED BRAND OF TÜRKİYE'S FUEL OIL SECTOR

Written by: Rıdvan Uçar (Sales and Marketing Asst. General Manager)

Introduction

What's the thing people on a long journey with their vehicle abstain from the most? Dirty toilets... What effect do dirty toilets have on public health? Numerous hazardous bacteria and microbes... Most of them set the ground for infectious diseases such as typhoid, diarrhea, and hepatitis.

So, isn't it surprising that a fuel distribution company from Türkiye tackles this and achieves permanent success?

OPET not only designed and maintained the cleanest toilets in fuel stations, but also delivered a massive public health program that made it to the news and went down to national history.

But how? Let's go back to the beginning of the story...

Founded by Öztürk family in 1992, OPET chose a different path from the growth strategy deployed by other fuel companies. Unlike the companies in the sector at that period, OPET preferred to start from small places and to expand to cities, thus having the chance to observe people's demand for service better and to create solutions. The number of stations increased day by day with the confidence and love of people. In late 2002, with the 50% share owned by Koç Holding Energy Group, OPET gave weight to infrastructure investments since its foundation and stood out with its social responsibility projects. OPET has become the fastest and the most consistently growing fuel company of the last decade with its strong infrastructure, down-to-earth vision, and faith in the nation.

Challenge

The lack of hygiene and sanitation standards in the Turkish fuel sector before OPET has been one of the primary problems. The biggest problem was the dirtiness of the toilets not just in stations, but in many common-use areas such as schools, airports, hospitals, restaurants, and mosques as well. A journey that is soon to turn into Türkiye's civilization project has started with a dialogue that **OPET Founding Board Member Nurten Öztürk** who has been a teacher for a long time before embarking on her career in the sector has witnessed in a toilet on a holiday eve.

"On a holiday eve, we were at Atatürk Airport for a flight to London. I went to the toilet. I overheard two foreign women talking in the toilet cabin. They were on their way back home after they visited Türkiye. They told me it was disgusting, very dirty. I waited to see who they were. When they opened the toilet door, I wasn't able to speak, because the toilet was so dirty that I failed to find a word for that. I felt incredibly upset. Throughout my voyage, I thought that we have got to do something, to save this country from this problem. The conclusion I have drawn was this: Creating a collective movement and focusing on resolving the problem," recalls Nurten Öztürk that day.

Solution

Nurten Öztürk introduced her project aimed at "clean toilets, healthy society" which she meticulously prepared as a project-oriented teacher, at the first OPET board meeting after that traumatic scene she witnessed at the airport. When Öztürk said, "Let's start a Clean Toilet Campaign which embraces the entire Türkiye and save this nation from this problem", some members said, "How is this possible Mrs Öztürk, isn't this a grueling project? Let's first choose some pilot stations or think about this for some more time". Fikret Öztürk, founder of OPET and originally a teacher like Nurten Öztürk, on the other hand, said "If Mrs Öztürk leads the project and visits every single station in person, this project will yield," and expressed his heartfelt support. In the wake of the meeting, the "Clean Toilet Campaign" was commenced, to subsequently brought up the said "toilet sanitation and hygiene" subject to Türkiye's agenda in 2000.

Target

Having been managed by OPET since 2000, the Clean Toilet Campaign as one longest-term social projects in Türkiye has targeted an important problem of the country. The principal purpose of the project was to raise awareness of the importance of toilet sanitation in human life and to popularize the consciousness of hygiene. Starting from its stations in the first place, OPET expanded the project throughout the nation and managed to make it permanent by manifesting its distinctiveness not only with standard corporate appearance and service quality but also with the importance it attaches to sanitation and hygiene at OPET stations.

First steps

After a preparation process of 1.5 months for the project, an invitation letter with the title "giant campaign" was sent to newspapers, journals, and television on March 20, 2000. During the press conference held on

March 23, Nurten Öztürk announced that the Clean Toilet Campaign was commenced initially at 44 fuel stations on highways and city centers, and then the project would be expanded nationwide following the pilot scheme. While OPET continued to provide training to its staff at fuel stations, toilets for the disabled were stipulated and diaper-changing units were added within the scope of the Clean Toilet Campaign.

In June 2000, OPET sponsored the organization "Anatolia the Cradle of Civilizations 2000" in Cappadocia and achieved great success with a work that would soon change foreign visitors' perception of toilets. Having set her heart on and worked night and day on the project, Nurten Öztürk installed portable toilets in the Cappadocia region and cleaned them together with her teams to change the visitors' perception of toilets in Türkiye. This time, "How can toilets in Türkiye be kept this clean," marveled the foreign visitors of the organization.

Expanded step by step and made it into textbooks.

Clean Toilet Campaign developed new expansions in line with the requirements of society, along with new collaborations. In 2003, "My Clean School Project" was implemented in all schools affiliated with the Istanbul Directorate of National Education, and the schools in every district were audited in liaison with OPET Perfection Ambassadors and OPET training teams and the school that took the first three place has been awarded. Owing to the persistent endeavors of Nurten Öztürk, the Ministry of National Education featured the campaign in some textbooks in 2006.

In late 2009, the campaign transformed to the "Loving is Protecting" project due to Swine Flu. All OPET stations and schools with training programs were protected with Bioshield - a disinfection application which inhibits the reproduction and transmission of microbes for 90 days. To set an agenda on epidemics and hygiene, there has been an emphasis via various communication channels on the danger created by our social habits such as kissing, handshaking, and hugging, which all facilitate the transfer of viruses.

During the COVID-19 pandemic in 2020, OPET stations featured various visual materials with warnings such as "Loving is Protecting - Timeout for Kissing/Handshaking" and posters and informative flyers with the title "Health First" that contained advice on hygiene against microbes, bacteria, and viruses were hung and handed out.

Applied the standards of the Turkish Standards Institute and expanded overseas.

OPET blazed new trails in 2012 with its works and leadership in hygiene and health. Turkish Standards Institute (TSI) made use of OPET's experience while setting new standards for public toilets. The new standards that were determined by OPET were approved and entered into force in the TSI Technical Committee's meeting on June 14, 2012.

The success achieved by the Clean Toilet Campaign went beyond the boundaries of Türkiye. OPET initially provided training for 4800 teachers and students in Mecca, Medina, Jeddah, and Riyadh upon an invitation from Saudi Arabia in May 2012. The next stop of the Clean Toilet Campaign has been Macedonia in April 23, 2013. There has been a sanitation and hygiene training with the participation of 750 students and 60 teachers at Tefeyyuz Primary School which is one of the oldest Turkish schools in the Balkans, providing Turkish education since 1884.

Health comes first.

When the Clean Toilet Campaign first got underway, the aim was to establish hygienic and healthy OPET stations. However, the interest and information demand of the society has become so intense in the upcoming years that OPET has carried its leadership in this field to schools, hospitals, municipalities, and all train stations of Turkish State Railways via trainings. An extensive collaboration with the Ministry of National Education started in 2019 and a nationwide sanitation and hygiene project has thus commenced.

With the cooperation of the Ministry of National Education General Directorate of Lifelong Learning, Turkish Union of Chambers and Commodity Exchanges Women Entrepreneurs Council and OPET, "Our Business is Clean Project" which started during the pandemic as a pilot scheme was expanded to all 81 provinces of Türkiye.

Meanwhile, OPET has introduced the "Spotless Future Begins at Schools" campaign in collaboration with the Ministry of National Education, and organized consciousness-raising and awareness training for the students in all public schools affiliated with the Ministry of National Education to establish permanent attainment as a behavioral pattern in terms of sanitation and hygiene. The "Spotless Future Begins at Schools" project has reached to approximately 19 million students and their parents with 1.2 million teachers in 61 thousand schools in the 2023-2024 school year.

Conclusion

Having been deemed worthy of numerous domestic and foreign awards since its outset, the Clean Toilet Campaign introduced a hygiene and sanitation standard to the fuel sector. As a company that is granted the Most Loved Brand of the Sector- Lovemark award, OPET has captured its customers' hearts, and its transformative power has set an example for other companies in the sector and companies from other sectors alike.

Analyzing the needs of the customers, centralizing its shareholders, and aiming social development while making a point of sincerity, OPET has raised a vital awareness by bringing up sanitation and hygiene to the agenda with Clean Toilet Campaign. OPET toilets have achieved the same standard in every corner of Türkiye.

The opinion leader of the OPET training and audit team and OPET social responsibility projects, Founding Board Member Nurten Öztürk has visited 78 provinces nationwide, provided 6482 hours of training, covered a distance of more than 7.5 million kilometers, and given one-on-one hygiene training to more than 12 million people within the scope of the project. OPET expanded the project to a wider framework through various collaborations. There has been training in public institutions, hospitals, schools, and any organization that made a request.

The project served as the best model possible for the fact that consciousness through education can go hand in hand with development in many places from schools and hospitals to public and private institutions. Of all research featuring brand perception, brand reputation, or social responsibility, the Clean Toilet Campaign is currently the most recognized and value-adding project.

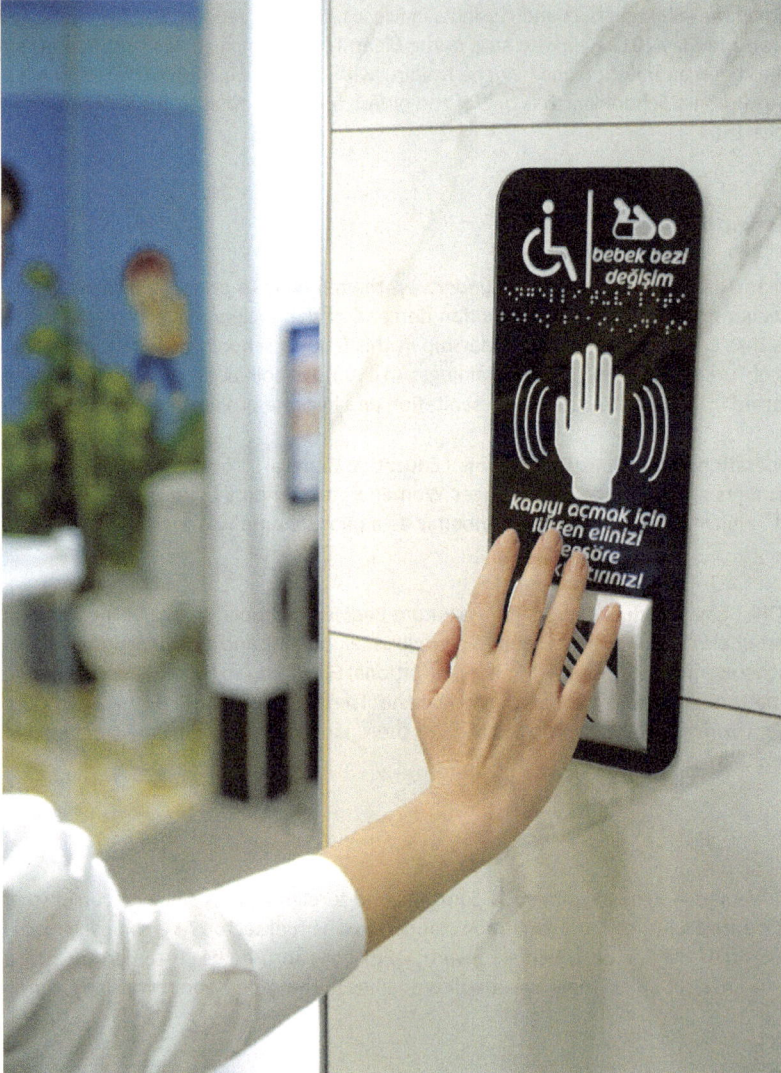

Questions to stimulate conversation on the case.

1. When you started the campaign, did you expect it to be this effective and popular?

We, OPET, have always emphasized the fact that we have started a long-term and permanent work with Clean Toilet Campaign since day one. While renewing our standards and stations, we have pioneered our sector as well. Our competitor have started to work on this subject after us. In 2012, Turkish Standards

Institution have exclusively consulted us while determining new standards for public toilets. The fact that we have designated the standards that are compulsory in all toilets including workplace and restaurant toilets manifests the importance of the point our project has arrived. If we haven't carried out Clean Toilet Campaign, we would still be seeing the infamous putrid toilets of the 2000's on highways. So, we anticipated this transformation when we have started this campaign.

2. Clean Toilet Campaign is one of the longest-running CSR projects in Türkiye. What is the secret for carrying out such a long-term and extensive project?

When we embarked for Clean Toilet Campaign, we have considered not only its economic but also the social and environmental effects in all stages, and we have created our road map with the aftermath of each step-in mind. We ensured continuity by frequently controlling the works through the tracking and inspection system we have established and restructured current works in line with the requirements. For any social responsibility project to achieve its purpose, it needs to fulfil the requirements of the society it exists within, to properly convey its purpose to society and gain back popular support, and also receive support and help from every level of the company. We are of the opinion that Clean Toilet Campaign, as it embodies all of these criteria, has created a social sensitivity and change about toilet sanitation and hygiene. When in such an intimate communication with the target audience, when in an endeavor to do something with one-on-one contact, you convey the same confidence and faith to the other party. Maybe this direct contact has been the thing that took this project to success.

3. What contribution did this project make to your group, your corporate reputation and culture?

As OPET, we tried to perfectly implement the project in our stations with our quality service approach and popularize the project throughout all levels of society. With our project, "Clean Toilets" have identified with our brand. We managed to take the perception of hygiene and sanitation in our station to top level. With "Clean Toilet Campaign", we aim to create a clean and healthy society. Toilets are a sign of civilization for a country. 90% of disease-causing microbes are directly or indirectly transmitted via toilets. Therefore, service sector, along with all institutions that undertake the task of servicing the public should be conscious and sensitive about this subject.

5. IMPLEMENTATION AND CONTROLLING IN THE MARKETING PLAN PROCESS

5.1 ORGANIZING AND IMPLEMENTING THE MARKETING PLAN

We have described and analyzed each of the ingredients of a typical marketing mix. In developing a marketing plan an organization will need to consider each of these elements, whilst at the same being cautious not to fall into the trap of viewing each ingredient in isolation. As already stated in the first chapter, marketing and the marketing tools must constantly be viewed as a collective whole and opportunities for synergy will only be exploited if it is regarded accordingly. Each ingredient of the mix should consistently reinforce the 'message' being conveyed by the others. To ensure that the plan does represent a coherent whole, it is of key importance that the organisation's approach to each of the marketing elements is presented in the plan in a clear and easy to read format. It should then become obvious whether ambiguities are present and corrective action can be taken (Hollensen and Opresnik, 2020).

5.1.1 THE PROCESS OF DEVELOPING THE INTERNATIONAL MARKETING PLAN

Basically, marketing planning is a rational sequence and a series of activities leading to the setting of marketing objectives and the formulation of plans for achieving them. Companies generally undergo a management process in developing marketing plans. In SMEs this process is usually informal. In larger, more diversified organisations, the process is often systematized (Hollensen and Opresnik, 2020).

DeFacto

THE JOURNEY OF DEFACTO FROM A CONTRACT MANUFACTURER TO A GLOBAL FASHION GIANT SPANNING 100 COUNTRIES

Written by: Barış Sönmez (General Manager of Retail and Marketing at DeFacto)

Introduction

- DeFacto's journey from a contract manufacturing firm to a global fashion giant operating in 100 countries is filled with numerous challenges and success stories. Founded in 2004 by the current Chairman of the Board Zeki Cemal Özen and CEO İhsan Ateş, DeFacto set out to revolutionize Turkish fashion by offering quality and original designs at affordable prices to consumers worldwide. Today, the brand reaches millions of customers in 100 countries through over 500 stores, online channels, and e-commerce platforms. Embracing renewal as a core cultural tenet, DeFacto stands as the pioneer of the "Accessible Fashion" concept and delivers quality products accessible to consumers from all walks of life.

Just 7 years after its foundation, DeFacto became the second-largest brand in the Turkish ready-to-wear sector and opened its first international store in Kazakhstan in 2012, followed by global expansion. As its operational footprint grew, a robust logistics network became essential to ensure the right products reached the right stores, leading to intensified efforts in this area.

One of the most significant steps to accelerate the brand's growth was the implementation of the state-of-the-art "ASRS Warehouse" in 2014. DeFacto's warehouse operations are conducted on a 50,000 square meter closed area located on a 100,000 square meter land in Çerkezköy. Additionally, there are 13 distribution centers abroad. This investment in infrastructure has played a significant role in DeFacto's steady growth.

- Another crucial step ensuring DeFacto's growth was the transfer of know-how from the right individuals and institutions. Collaborating with the most competent experts and institutions has been pivotal in producing and delivering the right collections to the right places for consumers. By transferring experienced names from the best retailers in the target countries, DeFacto has achieved significant gains. Today, DeFacto has transformed into a global fashion company, with nearly 30% of its revenue generated from international operations.

Retail is one of the most dynamic and innovation-driven sectors of the global economy, and it is heavily influenced by rapidly developing technologies and digital transformation. Recognizing this trend, DeFacto has positioned itself as a "Phygital" fashion brand by transforming its strength in physical retail through digitalization.

Closely following technological advancements and prioritizing technology investments, DeFacto established a technology company in 2015. Located in Yıldız Technical University Technopark, DeFacto Technology, with over 300 engineers, focuses on developing its software, managing DeFacto's IT operations in all countries, and conducting research and business development. These efforts have elevated DeFacto not only as a global fashion brand originating from Türkiye but also as one of Türkiye's largest technology companies. The widespread presence of DeFacto in online and offline channels and its operations in 100 countries

223

worldwide have enabled the accumulation of significant experience in omni-channel business processes. DeFacto Technology's primary focus is to develop systems that provide the best omni-channel and phygital experience for DeFacto customers through new-generation technologies and AI-supported applications. This commitment enables DeFacto to continuously enhance customer experience and offer pioneering solutions in the industry.

Focused on creating long-term, sustainable value for the industry, countries, and the world in which it operates, DeFacto improves its financial performance each year. Meanwhile, within its multi-stakeholder ecosystem, DeFacto aims to lead positive change across its entire value chain, primarily benefiting employees, customers, and suppliers. DeFacto is also committed to its societal and environmental obligations by being a signatory of the United Nations Global Compact, the Women's Empowerment Principles (WEPs), and a member of the Better Cotton Initiative.

Challenge

The goal is to grow by reaching more customers through increasing the number of stores, but focusing solely on opening new stores is not always easy, and achieving results can take a long time. While DeFacto has steadily increased the number of its stores, it successfully navigated a critical growth phase by establishing its infrastructure and making significant investments in digitalization as the world pivoted towards e-commerce. However, this was not enough...

How can we make better use of the existing resources of our brand which has strengthened its e-commerce capabilities and reached Türkiye and the rest of the world? How can we engage both existing and potential customers, and more importantly, how can we perfect the customer experience and strengthen the bonds between us and our customers?

Solution

DeFacto addresses these challenges by prioritizing the principle of personalized service and experience by adopting the vision of "Make customers fall in love!". The company has designed its omni-channel strategy and implemented a loyalty program to make the lives of its customers, each considered individually, easier. With an integrated marketing strategy based on the comprehensive analysis of customer data, DeFacto continues to focus on customer satisfaction by offering personalized product recommendations, payment alternatives, and various delivery options for a seamless customer experience.

Omni-channel Strategy

With technology investments forming the backbone of DeFacto's omni-channel efforts, the omni-channel structure introduced in 2016 has quickly gaining momentum, making DeFacto the first fashion brand in Türkiye to widely implement omni-channel practices. The integration of physical and virtual sales points proved to be one of the brand's most significant steps in its growth journey.

The omni-channel approach offers customers the opportunity to shop through various channels and methods, bridging online sales platforms with physical stores to provide a seamless shopping experience. Customers can shop independently of time and place thanks to omni-channel applications.

Another factor contributing to the success of DeFacto's omni-channel initiative is the use of both store and e-commerce stock together. By offering its entire collection in stores regardless of square footage, and simultaneously making all store inventories available to online customers beyond the traditional B2C warehouse stocks, the brand ensures a comprehensive inventory strategy. The first leg of this two-sided strategy, "Ship

From Store," keeps DeFacto store stocks available for online sales, offering warehouse and store inventories to customers simultaneously.

The second leg "PayAtStore," allows customers to easily order and have items delivered free of charge to their desired address for free if a product or its size or color is not available in the store.

The Click & Collect system was developed for customers facing difficulties in adjusting delivery times for their online orders. This system ensures that online orders are prepared at a chosen DeFacto store of the customer's choice, allowing them to pick up the order at their convenience without shipping fees.

In-store mobile payment is another unique feature in Türkiye, enabling customers to save time by making quick payments through the mobile app without waiting at the checkout or needing a POS device. Innovative alternative payment methods also allow customers to pay as they wish.

The omni-channel application also provides numerous conveniences for store employees. A significant facilitator in this regard is the "Retail Master" mobile application for its employees. This app allows DeFacto employees to perform all tasks through their smartphones without needing traditional handheld terminals. Additionally, with the Fitting Room QR project, customers who need assistance in the fitting room can quickly receive support from customer advisors.

Successfully implementing its omni-channel strategy in Türkiye, DeFacto has increased the efficiency of its stores while accelerating online growth by offering all stock to customers. DeFacto has also begun offering the omni-channel experience in prioritized countries outside Türkiye and plans to continue expanding this experience across all countries it operates in the coming period.

DeFacto Gift Club

With rapidly changing consumer behaviors and the increasing challenge of earning customer loyalty, loyalty programs have become critically important. DeFacto, committed to individualized customer engagement, launched its loyalty program in 2021. The mission was to offer personalized benefits but also to enhance DeFacto's brand perception. Launched in September of the same year, the DeFacto Gift Club enabled the brand to offer its customers more privileges and a personalized shopping experience. From its inception, this initiative garnered attention for its successful outcomes. As of June 2024, the program boasts 16 million members, with 75% being active customers. The relationship with customers has become continuous, evolving into a familial bond.

Members of the program benefit from Gift points, personalized offers, and discounts. Accessible through stores, the e-commerce platform, and the mobile app, the program offers additional rewards and Gift points during members' birthday and anniversary months. Additionally, models that learn from customers' shopping behaviors present the right product, at the right price, at the right time, enhancing satisfaction.

DeFacto Gift Club, designed to make members' lives easier, was established with a continuously evolving structure. The program maintains its dynamism through strategic brand collaborations and the ongoing addition of new customers. Having a positive impact in Türkiye and fostering mutual satisfaction between customers and the brand, the program has been rapidly expanding to priority countries since June 2024.

Conclusion

DeFacto continues to create economic and innovative value in all the regions it operates, driven by these efforts. The integration of innovative technologies with a focus on sustainability, quality, and benefit has led to marketing success. DeFacto Gift Club achieved a milestone in the Turkish fashion retail sector by surpassing 16 million registered members in just two and a half years.

Customers benefiting from the omni-channel application show a shopping frequency three times higher than those who shop exclusively from stores or online. Moreover, brand loyalty has shown a significant increase. DeFacto, Türkiye's global fashion brand, remains steadfast in its growth without being limited by square meters.

Questions to stimulate conversation on the case

1. **What were the biggest challenges encountered in DeFacto's omni-channel and loyalty program efforts?**

- Adapting all omni-channel processes simultaneously to our systems and business practices was a significant challenge, requiring us to develop everything in-house. We gained experience and learning in both software and operational areas. The Covid-19 pandemic shifted our customers' expectations, and we leveraged our operational flexibility accordingly. During lockdowns, we opened all our stores to online sales, continuing to serve our customers and maintain employment. We took all possible measures to ensure the health of our customers and employees, such as establishing regional hubs to consolidate orders from stores into single packages, providing a seamless experience.

- Managing our PayAtStore channel via web services proved to be challenging. We developed our application in-house, which continues to evolve based on our daily experiences. Today, after entering customer information, our application can make product recommendations based on their shopping habits.

- Adapting all omni-channel processes simultaneously to our systems and business practices was a significant challenge, requiring us to develop everything in-house. We gained experience and learning in both software and operational areas. The Covid-19 pandemic shifted our customers' expectations, and we leveraged our operational flexibility accordingly. During lockdowns, we opened all our stores to online sales, continuing to serve our customers and maintain employment. We took all possible measures to ensure the health of our customers and employees, such as establishing regional hubs to consolidate orders from stores into single packages, providing a seamless experience.

2. **What was the impact of these efforts on sales figures?**

- As a result of these initiatives, both our online and omni-channel sales continue to grow. By measuring the activity and frequency of Gift Club members, we can take action to enhance their engagement. Additionally, we assess the effectiveness of our campaigns based on this data and make necessary adjustments.

- Our multi-channel users show 1.5 times more activity and three times higher frequency compared to single-channel customers (e.g., only store or only online). Therefore, by increasing the number of customers using omni-channel applications and enabling them to fulfill more of their needs through DeFacto, we generate additional revenue. We expect omni-channel applications to account for more than 10% of total revenue in 2024.

3. **In the next 5 years, what results do you aim to achieve with these efforts?**

Our primary goal is to continually deliver a unique and superior omni-channel experience to our customers through ongoing initiatives and new endeavors. By upholding our leadership in the sector with top-notch omni-channel practices that ensure frictionless customer experiences, we anticipate achieving annual additional revenue growth of 10-15% over the next five years.

Furthermore, we plan to globally expand our loyalty program across all countries where we operate multi-channel operations, aiming to enroll all DeFacto customers worldwide into the Gift Club, thus reaching a customer base of 50 million. This strategic approach not only aims to foster a large community but also strives to elevate customer satisfaction to its pinnacle.

4.   What will be the next step in DeFacto's growth journey?

- DeFacto is far beyond where it started, having steadfastly achieved its goals to date and continuing to take confident steps toward future targets. We aim to advance our "Phygital Fashion Brand" by several steps, striving to become the world's best fashion brand at utilizing personalization. We will fully leverage global trends and the latest technological innovations, offering these advancements to our customers. We will maintain and strengthen the strong bonds we have established with our customers and extend this globally.

Links

Website: www.defacto.com

5.1.2 DECIDING ON THE INTERNATIONAL MARKETING MIX

Companies that operate in one or more foreign markets have to decide how much, if at all, to adapt their marketing mixes to local conditions. At one extreme are international companies that use a **standardised marketing mix**, selling largely the same products and services and applying the same marketing approaches world-wide. At the other end is an **adapted marketing mix**. In the latter case, the company adjusts the marketing mix elements to each target market, bearing more costs but aiming at a larger market share and return due to a more sophisticated and tailored marketing mix.

CASE STUDY
EVYAP

Written by: Leyla Şen (Corporate Communications Consultant, LEA Istanbul)

Introduction

In most countries, companies that reach the 100-year mark are rare—and getting rarer. The average lifespan of companies in the S&P 500 index was 33 years in 1965, but by 2020, this had decreased to 21 years. It is projected to drop further to just 15 years by 2027, driven by digital transformation, new business models, and shifting market dynamics. In Türkiye, a newly developed and highly entrepreneurial economy, 96% of companies fail to reach their tenth year.

In this article, we will explore the story of Evyap, a Turkish third-generation family business in the personal wash, personal care, and hygiene market, which has not only survived in a highly competitive environment but thrived.

First founded in 1927 as a small soap manufacturer, Evyap is today the leading local player in its market, with flagship brands such as Duru and Arko being well-recognized both domestically and internationally. It has expanded its operations to become an international FMCG brand with manufacturing facilities in Asia and North Africa, enabling it to serve international markets more effectively. It boasts state-of-the-art research

229

facilities which have allowed the company to continuously innovate and expand a diverse product range that includes bar and liquid soaps, shower gels, shampoos, shaving products, creams, lotions, perfumes and deodorants, baby nappies, wet wipes, toothpastes, and very recently pet care products—most of which it exports to 100 countries worldwide. Its new oleochemical production facilities are considered among the world's largest and most sophisticated, giving the company a significant competitive edge in the fast-growing Asian market.

Evyap has also fully embraced sustainability practices, integrating dry production, energy conservation, and zero waste practices into its manufacturing processes.

We believe that Evyap's story is an inspiration to family businesses everywhere. It shows that the right values and business practices can indeed ensure longevity, resilience, and continued growth even in markets dominated by very large global players. The values and practices established by the company's founder Mehmet Rıfat Evyap and upheld by successive generations of family members and professional management have helped create a company that is a source of pride and accomplishment not only to the Evyap family but also to its employees and their communities.

Challenges

Evyap's journey began in 1927 in Erzurum, a remote city in the very east of Türkiye. The Ottoman Empire had dissolved just three years prior, and the young Republic of Türkiye had inherited an impoverished nation, devastated by successive wars and epidemics. The country had no large-scale manufacturing capabilities, relying almost entirely on imported goods. Soap-making facilities were concentrated in Istanbul and the western regions of Türkiye, producing basic laundry, and washing soaps in small-scale soap kitchens and workshops. In Erzurum, the ingredients for soap making, such as olive oil, had to be brought overland from the country's western regions. Rapid urbanization and population growth also produced a rapid increase in the demand for soap, critical for health and hygiene. By 1930, there were around 50 soap workshops and small-scale factories across the country, with an annual production of between 20,000 to 24,000 tonnes.

At the same time, Türkiye's large population, developing economy, and rising incomes have made it an attractive market for multinational brands. Global giant Unilever entered the Turkish market in 1952 with its soap products, followed by Procter & Gamble, Johnson & Johnson, and others in subsequent years. Both P&G and Unilever remain Evyap's main competitors. The personal hygiene and care market worldwide is worth about USD 600 billion today. Product innovation and diversification are critical in all its segments, and consumers are faced with a bewildering array of brands and products across new retail and online channels.

Despite all these challenges, Evyap will celebrate its centenary in 2027 and remains a highly successful family business that continues to grow and expand. What did it do right?

"Always Do Better"

True entrepreneurs are curious and inquisitive people who enjoy learning and can recognize new opportunities. As a child, Mehmet Rıfat would watch soap being made at home, as this was quite common practice at the time. As a young man working as a notary assistant to his father, he met a Russian immigrant named Abdullah Hamidov, who had operated a soap factory in Kazan, today the capital of Tatarstan. Hamidov had fled to Erzurum during the Bolshevik Revolution of 1917. Mehmet Rıfat converted the family stables into a small factory and learned the intricacies of soap-making from Hamidov. Production started in 1927 with a single cauldron producing 8-10 tonnes.

A piece of advice from his notary father during those early days remained a guiding principle for him and became a core value passed down through the generations. Mehmet Rıfat's son, Fikret Evyap (1932-2022), later described this moment in these words: "One day, while my father was boiling soap, my grandfather visited. Seeing the cauldron, he asked how many bars it would produce. When told it would yield 20,000 bars, he said, 'That means you are signing a contract with 20,000 people. You must deliver on their expectations without disappointing them. If they like it the first time, they will pay for it again next time. Your soap should appeal to people because, as the most elevated among God's creatures, they deserve the best. If you are making soap for them, it must be of the highest quality.'"

This philosophy of earnest commitment to the needs and expectations of the customer became the foundation of Evyap's business ethos.

Today, the company's mission statement, "Always do better," is rooted in this commitment: Never compromise on quality, always keep improving, the customer deserves our best.

This principle was meticulously upheld by his sons, Fikret and Fethi Evyap, in transforming the company from a domestic entity into a multinational player. And it remains the core promise of Evyap, launching into the future under the stewardship of the third generation. These are the key factors that have contributed to Evyap's longevity and success:

1. Prioritizing Quality Above All

The three golden rules established by the founder to prioritize quality have guided Evyap's transformation from a local producer to an international FMCG company. Mehmed Evyap, a third-generation family member and Chairman of the Executive Board, describes these rules: "The first rule is to produce superior quality products and deliver them at a reasonable price. This means that if you build a solid foundation with quality, those who purchase the product will derive maximum benefit, resulting in loyalty. The second rule follows naturally: the reward for producing high-quality products is trust and loyalty. The third rule is that trust and loyalty require the best products, which necessitates new investments. We must reinvest our profits. These simple yet effective rules—good products generate customer loyalty, and customer loyalty demands good products—have sustained us for 97 years. Everyone at Evyap knows these three golden rules. I believe our success lies in them."

2. Maintaining Focus

Repetition breeds excellence. Evyap now has a very large product portfolio, but it has never lost its focus on personal wash, personal care and hygiene products. Ömer Evyap, a third-generation family member and Head of the Hygiene Group, explains the benefits of focus: "Just as a good tennis player perfects their game with 10,000 hours of practice, we have gained the experience to produce the best by focusing on the same field for 97 years. Today, with production facilities in three countries, sales, and marketing offices in over ten countries, and exports to over 100 countries, Evyap is among the world's leading personal care and hygiene companies. As we approach our 100th anniversary, I envision a future where Evyap, with its strong brands, continues to lead the market with innovative products, providing the best to consumers across an even broader geography."

3. Exceeding Customer Expectations

The founder's passion for soap and the subsequent generations' commitment to innovation enabled the company not just to meet but exceed customer expectations. His visionary approach led to the production of toilet soap—perhaps for the first time in Erzurum. Similarly, his keenness for innovation led to the production of lipsticks and cottonseed creams in Erzurum, a provincial city where such products were little known in the 1930s. Since then, the company has continued to innovate, constantly extending, and improving its product offering. Evyap's dedication to exceeding customer expectations has led to the foundation of a state-of-the-art R&D center, making the company the first R&D center-certified domestic manufacturer.

Instilling Family Values into Corporate Culture

The enduring success of a company relies on stable leadership, strong corporate culture, effective governance, and a clear mission that is well-executed. This is evident in Evyap's story, where a robust family and company culture has been pivotal. Evyap's business philosophy centers on responsible production, ethical practices, and valuing stakeholders. The founder, Mehmet Rıfat Evyap, embedded social responsibility into the company's core, ensuring a portion of profits is allocated to social causes.

As Evyap approaches its centenary in 2027, the family has refreshed its vision, mission, and values to resonate with younger generations while maintaining its essence. Ayşe Evyap Kadakal, a third-generation board member, explains that their new motto, "Always do better," is a modern interpretation of the founder's commitment to quality. "The essence of our vision, mission, and values remains the same. We simply updated them to be more relatable and understandable for the new generation. Our corporate promise, "Always do better," is a modern adaptation of our founder's advice to never compromise on quality and to produce superior products. The underlying principle is that we must always aim to do what is best for the future. We are responsible for developing and supporting what is right for our world and all living beings.

Therefore, we must be future-oriented. Our mission is to enrich personal and social life through our products. We strive to create opportunities that positively impact lives, supporting and inspiring people in their quest for a meaningful life, and passing this fundamental value on to future generations. We emphasize that our efforts should benefit not only people but the entire world."

4.   Responsibility to Stakeholders and the Ecosystem

Evyap's nearly 100 years of success is rooted in its strong commitment to social responsibility, which is embedded in the company's culture through a protocol that allocates a portion of profits to charitable causes. This dedication is reflected in various initiatives aimed at supporting disadvantaged groups, providing educational aid, and assisting those in need, including families, students, and individuals in prisons. Additionally, Evyap collaborates with disaster relief organizations and supports environmental welfare, demonstrating its focus on creating a positive impact on society and prioritizing stakeholder value over profit.

Conclusion

Evyap's nearly century-long journey is a testament to the enduring power of strong family values, unwavering commitment to quality, a single-minded focus on its area of expertise, a sincere dedication to customer needs and expectations, and a deep sense of social responsibility. By embedding these principles into its corporate culture and continuously adapting to changing market dynamics, Evyap has not only survived but thrived in a highly competitive global personal hygiene and care market. Its focus on innovation, ethical practices, and stakeholder engagement has enabled it to build a legacy that benefits its employees, customers, and the broader community. As Evyap approaches its 100th anniversary, it stands as an inspiring example of how a family business can achieve lasting success and make a meaningful impact on the world.

Summary

Evyap's journey from a small soap manufacturer in Erzurum to a global FMCG player is a testament to the power of unwavering commitment to quality, focus, and values. As the company approaches its centenary, it stands as an inspiring example of how family businesses can thrive in a competitive global market dominated by multinational giants. The company's success is built on a foundation of core principles established by its founder, Mehmet Rıfat Evyap, and diligently upheld by subsequent generations.

These principles - prioritising quality, maintaining focus, exceeding customer expectations, instilling family values into corporate culture, and demonstrating responsibility to stakeholders and the ecosystem - have not only ensured Evyap's longevity but have also driven its continuous growth and innovation.

As Evyap looks towards its next century, it remains committed to its motto "Always do better," adapting to new challenges while staying true to its foundational values. The company's story serves as an inspiration to family businesses worldwide, demonstrating that with the right values, practices, and a commitment to innovation, it is possible to build a legacy that contributes positively to society, the environment, and the global economy.

In an era where the lifespan of companies is decreasing, Evyap's enduring success offers valuable lessons on the importance of quality, focus, innovation, and social responsibility in building a sustainable and thriving business. As it continues to evolve and expand, Evyap remains a beacon of how traditional values can be harmoniously blended with modern business practices to create a company that is not just profitable, but also purposeful and impactful.

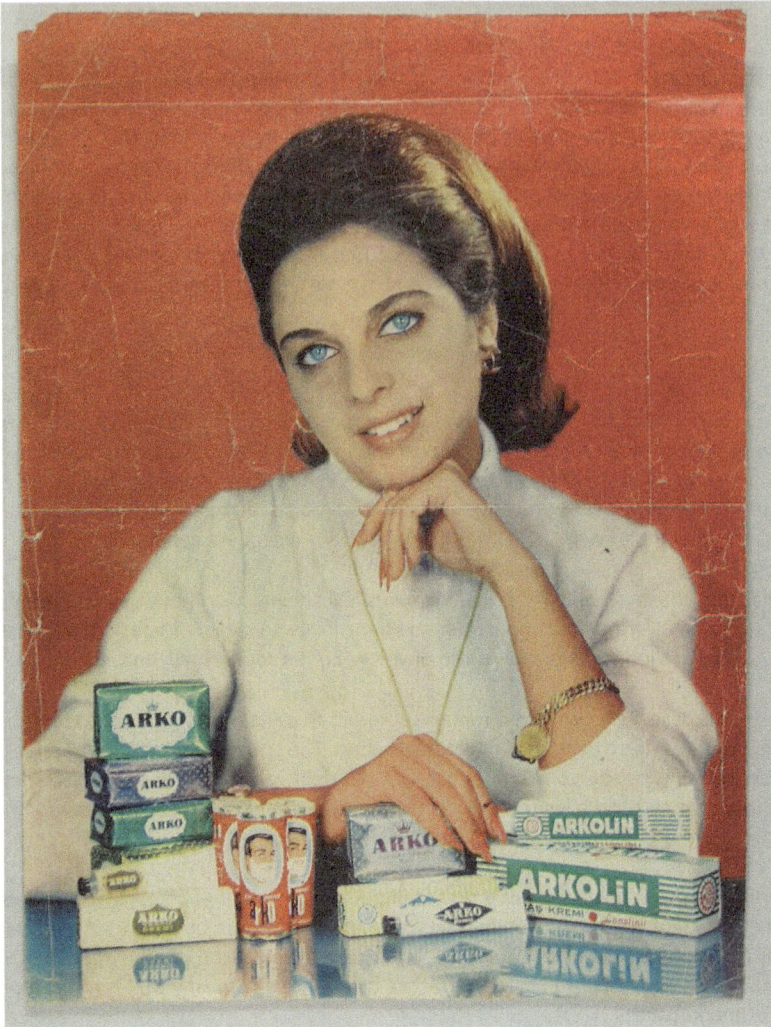

Questions to stimulate conversation on the case

1. **What key factors have contributed to Evyap's longevity and success in the highly competitive personal care and hygiene market?**

Evyap's success can be attributed to its unwavering commitment to quality, continuous innovation, and strong family values. The company's founder, Mehmet Rıfat Evyap, established core principles that have been upheld by successive generations, ensuring that customer expectations are always met or exceeded. Additionally, Evyap's focus on sustainability and social responsibility has helped build a loyal customer base and a positive corporate reputation.

2. **How has Evyap managed to maintain its focus on personal hygiene and care products while expanding its product portfolio and global presence?**

Despite its large product portfolio, Evyap has maintained its focus on personal wash, personal care, and hygiene products by leveraging its extensive experience and expertise in this field. The company has invested in state-of-the-art research and development facilities, allowing it to innovate continuously and improve its

236

offerings. This focus has enabled Evyap to expand its operations globally while staying true to its core mission of providing high-quality personal care products.

3. **In what ways has Evyap's commitment to social responsibility and sustainability practices impacted its business operations and growth?**

Evyap's commitment to social responsibility and sustainability has positively impacted its business operations by fostering a culture of ethical practices and stakeholder engagement. The company's protocol of allocating a portion of profits to charitable causes has helped build strong community relationships and a positive corporate image. By integrating sustainability practices such as dry production, energy conservation, and zero waste into its manufacturing processes, Evyap has also enhanced its operational efficiency and environmental stewardship, contributing to its long-term growth and success.

5.1.3 WRITING THE MARKETING PLAN DOCUMENT

Marketing planning is widely adopted by organisations from all sectors. The process of marketing planning integrates all elements of marketing management: marketing analysis, development of strategy and the implementation of the marketing mix. Marketing planning can, therefore, be regarded as a systematic process for assessing marketing opportunities and matching them with own resources and competences. In this respect, the process aids businesses to effectively develop, coordinate and control marketing activities. Basically, the major functions of the marketing plan are to determine where the company is, where it wants to go, and how it can get there. Marketing planning is able to fulfil these functions by driving the business through three sorts of activities: (a) analyzes of the internal and external situations, (b) development of marketing strategy, and (c) design and implementation of marketing programmes (Hollensen, 2006).

The marketing planning process is linked to planning in other functional areas and to overall corporate strategy. It takes place within the larger strategic marketing management process of the business. To survive and flourish, the business marketer must properly balance the firm's resources with the objectives and opportunities of the environment. Marketing planning is a continuous process that involves the active participation of other functional areas. The marketing plan itself is the written document that businesses develop to record the output of the marketing planning process. This document provides details of the analysis and strategic thinking that have been undertaken and outlines the marketing objectives, marketing mix and plan for execution and control. As such, the plan plays a key role in informing organisational members about the plan and any roles and responsibilities they possibly have within it. The plan also provides details of required resources and should highlight potential obstacles to the planning process, so that steps can be taken to overcome them. The marketing plan is a kind of road map, providing direction to help the business implement its strategies and achieve its objectives: the plan guides top management and all functional areas within the organisation.

Once the core marketing analyzes are complete, the strategy development process follows. The key during this phase is to base any decisions on a detailed and objective view from the analyzes. The most appropriate target markets will be identified, basis for competing and positioning strategies determined and detailed marketing objectives presented. As these choices will affect how the business proceeds in relation to its customers and competitors, there must be consistency with the company's general corporate strategy. The marketing strategy must also be realistic and sufficiently detailed to form the basis for the marketing programmes which follow.

The final stage of the marketing planning process involves the determination of marketing mix programs and their implementation. A detailed explanation is needed of precisely what marketing tasks must be undertaken, how, by whom and when. There needs to be a comprehensive rationale connecting these marketing mix recommendations with the analyzes and strategy preceding them.

Assuming that appropriate attention has been devoted to the marketing analyzes and marketing strategy that guide the marketing programs, managers must next ensure that adequate detail is provided to make the marketing mix genuinely implementable. This means that each component of the marketing program – product, price, promotion, distribution, and people – must be discussed separately and the tasks required to action it are fully explored.

Those involved in planning will usually prepare some form of written marketing plan document in which to explain the outputs of the process. The marketing plan provides a useful framework for the analytical and strategic thinking undertaken, the detailed marketing objectives and marketing programs, their implementation and control. Managers are able to refer back to the document for guidance and should regularly update it to ensure that a full record of the marketing planning activities is available. The document helps focus the views of senior management and explain the required marketing activities and target market strategy to other functional areas within the business, such as operations and finance (Dibb, 2002).

The key components of the marketing plan are the following (Hollensen and Opresnik, 2020):

1. Title page
2. Table of contents
3. Executive summary
4. Introduction and problem statement
5. Situational analysis
6. Marketing objectives
7. Marketing strategies
8. Marketing programs and action plans
9. Budgets
10. Implementation and control
11. Conclusion.

We shall now examine each section of the marketing plan structure in further detail (Hollensen and Opresnik, 2020).

5.1.3.1 Title Page

The title page is an identification document that provides the reader with the following essential information:

1. Legal name of business
2. Name of document ('Marketing Plan for …')
3. Date of preparation or modification of the document
4. Name, address, e-mail and phone number of the business or contact person
5. Name, address, e-mail and phone number of the individual or business who prepared the plan
6. The planning period

5.1.3.2 Table of Contents

This is the list of subjects covered in the marketing plan and where to find them.

5.1.3.3 Executive Summary

This gives busy executives and managers a rapid overview, in form of a concise summary of the key points in the marketing plan. This section encompasses a one-page summary of the basic factors involving the marketing of the product or service along with the results expected from implementing the plan.

5.1.3.4 Introduction and Problem Statement

The identification and clear presentation of the problem(s) or issue(s) facing the company is the most critical part of the introduction. Only a problem properly defined can be addressed. The marketer should shortly address the main problem in the marketing plan. The marketer needs to be on alert for symptoms parading as key issues and underlying problems. Strategic marketing problems are long-term, involve large sums of money, and affect multiple aspects of the firm.

5.1.3.5 Situational Analysis

Based on a comprehensive audit of the market environment, competitors, the market, products, and the company itself, this section provides a condensed view of the market (size, structure, and dynamics), prior to a detailed analysis of individual market segments, which form the heart of the marketing plan.

The process is based upon market segmentation – that is, homogeneous groups of customers with characteristics that can be exploited in marketing terms. This approach is taken because it is the one that is most valuable for managers in developing their businesses. The alternative product-oriented approach is hardly ever appropriate, given the varying requirements of the different customer groups in the market in which most organisations compete.

It is necessary to summarize the unit's present position in its major markets, in the form of a SWOT analysis for each major market segment, product, or business group. The word SWOT derives from the initial letters of the word's strengths, weaknesses, opportunities, and threats. The analysis includes the following issues (Hollensen and Opresnik, 2020):

The Firm and its Market

- Identification and evaluation of the competences in the company (key personnel, experience, skills and capabilities, and resources), in comparison with competitors.

- The structure of the marketing organisation (lines of authority, functions, and responsibilities).

- Description of the total potential market (i.e. potential customers).

- How does the company's product/service satisfy the needs of the market?

- Description of the particular customers to be targeted.

- Size of (a) total potential market (number of potential customers), and (b) the target market. Estimates should be supported with factual data.

- Growth potential of (a) total potential market, and (b) the target market. The marketer needs to look at local, national, and international markets. Estimates should be supported with factual data.

- The company's market share (firm's sales divided by the total market sales in per cent)

Competitive Environment

- Major competitors: name, location, and market share.

- Comparison of the company's product/service with that of the major competitors (brand name, quality, image, price, etc.).

- Comparison of the company with that of the major competitors (reputation, size, distribution channels, location, etc.).

- How easy is it for new competition to enter this market?

- What has the company learned from watching competition?

- Are competitors' sales increasing, decreasing, steady? Why?

Technological Environment

- How is technology affecting the product/service?

- How soon can it be expected to become obsolete?

- Is the company equipped to adapt quickly to changes?

Socio-Political Environment

- Description of the changing attitudes and trends. How flexible and responsive is the firm?

- New laws and regulations that may affect the business. What might be the financial impact?

From the SWOT analyzes, key issues that must be addressed. Marketers should summarize the company's internal and external assessment in form of a SWOT-matrix with the key points from the situation analysis.

5.1.3.6 Marketing Objectives

Within this section, the marketing objectives in terms of sales volume, market share, return on investment, or other objectives or goals should be stated precisely (e.g., 'To obtain a sales volume of 3.000 units equal to an increase in market share from 10 per cent to 15 per cent of total market, by the by the end of the next fiscal year.').

5.1.3.7 Marketing Strategies

The question addressed within this part is how to reach the company's objectives and goals? Which strategic models should be used (new market penetration, penetration, market development, etc.).

5.1.3.8 Marketing Programs and Action Plans

Marketing programs are the actionable means of achieving desired ends. They outline what needs to be done, how it will be done, when it will be done, and who will do it.

- How will the company implement the above strategy?

- Product/service: quality, branding, packaging, modifications, location of service, etc.

- Pricing: How will the firm price its product/service so that it will be competitive, yet profitable?

- Promotion/advertising: How, where, when, etc.

- Selling methods: Personal selling, mail-order, etc. The marketer must also include number of salespersons, training required, etc.

- Distribution methods

- Servicing of product

- Other: the marketer is supposed to add any other relevant information

5.1.3.9 Budgets

Having detailed the steps that will be necessary to achieve the marketing objectives, the writer of the plan should then be in a position to cost the various proposals and to derive an overall marketing budget for the planning period. Of course, in reality, this is not uncomplicated. Cost will certainly have been in the minds of marketing planners even before they commenced the marketing planning process. At the very least, the development of a suitable budget is likely in practice to have been an iterative process, with proposals being re-evaluated in the light of budgetary constraint.

There are a variety of ways of determining the marketing budget. Irrespective of the method actually used, in practice it would be usual to specify how the eventual budget has been allocated and to include such a specification in the marketing plan itself. It would also be typical for an allowance to be made for contingencies in the event that monitoring by the organisation suggests that the objectives will not be met. Sufficient resources should then exist for some form of corrective action to be taken.

A budget of cash flows should also be prepared. It identifies whether a company will have enough money to meet its cash requirements on a monthly basis. Some sales will be made in cash while others may be made on credit. Because sales made on credit will not result in the receipt of cash until a later date, they must not be recorded until the month in which the cash will actually be received. Therefore, the percentage of sales to be made in cash and the percentage to be made on credit must be estimated. The percentage of credit sales should be further broken down according to the business 'different collection periods (30 days, 60 days, etc.).

5.1.3.10 Implementation and Control

As soon as the plan has been implemented, the management will then have to take responsibility for monitoring the progress of the organisation towards the goals specified. Managers will also need to concern themselves with the costs that have been incurred at each stage of implementation and monitor these against the budget. Thus, control mechanisms need to be put into place to monitor:

- the actual sales achieved, against the budget.

- the actual costs incurred against those budgeted.

- the performance of individual services against budget

- the overall strategic direction that the organisation is taking – i.e., will the overall corporate objectives be achieved in a manner commensurate with the organisation's mission?

If variances are detected in any of these areas, corrective action should be initiated, if necessary, by utilizing resources allocated for contingency in the budget.

5.1.3.11 Conclusion

This section briefly concludes the problems stated in the beginning of the report, based on the analysis in the marketing plan. The conclusion is not a summary. The executive summary will normally also include the key results of the market analysis.

5.1.4 IMPLEMENTING THE MARKETING PLAN

Marketing strategy concerns the issues and challenges of *what* should happen and *why* it should happen. Implementation focuses on actions: *who* is responsible for different activities, *how* precisely the strategy should be carried out, *where* things will happen and when action will occur. No matter how well conceived a strategy and marketing plan might be, it will definitely fail if people are incapable of carrying out the necessary tasks to make the strategy actually work in the market. Consequently, implementation capability is an integral part of strategy formulation.

The implementation of a new strategy potentially entails profound effects on people in organisations. Unfortunately, most people most of the time are not open to change. It represents risk, uncertainty, and more effort than the regular day job. Therefore, the implementation of a strategic move is usually associated with the need for people to adapt to change. Therefore, the management of change is an essential ingredient in effective planning and implementation.

Even though the benefits of adopting marketing planning are well established, the effectiveness of the process is not definite. A range of barriers to successful marketing planning have been highlighted in the literature. Consequently, careful attention is essential to ensure that marketing planning is effectively implemented. The starting point should be an appreciation of the probable barriers, so that preventative and remedial action can be taken (Hollensen and Opresnik, 2020).

The recommendation is that marketers should use the following three solutions (Hollensen, 2006):

- **Solution 1**: provide the necessary infrastructure and resources for marketing planning activities.

- **Solution 2**: use a robust analytical process that is objective and complete in terms of the inclusion of the essential ingredients of marketing planning.

- **Solution 3**: devote managerial time and attention to the on-going management of the resulting plan's implementation.

5.1.5 DECIDING ON THE MARKETING ORGANIZATION

Marketing organization provides the framework in which marketing implementation takes place. The firm's organizational structure is a critical variable for the implementation of the company's marketing plans. The following summary highlights the main reasons for this (Hollensen, 2006):

- There may be difficulties in coordinating and controlling operating units of different sizes and levels of complexity.

- Personnel in different markets will have diverse abilities and expectations, and organizing such a heterogeneous group can be challenging.

- There may be excessive head-office control.

Effective marketing planning only comes about when the marketing strategy and organisational structure correspond. The elementary question 'Do we have the right organisation for our strategy?' is one that all chief executives should be asking. This question can be broken down into four 'basic' parts, the first two of which are concerned with the division of responsibilities amongst the labour force, whilst the remaining questions focus on coordination and control:

- What tasks are required to put the strategies into operation?

- To whom should these tasks be assigned?

- How interdependent are these tasks?

- How can the organisation be sure that the tasks assigned will be performed?

There is nothing like *the* correct answers, and consequently there are accurate structures for all organisations, but successful firms are those that tend to have organisational structures that fluently fit their specific needs in terms of corporate objectives, strategies, corporate culture, etc.

There are many ways in which a multinational company and marketing can be organised. The most relevant are the following organisational structure archetypes (Ellis-Chadwick and Jobber, 2016):

- no marketing department

- functional structure

- international division structure

- product-based structure

- geographic structure

- matrix structure

5.2 BUDGETING AND CONTROL

An organisation needs to budget in order to ensure that its expenditure does not exceed its planned income. Marketing control is an essential element of the marketing planning process because it provides a review of how well marketing objectives have been achieved. Consequently, this section will outline the need for a control system to supervise the marketing operations of the company (Hollensen and Opresnik, 2020).

5.2.1 MARKETING PRODUCTIVITY AND ECONOMIC RESULTS

The **productivity** of an operation is related to input resources how effectively in a process are transformed into economic results for the service provider and value for its customers. The traditional productivity conception has been developed for manufacturers of physical goods as a production efficiency concept. Existing productivity models and measurement instruments are also geared to the context of manufacturers. Moreover, they are based on assumptions that production and consumption are separate processes and that customers do not participate in the production process (Hollensen, 2006).

High productivity is commonly assumed to be a primary goal in so much as a productive operation is more likely to have lower costs. It is the close connection with the cost performance of an operation of process that accounts for the interest in understanding and measuring productivity. Although the definition of productivity appears straightforward, productivity can be difficult to deal with for different reasons, but first of first of all the outputs are usually expressed in different forms to the inputs. Outputs are often measured in physical terms such as units (e.g., cars produced), tonnes (of paper), kilowatts (of electricity), or value (Euros), for example. However, the inputs are usually physically different and include measures of people (numbers, skills, hours worked or costs), cost of input resources or marketing actions (Johnston and Jones, 2004).

Especially, the intangible nature of many services means that it is difficult to define and measure the service outputs being provided. The measurement and management of inputs and outputs is also complicated because of the simultaneous production and consumption of many services, as well as their perishability and heterogeneity, as service encounters are experienced differently by different people or even by the same people in different circumstances.

Because the service (production) process and service consumption are usually simultaneous processes, where customers participate actively, the resources or inputs used to produce services cannot be standardized more than to a certain level. It is difficult to relate a given number of inputs, in volume or value terms, to a given number of outputs. Frequently, it is even difficult to define 'one unit of service. 'According to the traditional manufacturing-related productivity concept, productivity is defined as the ratio between outputs produced and inputs used, given that the quality of the outputs is kept constant (the constant quality assumption).

Only if the quality of the production output is constant and there is no significant variation in the ratio between inputs used and outputs produced with these inputs, productivity can be measured with traditional methods.

Productivity cannot be understood without taking into account the interrelationship between the use of inputs or production resources and the perceived quality of the output produced with these resources. The interrelationship between internal efficiency and external efficiency is crucial for understanding and managing service productivity.

Marketing actions, such as advertising, service improvements, or new product launches, can help build long-term assets (e.g., brand equity, customer equity). These assets can be leveraged to deliver short-term profitability (Rust et al., 2004). Thus, marketing actions both create and leverage market-based assets. In this context, it is important to distinguish between the 'effectiveness 'and the 'efficiency 'of marketing actions. For example, price promotions can be efficient in that they deliver short-term revenues and cash flows. However, to the extent that they invite competitive actions and destroy long-term profitability and brand equity, they may not be effective. Consequently, a company needs to examine both tactical and strategic marketing actions and their implications (Hollensen, 2006).

Financial benefits from a specific marketing action can be evaluated in several ways. **Return on investment (ROI)** is a traditional approach to evaluating return relative to the expenditure required to obtain the return. Commonly used retrospectively to measure short-term return, ROI is controversial in the context of marketing effectiveness. Because many marketing expenditures play out over the long run, short-term ROI is often prejudicial against marketing expenditures. The correct usage of ROI measures in marketing requires an analysis of future cash flows.

Other financial impact measures include the internal rate of return, which is the discount rate that would make the discounted return exactly equal to the discounted expenditure; the net present value, which is the discounted return minus the net present value of the expenditure; and the economic value-added (EVA), which is the net operating profit minus the cost of capital.

Except for the non-financial metrics such as awareness, in each case the measures of financial impact weigh the return generated by the marketing action against the expenditure required to produce that return. The financial impact affects the financial position of the firm, as measured by profits, cash flow, and other measures of financial health.

5.2.2 MARKETING BUDGETING

The purpose of a **marketing budget** is to pull all the revenues and costs involved in marketing together into one comprehensive document. This is an important managerial tool that balances what is needed to be spent against what can be afforded and aids in the framework of prioritization. It is then used in monitoring the performance in practice.

Budgeting is also an organisation process that involves making forecasts based on the proposed marketing strategy. The forecasts then are used to construct a budgeted profit-and-loss statement (i.e., profitability). An important aspect of budgeting is deciding how to allocate the proposed investments across all of the anticipated programs within the marketing plan.

The marketing plans and the annual budget are interlinked in several ways – the sales forecast, the pricing policy, the marketing expenditure budget, and the allocation of resources. A budget is a detailed plan outlining the acquisition and use of financial and other resources over some given time period. The **annual budget** is commonly referred to as the `master budget`. Usually, it has three principal parts: the operating budget, the cash budget, and the capital expenditure budget. It is driven by the sales forecast. The budget plays a key role in an organisation by moving the organisation from an informal reaction method of management to a formal controlled system of management. It addition, it might act as a motivator and communicator, as well as for functional coordination and performance evaluation (Hollensen, 2006).

It is evident that the annual budget and the marketing plan are interwoven and should be part of the same process in organisations. The management implications are significant. An organisation works effectively when there is clear communication and coordination across functional lines. For effective implementation of an organisation's strategy, the firm must serve customers better than the competition. This implies that all management policies and systems should be continuously reviewed.

Regardless of the organisational level, control involves some form of profitability analysis as already mentioned above when discussing various marketing metrics. In brief, **profitability analysis** requires that analysts determine the costs associated with specific marketing activities to find out the profitability of such units as different market segments, products customer accounts, and distribution channels (intermediaries).

An array of measures (often referred to as **marketing metrics**) is available to marketing managers who wish to measure the effectiveness of their activities. However, it is often difficult to determine the exact contribution of marketing efforts because outcomes are usually dependent on multiple factors. For example, higher sales may be caused by increased and/or better advertising, a more motivated sales force, weaker competition, and so on. This makes it difficult to justify, for example, increased advertising expenditure, because it is difficult to quantify the effects of advertising.

Despite these issues, marketing is requested to become accountable for its activities. In order to assess performance of marketing activities, marketing managers are using marketing metrics, which are quantitative measures of the outcomes of marketing activities and expenditures (Hollensen and Opresnik, 2020).

5.2.3 CONTROLLING THE MARKETING PROGRAMME

At this point in the marketing planning process, the marketing plan is almost complete. The final step is to plan how the company will control the plan's implementation. Marketing control keeps both employees and activities on track, so the organisation continues in the direction outlined in the marketing plan. However, some employees in the organisation often view 'control 'as being negative because they tend to fear that the control process will be used to assess their performance and ultimately as a basis for 'punishment'.

In preparing a marketing plan, marketers have to plan for three types of marketing control: annual control, profitability control, and strategic control (Hollensen, 2006):

- **Annual control:** Because marketers generally formulate new marketing plans every year, they require annual plan control to assess the progress of the current year's marketing plan. This includes broad performance measures (e.g., sales results, market share results) to evaluate the company's overall effectiveness. If a company fails to achieve this year's marketing plan objectives, it will have difficulty achieving its long-term goals and mission. Although e.g., 'market share measures' are driven by sales performance, they reflect relative competitive standing. These measures aid senior managers gauge their organisation's competitive strength and situation over time.

- **Profitability control:** This assesses the organisation's progress and performance based on key profitability measures. The precise measures differ from company to company, but they frequently include ROI, contribution margin and net profit margins. Various companies measure the monthly and yearly profit-and-loss results of each product, line, and category, as well as each market or segment and each channel. By comparing profitability results over time, marketers can identify significant strengths and weaknesses and recognize problems and opportunities early. Closely related to profitability control, productivity control is measuring the efficiency of the e.g., the sales force, channels and logistics, and product management. The purpose is to measure profitability improvements through reduced costs or higher yield. As productivity is vital to the bottom line some companies appoint marketing controllers to establish marketing productivity standards. Noticeably, productivity control is connected not only with profitability but with customer relationships as well.

- **Strategic control:** This considers the organisation's effectiveness in managing the marketing function, in managing customer relationships, and in managing social responsibility and ethics issues. Whereas profitability control is applied monthly or more often, strategic control may be applied once or twice a year, or as needed to give top management a clearer picture of the organisation's performance in these strategic areas.

6. EXTERNAL ORIENTATION OF STRATEGIC MARKETING PLAN

In this chapter we focus on the decisive role of culture that will determine to what extent your marketing plan is effective in delivering value to target customers, retaining customers, and creating customers as loyal advocates.

Market orientation, in practice, is underpinned by a customer-centric culture that is shared across all functions and exists at all levels in the business. It has two connected components: a **customer mindset** and a related **set of behaviors** reflected in the decisions and practices that occur in all parts of the organization that affect customer experience and value.

6.1 THE DECISIVE IMPACT OF A CUSTOMER-CENTRIC CULTURE AND THE VITAL ROLE PLAYED BY MARKETING LEADERS

The discipline of modern marketing, first espoused by Philip Kotler, is centred on the philosophy that marketing's primary role is to create value that will satisfy current and future customer needs profitably.

This market-oriented philosophy was first practiced in large businesses by Proctor & Gamble (P&G) through development of product management and brand management organizational structures. The product manager was responsible for leading his or her brand profitably by influencing all parts of the organization to create and deliver products that satisfied customer needs at prices that consumers were prepared to pay. While many other fast-moving-consumer products companies followed P&G's lead, it seems the majority in other industries did not. It is only now in the age of disruption have we seen newer companies like Amazon, Salesforce, Adobe, and Google practice marketing in this sense where the whole organization is geared to creating and delivering value for customers. Also, many long-established companies like Lego, Mercedes-Benz, IKEA, and 3M, have now followed suit and built strong market-oriented businesses.

6.2 MARKET ORIENTATION AS A CULTURE THAT FOCUSES ON THE CUSTOMER

At the heart of market orientation in action is "**engagement**" - engaging customers with your brand, engaging the community with your purpose and engaging your colleagues in the business to deliver the value identified and expected. That process of engagement requires a culture based on a customer mindset and behaviors based on the idea that "**what's best for the customer is ultimately best for the business**". Marketing, traditionally led by CMOs and more recently by Chief Customer Officers has been primarily focused on engaging new customers. More recently their focus has embraced engaging communities. The typical "Achilles 'heel" in marketing has been, and still is, engaging with colleagues and people in the rest of the business and leading activities designed to retain existing customers. There is often not a deep understanding or commitment that customer and community engagement require buy-in and delivery by people in all parts of the business – **it is cultural! Nor do most marketing leaders have a methodology for doing it.**

The importance of market orientation as a **corporate customer culture** was highlighted in an empirical study by Homberg and Pflesser (2000) and the relevance of a culture that focused on customers and considered competitors (Homberg, Grozdanovic and Klarmann, 2007). The relationship between corporate culture, market orientation and innovativeness in Japanese firms was explored by Deshpande, Farley, and Webster

(1993). This work addressed the culture measurement issues and performance outcomes and provided a framework for measurement. A large amount of research has also been conducted to define and measure the relationships between organizational culture and performance - see for example Kotter and Heskett, 1992, Ogbonna and Harris, 2000 and Berson, Oreg and Dvir, 2005.

These studies, as well as observation by practitioners, lead us to conclude that corporate customer culture is a decisive driver of business performance.

While most senior corporate leaders intuitively agree that a customer focus is important to future business performance, they do not fully understand the critical requirement of a customer-focused *culture*. To effectively survive and prosper in today's environment, most organizations must have a **customer culture**. It has become clear that this is imperative to implementation of the strategic marketing plan and creating sustainable growth and profitability.

6.3 A CUSTOMER CULTURE IS NECESSARY TO IMPLEMENT THE MARKETING PLAN

The best marketing plans often fail due to lack of senior management buy-in, limited cross-functional collaboration, and a poor understanding of the business's marketing strategy. This issue worsens when key functions are internally focused and do not recognize or care that their role is to create and deliver value for customers. Marketers must not only embody a customer-centric culture but also lead their company in doing the same. Successful implementation of the marketing plan depends on it, as customer culture is essential to both business and marketing performance.

AKBANK

CASE STUDY
AKBANK

Written by: Beril Alakoç (Chief Brand and Communications Officer, Akbank)

Introduction

In 2021, Akbank, one of Türkiye's most renowned banks, began a transformative journey to revamp its youth marketing strategy. With a rich history of over 76 years, Akbank aimed to bring all its youth-focused initiatives together under one comprehensive strategy. Recognizing the long-term relationship potential of the young people—comprising 15.08%[1] of Türkiye's population—Akbank aimed to support this key segment in navigating economic challenges while building a foundation for future success.

This age group, often skeptical of traditional banks, needed more than financial services; they sought meaningful support and opportunities for personal growth. In response, Akbank redefined its approach by integrating customer segmentation with a focus on value creation. The bank's holistic strategy combined financial services, social responsibility initiatives, and marketing communication efforts, providing young people with real, tangible benefits.

By embracing a 360-degree marketing approach, Akbank not only addressed the immediate financial needs of young people but also empowered them with tools for personal development, creating a lasting, positive impact on their lives. This strategy positioned Akbank as a trusted partner, fostering long-term loyalty while helping youth achieve their goals—whether financial, educational, or social.

Challenges

Akbank faced a significant challenge: How to win over a youth segment that traditionally viewed banks as distant, formal, and disconnected from their realities? A global study showed that young people found dealing with financial institutions more stressful than major life events like divorce. Furthermore, the rise of fintech companies presented a competitive landscape, offering alternatives to traditional banking.

Akbank needed to offer real, tangible benefits that addressed both the financial needs and diverse personal development goals of the youth. Young people sought not just financial products but opportunities for growth, education, and social impact, areas that banks traditionally did not prioritize. Akbank's challenge was to create a comprehensive offering that aligned with these expectations while maintaining a competitive edge in the financial services sector.

---

[1] https://data.tuik.gov.tr/Bulten/Index?p=Istatistiklerle-Genclik-2023-53677#:~:text=Adrese%20Dayal%C4%B1%20N%C3%BCfus%20Kay%C4%B1t%20Si-stemi,872%20bin%2039%20ki%C5%9Fi%20oldu.

250

Youngster's first personal loan at Akbank

Solution

Akbank launched a holistic youth communication strategy, centralizing all its youth-related financial services, social responsibility projects, and marketing efforts. The strategy was built on three core principles:

Understand, Don't Act: Through social listening, Akbank realized that young generation doesn't want brands to 'act young,' but rather to demonstrate that they understand and support their concerns. This was the cornerstone of Akbank's communication strategy.

Offer Tangible Benefits: Economic realities made young people more pragmatic, driving them to seek real, immediate benefits from brands. In response, Akbank developed targeted, impactful projects to meet these needs.

- One in five young people is classified as "neither in employment nor education" (NEET)2.

- While 36% of young people are optimistic about their prospects, 39% believe their circumstances won't improve, and about a quarter remain undecided2.

Embrace Diversity: The strategy underscored Akbank's commitment to recognizing the individuality and diverse aspirations of young people. By promoting inclusivity and acknowledging the unique perspectives within this demographic, Akbank ensured its messaging resonated with a wide range of youth experiences and ambitions.

Young people place the highest importance on values like "honesty," "equality," and "defending human rights[2].

Creative Approach

Under the creative vision of Akbank's youth communication strategy, all initiatives were unified under a single, overarching campaign featuring Serenay Sarıkaya as the brand ambassador and the slogan "Aklın Yolu Çok" (Wisdom Takes Many Paths). This creative solution was not confined to just the financial aspects or university students but encompassed the entire youth engagement strategy, ensuring a cohesive and impactful connection with the target demographic.

- Serenay Sarıkaya, a prominent and relatable figure for young people, highlighted tailored financial products that addressed the unique needs of students, such as interest-free loans and exclusive benefits on digital platforms.

- The campaign's tagline, "Aklın Yolu Çok" reflected Akbank's commitment to celebrating the individuality of young people. Using visually striking kaleidoscopic imagery, the campaign highlighted the diverse aspirations of youth and how Akbank supported these through both financial and social means. This creative approach resonated deeply with the target audience.

- To reach the target audience, Akbank implemented a data-driven media strategy focused on the media habits of young people, utilizing television, mobile games, TikTok, and other youth-oriented platforms. This integrated approach resulted in over 1 billion impressions.

1. Financial Solutions

Akbank introduced several youth-centric financial products that directly addressed the needs and challenges of young people.

---

[2] https://konda.com.tr/uploads/genclik-ve-toplumsal-deg-erler-arastirma-raporu-4a14084372e7295eeefbb7da9136a27a7414c5b6222a12e294c62d1c7ce0a955.pdf

- Üniversiteli Akbanklı Program (Akbank's University Student Program): This initiative offered special benefits, such as interest-free loans on weekends and exclusive campaigns for the Axess Öğrenci Kartı (Student Card), making it easier for students to manage their financials.

- İlk Kredim (Youngsters' First Loan): This credit option, specifically designed for young people, provided a three-year, no-fee personal loan.

- Akbank's youth-oriented, innovative services also include free EFT/Transfer services and shared ATM access, providing hassle-free banking. To further support students, Akbank offers a 0% interest rate on overdraft accounts during weekends, giving them a flexible financial cushion. With the Axess Öğrenci Kartı (Student Card), students can earn up to 400 TL in cashback rewards. Additionally, Akbank provides a 50% refund on digital platform memberships, offering young customers valuable savings on everyday digital services."

The most notable achievement of the marketing campaigns was the 41% increase in Akbank's youth customer base, with the bank gaining 576,000 new young customers throughout the year in 2023. This surge not only surpassed expectations but also elevated the overall share of youth within Akbank's total customer segment from 15% to 17%. The Üniversiteli Akbanklı program played a pivotal role, enrolling 71,000 new students. İlk Kredim was used 45,000 times in 2023, representing a 206% increase over the previous year. In addition, Axess Öğrenci Kartı sales saw a dramatic 94% increase, reaching 16,000 units in 2023.

2. Social Solutions:

a- Education:

- Akbank Gençlik Akademisi (Akbank Youth Academy)

  Recognizing the importance of education and professional growth, Akbank launched the Akbank Gençlik Akademisi in 2021. This platform was designed to equip young people with the skills they need for the future, focusing on leadership, financial literacy, entrepreneurship, and personal development.

  By fostering both financial literacy and entrepreneurial thinking, the program aligned perfectly with the aspirations of young people, many of whom value opportunities for growth beyond the classroom. The academy also provided mentorship programs, pairing young participants with experienced professionals who could guide them through the early stages of their careers.

  Since its foundation the Akbank Gençlik Akademisi has been especially successful, reaching over 170,000 students across all 208 universities in the country. Participation increased by 116%, with 33,000 students benefiting from a wide range of educational programs, in 2023 compared to the previous year.

b- Volunteerism:

- Şehrin İyi Hali (The Good State of the City)

  Akbank is an institution known for its long-lasting and inspiring social benefit initiatives that contribute to society and drive change. The bank's social benefit efforts focus on four main areas: culture and arts, entrepreneurship, education, and volunteerism.

Akbank's Şehrin İyi Hali project was a key component in bridging the gap between the bank and youth through volunteerism. The program, launched in 2012, encourages young people to get involved in social responsibility initiatives. By offering them the opportunity to work with various NGOs, Akbank enabled them to make tangible contributions to society while fostering a sense of responsibility. Over the years, Şehrin İyi Hali has attracted more than 22,000 young volunteers.

In 2024, Akbank further expanded the initiative by organizing university campus tours and workshops designed to raise awareness about volunteerism and the value of giving back to society. The events, enriched with contributions from prominent figures serve to engage more young people across Türkiye . The program fosters a sense of community and provides young people with an avenue to develop leadership and organizational skills.

c- Art

- **Digital Art on Campus:**

Akbank continues to foster a deep appreciation for arts and culture within the community. Through initiatives that reach hundreds of art enthusiasts, Akbank maintains its pioneering role in promoting and expanding contemporary art in Türkiye. As one of the leading supporters of digital art, Akbank extends its efforts to university campuses with the "Digital Art on Campus" program. This initiative features digital art exhibitions, talks, film screenings, and workshops at various universities across Türkiye, aiming to connect students with prominent national and international digital artists.

- **Contemporary Art Education Program for Children and Youth**

The "Contemporary Art Education Program for Children and Youth," held at Akbank Art Beyoğlu, offers middle and high school students an opportunity to engage closely with contemporary artworks in gallery settings. The program fosters creativity and encourages artistic, cultural, and social exploration. Conducted in three stages, it combines both theoretical and practical components, allowing students to experience and deepen their understanding of contemporary art.

d – Entrepreneurship:

Akbank LAB, the bank's dedicated innovation and entrepreneurship hub, drives cutting-edge projects and solutions. It also provides programs tailored specifically for young people within this framework.

- **Akbank on Campus**

Through the "Akbank on Campus" competition, part of the Akbank Gençlik Akademisi, Akbank empowers young people to bring their projects to life in the fields of Sustainability and Social Impact, Innovation and Entrepreneurship, and Digital and Technology. Launched in 2022 and continuing into 2024, the program supports university clubs with training and mentorship. In 2023, students developed solutions for campus challenges, competing in these categories, with the top three projects awarded based on jury evaluations.

- **CaseCampus Bootcamp Live**

The CaseCampus Bootcamp Live Program, in partnership with Endeavor Türkiye, targets aspiring entrepreneurs. Each year, 75 young participants, including undergraduates, postgraduates, and recent graduates under 30, engage with successful entrepreneurs, academics, and investors. The program features case studies, workshops, and networking opportunities, and has connected with over 600 students to date.

- **StartUpCampus Program**

  Since 2018, Akbank and Endeavor Türkiye have collaborated on the StartUpCampus Program, rebranded as "Boost the Future" in 2021. This 10-week online program supports 12 technology entrepreneurs annually, offering training and mentoring through Akbank LAB to help scale their businesses and expand globally.

Fostering Resilience and Growth: Akbank's Commitment to Young People and Sustainability

Sustainability Approach:

When examining the United Nations Sustainable Development Goals (SDGs), it's clear that they address broader human-centered issues like decent work, economic growth, gender equality, and quality education, beyond just environmental concerns. Akbank views sustainability as a strategy that impacts all areas of life, not just emissions.

Under this strategy, Akbank supports sustainability through initiatives such as sustainable finance tools, mentorship for women entrepreneurs, Akbank Gençlik Akademisi, long-term support for the arts, and volunteerism. As part of this strategic approach, Akbank prioritizes youth-focused programs, empowering young people in innovation, entrepreneurship, and leadership.

Looking ahead, Akbank aims to further promote sustainable living across Türkiye with inclusive initiatives and communication.

- **Güzel Yarınlar Hareketi (Bright Tomorrows Initiative): A Corporate Social Responsibility Initiative Supporting Young People in Earthquake-Affected Regions**

  In 2023, Türkiye experienced one of the most devastating disasters in its history, as earthquakes struck various regions, leaving widespread destruction in their wake. Amidst this tragedy, the youth in the region faced not only physical but also psychological and educational challenges.

  In response to the earthquakes, Akbank, in partnership with TOG (Toplum Gönüllüleri Vakfı / Community Volunteers Foundation), launched the Güzel Yarınlar Hareketi to support young people in the five most affected cities. Recognizing the young's needs, Akbank and TOG designed a program that combined elements of education, technology, creativity, and psycho-social support to help them rebuild their futures.

  Over the course of one year, Akbank and TOG organized 690 workshops and nearly 1,200 hours of activities. These efforts reached 10,220 young participants, exceeding the initial target of 10,000.

  According to the Impact Monitoring and Evaluation Report of the Güzel Yarınlar Hareketi, the initiative positively influenced young people's outlook on the future. Participants showed improvements in initiative-taking and creativity, with a strengthened sense of "I can do it." The majority of participants left the centers feeling happy and peaceful, with 97.7% reporting positive emotions.

- **Dönüşümde Gelecek Var (The Future in Transformation): A CSR Initiative for Sustainability Through Upcycling and Vocational Training**

255

In addition to its youth engagement efforts, Akbank initiated a major sustainability project called Dönüşümde Gelecek Var. This project focused on upcycling office furniture from Akbank's headquarters and transforming it into functional items for kindergartens and schools in earthquake-affected regions.

The project had two core components:

- Upcycling for Schools: Rather than discarding old office furniture, Akbank repurposed these items into desks, bookshelves, and other essential furniture for schools in the earthquake-stricken regions. This approach not only reduced waste but also provided much-needed resources for communities in recovery.

- Vocational Training for Youth: Akbank partnered with a vocational high school in the region (İskenderun Mesleki ve Teknik Anadolu Lisesi) to train students in upcycling techniques. The bank established a workshop where students, alongside their teachers, used these techniques to build furniture for kindergarten children. These students gained valuable skills in sustainable manufacturing, learning how to transform discarded materials into high-quality products.

Dönüşümde Gelecek Var upcycled over 6700 pieces of furniture, which were donated to 415 schools. The project is expected to reach 650 schools and benefit nearly 290,000 students. This initiative not only demonstrated Akbank's commitment to sustainability but also provided young vocational students with hands-on experience in circular economy practices.

Strengthened Brand Perception

Akbank's efforts to align its brand with the values and needs of young people resulted in a marked improvement in youth perception scores. In 2023, market research revealed that the statement "Akbank is a bank that stands by young people" achieved a score of 36, putting the bank 7 points ahead of its closest competitor. This improved brand perception is a testament to Akbank's strategic approach to building trust and loyalty among the youth demographic[3].

---

[3] Future Bright, Reklam ve Marka Sağlığı Araştırması (2023). FY- Genç Hedef Kitle 18 – 25

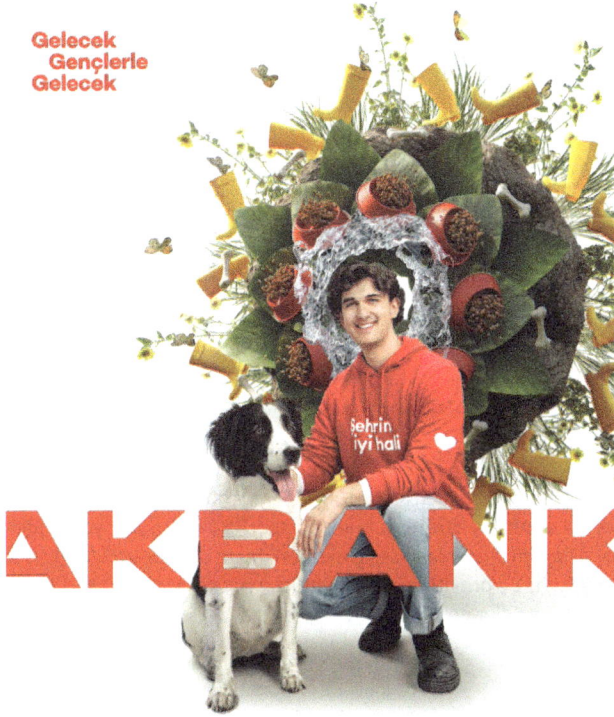

Gelecek
Gençlerle
Gelecek

AKBANK

Wisdom has many paths, my path is goodness

For volunteering projects

🔍 Şehrin İyi Hali | 🎤

Conclusion

Akbank's comprehensive youth engagement and sustainability strategy successfully addressed the challenges of connecting with a discerning and often skeptical youth demographic. By fostering long-term loyalty and delivering tangible value, the bank created mutual benefits for both its business and the young people it serves. Through tailored financial products, educational opportunities, and socially responsible initiatives, Akbank has positioned itself as a trusted partner for the next generation. At the same time, Akbank's marketing and communication efforts amplified the voices of young people, giving them visibility and a platform to be heard across society. These initiatives instilled hope and confidence in the youth, positioning Akbank as a bank that not only supports but actively empowers the next generation.

Questions to Stimulate Discussion

1.   **What were the most pressing needs of young people?**

Young people were primarily concerned with financial independence, personal growth, and access to opportunities. However, they often faced societal biases that unfairly portrayed them as unfocused or unrealistic in their aspirations. Despite these stereotypes, the reality is that young minds are full of innovative ideas and boundless dreams, but their ambitions are often constrained by a lack of resources.

2. Why is it crucial to address the challenges young people face?

With young people making up 15.5% of the population, they represent both a significant current consumer base and the future of the economy. Addressing their challenges—like financial instability and limited opportunities for personal growth—is key to building long-term loyalty. By helping them overcome these obstacles, brands like Akbank can empower them to succeed, shaping a generation that will drive future innovation and economic progress.

3. What were the key solutions Akbank implemented to engage with young people, and why were they effective?

By leveraging key marketing principles such as customer segmentation, value creation, and relationship marketing, Akbank developed a unified strategy tailored specifically to the youth demographic. The bank introduced initiatives offering interest-free loans, tailored financial products, and educational programs designed to empower the youth. By providing them with the necessary tools and opportunities, Akbank not only addressed their immediate financial and developmental needs but also stood by their side, enabling them to realize their full potential.

Case Highlights

Akbank's youth engagement and sustainability strategy successfully addressed the needs of the young people by consolidating existing initiatives and introducing new ones under a unified framework.

The Üniversiteli Akbanklı program provided practical financial solutions, such as interest-free loans and exclusive benefits on digital platforms, contributing to a 41% increase in the youth customer base. Akbank Gençlik Akademisi programs saw a 116% rise in participation in 2023 and have supported more than 170,000 students with leadership and vocational skills over the past three years. The Şehrin İyi Hali initiative attracted over 22,000 young volunteers, fostering a sense of community and social responsibility. In response to the 2023 earthquakes, the Güzel Yarınlar Hareketi supported more than 10,000 young people in disaster-affected regions through educational and creative workshops. Additionally, the Dönüşümde Gelecek Var project upcycled over 5,300 pieces of furniture for schools, providing vocational students with hands-on experience in sustainability practices. Through various initiatives, ranging from digital arts to entrepreneurship, Akbank demonstrated its commitment to sustainability with a strong focus on empowering young people.

By addressing both the financial and social needs of young people, Akbank also challenged societal biases that often portray youth as disengaged or unfocused. Akbank recognized that their ambitions are vast, though often limited by a lack of resources. By offering tangible opportunities and support, Akbank helped break down these barriers, positioning itself as a committed partner in their growth and success.

As a result, these initiatives strengthened Akbank's brand perception and amplified the voices of young people. Market research shows that young people now view Akbank as a bank that supports their needs by a score of 36, positioning it 7 points ahead of its competitors. By addressing both their immediate needs and long-term aspirations, Akbank has instilled hope and confidence in the next generation.

6.3.1 WHAT IS A CUSTOMER CULTURE?

" I came to see, in my time at IBM, that culture isn't just one aspect of the game – it is the game. In the end an organization is nothing more than the collective capacity of its people to create value." Lou Gerstner, former CEO of IBM

The authors conducted extensive research to find out why so many organizations are not customer focused. They found that when company leaders were asked if they were customer focused, most said "yes, of course, it is in our vision". When they asked what they meant by customer focus and how did it apply in their organizations there were many different answers – good customer service, well targeted offers to market segments, quick handling of customer complaints. It was clear that different people in the same organizations and across businesses had a different view as to what customer focus means. Also, there was a view that it applies specifically to frontline staff. There was a clear need to be able to define it, make it tangible and actionable.

First, we must distinguish between customer focus and customer culture. The term *customer focus* means different things to different people. It ranges in its meaning from "good customer service" across a spectrum to "ensuring that the whole organization, and not just frontline service staff, puts its customers first"— meaning understanding customers 'needs and doing what is right for the customer. In this last meaning, every department and every employee should share the same customer-focused vision. For this to occur, an organization must have a *culture* based on the belief that *what's best for the customer is best for the business*. It is this meaning of customer focus we call *customer culture*. In fact, to have real customer focus, you *must* have a customer culture.

Toyota embodies this thinking and has developed customer culture practices over many years. In its Lexus division it places great emphasis on having all staff focus on the customer's journey. What does this mean in practice? A great example comes from outlier cases that demonstrate just how far Lexus would go to make sure customers were satisfied. On rare occasions in Europe, families travelling in the French Alps have been stranded due to mechanical breakdown. Can you imagine what it would be like to breakdown in the middle of a mountain range? No doubt these families would be anxious for their safety and frustrated by the failure of their luxury vehicle. So, what was Lexus's answer to these extreme moments of truth? Lexus arranged to collect them by helicopter to take them to their destination. They understand that it is not about the car, it is about getting its customers to where they planned to be. As one insider said: "yes, of course we will fix the car, but our first priority is to ensure our customers get to their destination safely and on time."

Second, customer culture needs to be embedded in people and teams through orientation and induction, leadership, processes, rewards, key performance measures, a common language, and an expected way of doing things. What's more, customer culture comprises several practice disciplines—a shared set of behaviors and skills that can be developed, refined, and practiced, becoming habits that lead to better personal and business results.

Third, customer culture does not mean that a company responds to any and every request for improvements or new products and services that any and all customers say they want. This is usually impractical and unprofitable and does not allow the firm to focus on the customers it can best serve with superior value. **This is the reason marketing plans are developed**. Every business must have a clear strategy, value proposition, and target customers whose needs are understood and for whom superior value and experience are delivered. A strong customer culture is one that is clearly aligned to the company's marketing strategy and plan so that all managers and staff understand and respond to the current and future needs of targeted customers. It includes the clarity and skills to know when specific customers 'needs can't be met by the business and can better be served by competitors and to help customers to find a solution elsewhere. A customer culture is one in which people in a business interact with both customers and noncustomers in a way that shows they care—either by solving customers 'problems or by referring noncustomers to other companies that can meet their needs better.

Customer culture embodies shared values across the entire business that translates into behaviors in all functions that are aligned and committed to creating superior value for customers in a profitable way. A strong customer culture delivers a customer experience that is consistently excellent along the whole service chain. The ultimate aim is to have the customers make your business the centre for everything they do for your particular offering. Then your customers will be advocates of your business and your products and services. You won't have a sustainable organization unless you build the right culture—a *customer culture*.

Marketing has a pivotal role in organizational sustainability. The methodology and measurement tool that follows makes customer culture tangible and actionable. It acts as a valuable guide for marketing leaders to implement their strategies and lead organizational sustainability.

6.3.2 HOW CAN WE MAKE CUSTOMER CULTURE TANGIBLE AND ACTIONABLE?

The authors' research program was built on the prior work of empirical studies by market orientation academics and corporate culture researchers. It was built on the premise, supported by convincing evidence, that a strong customer culture drives positive future business performance. The authors set out to measure customer culture by staff behaviors with respect to customers – often described as, "What we do around here."

Figure 6.1 depicts customer-centric mindset and behaviors as the foundation for creating positive customer experiences that, in turn, provide customer satisfaction, loyalty and advocacy. These together drive sustainable revenue growth and profitability.

Key Metrics

Financials — BUSINESS PERFORMANCE

Customer Satisfaction Score
Net Promoter Score — CUSTOMER LOYALTY AND ADVOCACY

Customer Retention — CUSTOMER EXPERIENCE

Customer Culture Measurement
Market Responsiveness Index
Employee Engagement — CUSTOMER CULTURE
Customer Centric Mindset ➡ Customer Centric Behaviors ➡ Customer Centric Processes

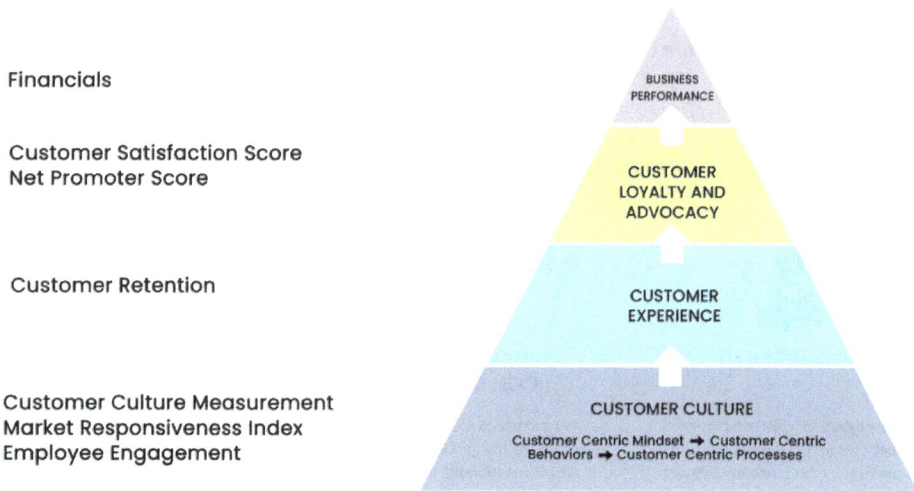

Figure 6.1: Customer Centric Behaviors Drive Customer Experience
Loyalty and Profitable Growth.

In our research we wanted to identify the tangible customer culture factors and their links to business results. We researched more than 100 companies and conducted quantitative and qualitative analysis to identify valid links.

The authors 'research found eight critical cultural disciplines of customer culture. These determine if a business can create customer advocates and win in the marketplace. They expose the risks that a company's capabilities will not support its strategy. These disciplines are also required to effectively implement the strategic marketing plan. The names given to these 8 disciplines and their associated behavior summaries are shown in Figures 6.2 and 6.3.

External Drivers: These behaviours lead to an understanding of "the market."

CUSTOMER INSIGHT
This measures the extent to which employees monitor, understand, and act on current customer needs and satisfaction.

CUSTOMER FORESIGHT
This measures the extent to which employees anticipate customer needs, recognize unspoken needs, consider future needs and take action to satisfy them.

COMPETITOR INSIGHT
This measures the extent to which employees monitor, understand, and act on current competitor activities and take action to incorporate these in their actions to improve customer experience.

COMPETITOR FORESIGHT
This measures the extent to which employees identify and consider possible future competitors and how they might affect the value that will be offered in the future.

PERIPHERAL VISION
The extent to which employees monitor understand and respond to trends in the larger environment (Political, Economic, Social, Technological, Environmental and Legal).

Figure 6.2: Five Externally Oriented Practice Disciplines.

Internal Enablers
These behaviours leverage employee action to successfully address customers needs

EMPOWERMENT
The extent to which employees are able to make decisions that are best for the customer without the explicit approval of senior leaders.

CROSS-FUNCTIONAL COLLABORATION
This measures the extent to which employees interact and collaborate cross—functionally. This includes spending time with people from other work groups, taking a cross—functional perspective, sharing information, and inviting contributions.

STRATEGIC ALIGNMENT
This measures the extent to which employees understand, attend to, and enact the vision, mission, objectives and strategic direction of the company in their day—to—day activities, specifically focusing on the customer.

Figure 6.3: Three Internally Enabling Practice Disciplines.

Customer culture is implemented through these 8 best practice disciplines—a set of behaviors and skills that can be developed, refined, and practiced, to become habits that lead to better personal and business results. The next section describes each of the 5 externally oriented disciplines and how they underpin the strategic marketing plan.

6.4 TYING THE 5 EXTERNALLY ORIENTED PRACTICES TO THE MARKETING PLAN

Each of these practice disciplines support the implementation of the strategic marketing plan.

6.4.1 THE CUSTOMER INSIGHT DISCIPLINE

For marketers this is at the heart of their strategies. The questions that need to be addressed and answered in the marketing plan should include:

Do we understand our current customers`needs? Do we know how satisfied or dissatisfied they are with our products or services? Do we act on this knowledge? Do we communicate to customers our actions resulting from their feedback?

Mercedes Benz asked customers a different question from the norm (What do you think of Mercedes Benz?) to obtain feedback on their needs by reversing the question and asking: "What do you think Mercedes Benz thinks of you?" Answers from customers brought new actionable feedback.

Marketing leaders have an important role to play in encouraging people in support functions like IT, HR and finance to gain experience with customers as a prompt for changes that can be made to enhance customer value and experience.

6.4.2 THE CUSTOMER FORESIGHT DISCIPLINE

This second customer discipline relates to a company's ability to obtain new customers profitably and anticipate future needs. Your company's ability to attract new customers is based on its customer foresight and its willingness and ability to embrace new ways of providing service. Will it lead the market by launching new services before customers recognize their own changing needs? The questions that need to be addressed and answered in the marketing plan should include:

Do we gather information on potential customers? Do we target them based on our opportunity for competitive advantage? Do we understand and invest in meeting future needs of prospective customers? Do we understand and act on needs that customer can`t express?

In the early 2000s Starbucks in the US could see the coming digital mobile revolution and was one of the first retail food companies to provide an App that would enable consumers to order their coffee before arriving at the shop. This led to club membership and enabled Starbucks to obtain data on customer preferences, strengthen customer relationships, attract new customers, and provide loyalty benefits.

Marketing has a leading role in identifying future needs and sharing foresight around who the future customers will be and what they will need.

6.4.3 THE COMPETITOR INSIGHT DISCIPLINE

Your company's understanding of its customers 'alternatives is crucial to its ability to compete. Competitor insight is reflected in workforce behaviors and prevalent activities that give the company a deep and dynamic understanding of its current competitors. Without these strong drivers, the company cannot stay in touch with its competitors 'strategies and is in danger of losing market share and profitability.

The questions that need to be addressed and answered in the marketing plan should include:

Do we as a company monitor, understand, and respond to our competitors 'strengths and weaknesses? Do we factor in competitors 'current strategies into our own strategies? Do we all understand how they contribute to the firm 's current value proposition and competitive advantage, and do we act to support it?

Virgin – Many of the Virgin businesses have arisen from their insight into markets where competitors have been poorly servicing customers. Virgin Airlines was launched at a time when US airlines and British airlines were renowned for bad customer experiences. A deep understanding of what value airlines are providing and what value consumers want was key to a successfully differentiated Virgin Airlines business based on customer service.

Marketing leaders make a vital contribution through development of value propositions that consider how the company 's offer is different and superior for particular customers. This needs to be understood by people in all parts of the business in terms of how they contribute.

6.4.4 THE COMPETITOR FORESIGHT DISCIPLINE

Competitor foresight relates to a company's ability to foresee new competitors that could impact its markets in the future. New innovative competitors have an impact on uncovering latent needs of customers and influencing their perception of their future needs. The questions that need to be addressed and answered in the marketing plan should include:

Do we consider potential competitors when making decisions about customers? Do we identify market shifts in order to foresee potential competitors? Do we all contribute to competitive intelligence relating to potential new competitors and how they might affect future customer needs?

There are many examples of technology companies that successfully pre-empt future competition by taking over emerging competitors or by introducing a new service before competitors. Google and Facebook are examples. Toyota with its early Hybrid cars pre-empted future competitors within its industry. However, Tesla has been the innovator for battery powered vehicles.

Marketing leaders play a key role in sharing possible future competitive scenarios as an input for employees in all functions to recognize the need for agility and new capability requirements to compete for the future.

6.4.5 THE PERIPHERAL VISION DISCIPLINE

Peripheral Vision, reflected in workforce behaviors, gives the company a deep and dynamic understanding of its broader external environment. Without these strong drivers, the company will miss opportunities and risk the loss of customers due to market and industry shifts. Changes in technology, economic conditions, government policies, and society all impact current and future customer needs. The questions that need to be addressed and answered in the marketing plan should include:

Do we monitor, understand, and respond to the political, economic, social, technological, and natural envi-ronment trends emerging on the periphery that could affect its customers and its business? Are all staff members encouraged to scan their respective fields of expertise for new ideas relevant to the changing ex-ternal environment? Do we act on this flow of new ideas?

Vodafone – As a mobile telecommunications company, Vodafone saw the merging of banking and mobile communications in Kenya and India where people stored and transferred their money on their mobile phones. As the banking markets became deregulated in these countries Vodafone applied for banking li-censes so they could service this growing market.

Marketing leaders can provide important inputs to the strategic planning process that identify the risks and opportunities to the business from pending external changes.

6.4.5.1 Tying the 3 Internally Enabling Practices to the Marketing Plan

The three internally enabling disciplines—*empowerment, cross-functional collaboration,* and *strategic align-ment* – are vital to the capability of all functions in the business to implement the strategic marketing plan. The plan needs to include how these practices will be strengthened to ensure the plan is effectively imple-mented.

Without strengths in these practice disciplines, the effective implementation of the plan will be compromised.

6.4.6 THE EMPOWERMENT DISCIPLINE

When we measure the customer-centric culture of organizations around the world, one of the recurring themes is a low score on "empowerment". Lack of empowerment – real or perceived – has a huge impact on the ability of frontline staff to solve a customer's problem and on support staff to help frontline staff do it easily and quickly. Lack of empowerment also has a big impact on costs and is seen in many ways – dupli-cation of work, mixed communication to customers, bottlenecks and slowdowns in customer service, and new product introductions - just to name a few.

For staff to be empowered to solve customer problems or rapidly respond to customers 'requests a business needs a culture that encourages staff to be accountable for ensuring a solution for the customer is delivered.

The questions that need to be addressed and answered in the marketing plan should include:

Are we empowered to make decisions that are best for the customer without the explicit approval of senior leaders? Can we challenge the way things are done for customers when we see a better way? Do we have to wait too long for approvals for improvements that will benefit customers or solve a particular customer's problem? Can we propose new ideas that will benefit customers?

There are good examples of empowerment in the hospitality industry. Disney and Ritz Carlton are great examples of companies where employees operate with a culture of making sure customers are happy and being empowered to quickly rectify any customer problems. We see this not only in frontline employees but also employees in support functions like housekeeping, maintenance, and accounts.

Marketing leaders can play an important role in encouraging others in different functions to suggest changes that can deliver greater value for customers.

6.4.7 THE CROSS-FUNCTIONAL COLLABORATION DISCIPLINE

Collaboration is another trait of workforce behavior that enables a strong customer culture and makes it possible for the company to transform the information generated by the externally oriented disciplines into value for customers and shareholders. Without strong cross-functional collaboration across a business, valuable information is squandered, and business opportunities are lost. Also, the impact of value delivered to customers is weakened. The questions that need to be addressed and answered in the marketing plan should include:

Do we in marketing with colleagues from different work groups share information and work together? Are we working cross-functionally to solve customer problems and deliver better service to customers? Are mechanisms in place to encourage cross-fertilization of ideas, practices, and value creation? Do people in the business receive individual recognition for initiating end-to-end solutions for the customer?

IKEA and LEGO are companies that have built their culture on strong cross-function teamwork and collaboration. They both foster cross-functional collaboration to ensure their products and services are effectively delivered to markets around the world.

This is an area where marketing leaders can improve by sharing customer insights, seeking ideas from people in other functions that can enhance customer experience and create more meaning for those in other functions as to why and how a customer-centred approach helps them and the business.

6.4.8 THE STRATEGIC ALIGNMENT DISCIPLINE

The final discipline of workforce behavior that enables a strong customer culture and makes it possible for the company to create and deliver value for customers and shareholders is its level of internal alignment. Without strong alignment within a business, there are inefficiencies that affect customers and lack of employee engagement that creates inconsistency and affects business performance and customer satisfaction. The questions that need to be addressed and answered in the marketing plan should include:

Is the firm's strategic direction discussed regularly in marketing and with all employees? How quickly are work group priorities changed when the firm's strategic plans change? Do we in marketing fully understand and buy in to the company's vision and values and see how it relates to us personally and how we work? Can all people in the business tell you how they are working differently to implement a customer-focused strategy?

Salesforce.com has a vision to help its customers succeed and values that align employees around that vision. Alignment is reinforced through its Dream force conferences held around the world where customers and their successes are stars of the show and large numbers of staff attend to interact with and listen to customers. Salesforce also reinforces alignment through visual cues in most meeting rooms and around its many buildings.

Marketing leaders have a vital role to play in helping people in all business functions understand the marketing and customer strategy and how they can support it more directly through stronger strategic alignment.

These eight disciplines represent behavioral disciplines that at their best, enable organizations to become number 1 in their markets. They can place companies where Amazon and Google are now placed – in a class of their own representing the yardstick of the most customer-centric and admirable companies in the world – as perceived by their customers and the community at large. This brings with it superior business performance.

Marketing leaders have a critical role to play in promoting customer culture and engaging all employees across the business to deliver better value for customers. They can provide the links between vision, values, strategy and customers.

6.5 HOW DO THESE 8 DISCIPLINES DRIVE BUSINESS PERFORMANCE?

These disciplines have a decisive impact on sales growth, profit growth, profitability, customer satisfaction, new-product success, and innovation. Figure 6.4 shows each discipline is a driver of particular business performance outcomes. The check marks in Figure 4 indicate validated quantitative relationships between the disciplines and business performance metrics. These customer culture disciplines predict better, sustainable business results. Each drives measurable improvements in sales, profitability, innovation and new-product or new-service success.

Disciplines	Customer Satisfaction	Innovation	New Product Success	Profit Growth	Profitability	Sale Revenue Growth
Customer Insight	✓	✓	✓			✓
Customer Foresight		✓				
Competitor Insight				✓	✓	✓
Competitor Foresight	✓	✓				
Peripheral Vision		✓				
Empowerment	✓	✓				
Cross-functional Collaboration	✓	✓	✓	✓	✓	✓
Strategic Alignment	✓	✓	✓	✓	✓	✓

Figure 6.4: Customer Culture Drivers of Business Outcomes.

6.6 HOW CAN WE MEASURE OUR LEVEL OF CUSTOMER CULTURE?

" *What's measured improves."* **Peter Drucker**

This applies to customer culture. No matter where you stand on the customer culture spectrum, start by measuring and benchmarking where you are now.

At the same time a measurement tool was created called the *Market Responsiveness Index (MRI)* to enable organizations to be benchmarked against the best – like Amazon, Virgin, Google, and Salesforce. Figure 6.5 shows a 100% score in each of the 8 disciplines representing the position a company would be if it was higher in all disciplines than all companies in our database – a hypothetical situation because we see different companies topping our database in different disciplines.

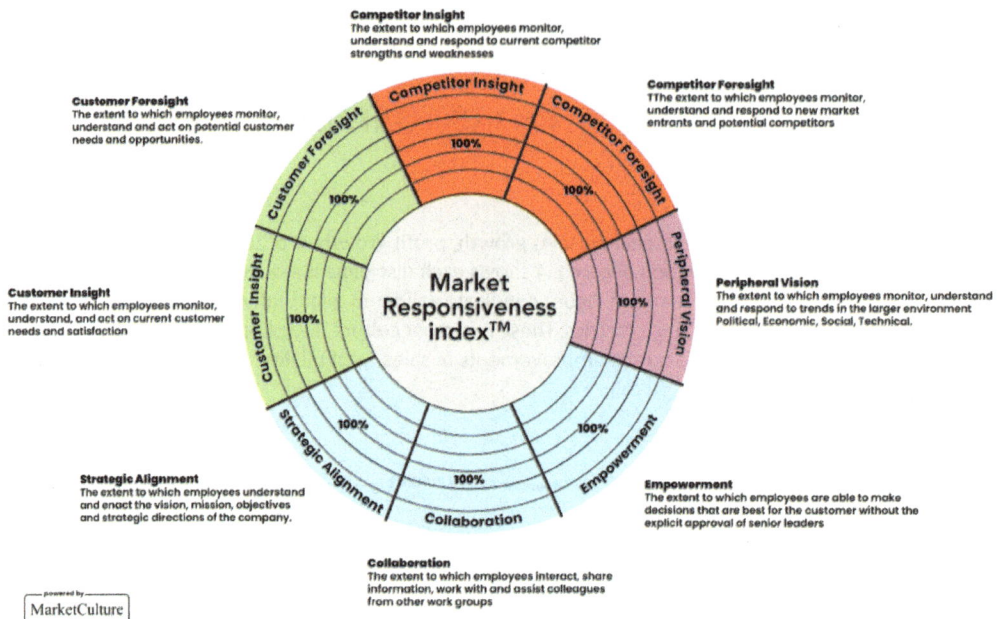

Competitor Insight
The extent to which employees monitor, understand and respond to current competitor strengths and weaknesses

Customer Foresight
The extent to which employees monitor, understand and act on potential customer needs and opportunities.

Competitor Foresight
TThe extent to which employees monitor, understand and respond to new market entrants and potential competitors

Customer Insight
The extent to which employees monitor, understand, and act on current customer needs and satisfaction

Peripheral Vision
The extent to which employees monitor, understand and respond to trends in the larger environment Political, Economic, Social, Technical.

Strategic Alignment
The extent to which employees understand and enact the vision, mission, objectives and strategic directions of the company.

Empowerment
The extent to which employees are able to make decisions that are best for the customer without the explicit approval of senior leaders

Collaboration
The extent to which employees interact, share information, work with and assist colleagues from other work groups

Figure 6.5: The 8 Disciplines of a Customer Culture.

By definition, a company's relative strengths and weaknesses exist only in comparison to those of its competitors. From our research we developed a measurement tool to benchmark a company's customer culture relative to a database of now more than 750 companies and more than 1000 business units of organizations in the Americas, UK, Europe, Middle East, Africa, and Asia/Pacific. This measures a business's customer cultural capabilities on the 8 disciplines, provides a risk assessment in relation to its strategy, and gives guidelines for action to strengthen the business's customer culture. **By taking this reality check business leaders can assess the ability that the organization has to implement its strategic marketing plan.**

• **The Market Responsiveness Index (MRI)** tool provides benchmarks as percentiles (similar to reported SAT results used by universities for student assessments) rather than raw scores on each of the eight cultural disciplines. The MRI measurement tool uses a survey assessment completed by all relevant staff in a company or in one or more business units. The result is a snapshot of where the overall company and each business unit stand compared with a large number of other businesses. It measures the behavioral heartbeat of the organization and the degree to which it has a customer culture and can respond to its markets and proactively engage market shifts.

The database includes businesses covering many industries that range from low to high customer culture on these 8 disciplines. The MRI may tell you, for example, that your company's ability to monitor, understand, and respond to its competitors 'strengths and weaknesses is in the 82nd percentile (better than four-fifths) of all companies in the benchmark database. This may be considered a relative strength, whereas customer insight at the 60th percentile could be improved significantly by introducing behaviors and processes designed to improve current customers 'experiences with your business.

Even in companies that have very strong customer cultures there is always room for improvement in one or more disciplines. Also, a company's profile is a moving target as businesses continue to improve and strengthen their customer culture.

6.7 WHAT DO HIGH PERFORMERS AND LOW PERFORMERS LOOK LIKE?

Figure 6.6 shows an example of the Market Responsiveness Index results of two real companies—one for a high-performing business, and the other for a low performer. The more shading reflects a stronger customer culture that drives better business performance. The *low-performing business* (depicted on the right side of Figure.6 6) shows low benchmarked scores on customer disciplines being the 34th percentile on customer insight and 4th percentile on customer foresight, which indicates significant risk on those factors.

Collaboration is above average at the 60th percentile, but very low scores on the other disciplines indicate a business that is predominantly internally focused. It would have many more customer detractors than advocates. It would have no competitive resilience and would experience declining profit margins and profitability if left unchanged.

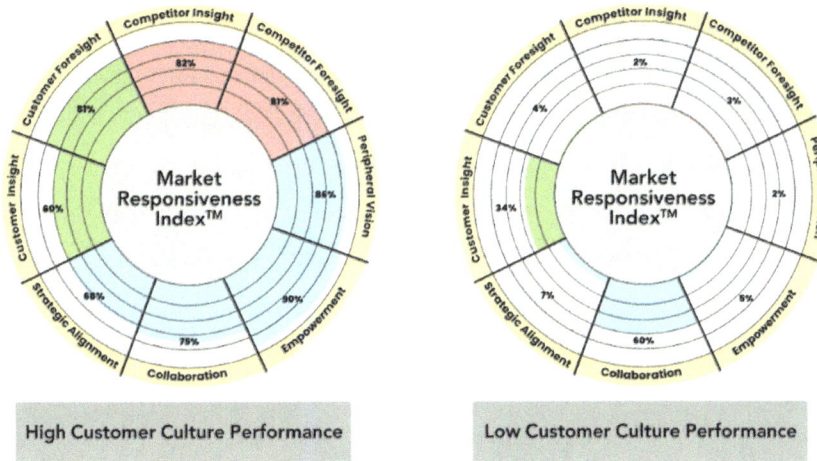

Figure 6.6: Profiles of 2 Businesses: High Performer (left) and Low Performer (right).

It is at high risk of losing customers and not having the capability of acquiring new ones profitably. Its cultural capability is completely unaligned with its strategy and its likelihood of achieving its objectives is very low.

The high-performer business is a manufacturer of medical devices and is the undisputed leader in its market. Prior to benchmarking it reported higher than average performance than its competitors in terms of sales and profit growth, and profitability for the previous three years. In the Figure 6.6 image on the left it shows this firm is relatively strong on all elements of customer culture which links to a sustainable competitive advantage. This business is highly likely to outperform its competitors for the foreseeable future if it maintains or adds to its customer culture strengths. It's one area of vulnerability may be customer insight that indicates a lesser emphasis on the needs and servicing of its current customers. This may open the way for an existing or new competitor to chip away at its customer base.

We have presented the evidence supporting the importance of customer culture to business performance. We understand how to measure it. We know what the 8 disciplines are to strengthen it. Marketing leaders have a pivotal role in leading it.

Marketing's Pivotal Role in Leading the Implementation of the Strategic Marketing Plan

"I would define Amazon by our big ideas, which are customer centricity, putting the customer at the centre of everything we do."

Jeff Bezos, CEO, Amazon

Jeff Bezos is today's quintessential marketing leader with his relentless eye on leading a sustainable customer-centric culture at Amazon.

The central philosophy of marketing in today's turbulent environment is embodied in organizations that act with a strong *customer culture*. Tomorrow's world requires it for sustained organizational success. Customers and communities need it now to fulfil their needs in a fast-changing world. Imagine if all organizations – for profit and non-profit – had strong customer cultures. Imagine what we could all achieve for our customers, our communities, our employees, our stockholders, and our world. Marketing, led by CEOs, CMOs, CCOs and indeed all corporate leaders, has a pivotal role in leading organizational sustainability and can use the 8 disciplines model and measurement tool to ensure that marketing plans are successfully implemented.

7. DISRUPTIVE DIGITAL MARKETING STRATEGIES

7.1 HARNESSING THE DIGITAL OPPORTUNITY

Digital Divide has become a commonly used term in the past few years, although in truth, it is a term that has its roots in a remote origin.

Since the late 1960s, organizations started to discuss how to make computers known to people. In 1991, the term "Digital Divide" was used for the first time in an official document, the High-Performance Computing Act.

This document has sanctioned the birth of the fibre-optic network, which later became the "Internet", which drastically conditioned the way of sharing information, knowing, and communicating.

The Internet has opened new frontiers in the possibilities of interaction between people and between companies, in the delivery of business, and channelling a marketing plan.

These new frontiers have had an incredible impact on every aspect of life before affecting the professional future - starting from 1970 and with a generational leap from 1990 - to govern the present day. A phenomenon that precisely has also highlighted the gap between wealth and poverty.

To better contextualize the assumption, think that from 1991 to 1996 the number of Personal Computers in the United States had a sales boom leading the number of PCs from 300,000 to over ten million. Those numbers symbolize a social trend that would inevitably have a decisive influence on seeing the world.

Therefore, in such a frenetic evolutionary time, it was impossible for everyone to adapt promptly. In the first instance, for social, personal, or cultural reasons. Secondly, due to the inability to respond to a market demand that pushed the purchase of products - such as Personal Computers - that were not within everyone's reach.

Today almost every home has a PC, a smartphone, and a smart TV - or more than one. Nevertheless, the problem now arises of a cultural gap that divides people and companies from a world made of digital opportunities.

That is what we define "Digital Divide", referring to the acknowledgment, access, and use that people and companies have on technologies and their impact.

Digital Divide is a gap identified in economic and social inequality in the ability to interact on the primary good of digital communication, represented by the flow of data.

In addition to the infrastructural one, this knowledge gap tends to have important and deleterious effects on several economies, which could instead reap enormous benefits from the web and digital in general.

It, therefore, becomes a paradox, a system where the web reveals itself as a tool that, by its intrinsic nature, possesses the gift of breaking down barriers and instead can prove to be castrating for an inappropriate and ready-to-use context.

That is, sadly, what emerged from the Covid-19 pandemic. On one side, countries, companies, and people with explicit knowledge of the digital opportunities and tools have switched with a "mouse click" to a digital-driven everyday life. On the other hand, in different parts of the world, similar players have struggled to open their minds, eyes, and business to this new, forced, digital era. Something that we already had, digital, was imposed on us as a solution and salvation to try to continue our lives in a "new normal".

The Digital Divide was an ever-present growth barrier and did not tend to diminish. With Covid-19, organizations had to jump right into digital without infrastructures and knowledge - in some cases - accelerating an inevitable but slow evolution.

Pandemic accelerated the awareness of how digital tools can be a trigger to seize new opportunities. It allows enterprises of all sizes to emerge from the crisis, and at the same time, give birth to start-ups that know how to exploit these new tools fully.

Trying to bring entrepreneurs closer to the world of digital communication is not easy. Even in pandemic time, the phrase often repeated was "we have always done it this way". In reality, the time has come that not embracing digital compromises the very existence of companies on the market.

Fortunately, a generation is growing up, the one defined as the "Generation Alpha". Among those digital natives are the entrepreneurs of tomorrow. They have one foot inside IT and the other inside the web, and who knows how they will use them when the time comes.

We speak of Generation Alpha, referring to people born and raised with digital technologies, such as computers, the Internet, smartphones, and tablets. An environment contaminated by the advent of electronics that has invested the new generations since 1985, leading the new professionals of the future to become entrepreneurs capable of using computers and social media effortlessly and by trial and error.

VitrA

VITRA TILES' GLOBAL LIGHTHOUSE NETWORK JOURNEY: ROOTED IN TRADITION, DRIVEN BY INNOVATION

Written by: VitrA Communications Team & Deniz Konuralp, (Sustainability Strategy and Communications Consultant)

Introduction

VitrA Tiles, one of the flagship companies of the Eczacıbaşı Group, has been at the forefront of the ceramics industry for over three decades. VitrA Tiles' three prominent brands—VitrA, Villeroy & Boch, and engers—reach consumers in nearly 90 countries, generating about 80% of the company's annual sales from international markets. The Eczacıbaşı Group, founded in 1942, established Türkiye's first modern pharmaceutical plant, ceramic sanitary ware plant and tissue paper plant. Today, aside from operating the world's largest ceramic sanitary ware plant under one roof, the Group is active in healthcare and consumer goods, driven by a commitment to stakeholder capitalism and the principles of the Fourth Industrial Revolution (4IR). VitrA Tiles exemplifies how a traditionally rooted industry can evolve, adapt, and lead in the modern global marketplace.

This case study demonstrates how the company's successful adoption of Industry 4.0 practices enhanced its competitive advantage both in manufacturing and marketing, leading to its invitation in December 2023 to become the first and only ceramic tile company inducted into the prestigious World Economic Forum's Global Lighthouse Network (GLN). This recognition places VitrA Tiles among an elite group of manufacturers setting the standard for the future of production through the comprehensive adoption of 4IR technologies.

Challenge

The ceramics industry is one of the world's oldest manufacturing sectors, deeply rooted in tradition and reliant on time-honoured methods. This is particularly true in the production of ceramic tiles, where the firing process demands vast amounts of heat, making it a highly energy-intensive segment. Adapting to modern advancements has been a slow process for the industry, but VitrA Tiles recognized the necessity of change to maintain its competitive edge and sustainability. The challenge was clear: how could VitrA Tiles, steeped in tradition, embrace digitalization and sustainability to remain a leader in the global ceramics market?

Solution

Murat Gölcü, IT Director and Digital Transformation Leader:
"Our journey to becoming a candidate for the Global Lighthouse Network was long and challenging, but the excitement of success at the end made it all worthwhile."

VitrA Tiles embarked on a comprehensive digital transformation journey, underpinned by a commitment to sustainability. This transformation was centred around the modernization of its

273

Bozüyük production facility, integrating advanced digital solutions to enhance operational efficiency and environmental stewardship.

Named the **DigiTile project,** this Industry 4.0 initiative integrated cutting-edge technologies, including cloud computing, artificial intelligence, big data, data analytics, and the Internet of Things (IoT), into VitrA Tiles' production processes. A custom-developed Manufacturing Execution System (MES) and an IoT infrastructure allowed seamless data transfer from production to the cloud, enabling real-time monitoring and optimization.

By focusing on intelligent process control, supported by AI and machine learning technologies, VitrA Tiles achieved a remarkable 20% improvement in Overall Equipment Effectiveness (OEE) across its digitalized production lines.

The DigiTile project led to a 50% reduction in waste—a notable achievement in an industry where material wastage has been a longstanding challenge. Additionally, **DigiTile's Industry 4.0 processes** enabled VitrA Tiles' production line to reduce energy consumption by nearly 15%, further showcasing the company's commitment to environmental responsibility.

Global Lighthouse Network: A Platform for Leadership and Collaboration

Mustafa Zeytin, Production Manager:
"Winning global recognition in my first year at VitrA Tiles has been a special honour, motivating us all to fully embrace Industry 4.0 and refine our business processes."

In December 2023, VitrA Tiles reached a significant milestone by becoming the first and only ceramic tile company to be inducted into the World Economic Forum's Global Lighthouse Network (GLN). This prestigious recognition places VitrA Tiles among a select group of global manufacturers that are setting new standards for the future of production through the adoption of 4IR technologies.

The Global Lighthouse Network is more than just an accolade; it is a collaborative platform where leading manufacturers share knowledge, experiences, and best practices. As a member of this network, VitrA Tiles joins 153 other global leaders dedicated to transforming factories, value chains, and business models. The network emphasizes the importance of collaboration in addressing the global challenges of the modern era, such as climate change, supply chain disruptions, and economic volatility. This exposure can help VitrA Tiles learn from the experiences of other companies, adapt successful strategies, and avoid potential pitfalls. This acknowledgment as a leader in digital transformation and sustainable manufacturing can build credibility with customers, partners, and investors, and open new business opportunities.

As a member of the GLN, VitrA Tiles can play a pivotal role in shaping the future of manufacturing standards on sustainable and digital manufacturing practices, with its induction—announced at the Davos Summit in January 2024—set to accelerate the company's efforts in driving innovation and sustainability across its operations.

Pioneering Sustainability in the Ceramic Tiles Sector

Musa Yılmaz, Factory Director:
"We aim to lead with a production methodology that respects nature and the environment, ensuring our facility produces at the highest standards."

Sustainability is a core principle for VitrA Tiles, shaping every aspect of its operations. The ceramics industry has traditionally been associated with energy consumption and environmental impact. However, VitrA Tiles has emerged as a leader in redefining responsible manufacturing within the sector. The company's commitment to sustainability is deeply integrated into its digital transformation initiatives, which have been instrumental in reducing its carbon footprint and setting new environmental standards.

VitrA Tiles' approach to sustainability is multifaceted, encompassing energy efficiency, waste reduction, and a circular economy approach to production. By implementing advanced technologies such as AI-driven production controls and real-time monitoring systems, VitrA Tiles' production line achieved a 15% reduction in energy consumption. The company's efforts in sustainability were demonstrated by a reduction of up to 60% in its overall manufacturing carbon footprint, with a 30% decrease specifically in production lines utilizing the DigiTile project. These achievements were made possible through the application of Industry 4.0 processes and investments in renewable energy.

These sustainability milestones not only contribute to the global fight against climate change but also provide VitrA Tiles with a competitive edge in a market increasingly driven by consumer demand for innovative products, concerns about climate change, and stricter regulatory requirements. As a member of the Global Lighthouse Network, VitrA Tiles plays a crucial role in the global conversation on sustainable manufacturing practices, sharing best practices and pioneering new approaches that align with its vision of a future where manufacturing is both efficient and environmentally responsible.

Harnessing AI and Machine Learning: Driving the Future of Manufacturing Excellence

Burçak Atay, Technical Services Manager:
"For VitrA, embracing Industry 4.0 means creating a data-driven culture that transforms how we do business and inspires other organizations in our community."

Artificial Intelligence (AI) and machine learning are the engines behind VitrA Tiles' transformative shift in production. These advanced technologies have enabled the company to implement intelligent production controls that continuously monitor and optimize manufacturing processes in real-time. This approach allows VitrA Tiles to fine-tune its operations with unparalleled precision, resulting in a manufacturing system that is both highly efficient and resilient in the face of global uncertainties.

During the COVID-19 pandemic, VitrA Tiles' AI-driven systems were crucial in maintaining production continuity with minimal revenue loss. While many manufacturers struggled, VitrA Tiles' ability to adapt swiftly and efficiently set it apart. This resilience underscores the company's technological expertise and forward-thinking approach to risk management and operational stability.

As AI and machine learning technologies continue to evolve, VitrA Tiles is poised to lead the ceramics industry into a new era of technological innovation. The company's ongoing investments in these areas are not merely about keeping pace with industry standards; they are about setting new benchmarks. By continually pushing the boundaries of what is possible, VitrA Tiles ensures it remains at the forefront of manufacturing excellence, consistently raising the bar.

Looking Ahead: Pioneering the Next Century of Innovation

Esra Çalpak, Industry Application Manager: "
Our ultimate goal is to achieve excellence in production by using resources respectfully and producing the world's best quality products."

As VitrA Tiles looks to the future, its commitment to innovation, sustainability, and excellence remains steadfast. The company's integration of Industry 4.0 technologies has set the stage for a future where digital transformation and environmental stewardship are deeply intertwined. In the coming years, VitrA Tiles aims to expand its influence across new markets, continuing to lead in Europe. The focus will be on deepening sustainability practices, reducing carbon footprints further, and enhancing product offerings with cutting-edge innovations.

VitrA Tiles envisions a future where it continues to set the global standard for ceramics manufacturing, leading the industry in sustainable practices and technological advancements. The company is excited to explore new frontiers in technology, product development, and market expansion, all while staying true to the values that have defined it for decades. As VitrA Tiles embarks on this next phase, it is confident that its efforts will shape the future of the industry and contribute to a more sustainable and innovative world.

Questions to stimulate conversation on the case:

1. **How did VitrA Tiles manage to integrate Industry 4.0 technologies into its traditional manufacturing processes while addressing sustainability challenges?**

VitrA Tiles successfully implemented Industry 4.0 technologies through its DigiTile project. The integration of AI, IoT, and cloud computing allowed the company to enhance operational efficiency, improve overall equipment effectiveness (OEE) by 20%, and reduce waste by 50%. These digital advancements also contributed to a 15% reduction in energy consumption, reflecting VitrA Tiles' commitment to sustainability.

2. **What benefits does VitrA Tiles gain from being inducted into the World Economic Forum's Global Lighthouse Network (GLN)?**

Membership in the Global Lighthouse Network not only serves as recognition of VitrA Tiles' leadership in adopting 4IR technologies but also provides a platform for knowledge sharing and collaboration with other global manufacturers. This exposure offers opportunities to learn from best practices, build credibility, and explore new business opportunities, all while contributing to global sustainability conversations.

3. **How has VitrA Tiles' commitment to sustainability influenced its competitive position in the global market?**

VitrA Tiles' emphasis on sustainability has set it apart in the ceramics industry. By reducing its carbon footprint by up to 60% and implementing eco-friendly production methods, the company has responded to growing consumer demand for sustainable products and met stricter regulatory standards. This focus on environmental responsibility not only enhances its brand image but also strengthens its competitive edge in the international market.

**Watch our journey unfold
—scan the QR code to see the full story.**

7.2 DISRUPTION AS A MINDSET

The scientific-technological system has been one of the fields on which digitization has had the most significant impact with a change in interaction. This transformation has seen the imposition of a massive flow of information and knowledge.

While companies have to digitize themselves to bridge the Digital Divide, on the other hand, new technologies have entered so much into our lives that they influence the value proposition of existing products and services. Digital transformation significantly modifies the old business models and creates the conditions for developing new ones.

This value-added influence has increased the potential of Digital Disruption in many industries. A change in the world of innovation that is experiencing a rapid rise, directly proportional to the increasing use of mobile devices for personal and work use. To arrive more quickly and follow the use of these devices, many companies have changed their methodologies for accessing content and conveying advertising. A necessary condition for maximum monetization in a constantly evolving system.

However, this does not mean more "homework" for entrepreneurs, but new business opportunities to be exploited, new skills to be created, and new jobs. The world of work today calls upon an army of professions in which technical and humanistic profiles must be blended, mixed in order to transform communication into an effective telematic means suitable for everyday technological tools.

Digital Disruption, therefore, affects all sectors and all their levels. What is now clear is that companies either change, or close.

Digital Disruption forces entrepreneurs to innovate their business model precisely because the working practices that have remained unchanged over the years are no longer reflected in this globalized and digitized context. Old business and marketing strategies have proved to be deleterious in the face of globalization. Many companies have found themselves inadequate in terms of time and methods, chasing digitization as a bus they do not want to lose.

Artificial Intelligence (AI) and Machine Learning (ML) are revolutionizing the way Turkish brands communicate with consumers by allowing personalized experiences, making better decisions, and optimizing marketing strategies. Large corporations in Türkiye like Hepsiburada and Trendyol have adopted AI for dynamic pricing and personalized recommendations that resulted in huge improvements in customer retention and engagement. Financial institutions such as Garanti BBVA and Akbank have already been using AI-driven chatbots in the regard of customer services, ensuring immediate support to their customers. However, the rest of the enterprises are not demonstrating strong AI adoptions due to its infancy stage. Nevertheless, many Turkish businesses have started exploring the tools enabled by artificial intelligence since the demand for data-driven insights started to increase. In turn, this unfolding familiarity with AI technologies is placing Türkiye in a unique position to make brands competitive by automating marketing tasks, hence making their decisions quicker and more informed.

In Türkiye, the rise of voice search and smart devices is changing consumer brand discovery and interaction. With more Turkish-language voice assistants becoming available with Google Assistant and Amazon Alexa leading the charge, consumers are using voice commands now to perform a range of tasks starting from product searches and price comparisons to placing orders. This means that Turkish brands seeking to remain visible within this shifting landscape will have to optimize their content for voice searches. As voice assistants increasingly dominate daily routines from home automation to shopping, voice optimization will turn out to be one of the most important parts of digital marketing strategies in Türkiye. The integration of voice-activated services also affords brands the opportunity to offer more personalized, hands free customer experiences.

Robots are being used in service marketing in Türkiye to increase customer experience and efficiency. This adoption is led by hospitality, retail, and banking. Service robots at Istanbul Airport, one of the world's busiest, provide passengers with information and help. Major Turkish banks, such as Ziraat Bankası and Garanti BBVA, are utilizing RPA to enhance service delivery and response times. Robots improve efficiency, but Turkish brands must reconcile automation with traditional Turkish hospitality. Businesses may reinforce Türkiye's hospitality culture by deploying robots to do tedious jobs so employees can focus on customer service. As service robots become increasingly popular in Türkiye, they should boost consumer satisfaction and brand loyalty.

Therefore, it is not only the products and services that must be influenced by Digital Disruption but the entrepreneurs themselves.

The more structured companies, those with Marketing Communication offices within them or with outsourced agencies, experience this disruption in a completely different way.It is not just a question of company size or resources but of knowledge related to opportunities, risks, costs, and benefits.

That is a kind of change that needs leadership as well as a correct mindset. The leader's task is to convey the overall vision at the appropriate time to create the necessary impetus for transformation.

A transformation occurs when strategy and leadership work together to change the shape of what the company does. The result is usually something different, more than just a renewal, and sometimes it is innovation.

7.3 BUSINESS TO CONSUMER VS. BUSINESS TO MASS

The Internet has become a major advertising and communication medium for all companies. Even if all kinds and sizes of businesses can take advantage of the same channels, their communication is very different.

The differentiation between B2C, B2B, and B2G is well known in the fundamentals of marketing and beyond. However, digital marketing has brought to the attention that big B2C companies communicate differently from small businesses, also included in B2C.

A digital marketing campaign by a large B2C company usually involves a huge budget and a punctual segmentation of audiences and buyer personas.

A small business more often invests a tiny amount of money, has a local target, and does not have the same knowledge, structure, people, and resources of a multinational company.

Those differences, which emerged significantly during the pandemic, led us to define a new class of companies, the so-called B2M - Business to Mass.

A B2M company is an organization whose communication and promotion are aimed at the mass market and therefore need to define a much more detailed digital marketing strategy.

Web 4.0 was also called the Symbiotic Web, the next internet evolution that deeply integrates AI, automatisms, and immersive technologies like Virtual Reality (VR), Augmented Reality (AR), and the Internet of Things (IoT) into daily living-especially among the young, tech-savvy consumer and enterprise alike. Web 4.0 technologies create new opportunities for companies in the Turkish market to engage with consumers in particularly personalized and engaging ways. Web 4.0 enables a more intuitive relationship between people and technology by leveraging AI to predict customer needs and deliver very personalized experiences. Today, Turkish brands use innovative technologies to create more intelligent and responsive digital landscapes.

For instance, companies could offer personalized promotions in real time by IoT devices or use AR to create interactive shopping experiences. This trend is very powerful, especially in industries like retail, real estate, and automobile, where virtual showrooms and product previews are a fast-catching idea. Web 4.0 develops further the principles of decentralization of Web 3.0 into more sophisticated, AI-driven interactions. Currently, Turkish enterprises are amalgamating blockchain technology with artificial intelligence to create a decentralized, safe, and autonomous marketing ecosystem.

Through smart contracts and tokenization, brands can establish trust and transparency in their interactions with consumers. Turkish businesses, particularly in the technology and finance sectors, have commenced experimentation with DeFi and blockchain-based marketing tactics, facilitating secure, efficient, and transparent interactions between clients and brands in the future.

7.4 ALPHA, A GENERATION OF CREATORS

As mentioned before, Generation Alpha is growing up in a world where the Internet and social media are entirely merged with the reality of everyday life. What adults have experienced during the pandemic, forced home with a monitor as a filter between them and their previous real life is the typical lifestyle of Gen Alpha.

These entrepreneurs, managers, employees, and professionals of the future not only fully embrace digital within their lives but also create content and interact with each other.

Before that, Gen Alpha will be a generation of customers. There are some indications that they already influence their parents and relatives to buy products for them, more than kids usually do. That is supposed to be directly related to the digitization of this generation and their smart houses.

A child can now use the smartphone to watch content, play games, access Amazon and other marketplace apps, choose what to buy, and complete a transaction if the payment methods are set.

That puts Gen Alpha already in the potential audience of B2M companies that, with digital marketing, can influence their desires and transfer the request to their parents or relatives.

The concept is not far from the well-known television ads of games, especially before Christmas, that encourage children to ask their parents for a specific gift. The difference is that Gen Alpha can buy the gift themselves. Moreover, they will create content on social media and influence other children.

Gen Z and Alpha are becoming the leading forces in the consumer layout of Türkiye, thereby changing the way brands take up digital marketing. Digital-forward, these generations believe in authenticity, social responsibility, and technological innovation. Branded engagements of Turkish brands with Gen Z through TikTok or Instagram prove that the key to success involves creating purpose-driven content that is authentic. Branded services from companies such as Getir and Beko resonate with the current audience by making their marketing strategies align with social causes, sustainability, and innovative digital experiences. Both Gen Z and Alpha wield a strong influence on family purchasing decisions; therefore, they are crucial targets for brands eager to achieve long-term customer loyalty. With regards to this young and influential purchaser, the Turkish brands are able to relate to them more effectively by emphasizing social responsibility and digital innovation.

Companies now need to communicate with a generation of creators and influencers that do not know a world without digital. Influencer marketing has taken one of the top positions in Turkish digital marketing, especially on platforms like Instagram and YouTube. Influencers like Danla Bilic and Duygu Özaslan really have a powerful role in shaping consumer behavior, mainly in verticals like fashion, beauty, and lifestyle. Turkish brands use collaborations with micro-influencers more and more with the purpose of devising authentic, hyper-local activities that resonate with their target audience. TikTok's rise in Türkiye took influencer marketing to another dimension by opening new opportunities for brands desiring to reach a younger audience through creating and participating in short-form content and go-viral trends. While Turkish influencers are increasingly building connected communities, brands can turn those tied relationships into fruitful campaigns toward better engagement and sales regarding their products or services, particularly toward Gen Z and Alpha.

7.5 GOING GLOBAL THROUGH DIGITAL MARKETING

In a time of market stagnation, there is often a tendency to reduce the budget for marketing and communication activities. Equally often, we read that this concept is wrong, and instead, it is necessary to increase the budget aimed at activities that can directly influence the turnover. It is a philosophy that finds home on the concept that stopping communicating cannot be a good signal in itself, consequently generating a not very productive impact on the system itself. What is less often read is that the budget would be spent on activities whose results can be measured, to be able to concentrate on the channels that bring the most revenues.

Digital Marketing is a new way of conceiving the relationship between companies and stakeholders through online channels.

The Turkish market moved very fast toward omnichannel strategies and even unified commerce, meaning a seamless experience for consumers across both digital and physical channels. Regarding that, brands like Mavi and LC Waikiki have combined their e-commerce platforms with the physical stores, creating one big shopping experience. Personalization plays an important role in this approach, as several Turkish brands use mobile apps, sending SMS, and personalized email marketing in order to reach their customers. Loyalty programs integrated with personalized content based on consumer behavior can really help Turkish companies have long-term relations with their customers. Thus, localized content and personalization will be critically important by region in the diversified consumer landscape of Türkiye to thrive in delivering relevant and meaningful experiences across all touchpoints.

The Internet becomes a door to the world, and the web represents a channel for exploring different and new markets.

Due to the pandemic, many companies have explored new markets with new products. That can be a risky decision if not part of a structured marketing plan. Web Marketing can help in choosing the markets and defining the offer, also allowing insertion into the new context at reduced costs. A significant advantage. Especially considering how difficult it is, by nature, to establish itself in a little-known market.

Optimizing resources increases the chances of success. This is one of the most revolutionary aspects of the concept of internationalization.

Furthermore, the product concept is changing and has already partially changed. The Internet has, in fact, changed the identity of an asset, adding value to the company's business. A process that takes shape in the integration of new digital tools, such as social media, which have even involved the customer in the creative and development process.

It should also not be forgotten that while traditional communication channels still respond to advertising logic, the web allows a bi-directional presence, offering the possibility to dialogue with potential customers and tell them about their company uniquely and creatively.

Another huge advantage of digital communication, not found in other media, is the possibility of varying strategies almost in real-time. If, on the one hand, the investment in terms of time is the same as for any communication activity, Web Marketing still offers the great advantage of being able to apply timely corrections without losing efficiency.

Covid-19 forced us to a contest where not being present on the web is equivalent to not being found. Being there means communicating 24 hours a day, 7 days a week, 365 days a year.

It, therefore, makes sense to ask what is the best solution to undertake for the approach - or the expansion of the share - to foreign markets. Small and Medium Enterprises often prefer to internationalize without external intervention, although this may require a significant economic outlay.

An approach more inclined to "Learning by doing" is one of the most used methods by SMEs, as it allows them to explore different scenarios and, above all, provides the certainty of containing costs. The latter often reveals itself as mere perception. It is easy for many companies, victims of this system, to find themselves using resources in a less productive way than they believe.

Trade fairs, for example, seemed to be the best method for acquiring foreign contacts before Covid-19, despite requiring a high organizational level and consistent budgets. During the pandemic, some companies first got confused on how to acquire more customers or new orders. Some other companies jumped into the "online bus" investing all their budget on e-commerce and marketplaces that did sell a lot for the first few months and then became never-ending costs. Again, the lack of a digital strategy, and maybe, of a marketing plan.

The first step should be to understand how digital can help to go global:

- through the web, it is possible to obtain information on the reference market without the need to travel to analyze the individual elements.

- monitoring and constant communication on the web channels allows the company to present itself to the market before, during and after a trade fair.

- correct use of social media helps to increase the collection of qualified contacts and to raise brand awareness on the market.

- creative use of video-call software allows companies to share content, build and maintain relationships with stakeholders, and virtually bring them to their manufacturing plants.

In general, the pandemic has confirmed that the web can help companies to approach international markets with a lower budget than traditional methods.

The Internet is certainly the right channel to start from to acquire qualified contacts and build lasting relationships, both with customers and intermediaries, also through a commercial network that can be managed through the web itself.

Social media, in particular, have overturned the concept of sales. Today, the customer decides what to buy, no longer the company who decides whom to sell to. However, this means that setting up good communication on the web will undoubtedly lead to acquiring contacts and selling without having to carry out "active" commercial activities.

Social commerce is swiftly gaining prominence in Türkiye, with platforms such as Instagram and TikTok providing integrated buying experiences. Turkish firms are utilizing these channels to establish dynamic and engaging shopping experiences, especially via influencer collaborations and livestream shopping events.

These events, motivated by the triumph of livestream shopping in China, are more prevalent during peak shopping seasons such as Black Friday and Bayram campaigns. Consumers in Türkiye appreciate the real-time interaction and entertainment value of livestream shopping, which combines social engagement with instant purchasing options. As more Turkish consumers turn to social media for shopping inspiration, brands can capitalize on this trend by creating immersive, interactive experiences that drive direct sales.

Picking up the phone and calling a newly purchased - or centuries-old - contact list means interrupting the customer's work and wasting an enormous amount of time.

Having to send an export manager abroad for a year, setting up an office if not a headquarters, involves enormous costs that SMEs can no longer cope with, at least in the first phase. Moreover, the pandemic has taught us that perhaps we can do without it.

Connecting outside the local market, building new international partnerships, and managing new synergies are therefore the next step in building the company's role outside the national territory. From this point, the capillarity process of one's business starts from an international point of view.

Thanks to the role of the web as a driver to safely take the road to internationalization, it is possible to:

- acquire qualified contacts - in target and interested in the product - at lower costs than traditional activities;

- obtain practical support for export managers who can cultivate relationships even at a distance;

- have the possibility to sell directly through e-commerce, without having to open physical stores;

- start facilitated management of communities through social media;

- identify an accelerator for traditional communication and marketing activities;

- take advantage of the flexibility of web channels which makes it possible to change strategy almost in real-time, in case there are variations in company dynamics, or it is necessary to apply corrections to the strategies in place;

- feed the collection of information of the reference market - geo-location, customer, economic trend - and expand the credibility in the international field and, consequently, in the local market.

The classic model of internationalization, still widely used, is using figures in the area - export managers - who have the function of an antenna, scouting, and market development.

To support those salespersons, companies usually activate participation in fairs, sponsorship of local events, and other activities based on the allocated budget. This model is expensive, and it is not hard to see why.

However, the model is still valid: people must man the territory. People talk to people and do business with people. This attitude will never change because it is human.

Where do web tools come into play? Their role is to bring people together and decide to meet to find out if they can develop a business.

If used correctly, social media talk about companies using a clear local language that the target audience well understands. That is the task of cross-cultural communication.

In recent years, Computer-Generated Imagery (CGI) has transformed the methods by which brands produce and disseminate advertising content. CGI is swiftly gaining traction in the Turkish market, especially in sectors such as fashion, automotive, and gaming. Prominent Turkish fashion labels such as Koton and Defacto have commenced the integration of CGI in their digital marketing, utilizing virtual models and 3D surroundings to augment product displays. The use of CGI allows Turkish brands to reach a tech-savvy audience, offering visually captivating experiences that attract Gen Z and younger consumers, who have a natural affinity for digital content. Moreover, CGI provides an opportunity for brands to save on production costs while maintaining high creative standards, making it an attractive option in Türkiye's competitive market. As Turkish consumers continue to embrace digital platforms, brands can leverage CGI to create immersive, futuristic advertising that stands out in a saturated marketplace.

It is possible to present the company in a new market through digital and support its activities as a local reality. In this way, users come into contact with the company, and the distrust of a player from another country is reduced.

7.6 CROSS-CULTURAL CONTENT

Content is the heart of the strategy. Whatever the channels defined and the budget available, the content makes the difference between convincing the customer and losing him forever.

The same care put into studying the product and making it should be used to talk about it, through texts, images, or videos, to convey the value offered by the product itself and those who create it.

To better understand how to proceed with the writing of content, it is helpful to check previous texts written by other people, with a localization of the hashtags related to the brand, product, or service in question. In addition to facilitating the work and providing essential insight into the direction to take, the user experience with which the web user already expresses his interest in a particular topic should not be underestimated. It could be the starting point to understand the most congenial shape or cut to make communication effective.

When talking about content for foreign markets, the need to communicate in the language of the target country should be taken into consideration and, above all, the importance of cross-cultural content.

Creating cross-cultural content means thinking about what the company needs to share and creating it considering the culture of the target country, the traditions, the idioms. Only in this way concrete results can be achieved. Typically, the best choice is to rely on a native speaker professional, even better if he/she resides in the country in question.

It should also be born in mind that when we talk about cross-cultural content, we are not referring only to the texts of the website, the social communication, or the company brochure, but also the photographs used, the illustrated contents such as infographics, up to the videos, or other multimedia content.

Even in B2B, where English is often used to communicate abroad, it is important to localize content to get results. Only after starting a business relationship, it will be possible to maintain contact in English. In any case, even the B2B customer appreciates that the foreign company shows interest in its culture, that it strives to communicate in its language. In some countries, it is a must to speak the customer's language, precisely for a cultural reason.

Pandemic compelled many companies to start an internationalization process and consolidate their presence in a foreign market. That means getting in touch with the culture of the country.

7.7 DIFFERENTIATE IN THE POST-PANDEMIC MARKET

Pandemic forced companies to digitize their processes and communication as well as approach foreign markets to survive.

In this "new-global" emerged the need for a simple concept to help companies differentiate from the competition. The Marketing Distinguo has been defined as a glue concept between brand positioning and Unique Selling Proposition. It is essential as it simplifies the marketing manager and communications agency's job, and it is reflected in the product/service and in the hallmarks of the company itself.

The method to define the Marketing Distinguo of a company or a product, or even a professional, starts from the simple keywords they use in communication and promotion. Terms like quality, flexibility, passion, leadership, and reliability are often used by entrepreneurs - mistakenly - to define brand positioning or USP. Since they do not clarify the benefits, the customer may receive by buying the product, the method can erase them completely. On the other hand, it is also true that if a company uses words like quality or reliability in its communication, it is certainly based on concrete foundations. That is precisely where the foundations of the Marketing Distinguo are found.

Examining the concrete characteristics of the product, the service, the company, the people, and the market in which it operates, is the only way to determine an objective comparison with competitors.

After eliminating the non-unique characteristics compared to the competition, what remains is the Marketing Distinguo. The unique and distinctive reason to buy that product.

After a company has found that, the creative execution will lead to a great USP.

On the other hand, sustainability has increasingly become a key focus of the Turks in the decision to buy and choice of brand. Companies such as Arçelik and Vestel have been in the front line, adopting environmentally friendly production processes and promoting sustainable product lines. A transparent approach to environmental impact and ethical behavior attracts an increasing number of Turkish customers, especially among the younger generation. Sustainability campaigns that emphasize the importance of waste reduction, energy efficiency, and ethical sourcing of materials find great resonance in Türkiye, where community and long-term thinking are highly valued. By embedding sustainability into their marketing strategies, brands please consumer preference and differentiate themselves within an increasingly competitive marketplace. In this regard, sustainability is one of the facets that will be central in the implementation of digital marketing strategy in Türkiye due to its adherence to all general global trends, reflecting respect for environmental stewardship imbued in the local culture.

7.8 THE NEED FOR A DIGITAL MARKETING STRATEGY

Digital channels should be a natural operational variation of the promotion strategy within the marketing plan. So, said, most companies - especially SMEs - do not have a written strategy, and they do not know how to decline it to digital or non-digital promotion activities.

Over the years, and especially following the pandemic, companies have found themselves without a strategy to communicate through the only channel available: digital. That has discharged the responsibility of the strategy towards the web agencies, accustomed above all to carrying out the operational part.

Web Marketing channels, particularly social media, can be an excellent promotional tool for companies if used correctly and supported by a strategy dedicated to the reference market.

There is no winning packaged strategy. Some guidelines help to choose and identify the most appropriate tools to achieve the result.

Having a digital strategy looks essential to have clear ideas and monitor investments over time and apply any corrective measures when strategic changes occur.

However, companies must keep in mind that no communication activity can guarantee results, whether web or traditional. This axiom is often little considered, but it can turn out to be a superficiality that cannot be ignored in the medium and long term. Hence a new awareness that better directs the quality of its investments. If the company is not sure of the result, it is undoubtedly necessary to better organize the investment. It is advisable to increase the success rate, trying to have as much control as possible on the budget invested. Thinking in this light can become doubly profitable, as the success of a campaign will probably result in good profitability without wasting costs. Otherwise, losses will be limited with due planning and, moreover, parameters will be obtained to reconstruct the following action plan. Perseverance, therefore, plays a fundamental role, without the chronological aspect becoming an enemy of the results.

Therefore, it is necessary to define a point of departure and arrival and identify the resources that serve the purpose. A good web strategy will appear as a clear path to success.

The starting point is to define a goal for the digital marketing strategy (Figure 7.1). The goal should be related to the company's business and not only to the - so-called - vanity metrics well known for those operating with social media. As the name suggests, these metrics are numbers such as likes, comments, or post views that feel good to look at but do not directly relate to the business goal.

The other elements composing the digital marketing strategy are:

- Key Performance Indicators
- Channels and activities
- Content
- Marketing Distinguo
- Product or service
- Mission
- Vision
- Purpose and values

To define or verify a company's digital marketing strategy, it is possible to use the Visual Communication Planner. This marketing canvas is accompanied by a set of questions to be answered to fill all the above elements of the strategy.

The strategy does not have a specific shape. It assumes that of the channels and markets on which it develops. It adapts to changes, to the situation it encounters. The perfect strategy is like water. Only by adapting to changing conditions, it achieves its goal.

For this reason, the strategy is not made by the perfect answers but the right questions.

Data privacy is a highly valued issue in the Turkish market, mainly after the enactment of KVKK. Turkish consumers are getting increasingly sensitive about their digital rights, and brands need to find a balance between strict privacy legislation and the need for open communication. Compliance with KVKK is way more than a legal obligation; it is an enabler of trust between the brand and Turkish consumers.. For Turkish businesses to win confidence in the local market, they must allow personalized experiences while maintaining privacy and security of data. Additionally, brands also need to consider the increasing regulations that are sure to affect their manner of engaging users digitally due to data regulation, let alone cookie consent laws.

sahibinden.com

BEYOND A MERE CLASSIFIED PLATFORM

Introduction

sahibinden.com carried the tradition of classified ads from print media in Turkey to the digital world, sparking a digital revolution. Today, it continues as one of Turkey's leading e-commerce and classified ad platforms, with an average of nearly 65 million users per month. With approximately 1,000 employees and nearly 8 million active listings, along with hundreds of thousands of product varieties, sahibinden.com impacts people's lives across a wide range of services and 10 categories, including Real Estate, Auto, Spare Parts Accessories, Hardware, and Tuning, Industrial and Heavy Equipment, Goods, Pets and Livestock, Jobs, and Professional Services, In Home Help, Services, and Experts, Tutors.

sahibinden.com started its journey under the Aksoy Group as Turkey's first and largest second-hand buying and selling platform exactly 24 years ago, with only 2,700 listings in total. When sahibinden.com was established in 2000, the internet was just starting to spread into Turkish households. Consequently, people were mostly using offline channels such as flea markets to buy and sell their second-hand items, while homes and cars were exchanged through automobile markets, real estate agents, and newspaper classified ads. This traditional classified ad practice confined people to shopping within a limited area, with few options and narrow price ranges. However, sahibinden.com revolutionized this process by moving it online, broadening the limits of shopping and making buying and selling more accessible. Today, sahibinden.com is a dynamic marketplace that facilitates thousands of transactions daily across diverse categories, including real estate, auto, and goods, in all 81 provinces of Turkey.

With its user-friendly interface, robust technological infrastructure, and commitment to high customer satisfaction, sahibinden.com has become the most preferred platform in Turkey for real estate and vehicles over the years. Beyond being just a classifieds platform, it has transformed into a platform where *"millions of people's dreams come true and thousands of new stories unfold every day"*, cultivating a unique brand culture.

Challenge

1.   Creating Behavioral Change to Digitize the Classified Ads Habit

In its early days, sahibinden.com faced the significant challenge of transitioning the established habit of classified ads to the digital realm. This required not only shifting consumers' perceptions of classified ads but, more importantly, changing their habitual approach to using them.

- **Creating an Experience Users Can Easily Adapt To:** The traditional experience of newspaper advertising involved multiple steps—preparing the text, mailing it to the newspaper, and awaiting approval—requiring effort and time. Similarly, buying and selling homes and cars had comparable challenges. To promote behavioral change, it was essential to create an experience that encouraging users to quickly adopt an easier method.

- **Ensuring High Customer Satisfaction:** In the early days of sahibinden.com, providing the first users with a fast, easy, and exceptional experience was crucial for generating word-of-mouth marketing and expanding the user network.

- **Staying Current in a Rapidly Changing World:** As the internet became widespread in households and accessible to millions, new developments were constantly integrating into daily life. To remain relevant in this evolving landscape, sahibinden.com needed to maintain an agile and dynamic platform, continuously updating itself to keep up with changes.

2. Maintaining Leadership Over the Long Term

After digitizing classified ads in Turkey, sahibinden.com became the most preferred platform for millions when it came to real estate and vehicles due to its communication campaigns. However, sustaining leadership in categories that were essential to people's lives presented its own set of challenges.

- **Becoming the Leading Brand:** As the leading name in real estate, vehicles, and goods, sahibinden.com sought to not only advance the sector but also pioneer technological innovations and set industry standards.

- **Maintaining Leadership in Consumer Perception:** It was aimed to remain the top choice for millions in Turkey for real estate and vehicle needs, preserving the position among the sector over the long term.

- **Evolving from a Needed Brand to a Beloved Brand:** Real estate and vehicles are essential categories that people need repeatedly during their lifetime, though not daily. To achieve consistent growth and maintain high traffic, we needed to transform from merely a destination for specific needs into a cherished brand that resonates with consumers.

sahibinden.com
Türkiye'nin En Büyük E-Ticaret Platformu

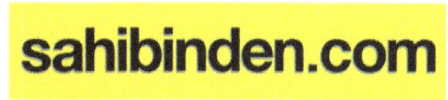

sahibinden.com

Solution

1. Creating Behavioral Change to Digitize the Classified Ads Habit:

- **Inspiration from the "Yellow Pages" of Traditional Advertising:** Consumers were accustomed to classified ads appearing in print media, often referred to as "yellow ads" or "yellow pages." Drawing inspiration from this familiar world, sahibinden.com aimed to remind consumers of the concept of classified advertising through its signature yellow color.

- **The Address Where You Find What You're Seeking with a Simple Interface & Seamless User Experience:** To encourage people to shift from the time-consuming and effort-intensive classic advertising to online classifieds, a user-friendly interface was designed. This interface allowed users to easily post ads or contact advertisers in just a few steps. With its robust technological infrastructure, detailed filtering options, and continuously updated features, sahibinden.com has become "The Address for Finding What You Need."

- **Pioneering Technological Innovations and Firsts:** As sahibinden.com expanded its reach and became more widespread across Turkey, it implemented technological advancements to meet user needs and preferences. For instance, it revolutionized the traditional ad-searching process—where users would search through daily newspapers for new listings—by notifying users of new listings via SMS. In 2002, "Secure e-Trade (GET)," was introduced allowing buyers to safely purchase shippable products with instant credit card payment directly on the site. In 2004, the launch of a Live Support hotline provided users with instant written assistance. In 2007, it enhanced security in online transactions by implementing the 3D Secure credit card payment feature. Continuously improving its platform based on user feedback, sahibinden.com became a pioneer that year for numerous services, including "Megafoto," "Verified via Mobile," and "Video Listings." As the pioneering address for classified advertising in Turkey, significant investments were made in technologies that developed and transformed the advertising sector. In the rapidly changing digital landscape, sahibinden.com has pioneered the development of the sector along with new technologies:

- In 2011, sahibinden.com launched Turkey's first mobile app in the e-commerce sector.

sahibinden.com

- By 2013, The "Property on Map" feature was launched allowing users to search for real estate on a map.

- In 2014, sahibinden.com renewed the "Experts and Services" category, creating a new platform to address the daily needs that require skill and labor-intensive work. This allowed sahibinden.com to connect users with a wide range of services, from home renovations and decoration to vehicle maintenance and transportation. That same year, ad posting via mobile devices feature was also introduced.

- In 2015, the "sahibindex Real Estate Index" tool was launched offering users Turkey's most comprehensive real estate market data service.

- In 2016, the "360-Degree Photo Listings" feature was launched allowing users to upload photos taken by 360-degree cameras to their listings.

- In 2017, sahibinden.com earned the title of R&D Center and continued to develop innovative projects. That same year, it "3D Tour" feature was introduced allowing users to explore real estate listings in detail and enhancing their overall experience.

- In 2018, sahibinden.com introduced an innovative service in the vehicle sector with its AI-based Car Recognition feature. This mobile feature allows users to take a photo of a car they are interested in and quickly obtain information about its make, model, and year.

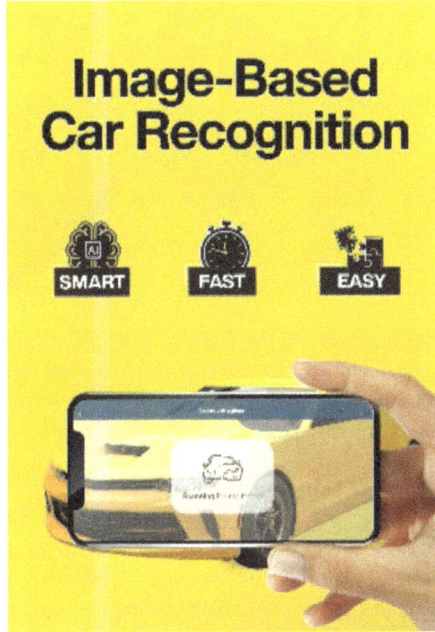

- By 2019, sahibinden.com increased its investments in the real estate and vehicle sectors by launching the Oto360 and Emlak360 projects.

- In 2020, sahibinden.com strengthened its technological infrastructure by establishing a cloud-based data center, positioning itself as a forward-thinking organization that leads the industry with its vision for the future.

- In 2022, Project Sales Offices were established for large-scale projects. To enhance speed and convenience for users in the real estate category, the S-Virtual Tour and subsequently the Listing Video product were launched.

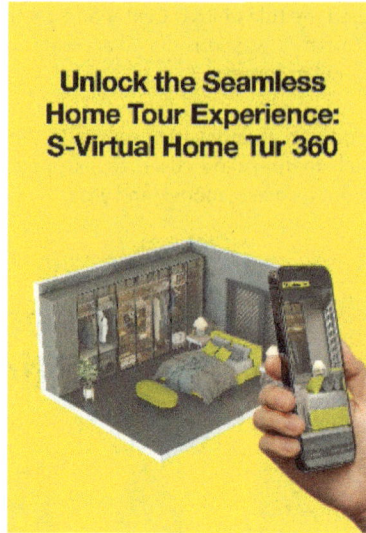

Unlock the Seamless Home Tour Experience: S-Virtual Home Tur 360

- In 2023, a B2B/C2B car sourcing platform for dealers - Otobid was established. Otobid, a first in Turkey, allows individual vehicle owners to list their cars for sale in an online auction environment, with participation from thousands of auto dealers across 81 provinces. This platform offers a fast, transparent, and reliable sales process.

2. Maintaining Leadership Over the Long Term

Memorable Through Playful Leadership Campaigns: To maintain its status as the top brand in consumers' minds, sahibinden.com consistently reinforced the message, "sahibinden.com is the address for buying, selling, renting, or searching." Over the years, the brand has kept a humorous and light-hearted tone in its communications, which strengthened its leadership image while adding a sense of approachability. In the "Probably Does Not Exist" campaign, the message was simple: "If you can't find the house or car, you're looking for on Sahibinden, it probably doesn't exist." This was humorously illustrated through scenarios where a cake was mistaken for a car or a cardboard house was taken for the real thing. This strong leadership message continues today with various clever and playful campaigns.

Not Just a Classifieds Platform, but Home for Millions of Stories: sahibinden.com's strong position in the real estate and vehicle categories made it the preferred address for millions of people dreaming of owning a home or car. On the 20th anniversary of its founding in 2020, a new campaign was launched. For the first time, "The place where dreams come true." message was communicated. This message was delivered through a film that told a touching story. A father sold his car to send his daughter to the school of her dreams. Years later, after becoming a successful businesswoman, the daughter bought the same car for her father. This campaign marked the start of a new direction for the brand's communication. It emphasized that sahibinden.com is not just a platform for transactions. It's a cultural touchstone in Turkey, a place where millions of stories come to life.

Consistently Leading in Employee Satisfaction: sahibinden.com prioritizes the health, happiness, and safety of its employees by ensuring a secure working environment in line with human rights and ethics-compliance policies. Employee satisfaction and career development are key focuses. To build an equitable, inclusive, and participatory company culture, sahibinden.com continuously develops communication methods and channels to listen, hear, and understand the employees. Employee experience initiatives are shaped by the feedback and suggestions received from the workforce, with the goal of creating environments where employees can perform at their best and work happily. The company has received the Great Place to Work award nine times, based on employee votes and evaluations. Additionally, it scored 83 points in the 2023

Happy Place to Work Survey (Turkey's Happiest Workplaces Survey), earning the Outstanding Employee Experience Certificate and Award.

The professional and passionate employees of sahibinden.com are dedicated to adding value to users' lives and delivering the best experiences through investments in innovation, digitalization, and a customer-focused service approach.

A Brand Embracing the Future: Through its strong technological infrastructure and innovative business model, sahibinden.com aims to contribute to the circular economy and environmental sustainability by enabling the reuse of second-hand products. Today, sahibinden.com is considered the backbone of the "second-hand ecosystem" when it comes to discussing the circular economy. The brand is committed to inspiring the industry and raising awareness in society with its environmental and social consciousness. Since 2021, sahibinden.com has been publishing the "Contribution of Second-Hand to Sustainability" report, measuring how users' preference for second-hand products contributes to sustainability and the circular economy. It is also one of the first e-commerce companies to sign the United Nations Women's Empowerment Principles and to earn the Green Office Certificate. Additionally, sahibinden.com is a member of LFCA (Leaders for Climate Action), which aims to create a carbon-neutral technology industry. The company has long been committed to internal efforts focused on energy conservation, renewable resources, and the conscious use of natural resources. As a signatory of the Women's Empowerment Principles (WEPs), sahibinden.com has also working towards publishing a Corporate Sustainability Report since the beginning of 2024.

Conclusion

Starting its journey in 2000 with just 2,700 listings, sahibinden.com has become "the address where dreams come true". Today, it touches the lives of millions of people in Turkey daily, offering a platform that users enjoy exploring as much as they would from a social media app. For many, browsing "Sahibinden" has become a hobby, and the platform opens doors to unique terminologies and uses in everyday language. From its inception, sahibinden.com has maintained the agility and dynamism of a startup with its continuously evolving business approach, enthusiasm, and communication tone. It consistently finds new ways to fulfill users' dreams and make their lives easier.

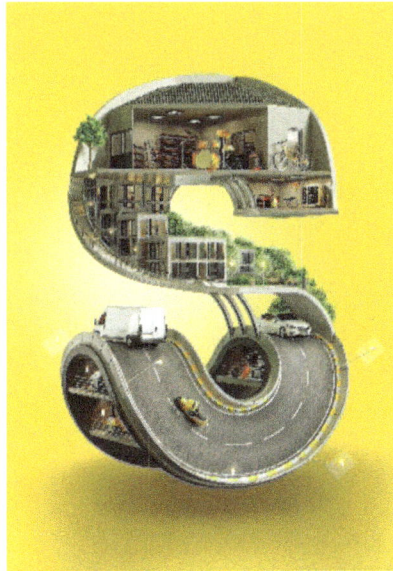

1.   How sahibinden.com encouraged consumers to transition from traditional to digital platforms?

sahibinden.com's digital platform allowed customers to access it 7/24, which encouraged them to migrate from traditional marketplaces to take advantage of the ease of anytime browsing and transactions. Also, the launch of a user-friendly mobile app allowed users to browse and post ads conveniently. sahibinden's interface design ensured ease of navigation, enabling even those unfamiliar with technology to comfortably browse and list items. The extensive search feature on sahibinden, lets users find listings that best suit their needs and interests, making it one of the most beneficial instruments for users.

Links and media

20.YIL: https://www.youtube.com/watch?v=a2mEkroSCwk
Sahibinden'in Sahibi Sizsiniz: https://www.youtube.com/watch?v=NKk8QlHoIew
Muhtemelen Yoktur :(2014-2018-2022)
https://www.youtube.com/watch?v=FvQPsMcodO0
https://www.youtube.com/watch?v=vvTmCYk7dh8
https://www.youtube.com/watch?v=7smDLJ4EtoI

7.9 ENHANCING OFFLINE PROMOTION

Digital marketing is much more than a communication revolution.

Referring to mere literary terminology, it would be more appropriate to think of an evolution so radical as to upset the methods and timing of interaction to the point of touching the contents.

Digital channels grew up alongside the so-called traditional communication. They expanded their boundaries, making them more blurred, but they did not erase them: people all over the world still leave their homes, buy magazines, and paper books, watch TV, and go to the cinema. They meet up, meet live, off social media platforms, hold meetings, tell stories, or share experiences. Even if online shops had an enormous growth during the pandemic, humans still buy in real shops, choose by touching the goods, nodding at the products, and are influenced by the position on the shelves and by the promotions at the point of sale. They still go to fairs. They meet their potential customers and partners, live, one to one, away from the web.

The streets of the whole planet are still dotted with dynamic and static outdoor advertising, such as streetside billboards or maxi-billboards that cover entire buildings.

On national, public, and private broadcasters, there are still thousands of commercials created according to the same logic that gave rise to the first television formats.

The evolution of virtual tools and interactions has reduced distances and facilitated interactions but has not replaced real contact nor traditional communication.

Thinking about Web Marketing as a strategic tool for companies, it is possible to arrive at the same conclusion. The starting point is, absurdly, the very end. It is undeniable that any business's final goal is the sale to the person and, consequently, the beginning must always be an analysis of the needs and the potential public market.

As long as the final subject of each trade is the human component - as is usual - the series of roads that pass through contact and free will, will be essential.

Hence, the acquisition of qualified contacts, online campaigns, and the generation of brand visibility do not entirely replace relational activities such as trade fairs, business meetings, and sector events.

These remain and, indeed, today they see the implementation of new communication channels to increase the appeal of a brand.

It, therefore, becomes easy to understand how, in this new digitized and globalized post-pandemic world, social media and online web activities are valuable tools for achieving goals that were previously difficult to reach.

The effectiveness of a fair, meetings or negotiations between countries increases credibility and success in a system where the information of a core business anticipates the work of personal promotion.

Before a meeting with a potential customer or partner, the research on the net allows companies to acquire valuable data and facilitate a happy outcome of the negotiation.

The analysis and study of the markets to approach, speaking of internationalization, via the web, miniaturizes financial exposures and maximizes efforts.

The World Wide Web can reveal itself as strategic in the evaluation and preparation upstream to get to know interlocutors, analyze their visible data and get a framework from which to extrapolate more valid strategies, all just a click away.

With a correct web reputation, it becomes even easier to arrange meetings: thanks to the recognition of the brand, distrust decreases, and doors open more easily.

In this sense, social media, in particular, became the secret weapon for export managers during the pandemic. Companies have learned to use the web to develop a helpful authority to approach fairs and missions differently. When the Brand Awareness process has been started correctly, then the contacts received already know the company's name and are more willing to start a negotiation.

8. THE RISE OF AI-DRIVEN METAHUMANS

Our technological world is going through a paradigm shift as never seen before in decades. The shift has gone so fast that most people do not realize it is happening. This process, which was introduced with Industry 4.0, this process is now shaped not only by automation, but also by advanced technologies such as artificial intelligence and machine learning. Mainstream media, academia and business leaders may still be talking about the digital transformation of the past, but the reality is that the full connectivity of Industry 4.0 is already part of our everyday lives.

Industry 3.0 digitalized and continues to convert data into bytes on cloud servers around the world. Industry 4.0 connects machines to machines using that data without going through human intervention. Robots have begun to talk to robots, bots to bots and systems to systems.

Analytics 4.0 rapidly followed. Data Science has entered the world of connections, data flowing through IoT, smartphone apps, smart home appliances, industrial sensors, and raw data from any smart device. Raw data from industrial sensors and all kinds of smart devices are now processed in a dynamic ecosystem and transformed into valuable insights. Today, data flows and connections are at the centre of innovation and pave the way for future technological developments.

The result is an accumulation wave of petabytes of data through billions of devices added to the billions of pieces (text, audio, and video) of data coming from social media. In less than a few years, it had become impossible for humans to process this data manually. Moreover, it had become nearly impossible to face these colossal amounts of data with classical software, including state-of-the-art 2015 artificial intelligence.

The big tech world could not survive without processing the incoming data in an age of efficiency, performance, and accountability.

In 2017, the Transformer solved the problem of processing massive datasets. Google produced a unique artificial intelligence industrialized model that could perform a wide range of tasks better than any other algorithm. Between 2017 and now, the architecture of Transformer models has reached the level of human baselines. OpenAI has taken this development a step further and introduced GPT-4 and beyond. This new generation of models *can effectively take on tasks, even in areas where they have not been trained before!*

All that remained was to add a physical form to these human-like algorithms and the concept of the AI-powered "meta-human" was born! Today, such systems are digital beings that can mimic human interactions and can be used in a variety of applications.

However, the most powerful and effective transformers are mainly *invisible*. They are deeply embedded in Google Search, YouTube, Facebook, and online software in general. These humanlike invisible and increasingly visible metahumans understand our language, images, and, most importantly, our behavior. They know who we are and thus possess an incredible marketing power. They can provide us with consumption recommendations but also influence us in many other ways.

We will first see how consumer-orientated AI is built on traditional marketing. Then we will explore the humanlike transformers we now call foundation models. Next, we will witness the rise of metahumans. Finally, we will peek into what could be the next steps.

8.1 THE MANUFACTURING OF THE "ALL-AMERICAN" BREAKFAST

Who would doubt today that bacon and eggs represent the "all-American" breakfast? Every restaurant, hotel, and millions of households in the US will defend bacon and eggs as a beacon of American culture. Yet this craving for bacon and eggs was artificially implanted in the "healthy diet" mind map of unconscious American consumers.

This marketing strategy began with Gustave Le Bon. Le Bon had already laid out the basic theory of crowd psychology in 1895 and how it can be manipulated in *Psychologie des Foules* ("Psychology of Crowds"). Thus, Le Bon already linked psychology and crowds.

Walter Lippman took these concepts further in 1922 in *Public Opinion*. He invented the term "the manufacture of consent." He explains how public opinion can be manipulated by manufacturing consent. He shows how it can be applied in economics, politics, and any domain involving public opinion. In one chapter, he lays the grounds for 21rst century AI-driven marketing in one simple phrase: "The old constants of our thinking have become variables." Lippman stresses the importance of leading the crowds in the right direction using *psychological propaganda* "not necessarily in the sinister meaning of the word alone."

Edward Bernay, Sigmund Freud's nephew, transformed early theory into a pragmatic theory that he successfully implemented for decades in *Propaganda* (1928). He found that the root of a human's decision laid in the opinions of those they trusted the most. He thus invented the concept of a "sponsoring committee."

20th-century marketing was born. The sponsoring committee would manufacture the consent of the crowds through advertisements and events.

One of Bernay's most significant successes is eaten by millions of Americans every day at breakfast.

In the 1920s, Beech-Nut Packing Company in the US experienced a brutal slump in bacon sales, one of their main products. The 19th century of hard-working labour requiring *heavy* calorie-packed breakfasts was over. Instead, Americans wanted to be slim. So, they ate a *light* breakfast with orange juice, some toast, and coffee. The 1920 American was slim, keen on exercising and trying to live a healthy life. Beech-Nut Packing Company needed to change that. And fast.

Edward Bernay was now a recognized expert of the manufacture of consent after having masterminded a campaign to convince young American men to go to war with the "evil huns" in WWI. At the time, few Americans wanted to fight. Edward Bernay, with many others, manipulated the public as described in *Propaganda*, 1928.

After his successful WWI campaign, Bernay had to convince Americans to go to war against healthy breakfasts. His goal was to convince Americans that a *heavy* breakfast was *healthier* than a *light* breakfast.

He first asked one physician to write to five thousand physicians to ask for them to confirm this. He received about four thousand five hundred written answers confirming that a heavy breakfast was healthier than a light breakfast.

He and his team then ran newspaper campaigns around the country, publicizing those heavier breakfasts were healthier. Headlines of newspapers stated that thousands of physicians advised eating a heavier breakfast to improve the health of children and adults. In short, fatter was better.

The articles used psychological manipulation inception techniques by stating here and there that bacon and eggs widely improved your healthy heavier breakfast.

Beech-Nut Packing Company's sales of bacon increased significantly. The myth of the "All-American" bacon-and-eggs breakfast is implanted in the minds of Americans to this very day, along with a wide range of sugar-packed food.

The transition from reality to hyper-reality had begun.

8.1.1 FROM REALITY TO HYPER-REALITY

After WWII, the word "propaganda" went out of fashion. However, the Ministry of Propaganda of the Third Reich proved the effectiveness of propaganda most evilly in the history of humanity.

The term "propaganda" was replaced by "public relations."

Today we do not use the word "manipulation" but "influencing" or "lobbying" in social media and media in general. "Lobbyists" are in every country and "influencers" on every social media platform.

The pre-WWII techniques have improved exponentially with the arrival of the World Wide Web, big data, and artificial intelligence.

Let's take a deep look into what we are dealing with. Then, we will use a smartphone camera to illustrate the paradigm change we are experiencing from reality to AI-driven hyper-reality.

Imagine you are taking a picture of your family. If you have a recent Google Pixel model or any other trendy brand, your camera emulates a physical camera with AI software. Suppose your family is standing there and one of the members of your family is blinking. Frustrating right? Like other similar brands, Google Pixel has a feature that will take video frames of the family until you press the button to take the photo. Then it will run powerful AI to choose the best images. It will process the colours, forms, and lighting.

In the end, the picture of your family at the precise moment you press the button to take the photo will look extraordinary. However, it is *not your family*! Your family is not perfect, with fantastic Hollywood-level photos. Your family contains flaws that often generate more emotions than a perfect image. We often smile at old pre-AI photos and say, "see how I closed my eyes to bother my parents!" Now, you are not looking at a moment but processed enhanced frames stacked up to make reality *automatically* better than what it is.

An AI-driven camera will not provide the reality of the moment but a manufactured cleansed hyper-reality of a family event.

Figure 8.1 sums up the process that takes us from reality to hyper-reality.

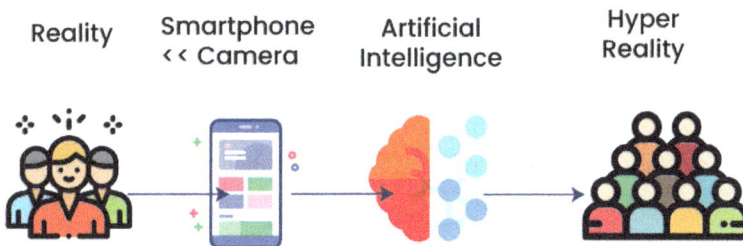

Reality　　Smartphone　　Artificial　　Hyper
　　　　　　<< Camera　　Intelligence　　Reality

Figure 8.1: From reality to hyper-reality.

The processing of reality to manufacture, or lightly put, "create," hyper-reality applies to almost every domain in our digital world: news, streaming, chats, and all forms of media and social media in general. About 90% of the world's population, around 7.5 billion people, own a smartphone. Everywhere we go, we see people on their smartphones, including us!

Humanity perceives reality through the prism of hyper-reality generated by cloud technology, big data, and artificial intelligence.

Figure 8.2 generalizes the paradigm of the industry 4.0 connected digital world we live in. We have created a digital hyper-reality map of the world through which we perceive reality.

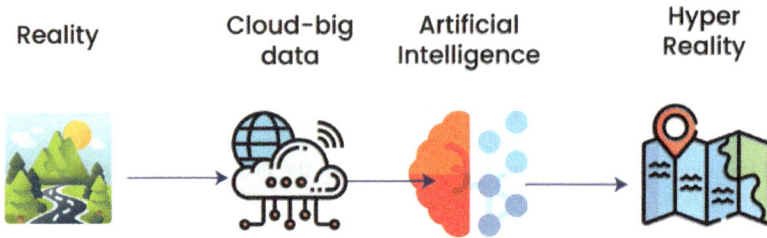

Reality   Cloud–big data   Artificial Intelligence   Hyper Reality

Figure 8.2: From reality to hyper-reality.

Building a digital world of hyper-reality is a step-by-step process in a pipeline. For example, in figure 8.3, you can see that a semantic sign (text, audio, video, signal, etc.) contains three components:

- **The Signifier.** The signifier is the physical part of a sign. In this era, it has become a difficult concept to understand! The signifier can be a word such as "cake," for example. But the word cake is not the cake! You cannot eat the word "cake." The map is not the territory.

- **Hyper-reality.** The hyper-reality layer of a sign has evolved beyond traditional media representations. Today, through technologies like the metaverse, virtual reality (VR), and augmented reality (AR), individuals can experience immersive digital environments that blend with real-world interactions. For instance, a teenager buying a pair of Nike shoes may now also buy a virtual pair of sneakers in the metaverse or even an NFT to display on their social media profiles. They are not just buying shoes but a full experience that transcends physical reality.

- **The signified.** In the age of algorithms and personalized media content, the signified has become nearly obsolete. Social media platforms curate content that appeals to users' preferences, reinforcing hyper-reality and creating digital echo chambers. With hyper-reality now omnipresent in the form of branded content, ideological narratives, and immersive digital experiences, reality itself is often overshadowed. Consumers interact more with digital representations and virtual identities than the actual world. Hyper-reality has almost replaced reality in many spheres, especially among younger generations. Digital items, such as NFTs and virtual identities, have become extensions of personal identity and status.

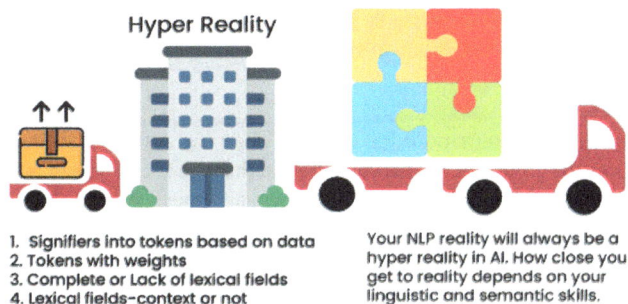

Sign=Signifier + Hyper Reality + Signified

Hyper Reality

1. Signifiers into tokens based on data
2. Tokens with weights
3. Complete or Lack of lexical fields
4. Lexical fields–context or not

Your NLP reality will always be a hyper reality in AI. How close you get to reality depends on your linguistic and semantic skills.

Figure 8.3: The hyperreality pipeline.

The vanishing representations of reality are progressively being replaced by hyper-reality:

- consumption on an e-commerce "store" is replacing the physical store. But this is not limited to a digital store. Thanks to augmented reality (AR) and virtual reality (VR) applications, it is now possible to experience a product digitally without going to a physical store. For example, with IKEA's AR app, a user can digitally place furniture in their room. Such applications take the shopping experience beyond the physical world.

- An e-commerce site such as Amazon is *not* an ordinary store. Instead, it is packed with algorithms that analyze our behavior and continuously suggest other items to purchase. Amazon offers a system that empowers hyper-reality with personalized recommendations, automated customer service (e.g. chatbots) and targeted advertising. Thus, the consumer not only shops, but also exists in a digital ecosystem where their behavior is constantly monitored and shaped.

Waiting time is becoming a deprecated concept. We can consume *continuously*:

- On Deezer or Spotify, we can consume one "record" after the other. So, there is no need to wait like in the old days when we had to purchase a record physically. Thus, the time to access music is zero. This increases not only the availability of music, but also users' expectation of instant gratification. Listeners can now consume content without waiting to discover new songs and create personal playlists.

- On Netflix or Prime Video, we can consume one video after the other. So, there is no need to *wait* to go to a physical theatre. Moreover, platforms keep the user in the content consumption cycle by constantly offering new series and movie recommendations by monitoring consumer behavior. This ensures uninterrupted consumption.

The excitation of the deprecation of waiting time is the force driving society into hyper-reality.

The old "signified" reality-driven relation with the "signifier" is melting by the day. So, the act of physically somewhere for something is for "old-timers."

Hyper-reality has become the new reality of our civilization:

- we don't need to waste time going somewhere for something;
- we avoid traffic jams, so it is even sustainable and green;
- we are not impeded by the unpleasantness of the physical world of consumption.

Soon, we will not be driving our cars physically anymore. Instead, we will be browsing online, attending virtual meetings, or having augmented reality (AR) experiences while going from one place to another as we do in public transportation or taxis.

The billions of hyper-reality representations (text, audio, video, signals) are stored on big data servers. As soon as this data touches the ground on the servers, they go through sophisticated AI-driven algorithms that analyze the data, your profile, your behavior, your location, and more. Advanced AI-driven algorithms use this data to deliver personalized content and services. Much more.

Google Search is driven by Foundation Models that we will go through in the next section. Google Search learns who you are through your web browsing. Each Google Search user obtains different pages when searching. These models analyze the subtleties of language with natural language processing (NLP) algorithms and provide customized experiences based on personal needs.

The World Wide Web (WWW) is a vast map of a territory we are losing touch with. But unfortunately, the map is not the territory. Hyper-reality is not reality. Nevertheless, by understanding the architecture of big tech AI, we can see the territory more clearly from this map.

The goal is to use AI as a tool by perfectly understanding it. Once you master AI, it becomes a fantastic tool that enhances our performances!

8.2 SUPERHUMAN AI: FOUNDATION MODELS

8.2.1 AI FOUNDATION MODELS

A Foundation Model is a transformer model that can perform natural language processing, computer vision, and any signal. Such models are revolutionizing artificial intelligence with their versatile learning capabilities and large-scale data analysis capacity. Transformer models have the following basic properties:

Multimodal learning: The ability to establish meaningful relationships between different types of data, such as words, images, sounds. For example, the capacity to recognize an image and produce text about it.Ability to generalize: Not only can they learn specific languages or tasks, but they also have the ability to use this knowledge in new and untrained tasks.Unlimited scalability: These models can be trained with virtually unlimited data and can be used for larger tasks.Performing complex tasks (Emergence): They can succeed even in tasks for which they have not been trained before, i.e. they show the ability to solve new tasks as they arise. Homogenization: The same model can perform a wide variety of tasks; it can translate between languages, analyze images, generate text and more. Our natural ecosystem or eco-human abilities are universal. Human operational activities can be divided into multiple functions, as shown in figure 8.4.

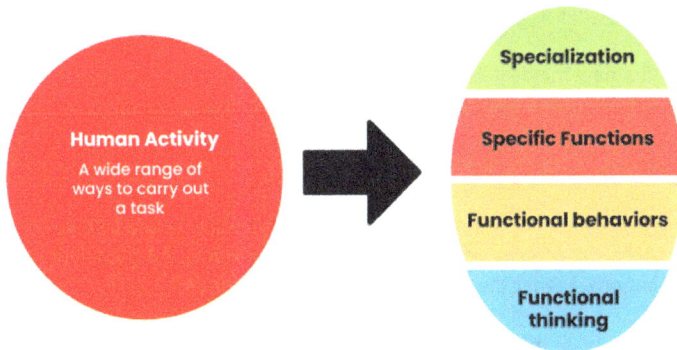

Figure 8.4: Splitting human activity into functions.

By dividing human activity into smaller identifiable repetitive tasks, AI can now reproduce and replace a wide range of functional and practical human tasks.

8.2.1.1 Tasks

A transformer model, such as GPT-4, or a fully trained baseline model, such as Google PaLM, has the capacity to perform an almost unlimited number of tasks. These models succeed not only in natural language processing, but also in multimodal tasks such as the integration and interpretation of visual and auditory signals. These capabilities of basic models go beyond understanding language demands and offer a wide range of applications to solve many complex problems. Artificial intelligence is becoming increasingly proficient in understanding not only our individual demands, but also in learning new tasks and combining them with prior knowledge. Naturally, these tasks cannot replace human analysis for complex tasks such as legal and medical documents. However, one slight mistake could lead to critical life-and-death situations.

However, transformer NLP tasks can perform a wide variety of tasks that exponentially increase a user's productivity. Therefore, there is no doubt that a corporation that possesses these tools has a competitive edge over its competitors.

The foundation model transformer does not train to perform specific tasks. Instead, a transformer learns how to understand a language. Then the system will generate sequences based on our ability to show it what to do. When the system predicts, it does not rely on data anymore. It uses its intelligence.

In this section, we will explore five tasks among others that you can invent through well-defined requests called "prompts." Prompts are natural language phrases we define to show the AI engine what we expect.

8.2.1.2 Summarizing

OpenAI GPT-4 and similar models can adapt summarization tasks to each person or audience. The ability to adjust the summarization style according to the audience's level of professional knowledge, language skills or the platform on which the summary will be used is a result of the advanced personalization features of such models. For example, the following text comes from one of my posts on LinkedIn:

"What will developers do in a world I4.0 of automated development? OpenAI GPT-3 automates everything, including writing code for OpenAI's API!

It is clear that without a new mindset and set of new skills, 2010 developers and data scientists will seem obsolete by the end of this decade even if they have a job (which is a great thing, of course!).

However, the exciting jobs will be for the happy few who adapted and work on the cutting edge, as always.

This post is part of my Analytics 4.0 sharing until the end of the poll I started last week. The poll has drawn 50,000 views, but I haven't seen comments of a clear vision of Industry 4.0-Analytics 4.0 that reflects the animated gif below that proves that the future lies beyond tools for us."

Now, suppose I want to explain this to a second grader. OpenAI accepts natural language requests. So, we have to write meaningful prompts to guide the AI GPT-3 or GPT-4 engine.

My second grader asked me what this passage means:

"What will developers do in a world I4.0 of automated development? OpenAI GPT-3 automates everything, including writing code for OpenAI's API!

It is clear that without a new mindset and set of new skills, 2010 developers and data scientists will seem obsolete by the end of this decade even if they have a job (which is a great thing, of course!).

However, the exciting jobs will be for the happy few who adapted and work on the cutting edge, as always.

This post is part of my Analytics 4.0 sharing until the end of the poll I started last week. The poll has drawn 50,000 views, but I haven't seen comments of a clear vision of Industry 4.0-Analytics 4.0 that reflects the animated gif below that proves that the future lies beyond tools for us."

I rephrased it for him, in plain language a second grader can understand.

We can see that:

- "My second grader asked..." is the initial prompt to explain what we expect.
- "What will developers do..." is the text I took from my LinkedIn post.
- "I rephrased it for him..." is an additional prompt to show the system what to do.
- The automatic output of the GPT-3 engine is rather impressive:

"It means that the future lies beyond the tools and that we should focus on the mindset and skills to work in an automated world."

The grammar is at a human level. The summary provides insights and sums up my ideas perfectly.

Summarizing with foundation models has become an asset for many software editors seeking new markets:

- Adapting summaries to the level of a reader, an audience, or a class.
- Fine-tune articles to make them more concise.
- And any other summarizing task you can imagine!
- Summarizing legal documents.

8.2.1.3 Notes to summary

Sometimes, we take quick notes during a meeting and then write an email, to sum up, the meeting.

First, we enter a prompt to tell the transformer model what we want:

Convert my shorthand into a first-hand account of the meeting:

Then, enter your notes:

profits up 10%, infrastructure ok, software bugged, beta-testing needed

Finally, I ask for the task expected:

Summary:

The output of the model focuses on precisely the issues to solve:

Company is doing well but needs to come up with a solution for the software bug, and more beta-testing.

Once again, we created the task with a prompt and could have created many other tasks we think of this way.

8.2.1.4 Question and Answer

Question and answering can prove quite practical if we clearly define what we expect and don't ask ambiguous questions.

We must follow the procedure. The first step is to use OpenAI's prompt to tell the transformer model what we expect:

I am a highly intelligent question answering bot. If you ask me a question that is rooted in truth, I will give you the answer. If you ask me a question that is nonsense, trickery, or has no clear answer, I will respond with "Unknown".

Then we ask each question beginning with "Q:" (Question), and the model will answer after "A:"

The following dialog shows that the system answers questions but also builds on the previous dialog.

I am a highly intelligent question answering bot. If you ask me a question that is rooted in truth, I will give you the answer. If you ask me a question that is nonsense, trickery, or has no clear answer, I will respond with "Unknown".

Q: Can you define artificial intelligence?
A: Artificial intelligence is the intelligence exhibited by machines or software.
Q: Can machine intelligence use semantic search?
A: Yes.
Q: Can you define semantic?
A: Semantic is the meaning of words.
Q: Give me an example of a semantic analysis of the word house?
A: A house is a building that is used as a home.
Q: What is a hypernym?
A: A hypernym is a word that is more generic than another word.
Q: What is the hypernym of house?
A: Dwelling.
Q: What is a higher hypernym of the previous word?
A: Shelter.

You will notice that the last question refers to the "previous" word not the actual word. And that the answer is correct.

A software editor can build endless chatbot dialogs based on this task.

8.2.1.5 Interview questions

Sometimes finding interview questions can be challenging. For example, imagine we have to create questions for a job interview for a machine learning candidate.

The first step consists in defining the prompt:

Create a list of questions for my job interview with a machine learning candidate:

The system generates the questions required:

1. What is your favourite machine learning algorithm?
2. What is the difference between supervised and unsupervised machine learning?
3. What is the difference between open and closed machine learning systems?

However, some additional definitions may be necessary. We can go back to the question-and-answer task for explanations with simple "Q:" prompts and note the answers shown in the following dialog.

The dialog begins with the prompt we went through in the previous task, and then we can obtain the definitions we need to prepare for the job interview:

"I am a highly intelligent question answering bot. If you ask me a question that is rooted in truth, I will give you the answer. If you ask me a question that is nonsense, trickery, or has no clear answer, I will respond with "Unknown".

Q: What is the difference between supervised and unsupervised machine learning?

A: Supervised machine learning is when you give the machine learning algorithm a set of data that has been labeled. Unsupervised machine learning is when you give the machine learning algorithm a set of data that has not been labeled.

Q: What is the difference between open and closed machine learning systems?

A: Open machine learning systems are systems that are open to the public. Closed machine learning systems are systems that are not open to the public."

To sum up this sometimes-complex task, transformers helped us:

- find questions for an interview
- go through the answers the transformers gave
- ask transformers to explain the definitions of the correct answers

We can see the time saved by the use of transformers.

8.2.1.6 Natural Language to Code

OpenAI trained a Codex, a GPT-3 transformer model, to generate code with natural language. But improvements have not been limited to Codex; newer models further optimize the code writing process, offering benefits such as minimizing errors, completing more complex projects faster, and speeding up debugging processes. Development time has impeded the progress of many projects up to now. Codex will take your teams to the next level and save incredible development time and project costs.

It seems impossible. However, reality has begun to exceed fiction. Let's take the case of the product manager. They want to show the development team the potential of Codex. The users have been asked to the meeting too to show them that, from now on, they can participate in product development!

Let's see how the job was done with Codex by a user!

First, the user enters a sentence in natural language:

Draw a small basketball and make it bounce around.

Codex does two things at the same time:

- It generates source code automatically

```
var ball = document.createElement('div'); ball.style.width = '50px'; ball.style.height = '50px'; ball.style.back-
groundColor = '#009900'; ball.style.position = 'absolute'; ball.style.left = '50px'; ball.style.top = '50px';
ball.style.borderRadius = '50%'; ball.style.webkitAnimation = 'bounce 1s infinite'; ball.style.animation = 'bounce
1s infinite'; document.body.appendChild(ball);
```

- It creates the page automatically

Now the user asks the program to bounce the code around:

bounce the ball around the window

Codex does two more things at the same time again:

- It generates source code to bounce the ball in the window:

```
var x = 0; var y = 0; var dx = 1; var dy = 1; var maxX = window.innerWidth - 50; var maxY = window.innerHeight
- 50; var interval = setInterval(function() { x += dx; y += dy; if (x > maxX) { dx = -1; } if (x < 0) { dx = 1; } if
(y > maxY) { dy = -1; } if (y < 0) { dy = 1; } ball.style.left = x + 'px'; ball.style.top = y + 'px'; }, 10);
```

- Then it bounces the ball in the window:

The user could continue to add lines and lines of natural-language-to-code functionality to the program.

The product manager has demonstrated that critical time can now be saved on each project.

Codex will significantly reduce the time to market many products.

What will developers do in a world I4.0 of automated development? Models like OpenAI Codex and GPT-4 even automate writing code for OpenAI APIs! It is clear that without a new mindset and set of new skills, 2010 developers and data scientists will seem obsolete by the end of this decade even if they have a job (which is a great thing, of course!).

However, exciting jobs will be there for those who adapted and work on the cutting edge, as always.

8.2.2 THE LIMITS OF FOUNDATION MODELS

Foundation models can generate hundreds of tasks based on a new generation of engineers' imagination, skills, and talent to design effective prompts.

It's not productive to analyze NLP Transformers measured purely in size. So the bigger it is, the smarter it is? So now Nvidia has a Megatron-Turing NLG 530B. Does that mean it's better or simply more powerful?

We can rightly wonder about the increasing size and if it would follow some kind of Moore's Law. Nvidia's Megatron-Turing possesses 530 billion parameters. We have 86 billion neurons but exponentially more in connections. This makes Nvidia's 530 billion parameter model tiny compared to our thinking capacity. So basically, we are still in the early days of this technology.

Power will solve basic human functions for specific micro-decisions and tasks.

Power will NOT solve the fundamental problem of reaching high-level human reasoning power. This will require SEMANTIC RULES injected automatically into transformers at a large scale.

For example, consider the following phrase: "A most dangerous game" (1924 novel by Connell).

In this context, a game can mean a dangerous game because a hunter is hunted by Zaroff, the hunter in the novel. However, a game can also mean a dangerous game (in the sense of what is hunted) because the hunted hunter becomes more dangerous than Zaroff. In this case, the hunted is the dangerous game that was initially supposed to be prey.

With OpenAI GPT-3, an otherwise extraordinary tool, this is how far you can go without injecting semantic rules:

Q: What does a dangerous game mean?
A: A dangerous game is a game that is likely to cause injury or death.
Q: But is there another meaning to game?
A: Yes, a game is a form of play or sport, especially a competitive one played according to rules and de-cided by skill, strength, or luck.
Q: Yes but if somebody is hunting, what's the game?
A: The game is the animal being hunted.
Q: So then what could a dangerous game mean in that sense?
A: A dangerous game could mean a game that is likely to cause injury or death.

We can conclude this experiment with another usage of the word "game": game over!

This version of OpenAI's transformers understands the subtility of a language as we can to a certain extent. The machine intelligence of transformers is enough to create powerful eCommerce applications.

8.2.3 EMBEDDED METAHUMAN RECOMMENDERS: ECOMMERCE

AI Technology has gone from analyzing marketing segments to personal profiling. Private data has gone far beyond the name, gender, address, location, phone number, credit card number, etc. That was in the old days!

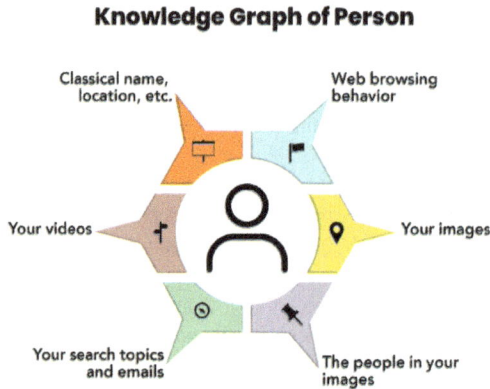

Figure 8.5: Knowledge graph.

Today, knowledge graphs make customized profiles of each person, as shown in figure 8.5. Knowledge graphs are built on top of big data. AI-driven recommenders have evolved significantly with the arrival of transformer models. As a result, they are deeply embedded in pipelines based that create and use knowledge graphs:

- A person browses on the web, purchases products, takes pictures, watches video, makes phone calls, texts others, and many other things.
- Every activity is tracked and stored in raw formats in big data.
- Classical algorithms, classical artificial intelligence, and transformers analyze the sequences of our behavior.
- Knowledge graphs are for each of us.
- Knowledge graphs are built for people similar to us.
- AI generates correlations between us and others.
- Recommenders, learn, train, and reach humanlike machine intelligence and predictions.

As a result, recommender systems evolve through the continuous learning of models with human-like intelligence, better meeting the needs of users and increasing the importance of issues such as personal privacy and data security.

Let's illustrate this with a few days of a person named X and machine intelligence named Y.

- X writes emails. Y parses the emails, classifies them, stores keywords, and more.

- X goes from one location to another. Y can track all the locations in one way or the other on smartphones through several apps.
- X watches a video on streaming platforms while waiting somewhere or in the evening. Y analyzes X's behavior and stores the sequences.
- X listens to music on streaming platforms. Y analyzes X's tastes and behavior.
- X makes purchases online. Y remembers them and learns for them.
- X continues to do things. Y learns from them.

Philip Kotler brought us from old production-to-market models the new consumer-driven innovative marketing.

Artificial intelligence has brought us from a consumer-driven market to a customized personal market for each person!

8.3 THE RISE OF AI-DRIVEN METAHUMANS

The goal of this section is to take you into the *opportunities* and *challenges* of letting a new species of metahumans enter our personal lives and workplaces.

AI-powered digital metahumans are emerging as a new *species* with digital face, voice and behavior simulations. Unfortunately, few people can see the difference between a well-generated digital face and a human face. It's so hard to believe that this section is built on practical examples you can visualize in a few clicks with absolutely no programming skills.

Metahumans are entering our society as a new species.

There is a **lack of training** millions of people worldwide to fit the *immediate* need of a company or a government organization. As a result, companies have often struggled to find the right profile for a job. A small company, for example, cannot afford to hire a USD 150,000 AI engineer to implement systems and train a small team of twenty employees. Likewise, that same small company might not afford to hire a consultant either.

Large corporations must constantly compete with competing entities to hire data scientists, legal advisors, and SMEs (Subject Matter Experts) in many domains.

An AI-driven metahuman trained as a foundation model and fine-tuned.

8.3.1 CREATING A HUMAN FACE

Generated Media, https://generated.photos/, offers digital human faces for many purposes such as advertisements, articles, documents, websites. One of the key advantages of using these AI-generated faces is the lack of copyright restrictions, meaning there are no royalties or licensing fees required. This makes it an attractive option for businesses and creators looking for affordable, royalty-free media solutions while maintaining flexibility in how they use these digital assets.

You can also use these images for valuable tasks:

- for psychological research on human expressions

- to generate billions of new faces and expressions to train AI-driven computer vision programs to recognize humans faces and expressions without using actual human private data

You can go online and create a human face with a few clicks:
https://generated.photos/face-generator/6169408f9f43fe000e4e0a3c

You can add human emotions and make these fake human faces happy, sad, neutral, surprised, and more. It seems exciting and provides new opportunities.

As always, technology comes with its share of dangers. For example, since social media platforms accept profiles without official ID, anybody can:

- Create a fake e-mail.
- Upload a fake photo.
- Create images simulating photos taken of dear fake friends.
- Invent a fake biography.

As a result, individuals can form real connections with others across the globe based on deception. This raises significant concerns about identity theft, fraud, and the potential for emotional manipulation. The consequences can lead to damaged relationships, misinformation, and a general erosion of trust in online interactions. In a world where digital identities are increasingly important, it becomes crucial for users to remain vigilant and discerning about whom they connect with online.

Even better, hackers can do all of this automatically. Digital human faces have already entered our lives, knowingly or unknowingly.

8.3.2 FULLY DIGITAL METAHUMANS

Digital human faces have become full-blown metahumans with a body, clothing, and behaviors. This new generation of metahumans has begun to enter video games and expand to advertisements, corporate videos, support lines, and more.

Epic Games occupies a large share of the video game market. Epic Games has developed Unreal Engine, one of the most powerful animation tools ever. You can now build a metahuman online with an Unreal Engine and import it into your video scenarios.

Developer skills are not required. To see how this is possible, you can simply click on the following link:
https://www.unrealengine.com/en-US/digital-humans

Once the metahuman has been integrated into a game, artificial intelligence functionality can be added. After that, the metahuman will act independently, with its features and a level of freedom in its behavior. In this game, the metahuman has weapons, for example, that are perfectly digitalized real-life weapons in very sophisticated details.

It has become increasingly difficult to distinguish reality from virtual fiction. In addition, augmented reality glasses are now available, making it nearly impossible to distinguish physical reality from digital reality.

The opportunities are endless if you take both AI and robots into account:

- metahumans for support lines and maintenance

- metahumans to ask a patient to describe symptoms and to do some first level AI analysis before contacting a physician
- first-aid suggestions
- first on-site recommendations when a fire begins
- assisting the elderly

With solid government regulations and law enforcement, we will learn how to adapt to the emergence of this new species.

8.3.3 DIGITAL HUMANS IN THE WORKPLACE

UneeQ offers corporate services for digital humans. The idea is to "revolutionize customer relations."

A digital human, or AI-driven metahuman, will interact with your customers at a scale never experienced before.

Often, when we contact a person in a corporation or a support line, we immediately feel the conversation's limits. The person is operating within a framework, and if we step beyond it, the situation escalates. Another person must be contacted, etc.

A digital AI-driven metahuman will provide a customized, deep, and meaningful interaction with a customer. Such interactions not only provide information, but also have the potential to create emotional connections, show empathy and enrich the user experience. In this way, brands can develop stronger relationships with their customers and increase their loyalty.

You can explore the field of customer interactions with absolutely no development skills by click on the following link: https://digitalhumans.com/

Metahumans will exist with no salary to pay. They can work 24/7 with no vacation. They are never sick or never go on strike. They will possess AI that equals and even exceeds human abilities in many cases. They will look deceiving humanlike. They will show emotions both in tone and in facial expressions.

This new species will inevitably exist beyond individual use. They will enter metaverses.

8.3.4 A METAHUMAN METAVERSE

Metahuman societies can be built in a metahuman metaverse. Thus, the market potential is limitless.

Alethea has created a metaverse in which metahumans can exist and thrive. You can create a metahuman and your own metaverse. Or you can join an existing metaverse.

The World Wide Web started with researchers sharing their documents.

A metaverse can be recreational, but it can also be educational, for example.

An educational metaverse can be built for children, teenagers, and adults who cannot access physical professors. In addition, MOOCs are limited in terms of interactions. Therefore, an educational metaverse could be powered by highly intelligent AI-driven metahumans that interact with students, teach, answer questions, summarize knowledge, and more.

You can explore a metaverse live in a few clicks on Alethea: https://alethea.ai/

It is up to governments to create a legal status for metahumans and metaverse societies, just as in the physical world. In an ethical framework, the potential will take us well into another era, possibly Industry 5.0.

8.4 TRANSHUMANISM, THE NEXT STEP?

Humans watch the evolution of artificial intelligence, increasing competition with their intelligence. In the old days, humans were enhanced and replaced by machines that were tools. Then came software as tools.

Artificial intelligence, metahumans, and robots challenge the integrity of the human brain. As a result, insidious questions keep coming up:

Are we smart enough for our world?

- What if AI metahuman software and robots take my job?
- What can I do about this?

The temptation to change humans has become a reality with new technologies like brain-computer interfaces and genetic engineering.

8.4.1 BRAIN-COMPUTER INTERFACES

Brain-Computer Interfaces (BCI) or Mind-Machine Interfaces (MMI) connects the brain to machines, enhancing humans.

In 2016, Elon Musk founded Neuralink with some other investors. Neuralink designs brain implants to enhance humans. OpenAI, the designer of foundation models, also co-founded by Elon Musk, shares the same offices in San Francisco.

The first step in Neuralink's implementation involves surgically operating on a human to install the **Link** device directly in the brain. This device connects the human brain to computers and mobile devices, utilizing micro-threads implanted in the brain to enable individuals to control electronic devices with their thoughts. One of the primary motivations behind developing brain implants is to assist people with paralysis, allowing them to regain some control over their environment and overcome disabilities.

It seems evident that at one point, Link will contain artificial intelligence in one form or another. At that point, super-intelligent humans with BCIs. might form an elite that can surpass 100%, biological humans.

Microsoft finances BCI research as well for augmented or virtual reality, for example. One of the examples they cite involves a worker on a shop floor using a BCI while their hands are busy. Many people will be tempted to increase their productivity with BCIs. Microsoft has dedicated its deep pocket resources on BCI:
https://www.microsoft.com/en-us/research/project/brain-computer-interfaces/

Samsung uses EEG technology for our mind to control tablets, smartphones, and other devices:
https://www.technologyreview.com/2013/04/19/253309/samsung-demos-a-tablet-controlled-by-your-brain/

NeuroSky is already commercializing EEG mind wave headsets:
https://www.amazon.com/dp/B07CXN8NKX/ref=cm_sw_r_tw_dp_WJBAMNJMJ7EP52CPVCYJ

The idea is to use mind wave technology for video games, toys, robots, and any device with remote control features.

8.4.2 GENETIC ENGINEERING

The incredible progress of medical science has demonstrated that artificial intelligence can contribute to progress. It also opens the door to genetic engineering.

Genetic engineering uses recombinant DNA (rDNA) to manipulate genes. Gene therapy will expand in the years to come because of its efficiency. First, however, bear in mind that AI Foundation Models are formidable sequence learners and predictors.

CRISPR (Clustered Regularly Interspaced Short Palindromic Repeats) is a cost-effective gene-editing tool. Research and possibly experiments have begun to engineer smart babies.

8.4.3 A NEW IDEOLOGY

Brain-Computer Interfaces (BCI) have entered the market, and artificial intelligence will undoubtedly become a key component.

Gene engineering has also entered the market, and artificial intelligence will contribute to its evolution.

Transhumanism with BCIs, gene engineering, and more technology to come can change the course of the human race. Will a new elite human species emerge, genetically enhanced, and using BCIs to control a wide range of devices:

https://www.technologyreview.com/2018/11/25/138962/exclusive-chinese-scientists-are-creating-crispr-babies/

Those who resist this movement initiated by Californian billionaires might appear as old-timers.

Suppose this new ideology embraced by many goes into effect. What will happen when an AI-driven hacker hacks the brain implant in a human? Will the person victim of this attack be at the mercy of the hacker? Could it cause brain damage?

Worse is the next step for a hacker-mind-control strategy? Could it start with "mind ads" in children playing video games with EEG detectors that read their minds or ours on smartphones? Then could we be hacked and brainwashed with subliminal ad scenarios?

Each of us will soon be faced with critical choices.

8.5 A PATH TO HUMAN-CENTERED AI

Artificial intelligence has enhanced productivity in all domains. For example, without AI algorithms, it would be nearly impossible to perform searches on the web, read scientific articles worldwide, communicate with each other through web applications, and more.

Web applications tend to reduce physical activity, which can be nefarious. However, AI-driven apps avoid using cars and reduce pollution. Cloud servers consume energy. But cloud servers do not consume the energy it would take to revert all our virtual activity into physical activity.

AI can be a great tool if we follow some common-sense principles.

8.5.1 COMMON-SENSE PRINCIPLES

AI-driven marketing can benefit humanity through the following principles:

- **Education**. Every human being should learn precisely what AI is, does, and can do, from children to CEOs, if each human being understands AI-driven recommender systems. You can then interact with AI-driven systems to your benefit.

- **Regulation**: The public must be informed by a clear message that AI is being used on them. This helps users to become more aware of data privacy and the protection of their personal information. Exactly the way we now get pop-ups for Cookies or big tech gets billion-dollar fines.

- **Humanity**. Big technology companies have an ethical responsibility to provide useful innovations for humanity. The limited use of technologies such as gene engineering and Brain-Computer Interfaces (BCI) should be encouraged for medical and ethical applications only.

- **Empathy**. Anything that AI can do is not the essence of humans. Humans love and have empathy. We should focus on that and never forget that. What's life without emotions? This should be at the center of marketing strategies. Emotions are the cornerstone of the connection between a brand and the consumer.

- **Ethics**. Cultural ethical values in different countries should be considered and diversity should be emphasized. No single company or country can dictate to the rest of the world what is best, so a common ethical ground should be established through international organisations.

- **Bias**. Bias must be based on scientific facts, not opinions. There are simple errors that can be corrected, such as tagging the image of a circle as a "rectangle" because of quality control errors. However, political, religious, and personal opinions require a careful approach that needs to be addressed by each country and culture.

- **AI as a tool**. AI is a fantastic tool for e-commerce, manufacturing, and supply chain management. AI generates tremendous productivity and profits. That is fine if it remains a tool outside our physical body and does not manipulate our minds.

- **Data Privacy.** Data privacy and security should be at the forefront of AI-supported marketing processes. Providing transparency about how users' data is collected and used increase's reliability.

- **Sustainability.** The contribution of AI applications to environmental sustainability is important. Marketing strategies should be designed to minimise environmental impacts.

- **Innovation and Adaptation.** Considering that AI is a constantly evolving technology, marketing strategies need to adapt rapidly to this change. Adoption of innovative methods provides competitive advantage.

You can use AI as a tool or become the tool of AI. The future of your integrity as a human being is in your hands.

9. LEADING BY INNOVATION & DESIGN: STRATEGIES AND VALUE CREATION

Innovation has been universally accepted to be the defining force in modern l'affaire business. Design being a form of and resource for innovation has gained currency in modern times more than ever. As the business structure and environment become increasingly challenging and complex, the adoption of design and innovation lead strategies for sustainable growth and development seem commonplace by more and more companies. As we navigate through COVID 19, economies, Firms and Individuals worldwide have been all efforts leveraging design thinking and innovations to cope with the unprecedented crisis. Designers have been busy with their design thinking and come up with innovative solutions.

DeBresson, one of the leading researchers in the field of innovation mentioned: "One of the most important achievements of contemporary economies and societies is the constant creation of new knowledge. Yet economic theory is still focusing on the problems central to a past epoch: universal scarcity. Economic analysis is still largely focused on the management of scarce resources, what the economists have termed the optimal allocation of factors. Yet the process which characterises today's economy is the creation of new factors."

Economics has long been dealing with issues of allocative efficiency and adaptive efficiency. But the modern economy seems highly characterised by the process of "creative destruction" and the creation of new factors. The celebrated world leading Economists from Adam Smith to Robert Solow, Ricardo, Marx, Marshall, Schumpeter and Keynes all have recognised the importance of innovation and the role it plays in long term growth and productivity. Even the celebrated critic of capitalist society, Karl Marx appreciated the importance of innovation and did mention in the communist Manifesto that "The Bourgeoisie (i.e., capitalism) cannot exist without constantly revolutionizing the instruments of production. Conservation of the old modes of production in unaltered form was, on the contrary, the first condition of existence for all earlier industrial classes. The bourgeoisie, during its rule of scarce one hundred years has created more massive and more colossal productive forces than have all preceding generations together. It has accomplished wonders far surpassing Egyptian pyramids, Roman aqueducts, and Gothic cathedrals..." [Marx and Engels, 1847].

We all know the contribution and the impact companies like Nokia made at one time to the Finnish economy and companies like Google, Microsoft, Facebook continue to do so in times today. The economics of creation and destruction have never been so visible. Have a look at the Unicorns and how they seem to be emerging worldwide, particularly in the USA, UK, India, and China. Unicorn is defined as a company with valuation of more than $ 1 billion There were less than 40 unicorns when venture capitalist Aileen Lee coined the term "Unicorn" in 2013. However, in 2021, one Unicorn emerges every three days.

If one looks around the incredible growth records of the free-market economies, one can easily establish the importance of innovation more than ever. Though the importance of allocative and adaptive efficiency has always been discussed, the changes in the market, technological conditions, augmenting competition; shortening product life cycles have forced the firms to develop the learning economies and creation of new factors.

Well did Schumpeter observe:

"The first thing to go is the traditional conception of the modus operandi of competition. Economists are at long last emerging from the state in which price competition was all they saw. As soon as quality competition and sales effort are admitted into the sacred precincts of theory, the price variable is ousted from its dominant position. However, it is still competition within a rigid pattern of invariant conditions, methods of production and forms of industrial organization in particular... that practically monopolizes attention. But in capitalist reality as distinguished from its textbook picture, it is not that kind of competition which counts but the competition from the new commodity, the new technology, the new source of supply, the new type

of organization which commands a decisive cost or quality advantage and which strikes not at the margins of the profits and the outputs of the existing firms but at their foundations and their very lives" (Schumpeter, 1939).

New product, new production function, new technology, new source of supply, new type of organisation are all outcomes of design and innovation ecology embedded with design thinking, value engineering, industrial and innovative linkages. As design happens to be the core of innovation, the question we may ask is how does design promote innovation? Could design be the basis for competitive advantage at the firm and economy level?

It is with this background that I would like to share how companies can lead by design and innovation and focus on some of the strategic prescriptions for value creation. I will do this by illustrating the following:

1. Micro and Macro impact of Design: How does design impact the firm and economy?

2. Building an Innovation Enterprise: What are the important elements of an innovative enterprise?

3. Building Innovation Conducive Culture: How does an enterprise create a cultural fit conducive to Innovation activities?

4. Design and Innovation: The Future Trends

5. The emergence of the design economy

9.1 MICRO AND MACRO IMPACT OF DESIGN

Executives worldwide seem to be focusing more on design aligned with their vision to enhance enterprise innovation capability and competence. After all, research findings do suggest that organizations with higher innovation intensity tend to perform relatively better. The competitive reality of the new age has brought design and innovation as the central focus. Shrinking product life cycles, shortening strategy life cycles, shifting values of the customers and the suppliers and changes in the marketplace demand the players change the rules of the game.

The American Heritage Dictionary (2000) defines 'design 'as "the purposeful or inventive arrangement of parts or details." According to OECD (1992), design is "the very core of innovation... the moment when a new object is imagined, devised, and shaped in prototype form."

According to Lorenz, "the old weapons for achieving real differentiation have become inadequate. No longer can comparative advantage be sustained for long through lower costs, or higher technologies. The design dimension is no longer an optional part of marketing and corporate strategy but should be at their very core."

Porter (1980) described 'price', 'focus', and 'differentiation 'as the basis for competitive strategy. Within this framework, 'Design 'offers differentiation in features including quality, robustness, precision, ease of use, product appeal, and price.

It is obvious that design actions create value. Better designs yield better business growth opportunities and results. A study by McKinsey & Company titled, "The Business Value of Design" tracked the design practices of 300 publicly listed companies over a five-year period in multiple countries and industries. " The report exhibited the correlation between best design practices and financial performance.

317

Design practices were identified along the four themes of the McKinsey Design Index (MDI):

1. Analytical leadership: Measuring and driving design performance with the same rigor as revenues and costs.

2. User Experience: Breaking down internal walls between physical, digital, and service design and focus on overall user experience.

3. Cross functional talent: Making user-centric design everyone's responsibility.

4. Continuous iteration: De-risking development by continually listening, testing, and iterating with end users.

The research findings produced:

1. A strong correlation between high MDI scores and superior business performance signifying that design performance leads to an increase in revenue and total returns to shareholders. Top-quartile MDI scorers had 32 percentage points higher revenue growth and 56 percentage points higher TRS growth for the period as a whole.

2. Good design matters in all industries.

3. The market disproportionately rewarded companies that truly stood out from the crowd.

Design impacts economies as well. According to a report by the Design Council, UK entitled "Design Economy 2018", the design economy generated £71.7 billion in gross value added (GVA), equivalent to 7.2% of the UK total GVA.

The report shared some of the findings as follows:

- Workers with a design element to their work were 41% more productive than the average.

- Those who invest in and use design strategically (though don't necessarily have a large proportion of designers in their workforce), the average output per employee is greater.

- The use of design within an organisation contributes to an increase in sales turnover, business competitiveness, and awareness and recognition of the brand and/or raises brand loyalty.

- Firms that invest in design are more likely to invest in other intangible assets such as R&D and get them working in synergy to generate new innovations and create additional value.

- Firms with any R&D or design functions or facilities in-house are significantly more likely than average to have developed completely new and original products, services, or processes.

- Design is a form of innovation.

9.2 BUILDING AN INNOVATIVE ENTERPRISE: THE VISION OF INNOVATION

The term Innovation was coined by the German Economist Riedel (1839) and sociologist De Tarde (1890). However, economics of innovation gained its importance only after the release of the Locus Classic "The Theory of Economic Development" by Schumpeter. He defined Innovation as:

- The introduction of a new good

- The introduction of a new method of production,

- The opening of a new market,

- The conquest of a new source of supply of raw materials or half-manufactured goods,

- The carrying out of the new organization of any industry

In Management Challenges for the 21st Century, Peter Drucker wrote: "One cannot manage change. One can only be ahead of it. In a period of upheavals, such as the one we are living in, change is the norm. To be sure, it is painful and risky and above all it requires a great deal of very hard work. But unless it is seen as the task of the organization to lead change, the organization … will not survive." In other words, in order to remain ahead of change companies must learn to encapsulate in their vision the commitment to build the global learning community, incubate new possibilities, manage the present and build the future.

The question remains as to how companies build an innovative enterprise. How do they build innovation culture within and across the value chain?

9.2.1 THE VISION OF INNOVATION

The concept of innovation has been derived from the theory of production (Frisch, 1930), as a change in production function or technique. The productive efficiency and adaptive efficiency have been major drivers of economic growth. The neoclassical economists emphasized "the study of how societies use scarce resources to produce valuable commodities and distribute them among different people," whereas the innovation economists focus on "the study of how societies create new forms of production, products and business models to expand wealth and quality of life." Innovation at the corporate level relates to the firm's capability vis-à-vis the new forms of production, products and business models. So how does the firm build, grow and develop its innovation competence or capability? What is the source of innovation? Where do the winning strategies or ground-breaking ideas come from?

As various studies suggest, many of the revolutionary ideas find their origin in the vision of a single individual (Gary Hamel). They come from visionaries like Bill Gates (Microsoft), Anita Roddick (The Body Shop), Andy Grove (Intel) and many others. Vision supports innovative growth strategies. It sets the stage for all kinds of innovation possibilities including product, process, market, and business innovation. The underlying principle of a solid foundation of creating an enterprise innovation framework is the ability to see through the discrete future outcomes and the ability to build the corporate ecosystem to achieve them.

**CASE STUDY
ZÜBER**

INNOVATING NATURALLY: "HOW ZÜBER REVOLUTIONIZED SNACKING INDUSTRY"

Written by: Züber Strategy and Marketing Team

Introduction

Züber is a trailblazing healthy snack brand from Türkiye, committed to authenticity and all-natural ingredients in a time when both food and life are becoming increasingly artificial and disconnected from reality. In a snack market dominated by processed ingredients and refined sugar, Züber offers delicious alternatives that **challenge** the status quo. From the start, the brand set out to debunk the myth that indulgence leads to regret or that healthy foods lack flavor, showing that mindful choices can be both satisfying and enjoyable. Züber's mission goes beyond creating snacks – it seeks to redefine the snacking experience, turning every choice and moment into an opportunity for a healthier future.

At its core, Züber rejects artificial ingredients and refined sugar. The company is dedicated to crafting snacks with high quality and all-natural ingredients that you can see and pronounce. The brand quickly established itself as the #1 choice in the healthy snacks market, creating new categories with high functional benefits. Once it became the go-to option for consumers seeking delicious, healthy alternatives, Züber shifted its focus toward expanding its influence across the broader snack sector. While staying true to its core principles of taste and a free-from formula, Züber set its sights on growing its presence across multiple snack market verticals. By 2020, the brand strategically transitioned into a comprehensive snack provider, recognizing the need to cater to a wider variety of tastes and occasions. This evolution led to the development of a diverse product portfolio beyond snack bars, shaped by extensive R&D efforts, close work with leading chefs and dietitians that highlighted Züber's commitment to innovation particularly during the COVID-19 pandemic when at-home snacking took on increased importance.

Züber's strategy involves expanding its product line to cater to different snacking and lifestyle needs. The range includes delicious fruit, protein, and granola bars as alternatives to traditional chocolate bars, indulgent Lokma fruit balls offering a healthier spin on classic flavors, and Noutos chickpea chips as a tasty substitute for conventional chips. Although the entire portfolio is perfectly suitable for kids, Züber introduced a Kids line in partnership with "Universal Studios Limited" and "Despicable Me" for further portion control targeting toddlers. Additionally, the brand offers wholesome peanut spreads, hazelnut cocoa spread Nutzilla, peanut cocoa cream Peanutzilla ensuring that every Züber product turns guilty pleasures into health-conscious delights. As a result, Züber is not only competing in the niche healthy snack category but also transforming the broader snack market, setting new standards, and demonstrating that passion can drive innovation to create better solutions.

Challenge

Züber's mission was rooted in addressing Türkiye's significant public health and nutritional challenges that underscored the urgent need for healthier eating options, giving Züber an opportunity to meet the rising demand for nutritious snacks to help counteract these trends.

According to 2016 World Health Organization (WHO) data, Türkiye had the highest adult obesity rate in Europe (32%), and COVID-19 worsened this with 60% of the population gaining 5-10% more weight (Özoğlu, 2021), which are all related with increased health risk. The widespread consumption of ultra-processed foods (UPFs) high in artificial ingredients and low in essential nutrients plays a major role in the obesity epidemic (Monteiro et al., 2013).

Higher consumption of UPFs has been linked to higher risks of serious health conditions, such as cancer and heart disease (Cordova et al., 2023). Other increased risks involve particularly Type 2 diabetes and mental health disorders (Lane et al., 2024). Artificial sweeteners are linked to a 26% higher risk of depression (Sam-uthpongtorn et al., 2023), while diets high in processed sweets are associated with increased symptoms in children with ADHD (Yan et al., 2023).

On the flip side, the lack of consumption of healthy foods like whole grains, nuts, seeds, and milk highlighted the need for comprehensive dietary interventions (GBD 2017 Diet Collaborators, 2018). Züber's dedication to offering tasty snacks made from all-natural, nutrient-dense ingredients with no refined sugar positioned the brand as a key player in addressing these nutritional gaps.

However, as Züber aimed to transition from a healthy snack brand to a comprehensive snack provider, it faced two significant challenges:

1. **Product Range Challenge: Can healthy really be tasty?**

Züber faced the challenge of reshaping consumer expectations that healthy snacks must come at the ex-pense of taste or indulgence. The brand aimed to demonstrate that consumers could enjoy delicious flavors without compromising on health, thereby bridging the gap between indulgence and nourishment.

Expanding beyond the "healthy snack" niche was necessary to challenge the norms of the broader snack category. Züber sought to redefine snacking by introducing products that are not only healthier but could directly compete with mainstream snack options in terms of taste, texture, and overall consumer appeal. This required the brand to position itself as a leader in both health-conscious and indulgent snacking, prov-ing that better-for-you choices can be just as satisfying.

2. **Communication Challenge: What is Züber and why should I care anyway?**

As Züber expanded its product offerings, the brand faced a major communication challenge. Züber not only needed to build brand awareness, for the brand itself, but also market awareness for healthier, free-from alternatives. To stand out in a crowded field of established competitors with hefty media budgets, Züber had to devise a clever, high-ROI marketing strategy.

The goal was to create a distinctive voice that resonated with both health-conscious consumers and those craving tasty, guilt-free snacks. By doing so, Züber aimed to broaden its appeal, boost market penetration, and drive growth in the snack market.

Solution

Becoming the Challenger Brand in the Snack Category:

1.   Portfolio Fulfillment Journey:

Züber's journey began in 2017 with a bold vision: to redefine the snack industry, starting with just four fruit bars. Since then, Züber has continuously expanded its range, introducing Veggie and Kidz series that cater to diverse motivations and occasions, with a dual focus on indulgence and health-conscious choices.

Züber's next breakthrough was the launch of Türkiye's most robust protein snack portfolio in both ball and bar forms, solidifying its market leadership. As the pandemic reshaped consumer behavior, the need for at-home snacking surged. In response, Züber conducted meticulous, insight-driven R&D and worked very closely with chefs and dietitians for the creation of Lokma – an innovative fruit ball that perfectly meeting this new demand and earned the NielsenIQ BASES Breakthrough Innovations 2022 award in the healthy snacks category.

Züber did not stop there. With the introduction of peanut-based spreads, Züber became a staple on breakfast tables and during energy breaks. Soon after, Noutos chickpea chips revolutionized the chips category, proving that chips could be both delicious and all-natural. The brand's magic touch extended to oat-based snacks with the launch of granola bars. Snack lovers rejoiced with the debut of palm oil-free, refined sugar-free, and additive & preservative-free hazelnut cocoa spread Nutzilla, and Peanutzilla, a smooth, creamy peanut butter with cocoa. These two treats are exceptionally delicious yet healthy choices for everyday snacking.

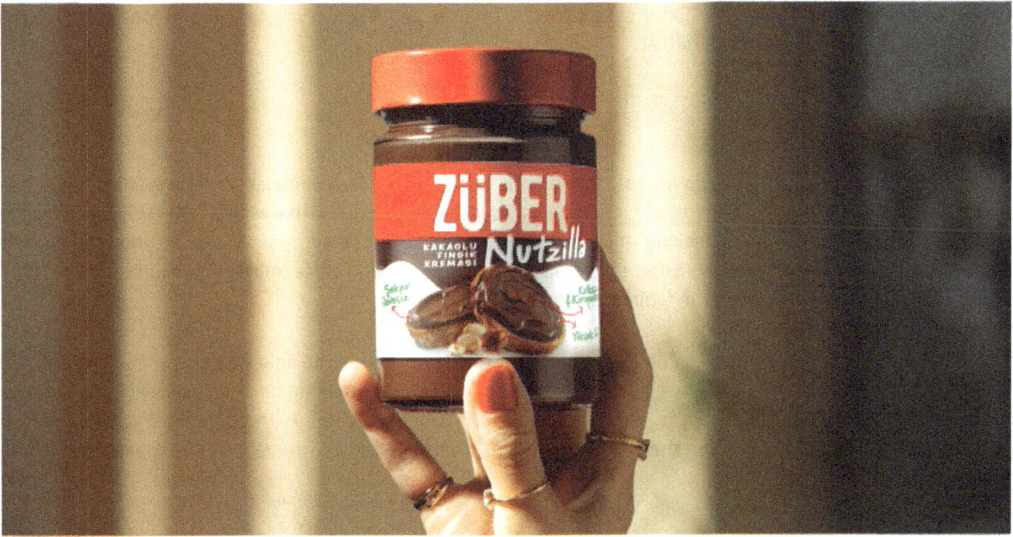

Züber has successfully expanded beyond traditional health bars into indulgent, health-conscious alternatives, directly competing with popular snacks by offering superior, healthier options. This strategic expansion aims to redefine indulgence and health-conscious choices within the category, democratizing healthy snacks for a broader audience and seamlessly fitting into familiar consumption occasions and taste preferences.

2. Communication Fulfillment Journey:

By 2023, after six years of market presence, Züber took a bold step to amplify its voice and redefine its brand narrative. A six-month, deep-dive market study across diverse cities revealed that consumers craved more than just healthier alternatives — they wanted Züber to emerge as a daring lifestyle brand challenging the status quo.

In response, Züber crafted a groundbreaking communication strategy centered on a manifesto film, designed to break away from the superficial marketing that saturates the industry. To capture authenticity and impact, Züber enlisted a directing duo renowned for their documentary work, who had previously avoided commercial projects. This choice ensured that the story felt genuine and unfiltered.

Defying conventional wisdom, which suggested that showing products being enjoyed by glamorous individuals would drive appetite and sales, Züber opted for a radical approach. The brand encouraged viewers to question the authenticity of both media portrayals and the snacks they consume. By highlighting how social media and entertainment often distort reality, Züber positioned its products as "real snacks" made with all-natural, additive-free ingredients. In the ad, only a few seconds were dedicated to Züber products, reinforcing the message of authenticity.

The campaign was further boosted by a collaboration with a well-known Turkish celebrity committed to a healthy lifestyle and social causes. This partnership significantly amplified the campaign's reach, generating 400 million views across Instagram, TikTok, and YouTube. As a result, Züber saw a substantial increase in brand awareness and a surge in retailer interest, with many offerings prime shelf space at no cost.

The two-minute commercial served as a powerful manifesto of Züber's vision, challenging industry norms and encouraging viewers to rethink their choices. It spotlighted Züber's diverse product range, especially its chips, while also featuring protein bars, fruit bars, granola bars, and hazelnut spreads. This approach effectively communicated that Züber's products are both healthy and delicious, strengthening its position as a transformative force in the snack industry.

Through this innovative strategy, Züber established itself as a significant challenger brand, dedicated to re-shaping the snack market for the better.

Conclusion

Züber's evolution from a niche player to a formidable force in the snack industry highlights its relentless commitment to innovation, authenticity, and consumer-driven growth. With over 50 SKUs across 8 categories, Züber redefined healthy snacking and shattered conventional barriers, proving that indulgence and health can coexist harmoniously. Emerging as a dominant brand on supermarket and discount retailer shelves, Züber leads the category in fruit and protein snacks.

This remarkable success embodies Züber's bold vision to revolutionize the snack industry, challenging the status quo and setting new benchmarks. Züber's journey proves that making better, healthier food choices is not only achievable but can also be incredibly delicious and satisfying. As the brand moves forward, it remains dedicated to transforming the snack landscape, creating a better future, one snack at a time.

1.   How did Züber's strategic approach enable it to challenge established norms in the snack industry?

Züber's strategic approach was marked by its willingness to defy the status quo and embrace bold risks. The brand did not just follow market trends; it relentlessly pushed to redefine and reinvent them. With a mindset rooted in continuous learning and fearless experimentation, Züber distinguished itself from the competition. This combination of boldness, meticulous planning, and execution, enabled Züber to challenge and gradually reshape industry standards, cementing its position as a trailblazing leader in the healthy snack market.

2.   How did Züber establish its role as a distinctive challenger in the industry?

Züber's bold vision and strategic positioning turned it into a game-changer in the snack industry. By deeply understanding the key drivers behind consumer decisions and predicting future trends, Züber crafted a strategy that went beyond quick wins. This research-driven approach helped create a unique identity that strongly resonated with people. Züber was not just launching products; it was building a foundation for long-term success by consistently exceeding expectations and breaking industry norms. Its striking communication strategy, highlighted by a daring image film, challenged both product standards and wider industry conventions. As a result, Züber has established itself as a trailblazing leader, setting new standards and redefining the market.

3.   In what ways did Züber's innovation strategy reshape consumer perceptions by blending indulgence with health in the snack market?

Züber's extensive R&D processes combined with a brave innovation strategy were essential to reshape consumer perceptions around healthy snacks. By introducing products like the award-winning Lokma fruit balls, which combined indulgent flavors with all-natural, health-conscious ingredients, Züber demonstrated that snacks could be both delicious and nutritious. This transparent, consumer-centric approach challenged the belief that indulgence, and health can't coexist, allowing their products to bridge the gap between flavor and nourishment. This success expanded Züber's market reach and helped set a new standard in the industry.

Case Highlights

Brand Overview

Züber is a pioneering healthy snack brand in Türkiye, transforming the snack industry by offering all-natural alternatives with no refined sugar in a market dominated by processed options. The brand's mission is to redefine snacking, showing healthy choices can be satisfying.

Strategic Innovation

Züber began its journey by focusing on all-natural, functional snacks within the healthy snack category. Recognizing evolving consumer demands, the brand expanded its product line to cater to a broader audience, blending indulgence with nourishment. Key innovations included the award-winning Lokma fruit balls, offering a healthier, fruity twist on traditional treats; Noutos chickpea chips challenging conventional savory snacks; the Kidz line featuring fun, healthy snacks for children, broadening appeal for families; Nutzilla, a palm oil-free, additive-free, no-added-sugar option in the hazelnut cocoa category; and Peanutzilla, a peanut and cocoa spread in butter form.

Communication Strategy:

To reinforce its brand positioning, Züber developed a communication strategy rooted in authenticity and consumer insight. Extensive market research revealed demand for snacks balancing health with indulgence. Züber's messaging emphasized its commitment to all-natural ingredients and real consumer connections, resonating deeply with its target audience. The brand's campaign, featuring documentary-style storytelling and genuine narratives, solidified its position as a challenger in the snack industry.

Market Impact:

Züber's innovative approach and communication efforts enabled the brand to transcend the niche healthy snack market and become a significant player in the broader snack industry. By maintaining a focus on all-natural, wholesome ingredients, Züber met the growing demand for healthier snacks and redefined what indulgence means in snacking.

Outcome:

With over 50 SKUs across eight categories and a growing market share, Züber has set new standards in the industry, proving that indulgence and nourishment can coexist, and establishing itself as a leader in better food choices.

Glossary:

- **WHO (World Health Organization):** A specialized agency of the United Nations responsible for international public health.

- **R&D (Research and Development):** The activities companies undertake to innovate and introduce new products and services.

- **SKUs (Stock Keeping Units):** A unique identifier for each distinct product and service that can be purchased.

- **Free-from formula:** A product formulation that excludes certain ingredients, typically allergens or artificial additives, to meet specific dietary needs or preferences.

- **UPFs (Ultra-Processed Foods):** *"Ultra-Processed Foods refers to food products that have a long list of ingredients, typically more than five, and contain food substances with no or rare culinary use or cosmetic additives, some of which have unrecognizable ingredients."* (Encyclopedia of Human Nutrition, 2023)

- **ADHD (Attention Deficit Hyperactivity Disorder):** As defined by the National Institute of Mental Health, *"attention-deficit/hyperactivity disorder (ADHD) is marked by an ongoing pattern of inattention and/or hyperactivity-impulsivity that interferes with functioning or development."*

References

Encyclopedia of Human Nutrition (4th ed.). (2023). Ultra-processed foods. *ScienceDirect.* https://www.sciencedirect.com/topics/nursing-and-health-professions/ultra-processed-foods

Global Burden of Disease 2017 Diet Collaborators. (2018). Health effects of dietary risks in 195 countries, 1990–2017: A systematic analysis for the Global Burden of Disease Study 2017. *The Lancet*, *393*(10184), 1958-1972. https://doi.org/10.1016/S0140-6736(19)30041-8

Lane, M. M., Gamage, E., Du, S., Ashtree, D. N., McGuinness, A. J., Gauci, S., et al. (2024). Ultra-processed food exposure and adverse health outcomes: Umbrella review of epidemiological meta-analyzes. *BMJ*, 384, e077310. https://doi.org/10.1136/bmj-2023-077310

Monteiro, C. A., Moubarac, J.-C., Cannon, G., Ng, S. W., & Popkin, B. (2013). Ultra-processed products are becoming dominant in the global food system. *Obesity Reviews*, *14*(Suppl. 2), 21-28. https://doi.org/10.1111/obr.12107

National Institute of Mental Health. (2024). Attention-deficit/hyperactivity disorder (ADHD). https://www.nimh.nih.gov/health/topics/attention-deficit-hyperactivity-disorder-adhd

NielsenIQ. (2022). *NIQ BASES Breakthrough Innovations 2022.* NielsenIQ.

Özoğlu, İ. N. (2021). Obezite, 21'inci yüzyılın en önemli sağlık sorunudur. *Yeşilay.* https://www.yesilay.org.tr/tr/makaleler/obezite-21inci-yuzyilin-en-onemli-saglik-sorunudur

Samuthpongtorn, C., Nguyen, L. H., Okereke, O. I., et al. (2023). Consumption of ultra-processed food and risk of depression. *JAMA Network Open*, 6(9), e2334770. https://doi.org/10.1001/jamanetworkopen.2023.34770

Yan, W., Lin, S., Wu, D., Shi, Y., Dou, L., & Li, X. (2023). Processed Food-Sweets Patterns and Related Behaviors with Attention Deficit Hyperactivity Disorder among Children: A Case-Control Study. *Nutrients*, *15*(5), 1254. https://doi.org/10.3390/nu15051254

9.2.2 THE VISION: SUPPORTING THE STRATEGIC INNOVATION PLANNING PROCESS

Schumpeter, "the father of Innovation Economics," assumed the innovative entrepreneur to be a rare heroic and exceptional person, of unusual visionary and "volitional" characteristics, who would generate disequilibrium.

Another forerunner Carl Menger, the founder of the "Austrian school" viewed the entrepreneur as the agent of equilibrium, the one who identifies an unsatisfied market, a surplus supply or demand. He engages in innovative activities to reconcile supply and demand through better/quicker use of information. Whichever theory the business communities follow, the importance of the vision cannot be over accentuated.

What makes the visionaries look into the future has been well addressed in the study by B.J. Loasby titled "Long Range Formal Planning in Perspective." Loasby points out three reasons:

1. To understand the future implications of the present decisions. What must a firm be prepared to do next year in order to gain the full advantage from what it decides to do now? What will be the effect of its current choice on the range of options available to it in the future?

2. To examine the present implications of the future events. i.e., to understand "what needs to be decided now in order to be prepared for what is expected to happen later on?"

3. To provide a basis for evaluation of their (managers) performance.

Innovation also emerges from normal economic activity. I have been researching in areas related to cluster analyzes and clustering of innovative activities. My study confronts the following hypothesis by reconciling inter industrial analysis with the study of innovative activities:

A. Innovations cluster in part of the economic space (Schumpeter,1937)

B. Varied linkages in everyday economic life tend to favour innovative linkages and clusters (Aitken 1985)

C. Innovative clusters and linkages may contribute to increase the division of labour (Smithian hypothesis)

The objective of the study is to demonstrate & identify the key locations of innovations, locate the innovative clusters, map the structure of innovative interactions, and establish patterns in clustering and innovative activity. Companies as many research findings support can leverage existing economic interdependence as shown by input output analysis and innovative linkages.

INDUSTRIAL LINKAGES, INNOVATION LINKAGES

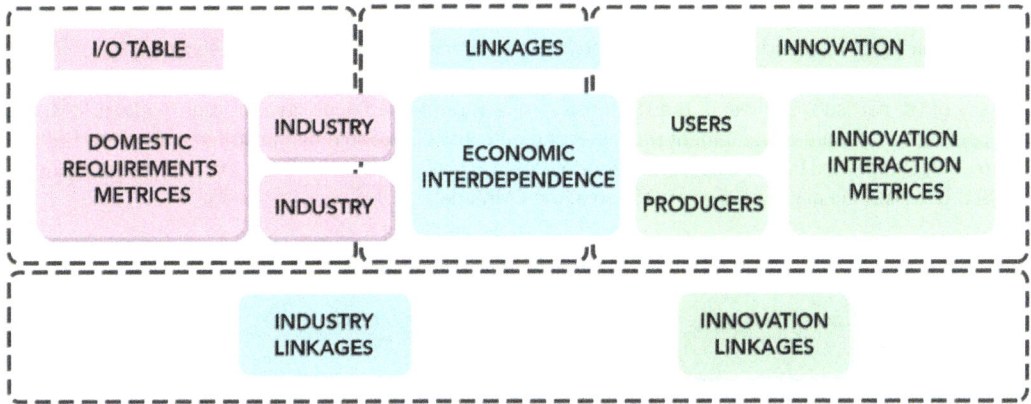

Figure 9.1 Industrial linkages, Innovation linkages

Innovation here refers to the innovative activities and not the proven innovations per se as it would be known only after the adoption and diffusion whether the innovation is incremental or radical. *Clustering of Innovative activities refers to the clusters that emerge out of various important interactions between the users and producers.*

An understanding of the following questions can well support enterprise innovation planning processes and embed them into design and innovation actions.

• How does Innovation emerge from normal economic activity?

• What is the structure of innovative interactions? Who are the main suppliers and users of innovative activities?

• Where do innovative acts exist in economic space and how their relative distribution in this space can be measured?

Various studies do show that innovation is a function of existing economic interdependence and innovative linkages that emerge due to producer-supplier interaction.

9.2.3 DEFINING THE "RESULTS" AND MANAGING INNOVATION PLANNING

Companies should build the competence to define the results they expect to achieve, build the culture of continuous search and modification, and adopt the attitude of "inventive future" (D. Gabor).

Managing by results is highly recommended by P.F. Drucker. This demands the corporate ability to leverage on today's level of knowledge and develop the normative forecasting to address the anticipated results.

9.2.4 INNOVATION CAPABILITY MATURITY MODEL: DESIGN AND ASSESSMENT FRAMEWORK

An innovation capability maturity model could be used as one of the effective instruments to design the innovation framework and explore the fit between a firm's capability areas and the construct itemsed.

Many of us, particularly those in the IT industry are aware of The Capability Maturity Model (CMM) that supports the software-development processes. An outcome of research by the Software Engineering Institute (SEI) and funded by the U.S. Department of Defense (DoD), The first version of CMM was published in 1991. To assess the maturity of a process area, the CMMI defines five maturity levels:

1. *Initial*: Process unpredictable, poorly controlled, and reactive

2. *Managed*: Processes characterized for projects and is often reactive

3. *Defined*: Processes characterized for the organization and is proactive

4. *Quantitative Managed*: Processes measured and controlled.

5. *Optimizing*: Focus on process improvement

Innovation Capability Maturity Models (ICMM) have been developed by some researchers for application in innovation management.

The ICMM v2 defines a structure of five maturity levels:

1. Ad hoc innovation: consumed with day-to-day operations, outputs are inconsistent and unpredictable.

2. Defined innovation: need to innovate identified and defined, outputs are inconsistent, but traceable

3. Supported innovation: practices, procedures and tools implemented, consistent outputs maintain market share.

4. Aligned innovation: integrated and aligned activities and resources, outputs are a source of consistent differentiation.

5. Synergized innovation: synchronization of activities and resources, outputs provide sustained competitive advantage

There exist some other ICMM models as well such as the model of Darell Mann that differentiates between the five levels of: seeding, championing, managing, strategizing, and venturing or the one based on Apple case studies that consists of five levels: discrete, established, strategic, optimized, and adaptive.

The innovation capability construct can be designed incorporating the innovation process (the innovation capability areas) and the innovation capability construct items. (H. Essmann and N. du Preez) In the model, the innovation capability areas include:

- Innovation process. The innovation lifecycle, i.e., the practices, procedures and activities vis-à-vis the idea generation, screening, feasibility assessment, development, and implementation and eventually to a stage of commercialization and operation

- Knowledge and competency mapping.

- The organizational support system. The factor endowments, the knowledge of technology and the markets and S3P — structure, strategy, systems, and people

The innovation capability and organizational constructs provide an effective mechanism for depicting the interrelations between the capability requirements and the organizational attributes. The construct items are as follows:

- Strategy and objectives. The mission and vision, short- and long-term objectives, etc.

- Function and processes in place. To drive the organisation closer to fulfilling its objectives, whether directly (such as valued-added processes) or indirectly (such as administrative and support processes).

- Organization and management.

- Data and information. Relating to the internal and external environments, the basis for all decision making (from complex strategic decisions to process decisions) and the (communication) link between all internal and external entities (individuals, production units, departments, management, suppliers, the market, etc.).

- Customers and suppliers.

As prescribed by H. Essmann and N. du Preez, the three maturity level descriptions in the model for this requirement are as follows:

1. Maturity Level 1: IP/SO1 L1. "Opportunities" of the future are based on extrapolations of the past.

2. Maturity Level 3: IP/SO1 L3. Initiatives to find latent opportunities are undertaken. Procedures have been developed and implemented, and the required outputs defined.

3. Maturity Level 5: IP/SO1 L5. Future Orientated scanning and exploring activities provide consistent strategic input. Procedures to identify latent opportunities are institutional.

9.2.5 THE POTENTIAL APPROACH TO ESTABLISHING INNOVATION

The companies need to undertake the following to establish innovation:

- Define the vision and ensure it is understood by one and all.

- Audit the enterprise's strategic business objectives and design pipeline to achieve them.

- Define design actions and innovation goals to support growth objectives.

- Identify source of innovation and the functional interlinkages

- Innovation capabilities requirement analysis for the future

- Design system thinking, process and strategic models to drive innovation.

- Create a family of metrics to measure the effectiveness and the efficiency of design led Innovation.

- Create cascading metrics that align business units, divisions, group, and lateral process capabilities.

- Analyze Strategies and metrics on an ongoing basis.

TAV
Airports
A member of Groupe ADP

CASE STUDY
TAV AIRPORTS

LOOKING FOR WAYS TO IMAGINE THE AIRPORT OF TOMORROW

Written by: Erhan Ustundag (Corporate Communications Director, TAV Airports)

Introduction

In 2024, global passenger traffic is expected to reach 9.7 billion, surpassing the 2019 level for the first time since the COVID-19 pandemic.

There is a strong correlation between GDP increase and the propensity to fly. Through technological changes and economic progress driven by globalization, air travel has become increasingly accessible to different parts of society across the globe. Deregulation of the industry diversified airline offers as legacy carriers were joined by low-costs and regionals. The hub-and-spoke system increased connectivity. Security became crucial in a global world without borders and faced with a changing nature of threats. The global passenger traffic exceeded 9 billion in 2019, in comparison to around 2 billion in the 1990s.

Driven largely by developing markets, passenger traffic is forecast to reach 20 billion by 2042. This growth will necessitate around USD 2.4 trillion in airport investments.

TAV Airports, a leading global brand in airport management, began operations in 2000 in Istanbul, Türkiye. Over the last two decades, the company established a portfolio of 15 airports in eight countries. Since 2012, it has been a part of Groupe ADP, the largest airport management group globally, serving more than 360 million passengers annually.

TAV Airports has a unique business model, whereby it provides services to passengers through its subsidiaries at every step of the value chain. It has airport operations in Türkiye, Georgia, North Macedonia, Saudi Arabia, Croatia, Kazakhstan, Latvia, and Tunisia. Including the products and services of its subsidiaries, TAV's global footprint comprises 110 airports in 33 countries.

Challenge

Facilitating global trade and tourism, aviation is highly sensitive to external risks as well as any trend with global implications. One such over-encompassing challenge is climate change, as it requires a complete overhaul of the industry transforming into zero-carbon operations. Faced with such a complex challenge, the *raison d'etre* of air travel needs to be reaffirmed.

Airport investments, by its very nature, need to have a long-term vision. They are planned and built according to long-term forecasts.

Today, faced with the challenge of climate change and the need to decarbonize the industry, the question is how to envision the airport of tomorrow and how to bring together the diverse interests of industry stakeholders for collaboration and collective action.

Solution

TAV Airports has been one of the early adopters of climate action in the industry. Ankara Esenboga, the gateway to the Turkish capital, was the first airport in the country to achieve carbon-neutral status in 2013, through the Airport Carbon Accreditation (ACA) program, setting industry standards. The same year TAV Airports was named among the "Climate Leaders" in Türkiye by the Carbon Disclosure Program (CDP). Additionally, meeting stringent criteria for ESG performance, TAV Airports was included in Borsa Istanbul's sustainability Index when it was established in 2014.

Faced with surmounting evidence, regulation on environmental, social, and governance issues started to gain prominence among governments and financial institutions by the second half of the 2010s. Groupe ADP and TAV Airports laid out their ambitions in a charter, titled "Airports 4 Trust", in 2021 in order to remain competitive and foster their leadership in the industry.

The charter comprised of two parts. The part addressing social issues is titled "thriving with local communities" and it underlines the commitment to create value for local stakeholders. The second part is entitled "protecting the environment" and it sets forth the below ambitions:

- Tend towards zero environmental impact operations within our scope of responsibility including concessionaires, which notably includes the commitment to reach carbon neutrality by 2030 at the latest.

- Participate actively in the aviation sector's environmental transition efforts and, when applicable, provide solutions airside,

- Promote the integration of each airport in a local resource system, favoring short circuits/routes, encouraging the circular economy, and promoting the production of resources on site,

- Build a greener future by reducing the environmental footprint of our project development activities.

This charter complemented a 5-year strategic planning and roadmap, the "Pioneers 2025". The efforts also included defining a common purpose and values by Groupe ADP and TAV Airports.

The common purpose driving the above-mentioned ambitions is as follows: "Welcome passengers, operate and imagine airports, in a responsible way and all around the world."

It embodies three strong beliefs:

- To be a hospitality expert in the service of travelers. The airport of the future must offer a seamless digital journey, high value-added services, and a personalized experience.

- To be an innovative group serving the infrastructures of tomorrow. The airport of the future must be an efficient one thanks to sustainable construction and operating methods.

- To be a multi-local group in service of local communities. The airport of the future must be a transportation and energy hub that is integrated into overall regional planning.

The "Pioneers 2025" roadmap is founded on three pillars: Digitalization, Hospitality, and Sustainability.

- Aiming at creating smart airports that will improve customer experience, support the development of the hospitality offer, and create additional revenues. Additionally, the program will help optimize operations, increase terminal capacity, optimize costs, and standardize processes.

- Continuously develop hospitality offers, through continuous evaluation of the changing needs of passengers and innovating to provide the best-in-class solutions.

- A comprehensive ESG strategy covering four areas: Complying with the highest international standards in corporate governance, minimizing the impact of operations on the environment, advancing flexibility, innovation, and competitive advantage with a focus on diversity and inclusion, and building long-term trust and cohesion with local stakeholders, reinforce the benefits of the airport activity for the local communities.

The communication plan to complement this strategic transformation focused on incorporating all the above-mentioned aspects in all areas of PR activities.

TAV Airports' business model is built on concessions and amid privatizations, airports are strategically important infrastructures for transportation networks. Therefore, governments and aviation authorities remain as important stakeholders. Lenders that finance airport development projects are crucial. The reputation and performance of TAV Airports in ESG plays an important role in getting and financing new projects.

As a service provider, TAV Airports employs more than 40 thousand people globally. Employee satisfaction as well as their role as brand ambassadors make effective internal communications a top priority. Passengers and airlines are the main customers of the provided services. Lastly, the public must be convinced that TAV Airports acts responsibly at every step.

Two main messages were developed to reflect such ambitions: "Changing the planet and the people for the better" and "The airport of tomorrow, today". Every communication is built around these messages on an asset base and at the corporate level. Brand equity assessment research was conducted in 2023 to assess brand attributes among stakeholders including corporate citizenship and leadership in environmental protection. It will be replicated to evaluate the effectiveness of efforts and adapt communication planning accordingly.

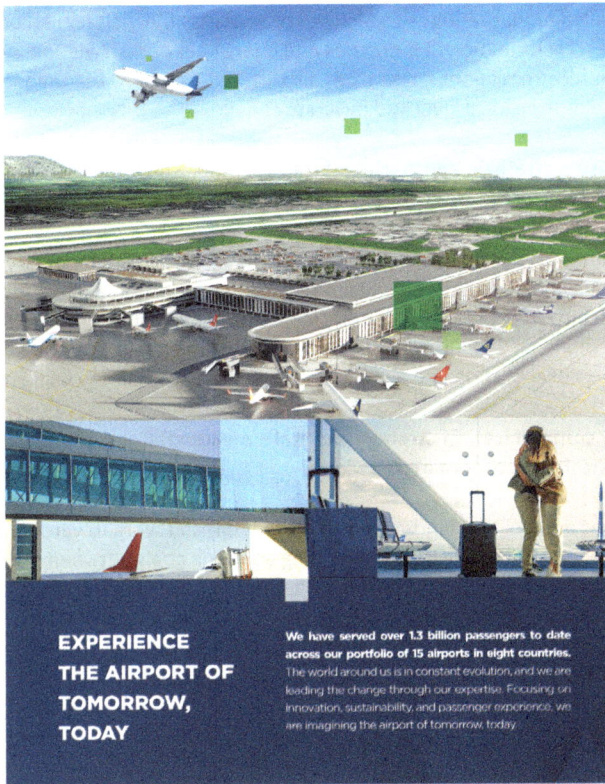

Conclusion

Aviation creates around 2% of global emissions. Airport activity is a very small part of that. Nevertheless, airports can play an important role in bringing together stakeholders for collective action and facilitating change.

It's important to note that complex transitions such as the decarbonization of activities require a clear vision and a clear strategy to walk towards the end goal. It is a long-term commitment which involves stewardship at top management and involving all stakeholders in a structured way.

Today, four airports in TAV Airports' portfolio have reached carbon neutral status, namely Ankara, Antalya, Enfidha, and İzmir. A roadmap is in place to make all assets carbon neutral by 2030. In addition to existing installations, a new solar power investment which will cover more than 30% of the electricity use in TAV's Turkish airports is on the way. The company will be net-zero by 2050 at the latest.

Finally, raising awareness about climate action and transformation into a zero-carbon industry as well as creating the tools for collaboration will remain at the core of TAV Airports' strategic approach.

Questions to stimulate conversation on the case

1. What role airports can play in the decarbonization efforts of the aviation industry?

337

Climate change is a challenge that requires collective action across the globe on an unprecedented level. It will require a complete transformation of industries and energy networks. Aviation is considered an energy intense industry. While most emissions come from aircraft, airports have the unique position to bring together industry stakeholders on local level and facilitate change.

2. How can we devise a strategic approach to bring together stakeholders with diversified needs to work towards tackling a long-term common goal such as climate change?

The fastest mode of commercial transportation, aviation is a highly regulated industry on a global scale. It is built on a complex organizational structure involving authorities on international and national level, aircraft manufacturers, airlines, airports et cetera. Currently it creates more than 87 million direct and indirect jobs, and approximately 4% of global GDP. In order to foster transformation, industry players need to adopt an approach of competitive collaboration and airports are in a unique position to facilitate this.

3. How can PR and communication strategy facilitate awareness and change for business transformation amid political and economic crosswinds?

Fluctuations in economic and political landscape can make it difficult work towards long-term goals. Communications efforts can create awareness by underlining common goals between stakeholders when they tend to focus on short term gains. Stories on common targets and collaborative action can build confidence, create new connections, and motivate stakeholders for transformative efforts.

9.2.6 THE TIMING OF INNOVATIVE OUTPUTS

One of the issues central to the competitive importance of innovation is its timing.

Sometimes it pays to be the pioneer and the first to the market, but more often it pays to be a relatively early adopter (Baumol, Blackman and Wolf, 1989) to receive the advantage of backwardness (Gerschenkron, 1962).

Where there are physical networks sometimes it pays more to be a late adopter when the whole network is already set up. Companies have to really understand the dynamics of the market and find out whether network externalities exist.

9.3 BUILDING AN INNOVATION CONDUCIVE CULTURE

As we understand, the concept of innovation has become the most important a la carte priority in the modern corporate world. Organizations today must be able to build a culture of innovation that absorbs and responds to the changes in technology and to the market conditions. The idea is to lead the change as the environment changes and to keep all the learning processes and efforts directed toward creating the new knowledge necessary to offer differentiated products at a relatively lower cost by innovating the product, process, market, or organization by leveraging the competencies and endowments of the enterprise.

An increasing number of researchers agree that a firm's intangible assets, including corporate culture, contribute to the overall value of the firm and drive organizational and technological capabilities and competencies.

arçelik

ARÇELİK TELVE: FIRST AUTOMATIC TURKISH COFFEE MACHINE INNOVATION

Written by: Fatma Dila Esen Tan (Brand & Marketing Communications)

Introduction

Arçelik was founded in Istanbul in 1955. By producing Türkiye's first washing machine in 1959 and the country's first refrigerator in 1960, it signaled its potential to become a powerful industrial giant. Over the years, it has continually aimed higher, developing, growing, and becoming the market leader in Türkiye's white goods sector. With the motto "Respecting the world, respected worldwide", Arçelik has expanded beyond borders and globalized. Arçelik, the leader in the white goods sector in Türkiye, introduces superior design and technology to consumers with an environmentally friendly and innovative approach. Producing white goods products across various categories—from refrigerators to washing machines, televisions to coffee makers—Arçelik has become a reliable partner for homes and businesses in Türkiye thanks to its wide range of products, dealers, and service network.

Arçelik is the local jewel of the global white goods company Beko which operates under Koç Holding—one of the most important entities in the history of the Republic of Türkiye— and is preparing to celebrate its 70th anniversary. With 55,000 employees, 22 brands, and subsidiaries in 58 countries, the company has become the second largest in the world and the largest in Europe in the white goods sector.

Committed to providing an excellent customer experience to its consumers through its extensive dealer and authorized service network, Arçelik continues to develop and grow in collaboration with its suppliers. By embracing the principles of responsible consumption and production under the sustainability framework, Arçelik uses the strength it derives from its homeland to make a positive global impact and create value for the planet and all of its stakeholders. The company aims to protect natural resources with the technologies it develops while also raising awareness in society. In line with its goal of becoming net zero by 2050, Arçelik encourages and supports its suppliers with the resources it provides. The company produces products that feature easy-to-use, energy-efficient, and innovative technologies. Arçelik is proud to be known as the "brand of firsts" and is also recognized as the inventor of the automatic Turkish Coffee Maker. This year, the brand celebrated the 20th anniversary of its automatic Turkish coffee machine named "Telve."

Challenge

In a world that evolves and changes day by day, brands that can adapt to these changes achieve success. Understanding consumer needs and adapting to shifting dynamics is crucial. Leveraging technology to closely follow global trends and capture new ones is one of the greatest challenges for any brand. Brands that introduce innovations in their industry are likely to see an increase in their technological brand perception. Understanding their consumers allows companies to quickly respond to rapidly changing needs, thereby strengthening their connection with them.

Emerging technology not only affects companies but also changes individuals' lives. People are increasingly interested in brands that make their lives easier. For brands, the goal becomes to produce fast and high-quality solutions that simplify life. It has become very important for many people to have access to high quality, enjoyable and quick coffee. Whether starting the day, working, taking a break, or chatting with friends, coffee often accompanies many pleasant moments. Turkish Coffee, one of the most important cultural values of Türkiye, is consumed widely. Its preparation generally involves mixing water and coffee in a coffee pot, then boiling and frothing it on the stove. It is then served with a thick foam in a Turkish coffee cup. Especially enjoyed by Turks, Turkish coffee is now consumed in many parts of the world. Arçelik pioneered a new technology by combining its innovation and R&D competencies with a cultural value.

How did Arçelik develop the first Turkish Coffee Machine to bring one of the most important cultural values of Türkiye, Turkish coffee, to coffee enthusiasts more quickly and deliciously?

Solution

Turkish coffee, with its rich history and unique flavor, is an indispensable part of Turkish culture. Additionally, Turkish coffee is one of the most ritualistic types of coffee. It is slowly brewed in a coffee pot on the stove, frothed, and then brewed again while being served. This repeated brewing ensures a rich foam in each cup. Turkish coffee has evolved into a cultural treasure. Since the Ottoman Empire, its taste, flavor, and manners of service have been preserved. It plays a key role in pleasant conversations, is served following exquisite meals, and is a delightful highlight of traditional Turkish engagement ceremonies. There are even Turkish sayings like "a cup of Turkish coffee has a memory of forty years." This is why it has become deeply embedded in Turkish culture and has evolved into a 500-year-old tradition.

Arçelik, a brand that values cultural heritage and introduces many innovations to consumers, first proposed the idea of combining the traditional Turkish coffee brewing method with innovation at the beginning of the 2000s. After months of research and development, initial steps were taken to bring this innovation to life. First, market research was conducted, and user habits were examined. Coffee culture, coffee consumption habits, and brewing techniques were researched. Surveys were conducted.

In 2004, Arçelik created a new product category by introducing the world's first automatic Turkish coffee machine, "Telve," to the market. Telve standardized the preparation of Turkish coffee using the traditional pot method and made brewing more practical. The creation of this groundbreaking product, which was

341

a first for both the brand and the world, established Arçelik as the pioneer of the first Turkish coffee machine. Arçelik gained significant recognition for its contribution to the evolution of Turkish coffee, a key element of Turkish culture and its flavors, on a global scale.

After introducing the world's first automatic Turkish coffee machine, Telve, in 2004, Arçelik updated its design in 2015, earning the Red Dot and Good Design awards. In 2017, Telve Pro, developed for the HORECA channel, provided the ability to brew up to 9 cups of Turkish coffee in three different settings, offering an ideal solution for high-usage establishments. In 2019, with a completely redesigned Telve, the machine prepared rich, frothy traditional Turkish coffee with a single touch, maintaining consistent taste and texture in every cup. The induction technology heats the pot evenly from all sides while the Cooksense® technology ensures a consistently rich foam with every brew. In 2024, Arçelik proudly celebrated the 20th anniversary of Telve, which dominates the market in its category. To celebrate Telve's 20th anniversary and its achievements, the brand launched a major communication campaign during this period with the slogan "Arçelik Telve for 20 years, in thousands of homes and hundreds of thousands of hearts".

At Arçelik, based on our experience in both the home electronics market and this product category, we embarked on developing Turkish coffee machines with certain essential features to ensure high performance and meet coffee enthusiasts' expectations. The goal was to elevate the coffee experience by providing a machine with superior features that deliver the same taste and enjoyment in every cup.

Quality & Flavor

The automatic brewing function of Turkish coffee machines ensures that coffee is brewed at the correct temperature and with perfect consistency. One of the most important elements of Turkish coffee's flavor is its rich foam. For a high-quality and enjoyable Turkish coffee experience, the coffee must be brewed to leave a generous foam on top. To achieve this, Arçelik developed foam detection technology called CookSense, which maintains the ideal foam level with each brew while extending the product's lifespan with dual sensors. Thanks to Spinjet technology, optimal mixing for foam formation is achieved before brewing. Antispill technology provides additional safety solutions to prevent coffee from overflowing during brewing. The Turkish Coffee Machine developed by Arçelik is protected by a total of 16 patents.

Ease of Use

A coffee machine should not only create enjoyable moments with its taste but also simplify the user's life. It should brew coffee quickly to the ideal flavor and be user-friendly. We developed a practical product with easily accessible buttons and a user-friendly interface. The use of easily cleanable parts enhances convenience. Another important feature is having a sufficiently large water reservoir, capable of preparing multiple cups of coffee. This feature becomes particularly valuable when considering the significance of serving Turkish coffee to guests in Turkish culture. The machine, featuring a water reservoir that is easy to remove and replace, and which alerts the user when water is low, enhances the enjoyment of Turkish coffee to a new level.

Safety

Arçelik's Telve Turkish Coffee Machine won the IF Design Award. In addition to its stylish design, Telve is also designed with kitchen safety in mind. Product safety is crucial for preventing potential accidents in the kitchen. An ideal Turkish coffee machine should have safety features like automatic shut-off, overflow prevention systems, and overheating protection. Arçelik coffee machines undergo much more rigorous testing conditions compared to competitors. Safety is one of Arçelik's top priorities.

Material Quality & Durability

During the manufacturing process, using durable and high-quality materials was a key focus. For long-lasting use, the machine must be made from high-quality materials. Stainless steel, durable plastic, and sturdy components enhance the machine's durability and provide trouble-free use for many years. It is also worth noting that material quality impacts the coffee's flavor.

With a Turkish coffee machine possessing these features, it is possible to elevate the coffee experience by ensuring the same taste and enjoyment in every cup.

Arçelik has continuously improved the Turkish Coffee Machine for over 20 years with new designs and technologies. Coffee machines are now produced in various colors to match different decors and offer size options to accommodate different kitchen spaces. Additionally, to ensure that consumers of all budgets can access this ideal Turkish coffee machine, the product range has been expanded and different products have been developed to offer various price options.

In 2021, Arçelik collaborated with one of Türkiye's well-known figures, Okan Bayülgen. The coffee documentary titled "Göz Açıp Kapayıncaya Kadar," featuring Okan Bayülgen in the lead role, was introduced to coffee enthusiasts. The highly acclaimed documentary received awards in the "Best Documentary" category at the Rome International Film Awards, as well as in the "Media Section - Content Focused Media Usage" and

"Durable Consumer Goods" categories at the 16th Felis Awards. Additionally, the documentary was selected as a success story among Google Case Studies within the Think with Google framework.

Conclusion

In 2004, Arçelik introduced the world's first automatic Turkish coffee machine, Telve, pioneering a new product category and leading the industry by embracing Turkish coffee culture. Since then, Arçelik has continued to enhance Telve with its R&D and innovative strength, continually adding value to Turkish coffee culture in line with consumer needs.

Arçelik Telve has received significant attention both in Türkiye and internationally due to its features. The device automates the traditional Turkish coffee brewing process with a single touch, simplifying the user's job. Additionally, its elegant and modern design adds an aesthetic touch to kitchens.

Telve has standardized the preparation of Turkish coffee using the traditional pot method and made the brewing process more practical. It is believed that Telve has taken on a crucial role in introducing Turkish coffee culture to the world. The innovation of Telve is considered one of the most important steps in Arçelik's journey to becoming a global brand.

Questions to stimulate conversation on the case

1. Why was developing the first Turkish Coffee Machine challenging?

Turkish coffee is a special beverage that requires a precise preparation ceremony and must be served with a rich foam. The amounts of coffee and water must be carefully measured; adding too much coffee or too little water will ruin the flavor and enjoyment. It also needs to be brewed with stirring, and served at the right moment when it has frothed sufficiently. Mastering the art of brewing Turkish coffee, which holds significant cultural importance, is a skill. Until Arçelik, achieving this with a machine was merely a dream. Developing the first Turkish coffee machine required a detailed research and development process due to the many critical nuances involved. Introducing Turkish coffee to consumers with a single button press to achieve the ideal consistency and flavor was a groundbreaking innovation. To produce coffee with the ideal froth and flavor, specific technologies needed to be developed. Through the foam detection technology CookSense, Arçelik successfully provided Turkish coffee with the perfect foam effortlessly to coffee enthusiasts. This special flavor, preserved for centuries, now makes users' lives easier and offers them moments of joy thanks to Arçelik Telve. Consequently, the product has earned a place on kitchen countertops. Satisfied consumers even rely on Telve for special occasions like engagement ceremonies, quickly serving delicious coffee to numerous guests.

2. What is the significance of developing the first Turkish Coffee Machine for Arçelik, and what motivated it?

Arçelik is one of the most valuable brands in the history of the Republic of Türkiye. With 70 years of experience, it has established a deep connection with consumers and has won the Lovemark award for 15 years. Throughout its 70-year history, Arçelik has aimed to be the brand of firsts by introducing many innovations to consumers and has achieved this numerous times. For a brand that proudly embodies successful domestic and local production, becoming the first to merge this important Turkish cultural flavor with technology was a significant achievement. Turkish coffee is not only a beverage, but also a way of socialising, a special element of Turkish cuisine with a deep-rooted history. Furthermore, by creating a new category in the industry, Arçelik compelled competing brands to consider producing similar products. As the pioneer of this category, Arçelik gained a competitive advantage and earned consumer trust and appreciation.

Links and media

www.arcelik.com.tr

Case Highlights

Arçelik is a white goods brand established in Türkiye in 1955. Part of Koç Holding, Arçelik has grown over the years into a global brand, committed to being a technology leader known for its innovations. One of its most significant achievements is developing and introducing the first Turkish Coffee Machine for coffee enthusiasts. The importance of this milestone lies primarily in the creation of a new product category, which led to the emergence of new competition in the market by setting a precedent for rival brands. Thanks to this pioneering product, named Telve, the process of making Turkish coffee, which is widely and frequently consumed, has been simplified and accelerated. Consumers can now achieve the ideal consistency and flavor of coffee with the push of a single button.

9.3.1 CULTURE AND INNOVATION

Wieland sees the culture of innovation as the institutions (norms, values, formal and informal) that have a significant influence on how the actors involved in an innovation process perceive economic and technical challenges and how that provides them with strategies to tackle these.

Herbig and Dunphy highlight the profound significance of a culture for the adoption of innovative technologies when they hold that "existing cultural conditions determine whether, when how and in what form new innovations will be adopted. If the behavior, ideas, and material apparatus which must accompany the use of innovation can affect improvements along lines already laid down in the culture, the possibilities of acceptance are much greater."

The impact of culture on innovative activities from ideation through commercialization and adoption/diffusion is profound.

9.3.2 INNOVATION MODELS

Research provides us with various models that organizations can follow to develop the innovation capability and sustain a competitive advantage. In each, the adoption of an innovation-friendly culture crosses functional areas and demands participation by all organizational/departmental players -- strategic and tactical, financial, and organizational. It's a pervasive cultural attitude that nurtures consistently innovative behavior and success. The cultural fit for innovation planning will determine the outcome for the entire enterprise.

9.3.3 EVOLUTION OF INNOVATION MODELS

The process of innovation needs clarity and understanding. Past models saw innovation as a linear sequence of functional activities. Either the opportunities surfaced out of research and got commercialized ('technology push") or the market signalled the opportunity, and the innovation was born ("need pull"). Ray Rothwell suggested that the nature of the innovation process has evolved from simple linear models to more complex interactive models.

Rothwell's Five Generations of Innovation model begins with first- and second-generation linear models and develops into a fifth-generation model touting systems integration, extensive networking, flexible and customized response, and continuous innovation. To implement this comprehensive model of innovation requires the organizational culture to be tuned and engineered accordingly.

9.3.4 THE CULTURE CANVAS

Bausor (1994) said the firm must be designed, it has to be engineered and that this is an ongoing process. Many CEOs of leading corporations indicate the biggest challenge they face while working in a consortium or alliance is trust related to the cultural fit. It is not a question of competence or delivery, but of the difficulty the team has in establishing cultural unity.

9.3.5 THE SOURCE OF INNOVATION

Peter Drucker argues that innovation is real work that can and should be managed like any other corporate function. To Drucker, the most innovative ideas come from methodically analyzing seven areas of opportunity – Unexpected Occurrences, Incongruities, Process Needs, Industry and Market Changes, Demographic

Changes, Changes in Perception and New Knowledge. Addressing these diverse areas of opportunity requires the support of an innovation-friendly culture across all functional areas to quickly identify and act on each internal and external opportunity for innovation.

Various models exist to explain how firms leverage technological capabilities and market capabilities for innovative activities. According to Abernathy -Clark Model, an innovation is regular if it conserves the existing technological and market capabilities, *niche* if it conserves technological capabilities but obsoletes market capabilities, *revolutionary* if it obsoletes technological capabilities but enhances market capabilities and *architectural* if both technological and market capabilities become obsolete. He also emphasised that market knowledge can be just as important as technological knowledge.

Henderson Clark Model considers products being made of components. Hence building them must require component knowledge and the linkages between them (architectural knowledge) An innovation can then impact either component knowledge or architectural knowledge or both.

9.3.6 THE ADOPTION OF INNOVATION

Herbig and Dunphy highlight the profound significance of culture to the adoption of innovative technologies when they said, "existing cultural conditions determine whether, when how and in what form new innovations will be adopted." We need to identify more fruitful ways to establish the culture of innovation to support the innovation research, policy, and practice. The organizational culture must consider the following:

- Innovation should be seen as a distributed process across many actors, firms and other organizations that are influenced by regulation, policy, and social pressure.

- The unit of analysis should not be restricted to a specific product/technology; it must look into the technological systems or regimes, and their evolution rather than management.

- The assumption that innovation is the consequence of coupling technological opportunity and market demand is too limited and needs to include the less obvious social concerns, expectations and pressures.

- The organizational culture should promote interaction with the other agents of innovation (e.g. Universities, corporations) to build and test new hypotheses and incubate new ideas.

- Distinctive competencies that enhance the corporate ability to adapt the skills necessary to leverage new technology and market changes.

- Mental models -- individual and organization-wide beliefs about the world and how to make sense of it must be dynamic in order to address the changing environment and/or competitive situation.

- The learning trap (a tendency to keep on doing the same thing even in situations where it is no longer effective) should be discouraged.

- Creativity must be nurtured and rewarded.

- The learning mechanism should enhance the market/technology sensing and foresight of an organization and its individuals.

9.3.7 SOCIO-CULTURAL DETERMINANTS OF INNOVATION

Companies are encouraged to engage in assessing the socio-cultural determinants of innovation (listed below) and how they relate to each other within their organization on an ongoing basis if they expect to instill a dynamic culture that is conducive to innovation. The consistent and methodical consideration of these factors as they pertain to innovation opportunities represents a culture-shift conducive to innovation.

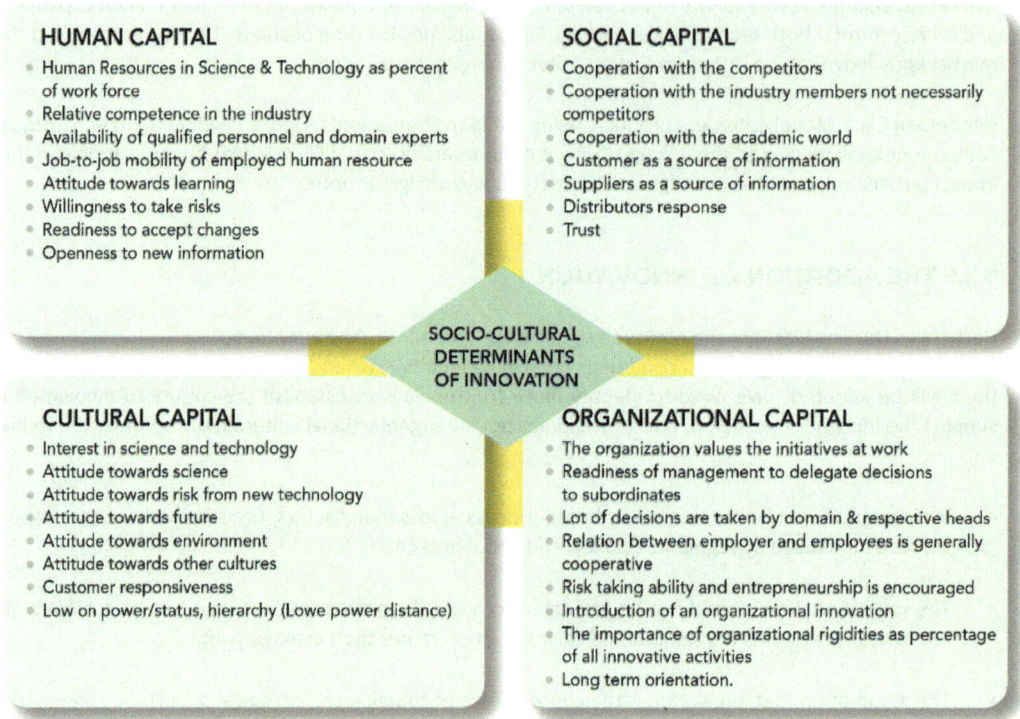

HUMAN CAPITAL

- Human Resources in Science & Technology as percent of work force
- Relative competence in the industry
- Availability of qualified personnel and domain experts
- Job-to-job mobility of employed human resource
- Attitude towards learning
- Willingness to take risks
- Readiness to accept changes
- Openness to new information

SOCIAL CAPITAL

- Cooperation with the competitors
- Cooperation with the industry members not necessarily competitors
- Cooperation with the academic world
- Customer as a source of information
- Suppliers as a source of information
- Distributors response
- Trust

SOCIO-CULTURAL DETERMINANTS OF INNOVATION

CULTURAL CAPITAL

- Interest in science and technology
- Attitude towards science
- Attitude towards risk from new technology
- Attitude towards future
- Attitude towards environment
- Attitude towards other cultures
- Customer responsiveness
- Low on power/status, hierarchy (Lowe power distance)

ORGANIZATIONAL CAPITAL

- The organization values the initiatives at work
- Readiness of management to delegate decisions to subordinates
- Lot of decisions are taken by domain & respective heads
- Relation between employer and employees is generally cooperative
- Risk taking ability and entrepreneurship is encouraged
- Introduction of an organizational innovation
- The importance of organizational rigidities as percentage of all innovative activities
- Long term orientation.

Figure 9.2 Socio-cultural determinants of innovation

Hofstede postulates that an "Innovation culture" is to be understood in terms of attitudes towards innovation, technology, exchange of knowledge, entrepreneurial activities, business, uncertainty and related behavior, and historical trajectories.

Companies who consistently nurture a culture of innovation will have the greatest opportunity to realize the benefits that innovation promises for the future.

Industry Insights: Education

Remote Learning Environment and Technology Enhanced Learning

Technology Enhanced Learning in a remote environment has not been new but its importance grew significantly in recent years mainly during the outbreak of COVID 19. As of March 2020, since the time COVID started, 89% of the World's student's population was at the learning loss with lockdowns in place, school closures and uncertainties and chaos building throughout the world economy. Educational institutions had to design a TEL ecosystem in a remote environment as there was no choice left.

The increasing importance of online education due to its reach and impact has led to an emergent learning ecosystem that needs meticulous design considerations and competence enhancing strategies to stay afloat. The industry seems to be characterised by the advent of ed-tech enterprises (EDx, Udemy, Coursera Upgrad, Unacademy and more), intelligent tutoring systems, AI enabled personalised education and assessment (Watson Classroom education), robotics assisted learning (Miko) and more such enterprises. Investment in ed-tech appears promising. As a result, many unicorns are born. The question arises whether online learning is going to be the next new normal. What should be the design strategy for these Ed-tech enterprises to remain competitive? How does one look at the future of learning and assessment?

Strings of debates and discussions have been around the subject of online learning. Some of the issues that appear more relevant in the current scenario though have been discussed in the past are:

1. How effective is online learning as compared to face-to-face instruction?

2. Does blended learning, i.e. supplementing face-to-face instruction with online instruction enhance learning?

3. What practices should be followed to make online learning more engaging and effective?

A report by the US Department of Education "Evaluation of Evidence-Based Practices in Online Learning: A Meta-Analysis and Review of Online Learning Studies" has shown that:

1. Students in online conditions performed modestly better, on average, then those learning the same material through traditional face-to-face instruction.

2. Instruction combining online and face-to-face elements had a larger advantage relative to purely face-to-face instruction than did purely online instruction.

3. Online learning can be enhanced by giving learners control of their interactions with media and prompting learner reflection.

Online Learning Experience: Design considerations

Given the current scenario, companies providing online learning need to design a learning ecosystem to maximise learning experiences and they must consider the differentiating factors embedded into their offerings by providing:

1. **Expository learning experiences**-content transmitted by a lecture, written material, or other mechanisms.

2. **Active learning-** in which the student has control of what and how he or she learns.

3. **Collaborative or interactive learning**-learning by interaction with one another and with a teacher or other sources.

In the next new normal, one will find more and more enterprises supporting all these types of learning:

- [ ] Expository instruction— knowledge transmission by digital devices.

- [ ] Active learning— knowledge building through inquiry-based manipulation of digital artifacts such as online drills, simulations, games, or micro worlds.

- [ ] Interactive learning— inquiry-based collaborative interaction with other learners with teachers becoming co-learners and acting as facilitators.

In addition to enhancing the learning experiences as mentioned above, innovating learners' engagement, personalised learning through cognitive computing and learning delivery models will be the differentiating factors.

KI Education

Kotler Impact (Ki) Education is one of the educational initiatives by the World Marketing Summit (WMS) and Kotler Impact Inc. The initiative plans to offer education programs under *Kotler Impact Education* by partnering with existing academic institutions worldwide to integrate high-quality globally benchmarked contemporary curriculum.

Kotler Business School - by setting up an independent campus to offer some short-term skill focused programs along with the Masters Program in design, Innovation and Marketing. The first such program is expected to be operational in Pune, India from the year 2022 before expanding its reach into other Asian countries.

Kotler School of Creative Industries -that will offer managerial programs in the fields of Industrial Design, Animation and Video Game.

We will leverage technology and KI's global ecosystem to deliver these programs in the fields of Creative industries, neuroscience, AI, IT and Neuromarketing. The programs will be offered in a blended mode leveraging the best of online and face-to-face instructions with an opportunity of pathways, for example in Switzerland or Japan.

Industry Insights: Creative Industries

Creative industries, particularly Video Game, Animation and VFX industry performed well during the Pandemic. The video game industry generated a revenue of almost $162.32 billion and is likely to reach a revenue value of $295.63 billion in 2026. The global esports audience is expected to reach a total of 456 million people. The total value of the Global Animation, VFX & Video Games industry was US$ 264 billion in 2019 whereas Most of the segments in the animation industry are growing at the rate of 2-3% Year on Year.

As the industry is lucrative but extremely volatile, companies have been trying to innovate their business models. In-app purchases, Market communication through Video Gaming, e-sports tournaments, AR/VR Content are on the rise. The competition landscape is very volatile. There have been Indie games making fortunes and AAA games that went bust. In such a scenario, the role of design thinking, design performance and the aligned business vision cannot be over accentuated.

Keeping in mind the risks associated with video game development, it would be nice to explore neuroscience for new game development to map the perceived responses of a game concept at an early stage so as to increase the probability of game success. One such project in pipeline that we propose is to use a tool called Synergetic Navigation System-an internet-based system for data acquisition, time-series analysis, and visualization of outcome and process data as well as analysis results currently used for real time monitoring of Psychotherapy sessions. SNS allows for the implementation of various questionnaires or coding systems. Data can be entered, and results can be checked by most web-compatible devices, including PCs, notebooks, tablets, or smartphones.

The idea is to develop a model wherein game designers can map potential gamers' reactions and responses to video game prototypes at an early stage and de-risk product development by continually listening, testing, and iterating with end users.

The same can be applied to industrial design.

9.4 DESIGN AND INNOVATION: THE FUTURE TRENDS

The pandemic has caused panic across the world. Countries all over the world have been trying to attune their responses to the ongoing pandemic and the unprecedented socio-economic and medical challenges. There exist many concerns such as:

- What will the next new normal look like?

- How do we look at the balance of economic growth and economic development?

- How do we restructure or design our businesses and economies?

- What are the challenges facing Individuals, firms and governments?

- Will it impact globalisation? Will reshoring replace offshoring?

- Can we begin to look beyond the theories of aggregate demand and aggregate supply?

- Will economic analysis take note of creation of new factors that characterise the modern economy rather than the allocation of existing factors?

Experts' opinions differ as to what caused COVID 19. Some see it as a consequence of mistreatment of habitat and wildlife, and some argue that the unprecedented pandemic owes to the rising global climate crisis. Scientists, epidemiologists, or ecologists may not achieve a consensus on the real cause of COVID 19, but the shock waves have created an alarm for the whole world to build a sustainable, resilient, fair, green, dependence-reducing economy.

In order to build a sustainable, green, enterprising economy, design will play a crucial role in future.

9.4.1 DESIGN TO LEVERAGE ON USER-PRODUCERS INTERACTION

Various studies suggest that Innovative interactions between the suppliers and users of innovative outcomes lead to clustering of innovative activities and provide for designing new products/processes or improving the existing products/processes including business model innovations.

Von Hippel and colleagues have highlighted the crucial role of users in innovation. Producers have knowledge about technical solutions and users about their needs, the context of use, and their own capabilities as users. Both sets of knowledge are characterized by "stickiness".

The recommended design strategy to leverage on user-producers interaction includes the following:

- Identify the lead users.

- Continual Research about their needs, the context of use.

- Embed the real issues into the design/solution brief .

- Explore various ideas and possible solutions.

- Visual communication on possible ideas and solutions.

- Work on the selected idea further with embedded feedback from lead users (formative design assessment).

- Build the prototypes (value engineering).

- Summative assessment.

- Product design and development.

9.4.2 DESIGN FOR DISRUPTION

As of November 2021, a total number of unicorn companies worldwide happen to be about 907 standing at a total cumulative valuation of about **$2,955B.** A study conducted in June 2020 by Charles Plant of Narwhal Project, a technology research company states that a Unicorn grows at a Compounded Annual Growth Rate of 75% for the first ten years.

How do these startups create such high valuations? How do they win investors' confidence? What if the growth rate falls? How can these enterprises become sustainable? Undoubtedly, these startups including the potential unicorns design their business offerings to address the unmet or underserved needs and create a niche for themselves.

Start-Up	Niche
AirBnB / Oyo	A new way of booking hotel rooms
Uber / Ola	Revolutionized shared mobility space without owning any fleet
Zomato / Swiggy	A new way of obtaining hotel food at home

Netflix / Zee5	Offered option of "on-demand" content consumption for a fee

They also create real value for investors, the ecosystem and the economy ranging from generating employment to creating a ripple effect across sectors. However, the challenge for these unicorns is to maintain the growth rate to increase revenue multiple, as their valuation is based on existing revenue and revenue multiple and not on the basis of their book value or profit multiple or discounted cash flow. They invest heavily into rapid growth building and accelerating strategies to win financial support by the prospective investors. But in order to become sustainable, they need to have design and innovation goals in place, without which it would be difficult to stay competitive as their valuation may decline due to declining growth rates.

Disruptive technologies or innovation became popular with the work of Clayton M. Christensen and his collaborators beginning in 1995. Disruptive innovation refers to a product or service designed for a new set of customers. The concept of disruptive innovation can be misleading if one talks of the product or service at a fixed point of time as the products and services may evolve over a period of time.

So how do we design for disruption?

- Identify how your design addresses the Market Scarcity.

- Address the end users' concerns.

- Identify the personas and develop the tasks to be accomplished to match with what they desire.

- Estimation of time to make the model profitable.

- Measure and analyze the cost drivers and revenue streams.

- Evaluation of selling strategies.

- SWOT analysis.

9.4.3 USER CENTRED AND HUMAN FACTORED DESIGN

"Science never appears so beautiful as when applied to the uses of human life." said Thomas Jefferson. There is no denial to the fact that Design must be user centred and human factored. Human Design Technology (HDT) is a design technology that synthesizes marketing research, ergonomics, cognitive science, industrial design, usability evaluation, and statistics (multiple valuable analysis), and forms appealing products that are friendly to humans (Yamaoka 2001).

Ergonomics that is how consumers interact with the products and anthropometry data -that deals with human measurements are of prime importance in product design.

Let me give you an example of user centred product. Based on the market research findings that children were spending more time on screen-based devices playing, a company came up with an idea of a playful learning robot-MIKO 2 that engages, educates and entertains kids. It is a healthy replacement for screen-based devices and focuses on learning and development of the child. Launched across the US, UK, India and the UAE with users from 90 plus countries, Miko 2 is a unique offering that self-initiates contextual topics

353

with children to enable conversational learning. MIKO2 today has registered over 70 million interactions and is witnessing an 80 % plus 30-day retention that surpasses any parallel product for Kids globally. Throughout the development of MIKO 2, children, their needs and behavior, have been at the core of its design.

To summarise, managing by design and innovation has never been as important before. Companies have to adopt design and innovation driven strategies embedded with user centred and human factored approaches to compete in the future.

9.5 THE EMERGENCE OF DESIGN ECONOMY

In modern business practices digitalisation, changes in global value chains and the green transition will be the key drivers. So, will be the emergence of design economy. The firm in the next new normal post COVID 19 will be characterised by the following:

- Increasing focus on design and innovation led business strategy.

- User experience at the core of product and process innovations

- Human factors & Usability engineering throughout the development process

- Embed Data driven computational design and analytics.

- Design and develop new experiences, digital solutions, products and services

- Build design metrics into product specifications.

- Sharing early prototypes with outsiders and celebrating embryonic ideas

- Design for sustainability i.e. the systematic development, testing, and international diffusion of methods and tools for the design of products with superior life cycles, improved eco efficiency and effectiveness (via intelligent materials and energy applications, integration of emerging product-technologies, and economic optimization)

- Circular activities-focused on eliminating waste and pollution, circulating products and materials. and regenerate nature. French automotive company Renault has initiated a drive to extend the life of vehicles and components and keep materials in use, thereby reducing the use use of virgin materials.

9.6 THE ROLE OF INNOVATION IN CUSTOMER VALUE CREATION

Innovation is recognized as the key to company performance, the country's economic growth, and achieving competitive advantage in an industry. Innovation contributes positively to the success of the company as well as to the increase in a country's living standards. It facilitates the adaptation and adjustment of companies to changing conditions and allows them to meet the changing needs of the market (Blackwell, 2006).

Innovation involves the introduction of new processes and structures as well as new products and services (Damanpour, 1991). In literature, researchers classify innovation as administrative innovations that focus on management processes, technical innovations that cover products and services, and radical innovations that represent radical change or incremental innovations that include gradual change (Gopalakrishnan and Damanpour, 1997). The positive impact of innovation on organizational performance and its important role in achieving success in organizations have been demonstrated in various studies (Hult et al., 2004; Mone et al., 1998). Similarly, studies in the literature have shown that firms that prioritize innovation, grow, and achieve high profitability (Li and Atuahene-Gima, 2001; Price, 1996). In addition, investment in innovation enables firms to improve their market positions (Baker and Sinkula, 2002). Seeing the significant contributions of innovation, Turkish companies prioritize innovation than ever before to achieve global competition, and in this process, they are inspired by innovative economies such as India, China, and Korea (Uzkurt, 2013).

Prahalad and Ramaswamy (2004), who introduced the concept of co-creation, emphasized that the firm and the customer create value together with a customer-focused approach. In today's competitive global market where consumers are constantly searching for value, innovation emerges as an indispensable element of success (Mahmoud et al., 2018). Some researchers classify co-creation as a form of open innovation (Frow et al., 2015) while others view co-creation as a category within open innovation (Barczak, 2012). The conceptualizations of the concept vary from customer involvement where they participate and contributes to the innovation (Frow et al., 2015), to active engagement of the customer in product design (Bogers et al., 2010), co-production (Vargo, 2008; Troye and Supphellen, 2012) and value creation (Payne and Frow, 2005).

Innovation provides solutions to customer needs and increases perceived customer value (Vargo and Lusch, 2004; Michel et al., 2008), and the value perceived by customers is more important than the innovation itself (Kandampully and Duddy, 1999). Therefore, firms need to determine current and future customer needs and provide innovative solutions to customers to achieve competitive advantage. Therefore, to be able to gain competitive advantage, firms increase their innovative capacities through mutual interaction and cooperation with their stakeholders. Thus, they can positively affect customer perceptions and market positions (De Jong et al., 2003).

Value creation for customers is possible with the determination of customer needs and their transformation into marketing innovations (Sanchez-Gutierrez et al., 2017). The transformation of customer needs into innovative marketing outputs is only possible with the establishment of relationships and collaboration with customers (Parahald and Ramaswamy, 2000; Ulaga and Eggert, 2006). Literature reveals that the innovation capacity of industrial clusters is supported by cooperation between companies (Storper, 1995).

Contrary to what is argued in the literature, Eraydın and Armatli-Köroğlu (2005) revealed that innovation in industrial clusters in Türkiye is faced with various difficulties due to the limitations in infrastructure, research and development systems and weak institutional connections. Authors stated that global networks are supported by local dynamics and transfer of tacit knowledge through informal communication is instrumental in industrial clusters in Türkiye. Consequently, despite these difficulties, Turkish firms that operate in industrial clusters have introduced significant innovations and demonstrated their competitive power in global markets as knowledge transfer enables industrial clusters to overcome their limitations and gain a competitive advantage in national and international markets.

10. DESIGNING VALUE

"Design is more than a feeling: it is a CEO-level priority for growth and long-term performance" – Mc Kinsey Design

Design is present everywhere in our lives. Step by step, daily, we come across examples of designs that either make our lives easier and more enjoyable or the exact opposite, whether it is products, services, interfaces, experiences, or even communications.

A chair is designed with an awkward seat height, making it uncomfortable for most users leading to back pain. That coffee machine with so many buttons and settings that it's a bit overwhelming. And that customer service hotline that puts you on hold for what feels like forever. It's no wonder we sometimes feel frustrated and have negative perceptions of the brand. A website that doesn't scale properly on mobile devices results in a poor browsing experience for many users. A company's social media account takes days to respond to customer inquiries, resulting in a perception of poor customer service. Moreover, the list goes on.

However, we are also familiar with iconic designs like the Swiss Army Knife, Google's unassuming homepage, Disneyland's visitor experience, and the frequent-flyer program that upgrades us to business class. This tech company regularly updates customers on the status of their orders, potential delays, and upcoming product releases, keeping them informed and engaged. The remarkable thing is that we praise the design and recollect every one of those brands because they have comforted us in some way.

We love it when life is simple. When we are given simple and precise instructions, it smoothens the process. When products work, services are efficient and experiences fulfilling. The iPhone's interface is known for its ease of use, simple gestures, and well-organized home screen, allowing users to navigate effortlessly. AirPods automatically pair with all Apple devices, switching seamlessly between iPhone, iPad, and MacBook. The setup is intuitive, with no complex pairing process, providing a hassle-free user experience. Dyson's cordless models offer the freedom to clean without being tethered to an outlet, making them convenient for users who need flexibility in cleaning different spaces. IKEA's flat-pack design allows for efficient packaging, reducing shipping costs and making it easier for customers to transport products home themselves.

Each set of examples produces a different consequence: we either love or dislike every one of those brands that offer us such diverse experiences. Good design draws a non-negotiable line between the two sets and expands how we perceive the value of the most empowering brands.

10.1 DESIGN CREATES VALUE

It can be reasonably assumed that most individuals do not possess expertise in the field of design. However, everybody shares a sixth sense that distinguishes what works and what does not. The process by which a particular design is created may be opaque, and the philosophical underpinnings of the designers may be unclear. However, the subjective response evoked by the design is a tangible and indisputable phenomenon. This simple and powerful concept is the heart of Human-Centered Design, or HCD.

Human-Centered Design (HCD) is a process and a set of techniques destined to create new solutions for the world. These solutions include products, services, spaces, experiences, organizations, and modes of interaction.

The reason why this process is called "human-centered" is the fact that, at this very moment, it is focused on the people for whom the new solutions are to be created. The HCD process starts by studying people's needs, perceptions of reality, and behaviors to which the solutions will benefit. The intention is to listen and

356

understand what these people want and need, even when they fail to know it themselves. That's what we call the desirability lens. Throughout the design process, we see the world from this perspective. To take the path towards solutions starting from desire means a significant change in design philosophies. Before, design had always followed the need for functionality, which is something taken for granted.

Once we have identified what is desirable, we start seeing solutions regarding what is feasible and what is viable. We will introduce these perspectives in detail during the last phases of the process.

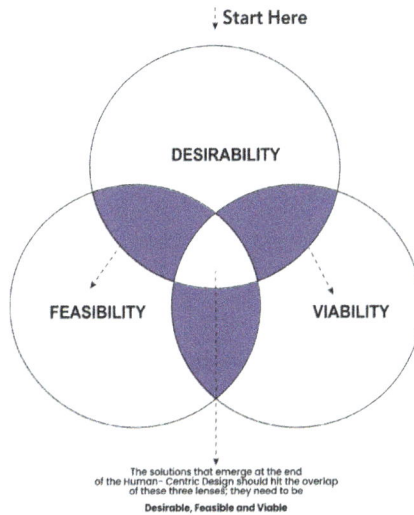

Figure 10.1 Human-Centric Design

The IDEO Approach

IDEO is a design and consulting firm with offices in the United States, England, Germany, Japan, and China. It was founded in Palo Alto, California, in 1991. Its methods for managing innovation have become very popular in the United States since 2004, especially the Design Thinking approach for designing products, services, environments, and digital experiences.

Considering the IDEO approach on the subject, we understand that solutions coming from an HCD project should fall precisely on the point that brings together the three worlds: what is desirable (what people want), what is feasible (what is possible in technical and organizational terms) and what is viable (what is economically achievable).

The approach to the innovation process consists of focusing, from the start, on the desirability of the solutions that are about to be created. In general, researchers, engineers, and marketing professionals begin working on the technical or financial aspects, but according to IDEO, we need to start with the desirability of having people want the products/services above anything else. That is where the difference lies.

This way of dealing with the problems that clients introduce to us allows companies to grow in the three exploration fields simultaneously, focusing on the future users of the product or service and making their experience and desire a priority.

"It isn't just a simple mode of design; it's a real management method of innovation, and it would be a mistake to leave it only in the hands of designers, which is why we must work in interdisciplinary teams" – Tim Brown, CEO IDEO.

Design Thinking has become a classic approach to design, accepted and adopted worldwide, establishing five distinctive stages of work.

Empathize: Contact the client and thoroughly learn about their perspective, going beyond mere quantitative studies. It is necessary to empathize and rely on qualitative techniques such as applied ethnography to understand the users and their context.

Define: analyzing the new definition of the problem that must be solved and choosing a standpoint.

Ideate: it is a different way to conceive creativity, and it consists of fostering creative trust to generate hundreds of ideas, narrow them down, and select the best.

Prototype: rapid creation of object solutions using crafting tools, pieces of cardboard, or any material available to symbolize the new product or service.

Test: to explain and experiment with the users.

Design Thinking is not a one-way method: the manager/client can go back to any of the stages anytime, which allows them to constantly readjust the teams to better focus on client satisfaction and the desirability of the final product.

It is a method that makes it possible to explore new territories, progressively gaining trust thanks to the knowledge acquired through trial and error. The key difference between design thinking and other innovation processes lies in their capacity to discover new insights, new needs, or problems, whether on the consumer's side or within the company.

The potential of Design Thinking lies in the remarkable efficiency of the empathy-definition combo: the process allows either the innovation team or the founders of a start-up to gain insight into the realities of the markets at an early stage. This insight enables them to gain a deeper understanding of the client's day-to-day experience, allowing them to redefine the problem more nuanced and comprehensively. This situation is compelling in a VUCA context (Volatility, Uncertainty, Complexity, and Ambiguity), and it outlines the demanding circumstances currently faced by businesses in the modern world.

Another aspect of this method worthy of mention is the prototype-test tandem. The possibility of re-doing the prototype according to the results from the test promotes learning from failure, which is one of the primary keys of the method: *fail early, fail fast, fail small*. Only then, learn and succeed.

10.2 THE HCD PROCESS

The HCD process begins with identifying a specific challenge that needs to be solved, and it goes through three main phases: HEAR, CREATE, and DELIVER. During the process, the team will go from specific observations to more abstract generalizations, finally going back to specific data by designing concrete solutions.

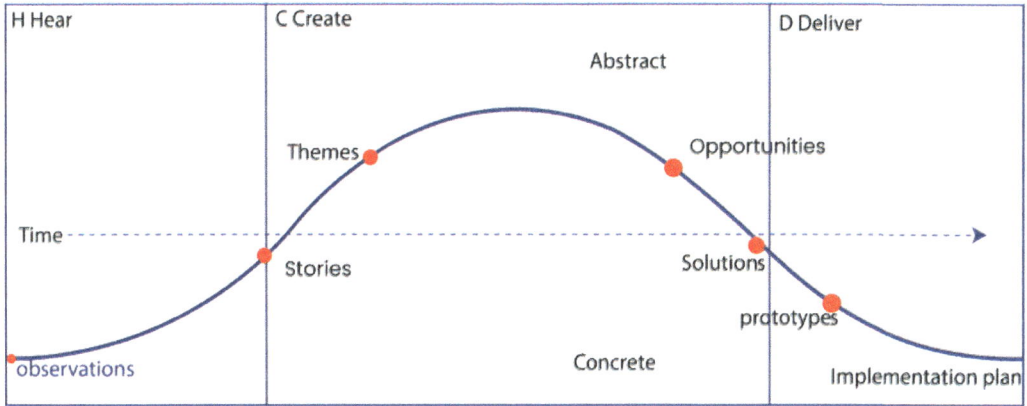

Figure 10.2 the HCD Process

10.2.1 BEST PRACTICES FOR INNOVATION

Having completed thousands of design challenges, IDEO has learned some rules that contribute to creating a more pro-innovation environment.

Multidisciplinary Team

The challenges are complex, and there is a good chance that others have already faced them. When problems are this intricate and challenging but have been previously studied, the possibilities of success will multiply if the manager gathers the right team.

The team is likely to perform better if it consists of a group of 3 to 8 individuals, one of whom will be the coordinator. Teams integrated by people from different disciplines and diverse educational backgrounds will generate more opportunities to come up with unexpected solutions since they will approach problems from various perspectives.

Designated Workspace

Having a workspace exclusively destined for the project contributes to the possibility of the team receiving permanent inspiration from pictures of the observations, diving into a world of allusive post-its, and following the progress of the project step by step.

Tight Schedules

Many people notice an improvement in their performance when they feel obliged to adjust to a deadline and strict schedules. Moreover, an innovation project will likely encourage more motivation and keep the team focused on its goal if it follows a beginning-middle-end structure.

10.2.2 HEAR PHASE

Hear Goals

Designing significant, innovative solutions that are useful for the community members starts by comprehending their needs, hopes, and aspirations regarding the future.

The HEAR stage provides the team with methods and advice on engaging people in their home environment, aiming to understand issues in depth.

As a goal, this stage must enlighten us on:

- Who to talk to
- How to empathize
- How to collect stories

Results

At the end of the HEAR phase, it will be necessary to prepare for fieldwork by completing the following worksheets on the Field Guide:

- Recruitment Plan
- Research Schedule
- Identity, Power, and Politics
- Group Interview Guide
- Individual Interview Guide

The outputs of this phase are:

- Listening to people's stories
- Observing the community members' reality
- A better understanding of their needs, obstacles, and limitations

"The strength of qualitative research lies in the depth of its comprehension instead of the extent of its reach."

10.2.3 CREATE PHASE

Create Goals

In order to shift from investigation to definite solutions, it is essential to travel across a process of synthesis and interpretation. On the one hand, this situation demands reducing and selecting information; on the other, it demands the transformation of our intuition of the current reality into creating opportunities for the future. This is the most abstract part of the process, which occurs when people's concrete needs turn into an acute intuition about the overall population and a system of models of interpretation created by the team.

Once the team has defined the opportunities, it can generate hundreds of solutions through brainstorming to concrete a few into prototypes later.

Solutions are exclusively created during this phase according to the client's desirability filter.

The CREATE Phase goals are:

- Interpreting data
- Identifying patterns
- Defining opportunities
- Creating solutions

There are four key activities in this phase:

- Synthesis
- Brainstorming
- Prototype
- Feedback

Synthesis is what makes what we have seen and heard during observations *meaningful*.

Synthesis transports us from inspiration to ideas, from stories to strategic orientations.

When gathering, editing, and condensing what we have learned, synthesis allows us to adopt a new perspective and identify our innovation opportunities.

A proven method to achieve unexpected innovations is brainstorming ideas, setting rules like differing opinions, or adapting to improve others' ideas.

Brainstorming makes our minds rise in the air unlimited. Generating unquestionably impracticable solutions often conjures up ideas that happen to be relevant and reasonable. It is necessary to come up with a hundred ideas (many mediocre) to find three solutions that are indeed on point.

Prototypes are a valuable method for putting solutions into practice quickly and economically. It consists of a technique that has been tested to learn how to design a good offer and to speed up a process that tends to spread its solutions to the rest of the world.

Creating prototypes means building for thinking, knowing that transforming ideas into tangible realities assists us in redefining and repeating ideas rapidly.

Creating many different prototypes that highlight varied aspects of one's products or services allows people's sincere opinions and stops the team from getting prematurely stuck on one idea alone.

Feedback is fundamental to the design process since it takes the constituents directly back to their core.

Furthermore, feedback leads to reiterating the most convincing solutions to the constituents.

DELIVER Phase

Once the design team has created many desirable solutions, it is time to consider making them feasible and viable. The DELIVER phase sets the path towards the implementation of the main ideas.

Presented here are ideas that can be useful for complementing the already-existent implementation process in the organization and for introducing changes to the solutions the way known before.

In the DELIVER Phase, the team will:

- Identify the necessary abilities.
- Create a financial sustainability plan.
- Develop a flow of innovative projects.
- Carry out pilot tests and impact evaluations.

10.2.4 WHAT IS THE VALUE OF DESIGN?

- To answer this question, we have decided to rely on what we consider to be the most extensive study by McKinsey Design, which has enabled people to understand, on a global scale, the nature of the design actions leaders can carry out to unlock the creation of value in their business. This research aimed not to start from scratch but to build upon and strengthen previous studies and measurements, such as those developed by the Design Management Institute.

- Over five years, design practices from 300 publicly listed companies were applied in several countries and industries. Design leaders and CEOs in the companies mentioned above were interviewed. McKinsey's field team collected over two million financial data and registered over 100,000 advanced design actions.

- Regression analysis unveiled the 12 actions that contributed most to financial improvement and sorted them into four significant themes.

- The four MANTRAS of good design described below are part of the McKinsey Design Index (MDI), which rates companies by how strong they are at design and, for the first time, how that connects with the financial performance of each company.

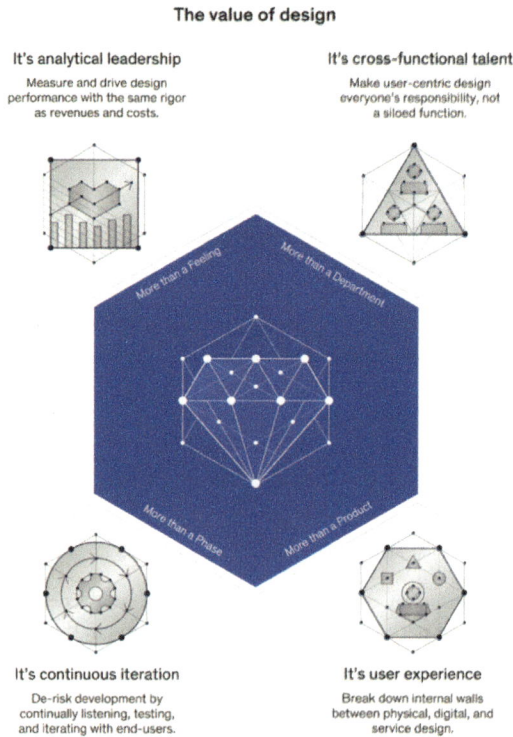

The value of design

It's analytical leadership
Measure and drive design performance with the same rigor as revenues and costs.

It's cross-functional talent
Make user-centric design everyone's responsibility, not a siloed function.

It's continuous iteration
De-risk development by continually listening, testing, and iterating with end-users.

It's user experience
Break down internal walls between physical, digital, and service design.

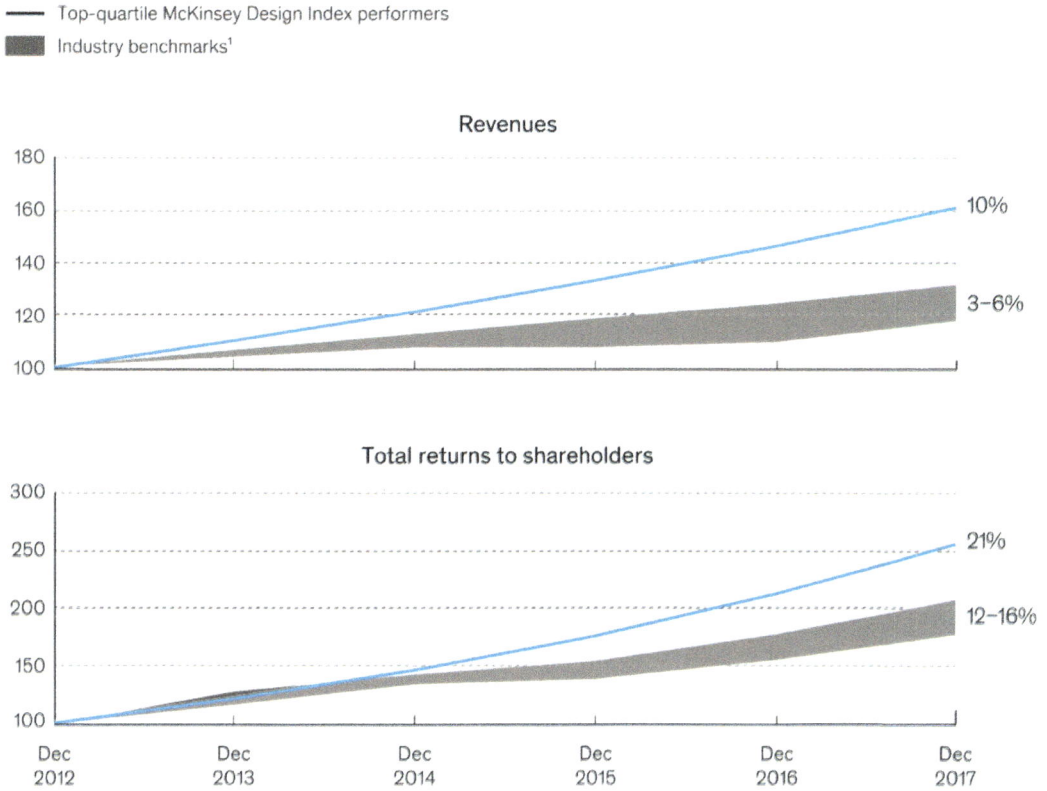

Figure 10.3 The value of design

Figure 10.4 McKinsey's Design Data

10.3 THE FOUR MANTRAS OF GOOD DESIGN

The four themes described below are part of the Mc Kinsey Design Index (MDI), which rates companies by how strong they are at design and, for the first time, how that connects with the financial performance of each company.

MANTRA # 1: MORE THAN CREATIVITY, IT'S ANALYTIC LEADERSHIP

The companies that performed best financially have understood that design is a top-management matter, and they have examined their design performance as thoroughly as they used to follow up on revenues and costs.

However, design leaders state they are treated as second-class executives in those companies with a lower performance rate. Design and leadership problems arise, such as being stuck in middle management. They are rarely promoted to the higher level. When they are, the senior executives make decisions based on intuition rather than concrete proof.

The designers themselves have been partly guilty in the past: they haven't always followed metrics or shown management in detail how their designs link up to achieving business goals. Their survey transparently shows, nonetheless, that the companies with the best financial performance are the ones that have combined design and business leadership through bold design, driven by a vision enclosed on the deliberations of their best teams.

A strong vision that explicitly commits organizations to design in the name of the client functions as a constant reminder to the top team.

IKEA works to "create a better daily life for numerous people".

As co-founder of Pixar Ed Catmull said to the readers in an interview on *Mc Kinsey Quarterly*, in order to continue surprising, the audience, his company encourages its teams to take risks in their new projects: Pixar considers that repeating the formula of past success is the main threat to surviving in the long term.

İlke Bigan, Partner at McKinsey & Company, stated in the State of Fashion 2022 report that 53% of companies focus on analytics to deliver more thoughtful and customer-centric design. Bigan added customers with products better adapted to their needs, and businesses with better total price sales meant less waste and more contribution to sustainability.

Of course, having beautiful Vision, Mission, and Value statements displayed on posters in the corporate headquarters office is not enough to accomplish sensibilization and deep understanding of the clients among higher executives.

On a leadership level, these companies are also curious about what the users need in contrast to what they say they want. One of the prime insurance corporate groups in France invites clients to their ordinary monthly meeting only to discuss what the value of the products and services means to *them*.

Toyota Great Britain transformed its customer feedback and decision-making methodology by establishing the ConsumerOne insight community. By situating the voice of the customer at the core of every decision, Toyota GB prioritized customer-centric innovation. The company gained valuable insights into the ConsumerOne platform, which enabled them to tailor their products and services to align with customer demands and preferences, enhancing overall satisfaction and loyalty.

The CEO of one of the largest banks in the world spends one day a month with bank clients and motivates all C-Suite members to do the same.

Through personal presentation or constant commitment to researchers, executives can be role models for their businesses and learn first-hand what excites and frustrates their clients the most.

Unilever proactively engages with its extensive customer base through its Open Innovation platform, a conduit for fostering collaboration. By leveraging the collective expertise of start-ups, academics, designers, and customers, Unilever employs co-creation to drive innovation in product development.

However, many companies acknowledge an alarming gap at the top of their organizations regarding understanding. In one survey, less than 5% of the interviewees said their leaders were likely to make objective design decisions – for example, to develop new products or enter new areas.

In an era of ubiquitous online tools and data-based comments from clients, the fact that design is not measured as thoroughly as timetables and costs is little but surprising. Companies can now incorporate design metrics like satisfaction rates and usability scores in the product specifications in the same way that they contemplate requirements for material quality or the relation between timelines and marketing goals.

The value of such accurate knowledge is significant: an online gaming company recently discovered that a solid 25% sales boost had followed a slight increase in its website's usability. Similarly, after launching its squeezable ketchup bottles, Heinz saw a 25% increase in sales for several years, outperforming its competitors by three times the margin despite being the market leader. Furthermore, the company unveiled improvements beyond these adjustments that had little to no additional impact on the user perception of value, so it resolved to avoid extra efforts that would have brought only mild additional profits.

MANTRA # 2: "IT'S THE USER EXPERIENCE STUPID"

The top performer companies adopt the whole user experience; they are determined to throw down the internal walls between physical, digital, and service design.

The importance of being user-centered signifies a broad vision of the spots where design can make a difference.

We live in a world where a smartphone can warn the user to leave early for the next appointment due to traffic jams, and the house can be updated on when the owner will be home to turn on the heat upon arrival.

The limits between products and services are merging into integrated experiences.

In practice, this often means mapping a customer trip across weak spots and potential sources of delight instead of starting by copy-pasting something others are already doing.

This design approach requires collecting solid customer data through first-hand observation and, more importantly, comprehending the underlying needs of potential users in their contexts.

These insights must be defended at every meeting. Nonetheless, barely 50% of the company's Mc Kinsey surveyed conducted user research before creating their first design ideas or specifications.

Combining physical products, digital tools, and "pure" services provides new opportunities for companies to capture this range of experiences.

A hotel, for example, might do more than just focus on the period between check-in and check-out (the service element) by promoting early interaction through social networks or their apps, utilizing a communication strategy based on sharing memories that connect their audience emotionally and encourage them to book again in the future.

A highly descriptive example is the CitizenM Hotel in Paris, near Gare de Lyon. Starting with their promise of *affordable luxury,* they guarantee a high-end experience without extreme costs. The key to success is guests' self-management, the best possible taste in common spaces design, digitalized processes, and warm and pleasant breakfast and bar areas. The rooms are not gigantic, but they are filled with modern design while also keeping things minimal through simple yet alluring gear – for example, installing a tablet with complete commands to control everything instead of one TV remote, one room temperature regulator, and six different electronic devices disconnected from one another.

Petit rooms like these do not make us feel restrained because of their size; on the contrary, they offer us an experience of comfort, cleanliness, good taste, and best-of-breed technology. People at the hotel realized they were still missing something, and it was the human touch of a friendly concierge at those two significant moments of truth, check-in and check-out, aiding guests who needed to modify their original bookings, managing special requests, facing, and clearing out concerns and in other words, adding a diligent touch of humanity when guests might need it the most. This symbolic gesture drove the hotel to a 7-point increase in NPS and a 5% rise in the short-term retention rate.

Companies fueled by design should not limit themselves to their ecosystem, especially not to their services or products. The best, most outstanding businesses nowadays think and act more broadly.

For example, ready-made meal businesses have become very popular among single workers who buy them on their way home after work. One food delivery company explored the possibility of partnering with Netflix to develop a one-click food ordering system accessible via a digital interface.

Mobile Payment services like Google Pay and Apple Pay resulted from an intention to think outside the limits and create more accessible ways to access cash. One solution is a piece of plastic in the wallet, but how much easier is it to use a device already in the pocket?

MANTRA # 3: "MORE THAN A DEPARTMENT, IT'S MULTIFUNCTIONAL TALENT"

The best-performing companies make user-centered designs that are everyone's responsibility, not just an isolated function. In the jaded portrait of traditional design departments, a group of tattooed, aloof people operates under the radar, secluded from the rest of the organization. Considered renegades or nonconformists by their colleagues, these employees in the portrait are protective of the access to their ideas, claiming they have been beaten up too frequently by close-minded engineers or marketing bosses unwilling to (if not incapable of) transforming designers' grand visions into reality. We are not suggesting that this stereotype is still common nor that other functions are necessarily to blame, but the one true thing is that it can be surprisingly resistant.

The typical mistake companies make is having their design team believe they belong to a privileged cluster where creativity and the company's future reside. They want to build a paramount design studio to boost the design community's excitement. In little to no time, every designer will move their desks inside the studio and deactivate the door access for the marketing, engineering, and quality teams. These movements dramatically reduce cooperative work and undermine the entire company's performance.

Overcoming isolating tendencies is extremely valuable. The strongest correlation we can find is one that links top financial performers with companies that ensure they can break down functional silos and integrate designers with other functions.

This was particularly remarkable in CPG companies, top-quartile firms recording annual increase rates 7% higher than other weaker companies.

Nurturing superior design talent -2% of the employees contributing significantly to each business- is another crucial dimension of the teamwork dynamic.

Conquering the right primary incentives is a part of this: the most remarkable design-driven companies were three times more likely to have specific incentive programs for their designers. These programs are linked to design results like user satisfaction metrics or grand prizes.

Nevertheless, the most important thing to remember is that keeping hold of great design talents means more than promising a big bonus or a career as a higher executive.

These carrot-and-stick schemes are not enough to retain the best design talent if they do not offer the freedom to work on passion-driven projects, time to participate in conferences with their pairs, and opportunities to stay in touch with the design community.

Talented designers in a CPG company with well-respected design credentials started to flee due to the time they were forced to invest in making PowerPoint presentations for the marketing team.

On the other hand, Spotify's appeal to top designers is often attributed to its culture of autonomy and connectivity and its effort to create an environment that is diverse, fun, and prompt to market.

Design is already expanding into various parts of the company: human-machine interactions, artificial intelligence, behavioral economics, and engineering psychology, without mentioning innovation and the development of new business models. Although it is not a new concept, the modern, hybrid "T-shaped" designers who work cross-functionally and simultaneously preserve their deep design knowledge will be the employees who are most likely to make a tangible impact through their work. They can only do so if they can count on the right tools, abilities, and infrastructure. This situation requires the type of design software, communication apps, thorough data analysis, and prototype-creation technologies that fuel productivity and speed up design iterations. All of which calls for time and investment.

There is another strong correlation between successful firms and companies that resisted the temptation of cutting down on research, prototype creation, or concept-generation budgets at the first sign of conflict. Formal design allocations must be met in association with design leaders instead of appearing as something that often happens as line elements in the engineering or marketing spending.

MANTRA # 4: "MORE THAN A PHASE, IT'S AN ONGOING ITERATION"

Design thrives in environments that encourage learning, testing, and interacting with users: practices that boost the probabilities of achieving great product and service improvement while simultaneously reducing the risk of big, costly mistakes. This approach breaks the mold of the normal one in many companies that still emphasize inflexible and irreversible phases of product development.

Silo-based organizations risk losing access to the consumer's voice or depending too much on one iteration of that voice.

Top results come from constantly combining quantitative research (like conjoint analysis) and qualitative research (such as ethnographic interviews) of the consumers. This information should be combined with reports from the market analytics area about the competitors' actions, patent scans for monitoring new technologies, business concerns pointed out by the finance team, and so on. Without these tensions and interactions, top development can end up in nothing, creating excellent work that never sees the light of day or gets to delight the customers.

In a successful effort to improve the user experience, a cruise company in Mc Kinsey's research spoke directly to the passengers, analyzed data to see what meals and activities had been the most popular at different times, and implemented AI algorithms in security cameras to identify inefficiencies in the ship design.

Different sources of inspiration merged at a medical technology company while speaking with a toy designer about physical ergonomics and a date-app designer about digital interface design.

These moves helped the company redefine a device to make it appealing to clients with limited dexterity.

Not only was the resultant product safer and easier to use, but it also contributed to a quick growth in market insertion at its launch. Despite the iteration value, it is known that more than 60% of the firms are using prototypes only for producing internal tests, a moment when it is already too late for the development process.

On the opposite side to this, the most successful firms consciously nurture a culture of sharing the prototypes with people who are not even clients, collecting embryonic ideas. They also discourage the type of design management that spends hours perfecting their first mock-ups or internal presentations.

The agile approach helps companies to shorten the time to market while finding improvement opportunities on the run. Taking the pole position in the competitive race toward being perceived as the most innovative company is usually better than having extraordinary products.

Apple led the way in finding market spots, occupying them with new products before any other competitor, and, once there, securing its dominant position by improving features and usability. This strategy has been the key to the company's success since the iPod days.

Furthermore, the Apple Watch is a perfect example of many products that have adjusted themselves to reflect how clients use them "in real life."

Design-centered companies realize that launching a product is not the end of the iteration. Almost every business problem found in software involves constantly updating the products post-launch.

10.4 WE DESIGN PERCEIVED VALUE

"What we think changes the way we perceive what we see".

Experience is a perception. This position puts us in a complex situation when deconstructing the information gathered from consumer research.

In traditional research, generalized, superficial results can conspire against our desired design input.

What we genuinely want to know and need to know about the consumer archetypes is how they perceive their experience with the brand. Nothing more, nothing less.

Perception is a construct built within the brain thanks to a superior mental process. Each person has a different mental setup and makes their path in understanding what they perceive.

Penti

CASE STUDY
PENTI

Written by: Mert Karaibrahimoğlu (CEO at Penti), Cristina Polini (CMO at Penti), Gizem Burcu Bağcı (Marketing Director at Penti), Ömür Kula (CEO at WWF Türkiye)

Chapter 1

Brand strength breeds from product strength

Penti was founded by the Kariyo family in 1950, to provide for the needs of a very specific female target audience – Female Teachers, who were required to wear nylon hosiery to work. Their need was so specific and high on demand, it was a strong business opportunity. Achieving to design the right quality for the right price, Penti took off fast as a female brand and became synonymous with "Teacher hosiery". This strong essence and brand baseline helped Penti grew, and the brand became more confident with its presence in women's life, every year. In 1980's Penti decided to further invest in its brand and started the first organized retail formation in the innerwear business in Türkiye, via opening its own shops throughout the country.

Today, Penti is the largest fully integrated hosiery manufacturer in Europe, with 100 million pairs of hosiery production capacity per year. Exporting to more than 60 different countries, Penti is also a strong business partner to brands like Marks & Spencer, Sainsbury, and Primark.

Penti's success is mainly because of its dedication to creating successful, right on spot products. With Ekotesk certified nylon hosiery that allow a 3 cm thinning, with the first lycra integrated nylon hosiery, Fit15, that revolutionized the hosiery market in Türkiye, with the menstruation underwear that helps women to liberate their ped consumptions, with its "no-wire" bra technology that created the "non-bra" movement, Penti has always been the most innovative brand in the market that addressed the needs of women at every stage of their lives for any motivation that they had. "My Size One Size" collection helped women feel confident in any size or shape they were in. Products that are not only rationally on spot, but also emotionally right in time allowed Penti to always act in alignment with female sensitivity. As a brand that understands women's bodies very well, Penti launched "mix & match" in the beach category based on the fact that the lower and upper body sizes are different, and this opportunity gave both comfort for the size and freedom for the combination." Magic Mama Bra" is added, a nursing bra produced with the technology used in menstrual support panties, which absorbs liquid, prevents leakage, and breathes thanks to its 3-layer special technique, to its maternity collection. Working on innovative products for the needs of women of all ages, Penti presented the Penti Aging collection called, made of a wearable collagen called **UMORFIL®** Nylon, which is made of collagen containing fabric made of fish scales, which has a moisturizing effect, giving elasticity to the skin, support to delay aging and reducing some signs of aging. This collection also benefits the physical needs of pre-menopausal / menopausal women.

Women in general are trend makers in leading opinions that change the world, especially when it comes to natural and sustainable solutions. Women not only want the best product for themselves but also want to make sure that the next generations are protected, and the world is well taken care of. Penti never saw this as a consumer trend only. It was a company-wide transformation decision from the beginning. In 2021, Penti signed the UN Global Compact and became the first fashion retail brand in Türkiye that gave solid promises and commitments for sustainability. Within the commitments, Penti has promised to transform 95 % of its cotton and polyester sourcing into sustainable resources until 2030. In parallel, Penti Hoisery manufacturing company, has invested in energy efficient high compressor machines and achieved a 660.000 kWh energy sufficiency with 200 tones of reduction in its CO_2 carbon emissions.

From first day on Penti's strength was all about creating the right product for the right business opportunity that would benefit women's everyday life. This was such a strong base, that in years, Penti grew fit, sound, and sustainable to become the strongest brand of women in Türkiye.

Chapter 2

Conquering the world of women

Since that initial spark that was ignited by the nylon hosiery, Penti has always been considered as a women's brand, who really gets what women need. Today, from innerwear to socks, beachwear, homewear, active and casualwear to kids and men categories, Penti is active in 34 countries with over 500 stores, serving the needs of almost every kind of woman for many occasions and their loved ones.

The idea behind this categoric expansion was all about becoming the "one stop shop" for women for their most intimate needs. Penti invested further and grew stronger in its expertise of knowing the female body better than anyone in the market. Perfect fit, perfect sizing with best quality material and price, Penti became the sole address of women, when they especially needed a trusted expert for their innerwear. This success eventually made Penti as a brand to rise to become the Lovemark in its category, winning the title for 3 consecutive years since 2021.

Women's rational needs regarding their body, stretched to their emotional needs and from that new product ideas emerged. Finding the right size for a bra, became one of the first steps of a woman's self-confidence and Penti helped every woman, in every one of its stores to make sure the awareness was built.

Thus, the women who started seeing Penti as the expert innerwear, "body genius", wanted more. They wanted to buy the first bra for their daughters, that was designed specifically for their age and needs.

As Penti built women's confidence further, women built Penti into a multi-category giant. Woman being at the center of the brand, brand offered solutions to all loved ones in a woman's life.

Penti, fast and capable, started to dominate all categories that women wanted expertise and fashion both at the same time. Both the company and the brand were so strong, there was a new phase that the brand needed to jump – to create a deeper and more meaningful connection with women, Penti started to unify behind a single brand idea and tone of voice, which would become more than just a product, but also a mindset, a purposeful vision.

Chapter 3

Women conquering the brand

As Penti became stronger, expectations from the brand grew bigger. Making fashion statements or defining trends in each category was not any longer enough to really deserve to be the Lovemark of women in Türkiye. It was obvious for Penti, from all the research and data that the brand created, that women wanted and needed one thing and one thing only – to be understood. However, Penti was not yet ready to be the spokesperson for its target audience nor it was yet that eager.

The relationship between Penti and women, was ready to move beyond the product. However, it was a delicate shift that required to define the relationship as well as grow it further into a more meaningful version. Women wanted Penti to be something for them, the brand was expected to be more expressive, more present in issues regarding women.

Penti always knew that having a strong core category like intimate, women wanted to feel understood and seen. Yet this was not only about women's physical beauty, but it was also about their untold, un-talked, mostly hidden needs and situations that required attention, help, and sometimes support.

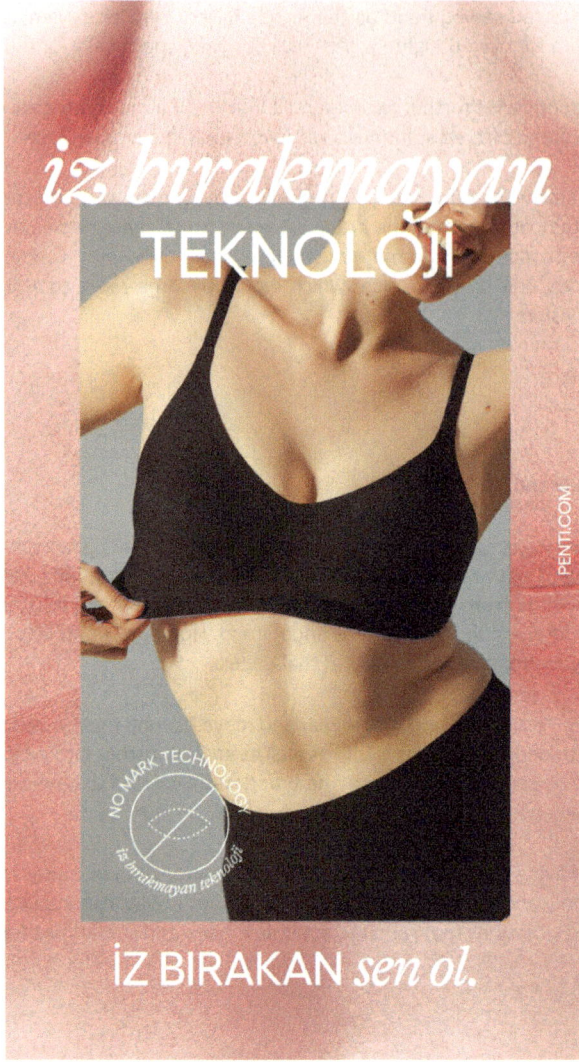

For the next phase of the brand, Penti stepped into the untold needs of women and the taboos around them. For the first time in Türkiye, Penti in prime-time TV, talked about menstruation as something "naturally normal". For the first time, Penti broke the taboo of menstruation being something to be hidden, nothing to be complained and showed women that they did understand them during this phase as well, and thus had the perfect product to serve them.

This first and very different communication strategy took Penti out of the product-driven and fashion-oriented, slightly silent, and non-opinionated territory of brand land and moved into the spotlight where now women had a reason to engage with the brand, deepening the relationship and starting to ask for more. Penti, was now ready to listen further and understand better what the women had to say or think.

This advertising campaign brought huge success. Penti was confirmed by far the number one Innerwear brand in top-of-mind awareness and the most used one by women in general. (Innerwear category top of mind awareness: 74%, total awareness 95%, at least once used our product ration 86% – 2024 stats representing of all Turkish women population.)

Chapter 4

Journey of becoming the most valuable women's brand of Türkiye

Changing the way Penti communicates itself to women, triggers other transformations. Penti, as a company, once starting to feel more confident about how already holistic and ready they are becoming more invested in achieving to be a real women's brand, with all their thinking, vision, and actions. Company's HR policy to sustainability commitments is all in line with empowering the female identity and preserving its energy. In 2021, Penti was named the "Best Employer" in both Türkiye and Europe and has been awarded with the title of "Great Place to Work" every year since 2021 in Türkiye. Penti has always carried its work culture forward, especially by being included in the "Best Places to Work for Women" list in 2024. Penti is already 90% women employed. It is one of the few companies that applied equal pay for men and women for similar titles and experiences. It is one of the few brands trying to change the patriarchic jargon of business life to a more equally represented language. Volunteers from Penti's staff, are actively participating in projects of gender equality. Penti was and is ready to promise that not only through its products but through its comradeship, that it will be there when women needed her. All this success is because of the meticulously ingrained Kyosei philosophy in the ways of working at Penti. The road to progress is through collaboration and lifting each other up for one common vision, like a family and this understanding has always pushed Penti forward, not only as a company but also as a community.

The way the women and issues regarding women were perceived was also at a changing period. Women were becoming more visible, stronger, and louder. With the mother nature also becoming louder about her needs, it was inevitable for brands like Penti to align themselves with such a change. New needs, new values and priorities were setting in, in a woman's life. Accepting her body, at any shape, size, or life stage, even at every mood, was becoming more important than ever. Solidarity and sisterhood were also rising.

Going further, Penti has now acting like a community brand, who has a joyful courage to pinpoint the needs of women while serving them with the right kind of solutions and help build their confidence. It all starts with their body and Penti knows this best. Feeling great in their own body, women need to make sure that they know their body, choose the right fit and size and material that will boost their self-belief from within.

Penti Club, though it is at its baby-steps period, will on its way to grow into the biggest women's club of Türkiye. We are trying to infuse inspiration to young and old women of Türkiye through our "Leave your Mark" Project by bringing women together with women who have left their mark in this world via their stories. We are right in front where it is time to speak up about violence against women. Every year, between November 25th to December 10th, we join forces with UNWomen to declare that we are here to fight with all violence against women via 16 days of consecutive activism. We are also here to make sure that breast health is a priority for women. We created the Palpbox Project to create awareness among women that self-scan is the most effective way for early diagnosis.

As Penti is growing stronger to become a purposeful women's brand, we know our role. We are here to unleash the inner power of womanhood by making sure that there is no single understanding regarding the female body beauty. We want to make sure that women are confident, comfortable, naturally beautiful and in harmony within their own bodies at every stage, occasion, mood and feeling in their lives. We will be relentless in designing products and services that enable this, and make sure that women have no barrier whatsoever to be able to do whatever her inner strength tells her to do.

Questions to stimulate conversation on the case

1. **In what ways did Penti utilize product innovation (e.g., Fit15, menstruation underwear, no-wire bras) to stay ahead of competitors and meet emerging consumer needs?)**

Penti has always been an expert when it's about the needs and expression of the woman body. For women to feel comfortable and thus confident in their own body, Penti has always been ahead of the game innovating on the form, fitness, and the shape of all kinds of innerwear and activewear. Penti works ahead of time to bring added-value solutions into the lives of women the fastest possible. Penti's offerings ensure women tos tay up to date in allignment with the evolving cultural values, the latest trends in fashion, advancements in tech, and by incorporating new techniques/fabrics in manufacturing, always earlier than its competitors can do. The main reason why Penti can do this is that Penti always really listen to the woman and understand her needs.

2. **How did Penti shift from being perceived as a product-driven brand to becoming a "Lovemark"?**

Penti shifted from a product-driven brand to a "Lovemark" by addressing women's emotional and untapped needs, like menstruation, body confidence, and maternity. It introduced empowering products such as no-wire bras and menstruation underwear, while engaging in societal issues like breast health and violence against women. By creating a consistent, purpose-driven voice and fostering community initiatives like Penti Club, the brand built a deeper emotional connection with women. This transition aligns with principles on brand loyalty and emotional branding by fostering trust, addressing holistic needs, and building lasting relationships beyond just products.

3. **How did Penti's communication strategies, such as addressing taboo topics like menstruation, help the brand deepen its connection with women, and what can this teach us about modern consumer behavior?**

- Penti's communication strategies, particularly addressing taboo topics like menstruation, helped deepen its connection with women by showing that the brand truly understood their needs and concerns. By openly discussing menstruation in its campaigns—something traditionally seen as taboo in Türkiye—Penti broke cultural barriers and empowered women to feel more comfortable and confident about their bodies. This bold move demonstrated empathy and a willingness to address topics that were often ignored, fostering a sense of trust and emotional connection with its audience.

- This approach also highlighted that modern consumers, especially women, seek brands that not only provide products but also understand their deeper emotional needs and are willing to engage in conversations about sensitive, personal issues. This shows us that addressing such untapped topics can build loyalty and deepen relationships, as consumers today are drawn to brands that are authentic, transparent, and aligned with their values, creating stronger emotional bonds.

- In essence, by moving beyond product promotion to meaningful discussions, Penti effectively aligned with modern consumer behavior, where emotional engagement and authenticity are key drivers of brand loyalty.

10.4.1 WHAT DOES IT MEAN TO UNDERSTAND THE CUSTOMER?

The extensive literature produced by Psychology and Biology has facilitated our understanding of the intricate nature of the perception process. Given the fact that this process is causally related to those of learning and memory, we can draw two conclusions: in the first place, the phenomenon is *intricate*; hence, we cannot fall for a simplistic answer to explain it. We are obliged to use a multi-dimensional model to decode the process and, most importantly, manage it. Business-wise, the understanding of the experience, however deep, means nothing if one cannot manage it like they would any other asset in the company.

The second conclusion is that we must acknowledge the understanding of consumers as the foundation stone in the experience design process, which also needs to be nourished by great human and social expertise. It is especially relevant to thoroughly know the filters through which consumers perceive their realities in general and their experience with the brand.

Therefore, comprehending the customers requires a strategic effort, and it is an ever-going process. It would be beneficial to have a similar display to that used in an ECG study, showing the subjects' feelings and thoughts in real-time. This situation would help us to identify any significant changes that could alter the ground hypothesis in our experience design.

The social era we currently live in highly improves the game for consumer comprehension. Access to real people's emotional states throughout their daily interactions had never been so at hand in the history of human behavior studies, as unimportant as it may seem at first glance.

The scoop that something changed in the customer's perception had never been so easy to get.

10.5 THE MENTAL MODEL

A foundation rock in Valué design, which we approach in this chapter following the Umuntu method, is understanding the client's mental model.

To put it into context, one can start with a technical definition of experience, according to which experience is considered the perception clients conform progressively through each interaction they have with the brand.

Nonetheless, when speaking of interaction, it is not in generic terms. Clients do not build perceptions during any sort of interaction. For instance, they do not do so merely in transactional interactions unless something misfortunate happens throughout the transaction. When this is the case, an operation that should have been simple transforms into a reason for frustration, leading the person to create an unpleasant perception.

It can be reasonably deduced that the initial and indispensable prerequisite for the existence of an experience is the interaction with the brand. The next step is emotion, which allows for no exceptions since it is the factor that cements the episode in the client's memory. Moreover, that remembrance is the subsequent step. Not in vain do we think of experience, among other ways, as "what we recall from what happened". A self-generated story we tell ourselves in each interaction with the brand that ultimately compiles a stock of episodes into a larger tale.

Now, let us concentrate again on the concept of experience as perception. In order to work on this, it is essential to undertake a detailed analysis and comprehension of the processes by which individuals construct their perceptions. Here is where the mental model inevitably comes into action. The mental model has to do with a superior psychological process that humans use to build perception, which develops throughout a series of associations within the brain and practically defines us as persons.

Hence, when referring to experience, we describe a personal phenomenon that is both human and brain based. Far behind lies the initial segment concept, slightly less than old-fashioned nowadays. Agreeing with that concept, we arranged clients into collectives with similar characteristics and studied them as a whole entity. The segment idea serves the purpose of discerning such criteria: demographic, social, psychological, and even geographic. However, it has reached a limit. The same limit will be the stepping stone to discovering the mental model archetype.

Inside the limbic brain in human beings is stored the perception machine we have come to call the *mental model*. It operates subconsciously through a process of attribution and signification of each archetype's experiences. This way, the mental model is sculpted out of the stone of every person's reference structure, their belief system, the stories they lived in the past, and the experiences that shaped them into who they are today.

Umuntu builds a schema of the mental model that allows us to collect information from projective research to use as a design input. In other words, it approaches something as complex as constructing perception practically, simplifying it into a four-dimension structure.

These dimensions conform to the nature of perception and could make it possible to acquire thorough, meaningful knowledge about people's perception, practically 60 or 70%. Among the information compiled in projective research are terms, references, words, and *verbatim* that constitute each person's unconscious. This verbal data stock is essential to go beyond transactional information and enlarge our perspective of the mental model study.

10.5.1 FIRST DIMENSION OF PERCEPTION: FUNCTIONAL

Everything starts with the functional dimension. The one explaining, precisely, the way things work – not just anything, but the brand the clients are interacting with, the one with which they construct experience-based perception. Customers rely on certain viewpoints when perceiving the different aspects of the brand's functionality.

The ability to communicate with a contact center or send a text via WhatsApp at any time, regardless of the situation, demonstrates the convenience and accessibility of these channels. These mentioned variables are going to be known from further on, as functionality describers; among which not only can accessibility be accounted for, but also response capability, employees' level and expertise, and *time* – even though time will prove to be a variable with plenty of extra considerations. Following up, we will see why the functional dimension integrates the *hard* edge of perception.

10.5.2 SECOND DIMENSION OF PERCEPTION: ECONOMIC

We are currently moving on to the economic dimension, which is the second *challenging* dimension, alongside functionality. The designation "black-and-white" is derived from the absence of a gradational spectrum of gray in either field. On the contrary, these disciplines demand clear and precise answers. Ambiguity is not a possibility when it comes to the Economy. In the experience with the brand, our brain interrogates us about the exact economic implication of such an experience. In addition to the official price, other factors, such as potential hidden costs that may arise later, or the cost-benefit ratio of traveling and transportation, must be considered.

Let us take the health field to name one case. If a professional casually changes the location of his or her appointments for a much more distant one, this change signifies an economic implication for the regular patient who is used to walking to the appointment and now has to decide on a transportation means with an additional cost.

The same applies to *time*, which, according to personal *verbatim*, can be thought of as a functional variable or an economic one: continuing with the health field example, if a patient attends an appointment somewhere more distant and is also faced with a sudden change of schedule, he or she might be forced to renounce their working day. If we picture the patient as a dependent middle-class worker who makes a living from what they earn daily, the implications of losing a whole one are too high.

10.5.3 THIRD DIMENSION OF PERCEPTION: EMOTIONAL

We now dive into the first *soft* dimension: the emotional dimension. It is far from wild to conceive this to be among the most important ones - perhaps, *the* most important - since it collects remainders from all the other dimensions and powerfully influences decision-making. Like a compass, the emotional dimension leads the brain to the north of clients' feelings and appreciation of their experience, making them lean towards one option.

Some of the most common emotional describer's worth mentioning are empathy, trust, and warmth. Instead of appearing in a pure state, feelings within the mental model result from an emotional driver, a trigger. When a customer's experience is frustrated by the lack of empathy of a brand member, the actual trigger is empathy. It is necessary to explore the depths of emotion inside the mental schema to get to their origin and find them in their final state, which is an *active* state of emotion.

10.5.4 FOURTH DIMENSION OF PERCEPTION: ASPIRATIONAL

Lastly, we find the aspirational dimension to finish up with the soft edge. Although sometimes the least known, the aspirational dimension frequently turns out to be perception's actual driver since aspiration stands for what people expect from the brand. If neither the experience nor the brand creates expectations, they become a commodity.

Therefore, such experience is the key to the fourth dimension. In the experience design process, expectation can be studied by considering the different, relevant client archetypes and observing how the selected describers express each one. An acceptable average number of variables or describers would be six, for example, and this applies perfectly to the rest of the dimensions. If the product for sale is a traveling credit card, describers will be different from an executive mom's perspective than those perceived by a stay-at-home man whose children are already grown up.

10.6 DIFFERENTIATION/RELEVANCE MATRIX

A determining tool for clarifying perception and mental model analysis and extracting crucial data is the differentiation/relevance matrix. This model consists of qualifying each mental model description in the different dimensions according to both variables. As the word implies, the relevance variable refers to the brand's importance and the client's experience. Differentiation concerns the uniqueness people perceive about what's expected and already known in the field.

Considering the measurement of each variable as a low/high indicator, inter-crossed with the low/high indicator of the complementary variable within a square-shaped diagram, we can highlight four analysis cardinal points: low relevance/low differentiation; low relevance/high differentiation; high relevance/low differentiation, and high/relevance/high differentiation. At first, what is noticed is that the critical cardinal points in the study are the bottom and the top: low relevance/low differentiation and high relevance/high differentiation. The first one addresses the basic requirements concerning the product or service, especially on a functional level. In experience design, it is necessary first to fulfill the basic needs to pursue the extraordinary. Nobody would be interested in whether a product is innovative or different if its prime features are underachieving, perform poorly, or are too difficult to get —when distribution and access fail.

The high relevance/high differentiation edge is positioned on the opposite side of the square diagram. It represents the singularity of the experience and aims to conquer the exceptional, following the customer's expectations and demands and considering what they perceive to be necessary. Of course, this situation has already successfully met the basic, indisputable requirements.

People's perception, as already seen, varies depending on each person's mental archetype. A tech-savvy college student who values the latest trends and innovations in gadgets will likely build a perception around high relevance/high differentiation differently than a retired individual on a fixed income who prioritizes affordability and practicality over cutting-edge features. The design challenge will be to create an experience for every perception model. Mastering this technique will allow the brand to load its design stock with privileged information. Thoroughly knowing the clients' appreciation scale within their personal perception machine changes the game for the value propositions that the brand will offer them through experience.

FLO GROUP

CASE STUDY
FLO GROUP

GROWTH MARKETING APPROACH IN A MULTI-BRAND AND OMNI-CHANNEL ORGANIZATION

About FLO GROUP

With a history spanning nearly 65 years, FLO GROUP has established itself as an omni-channel, multi-brand, customer-centric integrated retail company. Operating across the entire retail ecosystem—from production to distribution—FLO GROUP is the largest footwear retailer in Türkiye and ranks as the third largest in Europe.

The company operates in 28 countries across the CIS, Middle East, and North Africa regions, with over 800 stores in Türkiye and abroad. FLO GROUP directly employs nearly 15,000 people and indirectly provides jobs for approximately 70,000 more. Through an omni-channel business model, it reaches millions of consumers via retail stores, e-commerce platforms, and an extensive wholesale network. In 2023, these combined channels attracted 670 million visitors.

FLO GROUP's omni-channel approach, paired with its multi-brand business model, which includes leading brands in their segments, sets it apart from traditional retailers. Key brands like Kinetix and Polaris, which have accompanied generations in Türkiye, and the Italian brand Lumberjack, which joined the portfolio in 2012, have been pivotal in the company's global brand management. Since 2003, FLO GROUP has expanded its portfolio by securing regional licensing rights for global brands such as Dockers By Gerli and U.S. Polo ASSN. It continues its international expansion through strategic licensing agreements, including the acquisition of regional rights for Nine West, Lotto, and Reebok since 2019.

Implementing a business model with an omni-channel retail approach, FLO GROUP sold 53.1 million pairs of shoes in 2023 and welcomed around 700 million visitors across its multi-brand and monobrand stores, e-commerce activities, and widespread wholesale network.

The company's leading position in the Turkish market is reflected in FLO, which is Türkiye's top-of-mind shoe retailer, according to the IPSOS Brand Health Tracking Footwear Report. In addition, IN STREET and Sneakerbox, two sneaker and sportswear chains, further diversify the company's retail offering, alongside monobrand stores for Reebok, Nine West, and Lumberjack.

FLO GROUP's 360-degree integrated retailing strategy combines physical stores, e-commerce, and wholesale channels to drive both local and international growth. Alongside its proprietary e-commerce platforms, the company operates in global and local marketplaces, partners with wholesalers, and reaches consumers through its chain and monobrand stores.

FLO GROUP primarily targets young adult women and men aged 18-34, belonging to the BC1C2 socioeconomic segments. This demographic is fashion-conscious and values personal style, viewing clothing and footwear as key to self-expression. They prioritize convenience and speed in their shopping experience, favouring retailers that offer quick and efficient solutions. This group also looks for budget-friendly, high-quality products that deliver a strong price-performance balance. A wide variety of products, reliable customer service, and engaging campaigns are critical to securing their loyalty, both online and in physical stores.

Leveraging more than half a century of know-how and experience to continuously create value, FLO GROUP established a tech company within its own organization in 2023. Located at Yıldız Technical University Technopark, FLO Technology is a milestone achievement for the company, employing a tech team of 198 people as of March 31, 2024. This innovation hub has not only enhanced operational speed and efficiency but also bridged the gap between online and offline channels, offering a tech-driven omni-channel customer experience.

Committed to sustainability, FLO GROUP integrates economic, social, and environmental development throughout its entire ecosystem. The company aligns its efforts with the United Nations' Sustainable Development Goals (SDGs) and is an active member of the Global Compact, the Sustainable Development Association, and the Sustainability Academy.

FLO GROUP continues to enhance its sustainability performance, contributing to key SDGs such as Quality Education, Gender Equality, Affordable and Clean Energy, Decent Work and Economic Growth, Industry, Innovation and Infrastructure, Reduced Inequalities, Responsible Consumption and Production, Climate Action, and Partnerships for the Goals.

FLO GROUP fosters a diverse workforce in terms of both gender and age. The company, which has been listed among Capital Magazine's "100 Women-Friendly Companies" for several years, reported a 45.6% female employment rate in 2023, with 6,452 women in total. The company's workforce also reflects diversity across age groups: 3% Gen X, 58% Gen Y, and 39% Gen Z. In recognition of its human resources efforts, FLO GROUP received the "Respect for People Award" from Kariyer.net in 2020 and 2023.

Growth marketing approach and management

Understanding the needs and expectations of our customers with a 360-degree approach lies at the core of FLO GROUP's entire business model. Accordingly, we listen to our customers across all touchpoints in the four stages of customer lifecycle and analyze their demands and needs to manage our growth marketing efforts toward increasing value throughout the customer journey. The four stages of customer lifecycle and our approach are explained below.

Customer lifecycle – stage 1 – category users

At this stage, we track brand health metrics and market share in relation to our marketing communication investments and their impact on the target audience. Our goal is to leverage insights from two key surveys to pinpoint areas for brand development, attract category users to our stores, and increase sales of FLO GROUP brands, even in non-group retail outlets. The following surveys are instrumental in monitoring our performance:

Brand Health Survey

This survey measures the performance of FLO GROUP brands and competitors in key areas such as Top of Mind (TOM), Aided Top of Mind (TOMA), brand desire, purchase intention, and future buying tendencies. Additionally, it monitors preferred online and physical retail chains, as well as brands that the target audience prefers or has purchased. The survey specifically focuses on the audiences where brand investments have been made. Conducted monthly with a consistent sample, the brand health survey's results are analyzed and reported on a quarterly basis. At the end of each quarter, media and content strategies are adjusted based on the brand mindshare generated by our investments and those of competitors.

In addition, focus groups, qualitative surveys for specific target audiences, and pre- and post-advertising tests based on neuromarketing techniques are used to refine concepts and ideas that align with brand positioning strategies. These insights help advance creative content and scenarios. Target-specific evaluations are incorporated into media planning, ensuring that our brands reach the right audiences at the right time with tailored value propositions.

Market Share Survey

To better understand the competitive landscape and identify priority categories for investment, we conduct quarterly market share surveys. This survey collects data from a significant number of households each week, tracking the shoes purchased and feeding the information into our system for regular analysis. The insights derived from this analysis inform brand-specific growth strategies, investment decisions, and marketing actions across product groups.

In addition to these regular surveys, FLO GROUP conducts a comprehensive "usage and attitude study" every two years to gain deeper market insights. This study explores usage trends across different shoe categories, changes in these trends, key motivations behind store and channel preferences, and the extent to which FLO GROUP brands and competitors are favored within specific product groups in the past year. It also analyzes brand preferences among different demographic segments within the category user base.

Customer lifecycle – stage 2 – store visitors

The primary objective of our marketing investments is to increase traffic across both online and physical channels, thereby facilitating customer acquisition. It is essential to align meaningful communication investments with strategic brand content that mobilizes category users, driving store visits and engagement.

Tracking Store Visitors - We analyze visitor numbers using sensors placed at store entrances, comparing year-on-year data for stores that have been open the same number of days. This analysis is conducted monthly and segmented by store types (e.g., tourist, street, shopping mall, outlet, and discount stores), as well as by province and region. The insights gained guide our actions, including the development of special campaigns and tailored marketing support for stores that demonstrate lower traffic compared to the previous year or below-average traffic growth within their segment.

Exit Surveys – Biannual exit surveys are conducted in strategically selected stores that represent the wider Turkish market. These surveys aim to understand why visitors come to our stores, their shopping routes, expectations from the brand and store, their evaluation of product displays, and their experience with our service. Additionally, we seek to uncover the reasons behind customers' decisions to shop or not to shop. The feedback helps us assess both met and unmet customer expectations, allowing us to initiate product, service, and experience improvements across all functions as part of a corporate project. The effectiveness of these improvements is monitored through follow-up surveys.

Mystery Shopper Surveys – Quarterly mystery shopper surveys are conducted in all stores to measure service quality and evaluate the overall shopping experience across our retail chains. Each store is scored based on its performance within its respective region, and action plans are developed to enhance the customer service experience. The impact of these actions is tracked and reviewed on a quarterly basis.

Customer lifecycle – stage 3 – customer

Customer acquisition starts when the needs and expectations of store visitors are met with high-quality service. We categorize customers into two groups: **"New Customers,"** who are first-time shoppers of FLO GROUP brands, and **"Repeat Customers,"** who return to shop FLO GROUP brands again. We track the monthly data on new and repeat customers for each retail brand and compare performance across physical and online channels, taking targeted marketing actions as needed for each customer type.

New Customer Acquisition Cost is calculated by dividing marketing communication investments by the number of new customers acquired during the period when those investments were made. This metric is continuously monitored through a change chart that is segmented by category, brand, and product, allowing us to take necessary actions to optimize acquisition efforts.

Additionally, we conduct two surveys during the "customer" stage to better understand the service quality expectations across different functions within our company. These are detailed below:

Net Promoter Score (NPS) – After every purchase through any channel selling FLO GROUP brands, a single-question NPS survey is sent to customers. This survey uses the globally standardized 10-point scale, and customers who score us 6 or below are asked additional questions to better understand the reasons for their low scores. Insights from these surveys drive the design of improvement projects, with the outcomes continuously monitored through follow-up surveys using the same method.

Customer Service – Integrated Feedback Analysis - We have implemented an integrated feedback system, comprising various communication channels, to allow customers to share their opinions and reviews about our products and services through their preferred communication channel. Customers can choose to communicate via phone, chatbot, email, social media, Şikayetvar.com, or other review/complaint platforms. Customer service representatives respond to inquiries, requests, or complaints within 20 seconds across these channels. All customer feedback, along with NPS responses, is reviewed by the Customer Experience Committee, which convenes monthly and includes representatives from senior management. Emphasizing a customer-centric approach as a core value, the committee uses insights from the integrated feedback system as key performance indicators for service quality across all functions. These insights inform the development of customer-centric corporate projects, and relevant committees oversee the implementation and follow-up of these initiatives.

Customer lifecycle – stage 4 – loyal or lost customer

Maintaining customer retention is essential for enhancing customer lifetime value. As new customers move through all stages of the lifecycle, we target them with personalized communications and campaigns. These are tailored by analyzing purchasing behavior across multiple criteria, such as store, channel, product group, brand, pricing, variety, and timing. By leveraging these data-driven marketing efforts and insights from FLO GROUP's 26 million customers, we aim to achieve brand-specific growth by driving repeat purchases. FLO PLUS, our omni-channel loyalty program, plays a pivotal role in this strategy by offering various benefits that enhance customer value. The program allows us to collect product reviews, enrich customer data, and design exclusive campaigns for customers and their families and friends.

Preventing customer loss is equally critical at this stage. A "lost customer" is defined as one who has not made a purchase from FLO GROUP retail brands within the past year. The customer reacquisition program spans nine months after a customer is categorized as lost. During this period, customers receive communications with increasing frequency, offering different value propositions. If this program is unsuccessful, the customer is included in the Lost Customer Analysis.

Lost Customer – Lost Customer Analysis

This monthly survey is conducted using the Computer Assisted Telephone Interview (CATI) method with a large audience that significantly represents the lost customer base. The survey aims to determine whether lost customers have made shoe purchases within the past year, the brands they chose, and their reasons for those choices. Based on this information, we assess what actions are necessary to win these customers back to FLO GROUP brands. As with other surveys, the results are shared with the relevant functions and incorporated into broader corporate projects aimed at improving customer retention.

Appendix – FLO GROUP brands

FLO

Operating in the retail sector since 2001, the FLO brand has presence in 29 countries including Türkiye, in the CIS, the Middle East and North Africa regions, with 441 stores in the domestic and international markets along with online platforms in these countries as well as potential markets such as Morocco and Kazakhstan. Offering a rich selection of brands and a diverse product range with an accessible price strategy for all age groups and the whole family, FLO is the "First Choice of Moms." As a leader in the footwear and apparel segment with omni-channel shopping experience and an extensive retail network, FLO appeals to a wide target audience, starting with a younger demographic in the 18-34 age group, who seeks speed and convenience when shopping for shoes that complement their looks at accessible prices.

IN STREET

IN STREET entered the retail sector in 2014 under the FLO GROUP umbrella as a specialized retailer of sneakers and sportswear. IN STREET currently operates in 12 countries, serving consumers through 185 stores and online platforms. IN STREET's product and model selection includes popular and global brands such as Nike, Adidas, Reebok, Puma, Vans, Converse, and Skechers along with consumer favorites like Lumberjack and Lotto. Targeting young people in the 18-24 age group, IN STREET appeals to consumers who prefer comfort in daily life and activity.

SNEAKERBOX

Sneakerbox entered the Russian retail sector under the FLO GROUP umbrella with its first store opened in Moscow. Sneakerbox aims to specialize in sneakers and sportswear.

LUMBERJACK

Lumberjack, founded in 1945 in Italy, was added to FLO GROUP's brand portfolio in 2012. As a renowned Italian brand, Lumberjack sells millions of shoes in over 40 countries, primarily in Europe. Focusing on comfortable and durable shoes designed with urban and outdoor adventures in mind, the brand also offers active and sportswear collections. In addition to seven stores, including five monostores, Lotto also operates online sales channels in Türkiye and Italy. Lumberjack appeals particularly to the 25-45 age group with a range of designs for men and women.

KINETIX

Kinetix, founded in 1989 in Türkiye by FLO GROUP in response to the needs of the footwear consumers, has been offering sportswear collections since 2005. As a Türkiye-based sneaker and apparel brand, Kinetix is known for a range of trendy and comfortable products, primarily preferred by young people. Kinetix, a favorite of young people in the 15-25 age group, is highly recognized among global sportswear brands.

POLARIS

Polaris, families' favorite shoe brand since 2005, features a rich variety of traditional, modern, and stylish footwear across women's, men's, and kids' categories. Polaris, mostly preferred by families in C1-C2 socioeconomic segments, offers a wide product lineup.

NINE WEST

Nine West, loved by women around the world for its fashionable footwear, handbags, and jewelry, was founded in 1978 in New York City, taking its name from its address, 9 West 57th Street. Nine West entered the Turkish market in 1997 and joined the brand portfolio of FLO GROUP in 2019. As part of its the long-term strategic brand collaborations, FLO GROUP has expanded Nine West's licensing rights to 40 countries. In addition to 14 retail stores, Nine West products are also sold through mobile apps and e-commerce sites. Today, Nine West operates in more than 40 countries, primarily in Europe. Nine West offers a curated range of stylish and fashionable footwear, handbags, and accessories, appealing especially to women in the 25-34 age group.

REEBOK

Reebok, which joined FLO GROUP's portfolio of licensed brands in 2022, was founded in 1958 in the UK by Joe Foster and his brother Jeff as a small running shoe company with the ambition of tackling the athletics market. Today, Reebok designs, manufactures, distributes, and sells fitness, running and sportswear including clothing and accessories for women, men, and kids. FLO GROUP holds the licensing rights of the Reebok brand in 12 countries. Reebok, the choice of people who love to move, appeals particularly to the 16-50 age group with its focus on activity and experience.

LOTTO

Lotto was born in 1973 in the footwear district of Montebelluna, Italy. The sports footwear brand first launched with tennis shoes, later followed by basketball, volleyball, track, and field and lastly, soccer. With the addition of apparel and accessories to the product range, Lotto became a full-concept sports brand. FLO GROUP currently holds Lotto's licensing rights in 41 countries, offering aspirational shoe and sportswear collections. Lotto boasts more than half a century of experience and expertise in Italian design and functionality with products for various sports disciplines like football, tennis, basketball, and performance. Lotto appeals consumers in the 18-45 age group who lead active lives and love sports and movement.

U.S. POLO ASSN.

U.S. Polo Assn. brand products are authentic and officially sanctioned by the United States Polo Association, the national governing body for the sport of polo in the USA and Canada. Polo is considered among the oldest organized sports, played by royals and nobles. The inspiration derived from this sport and lifestyle comes to life in collections. The classic U.S. Polo Assn. colors and crest promote this style and reflect the spirit of the sport. Appealing to men, women, and children of all ages with unique, comfortable, and stylish models, U.S. Polo Assn. is a favorite among young people and families.

DOCKERS by GERLİ

Dockers by Gerli is a global shoe brand for active men who love the great outdoors and casual, dynamic, and confident looks. FLO Group first became a distributor of the brand in 2003 and later acquired licensed production rights. Dockers by Gerli shoes are the sturdy companions of men who want to be comfortable without compromising their stylish looks. Dockers by Gerli shoes are designed for men who seek casual comfort as a lifestyle.

KIZILAY

DOĞAL MADEN SUYU

CASE STUDY
KIZILAY MINERAL WATERS

REVITALIZING THE MINERAL WATER MARKET: KIZILAY MINERAL WATER'S STRATEGIC REBRANDING AND GROWTH JOURNEY

Written by: Rasime Yılmaz Ozman (Marketing Director at Kızılay Mineral Water)

Introduction

Kızılay Mineral Waters is a subsidiary of the Turkish Red Crescent Society (Türk Kızılay), which was established in 1868, and was donated to the Society by the Great Leader Atatürk in 1926 to generate sustainable revenue. All profits from the brand are directed to charitable causes through the Turkish Red Crescent, making it **the largest non-profit brand in Türkiye in this regard. The history of the water spring dates to** Phrygia in the 8th century BC. Natural mineral waters, known for their unique composition and health benefits, have been consumed for centuries across various cultures. Unlike regular drinking water, these waters originate from protected underground sources and undergo a natural filtration process that enriches them with essential minerals and trace elements. The specific geological conditions of the aquifers contribute to the distinct mineral profiles of each spring, making them unique. Kızılay Mineral Waters operates two natural springs and factories located in Afyonkarahisar and Erzincan, positioning it as one of the largest mineral water producers in the country with a production capacity of two billion bottles. It is also the only brand in Türkiye that sources from two different locations. The Afyonkarahisar Mineral Water is among the richest in total minerals (3,480 mg/L), while the Erzincan Mineral Water is the richest in magnesium content (317 mg/L) in the country. Since 2020, as the result of strategic investments, the brand has transformed a shrinking category into one of the fastest-growing beverage sectors. The subsidiary, known as "Kızılay Beverage" has expanded fivefold, becoming one of the largest contributors to the Turkish Red Crescent Society while offering consumers healthy, natural fruit-flavoured varieties that are free from preservatives. Additionally, Kızılay Mineral Waters, the oldest mineral water brand in the country, is committed to creating healthy alternatives in other beverage categories beyond mineral water. In 2024, the brand acquired an aseptic filling plant at Adana, and now offers healthy beverage options in the categories of turnip juice, lemonade, and iced tea, with postbiotic, preservative-free, and colorant-free varieties.

Challenge

Mineral waters are defined as waters that originate from natural sources and contain a minimum of 1,000 mg of minerals per liter. Despite TÜRKİYE being one of the world's richest countries in terms of mineral water resources, it has failed to effectively communicate this asset to both global and domestic audiences. Over the years, the category has become entrenched in consumers' minds as a "cheap beverage consumed after heavy meals," leading to a 10% contraction in the market in 2019 (Source: Nielsen Retail'19). This category, which never reached the expected market potential, was consistently undervalued on retail shelves. Competitive communication within the plain mineral water sector was limited and predominantly focused on the same benefits, such as alleviating indigestion and promoting stomach health. As a result, mineral water has been perceived by consumers primarily as a "soda" that addresses post-meal indigestion issues,

387

rather than as a health-enhancing drink rich in essential minerals (Source: Kalita Research, Mineral Water U&A 2019). The flavoured mineral water segment was characterized by numerous brands offering similar flavours, which failed to generate consumer excitement and they were perceived as alternatives for well-known carbonated soft drinks. Due to low demand, retailers provided limited shelf space for this category, which further contributed to its declining profitability and consumer preference. Consequently, the market continued to shrink.

Kızılay Mineral Water, a brand that has been in the market for nearly a century, has managed to maintain its presence in these market conditions but has seen a gradual decline, largely due to the emergence of new brands and insufficient investment in communication. The brand (just like the category itself) struggled to resonate with younger audiences and failed to adequately promote both the unique characteristics of its water sources and the fact that all profits are donated to charity. There was a pressing need for a communication strategy that would not only enhance the perceived value of the category but also drive brand growth and differentiation in the market.

Solution

To revitalize the mineral water category and reposition Kızılay Beverage within the market, a strategic intervention was necessary. Post-pandemic consumer behavior highlighted a global and national surge in the "Health & Wellness" trend. This shift towards adopting healthier lifestyles provided a strategic opening for growth in the Turkish market. The path to expansion involved redefining the perception of mineral water in consumers' minds by emphasizing its health benefits. Given Türkiye's status as one of the world's richest countries in terms of mineral water resources, Kızılay Mineral Waters, as the most established and authoritative brand in the country, identified its strategy by first educating the domestic market about these valuable resources, followed by international outreach. The brand aimed to reposition mineral water from being perceived merely as a basic beverage to being recognized as a high-value product with significant health benefits. The strategic plan was structured around the following key areas of focus:

To elevate the mineral water category, it was essential to address the gap in awareness regarding its health benefits, both among consumers and within the expert community. Despite being one of the healthiest beverage alternatives globally, the awareness of mineral water's advantages was insufficient, even among those who were expected to be knowledgeable. The lack of academic research on mineral water was a significant barrier; many experts, including nutritionists, doctors, and academicians, were not fully informed about the nature and benefits of mineral water. Interviews conducted with universities and various professional associations revealed that there was a widespread lack of detailed knowledge about these resources in Türkiye. The health impacts of these resources were not sufficiently recognized by informed professionals. The scarcity of scientific literature led to the dominance of general, often superficial, information in the public consciousness. Therefore, it became evident that a focused communication strategy targeting experts was necessary to bridge this knowledge gap and foster a deeper understanding of mineral water's health benefits.

For the brand, Kızılay Mineral Waters, the only brand with two distinct sources, had not effectively highlighted this unique aspect in its communication strategy, nor had it educated consumers about the origins of its waters. In contemplating the question, "What benefits could set the brand apart within the category?" it became clear that embedding the concept of "different source, different benefit" in consumers' minds would not only differentiate the brand from its competitors but also enhance the overall perception of the mineral water category. Research indicated that consumers generally assumed each brand had a single source and were unaware that the distinct flavours of the brands were due to variations in mineral content. Furthermore, the health benefits of these minerals were not prominent in consumers' perceptions. To enhance the perception of naturalness, the strategy adopted was to emphasize products that reflect the unique characteristics of their sources. The communication campaign would focus on convincing consumers of these benefits by clearly explaining the health advantages of Kızılay Mineral Waters. Therefore, an awareness campaign was deemed necessary to achieve these objectives.

As Kızılay Mineral Waters, we represent the largest purpose-driven brand in the country. Unlike many other entities, 100% of our profits are donated to the Turkish Red Crescent Society, a practice initiated by Atatürk in 1926 to ensure sustainable funding for the organization. Recognizing the value of being a purpose-driven brand, particularly among younger consumers, we understood the importance of effectively communicating this aspect. Research revealed that the brand's commitment to charitable giving was not widely known among consumers. To address this, it was crucial **to enhance awareness of the fact that every bottle purchased contributes to a greater good**. Therefore, a strategic communication plan focused on conveying this **"goodness"** was necessary to highlight the brand's unique contribution to social welfare and to strengthen its appeal among consumers.

Communication Strategies

Expert Communication: The www.madensuyu.org platform was established in collaboration with a scientific board comprising esteemed academics from various universities across Türkiye. This initiative was supported by a dedicated fund for research and publication on mineral water. The platform publishes academic articles and provides daily content for consumers with editorial assistance, catering to all brands within the mineral water category. This approach created a resource that serves both the scientific community and the general public.

Additionally, the content developed from this platform contributed to the book *"Miracle Drink: Mineral Water"*, and the inaugural International Mineral Water Congress was held in 2020. This congress, which is set to occur for the third time this year, gathered key stakeholders including scientists, industry representatives, academicians, mineral water brands, suppliers, and retailers from Türkiye and around the world. The congress featured prominent speakers discussing various topics such as the health benefits and applications of mineral water, national and global mineral water policies, industry dynamics, and investment opportunities. The event received significant media attention. Post-congress, booklets featuring papers from participating universities were produced and disseminated through the platform.

Since 2020, numerous scientific studies on mineral water have been conducted, with ongoing research in progress. Nutritionists are increasingly promoting mineral water through social media platforms. Importantly, the www.madensuyu.org platform has established itself as a reliable source of information on mineral water across various specialties, supporting the entire sector with authoritative and comprehensive resources.

Integrated Advertising Campaign

The objective of the integrated advertising campaign was to educate consumers about the distinct types of Kızılay Mineral Water, specifically highlighting the differences in content and benefits of our two plain mineral water varieties. This task presented a challenge due to the need to convey new information to a broad audience.

Before launching the comprehensive 360-degree campaign, we implemented a packaging redesign to enhance visibility. We prominently featured the unique attributes of our Afyonkarahisar and Erzincan products on their respective labels. The Kızılay Afyonkarahisar product was labelled as "RICH WITH MINERALS," while the Kızılay Erzincan product was designated as "RICH WITH MAGNESIUM." This strategic labelling aimed to draw attention by positioning the two variants side by side across all marketing channels.

Our approach was based on the premise that consumers would encounter two distinct plain mineral waters from Kızılay side by side on the shelf for the first time and question, "Why does Kızılay offer two plain mineral waters?" This inquiry would prompt them to explore the "RIch Magnesium" and "Rich Mineral" messaging on the packaging. We anticipated that once consumers reviewed the mineral content on the labels, they would prefer our brand, given that we offer the richest mineral products in the country. This strategy not only enhanced consumer awareness but also reinforced Kızılay's positioning as an expert brand within the mineral water category.

For our initial campaign, we selected a familiar, engaging, and youth-oriented profile, leveraging a well-known celebrity to enhance appeal. The campaign aimed to address health benefits, using a fun and educational approach to guide consumers on which type of Kızılay Mineral Water to choose based on specific health benefits.

We developed the communication framework around the theme of "goodness," consistent with the Turkish Red Crescent Society's longstanding focus. The campaign featured the tagline "Kızılay Erzincan/Afyonkarahisar is good for you," emphasizing the health benefits associated with each source.

The campaign consisted of three primary commercials and a tag-on. The commercials highlighted the unique attributes of each mineral water type: "Rich Magnesium is beneficial for heart and muscle health. Kızılay Erzincan with Rich Magnesium is good for you," and "Rich Minerals support nerve and stomach health. Kızılay Afyonkarahisar with Rich Minerals is good for you."

In each film, we reinforced our connection to the Turkish Red Crescent Society by incorporating the tagline "Kızılay, for Goodness" along with our jingle, and the tag-on reiterated that all profits are directed towards charitable causes through the Turkish Red Crescent Society. This approach aimed to simultaneously inform and engage consumers while underscoring our commitment to social responsibility.

In addition to our plain mineral water offerings, we expanded our Flavored Mineral Water category to include products with entirely natural flavors and no preservatives. These flavoured waters were produced from our Erzincan source, incorporating rich magnesium content.

To support this diversification, we designed a follow-up campaign featuring the same popular celebrity, aiming to draw consumer attention to the new fruit flavor varieties that had not previously been available in the category. The introduction of these new flavors on the shelves prompted consumers to reconsider their preferences, particularly in the context of the post-pandemic emphasis on healthy beverages.

Research indicated that health-conscious choices were increasingly influencing consumer preferences, even among younger demographics. By aligning our campaign with these emerging health trends, the mineral water category experienced significant growth, becoming one of the fastest-growing segments within the non-alcoholic beverage market.

In our 360-degree campaigns, we employed a comprehensive strategy integrating both online and offline channels with a focus on television-based communication. To enhance reach and awareness in alignment with our target audience's viewing habits, our media plan prioritized television. Recognizing the significance of the female demographic for our brand, we strategically placed our advertisements in high-performance programs and those featuring health-related content, utilizing TV sub-bands to highlight product benefits.

For the male audience, we targeted sports programs with high viewership to maximize impact. In our radio campaigns, we communicated the health benefits of minerals and magnesium, emphasizing their positive effects on stomach health, digestion, muscle function, and heart health. In the flavoured mineral water segment, we highlighted product attributes such as variety, preservative-free formulations, and high magnesium content.

To broaden our reach, we implemented a robust digital media strategy, targeting previously unreachable segments. We aired different versions of our commercials on Facebook, Instagram, and YouTube, tailoring the length and format to each platform's content consumption habits. In display advertising, we utilized personalized rich media placements across various content categories, including news, sports, women's interests, music, gaming, food, series & entertainment, and lifestyle.

Additionally, we organized extensive tasting events in retail environments to allow consumers to sample our product varieties. We deployed specialized visual materials in markets to enhance shelf presence. Furthermore, we established close connections with the press by arranging factory tours and distributing customized press kits to share our brand story effectively.

Conclusion

Since 2020, the mineral water category has experienced sustained growth within the soft beverages industry. The flavored mineral water segment, in particular, has begun capturing market share from carbonated beverages. Research has shown that consumers prefer flavored mineral water for its perceived health benefits. The www.madensuyu.org platform has become a pivotal resource for all brands, and the International Mineral Water Congresses initiated by Kızılay Mineral Waters have been adopted by MASUDER (Mineral Water Association), evolving into a collaborative event hosted by industry players across the country.

The allocation of shelf space for mineral water at retails has increased, reflecting the category's growth. Kızılay Mineral Waters has gained recognition for its unique resources, with Kızılay Erzincan Mineral Water emerging as a sought-after product among athletes, health-conscious individuals, and the elderly. According to post-commercial research, consumer awareness and engagement with Kızılay Mineral Waters improved significantly. Responses to the question, "Have you learned anything new about Kızılay Mineral Water from the commercial?" were predominantly positive, with new information performance scoring 4.56 out of 5 (Benchmark: 3.80) (Source: Kantar, Kızılay Adnow Study Results, March 2021). Additionally, the commercials demonstrated above-average effectiveness in driving sales, scoring 3.31 out of 4 (Benchmark: 2.96) (Source: Kantar, Kızılay Adnow Study Results, March 2021).

Brand Health reports indicate that Kızılay Mineral Waters achieved leadership in awareness scores, with its brand image enhanced through terms such as "rich magnesium," "naturalness," and "goodness" (Source: BHT Kantar/IPSOS 2021 – 2023). A comparative analysis revealed a 37.4% increase in plain mineral water sales following the campaign (Source: Kızılay Mineral Water Domestic Sales Data, 2020-2021). The brand's success has extended beyond national borders, with Kızılay Beverage expanding its exports to numerous countries across five continents. This growth has solidified Kızılay Beverage's position as a major donor to the Turkish Red Crescent Association. Committed to its Health/Wellness mission, the brand continues to innovate and expand its product portfolio while investing in diverse categories.

Questions to stimulate conversation on the case

1. **How did the strategic emphasis on mineral water's unique health benefits contribute to revitalizing the category while differentiating Kızılay Mineral Waters from competition, and what impact did this approach have on consumer perceptions and market growth?**

The strategic emphasis on the unique health benefits of mineral water played a pivotal role in revitalizing the category and differentiating Kızılay Mineral Waters from its competitors. When Kızılay Mineral Waters first introduced Afyonkarahisar and Erzincan still mineral waters side by side on the shelves, it sparked consumer curiosity about minerals. The consumer, previously downgrading the category to "just soda," began questioning, "Why does Kızılay have two still mineral waters?" This led to increased label reading and awareness of mineral content. By highlighting the specific benefits of minerals in communications, the category was repositioned in the consumer's mind. With heightened mineral awareness from label information, consumers became more informed and chose Kızılay Mineral Waters, which boasts the richest selection of minerals and magnesium among its offerings. Focusing on health benefits increased consumer interest and preference, capturing a share of the "Non-Alcoholic Beverages" market each year since 2020. Moreover, this strategy not only differentiated Kızılay Mineral Waters as an industry expert but also strengthened its market position and supported overall sales growth.

2. In what ways did the integration of charitable contributions into Kızılay Mineral Waters' brand messaging enhance its appeal among different consumer segments?

Integrating charitable contributions into Kızılay Mineral Waters' brand messaging significantly enhanced its appeal across various consumer segments, particularly among socially conscious and younger demographics. By emphasizing that all profits are donated to the Turkish Red Crescent Society, the brand effectively communicated its commitment to social good, which resonated with consumers seeking to support purposeful brands. This strategy not only reinforced Kızılay's unique positioning but also differentiated it in a crowded market.

3. How can similar strategies be applied to other brands seeking to leverage social responsibility for market differentiation?

It is always fruitful for a brand to align their social responsibility efforts with their core values and clearly communicating these contributions to consumers. This alignment helps build a strong emotional connection with the brand, fostering customer loyalty and enhancing market differentiation.

On the other hand, Kızılay Beverage case is unique on its nature. The brand name carries the Society's name as "Kızılay". The brand is literally owned by Red Crescend. It is not a social responsibility project, it is not a charity of some percent donation, it is not a periodical charity support. The organic 100% connection between the brand and the Society makes the case unique, believable, trustworthy.

10.6.1 THE ROUTE TO VALUE

The Umuntu process of creating value through design is a method that meets the goals formerly described in the processes of Design Thinking and the HCD process by Ideo.

To better illustrate the process, we like to represent it as a sequence of stages that might equal a route, traveling across different territories, where certain milestones and design goals are progressively achieved. That is why we have called it the "Route to Value".

The territories are delineated according to whether they are developed on the client's side, the brand's side, or in an intermediate manner to both.

The client territory triggers processes that happen in a way we couldn't control were it not because of integrating these events into the design process. An example of this is the moment when the client shapes their perception. This situation occurs entirely in the client's zone, and we are supposed to enter it, capture the essential information, and move on to the next stage.

To simplify the idea of the client territory, we could say that this zone compiles all the activities or processes that unravel within the client's mind. In our example, these are three: their goals or expectations, the pain they are undergoing, and the profits they will gain after the design process.

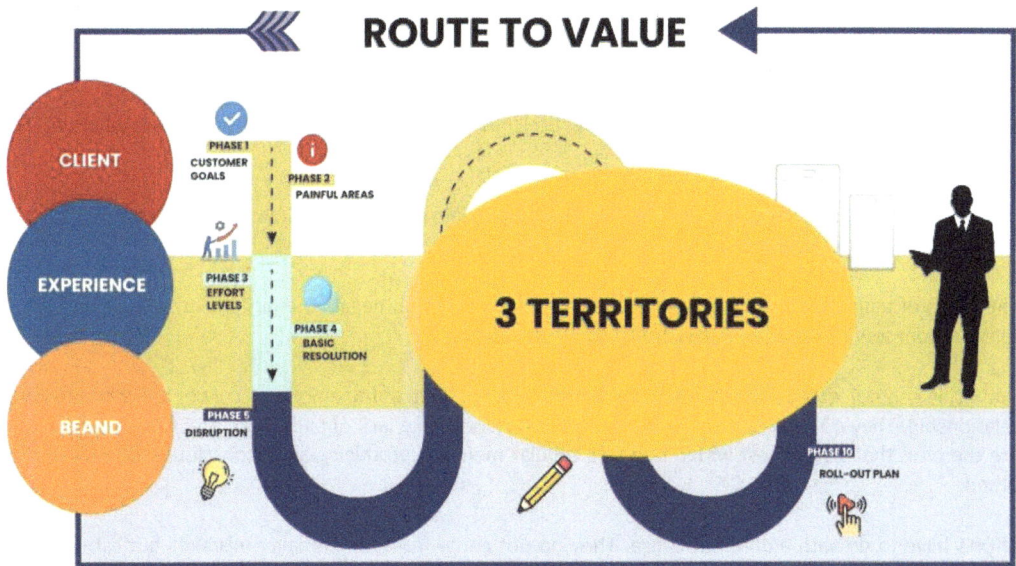

Figure 10.5 Route to Value

Conversely, we find ourselves across the brand or organization territory. The activities or constructions for which the company is exclusively responsible are stored here. There is no intervention from the clients whatsoever. Usually, it consists of internal processes, planning activities, innovation, and managing the resources we will use during the process.

393

10.6.2 STARTING THE JOURNEY

Our trip begins within client territory, the first stage being **client goals**.

Here, the client research team will face the challenge of unravelling what the client desires to achieve, what his wishes are (let's not forget the importance of desirability according to IDEO), and what he seeks when joining our brand's journey.

A shallow glance at the client's desires inevitably leads to mediocre designs because the design machine builds upon whatever input we provide it with. If we generate profound insights from the customer the designer's team will be able to produce an output of remarkable value. If we provide it with nothing but the basics, the results will be less than the lowest expectations.

On the way to detecting what the client wants, we run into one difficulty. What happens when the client doesn't know what they want? As Henry Ford used to say, had he asked clients what they wanted back in the day, they would have answered *a faster horse.*

Beyond the power of synthesis contained in it, this statement takes us into a field where the valid key to our problem awaits. How do our clients perceive reality? What is the mental model through which they perceive their experiences and determine their expectations?

In forming perceptions, each individual engages in a process of self-reference. Therefore, exercising empathy to conquer the client's territory actively is necessary. Cultivating receptivity to our clients' sentiments is essential to transforming our comprehension into design-related input, creating value.

Knowing the client also implies comprehending their feelings about their interactions within what we decided to call the experience territory.

Herein, the first two significant discoveries are the clients' **pain points** and their **levels of effort**. Even though we may tend to mix these two up, they are not always wholly connected.

The areas of pain are those interactions with the brand in which negative emotions arise, mainly due to tension from service mistakes or functional problems.

Brands, in general, except for those top performers, are unaware of the emotional cost of the friction in the relationship. They do not realize that this provokes emotions like lack of trust, fear, and frustration, which are the ones that last longest within people's cellular memory, producing an unconscious rejection of the brand.

Efforts have to do with a different cause. They do not come from functionality mistakes but rather from design flaws. In these cases, the organization wrongly chooses longer more intricate paths for experimenting with the brand, forcing the client to make a much more considerable effort than they intended.

The levels of effort are essential to understanding why our clients are abandoned because they do not last over time. Clients may agree to a particular spectrum of effort when they feel motivated by novelty or excited to live a new experience with a brand. Once past this stage, the effort becomes more unbearable, resulting in an impenetrable barrier that blocks the decision to continue with the brand.

Having thoroughly understood these two aspects of interactions with the brand, what comes into play is the art of **solving problems** to clear out the tension in the relationship.

It is almost a hygienic task, removing from the process anything that may cause pain or subdue the client to an unacceptable level of effort. Nevertheless, at the same time, it means preparing the field for our innovation teams to be able to suggest otherwise unthinkable options that will surprise the client, delight them, and invite them to keep on walking together through the route to value.

We call this stage the **disruption** because it corresponds to the moment when we need to think outside the box and bring about applicable innovations that will change specific ground rules of the relationship with the client.

Typically, in our co-creation workshops, we invite people from different areas of the company and participants from the outside who have no cultural restraints and can perform as the clients' advocates with no biases.

At this stage, we don't worry too much about the *how* as we do about the *why*. Nobody should be concerned about whether they will get corporate's approval, or the finance department will grant them the funds they need to make things happen. It's time to dream about that ideal world we want our clients to live in from now on.

As previously discussed in the context of Design Thinking, data-based empathy represents a crucial aspect of cultivating the sensitivity required to conceptualize the experiences of individuals from diverse backgrounds. Sensitivity comes from having felt the client's pain in our skin only to see it reflected on numbers that teach us just how frequent this symptom was in every client's experience.

Coming up with mechanisms for creating exceptional value is necessary but not enough. It's time to imagine how we want to take our client, what we call the **ideal journey.**

This ideal journey comes from modifying the current story and applying the innovations that originated in the disruption stage. It is not an imaginary journey. Our deep, emphatic knowledge of our clients' tender full stories commits us to designing a route that widely surpasses the current version but is also very feasible and viable since it gets progressively closer to the stage of idea implementation. Dreams shouldn't take us towards the edge of a rainbow that overwhelms us because of its beauty *and* its impossibility to be conquered.

The ideal journey has one purpose: to show us exactly what **experiential gain** the client will get from their trip with our brand. This phase cannot rely on merely functional profit such as "speed at opening a bank account", or "diligent, efficient attention when solving a problem", or guaranteeing "easy access" to our platforms. All these benefits are significant but, again, not enough. They meet the goal of achieving the expected minimum. The foundation of an exceptional experience profit lies in the fact that, after reaching the expected functional minimum, we must guarantee an emotional comeback or aspirations that imprint the experience on people's memory and make them want to repeat it, share it, and make foundation stories into a part of their lives. It seems ambitious, but it isn't. If we don't see things through this viewpoint, the result will always be mediocre and perish in the sea of unfulfilled expectations.

We must fully prepare to enter the prototyping stage to avoid these distortions of the ideal image and reduce the weight of subjectiveness or the effects of designer prejudice.

Here, we can mock up the ideal trip and transform it into a 3D model that we can exhibit to real people, as accurate as our clients. They will be able to provide us with a critical opinion, and they can take us back to previous stages to correct interpretation or design mistakes, helping us prevent worse evils in case those unchecked designs see the light of day and are offered to clients on a massive scale, compromising the company's profits, Brand image, and reputation.

Once granted the green light, we will move towards transformation. To do that, we have to carry out the **service components inventory**, a concept we define as a complex system of new or redesigned processes, technologies, and human attitudes that will make the service possible and bring life to the ideal experience just the way we dreamed it along the design phase and the way we want to deliver it at every touch point.

These design tools allow us to shape the stages where the experience will happen, acknowledging every physical evidence that will influence human perception.

The overall detailed information is the input to transform our experience design into an implementation plan that will now take us to the thorough explanation of *who* is going to be responsible for doing *what*, describing *how* they will do it and in what timeframes they will do it, what costs will they have and what resource team will they use.

The **implementation plan** is the final stage and the key to this design story. It is the moment of truth, paraphrasing an expression we love to use to explain the customer *journey*. Here, we create the guiding roadmap to guide us through the challenging path toward such a substantial transformation.

Experience design without the power of transformation is only a dream, in the middle of which we awake to face reality. We must listen to our intuition of what we need to do and gather enough strength, enthusiasm, and leadership to step up and make a change.

Experience design is about changing reality and creating value.

Those who devote themselves to Experience Design do it for a straightforward purpose: "to change society, making a positive impact on people's perspectives, even if it isn't beyond the limits of their interactions with a brand."

A vital idea inspires us. *Creating value is improving people's lives.* That's the horizon to which we're heading without rushing, without pausing.

10.7 KEY FINDINGS ABOUT GOOD DESIGN

Finally, we can conclude that when we talk about creating value through experience design, there are four key areas companies need to master in order to join the Mount Olympus of design.

Companies focusing on these four priorities boost their probability of becoming more creative organizations, keen on designing consistent and remarkable products and services, and experts in building long-lasting and profitable relationships with their clients.

Top performers firms in design enjoy benefits and prizes as appealing as doubling income growth and the performance of the shareholders over their competitors in the industry.

We are not only talking about building more excellent products, which they do. We discuss being the right fit for desirability, usability, and relevance.

Firstly, when at the organization's peak, the advice is to adopt an analytic approach to design, measuring, and leading the company's performance in this area as thoroughly as how the firm devotes itself to revenues and costs.

Secondly, make sure to put user experience on the table and focus on the company culture by smoothing the internal barriers (between physical products and digital services and interactions, for example) that are non-existent to clients.

In the third place, nurse the team by choosing people with top design abilities and empowering them in cross-functional groups that can assume the collective responsibility of improving the user experience and maintaining its members' functional connections.

Finally, it analyzes, tests, and learns rapidly, incorporating user knowledge from the first idea until after the final launch. Design is a corporate philosophy more than a methodology. It is a way to understand different customers' minds and perceptions, and it is a leadership strategy to align the entire company's people behind inspiring goals and establish an ongoing process that will transform the business, people's lives, and, ultimately, the world where we live. Nothing more, nothing less.

11. REMODELLING THE MARKETING RESEARCH

The secret of change is to focus all of your energy, not on fighting the old, but building on the new". Socrates

11.1 NEED FOR MARKETING RESEARCH

The business world is continuously changing and both human nature and behavior have evolved based on the many changes in world dynamics. This has created a new demand and supply situation to cater to human needs and desires. Marketing experts must come up with newer innovations. If we want to know about our business; both failures and successes, we need to know the root causes by collecting pertinent information. This is how the discipline of marketing research began since the early days of civilization.

Marketing research is not only for business students and academics but also for all professionals and non-professionals. It is for those who value learning and wish to keep updated with knowledge about the ever-changing world dynamics. This also helps them to improve their own lives and keep fit for survival 24/7.

The success of a brand is contingent upon several factors, including the ability to produce unique products utilizing the latest technology. However, this alone is insufficient. To achieve the desired profit, a brand must also possess an in-depth understanding of its customers, their expectations, and the capabilities of its competitors. Without this knowledge, a brand's success will be limited to mere production. Undoubtedly, the most crucial activity at this juncture is marketing research. Numerous successful brands that have neglected the significance of marketing research have committed various missteps on a global scale and have become vulnerable to their competitors.

In the context of the contemporary business environment, which is characterized by intense competition, marketing research represents a strategic instrument for the sustained success of businesses. It informs businesses across a range of domains, from the understanding of consumer behavior and the examination of market competition to the identification of market trends and the making of strategic decisions. Consequently, the utilization of data-driven and evidence-based marketing research represents a crucial factor for businesses to survive in the current economic landscape and to foster their growth and development.

Market research is an essential component in generating ideas and knowledge about products and services. Research benefits businesses and it is a means to understand issues and increase public awareness. In today's world, all successful companies invest in research and development. This is known as R&D and it helps businesses secure an advantage over their competitors by discovering how to make things happen more efficiently and profitably and therefore, differentiate their offerings from those of their competitors which can raise the company's market value and help them to become sustainable.

Business leaders and marketers often need to gather evidence-based information to reduce risk in managerial decision-making. They need information (more commonly used term "data"), through systematic inquiry on a variety of business essentials, which evolves constantly around the customers and consumers. Understanding consumers' buying and usage behavior is essential, including their satisfaction, acceptance, and even their rejections. It is also important to understand their knowledge, attitude, practice, and behavior (KAPB) regarding products or services.

A primary objective for many leading businesses is creating, developing, and maintaining customer-centric organizations. This vision is translated into mission, goals, and strategic practices, which are the key to success and long-term growth. Marketing research, which is fundamental to this process, enables marketers to create a strategic roadmap by gaining a comprehensive understanding of consumers' needs and expectations. By employing systematic and data-driven market research, businesses can make informed decisions, gain a competitive advantage, and respond effectively to changes in the market. Consequently, marketing research is not merely a tool; it is a strategic imperative that shapes the sustainable success of businesses.

Dr. Linden Brown (Brown 2013), one of the leading experts on customer-centric culture said "Business success in competitive industries is dependent on having satisfied customers and on the ability to keep them. To do this we need to understand the customers 'rules that determine whether we will retain them?" He further shared the customers 'rules, which include:

- Understand my current needs (listening, sharing, cocreating).
- Show me your authenticity in solving my problems.
- Give me something in value.
- Keep me engaged with new things I value.
- Help me solve my problems.
- Show me what I will need in the future. They focused on the customers and competitors as well.

It is important to know why many companies become either a success or failure. The current COVID pandemic has shown us how few companies have won in the marketplace and a few have perished forever. Amazon and Uber are among the few success stories. It is not only analyzing the COVID-induced crisis but also analyzing the customer's needs and the role and presence of their competitors. They considered their competitors as a very critical part of the industry. Social media and digital literacy, especially among the younger generations, have made the business journey more critical and complicated than ever before. We need to understand the competitive environment and track their footprints to determine how they are offering alternatives and how these may attract customers.

11.1.1 WITHOUT RESEARCH, THERE IS NO WAY OUT!

Today we are not as interested in knowing "How to succeed in business?" but rather "How do we sustain and stay successful in the competitive world of business?" This is essential, especially during and post COVID. The business entrepreneurs are desperately keen to learn from market researchers and business leaders. Considering the global socio-economic scenario, perhaps the business world, including the big names in global businesses, are struggling to reach their revenue and operating income targets by implementing improved strategy. Evidence-based authentic data is, therefore, extremely crucial for survival and sustainability.

The advent of the pandemic has precipitated a profound shift in consumer behavior. The digitalization process has accelerated, e-commerce has increased, and there has been a differentiation in consumer priorities. The utilization of marketing research enables businesses to gain a deeper comprehension of customer expectations through the analysis of these changes. Consequently, products and services are developed to the novel needs and demands of consumers. To illustrate, creating user-friendly e-commerce platforms for consumers who conduct a greater proportion of their shopping online is a need that can be identified through marketing research.

The sustainability of businesses is contingent upon the capacity to not only anticipate current market conditions but also to project future trends. Marketing research uncovers emerging trends within the sector, technological advancements, and shifts in consumer preferences. The data thus enables businesses to innovate and adapt to changing trends. Long-term trends, such as the growing demand for environmentally friendly products or the proliferation of digital services, can be identified at an early stage through the utilization of marketing research.

At no other time in our history, COVID has forced us into paying attention to measuring ROI (return on investment) and calculating financial return for all expenses and investments. We also calculate economic return, understanding how our hard-earned money, time and energy can save our people and planet. For all of these exercises, we need to apply our market research skills and knowledge.

The marketing Guru Professor Philip Kotler said "marketing research is the systematic design, collection, analysis, and reporting of data relevant to a specific marketing situation facing an organization. It gives marketers insights into customer motivations, purchase behavior, and satisfaction. It can help them to assess market potential and market share or to measure the effectiveness of pricing, product, distribution, and promotional activities." (Kotler 2010)

11.2 PURPOSE OF MARKETING RESEARCH

The fundamental purpose of marketing research is to facilitate the formulation of strategic decisions by providing businesses with a more comprehensive understanding of the opportunities and threats inherent in the market. This process encompasses the comprehension of consumer needs and expectations, market segmentation, and target audience analysis. Concurrently, the analysis of competitors' strategies and market positions represents an additional objective of marketing research, aimed at gaining a competitive advantage. Moreover, the ability to anticipate market trends and evolving consumer behavior enables businesses to adapt to innovations more effectively. In addition, the objective of marketing research is to enhance customer satisfaction and foster brand loyalty. Marketing research is an ongoing process that commences at the conceptualization stage of a product's development and continues through to the post-purchase phase. Consequently, it is subject to a variety of purposes. The different purposes of marketing research are exploratory, causal, diagnostic, descriptive, predictive, deductive, and inductive.

- **Exploratory research** is done not to find the final and conclusive answers to the research questions, but rather to explore the preliminary solutions helping to create a detailed design of the study. It involves gathering preliminary information to define and understand the problem faced by marketers. Researchers carry out exploratory research to finalize the approach (such as quantitative or qualitative). The findings from exploratory research help the researcher to change or modify the design as originally planned. Precisely it can be said that it forms the basis of a more conclusive research. Sometimes, it is also used for making quick business and strategic decisions and managing time and budget.

- **Causal research** investigates the cause-relationships among different variables. It is also termed explanatory research. It determines the variation in the variable which may influence the difference in other variable(s) and how they impact each other. The researcher tries to find the cause-and-effect relationships by testing different hypotheses. Causal research is always complex, especially when experimenting the behavioral issues such as perception, attitude, motivations, emotions, etc.

- **Diagnostic research** analyzes the data of a given situation exhaustively and tries to find the relationships of the variables and facts or occurrences as found in the data. To generate ideas for certain investigations, especially pinpointing the root cause of any problem impacting the growth and sustainability of particular products and services in particular market segments, this type of research helps identify factors that influence or intervene in a specific situation or consequence.

- **Descriptive research** is used to understand the behavior of the sample population. The purpose includes describing, analyzing and validating the findings. Descriptive studies attempt to determine the "who, what, where, when, or how much" of the research questions. Unlike exploratory research, the approach is more structured and describes existing attitudes and behavior of the consumers toward specific products or services. Descriptive research may be cross-sectional or longitudinal in nature. It can help researchers obtain historic trends on sales in the industry, the market potential for a product, consumers 'attitudes, trend analysis and forecasting, demographic profiles, and so on. Consumer research and opinion polls are also part of descriptive research.

- **Predictive research** in marketing is about analyzing (measuring) and predicting (forecasting) the future of the existing products and services or to be offered. Researchers use and analyze data from the primary or secondary data sets and to find patterns and predict possible future outcomes or trends. Predictive research helps to understand the possibility of the changes in the overall marketing situation, impacting on demand and supply situation due to changes in the consumers behavior. For example, working from home during the COVID pandemic, will there be any mid to long-term impact on consumer behavior especially on housing, automobiles, education and so on. Financial analysts have tried to assess the relationship between income and propensity to purchase digital products and other products and services triggered by the pandemic.

- **Deductive research** also deductive reasoning or deductive logic, is the process of reasoning from one or more statements (premises which are generally considered as true) or starting from a theory followed by a preposition of the hypothesis tested through empirical data therefore, reaching to a logical conclusion. The basic steps include (1) analyze existing theory, (2) formulate theories (proposing relationship between different specific variables), (3) test of hypothesis using various statistical methods such as regression, correlation, mean, median, mode and testing theories), (4) analysis of research results and (5) modification of hypothesis, if needed based on analysis.

- **Inductive research** is distinct from deductive reasoning. It is a process of reasoning where the data or observations are synthesized to form a general principle and reaching to a conclusion. It. In inductive research, market researchers try to discover various patterns or trends of consumer behaviors through observation. On the contrary, during deductive research, the researchers use observation, aiming to validate the patterns or trends.

11.3 RESEARCH PROCESS

Before carrying out any research projects, the researcher prepares and finalizes the proposal which includes the detailed design and implementation plan. This process describes how marketing research is designed and implemented and helps to guide the execution of a research project. As we know the research process is a systematic way in which the researcher follows certain steps to implement the approved design and thereby reaching to the ultimate project goal(s). The steps are as below:

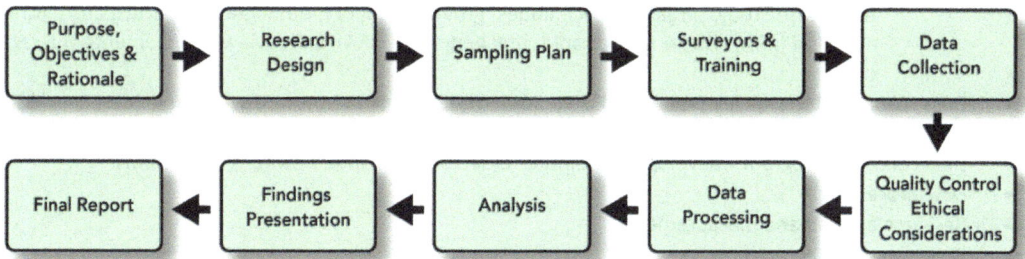

Figure 11.1 Research Process

401

11.3.1 RESEARCH PURPOSE/RESEARCH PROBLEM, OBJECTIVES AND RATIONALE

There should be a purpose of any research project and therefore, a researcher may have a series of questions that need to be answered by conducting scientific research. A significant number of researchers consider this stage to be the most pivotal and prioritized phase in the marketing research process. As the research problem or purpose also determines the research objectives, the type of design, the method of data collection, the type of analysis and how to make interpretations, it is crucial to ensure that these elements are aligned with the research problem. It is therefore of great importance to define the problem accurately. It is fundamental for the researcher to comprehend a better understanding of the existing situation or problem faced or anticipated by the firm or organization. While framing the purpose(s), the researcher formulates the broad and specific objectives essential for decision-making, leading to the completion of the research study. It is also important to know the rationale of the study. The steps involve:

- Purpose statement/study purpose(s)
- Problem identification/statement
- Delineating research objectives (broad and specific objectives)
- Stating research hypothesis
- Defining the scope of the study
  - Rationale of the study

11.3.2 RESEARCH DESIGN

The research design is a step-by-step plan, or a road map followed by a researcher to accomplish a scientific study efficiently. Research design refers to the overall strategy developed to carry out a research project that describes a "neat and crisp" and logical roadmap to undertake research question(s) through addressing the research problem, questions, objectives, and/or hypothesis and implementing through the processes of data collection, processing, interpretation, analysis, presentation, and discussion of findings.

Researchers can select different research design types depending on the nature of the study. However, every design must contain the following essentials.

- Identification of the research methodology - exploratory, descriptive, or causal research, ethnographic, experimental, quasi-experimental, randomized control trial (RCT), action research etc.
- Sampling design
- Source of data collection: primary and/or secondary research
  - Primary data collection can be qualitative, quantitative in nature or mixed method (combining both quantitative and qualitative for better findings):
    - *Quantitative* – survey, experimentation, systematic observation, and retail audit.
    - Qualitative – in-depth interviews, key informant interviews, focus group discussion, observations, case study, projective techniques, grounded theory, ethnography, participatory rural appraisal (PRA) also known as rapid rural appraisal - RRA), and review of documents and records.
- Data collection tools development and pretesting – questionnaire and/or discussion guides, checklist, etc.
- Data collecting program – developing computer-aided personal interview (CAPI) programs.
- Data processing.
- Research analysis and measurement.
- Report and presentation.
- Timeline.

11.3.3 SAMPLING PLAN

In research, a sampling plan is a base from where the researcher which the research begins the project or the study. A sampling plan encompasses the major component of data collection – the samples or sample population. This sampling unit, therefore, represents the total population drawn from the sampling frame (the entire selected population).

The sampling plan comprises three major decisions:

- **Sampling unit:** It is the first and main decision point to be taken that initiates the research. We need to pinpoint who should be the sampling unit. For example, in understanding the level of digital literacy in the agricultural sector, the sampling unit should be the farmers, the main contributors in this sector/industry.

- **Sample size:** The researchers consider the second decision to be determining the sample size (i.e. number of units/objects to be surveyed/interviewed). The required sample size is estimated by the researchers, generally by using statistical formulas and experience.

- **Sampling methods:** The final decision that completes the sampling plan is finalizing the sampling method or approach. There are different sampling methods in statistics. To collect reliable and accurate data, the researchers use the appropriate sampling method based on the nature of the study, characteristics of the samples, and study objectives. Broadly, the sampling method may be probabilistic or non-probabilistic.

While designing the sampling plan, the researcher considers the following factors (Andaleeb and Hasan 2017):

- Geographic location – rural, urban, metro, etc.
- Demographic characteristics – education, gender, income, occupation, age, etc.
- Psychographics–personality, values, opinions, attitudes, interests, and lifestyles

11.3.4 DATA COLLECTION

This is an important component of research. Many researchers say "data is the heart of research"; quality data yields the best result. It is the systematic process of collecting information on selected variables and thereby enables to capturing the appropriate and credible responses to the relevant questions. The methods used for data collection depend on the research design. The different widely used methods include:

- Personal interviews also called face-to-face interviews, using traditional pen and paper
- Computer-aided personal interview (CAPI)
- Online interviews using a website, using online links for data collection.
- Telephone/mobile interviews, using a computerized random dialing system.
- Mail surveys.

Researchers develop data collection instruments (popularly called questionnaires, focus group guides, depth interview/observation checklists, etc.).

11.3.5 DATA PROCESSING AND ANALYSIS

Once the data is collected, the data analysis team transforms the raw data into meaningful information fitting with the study objectives. Different software such as FoxPro, Quantum, or Excel are used for data entry and processing. Once the raw data is checked and cleaned, advanced analysis is conducted through statistical packages like SPSS, Tableau, Minitab, etc. The Statistician / Research Analyst provides inputs at various stages of data processing and analysis, such as editing all the completed interviews, which includes coding of open-ended questions, creating NETs, weighting, identification details and consistency checks. The analyst creates a final data file (e.g., using SPSS, ASCII etc. with variables and values) with appropriate banner points demonstrated in the Tabplan.

11.3.6 RESEARCH REPORT AND PRESENTATION

This is the final stage of any research project. The purpose is to prepare and present the research findings to the researcher and/or sponsors. The report contains several chapters based on the purpose and requirements, such as:

- Background (purposes, objectives, rationale etc.)
- Methodology and implementation
- Findings
- Conclusions
- Recommendations.

The research sponsors often require the presentation of the salient findings for their audience and stakeholders. There are many presentation platforms; and PowerPoint is a widely used platform for many years. In addition, other platforms include Gsuite, Prezi.com, Emaze etc. Emaze is said to be the future of online presentations because of its outstanding features. The online presentation has become more popular because of the recent trend of "working from home or anywhere" introduced due to the COVID pandemic.

11.3.7 QUALITY ASSURANCE AND ETHICAL CONSIDERATIONS

The researcher or the agency has to strictly affirm the quality control issues and ethical considerations. For example, ResInt Canada – an international market research agency incorporates "not harm" practices into the planning, implementation, and follow-through of each project. In addition, they consider all conceivable and practical steps to avoid exposing its personnel, participants in the project, and their communities to additional risks through our actions.

This applies to the conduct of their research, to the period following data collection, and after the completion of the research including any publication, dissemination, or sharing of data, analysis, reports, or presentations. They strongly believe in protecting the rights and confidentiality of the respondents. To protect the rights of the respondents, before approaching them for the detailed interview, their oral and written consent to participate in the interviews will be obtained.

They also provide full and correct information regarding the purpose of the study, the nature of information required, the benefits of the study, confidentiality to be maintained, and freedom to be exercised by the respondents during the interviews. ResInt also follows all ethical standards as approved by ResInt Canada, such as freedom of participation and withdrawal by the respondents at any point of time, ensuring non-discrimination in respondent selection, diversity, equity and inclusion (DEI), multi-cultural values, and showing mutual dignity and respect.

On the other hand, to prevent a variety of unfavorable circumstances for those participating in research, ethics committees have been established in numerous countries around the world. Researchers are required to obtain permission from an ethics committee before conducting any research within a community.

Before any survey, the researcher must ensure the following ethical considerations:

- Greet the respondents and treating the respondents with respect and dignity
- Seek cooperation from the respondents
- Respondent's identity must be protected, and information collected must not be shared with others without his/her written permission. Respondents also have the right to require that personal information be deleted after use.
- Respondents must not be harassed or embarrassed while gathering data.
- Respondents have the right not to participate and have the right to stop participating in a research study at any time.

11.4 SOURCES OF INFORMATION

There are basically three types of information sources, as narrated below:

- **Primary sources** are the original data (also called primary data before publication) on which all other sources are based, considered as original works, such as surveys, focus group discussions, in-depth interviews, etc.

- **Secondary research sources** are those that are already published in different journals, books, or posted on websites.

- Tertiary sources are the sources created to help locate primary and secondary sources. These are available in the published directories, official indexes, databases etc. Due to digital advancements, tertiary sources are widely available on the internet (e.g. Google, Amazon etc.)

Secondary Data. Secondary data are data previously collected by other researchers for any purpose and the findings/reports are published or publicly available.

Advantages and disadvantages of different sources

Sources	Advantages	Disadvantages
Primary	Answers a specific research question Data is current The source of data is known Privacy can be maintained	Expensive due to translating language and meaning (coding) Sometimes respondents are reluctant to answer lengthy interviews Sampling challenges and data-gathering difficulties (especially during political opinion polls)

Secondary	Saves time and money Aids in providing direction for primary data collection Helps design similar research studies (e.g. pinpoints people to approach) Serves as a basis of comparison for other data	May not give adequate or required information May not match entirely the requirement The quality and accuracy of data may be questioned

Source: Andaleeb and Hasan 2017

Difference between Quantitative and Qualitative Research

Feature	Qualitative	Quantitative
Type of research	Exploratory	Descriptive/causal
Focus of research	Understand and interpret	Describe, explain and predict
Sample size	Small	Large
Sample design/sampling	Non-probability, purposive	Probability
Research design	May adjust during the study	Finalized before launching the study
Types of questions	Unstructured	Structured
Type of analysis	Subjective, involves researchers' deeper qualitative involvement	Objective, statistical, computerized analysis
Generalizability	Limited	High
Ontological orientation	Constructionism	Objectivism
Epistemological orientation	Interpretivism	Natural science model, in particular, positivism

Source: Cooper and Schindler 2011, Bryman 2004

11.5 QUALITATIVE RESEARCH

Qualitative research is becoming more popular among business managers, compared to large-scale surveys. It comprises collecting and analyzing of non-numerical data to understand deep-rooted behavioral issues, such as concepts, opinions, attitudes, values and/or experiences, to capture deeper insights of the problem or generate innovative ideas for decision-making or research.

As we know, business managers and/or academic researchers usually research to understand two important questions – how and why things happen (Andaleeb and Hasan 2017). For example, during the COVID pandemic, millions of people died. Universities and research agencies have numeric data on the percentage of people who died in different countries, by age, language, race, gender and so on. If the researcher or business manager of any pharmaceutical company wants to understand the behavioral issues (such as attitude, perception, motivations, rejections etc.) that trigger the "not to use mask" or "use sanitizer" of certain ethnic groups that drive their behaviors; qualitative approach would the better solution for obtaining the required answers.

While qualitative research data collection and analysis can be careful and rigorous, most practitioners regard qualitative research may be probed more deeply. Qualitative researchers seek to understand research participants rather than to fit their answers into predetermined categories with little room for qualifying or explaining their choices (Hair et.al, 2017).

Different approaches of qualitative research include focus group discussions, in-depth interviews, observation, and case studies. Some of the applied disciplines of qualitative research are grounded theory, ethnography, and action research.

11.5.1 TYPES OF QUALITATIVE RESEARCH

Individual Depth Interviews (IDI) usually involve one-on-one interviews. Since depth interviews are conducted for deeper understanding and insights, experienced and skilled researchers or interviewers are usually involved. Usually, the IDI takes from 30 minutes to a few hours to complete depending on the nature and objective of the study. The interviews may be face-to-face, through telephone, or through the use of technologies like Zoom, WebEx, Skype etc.

Focus Group Discussion (FGDs) - popularly known as Focus Group Discussion or FGD, is one of the most popular and widely used qualitative techniques by social and market researchers. It is a group discussion among a small number of demographically similar participants. Ideally, there are around 6 to 10 participants in each FGD, led by an experienced and skilled moderator. The discussions can be guided or open and take around 90 to 120 minutes to complete. The participants often sit in a circle or round table setting with equal opportunity provided to all the participants to speak. More often, with the permission of the participants, the FGDs are recorded or observed by the experts through one-way mirror or CCTV cameras. (Andaleeb and Hasan 2017)

FGD sequence includes:

- **Self-introduction** - introduction of the participants and the moderators

- **Warm-up and ground rule** – the moderator starts with creating a warm-up situation. Shares the ground rules such as purpose, objectives, equal opportunity and right to express, nothing right or wrong to share their views, open, ethics, etc. Also seek permissions if recording or photographs are needed.

- **Discussion** – getting into the main discussion.

- **Sum-up** – summing up of the discussion.

Currently, during COVID, virtual FGDs have become quite popular and is conducted on Zoom, WebEx or even through WhatsApp.

Case Studies: Case studies are sometimes effective tools of qualitative research, used to understand specific phenomenon experienced by any individual, group or organization. The case may typify the success or failures of any entity that occurred at a point in time or over a longer period. It is often used in conjunction with the critical incident method in which participants are asked to describe instances of, for example, especially good or bad service experiences. In case studies, participants describe or explain situations in which they decided or solved a problem. However, problems of telescoping, selective perception, and social desirability make this method inferior to observation, shop-along, and participant observation. The researcher often disguises the case for privacy reasons.

Observation: It is another effective qualitative research tool, often used in marketing and the social sciences. This technique is used to observe the phenomena in their natural setting. Ethnographers widely use this technique to understand behavioral issues, such as attitude, perception, motivations etc. Researchers observe something related to products and services or consumers' behaviors or someone carefully to gain deeper insights.

Ethnographic Research: ethnography came from a Greek word meaning "folk, people, nation" and "I write". It is a branch of anthropology and the systematic study of individual cultures, conducted in a field setting. Ethnography explores cultural phenomena and examines the behavior of the participants in a given social context.

Most qualitative methods do not allow researchers to see consumers in their natural setting. Ethnography, however, is a distinct form of qualitative data collection that seeks to understand how social and cultural influences affect people's behavior and experiences (Hair et.al, 2017). This type of research is found to be very effective for market research involving product design and development, segmentation and positioning, advertising, and designing communication campaigns.

As a consequence of technological advancements, social media has become an integral aspect of contemporary life, prompting researchers to explore novel domains. This has led to the emergence of a new concept, netnography.

Netnography is an observational research technique that requires deep engagement with one or more social media communities. What differentiates netnography from other social media research techniques is the extensive contact and analysis of online communities and the use of participant observation (Hair et.al, 2017). It is a method of analysis that examines the behaviors, interactions, ideas, and community-building processes of people in online contexts. The data collected in online environments, including blogs, social media sites, forums, and user comments, is employed to gain insight into brand perception and consumer behavior. It is an especially effective method for understanding consumer attitudes and concerns, particularly in the context of the digital world. By monitoring real-time feedback from customers and identifying emerging trends, brands can develop strategies to address consumer needs and desires expressed in digital environments. The low cost and comprehensive nature of netnography have contributed to its growing popularity in the digital age.

Participatory Rural Appraisal (PRA): This appraisal is an approach widely used by social researchers, especially for non-government organizations (NGOs) and international organizations involved in development activities concerning health and nutrition, poverty alleviation, gender and discrimination, microfinance and poverty alleviation, education etc. The approach aims to incorporate the knowledge, attitudes, opinions, behaviors, and practices of the rural people in the planning and implementation of various development projects and programs. PRA is also known as Rapid Rural Appraisals (RRA).

Projective Techniques: Projective techniques are used to understand the hidden or suppressed meanings of particular research issues. Some of the most used techniques are stated below as narrated by Andaleeb and Hasan (2017) in their book on Strategic Marketing Management in Asia.

- **Word or picture association** – in any group discussion or IDIs, researchers may ask any participant to match his/her understanding, experiences, perceptions, or emotions about the research topics being investigated. For example, "If someone asks you to explain about "doctors" or "hospitals" what comes to your mind?"

- **Sentence completion** – researchers provide incomplete sentences and ask the participants to complete it based on their understanding, experiences, perceptions, or emotions. Thus, the researcher offers a "clue" to the participants as in" "Chinese food is generally very …." or "Lux soap is usually chosen because …"

- **Personification** – Researchers sometimes ask the participants to imagine any inanimate object and fit that with the character, traits, demographics and/or personalities of a human being; for example, "if the Lux brand of soap was a person, what type of person would it be?"

- **Cartoons** – Researchers employ ambiguous cartoons and then ask the participants to complete the although-t bubble attached to a character in the cartoons; for example – in a drawing of a boy and a girl standing in front of Pizza Hut "What are these people saying?"

- **Imagination exercises** – The participants are asked to relate a product, brand, person or organization with another entity; for example, "if your college was a car, what type of car would it be?"

- **Semantic mapping** – A 4-quadrant map is presented to the participants where different variables (such as brands, product components, or organizations) anchor two different axes (X and Y); the participants then spatially place these variables within the four quadrants. Thereafter, a discussion can ensue.

11.6 QUANTITATIVE RESEARCH

The quantitative research may be described as the collection of numerical data. It exhibits the relationship between theory and research as deductive, with a preference for a natural science approach, and as having an objectivist conception of social reality. (Bryman, A 2004). It measures consumers `knowledge, opinions, attitudes, and behavior and therefore attempts to obtain precise answers for questions related to *how much, how often, how many, when* and *who.*

Quantitative research acts on (a) converting observations/responses to a numeric value/numbers, (b) hypotheses testing (using statistical tests), (c) using charts, bar graphs, etc. in explain findings, and (d) narrating the relationships among variables quantitatively.

11.6.1 QUESTIONNAIRE DESIGN

Questionnaires are used to conduct interviews with respondents to produce quantitative or qualitative data and information. There are different forms of questionnaires such as open-ended, closed-ended, dichotomous and multiple choices. A questionnaire comprises of several questions designed to obtain the required information from the respondents. Examples are shown in the following box (Andaleeb and Hasan 2017):

The questions can be (a) close-ended (dichotomous) which measures questions that offer two mutually exclusive and exhaustive alternatives, (b) Close-ended (multiple responses) and (c) open-ended which provides no structure for a response and the respondent can answer freely. Examples are given below.

11.6.1.1 Examples from a questionnaire

Q. No.	Questions	Possible responses (Don't prompt)	Example
1	Do you own Mobile phone?	Yes (continue)	Close-ended (dichotomous) 2
		No (Go to demographic profile section)	
2	What type of mobile phone you have. (Single response)	Smartphone	Close-ended (Multiple response)
		Feature phone	
		Basic	
3	Why don't you have mobile phone?	Note verbatim:	Open ended

11.6.1.2 Question content

It is first and foremost considerations while designing and crafting the questionnaire.

- Purposeful – does this question match the study objective.
- Interesting - should this question be interesting to the respondent?
- Incomplete or unfocused– is the question complete and explains the purpose?
- Double-barreled question – does the question seek more than one answer from one question?
- Precision- does the question ask precisely what we want and need to know?
- Can the respondent answer adequately, considering time for thought, accuracy, presumed knowledge, recall and memory decay, and objectivity?
- Sensitive information– is there any sensitive issues, which will offend the respondent?
- Wording, and sequencing of sentences – unbiased clear explicit and concise?
- Is there any leading question?

11.6.1.3 Interviewer errors

- Sampling error (wrong selection of the respondents)
- Non-cooperation from the respondents (interviewer fails to secure cooperation)
- Data recording error (wrongly punched or recorded)
- Fail to create interview congenial environment during the interview.

- Cheating or falsification or influencing the respondents

11.7 INFORMED CONSENT

Before initiating the interview process, the surveyor, as a part of research ethics, will introduce him/herself and will seek consent to continue interviews. A sample of informed consent is given below (it was used by ResInt Canada in one of their projects on digital literacy among farmers and other stakeholders in August 2021).

Greetings! I am .... a Field Investigator working for ResInt Canada – a registered and reputed research company. Currently, we are conducting a national survey among the adult population to explore the opinions of people on how they use mobile technology, access information, and their digital literacy. We will be interviewing a few hundred people in different districts. The findings of this survey will be used for developmental programs and research. All information you provide will be kept strictly confidential. Participation in this survey is voluntary and it is entirely up to you to participate in the survey. You may refuse to answer any or all the questions. We hope that you will take part in this survey as your participation is important. It usually takes 20-30 minutes to complete this interview. Should you have any further queries you may contact ResInt.

Example of self-introduction and permission taken by an interviewer before a survey by ResInt Canada - a global research agency in South Asia:

"I _____, take an oath to this effect that I did not know the name and address of the above-mentioned person before taking this interview. Before asking the question, I followed the condition of ResInt Canada to conduct the interview. All the information collected in this questionnaire are correct and true. No dishonest means were followed to conduct the interview and information was collected according to preconditioned rules."

_____
Signature of Interviewer

11.8 CRITERIA FOR GOOD RESEARCH

To conduct any study appropriately, the study must meet all the common ground of the scientific method employed by the researcher. Good research will generate accurate, reliable, and dependable data and should ensure the following points.

- Research purpose defined and delineated properly.
- Research process detailed.
- Research design thoroughly planned.
- Sample size appropriately estimated.
- Sampling design clearly considered.
- Sample selection process stated.
- Questionnaire well-crafted and pretested.
- Selecting the skilled and trained surveyors.
- Ensuring quality control.

- High ethical standards.
- Confidentiality maintained.
- Limitations frankly revealed.
- Adequate analysis for decision maker's needs.
- Findings presented unambiguously.
- Conclusion justified.
- Researcher's experience reflected.

11.9 WRITING RESEARCH PROPOSAL

A research proposal is a document prepared by an individual or company/organization proposing a research project to be carried out by the individual or company/organization. It is an offer to conduct research on a specific topic (products or services) to a potential buyer or sponsor. It constitutes two offers – technical and financial.

Usually, the proposal contains the following sections:

A: Technical Proposal

- Background
- Objectives and hypotheses
- Rationale
- Research methodology
    o Methods (quantitative or qualitative or mixed-method)
    o Samples (sampling unit)
    o Sampling frame, population
    o Sampling design
    o Sample size
- Implementation
    o Respondent's characteristics and selection process
    o Geographic location
    o Questionnaire pretest and finalization
    o Surveyors selection (for quantitative)
    o Recruiters, moderators, etc (qualitative approach)
    o Training of the surveyors and other field team
    o Data collection approach (quantitative ad/or qualitative)
    o Quality control
    o Data processing (including programming for CAPI)
    o Team composition
    o Ethical considerations and confidentiality
    o Raw data/findings
- Presentation of findings
- Report (sharing with the sponsor for feedback and approval)
- Timeline

B: Financial Proposal

- Item-wise cost estimates
- Payment structure with bank details

11.10 RESEARCH IN ACTION

LC Waikiki is a market-leading brand in the Turkish fashion industry, and the company places considerable emphasis on market research as a means of maintaining and developing this position. The research conducted by the brand to gain insight into consumer behavior informs a multitude of decisions, from the formulation of product strategy to the development of marketing campaigns. LC Waikiki has a broad consumer appeal within the affordable fashion sector. The objective of the market research conducted by the brand is to provide a comprehensive analysis of consumer shopping habits and expectations. In particular, the interest of Turkish consumers in fast fashion trends and their preference for budget-friendly products have informed LC Waikiki's product strategies. Furthermore, the research has revealed behavioral trends, such as consumers' frequent store visits but mostly waiting for discount periods. The objective of the company's market research was to gain insight into the price sensitivity of consumers in Türkiye.

The research revealed that consumers in middle- and low-income groups tend to be price-oriented. By these findings, LC Waikiki has devised product categories encompassing a diverse range of price points and regularly conducts promotional discounts. This strategy facilitated the expansion of the brand's consumer base and the establishment of a robust connection with price-sensitive consumers. Furthermore, the company conducted market research to segment its consumer base, thereby enhancing the efficacy of its marketing strategies. To illustrate, an investigation was conducted into the impact of high-demand product categories on mothers in the context of children's wear. In the context of women's and men's clothing, consumer trends and purchasing habits were subjected to analysis across a range of defined segments. The earlier segmentation enabled LC Waikiki to develop customized product and campaign strategies for disparate consumer groups. LC Waikiki's comprehensive market research facilitates the formulation of strategic decisions that are grounded in consumer needs. In particular, the analysis of price sensitivity and fast fashion demands has enabled the brand to reach a significant consumer base. Concurrently, an examination of both online and physical store experiences prompted the brand to expand its e-commerce operations.

LC Waikiki employs market research methodologies to gain insight into the customer relationship with the brand, with a focus on customer satisfaction and loyalty. The objective of these studies is to ascertain which factors are of significance to the brand's loyal customer base and to identify the influences on their purchasing decisions. LC Waikiki implements enhancements in several key areas, including product quality, pricing strategy, store experience and customer service, to enhance customer satisfaction. To illustrate, a variety of loyalty programs have been devised by customer expectations regarding discounts and post-purchase service feedback (Kocabaş, 2018).

Hair, Jr., Joseph F., Celsi, Mary Wolfinbarger, Ortinau, David J., Bush, Robert P. (2017). *Essentials of marketing research (4th ed.)*. New York: McGraw-Hill Irwin.

Kocabaş, F. (2018). LC Waikiki'nin Tüketici Davranışlarına Yönelik Stratejileri. *Moda ve Pazarlama Araştırmaları.*

12. BETTER WORLD THROUGH SOCIALPRENEURSHIP

'When your business performs its job and benefits the stakeholders and society at the same time, directly or indirectly, that state is called Socialpreneurship.'

Fifty years back, when Milton Friedman was asked what the role of business in society is. He answered: "There is one and only one social responsibility of business—to use its resources and engage in activities designed to increase its profits."

The primitive business's methodology has been straightforward, you manufacture the product or announce the service, sell it and earn money. You market the business activity smartly to the right customers, and you make profits. You increase the business and make more profits, thus many ways to improve the monies for shareholders.

During this basic business approach, it is never considered how much harm the commercial activity is doing to stakeholders or society, directly and indirectly. For the first time, this basic business approach provokes thinking to change when the same activity starts causing damage in the supply chain, and repercussions are faced in the form of lower earnings. It's like a vicious cycle of direct & indirect side effects of the business, which hurts the financial viability.

Breaking free of this vicious cycle is only possible when the approach to doing business is reformed completely.

Through Entrepreneurship, we took risks, made profits, made shareholders happy, businesses thrived, and people got jobs, but then definitely something went wrong; what's the reason that many companies couldn't continue for long, customers moving to another brand?

12.1 THE CORE OF SOCIALPRENEURSHIP

The world we live in is a global enterprise, where every entity cares for one another, works, and stays in complete harmony. When we talk about the business world, we care for our businesses, we care for our suppliers, we care for our employees, we care for our shareholders, we care for our stakeholders, and we care for society. When we miss watching for anyone involved in the process, it may bring us some short-term profits, but we cannot expect stable profitability in the long run.

Even in real life, its nature's phenomena that do good, have good. What goes around comes around. So, what does the miracle of care require? It requires our collaboration, cooperation, and alliance, among all the parties involved in making this world a better place.

The term "socialpreneurship" refers to a strategy that prioritizes solving social problems over making money. It combines the ideas of goodwill, connected to non-governmental groups, with profit, associated with the corporate sector. Bringing about change in a variety of domains, such as human rights, education, health, and the environment, is the aim of social entrepreneurship. Experts view social entrepreneurship as the "business model of the future" because it can recognize and take advantage of chances for growth, especially in the face of challenges that have an impact on the environment and larger society (Enser, 2022). Social enterprises combine entrepreneurial strategy with social purpose, aiming to generate non-economic outcomes. They are self-financing, independent, and innovative in trading goods and services to address unmet needs. They may be described as hybrid organizations, autonomous and trading, potentially generating profit, employing people, and engaging volunteers. A benchmark for social enterprises is 50%. They are self-financed, independent, and reliant on donations and philanthropy, employing people and engaging volunteers to pursue their social purpose (Haugh, 2005).

12.1.1 MANAGING SOCIALPRENEURSHIP PROGRAMS

A social enterprise must be sustainable. Regardless of the merits of a given project, if it is not sustainable, it cannot contribute to societal benefit. This is due to its inability to facilitate the requisite transformation. It is therefore imperative that the projects and investments made for social entrepreneurship continue until the current situation improves irreversibly, and that they are updated as necessary. It is therefore imperative that social enterprises are not solely reliant on donations or the input of volunteers, but rather that they can generate their resources. The pursuit of profit is a fundamental aspect of sustainability in social enterprises (Enser, 2022).

An example is where a company surpasses its role to help people in pain and welcome new interns and start-ups in the industry. And it is sharing its secret with rivals as well, and thus it is increasing the market size. The name of the company is Medtronic. Medtronic is healthcare and biomedical engineering company, and it decided to play its role very impactful in a unique way. It has a ventilator that is portable, compact, and lightweight. This can be used under various circumstances in various environments. What Medtronic did that, it has offered its design, specifications, manuals, document, and coding free of cost. This is indeed a massive step by a profit-making corporation that offers its licensed product for free, even for a fixed time.

While social enterprises are driven by a social mission to create positive change and value, they also generate economic value through the design of their business models. As indicated by the Türkiye Social Entrepreneurship Ecosystem Situation Analysis, social enterprises represent 10% of enterprises within the European Union and provide employment opportunities for 11 million individuals. Since its emergence in the 1980s and its subsequent growth in Türkiye over the past 15 years, the social enterprise ecosystem has continued to evolve, yet remains in a developmental phase in Türkiye (Mengüç, 2022).

As indicated in the research report entitled 'State of Social Enterprises in Türkiye', there are approximately 9,000 social enterprises currently in operation within Türkiye. One such enterprise is TOYİ, which facilitates the transformation of all objects into toys and provides children with the means to express their creativity through play kits. This social enterprise employs the pedagogical benefits of play to impart fundamental competencies to children, including problem-solving abilities and the capacity to articulate emotions. It devises toy kits to foster the growth of productive and self-assured individuals, endowed with a well-developed imagination and creativity. A comparable example can be provided by Otsimo. It is a social enterprise that develops free educational games for children with special needs, such as autism and Down syndrome. Additionally, it provides a control system for parents to monitor their children's development (Kılıç, 2021). The program enables children to gain language development, social skills, and basic academic skills through the utilization of gamified and scientifically based educational practices. Otsimo's objective is to provide equal educational opportunities, particularly for children from economically disadvantaged backgrounds. It offers its services free of charge to these children and their families. The application employs an interactive and engaging approach to capture the attention of children with autism and facilitate their learning process. The application provides data-driven feedback for parents and teachers, enabling them to track their child's progress. Furthermore, it collaborates with special education specialists and psychologists in the development of its content. This initiative, which originated in Türkiye, rapidly achieved a significant global reach, garnering substantial support from prominent technology companies such as Google and Facebook. Otsimo has been successful in reaching a greater number of children by forming partnerships with international organizations such as UNICEF. In addition to making a valuable contribution to the education of individuals with autism, the company has developed an innovative and sustainable model for the provision of educational services (otsimo.com).

One illustrative example of social entrepreneurship in Türkiye is the 'Askıda Ne Var' project. This project is a social initiative that enables university students to benefit from a range of products and services, including food, clothing, theatre and concert tickets, books, magazines, and internships abroad, without paying a fee. The project's objective is to facilitate the personal and professional development of university students, to create a brighter future. It is exclusively available to undergraduate students enrolled in universities in Türkiye (Enser, 2022).

An additional case in point is the 'Surplus Food' project, which facilitates the utilization of unsaleable food-stuffs and integrates idle products into the economy, environment, and society. The social enterprise maintains its activities with a particular focus on the United Nations' Sustainable Development Goals, namely "Climate Action," "Zero Hunger," and "Responsible Production and Consumption." Moreover, 'Surplus Food' was selected by the United Nations Development Programme (UNDP) as one of nine initiatives to receive global support (Kılıç, 2021).

12.2 THE SOCIALPRENEURSHIP GUIDE TO SUSTAINABLE BUSINESSES

On Jan 16, 2020, Seattle-based Microsoft announced it to become carbon-negative by 2030. It promised that by 2050, it would remove all the carbon emitted directly or indirectly since its foundation in 1975. Microsoft allocated a 1-billion-dollar innovation fund to accelerate the global development of carbon reduction, and its capture and removal technologies to achieve this target. Microsoft promised to launch such technology to help its customers and suppliers reduce their carbon footprint. Last but not least, Carbon reduction would be an explicit aspect of their procurement processes for their supply chain, and the company will use its voice and advocacy to support public policy that will accelerate carbon reduction and removal opportunities.

Right after one month after the announcement by Microsoft, Jeff announced the launch of the Bezos Earth fund from 2020 summer to fight climate change. Highlights were the funding of scientists, activists, NGOs, anyone who can reduce the devastating effects of climate change. Jeff expressed his belief that the earth can be saved only by the joint efforts of all: big companies, small companies, Governments, global organizations, and individuals. After this announcement where Jeff pledged 8% of his total wealth, Amazon employees expressed unhappiness. They were expecting much more from him; they wanted him to do more. Before this initiative, His only most significant contribution so far had been $ 2 billion to help homeless families & fund schools in 2018. He didn't sign the 'Giving Pledge 'under which the rich donate half of their wealth during their lifetime to society.

Later, Amazon CEO and Founder Jeff Bezos donated $100 million to Feeding America. Amazon launched the $20 million AWS Diagnostic Initiative to accelerate COVID-19 research. In Europe, Amazon committed €21 million (almost USD 23 million) to support those most affected by the COVID-19 pandemic. It hired 175,000 additional full- and part-time employees. It has worked with food banks in 25 cities to deliver 6 million meals to underserved and vulnerable populations. It is donating $5 million in Amazon devices globally to those in need and donating 8,200 laptops to Seattle Public Schools students who do not have access to a machine at home. The Amazon Future Engineer program is donating 4,000 laptops to high school students across the U.S. and making new online computer science resources, including exam prep, accessible.

It's just not about the monetary donations; companies have been seen donating personal protective equipment (PPE) or other critical supplies, whether that is a mask, plane, or portable cell tower, contributing infrastructure, expertise, logistics, transportation, manufacturing equipment, or space, converting production lines and manufacturing additional critical supplies, Conducting clinical research, sharing data and technology, taking measures to keep workers employed, paid, and insured, helping customers get the products and financial assistance they need, doing something beyond its standard workflow and what is necessary for the company's survival as well.

12.3 THE WAY FORWARD FOR BUSINESSES

They need to upgrade to Socialpreneurship. It cares for everyone's benefit! Businesses don't need to take away future generations' ability to meet their own; profits co-exist with social purpose, satisfying all stakeholders.

Socialpreneurship is defined as a business approach that benefits the stakeholders directly, bringing benefits, ease and positive impact with its application, making this world a better place with every passing step and time, even much before earning profits. Socialpreneurship is THE NEED for a better future, satisfying Profit with Living Beings and Planet Needs. Under the approach of Socialpreneurship, businesses don't have to wait or rely on CSR (Corporate Social Responsibility) activities to exhibit their positive mindset or impacts on society.

Freidman's stance on business roles is no longer valid.

In 2019, Business Roundtable released a new "Statement on the purpose of a corporation," signed by 181 CEOs committed to leading their companies to benefit all stakeholders—customers, employees, suppliers, communities, and shareholders. The statement outlined a modern standard for corporate responsibility, i.e., we share a fundamental commitment to all our stakeholders - customers, employees, suppliers, communities, and shareholders.

Businesses need to expand their horizon from business focus to society, nation, and world. Customers won't remember entrepreneurs, but they will remember Socialpreneurs, who give them priority. Customers won't remember a brand not driven by a mission, cause, purpose, or belief! If you believe in something, people will believe in your faith and support, you with blood, sweat and tears, not for the only paycheck. Rebrand to aspirational brands, even an aesthetic brand serves no purpose until and unless it's sustainable. There is an inextricable link between purpose and profit. A better world means better profits.

Consumers today have become more sensitive than ever to the ethical practices of companies. From this perspective, socialpreneurship emerges as a key element in positioning companies as institutions that contribute to social welfare by emphasizing social and environmental responsibility. Companies that embrace the concept of socialpreneurship, which prioritizes sustainability, inclusivity, social impact, and creating social value (Dees, 1998), organize their overall marketing communication and strategies around these important values. Companies that emphasize their social impact through their narratives establish more effective connections and increase their interactions with socially conscious consumers.

Consumers form emotional bonds with brands that contribute to causes they care about, and they tend to share their positive experiences with others, become loyal consumers, and even become brand advocates. Supporting companies that contribute to these causes encourages the sense of becoming a part of something more important than just making a purchase. Social entrepreneurial companies can be considered hybrid organizations as they pursue both financial sustainability and ensuring social value (Doherty et al., 2014).

In addition, companies that cooperate with NGOs, environmental organizations, or other institutions that support social causes will have a broader positive impact and amplify their influence over socially conscious customers. These collaborations will contribute companies to gaining a competitive advantage by differentiating themselves in saturated markets by establishing a bond beyond a commercial relationship with the customers. Therefore, socialpreneurs create social impact by exploiting moral responsibilities while fulfilling their commercial responsibilities toward their stakeholders (Schaltegger and Wagner, 2011). Therefore, the integration of social impact into marketing strategies is of great importance in terms of enhancing marketing efforts, fostering relationships with consumers, gaining legitimacy (Vanhamme et al., 2012), building a social corporate identity (Berger et al., 2006), and strengthening the brand image. Government policies in Türkiye are trying to increase entrepreneurial activities (Karadeniz, 2010) and this supports entrepreneurs while also encouraging social entrepreneurship activities (Uygur et al, 2015). Social enterprises in Türkiye, especially those founded by women, both create economic wealth and address the social problems of the country (Uygur et al, 2015).

beko

WOMEN'S DEALER PROJECT

Written by: Nazlı Yılmaz (Brand & Marketing Commuınications)

Introduction

Beko Türkiye: The Promise of Social Health and Gender Equality

Beko, founded in 1955, is a global brand that reaches millions of users in global markets with its wide range of products of white goods to built-in appliances, from small household appliances to air conditioners. It offers smart solutions that will support the health of individuals, society, and the world, and make people's lives easier with its human and environmentally focused technologies. It is a leading brand operating in more than 135 countries and has market leadership in countries such as the UK, Romania, and Poland. It is the second largest durable household consumer brand in Türkiye.

Beko, which has determined its purpose of existence as "supporting healthy living", focuses on healthy individuals, healthy societies, and a healthy world by creating awareness in this area. It launched the Women's Dealer project in 2019 in order to support equal opportunities for a healthy society. With the Women Dealers project, Beko aimed to contribute to gender equality by supporting women's employment and entrepreneurship and to break down gender stereotypes regarding professions in society.

Challenge

Gender Inequality in Business

Beko, one of Türkiye's leading white goods brands, has more than 1,000 dealers across the country. Since the majority of these dealers are men, there was a perception that "dealership is a job specific to men." In addition to gender-based stereotypes that are also common among other occupational groups, another important factor that motivated Beko was the low rate of women in the employer and entrepreneur ecosystem. According to 2018 TÜİK data, the rate of women among employers was only 9%.

The results of the research "Women's Place in Society and Employment" (2021) conducted by Konda in collaboration with Beko also revealed similar results. According to the results of the research, the roles assigned to women and the stereotypes about women are one of the important obstacles to women entrepreneurs. Women's success can be defined through being a good mother, having good manners, happiness, and beauty/physical appearance. Regardless of employment status, men are more likely to define women's success through being a good mother and a good wife.

419

According to the same research results, among the difficulties faced by women entrepreneurs are economic reasons as much as the roles assigned to women. Although women invest all their savings when starting a business, sometimes this amount is not enough. In this case, a house or car is mortgaged, or financial support is received from the family.

In addition to all this information, when only employees with entrepreneurial experience are examined, the rate of women continuing the business they have established is higher than that of men (65%), with 73%. It is also seen in the concrete results that women are more successful when given the opportunity. Because more than three-quarters of women who work say that they can dedicate their lives to a job they love and believe in. Women entrepreneurs also have competencies such as being hard-working, being open to learning and development, loving the challenge, being self-confident and taking confident steps instead of taking risks.

For all these reasons, Beko concluded that breaking the perception that "dealership is men's job" and encouraging women financially and spiritually to become strong and successful entrepreneurs is one of the leading needs for a healthy society.

Solution

Women Dealer Project

In the face of this challenge, Beko aimed to break the perception of "Dealership is a job for men" with the principle of "equal opportunities for a healthy society" and the gender equality vision of Koç Holding, to which it is affiliated. In this direction, the Women Dealer Project was launched in 2019. The first goal of the project was determined to reach 100 women dealers.

According to Konda's research, there is a difference between women and men in terms of support received from their families in education and work life. It has been observed that men receive more support from their families in education and work life compared to women. Led by this information, the primary goal of the project was to increase women's power in social and economic life and to ensure that women become successful entrepreneurs by providing material and moral support. Beko aimed to transfer its experience and power in the dealer channel to women entrepreneurs. A package containing additional opportunities that will facilitate women who want to become Beko dealers by providing positive discrimination has been prepared. Within this scope, many privileges have been provided to women entrepreneurs who want to open a dealership, from finding a suitable store location to rent support, from store decoration to premium support for employees, additional display packages and a free POS machine. Mentorship and training support has also been provided to female dealer candidates. For the dealer channel, comprehensive training has been provided on product, finance, sales, accounting, and business administration through the Retail Academy operating within Arçelik Türkiye. Beko aims to offer women a sustainable and long-term investment opportunity.

An online application form has been created on the beko.com.tr website (www.beko.com.tr/100kadinbayi) for applications to be made within the scope of the Beko project.

Women's Solidarity

Beko dealer women share their feelings and experiences in a communication group established via social media and internal communication channels. In constant and close communication, dealer women frequently come together face to face to give each other strength and inspiration. With the women dealer meetings regularly held every year, it is aimed to ensure that dealer women learn the company's vision and priorities and strengthen their communication with each other.

Communication and Visibility

Communication support is also provided to women dealers who enter the ecosystem to make their voices heard. The project was introduced by using photos of real women dealers all over Türkiye, using outdoor advertisements and radio communications, and it was aimed to inspire women entrepreneurs. In 2023, the 100th year of the Republic of Türkiye, the project found a response in the society and the first goal was achieved; the number of female dealers has reached 100. Then, the project was taken one step further and the name of the project was changed from "100 Women Dealers" to "Her Business, Her Power", by aiming to reach a wider audience. For this purpose, an advertising film was prepared that did not only focus on dealerships but also aimed to stand against gender taboos in the minds of the society. It was aimed to create a significant impact in the society with 360-degree communication activities based on the advertising film.

Beko's advertising communication focused on the set of behaviors experienced since childhood, which underlies the taboo of "women's work – men's work" accepted in society. Women were doing jobs attributed to them by those around them, "taught" since childhood, and it was seen that there was a perception of what women's work was. This situation indicated the area in which Beko aimed to create awareness in society. Beko, which opposed the separation of daily housework and professions into "men" and "women" in society, also showed this in its commercial. In the communication opposing the distinction between women's work and men's work, sexist jobs imposed on a woman by her environment from childhood were centered, and sexist stereotypes that everyone, men, and women, heard and normalized in their lives were clearly depicted. The main character questions and rejects the stereotypes imposed on her. Later, it is seen that the main character became a Beko dealer in her adulthood, and she ends the film by telling her daughter that, contrary to what she was told, her job was to be a strong woman who could stand on her own feet and that she should do the job of her dreams. Beko has also emphasized the gender equality it has adopted under the umbrella of social health by expressing that women's work is not housework, but **women's work is women's power** in its communication language. The commercial was broadcast on television and all social media channels and achieved high levels of access and impressions. In addition, deepening content containing different messages was prepared with data pools created from those who watched the commercials, and people were directed to the website for application. In order to spread the awareness that was intended to be created with the commercial, a roadshow was held in 16 provinces under the leadership of the TOBB Women Entrepreneurs Board of Türkiye with many major collaborations including TOBB within the scope of the project.

- https://www.youtube.com/watch?v=e5KYP8hSwVg

Within the scope of the project, cooperation was made with various institutions and organizations such as KOSGEB*, TOBB** in order to reach and provide opportunities to more women. In order to reach 7,000 women entrepreneurs within TOBB and prepare them for commercial life, marketing training was provided through the Arçelik retail team. Free professional consultancy services were provided so that women entrepreneurs could receive financial support from institutions such as KOSGEB, İŞKUR****, SGK****.

Result

Awards, Awareness on Gender Equality, and Impact on Turkish Economy

It has been observed that the project studies and project-specific collaborations and communication practices have found a response in society. By the middle of 2024, the current number of women dealers has increased to 119, the current number of stores to 141, the number of women dealers in 41 provinces, and the number of people employed has increased to 512 (52% of which are women employees). With this project, job opportunities are provided not only for women entrepreneurs but also for women employees, increasing the multiplier effect of the project. The project has shed light on social awareness over time thanks to communication support. After the launch communication in March 2022, the total number of applications increased by 159%. After the campaign, according to the Q1 2021 form filling data, the 2022 Q1 application form filling rate changed by 310% (2021 Q1 vs 2022 Q1).

In addition to all the results, the project and its communication activities have won many prestigious national and international awards within the scope of gender equality from leading companies in the sector, such as the Türkiye Sustainable Business Awards, Women-Friendly Brands Award, TİSK***** Common Future Award, CSR****** Türkiye's Gold Success Award, Stevie Awards, Kristal Elma and Felis.

The Beko Women Dealership Project inspires women entrepreneurs around the world as part of the UN Women's Generation Equality Platform's Action Coalition Initiative and is a part of commitments led by Koç Holding. With this project, Beko has committed to increasing the number of women dealers to 150 by March 2026. The project continues to grow.

Questions to stimulate the case

1. What was one of the primary barriers to societal health in the business world?

One of the primary barriers in the business world was the gender inequality. The biggest challenge women encountered in business life was gender-based stereotypes and societal expectations. Stereotypes and roles assigned by society to women created significant barriers to women's success in entrepreneurship and employment. Societal perceptions often defined women's success in terms of traditional roles such as being a good mother or wife, rather than their professional achievements. Additionally, women faced economic challenges such as insufficient financial resources and lack of family support compared to their male counterparts. These obstacles collectively hindered women's ability to establish and sustain their businesses.

1. Top of Form
2. Bottom of Form
3. How did Beko take action for support a healthy society?

Beko firstly focused on the inequality in business life by launching the Women Dealers Project, aimed at promoting empowering women in the business world. This initiative was designed to challenge and change the perception that dealership roles are exclusively for men. By offering financial and moral support, mentorship, and additional resources such as store location assistance and training, Beko sought to increase women's presence and success in the dealership sector by underlining women's bsiness as their power.

Links and media

Website: https://www.beko.com.tr/kadinin-isi-gucu

Case Highlights

Beko, a leading global home appliance brand, launched the Women Dealer Project in 2019 for raising awareness to gender equality by focusing on healthy society. The project was initiated to challenge gender inequality by emphasizing disparity in business life. Beko supports women entrepreneurs by offering financial aid, mentorship, and training to break the perception of "Dealership is a job for men". Beko's efforts were firstly establishing a network of 100 female dealers, which expanded after achieving, under the new name "Her Business, Her Power," aiming to reach a wider audience with 360-degree communication activities based on the advertising film. The initiative has successfully increased the number of women dealers, enhanced job opportunities, and garnered significant awards, reflecting its positive impact on gender equality.

CASE STUDY
THE TURKISH RED CRESCENT

A NEW PERSPECTIVE ON DONOR RELATIONS: THE 3S-3P-3R MODEL

Written by: Cengizhan Salih (Donor Relations and Fundraising Director of TRC)

Introduction

The Turkish Red Crescent (TRC) is Türkiye's oldest, most respected, and largest non-profit humanitarian organization. Founded in 1868, TRC aims to enhance individual and community resilience and alleviate suffering while preserving human dignity. As a member of the International Federation of Red Cross and Red Crescent Societies (IFRC), TRC provides aid to those in need across Türkiye and worldwide, contributing to social welfare by offering shelter, food, and healthcare support. Its services span a broad spectrum, including blood donation, disaster response, international aid, migration and refugee services, social services, education, and youth programs.

Challenge

Today, non-profits are key players in global socio-economic and even political change. They respond to societal needs by operating across various areas, from humanitarian aid to environmental protection, education, and health. However, many still view "marketing" and "donor relations" narrowly or rely on traditional approaches. Non-profits depend heavily on donors to fund their projects and services. Without a steady flow of donations, sustaining their activities becomes difficult. Strong donor relationships ensure sustainability, enabling long-term planning.

Beyond Profit: The Unique Aspects Challenges of Nonprofits

It's crucial to understand that non-profits differ significantly from commercial enterprises. Their goal isn't profit but solving societal issues. They focus on the societal impact rather than the benefits of their products or services, aiming to raise resources for change and awareness, not for sales or profitability. Unlike businesses that offer tangible benefits to customers, non-profits provide material benefits to those in need and moral satisfaction to donors. With limited resources and less information about their donors, they must develop the most effective marketing strategies and well-formulated "donor relations strategies." But what does such a strategy entail, and how is it shaped?

Solution

Various models have been developed to enhance customer experience, helping companies better understand and satisfy their customers. Notable examples include the IDIC Model, Customer Experience Pyramid, Six Pillars of Customer Experience, McKinsey's Customer Experience Pyramid, Gartner's CRM Implementation Model, Customer Lifecycle Management, and Customer Journey Mapping. These models aim to optimize customer relations, increase satisfaction, offer better products and services, outshine competitors, and build long-term, valuable relationships.

However, non-profits have different needs than commercial enterprises, making these models less suitable. For example, they may fall short in customizing the donor experience, designing unique donor journeys, creating memorable and inspiring experiences, transforming donors into advocates, and capturing individual differences. While each model has strengths and weaknesses, a comprehensive framework covering all these aspects is lacking.

Surpassing Traditional Models: Introducing the 3S-3P-3R Model for Nonprofits

Our proposal for the development of the third sector is the 3S-3P-3R model, a new and unique approach strengthened to create a more effective donor experience. The proposed model offers a comprehensive approach designed to optimize and deepen donor relations for non-profit organizations.

Figure 1: Empowering Donor Relationships: The 3S-3P-3R Model

Abbr.	Component	Description
3S	Sharing	Sharing information, emotions, and experiences with donors (at a satisfying level)
	Satisfaction	Donor satisfaction with service, process, and communication (positive communication)
	Solution Oriented	Solution-oriented communication in response to donor requests
3P	Pursuit	Tracking donor requests and donations, inquiring about their status
	Period	Utilizing and finalizing donations within the promised period
	Proactive Listening	Actively listening to donors (their wishes and ideas)
3R	Relation on Trust	Establishing a trust relationship with donors
	Rewarding	Rewarding donors and expressing gratitude
	Reachable	Ensuring that donor relationship managers and the organization are easily accessible and reachable

The 3S *(Sharing, Satisfaction, Solution-Oriented)* formula emphasizes not only sharing information with donors but also emotions and experiences, ensuring they are satisfied with the services, processes, and communications they receive, and fostering positive, solution-oriented interactions. This approach strengthens donors' bonds with the organization while meeting their expectations.

For example, many non-profits collect donations to build water wells in areas with limited access to clean water. The Turkish Red Crescent (TRC) also builds wells and raises funds for this purpose. When the TRC's donor relations team discusses these projects with donors, they don't just share the well's location, technical details, or costs. They also convey the benefits the well brings to people, animals, and agriculture. During well openings, donors are connected via video conferencing to witness the event, allowing them to feel the joy and excitement first-hand, as if they were there. This transfer of **emotion and experience**, alongside information, is a powerful method of strengthening donor ties with the organization.

Ensuring donors are satisfied with the services they receive, and the pre-, during-, and post-donation processes, as well as their interactions with organization representatives, is crucial for building strong donor relationships. This involves reviewing processes, collecting feedback, and optimizing services, processes, and communication approaches to meet donor needs and expectations. For example, the TRC's teams responsible for developing donation products and systems, in line with the 3S-3P-3R model's donor relations

425

strategy, created a feedback system to gather post-donation feedback from donors. Donor satisfaction with the process is regularly tracked, and ratings are monitored (see Figures 1 and 2). Similarly, data from the 168 Call Centre is analyzed, and areas for improvement are identified based on findings.

Figure 2: Score Distribution of Ease of Making a Donation

(1: Very Difficult, 10 Very Easy)

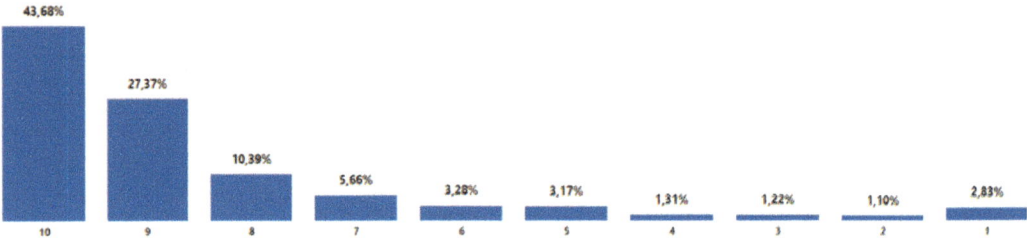

Figure 3: Monthly Change in Ease of Making Donations

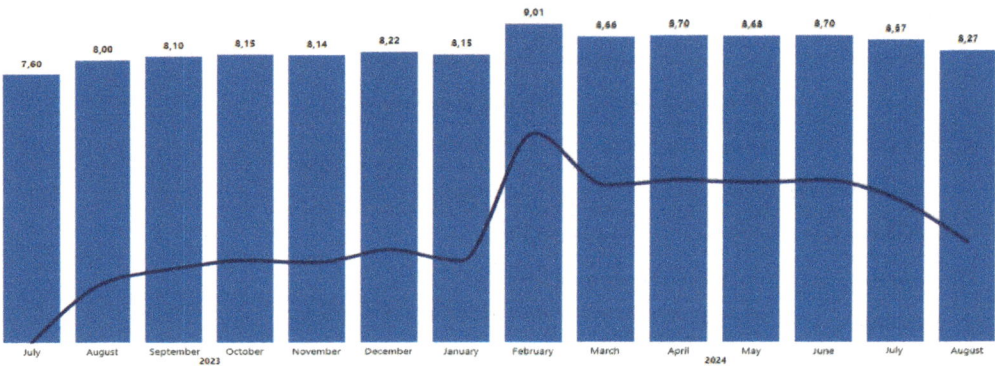

Like anyone with a request, donors expect solution-oriented language and approaches. Solution-oriented communication involves addressing issues with a positive, supportive, and proactive attitude. Instead of saying, *"This issue isn't related to us,"* a response like, *"We'll take immediate action to resolve this,"* or *"We understand this issue bothers you, and we're here to resolve it,"* exemplifies positive, solution-focused communication. Training staff who interact with donors in this approach can significantly benefit your organization.

The 3P *(Pursuit, Period, Proactive Listening)* formula involves tracking donor requests and donations, ensuring funds are used within the promised timeframe, and actively listening to donor wishes and ideas. This approach makes donors feel valued while enhancing the organization's transparency and accountability.

Tracking donor requests and donations, the first component, enables strong, long-term relationships. At the TRC Donor Relations and Resource Development Directorate, we strive to track these in several ways. For example, requests received through the Call Center are logged in the CRM system and forwarded to relevant departments for resolution. From the moment they are forwarded, the resolution time begins, which is also one of the performance indicators for our departments.

Figure 4: Directorate Based Donor Requests and Response Times Monitoring Screen

(01.01.2024 - 30.06.2024)

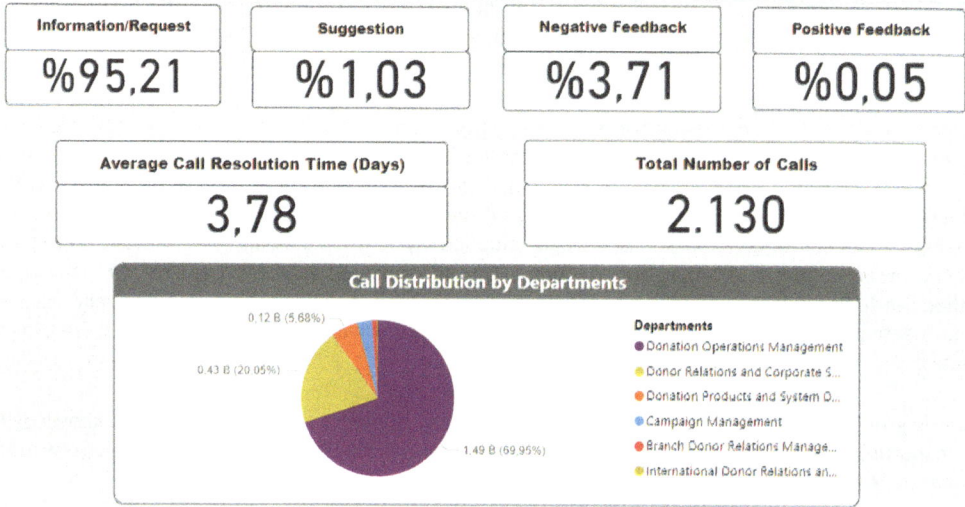

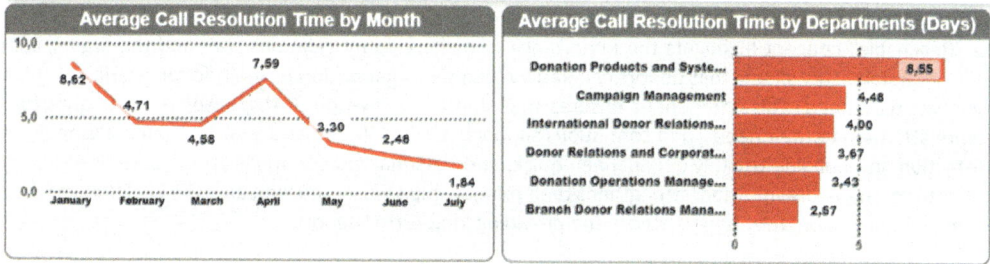

Information/Request	Suggestion	Negative Feedback	Positive Feedback
%95,21	%1,03	%3,71	%0,05

Average Call Resolution Time (Days)	Total Number of Calls
3,78	2.130

Call Distribution by Departments

0,12 B (5.68%)
0.43 B (20.05%)
1,49 B (69.95%)

Departments
- Donation Operations Management
- Donor Relations and Corporate S...
- Donation Products and System D...
- Campaign Management
- Branch Donor Relations Manage...
- International Donor Relations an...

Figure 5: Average Call Closing Time by Directorate and Change in Overall Average

(01.01.2024 - 30.06.2024)

Average Call Resolution Time by Month

	January	February	March	April	May	June	July
	8,62	4,71	4,58	7,59	3,30	2,48	1,84

Average Call Resolution Time by Departments (Days)

Department	Days
Donation Products and Syste....	8,55
Campaign Management	4,48
International Donor Relations...	4,00
Donor Relations and Corporat...	3,67
Donation Operations Manage...	3,43
Branch Donor Relations Mana...	2,57

At TRC, donor relations are managed through a donor portfolio system. Each staff member responsible for donor relations manages a specific portfolio of donors, addressing their needs, requests, and complaints. These donors are provided with a direct phone line to their portfolio manager, rather than having to contact the Call Centre. The portfolio manager also closely monitors these donors' contributions and keeps them informed of developments.

The "Period" concept refers to utilizing donations and completing projects within the promised timeframe. This ensures that donors see tangible results from their contributions within a set period, boosting their trust. Whether specified in a contract or verbally, using donations within the agreed timeframe enhances donor confidence and encourages continued support.

Proactive listening means actively listening to donors' wishes and ideas, going beyond just hearing them to fully understanding, evaluating, and responding appropriately. The well-known saying, *"We have two ears and one mouth so that we can listen twice as much as we speak,"* perfectly illustrates this concept. At TRC, donor relations staff send digital surveys to their portfolio donors, measuring satisfaction and identifying proactive listeners.

The 3R (*Relation on Trust, Rewarding, Reachable*) formula emphasizes building a trust-based relationship with donors, recognizing, and rewarding their contributions, and ensuring that both the organization and donor relations staff are easily accessible. These elements are crucial for establishing long-term, sustainable donor relationships.

In today's world, the dynamics of donor relations are rapidly changing. The traditional concept of loyalty is being replaced by emotional bonds and **trust**, which are deeper and more meaningful connections. As we increasingly understand that humans are "**emotional**" rather than "**rational**" beings, it becomes clear that building emotional bonds and trust is more important than cultivating loyalty. Indeed, if we had to choose only one component for donor relations, it would undoubtedly be trust. Building this trust starts with transparency, proactive communication, and accountability. TRC strives to establish this trust through various methods, including a donor portfolio management system, communication automation, specially designed donor meeting rooms, live broadcasts of donation use, and personalized reports, all of which are proving effective.

Rewarding refers to thanking, recognizing, and appreciating donors. Essentially, it means acknowledging their contributions, expressing how valuable their support is, and showing gratitude. An effective rewarding strategy increases donor satisfaction and loyalty, encouraging them to donate again.

At TRC, we make it a point to thank every donor who shares at least one contact detail with us. We have set up SMS and email automation systems for this purpose. Additionally, donations exceeding a certain amount trigger an email notification to us, prompting appropriate staff, from the highest level down, to make a thank-you call. We also visit donors with specially designed gifts to express our gratitude. Depending on the significance of the donation, we may also thank them publicly on social media, showcasing their exemplary behavior.

The "Reachable" concept highlights the importance of making donor relations staff and the organization easily accessible. This means that donors can easily reach the organization or their donor relations contact whenever they need. This component ensures that donors receive quick responses to their questions, prompt attention to their needs, and continuous support. Accessibility plays a vital role in increasing donor satisfaction and building trust. Multi-channel, quick, and personalized communication makes it easier for donors to reach the organization, strengthens their relationship with it, and increases the likelihood of them recommending the organization to others and providing long-term support.

In this regard, TRC has established various communication and accessibility channels, including "social media messaging, a call centre, web chat, and WhatsApp." Additionally, if callers to the call centre encounter busy lines and prefer not to wait, they are offered a *"press X if you don't want to wait, and we'll call you back"* option. Donor relations staff are also equipped with dedicated phones and lines, offering personalized, closer service to donors. With over 500 branches across Türkiye's 81 provinces, TRC demonstrates its commitment to being always accessible and reachable and from any location.

Conclusion

Ultimately, this model addresses the challenges that non-profit organizations face in managing donor relationships, recognizing the shortcomings of other models in use, and proposes a strengthened new model formulated as 3P-3S-3R. This model offers a strategic approach and a 360-degree perspective for building deeper, more meaningful, and trust-based relationships with donors, allowing non-profit organizations to establish personalized, long-term connections with their donors. The 3S-3P-3R model stands out as a holistic proposition for any non-profit organization that seeks to cultivate solution-oriented and proactive communication, maintain relevance through continuous feedback and improvement cycles, capitalize on opportunities for quick adaptation, and fully embrace the importance of trust-building.

Questions to stimulate conversation on the case

1. Why is donor relationship management so crucial for non-profit organizations?

Donor relationship management is vital for non-profit organizations because they rely on donor support to sustain their operations and serve the community. Strong and sustainable donor relationships ensure the continuity of financial resources and extend the organization's mission to a broader audience, thereby increasing its societal impact.

2. Can donor relationship management for non-profit organizations be managed with the same approach as customer relationship management in commercial companies?

The management of donor relationships in non-profit organizations differs from customer relationship management in commercial companies. While commercial companies focus on retaining customers and generating profit, non-profit organizations aim to build long-term, trust-based relationships with donors. Therefore, each approach requires its own distinct strategies.

3. What differentiates the 3S-3P-3R model from other customer relationship management models?

The 3S-3P-3R model differs from others by offering a 360-degree perspective on donor relationships. It centres on trust rather than loyalty, promoting the establishment of personalized, long-term relationships with donors. It emphasizes the power of proactive communication, staying current through continuous feedback and improvement cycles, and providing innovative solutions that meet donors' expectations without missing opportunities for quick adaptation.

KidZania

EXPERIENTIAL MARKETING AND TECHNOLOGY CHALLENGE AT KİDZANİA İSTANBUL

Written by: Ebru Timur (KidZania Istanbul Board Member & CEO)

Introduction

KidZania was founded 25 years ago, in 1999, by Xavier Lopez Ancona, an unconventional and visionary entrepreneur in Mexico City, as a safe experiential space where children can "learn by having fun". KidZania, which offers a professional experience in a real city life from its streets to avenues, factories, theatre and square, is a Children's Country with its own culture from anthem to dance, architecture to language. Today, with a success story that surpasses the dreams of its founder, KidZania offers children the opportunity to experience more than 100 occupational groups, welcomes millions of children every year in 28 cities in 17 countries, including Türkiye, and supports the solid foundations of the steps children will take in their adult lives.

KidZania's foundational concept of 'Edutainment,' or 'learning through fun,' serves as an innovative education model of the 21st century, ensuring that what children learn through experiential learning is permanent. At KidZania, children learn by getting involved through experience, discover themselves, and with the inspiration KidZania offers them, their imagination is strengthened and their self-confidence increases. KidZania provides an environment for children to discover their own interests and contributes to their cognitive and social development. In a city life where they are together with their peers, children socialize and develop various skills and values, ranging from financial literacy to teamwork, analytical thinking to motor skills, ethical awareness to a sense of responsibility and from self-confidence to solidarity.

With its success graph that stands out in the global network, KidZania Istanbul stands out as a unique KidZania city where children experience education and entertainment together since its launch in 2014. On its way to inspire the next generation, KidZania offers thousands of children the experience of learning with fun free of charge every year in cooperation with disadvantaged children, recognizing the right of every child. With its wide range of more than 100 professions and business lines, KidZania Istanbul realizes a real city life for children together with its purpose partners, the leading institutions, and organizations of the sector. For the most up-to-date technical and equipment information about the professions in the city, the references of the purpose partners are used. KidZania Istanbul observes UN sustainability principles, especially the main topics of environment and gender equality, in both city and company management. In addition to being a Global Compact supporter, it also takes an active role in platforms such as Lead Türkiye and Sales Network Women in Sales. While raising awareness on sustainability, environment, and gender equality through experiential means with its cause partners, it aims to strengthen their belief that they can do any profession regardless of socio-economic level, status, and gender.

430

Challenge

Born in the early 2010s, children of the Alpha generation have a distinct advantage over previous generations in terms of access to information. Growing up intertwined with technology, this generation has the ability to make more informed and original decisions while shaping their perspectives on the world, their career choices, and their dreams.

With the rapid development of technology, the flow of information has also gained a dizzying speed. In this context, every piece of information and every sharing require verification of accuracy. KidZania Istanbul comes into play at this point; it enhances the experiential learning process for children by blending information with entertainment, helping it become internalized and permanent. KidZania Istanbul invites the Alpha generation, born into technology and their families to safe and hygienic spaces that meet their need for socialization, where they can connect with their peers and engage in individual experiences.

KidZania Istanbul's ever-increasing number of visitors demonstrates the power of physical experiences, even in this age of digitalization. Hosting global guests, KidZania Istanbul provides children with permanent learning opportunities and provides brands with in-depth interaction with children and families. With the sense of reality that makes KidZania unique, children develop cognitive and social skills such as teamwork, financial literacy, communication, responsibility, and self-confidence while perfectly performing their roles in the city. In this context, KidZania is positioned as a unique learning-through-fun center that leaves a lasting impact on brands. Experiences in the city, which mirror the real world, create lasting memories in children's minds and lets KidZania to be in a position of unrivaled in experiential marketing.

431

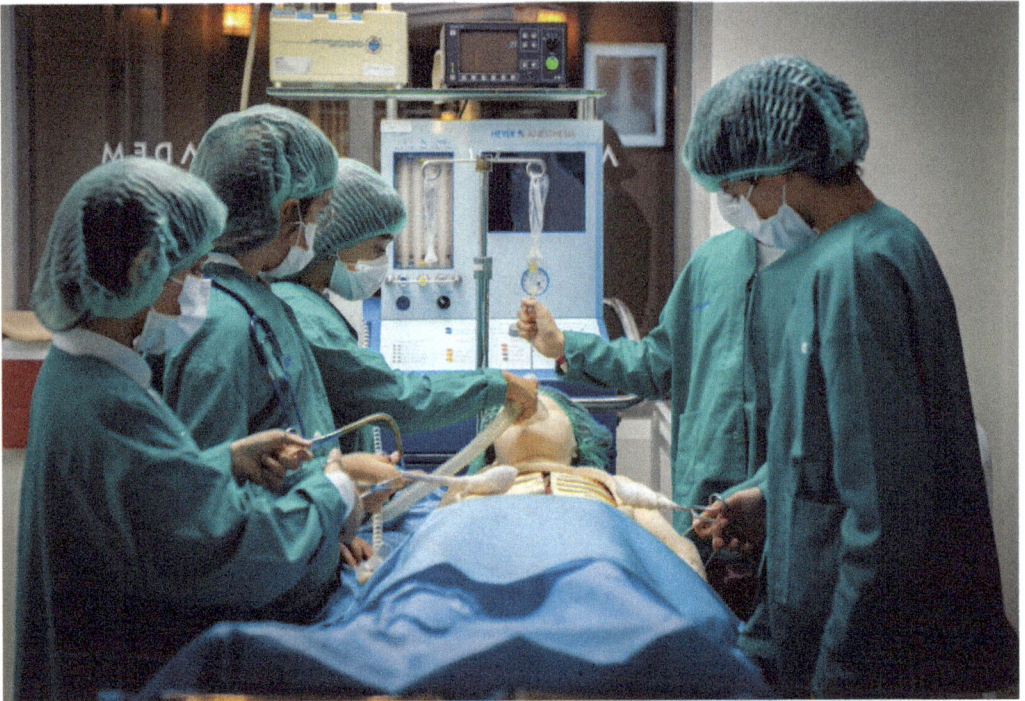

Solution

The concepts of "reality" and "participation," two key components of experiential marketing, come to life in a tangible way at KidZania Istanbul. Through realistic roles and occupational experiences, children have the opportunity to blend their imagination with the real world. The experiences gained through these activities become more meaningful and lasting. Their active participation makes these experiences more personal and impactful. As children assume various roles at KidZania Istanbul, their connection with the brands strengthens, and their experiences enhance their trust in those brands. Consequently, becoming a KidZania purpose partner contributes to the long-term reputation of brands.

The interactive experiences offered at KidZania Istanbul allow children to discover their own interests and talents by experiencing various professions such as scientists, teachers, firefighters, and bankers. This process offers both an inspiring and fun learning journey for children. Each experience in the city gives children a sense of reality by making them experience real-life scenarios.

The feeling of reality in the city is at the heart of deep and internalized learning at KidZania Istanbul. This sense of reality is created through realistic portrayals of professions and daily life practices that reflect the functioning of the city and with the presence of real brands. Purpose partners—leading brands in their sectors—are integrated into the activity areas with their authentic corporate identities. Simulated workplaces (such as factories, laboratories, hospitals, workshops, clinics, R&D centres, radio stations, television studios and newspapers) along with professional costumes, uniforms, equipment, and processes offer children the chance to experience various professions. Purpose partners are represented in the city, either in areas that correspond to their specific lines of business or through content that aligns with their brand promises or social responsibility initiatives. With the backing of KidZania Istanbul's purpose partner brands, information is conveyed in an up-to-date, accurate and reliable manner throughout all city experiences. Children are provided with unique learning and development opportunities that are unavailable elsewhere.

While KidZania Istanbul offers unforgettable experiences to children and their families, it continues to increase the power and impact of its purpose partner brands day by day. The

results of the "Consumer Experience Journey Research" conducted at KidZania Istanbul clearly reveal that the experiences at KidZania Istanbul leave lasting traces in the minds of children. The research shows that children who spend time at KidZania Istanbul remember the brands in the city 100 percent of the time and families remember the brands that offer this service to their children, 98 percent of the time. This reveals the brand's strong impact on children and families and its success in building loyalty.

The 2023 study "Future Consumers: The Future, Dreams and Realities" research report, more than half of the children remember the brands they experienced at KidZania Istanbul. Unassisted, they name the brand they see at KidZania as their favourite brand. The experiences they have in the city create lifelong, lasting memories for children and their families and help children's development processes and build their future identities.

Studies conducted globally and in Türkiye highlight the power of experiences in raising awareness among children. For example, thanks to the realistic experiences at KidZania Istanbul, children can concretely imagine being a scientist, teacher, firefighter, banker, or any other profession. These experiences also help children make more informed career choices. KidZania Istanbul and its purpose partners inspire and contribute to the development of future doctors, financiers, firefighters, artists, and leaders in various fields in Türkiye.

KidZania Istanbul enables children to better understand their role models and take strong steps in their lives with the valuable experiences it offers with purpose partners. All activities and experiences in the city fulfil children's need to be individuals, increase their self-confidence and contribute to the development of their social skills.

Conclusion

KidZania Istanbul offers an extraordinary learning environment for children by effectively implementing the cornerstones of experiential marketing, particularly the principles of 'reality' and 'participation.' The real-life scenarios presented here allow children to gain concrete skills by actively engaging in various professions while having fun. Through this experiential approach, children's access to accurate and reliable information is directly linked to real life, resulting in lasting interaction and learning.

Experiential marketing is an innovative strategy that enables children to discover the world in a realistic and interactive way. KidZania Istanbul, with its "reality" and "participation" oriented approach, offers children the opportunity to bring their imagination together with the real world. Children are involved in a journey of "social learning" and "self-discovery" by gaining valuable skills that they will use for a lifetime along with a fun experience.

Experiential marketing is an innovative strategy that allows children to explore the world in a realistic and interactive way. KidZania Istanbul, with its focus on "reality" and "participation" provides children the opportunity to merge their imagination with the real world. Through this journey of "social learning" and "self-discovery" children gain valuable skills they will use for a lifetime, all while enjoying a fun experience.

Children and families create unforgettable memories during the average of 5 hours spent at KidZania. When they meet KidZania Istanbul's purpose partner brands in real life, the positive experiences they've had enhance their interactions with these brands, making them strong and

long-lasting. With these lasting effects, KidZania Istanbul not only contributes to brand trust and reputation but also strengthens its unique position in experiential marketing.

Questions to stimulate conversation on the case

1. **What are KidZania Istanbul's experiential marketing strategies and how can their impact on children be defined?**

KidZania Istanbul adopts a strategy based on the core principles of experiential marketing: "reality" and "participation." With this approach, KidZania Istanbul provides children a safe environment where they actively engage in various professions and social roles by presenting real-life scenarios featuring real brands. These experiences, created in realistic spaces and through role play with purpose partner brands, allow children to have fun while also understanding the real-world equivalents of these roles. This method enables children to acquire knowledge, skills and values related to professions and life. By offering meaningful and lasting learning through realistic roles, it also gives brands the opportunity to engage positively with both children and families. This positive learning experience strengthens the connections that brands establish with children and their families.

2. **How is KidZania Istanbul's survival and challenge in the world of technology shaped?**

To remain competitive in the rapidly evolving world of technology, KidZania Istanbul integrates the latest technology into its daily operations. On the other hand, when it comes to children, rapidly developing technology brings risks and threats. Research indicates that when children's use of technology is not properly guided, it can lead to negative consequences such as social isolation, distraction, and physical health issues. The constant need to verify the reliability and accuracy of information accessed through technology, along with the prevalence of disinformation, creates an environment where children are left vulnerable.

In the research we conducted as KidZania Istanbul, the technology usage habits of children across Türkiye and the possible risks of these habits were analyzed. According to the results of the research, children spend an average of 163 minutes a day in front of the screen and this time increases with increasing age. As stated in the "Screen Time Guidelines by Age" conducted by the American Academy of Pediatrics (AAP) and the

World Health Organization (WHO), for the physical and mental health development of children, screen time should be limited to 1 hour a day for children aged 3-5, 1 to 1.5 hours a day for children aged 6-10 and 2 hours a day for children aged 11-13.

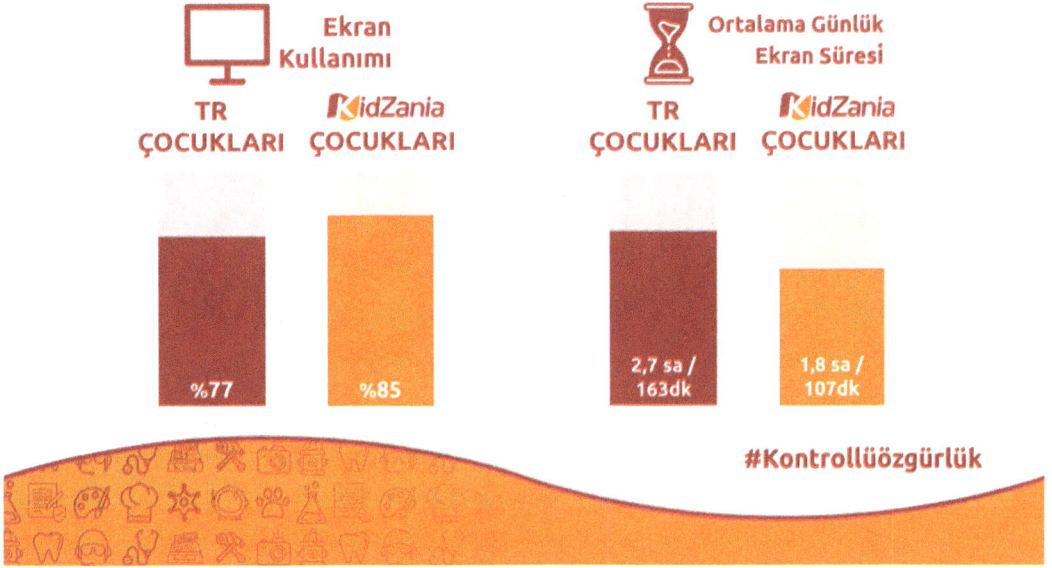

Ekran Kullanımı

TR ÇOCUKLARI — %77
KidZania ÇOCUKLARI — %85

Ortalama Günlük Ekran Süresi

TR ÇOCUKLARI — 2,7 sa / 163dk
KidZania ÇOCUKLARI — 1,8 sa / 107dk

#Kontrollüözgürlük

KidZania Istanbul's challenge is to provide a real, reliable, and unique learning experience through fun in a 10,000-square-meter area (city) designed specifically for children. Activities are tailored to support the cognitive and physical development of children aged 1 to 14. Unlike technology, which needs to be used in a controlled and supervised manner, KidZania allows children to safely explore the professions they are interested in, experiencing the reality of these roles through authentic costumes and equipment. As they engage with their peers, their socialization and communication skills are strengthened. They learn how to initiate and maintain conversations and solve problems collaboratively, all while observing and imitating others in a social learning environment. The involvement of real-life brands representing various professions further enhances children's and families' interactions with these brands, fostering.

awareness of their identity, services and promises. In this way, KidZania Istanbul offers brands a unique opportunity for experiential marketing.

3. **In a fully digitalized world, how does KidZania Istanbul continue to attract both global and local visitors?**

In this age where digitalization has entered our lives in every aspect, the secret of KidZania Istanbul's success lies in the reality experience it offers. Unlike other marketing strategies that are limited to digital platforms, KidZania Istanbul, which continues to host global guests, offers a world where children can touch, feel, and experience. This physical and experiential learning approach deeply develops children's cognitive and social skills, leaving lasting traces in their minds far beyond digital content. Offering the opportunity to experience the real world, KidZania stimulates children's imagination and creates a strong bond based on trust for brands. With this sense of reality and unique experiences, KidZania has an unrivaled position in the sector and continues to attract visitors of all ages, setting a global example in both education and entertainment.

Summary

KidZania Istanbul's extensive research and data clearly show that children are inspired by their existing knowledge and experiences and seek new learning opportunities. The dynamic edutainment model offered by KidZania encourages children to start with familiar activities and make in-depth discoveries in areas they are curious about and have not experienced before.

The new generation is a generation that has grown up intertwined with technology. However, despite being under the intense influence of technology, children still come running to KidZania and have fun and learn with real experiences here. The real-life simulations offered by KidZania Istanbul go beyond conventional marketing and create a lasting and meaningful impact on children's education and development processes.

These unique experiences at KidZania Istanbul maximize children's self-confidence with a sense of "I can". In this process, children acquire lifelong skills and values such as analytical thinking, taking responsibility, social sensitivity, communication, and teamwork. KidZania plays a unique role as an experience space that prepares children not only for the future but also for the present.

The experiences offered at KidZania Istanbul create unforgettable memories for children and parents. Here, children have real-world experiences that they will remember for the rest of their lives, while establishing a deep bond with the brands they meet in the process.

The brands experienced at KidZania Istanbul leave lasting memories in the minds of children and their families. KidZania Istanbul offers a unique long-term experiential marketing opportunity for brands' communication strategies for customer loyalty, trust and reputation management and corporate social responsibility visions. Being a KidZania Istanbul purpose partner gives brands the opportunity to establish a long-term interaction with children and their families, a relationship that will last for generations.

** Consumer Experience Journey Research, 2017 Argus Brand Development & Marketing Insight Company

** Future Consumers: Future, Dreams and Realities Survey, 2023 Future Bright Group

13. ADAPTIVE PUBLIC POLICY AND MARKETING DURING COVID-19

The nature of pandemics demands that we factor multiple perspectives – spanning history, philosophy, geo-politics, sociology – to make sense of how to implement macro-marketing a pandemic. This summary specifically focuses on mis-assigned labelling of pandemics and its representational repercussions for dehumanizing rhetoric. Given that at times of pandemics, people become predisposed to scapegoating, we highlight the urgency for marketers and policy makers for a more mindful approach to marketing and management. Specifically, this study raises concerns of using labels such as the Chinese or Wuhan virus for Covid-19 and using social psychology theories, details the aetiology of such constructions. In doing so, this study proposes for a more emancipatory approach to understanding the issue of nomenclature for infectious diseases, one which operates beyond the mere name effect of such diseases. Examples are provided from several countries to demonstrate best practice and standalone cases such as the United Kingdom's galvanizing efforts around its health services.

Covid-19 has splintered open a multitude of unprecedented challenges at local, national, and international level. Amidst this global crisis we are reminded yet again (Bashford, 2003; 2006) of the imperative to destigmatize pandemics (Satel, 2020). Currently, we have witnessed this stigmatization at multiple levels. Take for instance, calling the virus the "Wuhan" or "Chinese" virus by segments in the US and the concomitant and growing Americanization of the virus by some Chinese commentators, or "Jihad Virus" by populist voices in India. Conditioning public perceptions of the "other" with an infectious disease is nothing new (Bashford, 2003; 2006; Aaltola, 2011). History is replete with the fusion of "bio-medical and politico-military languages of defence, immunity, resistance and invasion, of the body, the community and the nation" (Bashford, 2003, p. 4). Public perceptions of pandemics can become conditioned with "scapegoats" and the "other" as causal agents, and have served to capitulate ideological agendas, often evading individual and collective conscious processing (Laidlaw and Moffatt, 2019). Indeed, disease control has a rich tradition of enabling states to "govern" not only "this side" but also "that side, of the border as well" (Bashford, 2007, p. 2) but the historical genealogy of de-humanizing rhetoric in managing pandemics and in general, has shown that it can spiral into hate, discrimination, torture and pre-emptive attacks (Bashford, 2006; Bain et al, 2014). Whilst we note that the frontline of destigmatizing pandemics is the nomenclature, we also highlight the need for the wider framing around the pandemic's discourse as just as essential to evaluate.

Until as recently as 2015, the common practice has been to name bacterial and viral infections by the location of origin but in 2015, the World Health Organisation (WHO) recognized the inherent risks of such an approach and proposed a new set of labelling guidelines. As Dr Keiji Fukuda (2015), Assistant Director-General for Health Security, WHO, stated: "This may seem like a trivial issue to some, but disease names really do matter to the people who are directly affected. We've seen certain disease names provoke a backlash against members of particular religious or ethnic communities, create unjustified barriers to travel, commerce and trade, and trigger needless slaughtering of food animals. This can have serious consequences for peoples 'lives and livelihoods" (WHO, 2015). The new practice guidelines stipulate disease names should adopt generic descriptors (e.g., respiratory disease, watery diarrhoea, etc), or more specific nomenclature based on the manifestation of the disease, based on who it targets, its severity or seasonality (e.g., progressive winter, etc) or when the pathogen is known, to include its causal agent within the nomenclature (e.g., coronavirus, salmonella, etc). The traditional convention of using geographical locations (e.g., Middle East Respiratory Syndrome) or species of animals is discouraged, as is people's names or cultural references. The nefarious nature of governing pandemics complicates the fusion of defence against pandemic fears as coupled with the 'other 'further. Whilst nomenclature is a critical first line of defence against this maladaptive ideography from developing, the polysemic nature of pandemics predisposes 'othering 'schema to develop.

This study therefore seeks to provide an overview of why and how dehumanizing rhetoric can emerge during a pandemic. We shift the focus from nomenclature alone to the wider discourse of conditioning "others" with pandemics. We argue that history is replete with such geo-politicising of pandemics and if the global community is to avoid the mistakes of the past, then these dynamics must be factored in governing them. The rest of this overview is structured as follows. First, we overview the polysemy of pandemics. Second, we detail how two inter-related theoretical streams – enemy image construction theory and Terror Management Theory (Greenberg et al, 1986) – can explain how and why scapegoating can become almost 'natural ' responses to pandemics and therefore the urgency to ameliorate these dynamics from the onset. We integrate the notion of constabulary functions (Burke, 1938) as rhetorical devices for managing publics (Jack, 2008), as complementing our understanding of garnering public unification in terms of a pandemic. Fourth, we offer a brief review of (mis)managing collective self-esteem during the current pandemic, citing the USA and the UK as comparative cases. Finally, we offer the lens of empathy-based communications as a solution to the current crisis, both for inter and intra state governance.

Whilst numerous studies exist detailing the polysemic dynamics of pandemics, and a rich repertoire detailing the geo-political nature of pandemics, we make a humble addition to this body of knowledge from a marketing management perspective. Whilst and we hope a raft of studies will emerge on facilitating the global, national, and local social marketing of pandemics, and studies from an organisational and consumer perspective, we intend to contribute to the debate in emancipatory and mindful marketing for policy makers. We feel the polysemic nature of pandemics predisposes their governance to geo-political framing, and therefore policymakers should ensure the slippery slope of conditioning pandemics, advertently or inadvertently, is monitored, evaluated, and controlled for. We provide next a backdrop to understanding pandemics as polysemic in nature. We hope this review provides others to understand the multi-dimensional nature of pandemics as extending beyond the causal virus to the socio-cultural and geo-political associations that can and do ensue.

13.1 A POLYSEMIC PERSPECTIVE ON THE LABELLING OF PANDEMICS.

Pandemic scares are polysemous in nature, in that they intersect between multiple layers of reality and as a result, are often not clear to conscious processing at both the individual and collective level (Aaltola, 2011). Indeed, perceptions of risk are if anything but objective but during a pandemic - compounded by fear, threat and confusion - subjectivity is amplified. Individual level anxieties are coupled to the social or collective body and therefore perceptions of risk during a pandemic are inherently socio-culturally mediated. As Durodie (2012. p. 2) clarifies, pandemic related risk perceptions are:

impacted upon by a vast number of social, cultural and political variables, such as the cumulative impact upon our imagination of books, television programmes and films that project dystopian – or positive – visions of the present and the future, as well as our interpretation and understanding – or not – of the forces and actors shaping our lives, as well as whether we believe – rightly or wrongly – that the authorities have ever been mistaken about a crisis before.

Given its polysemous nature, people don't necessarily react, and contrary to what we might expect, to perceptions of disease and death in the same way. A one glove fits all approach therefore omits the complexity of how different cultures process pandemic scares. Perceptions of pandemics are influenced by different learning histories, socialization processes and cultural dispositions of individuals (Chapman and Wyckoff, 1981). Aaltola (2012) digresses these complex representational properties of 'pandemic scares 'and coined the phrase 'politisomatics '(i.e., politico-somatics) to refer to how individual somatic-level anxieties related to disease and mortality, become fused with the "hierarchical interconnectedness of the global polity" (Aaltola, 1999, p. 235). The ontological security, or the sense of security and safety individuals feel in an unpredictable world (Browning, 2013), becomes coupled with world related 'pains', often shaped by the framing of state centric prevalent political imageries and the ideological agendas embedded in them (Aaltola, 2012). Therefore, actual and feared global political pains, in essence can transcend and become embodied at the level of individual body pain. In politico-somaticizing pandemics, Aaltola (2012) is introducing the macro political dimension, or power-political embodiments, to understanding the management of pandemics at the individual level. Developing the work of Susan Sontag (1988) who observed the nature of pandemics, as crystallizing epochal individual and political fears, Aaltola (2012) argues that such embodied macro-level imageries, anxieties, and vulnerabilities become infused at the micro-level. Effectively, pandemics become as 'scary 'as they do because individuals embody the "prevailing declining imageries and… other historically conditioned sensibilities, insecurities and vulnerabilities". It is for this reason, that during pandemics and any substantial collective crisis, states and indeed supra national bodies, employ a complex trajectory of 'constabulary functions '(Laidlaw and Moffatt, 2019), or the set of rhetorical strategies to create order out of disorder (Burke, 1937; Jack, 2008).

Pandemic scares can thus be explained as polito-somatic in that individual anxieties can become coupled to "images of political decline and regression of the prevailing world order as a hegemonic embodiment". Pandemic imagination is therefore anchored, in Watts (1999, p. 10) described as a "configuration of temporal sensibilities and institutional anxieties". Central to the type of social configuration emerging from pandemic scares is the infusion of apocalyptic tropes, largely emanating from media and policy making narratives but taping into and reifying deep seated cultural anxieties (Watts, 1999). These tropes serve to shift pandemics from being imminent to immanent or creating the "perception of an event as already in the process of happening even though it is yet to come" and whereby "a profound sense of instability and insecurity takes root, a feeling that can result in sweeping interventions" (ibid. p. 62). One can only imagine of the number of regulations passed through, in the name of the public without public awareness or consent, during the global management of Covid-19 for precisely the same reason. Using Kermode's (2000) logic of Kairos - or a turning point which condenses the past, present and future into a meaningful relation - Watt (1999) suggests such pandemic Kairos moments become experienced as prophetic visions for the public, i.e., utopian imaginings and transformations or the renewal of the body and its embodied body politic (Gomel, 2004). In essence, the global 'lockdown 'globally during 2020, was one such Kairos moment, during which the destruction of the old – the overcoming of the pestilence of the pandemic – for many became positioned with a seductive ideological brave new world (Gomel, 2004), and therefore a re-generation of the social body, or the "new norm" as public and social policy in several countries marketed this change.

What emerges is a renewal of what Buck-Morss (2002) described as the dreamworld, or the collective mental state and analytical concept related to "modernity as re-enchantment of the world" and its associative "expressions of a utopian desire for social arrangements that transcend existing forms" (ibid. x-xi). Adherents of such utopian worldviews, more common in secular societies who view progress linearly, typically hold that 'progressive hope '(Rutjens et al, 2009) or the faith that things will get better than they were before, i.e. the 'new normal', "would ultimately lead to a utopian society" (ibid. p. 540). Moreover, the defence of such 'progressive hope 'worldviews amplify when individuals perceive threats to their mortality (Rutjens et al, 2009), since in the face of mortality-salient threats, affiliation to in-group worldviews buffers against anxiety caused by mortality-salient cues (Greenberg et al, 1988). Pursuits of these dreamworlds, and the underpinning worldviews which shape them can take a dangerous turn when their energy is misused by instrumental structures of power (Buck-Morss, 2000). If the perceived threat to one's mortality is great enough, support for worldviews and associated dreamworlds can accumulate to the point of ethical blindness, or the "temporary inability of a decision maker to see the ethical dimension of a decision at stake" (Palazzo et al. 2012, p. 325), especially if the perceived threat is conditioned to out-groups (Greenberg et al, 1988). Social identity theory (Tajfel and Turner, 1979) supports this assertion since positive in-group self-evaluations and negative out-group evaluations have self-protective and self-enhancing functions, nominally at the level of self-esteem (Turner et al, 1987). The danger of course with such dynamics is that they can cause "good people to behave in pathological ways that are alien to their nature" (Zimbardo 2007, p. 195). Herein lies the challenge of fostering a humanized, emancipatory, and transformative pathway for the collective community, immersed in the rapture of confusion and uncertainty of Kairos, to adopt.

The nature of pandemics as polysemous points to a much more complicated debate than merely destigmatizing nomenclature alone. Whilst neutralising the name of a disease is an essential foundation in adaptive governance of a pandemic, it represents the surface of a deeper body of anxieties and associated copying pathways, which can turn in either adaptive or maladaptive directions. More so than normally, the direction of self-esteem recovery in times of crisis should be averted away from scapegoating targets to a unifying discourse of collective self-esteem. Given the dangers of spill over into de-humanizing out-groups when under perceived threat, the need to effectively manage communal self-esteem could not be more critical. We provide further theoretical discussion of (mis)managing this collective self-esteem.

13.2 MANAGING COLLECTIVE SELF-ESTEEM

The challenge to avert the in-out group bridge from expanding during a crisis is therefore critical enhance collective self-esteem and therefore pro-social interventions. A universal need, self-esteem is "achieved by excelling in activities valued by one's peer group or society and gaining the respect of actors whose opinions matter" (Lebow 2008, p. 61). Since self-esteem and national or even civilizational identity can become inter-wined (Browning, 2013), the celebration of national projects during a crisis can therefore buffer against anxiety caused by the impending sense of fear from a pandemic. Developing a communal sense of purpose, by fostering empathy for collective members, is central to this type of collective self-esteem governance. In the recent formulation of Phronetic marketing (Kotler and Komori, 2020), the father of modern marketing and the CEO of FujiFilm, explains how FujiFilm survived and thrived through disruption and chaos by galvanising a common purpose for its workforce of ninety thousand employees, almost all demotivated with the fear of liquidation, by fostering empathetic orientation between employees. This, in turn activated employee self-esteem and generated greater creativity to formulate social innovations to keep FujiFilm ahead of the mar-ketplace curve. Whilst the Kotler-Komori way is an organisational approach, the lessons of empathy and mindful marketing are the same for fostering goodwill between people in confusion, fear and panic and emerging stronger as a result through adaptive transcendence (Hyman et al, 2020; Shabbir et al, 2021).

Moreover, the evolutionary flourishing of humanity has been attributed to cross-group Corporation and singularly, this has been attributed to humanity's capacity for empathy (Zaki and Ochsner, 2012). Not sur-prisingly therefore, fostering empathy is considered central in rehumanising others and conflict resolution (e.g., Halpern and Weinstein, 2004; Bonds, 2009; Paul and Decker, 2013). Empathising, or imagining the other person's perspective (Halpern and Weinstein, 2004), also necessitates "on recognising that the other has a mind" like one's own (Fiske, 2019; p. 31). The association of zoomorphic metaphors for "others" has a nefarious history beyond the scope of this study but the primal examples being Western colonialism's usage of the "negro-ape" metaphor (Lott, 1999) and the notorious Nazi rhetoric of Jews as the "vermin of humanity" (Mieder, 1982). A more recent example includes press descriptions of immigrants as "aliens" or "parasites" (Musolf, 2015).

The UK's efforts to place the needs of the NHS at 'centre point 'in the discourse surrounding the pandemic was therefore logical from several perspectives. On the one hand it provided awareness of the immediate need for capacity management of intensive care units available at any one given time but at a polysemic level, it provided a unifying and collective self-esteem at the level of the social body. Given the polysemy of pandemics, the UK government was able to leverage empathy for NHS staff to create collective self-esteem. This therefore can also be viewed as a convenient and necessary constabulary function to channel national momentum to avoid misdirection in social attitudes, i.e., towards scapegoating for instance. The fact that over 750,000 people responded to calls for volunteering to help the NHS during the current crisis is testa-ment of the unifying momentum created by anchoring the need of the NHS as a collective duty and responsibility. The government's behavioral call to action for its public mantra rests on "Stay at Home. Pro-tect the NHS. Save Lives" further fusion of salvation of the self with the collective body as expressed through the communal connection that the NHS is for the British public. As did the national call to show appreciation to the staff of the NHS at 8pm of the 26th of March. For Laidlaw and Moffatt (2019), positioning heroes, and typically healthcare staff during a pandemic is vital for channelling public anxieties in an adaptive direction. Moreover, the UK media avoided the type of stigmatizing tropes emerging from segments in the US hierar-chy. In comparison, many states such as the U.S., Brazil, Russia, and India did not demonstrate a unified approach and instead were characterised by either divisionary or scapegoating rhetoric (Shabbir et al, 2021). Pandemic management, and its marketing, should ideally be decoupled from identity politics. Unfortunately, in many states this was not the case and instead collective narcissism was allowed to flourish. Collective narcissism has since been shown to weaker effects on collective goodwill during Covid (Van Bavel and Boggio 2020).

Sticking to U.K.'s example, the conditioning of the public to preserving their own health with the collective of the NHS was particularly, and at least initially (Shabbir et al, 2021), robust in engineering transcendence or 'symbolic bridging and merging '(Burke, 1937; Jack, 2008; Laidlaw and Moffatt, 2019). Transcendence encourages the conversion of old negatives to new positives. By educating the public of the intensive bed shortage, to self-care through isolation so not to spread the virus and inundate the NHS, the public engaged in a new mode of collective and civic responsibility. The fostering of a communal spirit during a crisis also fends off against alienation or cultural lag. Cultural lag or alienation denotes to a sense of dispossession and spiritual and material isolation from the unifying frame from the state (Burke, 1937; Jack, 2008; Laidlaw and Moffatt, 2019). Of course, alienation of those hesitant to Covid compliance has amplified since the early stages of lockdown, an effect this study believes is reflective of a breakdown in inclusive symbolic bridging, i.e., poorly designed communications which fail to capture the trust of a diverse mix of opinions in the population. The role of the third sector here is critical in fostering acts of community volunteering to ensure those most at risk of alienation are kept 'within the safety net'. The UK government and indeed others are advised to not let such alienated sub-groups fall by the 'wayside', or indeed become the demonised "other". The pursuit of collective resilience should not come at the expense of alienating sub-groups, especially those that are most vulnerable in society.

A second round of communal momentum building and yet a third, and numerous more would therefore be required to ensure that everyone within society is enabled towards emancipatory transcendence. Specific reassurances may need to be afforded to vulnerable sub-groups and their gatekeepers. Maladaptive trends such as the spike in calls to Childline, a service for children who are being abused in the U.K (Hockaday, 2020) is but one example from a myriad of where the most vulnerable in society have been neglected by a lack of inclusive pandemic preparedness. Specific campaigns for instance celebrated again at the collective level, to ensure optimal support, for teachers and children or for the third sector, and its multitude of beneficiaries, may be warranted in countries to remind the wider strata of society of groups at risk. While we have extolled the U.K.'s example of collectiveness around its NHS, a subsequent breakdown in collective trust due to confused messaging regressed some of this goodwill (Hyman et al, 2020; Wardman, 2020). It is therefore critical to sustain momentum around inclusive and collective communications.

13.2.1 MISMANAGING COLLECTIVE SELF-ESTEEM

Out-groups who are seen to challenge one's worldview, especially under conditions where mortality is made salient, as in during a pandemic, compromise the buffering function of one's worldview and self-esteem (Greenberg et al, 1988). Consequently, to reduce anxiety, people may manage such threats, by derogating, dehumanizing, or vilifying threatening out-groups "or, if the threat is sufficiently strong, simply exterminating them" (Pyszczynski et al, 2008, p. 318). The consensus in enemy image constriction theory supports this perspective further since the formation of the enemy image is closely tied to the origins and consequences of group stereotypes (Alexander et al, 1999). As Vuorinen (2012) explains, "inventing an enemy begins, paradoxically, with the invention of the self" by fostering the human tendency to "define the self as good and the opposing other as less" (p. 1). A Psychodynamic explanation of projection and displacement, often used to account for the development of "otherness" in enemy image theory (Vuorinen, 2012), goes yet further. This approach argues that in order to protect the mental self, people who are unable to deal on a conscious" level with their anxieties and hostilities" (Silverstein, 1089, p. 905) especially those related to what is "considered evil, destructive or weak" may project or displace them on to a socially accepted source of hostility and fear" (p. 905). Covid 19 unfortunately has witnessed too many of such mal-adaptive cases of scapegoating others. The use of the 'Jihadi Virus 'term in India for instance displaced insecurities of populist segments towards Muslim minorities.

The mutual dehumanization between segments in the US and China witnessed its own vicious 'infodemic' —spiralling into a blame game on both sides, with each accusing the other of having manufactured the virus and amplified across respective social media landscapes. For the Chinese, this emerged after its celebrated doctor Zhong Nanshan stated in a press conference (27th February) that the "virus may not have originated in China". Subsequently, high profile Chinese officials including the Chinese ambassador to South Africa and a Foreign Office spokesperson declared the same. A flurry of Chinese social media sentiments followed. In the US, the New York times in a tweet (24th January) referred to the virus as the "Wuhan virus" – a term which it has subsequently (since the 10th of March) declared as racist. The term in variant forms, Chinese and 'Kung Flu' included, proliferated in its use across the US media and online landscapes. From US Secretary of State Michael Pompeo and President to Donald Trump to numerous Republican Senators, to countless media commentaries, the terminology became close to mainstream within Republican quarters.

The stark reality of promulgating Covid-19 as the "Chinese virus" even raised alarm bells with the FBI. Josh Margolin from ABC News (2020) reports: "The FBI assesses hate crime incidents against Asian Americans likely will surge across the United States, due to the spread of coronavirus disease... endangering Asian American communities... based on the assumption that a portion of the US public will associate COVID-19 with China and Asian American populations." A report by Atlanta Council's Digital Forensic Research (DFR) lab reported that some U.S politicians are exploiting anti-Coronavirus fears with anti-Chinese "dog whistles", or 'coded language that can be used to denigrate a group while publicly denying you are doing it '(DFR, 2020). The DFR's analysis of social media engagement demonstrated a clear amplification, namely through retweets and resharing, linked to instances when Republican Senators and President Trump have publicly dog whistled such terms. For instance, within an hour of Republican Senator Paul Gosar's infamous tweet (March 8th) describing the virus as the "Wuhan virus, the term was retweeted 24,049 times within an hour. A concomitant rise in anti-Chinese and anti-Asian online hate crimes is emerging with the Chinese Affirmative Action group reporting 550 incidents of hate and discriminatory comments already reported (Donaghue, 2020).

Xenophobia in Europe also witnessed a rise, with for instance a French front-page headline on the Courier Picard declaring "Alerte Jaune" (Yellow Alert) and reports of hotels and restaurants in Italy having barred Chinese people specifically. The amplified immediacy of the threat presented by the pandemic by some media pundits, and indeed policy makers, therefore needs to be offset by ensuring that threat levels do not reach a threshold whereby a side effect becomes defining the self by vilifying the "other". Here, the UK's media has, by and large, adopted a coherent policy of not using the "Chinese virus" nomenclature but this does not by any means, that a maladaptive response is pre-empted. Given the propensity for people to develop such mal-adaptive coping strategies during a pandemic is amplified (Gilmore and Sommerville, 1994) and history, replete with the strategic use of scapegoating during times of pandemics for leveraging ideological identity projects for instance (Bashford, 2004; 2006), the slippery slope of state frames to "panic" and use scapegoats as constabulary functions to avert the public's gaze towards their own weaknesses, is a real danger during a pandemic.

Medical ethicists, Gilmore, and Somerville (1994) note that when segments of the population under threat enter denial (and therefore alienation), "symbolic processes of scapegoating" can take form since such individuals have rejected the adaptive copying frames from the state and are essentially on the lookout for someone to blame. By encouraging such tropes, politicians and policy makers are activating the alienated group. Dangerously, the bridge to collective utopia and emergence from the crisis, enters an acceptance and endorsement of dystopia preceding the emergence to recovery. To achieve the collective dream project, some have to be sacrificed is the worst-case scenario when politicians actively promote stigmatizing tropes during a pandemic, or neglect those most at risk from developing such attitudes, i.e., the alienated. The spikes in gun sales in some US states, in the advent of the virus, should give caution to US policy makers, since such sub-groups are essentially alienated to the communal collective transcendency approach and therefore more predisposed to scapegoating behaviors. Whilst Donald Trump has cited the Chinese rhetoric of Americanising the virus, as justifying his insistence to use the "Chinese virus" metaphor, the risk of a domino effect developing within alienated communities has to be leveraged. Similarly, the Chinese hierarchy are well advised to avoid 'Americanising the viruses to avoid a spiralling of mutual de-humanization. Whilst both rhetors may be using mutual de-humanization to manage their own public perceptions at home, as mutual constabulary functions, the targets on the receiving end of such mutual rhetoric are likely to be primarily American Asians and Americans in China. Moreover, the growing xenophobia may serve to additionally mask and therefore create an ethical blind spot towards the marginalised and vulnerable within society.

Concerns in Europe of a rising 'social bomb '(Ferguson, 2020) for instance remind us of this concern. Francesco Rocco, head of the International Federation of Red Cross and Red Crescent Societies noted, "We have a lot living very marginalised, in the so-called black hole of society... this is a social bomb that can explode at any moment because they don't have any way to have an income". Rocco further warned of the risk of suicide increasing amongst the most vulnerable forced to isolate on their own (Ferguson, 2020). It is when groups feel dispossessed that they are most predisposed to engineering maladaptive responses, and for some sub-groups - this may involve scapegoating. Hence the dangers of providing "dog whistles" against an 'out-group 'during a pandemic - the potent cocktail of marginalisation and ideology but needs a spark for the spiral of de-humanization to take hold. Moreover, marginalization extends to other sub-groups and diseases. Reporting in the Namibian, Arlana Shikongo (11th March 2020) reports that despite 332 cases of Hepatitis E reported since the start of 2020, and no casualties from Covid-19, the health ministry's resources are being placed towards managing Covid-19, at the expense of the acute Hep E crisis in the country. Good governance of Covid-19, above all else, should not fall prey into victim to the polysemy of pandemics.

13.3 REHUMANIZATION: ENDNOTE

To foster the type of nation level and cross nation level collective spirit needed during a pandemic, media outlets and indeed social media channels should actively discourage dehumanizing rhetoric as should regulators. Evidence of anti-European rhetoric is emerging in the British press and media for instance with headlines such as "The EU's cack-handed response to coronavirus is proof we were right to get out" (or "Coronavirus shows Brussels true colours as 'very weak EU institution 'crushed by crisis". Whilst such headlines may offer some temporary measure to shield the British public from gazing inwards into its own state of play in relation to Covid-19, a global problem demands a global empathetic orientation. Here, the UN and the WHO have a role to play in fostering this orientation of nations towards each other, and towards their own publics, especially the vulnerable in society.

Given the new brave world we enter with Covid-19, we propose a braver than the current interventions proposed by state and international leadership. This short treatise proposes the use of Oelofsen's (2009) rehumanization process at intra and interstate levels. Oelofsen (2009) suggested Lugones's (1987) mental 'world travel', to mentally transport oneself into another's world to "take [his or her] perspective" (ibid, p. 17). This form of imagining the situation of another has already been adopted by the UK, to foster empathy and identification with the NHS staff – we propose extending the realm of this to all sub-groups within the state, especially the most vulnerable but also, and critically, to those hesitant of vaccinating, and extending it beyond the borders to other states and their situations. A multi-dimensional influx of empathy or mindful marketing to let empathy run its own course of proposed. People become indifferent to others when they render other's lives invisible and therefore imaginative empathy allows one to grasp the reality experienced by others as a possibility for oneself, even when there are substantial differences (Oelofsen, 2009). Much more work needs to be done to digress some of the issues raised in this short review. Covid-19 and its management may well dominate every sector, academia included for a generation but by this small contribution we encourage an emancipatory approach. Numerous good example case studies from The Netherlands provide good case studies for students in national marketing during Covid-19 on how to galvanise the collective goodwill of citizenship. Marketing and management as disciplines will also need to reflect within, and approach pandemics, as indeed other disciples as essentially polysemic in nature. Given this polysemy, an emancipatory logic of freeing silenced voices should be prioritised so that we as a generation at an epochal moment do indeed make the future more prepared, more empathetic, and more mindful of how and why we communicate the way do during a time of crisis.

14. MARKETERS WITHOUT BORDERS

"Our marketing doesn't work." And I ask: "Why don't you hire a marketing consultant to help you?" They say: "It's too expensive."

The result is that many start-ups and companies do no marketing or poor marketing and lack a budget to pay for professional marketing help.

It's like the complaints of a group of sick persons. "Why don't you get a doctor?" "But we can't afford a doctor!" I say: "Why don't you try Doctors without Borders."

Let's look at the story of Doctors without Borders before we talk about Marketers without Borders. Here is an abbreviated sketch drawn from their account of their history.

In May 1968, a group of young doctors decided to go and help victims of wars and major disasters. This new brand of humanitarianism would reinvent the concept of emergency aid. They were to become Médecins Sans Frontières (MSF), known internationally in English as Doctors Without Borders. French TV was broadcasting scenes of children dying from hunger in remote corners of the world. In southern Nigeria, the province of Biafra was surrounded by the Nigerian army and the Biafran people were decimated by famine. The French Red Cross issued an appeal for volunteers. For a number of years, Max Recamier and Pascal Greletty-Bosviel—volunteer doctors with the International Committee of the Red Cross (ICRC) in Geneva—had been regularly intervening in armed conflicts.

A team of six set off to Biafra: two doctors—Max Recamier and Bernard Kouchner—as well as two clinicians and two nurses. These fledgling doctors found themselves having to provide war surgery in hospitals that were regularly targeted by the Nigerian armed forces.

In the following three years, other doctors began to speak up. These doctors, or "Biafrans," as they were known, began to lay the foundations for a new and questioning form of humanitarianism that would ignore political or religious boundaries, and prioritize the welfare of those suffering.

In 1971, Raymond Borel and Philippe Bernier, journalists from the medical review Tonus, issued an appeal to establish a band of doctors to help people suffering in the midst and wake of major disasters.

MSF was officially created on December 22, 1971. At the time, 300 volunteers made up the organization: doctors, nurses, and other staff, including the 13 founding doctors and journalists.

It became readily apparent that preparation was lacking, doctors were left unsupported, and supply chains were tangled. Some doctors wanted to stay a small commando unit of emergency doctors—and others who wanted to get organized."

In 1979, a vote was made on whether MSF should become more organized or remain a band of guerrilla doctors. Eighty percent voted in favour of the former. From this point, the new "realist" leadership of MSF would help transform MSF into the professional organization it is today.

In 2023, Türkiye and Syria have suffered from devastating earthquakes. It was again Doctors without Borders who had provided humanitarian help North West Syria. Although Türkiye is not registered to the system, Doctors without Borders collaborated with local partner organizations to help Türkiye as well.

As of 2024, MSF has 68,000 people working for them in over 77 countries across the world. Since its founding, MSF has treated over a hundred million patients. Even though one of the backbones of its funding is coming from donations; MSF maintained its institutional and financial independence offering effective and timely medical to those who need it most.

14.1 MARKETERS WITHOUT BORDERS

Marketers without Borders (MWB) would need to develop its own history and purpose. It starts with the idea that many start-ups and companies are dissatisfied with their marketing efforts and need help. They don't know where to get it and they can't afford it. To respond, we recognize that there are many professional and experienced marketers along with many academic marketers who might volunteer their time to look at tough company marketing problems and suggest remedies. Each volunteer would list his or her specialties and experiences.

Marketers without Borders would initially be tested in a small Turkish city. Suppose the city is Nazilli, Aydin, population approximately 160,000. The city has some industrial companies, many restaurants, and several cultural organizations. The following announcement is prepared and circulated in Nazilli, Aydin.

IS YOUR STARTUP OR COMPANY SATISFIED WITH ITS MARKETING? IF NOT, CONTACT **MARKETERS WITHOUT BORDERS**. PHONE NUMBER.

Each caller is told that everything will be confidential. The MWB agent asked the calling organization to briefly describe its business, marketing system and strategy, along with marketing questions that the caller has. The MWB agent tells the caller that an appropriate volunteer will be identified, and that person will call the caller and arrange for further discussion or a meeting.

If the caller is satisfied to work with the volunteer, the caller signs a statement that this caller's company takes full responsibility for whatever it decides to do with the MWB's advice, with no liability attached to the volunteer or MWB. The MWB volunteer signs a statement that he or she will hold confidential all facts about the company.

At the end of each engagement, the MWB volunteer writes up the major findings and advice without identifying the specific company. This goes into a case file that volunteers can look at for new ideas.

If the engagement leads to positive results, the caller company might want to show its appreciation to the volunteer or MWB itself. This is up to the parties themselves. The caller company might make an appreciation payment to the MWB volunteer and even ask the volunteer to give further advice on a paid basis. The calling company might donate to MWB to help MWB grow and cover its expenses.

If the results are positive in Nazilli, Aydin, this means that Nazilli's organizations have become better marketing performers and that Nazilli has experienced economic growth and improved livelihoods.

Now it is time for MWB to expand to other cities and learn more on attracting client companies, in attracting excellent volunteer marketers, and in raising money to expand abroad. If MWB is successful, one could imagine MWB branches all over the world. If more companies around the world learn how to use marketing more effectively, marketing will perform as a positive change agent and a force in global economic growth.

14.1.1 ISSUES TO BE RESOLVED

The first issue is that existing paid marketing consultants will oppose to this new disruptive competition. They might get legislators to rule against using unlicensed volunteer marketing advisors. They might publicize cases of poor marketing advice coming from MWB volunteers. The same happened early in Doctors

Without Borders with the charge that some poorly trained doctors were doing more harm than good. This means that MWB must be careful in their choice of marketing volunteers to match to company situations.

The second issue is how centralized or decentralized MWB should be. If MWB is highly centralized in setting standards, raising money, and choosing volunteers, this will protect its reputation better. If MWB is highly decentralized, then each branch is fairly free to set up its own standards and some shady practices might take place in certain locations.

The third issue: "What is good marketing advice?" Three experienced marketers might look at the same client situation and end up giving three different judgments of what the client should do. If the three marketers, then compared and discussed their ideas, they might come to agree on the best advice. But MWB is not set up to send three volunteers to work with the client. Overtime, MWB will get an idea about which volunteers are creating the most value for their clients. And overtime, MWB might run classes for marketing volunteers on the most recent developments in marketing and a review of recent cases that were successfully carried out.

14.1.2 CONCLUSION

At this time, Marketers without Borders does not exist. It is just an idea that might contribute to raising marketing's profile and positive impact on the performance of start-ups and existing companies. To get it further developed, I would be happy to receive written comments to improve the idea. With luck, I will also hear from a few marketers who would like to take over the idea, set up MWB, and move it through a number of cities, learning along the way, and launching MWB more visibly around the world.

14.2 LIFE AFTER COVID

Lockdowns, quarantines, masks, and social distancing had ended in late 2021 and people returned back to their normal lives. But has everything returned back to normal? Did Covid changed some tendencies of people. Is new normal, a relatively new normal?

14.2.1 THE "OLD NORMAL"

People would travel to and from work in their car or in public transportation. They didn't mind a crowded bus or train. They worked in a factory or office from 9 to 5. At home, in the evening, they enjoyed familiar food. They watched the news. They would watch a Monday evening football game. They would retire. Their weekend would be filled with going to parks, doing various tasks, joining friends at a restaurant, or enjoying a barbeque with friends.

During the Covid period, If we took a vote, most people would vote to resume this lifestyle. Now after the Covid period, what a blessing not to worry about germs, shaking hands, hugging a friend, going to see a movie, or attending a political rally.

Yet some people will vote against returning to this old normal. They never liked it. There was too much drinking and fake sociability. People ate too much and gained weight. Their viewed their work life as tedious. They didn't like the long commute to and from work. Everyday seemed like Sameday with lots of hustle and at the end of the week a total burnout.

14.2.2 THERE ARE MANY NEW NORMALS

When Covid period finished, people returned to the old norm lifestyle or to what life style lived before Covid. It doesn't make sense to say that most people favored new normal to the old normal. There isn't one new normal. One only needs to ask persons what they would want if they didn't return to the old normal. There are many elements that can make made up a new normal. Here are some elements that some people would want their new normal to have:

- A place where one can live near their work or easily reach by bicycle or scooter.
- A place with good public transportation and fewer cars to pollute the air.
- A place growing more local food, even where households can grow some of their own food.
- A place carrying on local manufacturing of common items, so these items don't have to be ordered from the Far East.
- A place where food stores and restaurants offer healthier food.
- A place where companies carry on their business without their people needing to do much air travel.
- A place that invests in beautifying the surroundings, where many people garden and put a high value on communing with nature.
- A place that puts a high value on good air and water.
- A place with public schools that gets kids to love going to school and learning new things and new skills.
- A place that values science, has a good local college doing research to improve things.
- A place that welcomes different religious and spiritual groups and practices.
- A place that welcomes and respects different racial and ethnic groups.
- A place widespread and affordable 5G broadband.
- A place investing in solar and wind energy and mostly electric cars.
- A place with good and affordable medical services.
- A place where everyone cares about improving the environment, recycling, reusing, and eliminating waste.
- A place where people can find or build good housing at an affordable price.

People started to understand the vital place of fresh air, freedom of roaming and socializing in their lives. Even if they work and hustle in the most crowded area of Istanbul with an overloaded white-collar lifestyle or earning their life with agriculture in a small town of Türkiye; most people realized those vital components of "old normal".

After a whole nation of people have gone through a dark period, a period of "enforced stay-at home," of little sociability, of high unemployment, of a high number of deaths, they get new ideas about what matters and what constitutes a good life. People became conscious of many different lifestyles. Here are five different "new normal" lifestyles that depart from the "old normal."

14.2.2.1 Five Different 'New Normal" Lifestyles

First, a number of consumers are becoming *life simplifiers,* persons who want to eat less and buy less. They are reacting to the clutter of "stuff". They want to downsize their possessions, many of which lie around unused and unnecessary. Some life-simplifiers are less interested in owning goods such as cars or even homes; they prefer renting to buying and owning. They prefer a "minimalist" lifestyle. As e-commerce has grown dramatically during the Covid period, C2C e-commerce has also grown sharply. C2C or consumer-to-consumer e-commerce enables any consumer to become seller. Dolap, a Trendyol owned C2C e-commerce platform, reached to 1.4 million users as of 2024. This gives minimalists to get rid of some of their products and create a second income opportunity as well.

Second, another group of consumers are *Degrowth activists* who feel that too much time and effort go into consuming. This feeling is captured in William Wordworth's poem,

"The world is too much with us…
Getting and spending, we lay waste our powers:
Little we see in Nature that is ours.
We have given our hearts away, a sordid boon!"

Degrowth activists worry that consumption will outpace the carrying capacity of the earth. In 1970, the world population was 3.7 billion. By 2011, the world population grew to 7.0 billion. Today (2020) the world population stands at 7.7 billion. Today (2024) the world population stands around approximately 8.2 billion. The U.N. expects the world population to grow to 9.8 billion by 2050. The nightmare would be that the earth cannot feed so many people. The amount of arable land is limited and the topsoil is getting poorer. Istanbul's population is now more than 16 million officially, which is claimed to be even higher with unregistered people. In 1950, Istanbul's population was less than one million. It is a very intensive growth which makes Istanbul a very population dense city, considering the cities' small land relatively to it's significance.

Several areas in our oceans are dead zones with no living marine life. Degrowth activists call for conservation and reducing our material needs. They worry about the people in the emerging poor nations aspiring to achieve the same standard of living found in advanced countries, something that is not possible. They see greedy producers and marketers doing their best to create "false and unsustainable needs."

14.2.3 CONCLUSION

There were lots of talk about the life after Covid during that period. Many people enjoyed returning to their normal life after the Covid. People led many types of lives but there was a dominant type that we can call the old normal. Many people enjoyed returning to the old normal. But many others either didn't like the old normal or didn't live the old normal.

Now more people are aware of the value of the places where they can live out some values that offer them more hope and satisfaction.

More people became conscious of climate change, income inequality, poverty, hunger, homelessness, poor living accommodations, racism, guns, and other issues. People increasingly favor political candidates who offer some new solutions to these social problems Source: Published online in The Marketing Journal, July 2020.

14.3 EMPOWER US!

The world is in shambles. There is a perfect storm of poverty, income inequality, greed, corruption, racial and ethnic segregation, tribalism. The coronavirus pandemic created huge levels of infection, death, and depression. People are divided rather than united. The planet is dangerously heating up. Business leadership seems largely preoccupied with profits, not social issues. Government is dysfunctional and if anything, showing authoritarian tendencies.

Is there any way to bring order and happiness back into this dysfunctional world?

Crises proposed building better systems of capitalism and democracy, all moved by the spirit of the Common Good.

The authors call for transforming Old Power into New Power. They say "Old Power favours exclusivity, competition, and authority, while the New Power rests on open-source collaboration, sharing, and crowd wisdom. The Old Power is protected by secrecy and confidentiality, while the New Power requires radical transparency. The practices associated with Old Power are managerialism, institutionalism, unquestioning loyalty, and long-term affiliation, while the New Power relies on self-organization, networked governance, conditional affiliation, and participation. Power affects each stage of the Strategic Transformation process."

EmPower Us! will fill you with hope, purpose, and action. More people are challenging injustice and protest the mismanagement of our shared planetary resources. Young people, women, ethnic and other groups are protesting the broken world condition. You will learn about many Catalytic people and communities. The authors describe the inspiring work and values of particular companies – Starbucks, Unilever, Patagonia, Zappos, Ben & Jerry, Ikea, Nike – in running resilient, caring, and creative enterprises. The authors describe the brilliant work of Catalytic individuals – Richard Branson, Elon Musk, Jeff Bezos, and many others – in innovating fulfilling enterprises and enriching our standard of living.

EmPower Us! Provides a wake-up call with 12 Guidelines to shape and motivate the work of caring individuals and organizations. We need to live TEST values (Trust, Empathy, Sustainability, and Transparency) and drive them into our economic, social, and political interactions with our institutions.

The book describes what it would take to change both ourselves and our institutions to generate transformative decisions that reflect the needs of customers, employees, citizens, and communities. The path for people is to collaborate more with others who are working to create a better world. Values provide the foundation and Purpose translates these values into action and drives transformation.

The book provides a roadmap to transforming the world in a more loving and caring world filled with Harmony. The authors call for "a balance between what we think (Head), what we do (Hands), what we feel (Heart), and what we Hope (Purpose and Intent)." They want to bridge the gap between generations, cultures, nations, leaders, and the people they represent. They describe a set of values, models, and best practices to build an equitable economy and a sustainable future.

14.4 THE CONSUMER IN THE AGE OF CORONAVIRUS

The coronavirus COVID-19 effected the world dramatically creating a path of death and destruction. The world went through the danger of falling into a Great Depression, with millions of unemployed workers across the globe. Such crises mostly hit the poor – both in terms of health and economics; many cannot even afford to wash their hands because of the lack of water.

Businesses closed down, and people were urged to stay home, practiced social distancing, and vigorously washed their hands. People were stocking up on all kinds of food and sundries that were part of daily living. Some were hoarding masks, toilet paper, and other necessities should COVID-19 linger on for weeks, months, or years. Turkish Economic Stability Development included 100 billion Turkish Liras during the Covid 19 period.

This period of deprivation and anxiety ushered new consumer attitudes and behaviors that changed the nature of today's Capitalism. Covid period did not only change perception of consumers for the wellbeing of mankind and nature. Covid also changed people's tendency towards e-commerce. As they could not go outside to fulfill their daily needs, they got used to use e-commerce. Finally, citizens re-examined what they consume, how much they consume, and how all this is influenced by class issues and inequality. Citizens need to re-examine our Capitalist assumptions and emerge from this terrible period with a new, more equitable form of Capitalism.

14.4.1 CAPITALISM'S DEPENDENCE ON ENDLESS CONSUMING

Let's begin by taking a long view back to the emergence of the Industrial Revolution.

The Industrial Revolution of the 19th century greatly increased the number of goods and services available to the world's population. The steam engine, railroads, new machinery and factories, and improved agriculture greatly increased the economy's productive capacity. More production inevitably is more consumption. More consumption led to more investment. More investment increased production in an ever-expanding world of goods.

Citizens delighted in the availability of more goods and choices. They could individualize their personalities through their choices of food, clothing, and shelter. They could shop endlessly and marvel at the innovative offerings of the producers.

Citizens increasingly turned into consumers. Consuming became a lifestyle and culture. Producers profited greatly from the increasing number of active consumers. Producers were eager to stimulate more demand and more consumption. They turned to print advertising and sales calls, and as new media arose, they turned to telephone marketing, radio marketing, TV marketing, and Internet marketing. With the ease of buying products from e-commerce, which consumers had to get used to during Covid period, consumption increased even more. Business firms would profit from the degree they could expand consumer desire and purchasing.

From the beginning, some onlookers had misgivings about the rise of consumerism. Many religious leaders saw the growing interest of citizens in material goods as competing with religious attention and spiritual values. The legacy of puritanical values kept certain population groups from acquiring too many goods and getting into too much debt. Some citizens were particularly critical of wealthy consumers who used goods to flaunt their wealth. The economist Thorsten Veblen was the first to write about "conspicuous consumption" that he saw as a malady taking people away from more meditative lifestyles. In *The Theory of the Leisure Class,* Veblen exposed this sickness of status display. Had he lived long enough, he would have been aghast at the news that the former first lady of the Philippines, Imelda Marcos, owned 3,000 pairs of shoes that languished in storage since her exile from the Philippines. Especially with the dramatic rise of e-commerce, impulsive buying became even easier. We can see lots of white-collar Turkish people who tend to buy something impulsively from Trendyol, Hepsiburada or N11 in between their meetings, busy times; sometimes hedonically.

14.4.2 THE GROWING NUMBER OF ANTI-CONSUMERISTS

People or organizations that reject consumerism, which is a social and economic structure that promotes the acquisition and consumption of things and services in ever-increasing quantities, are known as anti-consumerists. People who oppose consumerism contend that it harms the environment, creates social inequity, and promotes the pursuit of material objects at the expense of deeper connections and experiences. They might support legislation that limits the impact of consumerism on society, promote ecological lifestyles, or advocate for alternative economic systems.

The rise in anti-consumerists can be attributed to a number of factors. These are a few potential causes:

Environmental issues: As people become more aware of the effects of climate change and resource depletion, they are paying more attention to their own consumption habits and seeking for ways to leave a smaller environmental imprint. Many people regard anti-consumerism as a method to lessen their impact on the environment.

Capitalism is criticized by certain people who believe that consumerism is a symptom of capitalism's larger issues, such as economic injustice, worker exploitation, and environmental damage. Interest in alternatives to consumerism is increasing along with criticism of capitalism.

Social and cultural changes: In recent years, there has been a rising realization that happiness and contentment may not always result from the pursuit of material objects and the increase of riches. As a result, a lot of individuals are looking for other strategies to give their lives meaning and purpose.

Online communities: The internet has made it easier than ever for people with similar interests to get in touch and exchange ideas. Especially with the rise of opinion sharing communities like Twitter, Quora or Reddit in the age of social media, the strength communities have been escalated even more. This boost has contributed to the development of a sense of community and support for anti-consumerism, which has in turn helped the movement flourish.

14.4.3 HOW BUSINESSES SUSTAIN THE CONSUMER SENTIMENT

Business firms have an intrinsic interest in endlessly expanding consumption for the purpose of higher profits. They rely on three disciplines to boost consumption and brand preference. The first is *innovation* to produce attractive new products and brands to enchant customer interest and purchase. Now as of 2024, the smart phone market has three screen foldable phones, which is an innovation for the consumers who wants to have the combination of a tablet and a smart phone. The second is *marketing* that supplies the tools to reach consumers and motivate and facilitate their purchasing. Especially with digitalization and Covid-19 enhanced dramatic rise of E-Commerce, it is now way easier to access to the consumers. The third discipline is *credit* to enable people to buy more than they could normally buy on their low incomes. This tendency increases the gap between high income and low-income consumers since low-income consumers spend the liras that they do not even have with taking loans, while high income people earn from bank interests. Businesses aim to make consumption our way of life. To keep their productive equipment and factories going, they must ritualize some consumer behavior. Days like Back-to-School Discounts, Black Friday, 11.11. are partly promoted to stimulate more purchasing. Businesses want not only to purchase of their goods but fast consumption so that objects burn up, wear out, and are discarded at an ever-increasing rate.

Businesses use advertising to create a hyper-real world of must-have products that claim to deliver happiness and well-being. Businesses refashion commodities into compelling brands that can bring meaning into the consumer's life. One's brand choices send a signal of who the person is and what he or she values. Brands bring strangers together to share carefully designed images and meanings.

14.4.3.1 How Will Anti-Consumerism Change Capitalism

Capitalism is an economic system devoted to continuous and unending growth. It makes two assumptions: (1) people have an unlimited appetite for more and more goods and (2) the earth has unlimited resources to support unlimited growth. Both of these are now questioned. First, many people become jaded and satiated by the effort to continuously consume more goods. Second, the earth's resources are finite, not infinite, and could not meet the needs of a growing world population that comes with growing material needs.

Until now, most countries have used only one measure to assess the performance of their economy. That measure is the Gross Domestic Product (GDP). GDP measures the total value of the goods and services produced in a given year by the country's economy. What it doesn't measure is whether GDP growth has been accompanied by a growth in people's well-being or happiness.

We can imagine a case where GDP grows by 2 or 3 percent by workers working very hard and even at over-time. They only have two weeks of vacation a year. They have little time for leisure or renewal.

As the automobile prices increased more than %100 percent within one year in Türkiye, it is getting more and more difficult to buy a car for people in Türkiye. There is no need to even talk about buying a home to live. Even just buying a smart phone or a computer costs a monthly salary. So, people who would like to buy something to increase their welfare might end up being in a huge dept. In such a case, we would guess that GDP went up but the nation's average well-being and happiness went down.

We badly need to add new measures of the impact of economic growth. Some countries are now preparing an annual measure of Gross Domestic Happiness (GDH) or Gross Domestic Well-Being (GDW). Is our addiction to consuming, consuming us?

Part of the problem of economic growth is that the fruits of gains in productivity are not shared equitably. This is obvious in a country with a growing number of billionaires and a great number of poor workers. Many CEOs are paid 300 times what their average worker earns, and some take home as much as 1100 times the average worker. The economic system is rigged. Corporations have succeeded in emasculating trade unions and leaving workers with no say in what they or their bosses should be paid. In terms of income inequality, Türkiye is number one with 42.6 coefficient compared to 29.6 of European Union.

Even some billionaires are unhappy with this greatly lopsided pay arrangement. Bill Gates and Warren Buffet have publicly called for raising the top income tax rate. One citizen billionaire, Nick Hanauer has spoken about this on TED. He warns his fellow billionaires that "the pitchforks are coming." He pleads with them to pay higher wages and taxes and share more of the productivity gains with the working class. The working class should earn enough to eat well, pay rent, and retire with adequate savings. Today there are too many workers who couldn't muster $400 to pay for a pressing payment they must make.

14.4.4 CAPITALISM AND COVID-19 CRISIS

Capitalism will change for other reasons as well. If more consumers decide to be anti-consumerists, they will spend less. Their spending has traditionally supported 70 percent of the economy. If this goes down, our economy contracts in size. A slowdown in economic growth will lead to more unemployment. Add the fact that more jobs are being lost to AI and robots. AI programs like ChatGPT and others took a significant step from 2022 to 2024. This will require Capitalism to spend more on unemployment insurance, Social Security, food stamps, food kitchens, and social assistance.

Capitalism will have to print more money. More trillions will have to be spent. This means huge deficits that can't be covered by existing tax revenues. To the extent possible, tax rates will have to be dramatically increased. The lives of the rich are normally not affected by the grief and hardship of the poor. But now it is time for the rich to pay more and share more. In our current crisis, CEOs and their highly paid staffs have to take a cut in their pay. Boeing's executives recently set an example by saying they will work with no pay during the coming crisis.

With the COVID-19 period, Capitalism needed a new stage. Some consumers tended be more careful about their consumption, however some got used to impulsive buying with getting more used to e-commerce. Here are some factors about post COVID-19 era:

1. Some weaker companies and brands or companies of some unlucky markets like restaurants vanished. Consumers needed to find reliable and satisfying replacement brands.

2. The Coronavirus made us aware of how fragile our health is. We can catch colds easily in crowds. We must stop shaking hands when we meet and greet. We need to eat more healthy foods to have a greater resistance to germs and flus.

3. We are shocked by the inadequacy of world's health system and its great cost. We need to stay out of the hospital and play safe.

4. The sudden loss of jobs remained a trauma even after workers get jobs back. Most of them now spend and save their money more carefully.

5. Staying home led many consumers to become producers of their own food needs. More home cooking, more gardening to grow vegetables and herbs. Less eating out.

6. We place more value on the needs of our family, friends, and community. We use social media to urge our families and friends to choose good and healthy foods and buy more sensible clothing and other goods.

7. We want brands will spell out their greater purpose and how each is serving the common good.

8. People became more conscious of the fragility of the planet, of air and water pollution, of water shortages, and other problems.

More people seek to achieve a better balance between work, family and leisure. Many moves from an addiction to materialism to sensing other paths to a good life. They will move to post-consumerism. For some people, considering the low income-high rent situation in Türkiye and understanding the value of natural and healthy lifestyle; more people started to move to country lifestyle, developing their own foods and living out of burnout and consumption culture of big city life.

Capitalism remains the best engine for efficient economic growth. It also can be the best engine for equitable economic growth. It doesn't change to socialism when we raise taxes on the rich. We have given up on the false economic doctrine that the poor win when the rich get richer. Actually, the rich will get richer mainly by leaving more money in the hands of working-class families to spend.

As the Coronavirus crisis has shown us, a robust public health system is in the best interest of all – rich and poor alike. It is time to rethink and rewire Capitalism and transform it into a more equitable form – based on democracy and social justice. We are all in this together.

14.5 THE ECONOMY AFTER COVID

After the COVID period consumers did not exactly continue their old shopping habits. In Wuhan, China where the coronavirus first struck, consumers remained extremely cautious when the government lifted travel and other restrictions. Many were afraid to go outside. A few started to go into groceries to get their supplies. A few started to order and pick up food from pizza stores and restaurants. Some started to venture into fast food outlets and a few dining restaurants that opened their doors. Not many ventured into shopping malls, especially since many businesses in these malls remained closed.

14.5.1 DEVELOPMENTS

After COVID period there has been changes in consumer behaviors, shopping behaviors and employment positions. Here are some of these observations:

1. Businesses that kept communicating with their customers and that acted with urgency and service during the crisis has been the first to realize strong business growth. These businesses were trusted to satisfy their former customers and employees.

2. Consumers found out that some brands and stores have disappeared and that they need to choose new brands and stores. A recent McKinsey study in China found that 33 percent of Chinese consumers had switched brands during Covid-19 and 20 percent planned to stick to these switched brands. Businesses that are aggressive in their pricing and promotion have won customers who have lost their former brands.

3. Many consumers might carry a new consciousness about being healthy that will affect their food and brand choices. They heard that many persons who died from coronavirus were weak from overweight, diabetes, and heart and lung problems. Some consumers might decide to avoid or minimize meat consumption and switch to vegetarian or vegan diets.

4. Consumers did not have a chance to shop from physical stores during the COVID period. Both for their impulsive purchases like buying more and more t-shirts from Trendyol or for buying their daily needs like supermarket shopping; there was no other chance than using e-commerce. So, consumers got used to shop from e-commerce. This did not change after the COVID period. People got used to e-commerce even more. Businesses started to invest more on e-commerce and its logistics, spread their consumer network to further cities or countries. Percentage of e-commerce among all trade activities has increased dramatically during and after the COVID period.

5. Businesses need to rethink their product and service strategies and their media relationships and output. They must research emerging changes in consumer attitudes and behavior brought about by the coronavirus. They must recognize a new landscape of competitors. A company might have to make changes in its value proposition, product lines, market segments and geographical areas. Multinational companies need a different reopening strategy for each customer nation based on that nation's experience during the coronavirus. Businesses need to invest in social and community programs and in personalization to attract and retain loyal customers.

14.5.2 CONCLUSION

Recent era has been the time for the world's nations to cooperate and help each other curb the growth of this enemy. This enemy makes old style fighting between nations seem absurd and senseless. Maybe the coronavirus has moved the world to finally get serious about building peace and goodwill among nations.

The coronavirus has highlighted the need to restructure capitalism to serve more people not only with jobs but with institutions delivering better health, education, and family care. The coronavirus has highlighted other needs as well. More attention needs to be paid to how technology and innovation can improve our lives. How can technology improve grocery buying, banking, online meetings and conferences? There has already been a huge tendency towards leaning to technological tools whether it is about grocery buying, banking, meeting or just impulsive e-commerce buying. And for the medical side of these; how can innovation lead to better vaccines and drugs to cure, tests for antibodies, and methods of sanitizing and raising the level of hygiene and cleanliness in many parts of the world? These are issues that the world faced as an issue.

15. THE NEW MARKETING NORMAL: DIGITIZED, DISRUPTED, AND READY FOR UPSKILLING & UPSCALING

In today's world, marketing has evolved far beyond simply selling products or services. It's about creating a lasting, positive impact on society, the environment, and the lives of individuals—each one of us. As a result, more companies are embracing social responsibility and engaging in meaningful initiatives that support various communities and causes. This growing trend not only benefits society and the environment but also helps businesses build strong brand reputations and foster deep customer loyalty.

Take, for instance, companies that focus on supporting underprivileged and marginalized communities. By aligning their marketing strategies with social responsibility, they are not only driving revenue but also making a significant difference in people's lives. *Impact-driven marketing* is becoming a powerful tool—not just for profit, but for creating real change.

This chapter explores the global perspective on how companies are making a difference through their marketing efforts. It also highlights exemplary cases of businesses using marketing as a force for good, leaving a meaningful and lasting impact.

15.1 EMBRACING IMPACT AS A PART OF MARKETING STRATEGY

Today, we are witnessing a profound shift in how companies engage with their stakeholders. Businesses are increasingly communicating the message of making a meaningful impact, and their involvement in broader societal issues has never been more prominent. More organizations are eager to influence various aspects of society, and we are seeing a remarkable surge in companies embracing impact as a central part of their mission, vision, and daily operations.

Impact, in its various forms and methods of measurement, is becoming a critical component—if not the very heart—of Integrated Marketing Communications (IMC). As a result, it is no longer just an additional consideration but a driving force that shapes how companies connect with their audiences and contribute to the world around them.

Making a social impact extends far beyond the traditional—and often outdated—concept of Corporate Social Responsibility (CSR), which has been prevalent since the 1970s (ACCP, 2022). Today's global challenges demand more than sporadic, surface-level CSR initiatives. The current CSR policies and strategies often fall short of enabling companies to create a lasting impact on a larger scale.

True social impact requires businesses to focus on work that is sustainable, intentional, and systemically geared toward addressing both local and global community needs. It's not about isolated, one-off projects but about embedding positive social change into the fabric of the company, across all departments and at every level of operation. Companies that prioritize this holistic approach to impact will be the ones that not only thrive but also create long-term, systemic change in a world that is facing unprecedented challenges.

To truly make an impact, companies must carefully evaluate their clients, projects, and suppliers through the lens of the impact they generate. Though measuring impact remains a challenging and evolving process, more businesses are making strides in this direction. By prioritizing *impact-driven criteria*, companies can ensure that their partnerships and operations align with their broader mission of creating positive change.

In the next section, we will explore the different types of impact a company can make, from social and environmental contributions to economic and cultural influence, and how these can be measured and integrated into their overall business strategy.

15.1.1 TYPES OF IMPACT A COMPANY CAN MAKE

There are countless ways companies can make a meaningful impact, benefiting not only their integrated marketing communications but, more importantly, their customers and the message they convey to the world. While social impact initiatives have existed for decades, they are being emphasized and valued today more than ever before. Companies are increasingly stepping up to address both local and global community needs.

Here are five powerful examples of initiatives that focus on serving local communities and addressing critical societal challenges:

1. **Combating World Hunger**: Providing sustainable solutions to food insecurity and malnutrition.

2. **Fighting Against Human Trafficking**: Supporting efforts to end exploitation and protect vulnerable populations.

3. **Championing Social Inclusion and Talent Management for Refugees**: Offering opportunities for integration and employment to displaced individuals.

4. **Access to Clean Water**: Ensuring communities have access to safe and sustainable water sources.

5. **Education for Women and Girls**: Promoting equal access to education to empower future generations.

These activities showcase the many ways businesses can address pressing community needs, while also strengthening their brand values and making a lasting social impact.

Acting on behalf of communities in the poorest countries, particularly within Bottom of the Pyramid (BoP) markets (See Figure 15.1), enables companies to gain credibility and develop a deep sensitivity to local issues. By addressing the unique challenges these communities face, businesses not only make a meaningful impact but also establish trust and authenticity. This engagement demonstrates a commitment to long-term, sustainable solutions, fostering strong relationships with these communities while simultaneously enhancing the company's social responsibility and brand image.

In BoP markets, the focus is not just on selling products but on creating value that can uplift local economies, improve living conditions, and drive social progress.

The World's 15 Poorest Countries

GDP per capita using Purchasing Power Parity (PPP)

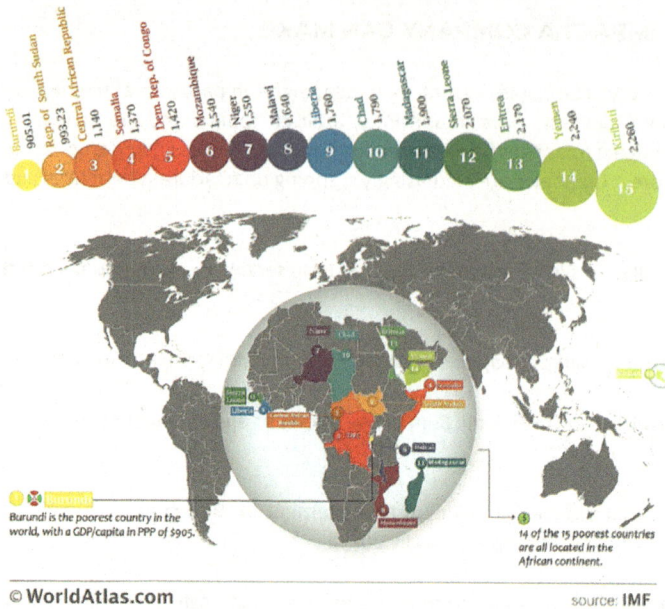

Figure 15.1: The world's 15 poorest countries, as well as their locations and GDP/Capita.

It is not only the responsibility of governments or non-profit organizations (NGOs) to fund projects with transformational impacts on communities; companies operating in these regions also have an obligation. Businesses must invest in initiatives that target the most vulnerable populations, collecting and analyzing critical data to ensure these programs are effective. By doing so, companies can, like the World Bank Group, help direct resources to those who need them most.

In this way, companies become co-responsible for laying the foundation for long-term prosperity, ensuring that future generations can thrive. This shared responsibility signals a shift toward a more inclusive and sustainable approach, where businesses play a crucial role in shaping a better world for all.

Activity for underprivileged community	Organizer	Description
Combating world hunger	Elon Musk	Elon Musk vowed to donate 6 billion of Tesla stock if the World Food Programme could describe how 6 billion would solve world hunger. (Lu, 2021)
	Half United	Half United is an organization that is fighting against hunger. Half United is committed to giving meals to children in need for every product purchased. The organization fights hunger by partnering with

458

		community gardens, volunteering with food banks, and providing meals to needy families. (Half United, n.d.)
Fighting against human trafficking	Tim Tebow Foundation & Reebok	Tim Tebow attempts to put a hold on human trafficking and child exploitation. Tim set up a rescue team in 2020 helping countless human traffic and child exploitation victims around the world. (Tim Tebow Foundation, n.d.). Tim Tebows collaborates with The Reebok Foundation desires to close the fitness gap by bringing fitness to disadvantaged populations and working closely with organizations that are defying convention by using fitness as a tool for the social charge. (Tim Tebow Foundation, n.d.)
	Airbnb	Airbnb has partnered with Polaris to strengthen the community's understanding of human trafficking and learn about red flags and how to respond if a potential human trafficking situation is encountered. In addition, a National Human Trafficking Hotline has been set up. Airbnb set up a community policy in multiple languages to further improve the understanding of the community and recognize signs. (Airbnb, n.d.)
Championing social inclusion and talent management of refugees	Accenture Refugee Hub	The Refugee Talent Hub is an initiative that brings refugees and employers together. As many refugees face difficulties to find a job, the Refugee Talent Hub is looking to close the gap. A network was missing to connect promising refugees with potential employers. With Refugee Talent Hub the refugee can connect with an employer, with paid jobs as the goal. (Refugee Talent Hub, n.d.)
	Consul-Tech	Consul-Tech is a training and consulting agency that focuses on helping individuals grow, evolve, and adapt to various challenges. Their primary aim is to assist newcomers and migrant clients in adjusting to Dutch culture and the labour market efficiently. By collaborating with multiple organizations and companies, they facilitate seamless integration for foreigners. Consul-Tech emphasizes personal training and growth, enabling individuals to access the best opportunities for self-development. They believe in the power of learning, which can help people achieve professional and personal success while overcoming challenges (Consul-Tech, 2023).
Access to clean water	Dopper	Dopper provides access to clean water in Nepal. For instance, by investing in local entrepreneurs. The project already provided water to 9.000 students in 2020. (Dopper in Nepal, n.d.)
	World Vision & Coca-Cola	Coca-Cola funded drinking water for 23.232 students at 95 schools in India. Improved water access, sanitation, and hygiene. (Partnership With Coca-Cola, n.d.)
Education for women and girls	Patagonia	Patagonia provides education programs in Chili through its non-profit entity, the Education Frontiers Institute. Providing learning experiences on partnering high schools, universities, camps, and other organizations. (Patagonia Frontiers, n.d.)
	Always	The Always Keeping Girls in School program reaches vulnerable girls with essential puberty and confidence education and donations of pads so that they can commit to their education and future. Since 2008, the

		program has reached over 200,000 girls and donated over 13 million pads in South Africa, Kenya, and Nigeria. (Always, n.d.)

Table 1: Overview of selected activities for underprivileged communities.

15.1.2 WAYS TO MEASURE MARKETING IMPACT

In today's digitized business environment, it has become easier to track a company's commitment to social impact, from dedicating time and skills to allocating a significant portion of profits toward positive societal change—regardless of geography or sector. As a result, businesses committed to social impact are now expected to address societal challenges more actively than ever before.

In 2019, *The Financial Times* published a comprehensive overview of best practices in sustainability, ethics, and social purpose, showcasing how business schools worldwide are contributing to these efforts. Many of the highlighted projects were developed in close collaboration with companies, underscoring the importance of partnership in tackling global challenges. These projects, which spanned research, teaching, student initiatives, and operations, naturally became part of the companies' integrated marketing communications once successfully completed.

To further recognize and promote these efforts, *The Financial Times* followed up with the Responsible Business Education Awards, celebrating the most impactful and innovative collaborations that advance sustainability and ethical business practices.

Field	Business School	Description
Research	INSEAD (FR)	Publishes cutting-edge research on sustainable models, inclusion, and well-being, including the book Blue Ocean Shift. It applies business methods to mitigate poverty and improve education and health in developing countries, works on global humanitarian logistics, and researches the issues of gender and diversity.
Teaching	MIT: Sloan School (US)	The USA Lab has an action learning course that sends students into rural communities to work with non-profits and community groups to try to solve pressing social challenges such as difficulty obtaining credit and childcare and how to revitalize a dying downtown area. The Sustainable Business Laboratory asks how to translate sustainability challenges into future business opportunities.
	Northwestern University: Kellogg (US)	A total of 60 percent of students enrolled in at least one social impact elective, and 18 percent took three or more. The Social Impact Pathway recognizes social change may come through different professional tracks and offers 34 courses, including impact investing and sustainable finance and medical technologies in developing countries. The Education Consulting Lab provides students with the opportunity to research and interview senior administrators in schools and other educational organizations.
	Rotterdam School of	Project time spans the last three months of the MBA. Student teams use 'design thinking' to formulate a challenge, generate ideas, and come up

	Management, Erasmus University. (NL)	with a creative solution with measurable impact linked to sustainable development goals. The 'I WILL' goal-setting programme ends with students formulating a personal statement which is printed on cards and shown during graduation.
Student projects	North Carolina State University: Poole College of Management (US)	The B Corp Clinic connects students to local and global for-profit businesses to help improve their environmental and social impact. Companies are matched with interdisciplinary, cross-university teams of students from different universities. More than 280 students have contributed 7,000 hours. A total of 83 percent of the team leads were women. The clinic is being replicated at academic institutions across the US.
Operations	Harvard Business School (US)	A sustainability plan has halved greenhouse gas emissions since 2006 while the campus has grown. Initiatives include eight green roofs to absorb rainfall, three of which grow vegetables that contribute to the greater plant-based foods on offer in the canteen. New software monitors heating and cooling systems to reduce energy use.

Table 2 How business schools, in collaboration with companies, engage in making a social impact.

Source: Jack (2019), Social Purpose: how business schools around the world measure up, Financial Times

15.1.3 INCREASING INVOLVEMENT OF COMPANIES ACROSS THE WORLD IN MAKING AN IMPACT

Social activities play a crucial role in shaping the impact and initiatives led by companies. These activities encompass a wide range of programs and projects related to social, environmental, and economic sustainability, designed to create positive change. By engaging in such initiatives, companies not only contribute to the greater good but also enhance their image and build goodwill with customers and other stakeholders.

Common examples of corporate social activities include charitable donations, employee volunteering, community development, environmental conservation, and sustainability efforts. These initiatives demonstrate a company's commitment to making a difference, which resonates with consumers.

In fact, companies that prioritize social responsibility often see significant business benefits. A study by Nielsen found that 55% of consumers are willing to pay more for products and services offered by socially responsible companies (Wertz, 2021). This highlights that social responsibility is not just beneficial for society and the environment, but also strengthens a company's reputation and fosters customer loyalty— proving that doing good can also be good for business.

Several companies around the world are making significant strides in creating a sustainable future and engaging in impactful activities. One standout example is *Dopper*, a company known for its innovative approach to reducing plastic waste. Recently, Dopper launched the world's first Cradle to Cradle Certified® Gold bottle collection, made of 85% waste materials. Their mission goes beyond just producing reusable water bottles; they are committed to raising awareness about plastic pollution and promoting sustainable alternatives.

One of Dopper's key initiatives, the *Dopper Wave*, mobilizes volunteers to clean plastic waste from beaches and oceans globally. The company also partners with local governments and organizations to promote sustainable practices and reduce plastic waste in communities. As a certified B Corp, Dopper meets rigorous social and environmental standards, using their business as a force for good. In collaboration with Albert Heijn, Dopper has also launched a new campaign that installs Dopper Water Taps in select stores, encouraging people to drink water from refillable bottles. This initiative began on World Water Day, providing free tap water to shoppers and reducing plastic use.

Another excellent example of impactful business practices is *Google*, which has long been committed to supporting underserved communities. In March 2023, Google pledged $50 million through their Google.org Impact Challenge to support organizations working on education and economic opportunities for these communities. The funds are distributed among ten organizations, including *Code for America*, which helps low-income families access essential government services, and *Khan Academy*, which provides free online educational resources. This donation follows Google's previous significant contributions, such as a $2 billion pledge to tackle the San Francisco Bay Area housing crisis and a $100 million donation for COVID-19 relief efforts.

These companies serve as prime examples of how businesses can leverage their resources and influence to create positive social change. As more organizations claim to prioritize social impact, the challenge will be to ensure that their efforts are genuine and truly contribute to lasting, positive change—a topic we will explore next.

15.2 MAKING AN IMPACT THROUGH POSITIVE CHANGE

Making positive change has become a popular and effective strategy for companies to appeal to customers and engage a broader range of stakeholders. Companies are now focusing on creating brand communities around their products and services, activating their purpose and impact, involving influencers in meaningful strategies aimed at making a difference, ensuring transparency in their supply chains, and participating in thematic events or festivals cantered on social impact.

15.2.1 BRAND COMMUNITIES

To make a meaningful impact, companies are increasingly dedicated to building vibrant brand communities around their products and services. A brand community is more than just a space; it's a dynamic environment—especially with the rise of the *Metaverse*—where individuals with a shared emotional connection to a brand can come together and engage not only with the brand but also with one another.

These communities foster a sense of belonging and loyalty, transforming customers into passionate advocates. By creating these connections, companies can cultivate relationships that go beyond transactions, enriching the overall experience for everyone involved.

An increasing body of psychological research reveals just how deeply ingrained the need for connection is in humans. Social connections are not merely desirable; they are essential for our happiness and success. According to Dr. Matthew D. Lieberman, Ph.D., director of UCLA's Neuroscience Lab, the human brain is most rewarded when we engage meaningfully with others, far more than with power or other intrinsic motivations like money and celebrity.

The effects of social isolation can be profound, leading to cognitive decline. Prolonged seclusion can degrade brain function, causing the hippocampus—the area responsible for learning and memory—to shrink. This highlights the vital importance of social interactions, reinforcing the notion that fostering connections is crucial for both our mental well-being and our overall quality of life. In this context, the role of brand communities becomes even more significant, as they offer individuals a chance to connect, share experiences, and thrive together.

In today's business landscape, the term "community" frequently emphasizes interactions over a genuine sense of belonging. For companies, building a community is not just a strategy; it's a vital way to cultivate customer loyalty. Brand communities have emerged as essential marketing tools, especially in the direct-to-consumer sector, where businesses rely heavily on social media and personal referrals to attract new customers.

By fostering these communities, brands can generate excitement and buzz around their products, creating an engaged audience eager to participate in the brand's journey. Members of these communities often play an active role, providing valuable feedback on product development and even getting the chance to test new samples before they hit the market. This collaborative approach not only strengthens the bond between the brand and its customers but also helps shape products that resonate more deeply with the audience's needs and preferences. Ultimately, cultivating a brand community enhances customer relationships and drives long-term success.

Traditionally, the relationship between companies and consumers was characterized by a transactional and impersonal dynamic. Customers would receive promotional catalogs or coupons in the mail every few months, but this approach left much to be desired in terms of communication and engagement. Today, passive consumerism is no longer sufficient.

Modern companies strive to keep customers actively engaged well beyond the initial purchase of their products. Brands now create vibrant communities on social media and their websites, allowing customers to become fans, share their experiences, and connect through private chat channels. They also host events to foster deeper interactions.

Building such a community not only enhances customer loyalty but also enables companies to benefit from organic word-of-mouth marketing. Enthusiastic product users promote their acquisitions on social media, generating buzz and providing valuable free publicity for the brand. This shift towards community-driven engagement transforms customers into advocates, amplifying the brand's reach and influence in a highly competitive marketplace.

To keep customers engaged, brands organize activities to unite and **create an entire brand community**.

One of the most popular ways brands foster engagement is by creating *online forums.* Many brand communities feature these forums, allowing customers to discuss topics related to the brand, share tips and advice, and connect with others who share similar interests.

In these vibrant online spaces, members can ask questions, seek recommendations, and engage in meaningful conversations. Often, representatives from the company are also present, answering questions about products and sharing insights into upcoming innovations. This direct interaction not only enhances the customer experience but also builds trust and credibility. By facilitating these discussions, brands create a sense of community and belonging, empowering customers to feel more connected to the brand and each other.

One of the most effective activities brands can undertake is creating a dedicated page or group on popular social networks. This approach facilitates easy access to information for customers while fostering a closer connection through diverse content.

Brands often establish social media groups where customers can engage with one another, share photos and stories, and stay updated on new products and upcoming events. These interactive spaces encourage community building and create a platform for authentic conversations among members. Additionally, brand representatives frequently participate in these groups, answering questions and providing insights about products and innovations. This direct engagement not only enhances the customer experience but also strengthens brand loyalty by making customers feel heard and valued within the community.

Brands recognize the importance of fostering community both online and offline, offering opportunities for real-life interactions. Many brand communities organize *events* such as product launches, workshops, and meetups, allowing customers to connect face-to-face and engage with the brand in a more immersive and personal way.

These events create a vibrant atmosphere where customers can share their experiences, learn more about the brand, and build lasting relationships with fellow enthusiasts. Attendees often leave with a deeper understanding of the brand's values and products, enhancing their overall loyalty. By facilitating these real-world connections, brands not only strengthen their communities but also create memorable experiences that resonate with their customers long after the event concludes.

Another effective strategy to boost audience engagement is through challenges and contests that encourage customers to participate and promote new products on their social networks. Brands can design games or creative challenges that inspire customers to interact with the brand in a fun and innovative way.

For instance, a clothing brand might host a design contest where customers are invited to submit their clothing designs for a chance to win a prize. This not only fosters creativity but also allows participants to feel a sense of ownership and connection to the brand. Such initiatives generate excitement and buzz, as customers share their entries on social media, amplifying the brand's reach and visibility. By engaging customers in these dynamic activities, brands can cultivate a lively community that celebrates creativity and strengthens customer loyalty.

When brands want to attract customers and make them permanent, they develop a loyalty system that encourages the audience to buy and use their products. Many brand communities offer loyalty programs that reward customers for engaging with the brand, such as making purchases or referring friends.

In recent years, companies have increasingly recognized the immense value of building and incentivizing brand communities. By allocating a dedicated budget toward community development, businesses can cultivate a loyal customer base, enhance engagement with their brand, and ultimately drive sales.

Investing in community building creates a space where customers feel valued and connected, leading to stronger emotional ties to the brand. Engaged communities are more likely to advocate for the brand, share their positive experiences, and influence potential customers. This organic word-of-mouth marketing can significantly amplify the brand's reach and credibility.

Furthermore, fostering a sense of belonging encourages customers to participate in events, contests, and discussions, deepening their connection to the brand. As these communities grow, they not only become a source of feedback and innovation but also serve as a powerful driver of sustained business success.

Companies incentivize their communities by offering exclusive discounts or promotions to community members as incentives to engage. Such deals and promotions primarily encourage customers to make purchases and make them feel exceptional.

Another tactic is to offer community members early access to new products or services. Giving customers a sneak peek before the public makes them feel part of an inner circle and can provide feedback to the brand before the wider launch.

Companies may also reward or recognize active community members who contribute valuable content or help others. Such rewards may include social media shoutouts, exclusive VIP event invitations, or even free products.

Incentivizing community members can also involve hosting events or meetups that unite people and strengthen the sense of community. Such incentives include hosting product demos, workshops, or social events like happy hours or dinners.

Allocating the budget toward incentivizing brand communities can increase customer loyalty, engagement, and sales. By providing value to customers beyond just the products or services, companies can foster a deeper connection with their audience and create a strong community of brand advocates.

Table 1 Selection of 20 Impactful Brand Communities and Why They Are Successful.

Brand Community	Justication for being impactful and succesful
Airbnb	One of those subjects that almost everyone enjoys discussing is travel, particularly now that the world is so much more accessible. This is why the Airbnb host community thrives by providing a forum for people to form bonds, gain insight into one another's cultures, and improve as hosts.
Apple	By providing a forum for feedback, self-service assistance, and knowledge-sharing across one of the busiest fan communities in the world, Apple Support Communities increase customer success. It increases user-generated content engagement and uses gamification to reward and promote helpful involvement.
Being Girl (Proctor and Gamble)	It connects and helps girls discover the answers to the challenging questions that come with growing up. Like a virtual big sister, the group promotes open dialogue and offers members the chance to seek Anna's guidance on issues like relationships, eating disorders, acne, and menstruation.
Charlie Hustle	Their success bases on the fact of rooting for one's favorite team instantly forges relationships with other ardent supporters, and Charlie Hustle has capitalized on this to build their brand community.
Disney	Disney has done its best to promote their corporation as a full-service entertainment provider, not just a media outlet. Their movies and stories, featuring well-known characters, are the ideal way to establish enduring emotional connections with each of their clients, no matter where they are in the world.
Figment (Random House)	Highly engaged people promote their favorite brands by writing honest and sincere reviews of the goods they use, which serves several purposes for other community members. It demonstrates how concentrating on, extremely engaged niches within their consumers can help all consumer-facing firms create branded community involvement.
Glow Recipe	The goal of Glow Recipe is to make skincare enjoyable for its clients by offering all-natural, fruit-inspired skin care products. Everything a buyer could possibly want to know about their products is available on their website, including quizzes that

	recommend skincare products, tutorial videos, and user reviews. Even a Glowipedia has been added to help consumers obtain their desired look perfectly.
GymShark	They make it simple for both new and recurring customers to get involved in their community by using their Gymshark Central blog as a central hub, where customers can find information whenever they want.
Harley Davidson	The Harley Owners Club functions by strengthening the sense of community among its followers and granting them access to special perks like invitations to official events, chapter membership in local areas, and extra services like roadside assistance. Together, these initiatives foster brand loyalty and improve Harley-Davidson motorcycle ownership.
Itzy Ritzy	Itzy Ritzy developed a value-added marketing approach using various forms of content, and as a result, it has emerged as a top source for information on parenting, covering everything from diaper bags to teething gadgets.
Lego	Consumers adore having a say in how the goods they use are developed, and the Lego Ideas community gives them that ability. Creative enthusiasts can choose what they want to see on the shelves next thanks to the ability for members to submit their product ideas and the start of competitions. Lego has been successful in developing a network that fosters product ideation.
Lululemon Athletica	The foundation of Lululemon's extensive product line is elegant yoga clothing, and the company's brand community is cantered on enabling its users to live active, healthy lives.
Oracle	Oracle Community links the platform's millions of users, whether they utilize it for personal or professional purposes. Users can post issues in specific forums and work together to find solutions. Users can create their own networks, set up meetings, and even exchange personal tales and start their own organizations.
PlayStation	In addition to being one of the largest communities of professional gamers, PlayStation Plus is also an advocacy community made up of eSports fans, enthusiasts, and top industry influencers. The community's ability to recognize its most valuable members and provide a forum for exchanging advice and setting up online play sessions will determine its level of success.
Polaroid	The brand community at Polaroid has developed over the years and is based on letting its members know through its loyalty program how much they are valued.
Red Bull	To tell fans about events ranging from music festivals to eSports, the Red Bull community leverages the power of social networking, sponsorship, and word-of-mouth promotion. To forge tighter ties with customers and progress its vibrant and vivacious image, the company frequently modifies its marketing plan. This makes it a fantastic example of an online brand community.
Rod Stryker	Sanctuary app has been successful in its mission to open Rod Stryker's trainings and unite its members in a mobile-first social area where they can communicate with one another and make new friends.
Sephora	The most recent beauty advice is always sought after from Instagram influencers or friends and family. Sephora was able to build a community experience that is

	seamless, immersive, and encourages conversational buying by combining their existing community resources, such as Beauty Board, Beauty Talk, and Ratings and Reviews.
Starbucks	Starbucks focuses on small details that help make inclusion in the brand community something felt by everyone, not just the customers that come in to get a drink.
The SAP Community Network	Huge multinationals like Disney and Bose and countless small and medium-sized firms are all able to engage and gain from one another as community members thanks to the SCN. The actual secret to the community's success is how many people are actively involved and eager to lend their time and knowledge to the network's expansion.

One fascinating example of creating a brand community is the German company Hornbach. As a home improvement and gardening retailer, Hornbach offers a wide array of products and services at competitive prices. While the company promotes its low prices as part of its brand appeal, it's crucial to recognize that offering affordable products alone doesn't equate to making a genuine social impact.

Hornbach goes beyond pricing strategies by actively taking steps to reduce its environmental footprint and promote sustainability. They have implemented energy-efficient lighting in their stores, minimized the use of plastic packaging, and introduced a variety of sustainable products. These initiatives not only demonstrate Hornbach's commitment to environmental responsibility but also resonate with consumers who value sustainability.

By fostering a community around these values, Hornbach connects with customers who share their passion for environmental stewardship. This approach creates a loyal customer base that feels aligned with the brand's mission, ultimately enhancing engagement, and driving long-term success.

Additionally, Hornbach has supported various community initiatives and social projects. For example, they have donated products and resources to community gardens, supported local schools and charities, and partnered with organizations to promote social inclusion and diversity. While Hornbach's low pricing strategy may attract budget-conscious customers and potentially benefit the financially disadvantaged, it is vital to consider their business practices' broader social and environmental impact.

Hornbach is committed to always offering the lowest price and returning money to customers who have paid too much. At first glance, this may seem like a simple pricing strategy, but it can potentially make a significant social impact. By offering the lowest price, Hornbach ensures its products are accessible and affordable to a broader range of customers, including those with lower incomes. Such practice could help to reduce economic inequality and provide greater access to essential goods for people who might otherwise struggle to afford them. Furthermore, by returning money to customers who paid too much, Hornbach demonstrates a commitment to **fairness and honesty** in its business practices. Adhering to such values can build customer trust and loyalty, increasing customer satisfaction and brand loyalty in the long term. From a social impact perspective, Hornback's commitment to always offering the lowest price and returning money to customers who paid too much aligns with several fundamental principles of corporate responsibility, including fairness, transparency, and accessibility. By prioritizing these values in its business practices, Hornbach has the potential to impact society and the environment positively. Of course, this approach has potential challenges and drawbacks, such as reduced profit margins and increased competition. However, if executed effectively and with a clear focus on social responsibility, this strategy could help to position Hornbach as a leader in the retail industry and set an example for other companies to follow.

Table 2: Selection of the companies making a social impact and a short description of their activities for their brand communities.

Company	Industry	Social impact activities
Airbnb	Travel and hospitality	Committed to promoting cultural exchange and creating opportunities for people to connect with others from around the world.
Allbirds	Apparel and footwear	Committed to sustainability and has implemented initiatives to reduce its carbon footprint and promote environmental responsibility.
Amazon	Retail	Committed to sustainability and has implemented initiatives to reduce its carbon footprint and promote environmental responsibility
Ben & Jerry's	Food and beverages	Committed to social responsibility and has implemented initiatives to promote diversity, equity, and inclusion within its workforce.
Bombas	An apparel company	For every sock sold, a pair of socks is donated to someone in need.
Brandless	A household goods company	Donates a meal to Feeding America® with every order
Coca-Cola	A beverage company	Focusses strongly on sustainability and is committed to reducing its carbon footprint and promoting environmental responsibility.
Ford	Automotive	Committed to reducing its carbon footprint and promoting sustainability through the development of electric and hybrid vehicles.
Google	Technology	Strongly focusses on education and is committed to creating opportunities for students to learn and innovate.
Microsoft	Technology company	Committed to empowering people through technology, promoting digital inclusion and improving access to technology in underserved communities.
Patagonia	Apparel	Committed to sustainability and has implemented initiatives to reduce its carbon footprint and promote environmental responsibility.
Procter & Gamble	Consumer goods	Committed to sustainability and has implemented initiatives to reduce its carbon footprint and promote environmental responsibility.
Salesforce	Technology	Committed to social responsibility and has implemented initiatives to promote diversity, equity, and inclusion within its workforce.
Savhera	A wellness company	Creates organic essential oils and products that create dignified employment for survivors of sexual exploitation around the world.

Starbucks	A food and beverage company	Committed to social responsibility and has implemented initiatives to promote diversity, equity, and inclusion within its workforce.
Tesla	Automotive	Committed to reducing its carbon footprint and promoting sustainability through the development of electric vehicles and renewable energy solutions.
The Body Shop	Beauty and personal care	Committed to social responsibility and has implemented initiatives to promote fair trade, ethical sourcing, and sustainable manufacturing practices.
Toms	Apparel and footwear	Committed to social responsibility and has implemented initiatives to promote social justice and provide shoes to children in need.
Unilever	Consumer goods	Committed to sustainability and has implemented initiatives to reduce its carbon footprint and promote environmental responsibility.
Vida Bars	Social impact enterprise	Provides eco-friendly personal care products free of harsh chemicals, as well as a passion for positively impacting on our world.
Warby Parker	Retail and eyewear	Committed to social responsibility and has implemented initiatives to promote access to affordable eyewear for underserved communities.
Zillow	Real estate	Committed to promoting affordable housing and has implemented initiatives to help people find affordable housing options.

15.2.2 PURPOSE AND IMPACT ACTIVATION

Often companies need help with their organizational structure and mindsets, unable to activate their purpose to their fullest potential and make a positive impact. There is a noticeable trend involving other businesses or private consultants for true purpose discovery and activation for positive impact.

One of the change-makers and purpose activators is *Sophie Wisbrun-Overakker*, Nature Positive Change Catalyst and Founder of Doing Business Doing Good (DBDG). Sophie is a purpose-to-impact accelerator for conscious business leaders who want to leave a regenerative legacy. Sophie guides them from strategy to impact on their regeneration journey to accelerate toward becoming nature positive. She empowers them to lead from purpose and implement love for nature and life in every aspect of their business. For 15 years, Sophie worked as an international sustainability leader and marketing director in companies like Procter & Gamble and Novartis. Her work as a sustainable change-maker and the first pioneer to accelerate sustainable transformation was awarded several times.

Sophie founded Doing Business Doing Good (DBDG), a Best for the World B Corp that empowers leaders and companies to become a regenerative force for good. DBDG offers in-company sustainable transformation programs, B Corp certification guidance, training, keynotes, workshops, coaching, and nature retreats. Sophie is a trusted sparring partner for CEOs and their teams, leading in-company transformation programs from purpose to more positive impact-making. She also empowered leaders across companies through her proven Purpose to Impact coaching programs to reconnect to their Soul Purpose and create positive impacts in their life and work. She launched the first Virtual Global Sustainability Summit (2017) with 30 sustainability experts, inspiring thousands of business leaders to use their work and business as a force for good.

Sophie works with CEOs of SMEs across industries and countries who are regenerative pioneers or are starting the regeneration journey. For example, she has been guiding the Dutch Retailer Xenos to develop a nature-positive vision and become a lighthouse for sustainable retailing. She also empowered a coffee and tea company, We Wonder Company, to embrace a purpose igniting a climate-positive movement turning every cup into a "good" cup.

Sophie has developed several methods to create a regenerative business for the thriving of all of life. We will highlight here her Regenerative Approach to building a Purposeful brand. She calls it the "Nature Positive Brand Building Model." (Source: How to build a purposeful brand by Sophie Wisbrun-Overakker).

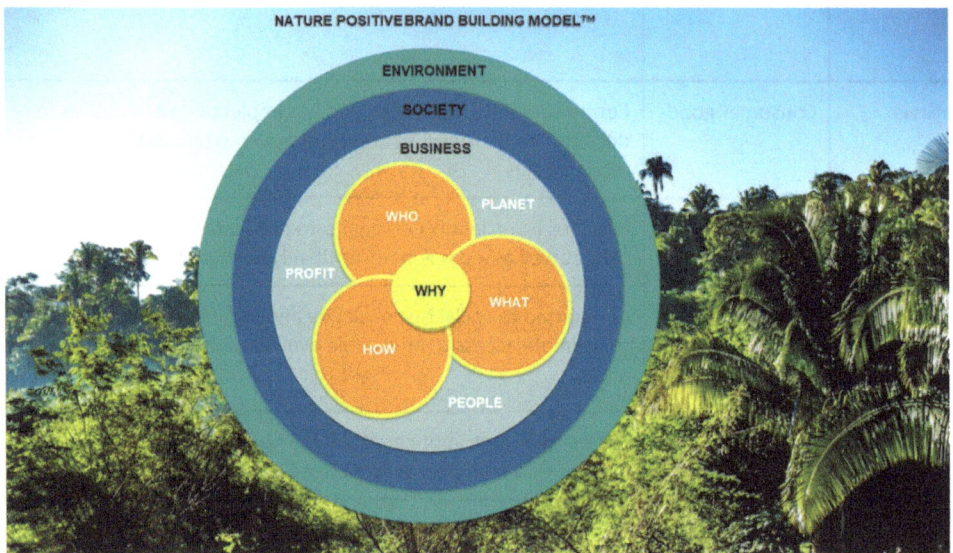

Figure 15.2: Selection of the companies making a social impact and a short description of their activities for their brand communities.

From Purpose to Impact in 5 Steps

Activating a Purpose is not easy, certainly not for brands that have existed for years. How do you integrate purpose into managing the daily business? Moreover, how do you ensure that the purpose becomes part of the DNA of your brand and organization, and most importantly, how does it connect to the individual purposes of your employees?

The majority of organizations have realized that brands must make a positive impact on society that goes beyond just business results. Because of this, many companies have tried to discover their purpose with many beautiful phrases and intentions as a result.

However, in practice, the next step to implement the purpose - bringing it to life in daily business choices and everything is done with the brand - needs to be made, or at least not consistently and authentically.

Because of this, it is, most of the time, not a whole purposeful story, and the total picture of what the brand stands for do not make sense.

Ultimately, it is not about having a Purpose but what you do with it! Which societal problem do you solve, and how well do you integrate and activate it? For example, it is challenging to understand when a brand claims to stand for a greener world and then its next plastic packaging is put on the shelf.

Having a Purpose is, in that case, nothing more than "marketing icing on the cake," which consumers and influencers mercilessly see through. The credibility and confidence in the brand and company will drop, and there goes the business result!

Activating a brand's and organization's purpose can be done in five steps, based on the Nature Positive Brand Building Method™. This new brand-building view ensures that the purpose is brought to life in every step of brand-building management, like a golden thread. It is based on multiple marketing frameworks, over two decades of experience as a marketing and sustainability executive, integrating multiple sustainability frameworks that address the nested interdependency of business interconnected with society and the environment.

Step 1: WHY - Purpose Discovery & Engagement

It starts with discovering the authentic Brand Purpose, the company's true nature, and the Why. Which societal problem is the brand trying to solve that is fundamental to its core business reason for being? Next, it is crucial to ensure that this purpose is lived by the leadership team, embraced by the employees, and integrated into their daily work.

Step 2: WHO - Understanding your stakeholders

Whom do you exist for, and what problem do you solve for them? On the one hand, this is about your customer: Who is your target group? What are their needs and challenges that you solve for them? On the other hand, it is about all your other stakeholders. Who are they? Do they know what you stand for, and do you actively involve them in achieving your vision?

Step 3: WHAT - Positive Value Proposition

When you have a clear picture of WHO you are for and what problem you solve for them, the next step is to build a positive value proposition. In short, WHAT you offer. This means integrating your purpose into the brand strategy, product portfolio, innovations, and other brand initiatives.

Step 4: HOW - Perfect Execution

The subsequent stage to activate the purpose in practice is in the HOW - in short, what your stakeholders see and hear from you. To ensure the overall brand picture makes sense in the execution, it comes down to 3 elements: 1. Communication strategy, 2. Stories you tell and claims you make, 3. Where and when do you tell them?

This only applies to companies with large marketing budgets. What does every person who answers the telephone in your company say? Which story does he or she convey?

Step 5: IMPACT - Measuring and Monitoring Positive Impact

The last and recurring step to implement purpose in everything from the brand is measuring and monitoring the results and the positive impact. Has the planned positive impact on business results, people, the environment, and society been achieved? Because eventually, the main goal of having a Purpose is to realize a positive impact for a better world.

Purpose gives you wings!

People behind brands have a huge opportunity to impact society, the environment, and business results positively.

Having and activating a strong, authentic Brand Purpose is the core, everything binding, often still missing, ingredient.

When people feel, they are contributing to something bigger and can create a positive impact, they become more motivated, fulfilled, energized, and perform better.

Purpose gives them wings.

Another example of involving external companies for purpose activation and making an impact is Good Up, the all-in-one employee engagement platform that lets employees' team up to start and join initiatives they care about and make their business more sustainable, socially responsible, fair & inclusive. Employees, while activated through Good Up, can make an impact in four core areas (1) Sustainability, employees work together and innovate to reduce the environmental impact of their company's operations, (2) Social impact, employees identify and address social issues that are important to them and align with their company's values, (3) Diversity, employees can work together to create a culture that values diversity, equity, inclusion and belonging (DEIB), and (4) Wellbeing, activities that are designed to promote the physical, mental, and emotional health of employees in the workplace.

15.2.3 INFLUENCERS INVOLVEMENT

Marketing influencers are increasingly becoming a powerful vehicle for companies to highlight their social impact. Influencer content encompasses any marketing material created or published by influencers, regardless of their size, niche, or platform. This content often feels more organic and authentic compared to traditional high-quality advertisements, effectively fostering a sense of trust and social credibility through digital word-of-mouth.

From unboxing videos and product reviews to viral TikTok trends, influencer marketing leverages relatable experiences that resonate with audiences. This approach allows consumers to see real people using and enjoying products, creating a more genuine connection.

Moreover, influencer marketing can be a more cost-effective strategy. The expense often depends on the influencer's size and the target audience the brand wants to reach. Engaging with micro-influencers—those with smaller but highly engaged followings—can be particularly beneficial. These influencers often cultivate close relationships with their audiences, making their endorsements feel more personal and impactful. By tapping into these authentic voices, brands can amplify their social impact messaging while building meaningful connections with potential customers.

Table 4 shows the ranking of influencers made by making use of AI software (per March 2023) (Crain, 2022)

Table 3 Global influencers and examples of their involvement in social impact activities
as of 1ˢᵗ March 2023 (as of 1ˢᵗ March 2023)

Influencer	Two channels with the highest number of followers	Involvement in social impact
Seth Godin	Twitter: 758.4K Facebook: 526K	Seth Godin promotes the charity: water. Trying to take a step in solving the water crisis.
Neil Patel	YouTube: 1.14M Facebook: 1M	Neil Patel promotes charity: water. Promoting a cause that provides clean and safe drinking water to people in developing nations and provides tracking service to see the progress.
Mark Schaefer	LinkedIn: 30K Twitter 169.9K	Is a board member of the Habitat for Humanity non-profit organization. The organization tries to overcome the chronic lack of decent housing in the world's poorest communities.
Gary Vaynerchuk	TikTok 14.9M Instagram: 10M	Board member on the pencils of promise non-profit organization. An organization that empowers communities through education. "We believe every child should have access to quality education" (Pencils of Promise, 2023)

Every country has a unique landscape of influencers who significantly impact marketing and its surrounding culture. These influencers, varying in size and niche, can shape consumer perceptions, drive trends, and promote brands in ways that resonate deeply with local audiences.

In some regions, influencers may focus on fashion, beauty, or lifestyle, while in others, they might emphasize technology, travel, or sustainability. Their ability to connect authentically with their followers allows them to sway opinions and encourage purchasing decisions, making them valuable partners for brands looking to enhance their marketing strategies.

Moreover, local influencers often understand the cultural nuances and preferences of their audiences, allowing them to tailor their messaging effectively. This localization can lead to higher engagement rates and a more significant impact on brand visibility. As a result, companies looking to expand their reach must consider the diverse array of influencers available in each market, leveraging their influence to create meaningful connections with consumers.

15.2.4 ENHANCING TRANSPARENCY

Supply chain transparency is becoming increasingly crucial for companies committed to making a positive impact on society and the environment. In today's landscape, transparency within supply chains has reached unprecedented levels. Companies are now more likely to partner with suppliers and vendors who prioritize environmental responsibility, ensure workers receive a living wage, and refrain from supporting harmful social policies.

One of the significant benefits of supply chain transparency is increased accountability. A survey conducted by the Sustainable Supply Chain Foundation revealed that 81% of companies prioritizing sustainability have experienced heightened accountability by disclosing information about their supply chains. This commitment not only enhances labor conditions and reduces environmental impacts but also fosters greater trust among consumers and stakeholders.

By actively sharing their supply chain practices, companies can demonstrate their dedication to ethical and sustainable operations. This transparency not only builds consumer confidence but also encourages other businesses to adopt similar practices, ultimately driving a collective movement toward responsible sourcing and manufacturing. As consumers become more aware of the origins of their products, companies that prioritize supply chain transparency will be well-positioned to thrive in an increasingly conscientious marketplace.

Another significant impact of supply chain transparency is increased efficiency. Companies that maintain a clear understanding of their supply chains can pinpoint areas for improvement and streamline their operations effectively. For example, Walmart's sustainability index program evaluates suppliers based on sustainability metrics, leading to impressive outcomes such as a 20% reduction in packaging and $200 million in cost savings.

By assessing and optimizing their supply chain processes, businesses can not only enhance operational efficiency but also minimize waste and reduce costs. This proactive approach allows companies to respond more agilely to market demands and consumer preferences while fostering sustainable practices. As organizations become more transparent about their supply chains, they are better equipped to identify inefficiencies and implement solutions that benefit both their bottom line and the environment. Ultimately, this transparency not only drives business success but also contributes to a more sustainable future for all stakeholders involved.

Transparency can also be a catalyst for innovation. By gaining a deeper understanding of the environmental and social impacts of their supply chains, companies can uncover new opportunities for sustainable business practices. A prime example of this is Patagonia's Footprint Chronicles, which enables consumers to trace the entire supply chain of their products. This initiative not only enhances customer trust but also leads to the identification of more sustainable materials and production methods.

Through this transparent approach, Patagonia has been able to innovate by exploring alternative materials, reducing waste, and improving overall product sustainability. Such initiatives empower companies to make informed decisions that align with their values and the expectations of their customers. As businesses commit to transparency, they not only foster a culture of accountability but also inspire creative solutions that can drive the industry toward a more sustainable future. This cycle of transparency and innovation ultimately benefits not only the companies but also the environment and society as a whole.

However, there are potential downsides to supply chain transparency that companies must navigate carefully. Some businesses may hesitate to disclose information due to concerns about competition, intellectual property, or confidentiality. The fear of revealing sensitive data can lead to reluctance in fully embracing transparency, as companies strive to protect their competitive advantage.

Additionally, there is a risk that consumers may become overwhelmed by an excess of information. If the data provided is not clearly presented or is inaccurate, it can lead to confusion rather than clarity, undermining the very trust that transparency aims to build. Consumers may struggle to discern what is truly relevant, which could dilute the impact of the company's sustainability efforts.

To mitigate these risks, companies must strike a balance between transparency and confidentiality. They should aim to communicate their supply chain practices in a clear, concise, and meaningful way, ensuring that the information is accessible and easily understood. By doing so, they can foster consumer trust while still safeguarding their competitive edge.

Despite these challenges, the benefits of supply chain transparency are significant. A survey by Cone Communications found that 89% of consumers are more likely to buy from a company that supports social or environmental issues. Therefore, companies prioritizing supply chain transparency are more likely to attract and retain customers, build trust, and contribute to a more sustainable future.

Notably, more events, conferences, and festivals are happening around the impact theme to make a bigger societal footprint and train leaders.

Is making an impact through marketing strategy authentic, or is it just a new buzzword?

Companies should prioritize making a meaningful impact rather than merely focusing on their product offerings. Analyzing the right data—such as offline store-level sales data—is crucial in this endeavour. When marketers collect and analyze accurate data, they can uncover deeper insights and make real-time enhancements to their campaigns.

Furthermore, connecting viewing habits with purchase behavior can significantly improve a company's Return on Advertising Spend (ROAS). In today's competitive landscape, having a substantial media budget is no longer enough. What truly matters is crafting the right marketing strategy that fosters a genuine understanding of and engagement with target consumers (Schwarz, 2019). By shifting their focus toward impactful marketing practices, companies can create lasting connections with their audiences while driving growth and success.

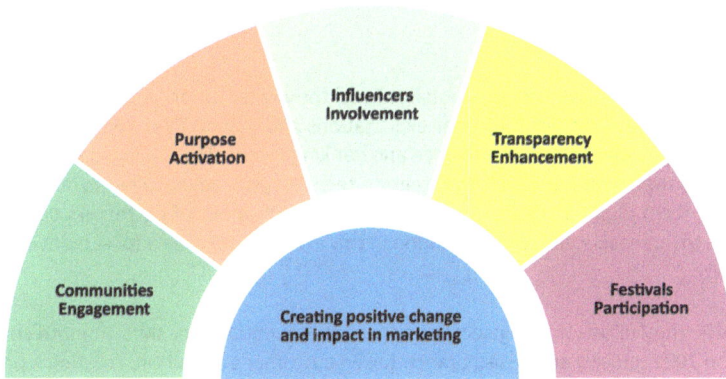

Figure 15.3: Five ways to create positive change and impact in marketing.

We all can learn from **Patagonia**! Positive impact happens not only through gatherings but also through exceptional decisions of company owners. Patagonia's billionaire owner, Yvon Chouinard, gave away a company to fight the climate crisis. Patagonia is a clothing company that is committed to sustainability and environmental conservation. The company's mission is to build the best product while causing no unnecessary harm and using business to inspire and implement solutions to the ecological crisis. Patagonia receives lots of attention for its environmental initiatives, including using recycled materials in its products, supporting grassroots environmental organizations, and advocating for the protection of public lands. With a team of lawyers, Chouinard structured the company to allow Patagonia to operate as a non-profit organization. With this new structure, every dollar received will go to the Holdfast Collective, which will use all the money earned to battle the environmental problem, and support thriving communities, as soon as possible (McCormick, 2022).

CASE STUDY
BURGAN BANK TÜRKİYE

Writen by: Halil Özcan, Burgan Bank Digital Banking Executive Vice President

Introduction

Established in 1989, Burgan Bank is one of the Türkiye's most prestigious financial institutions in the areas of retail, corporate and investment banking. Backed by a majority shareholder who is closely familiar with the MENA region and its dynamics as a rising center of the world, Burgan Bank Türkiye, puts its customer's goals in the centre of its banking activities, and conducts its business activities based on "banking focused on you" approach. ON Digital Banking was launched by Burgan Bank in October 2021 with a brand approach that emphasizes simplicity and clarity in banking services. ON Digital Banking aims to create a banking ecosystem that offers ease and simplicity as its operating model, providing comfort and convenience to its customers. For us, being a brand that values customer success as much as its own is one of our top priorities.

Challenge:

Over the past 10-15 years, in parallel with global trends, the digitalization process in Türkiye has brought about a significant transformation in consumer expectations and habits. The most noticeable reflections of this transformation have been seen in the finance and banking sector. The Turkish banking sector, thanks to its dynamic structure that allows it to quickly integrate technological advancements into its systems, accelerated its investments in digital banking. As a result, while the number of customers using digital banking services continues to increase steadily, competition in this area has become a focal point of the finance and banking ecosystem.

During this process, the Turkish banking sector underwent a revolutionary shift. Remote customer acquisition, introduced in 2021, quickly surpassed branch-based customer acquisition, creating a profound change in both the sector and consumer perceptions of traditional banking.

This transformation provided Burgan Bank, which has a strong presence in commercial, corporate, and investment banking with a limited branch network, the opportunity to transfer its expertise and competence into retail banking, creating the opportunity to compete with larger and older banks in the sector. At this point, to meet users' expectations of accessing a comprehensive range of products and services without the need to visit a physical branch, Burgan Bank launched ON Digital Banking to serve its customers.

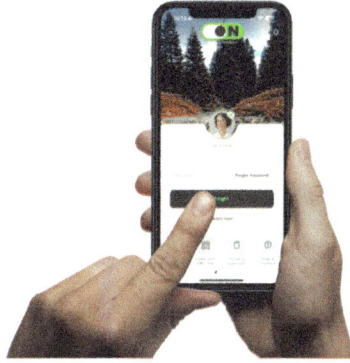

Solution

While creating the ON Digital Banking, we constructed our methodology to create our roadmap via insights by 4 pillars which were in-depth market research (ZMET Research, in-depth interviews, and other competitors' mobile banking users), strategy building (strategy meetings, Exco interviews and workshops), value proposition creation (Product/Service/Campaign offerings, IT Development Phase) and brand generation (Logo and brand identity). To bring 'ON' to the core of retail banking we aimed to best-in-class customer experience, robust product portfolio and continuous profitable growth & sales.

Our market research showed current digital banking approaches in the market had pain points (OFF) like privilege to larger deposits, welcome rates, complex mobile applications, and control at banks. And as ON we converted OFF points of digital banking to ON's with always free of charge transaction, financial technologies, privilege to all deposit sizes, always on competitive rates, and putting customers' needs at core, by creating a win-win ecosystem.

As digital banks mostly serve as a secondary bank for customers, due to customers choosing their main bank as their salary bank, we set our target audience as white-collar professionals aged 25-45 with a steady income, by offering additional promotions without requiring them to switch their main salary bank.

As a new generation Digital Bank, we offer full-fledged banking services to our customer available 24/7. There are only a few steps for consumers to become an ON'ner. After downloading the ON Mobile app, consumers can become a customer within minutes via RKYC process and immediately start benefiting from ON's advantages. Both our campaigns and the products create advantageous financial ecosystem for our customers. With our loyalty programs such as Earn with ON, ON Plus we are enabling our customers to benefit from cashbacks and additional interest rates to their overnight accounts. Additionally, through partnerships in various sectors such as e-commerce, restaurants, car rentals, and vacations, we provide customers with discounts and advantages. This not only enhances customer loyalty but also positions our bank as one of the best options for consumers, even if they don't choose us as their primary salary bank. While offering daily banking products to our customers we are also offering innovative services such as AI-based investment products, ON Fund Universe and ON Robo that we provide customers opportunity to analyze funds, instantly evaluate the most suitable investment opportunities, and track their portfolio while easily accessing their investment statements.

In all our communication and marketing strategies, we closely follow trends and adopt a performance-based approach. Our communication and marketing understanding is built on a holistic perspective. Furthermore, we believe that long-term collaborations with media channels, rather than one-time efforts, have played a significant role in the results we've achieved. In 2023, with our comprehensive 360-degree advertising campaign, we launched three different commercials to enhance our brand awareness and strengthen our brand identity through our embraced easy banking concept promising no commissions as long as the world turns. With our advertising investments, we have also achieved very effective results in brand awareness and customer acquisition.

BANKING IS
COMFORTABLE WITH ON!

Conclusion

In a highly competitive digital banking ecosystem in Türkiye, we have reached 1 million customers with a 56% increase in our customer base since the beginning of this year. According to the August 2024 Remote Customer Acquisition Market Share report published by the TBB, which includes a total of 19 banks, including large and medium-sized banks, our market share in remote customer acquisition increased by 23%, significantly exceeding the sector growth of 2% compared to the previous month.

As of September 2024, our loan volume grew by 33%, and our deposit volume increased by 86% compared to the same period last year. In terms of investment products, our fund size growth rate over the past year was 395%, while our fund income growth rate reached 240%.

To date, we have collaborated with brands from 18 different sectors, launching over 80 campaigns that have provided our customers with discounts and benefits.

So far, as ON Digital Banking, we have been honoured with 15 prestigious awards on a global scale, such as the World's Best Digital Bank Awards 2023, W3 Awards 2023, International Business Magazine Awards 2023, PSM Awards 2023, World Business Outlook Awards 2023, International Business Magazine Awards 2024, Global Brands Awards 2024, and World Business Outlook Awards 2024.

In terms of brand awareness, when comparing the results of our brand research conducted in December 2022 with our brand research conducted in June 2024, we observed significant progress. According to these results, our top-of-mind awareness increased from 1% to 13%, total spontaneous awareness rose from 12% to 31%, and our total brand awareness climbed from 61% to 65% over the 1.5-year period. Another important finding from our latest research is that a high percentage of people heard about us from their close acquaintances. In this respect, it can be said that we have created a strong word-of-mouth effect as a natural result of the quality of services we offer and our advertising investments.

In conclusion, ON, the digital banking brand launched by Burgan Bank in a highly competitive field, has become a leader in innovative practices in the industry in just three short years, bringing a fresh perspective to the new-generation banking approach. The increase in customer numbers, brand awareness, and financial results all reflect that ON's strength comes from its efforts and investments to understand customer expectations and needs, as well as sector dynamics and trends.

Questions to stimulate conversation on the case

1.   **What strategies did ON Digital Banking use to differentiate itself from competitors?**

ON focused on converting the "OFF" points of banking sector (complex processes, limited privileges) into "ON" advantages, such as always-free transactions, competitive rates, and accessible services for all deposit sizes. It created a win-win ecosystem by prioritizing customer needs and simplifying processes. ON also used innovative services like AI-based investment tools and customer loyalty programs to enhance the overall experience.

2.   **How did ON Digital Banking increase its brand awareness and customer base?**

ON employed a comprehensive communication and marketing strategy, including 360-degree advertising campaigns, to increase brand awareness. By launching three commercials and emphasizing a "no-commission" approach, ON positioned itself as a simple and customer-friendly banking option. Its collaborations with various brands and loyalty programs further contributed to customer retention and growth, leading to a 56% increase in its customer base.

3.   **What role did innovation play in ON Digital Banking's success?**

Innovation was at the core of ON's strategy, offering AI-driven investment products, seamless mobile banking, and personalized financial services. By addressing key customer pain points and leveraging technology, ON differentiated itself from traditional banks and competitors. This focus on innovation helped ON achieve rapid growth in customer numbers, loan volume, and deposits while receiving numerous industry awards.

Links and media

https://on.com.tr/en

Case Highlights

ON Digital Banking was launched by Burgan Bank in October 2021, with an emphasis on simplicity and clarity in banking services. Developed in response to the increasing demand for digital banking services and changing consumer expectations, ON aims to offer users an easy and seamless banking experience. For this purpose, a brand strategy was developed based on in-depth market research and customer insights.

In the highly competitive Turkish digital banking sector, ON has successfully differentiated itself by offering innovative financial technologies, commission free transaction options, and products that provide advantages for all deposit amounts. ON primarily targets white-collar professionals, strengthening its position by offering additional benefits without requiring them to switch their main salary bank.

The success of ON is based on a business model focused on customer needs, AI-supported investment products, extensive campaign collaborations, and innovative services. Furthermore, comprehensive advertising campaigns have increased brand awareness and significantly expanded its customer base. In three years, ON has reached 1 million customers and, in the past year alone, has grown its loan volume by 33% and deposit volume by 86%. As a result, ON Digital Banking has become a leading brand in the digital banking sector in Türkiye within 3 years.

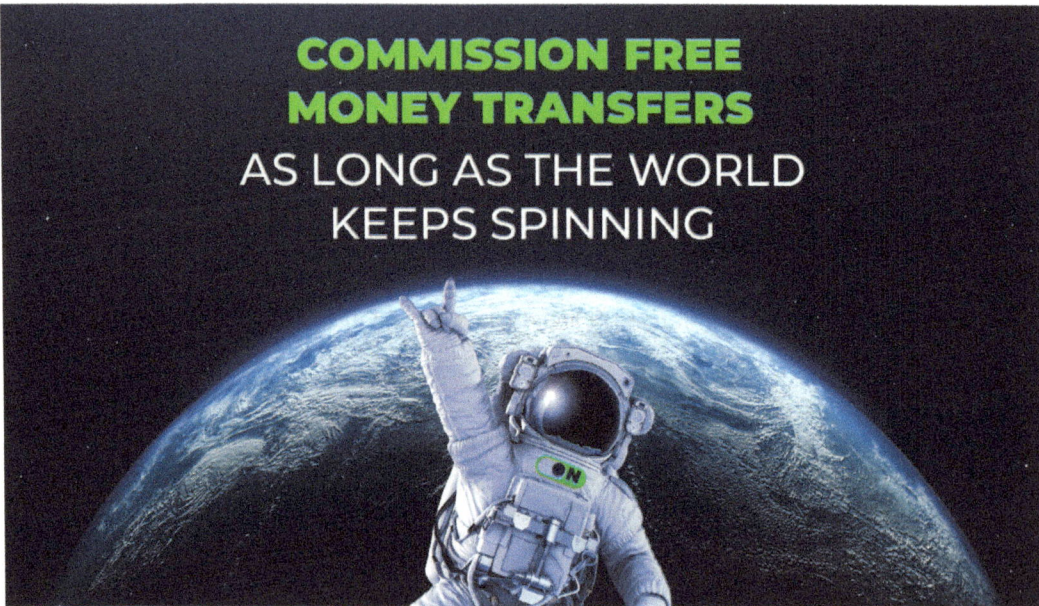

15.3 HOW TO MOVE FURTHER WITH MARKETING NORMAL

The mismatch between the positive change that deserves attention, and the rushing world and marketing developments is noticeable. They can be used for good if with reflection, not in a rush, stimulating way of thinking, the customer being critical, etc., yet trends in marketing fool people and customers. For instance, DeGrowth is popularized requires a different marketing approach and is increasingly present in marketing campaigns. Degrowth means shrinking rather than growing economies, so we use less of the world's energy and resources and put well-being ahead of profit. By pursuing degrowth policies, economies can help themselves, their citizens, and the planet by becoming more sustainable. DeGrowth's actions might include buying less stuff, growing your food, and using empty houses instead of building new ones (World Economic Forum, 2022). Recently Jason Hickel visited the Dutch parliament, giving directions to policymakers to strengthen the Degrowth thinking within Dutch politics. Hickel wants to focus on human welfare instead of economic growth, while food and affordable housing are still issues. Jason Hickel emphasizes focusing on the forms of production we want and how we want to improve it, and what forms are destructive and not as important. As Antonio Guterres, the current Secretary-General of the United Nations, emphasized, Eden on Earth is not there anymore, so we all need to write our letters for Life on Earth.

15.4 TRENDS IN MARKETING AND THEIR SOCIAL MEANING

Entrepreneur (2023) listed **five** significant trends in marketing in 2023: (1) The rise of augmented reality, 2. The power of personalization 3. The emergence of micro-influencers 4. The importance of employee advocacy 5. The growth of visual content (Hall, 2022a) listed **four** significant trends in marketing in 2023: 1. Influencers are becoming established ambassadors. 2. Interactive content is giving static posts a run for their money. 3. Video posts are increasing on social media. 4.AI is gathering more accurate data. KPMG provides five 2023 media trends: 1. Increased cost pressures on the media consumer due to economic conditions. 2. Continued consolidation within the streaming space, both intercompany and intra-company. 3. Advertising markets will be challenged, with the predicted growth far less than last year's pace. 4. Sports teams will continue to be a vibrant market, with an active M&A market combined with the emergence of direct-to-consumer sports offerings and niche sports proliferation. Media companies will refocus on profitability (KPMG, 2022) (See Figure 15.10).

Table 4: Overview of major marketing trends in 2023 and examples of social impact

	Trend	Short description	Examples
1	Influencers are becoming established brand ambassadors.	Influencers leverage impact by promoting a company's brands and products to audiences who already trust them.	Fitness YouTubers (Stan Browney) sponsored by My protein; IT brands sponsoring gamers.
2	Interactive content is giving static posts a run for their money.	People are having more and more trouble with watching long videos and want content that's interactive. It's the shorter 15 sec. that is working out.	Instagram reels; TikTok

3	Video posts are increasing on social media.	People are becoming more drawn towards video's that for instance replicate live experiences.	Short videos of house tours, on e.g., TikTok YouTube, and Instagram.
4	AI is generating more accurate data.	Marketers are beginning to take data from messaging platforms and automated technologies, such as heatmaps to guide their strategies.	Chat GPT; AI behind posts scheduling platforms (buffer, later, MailChimp); Automated customer support; Content creation
5	The rise of augmented reality	Businesses can add a different dimension to their customer experience by providing an augmented reality. It allows the customer to experience the product from home.	VR room tour; Google 360 virtual tour.
6	The power of personalization.	With analytics it becomes easier to target the customer. With personalized messages, emails, and sending relevant offers the customer experience, customer loyalty, and higher engagement can be stimulated.	Sending personal emails with MailChimp; Targeting with a personalized pop-up.
7	The emergence of micro-influencers.	Everyday people with a large following that promote sponsored content from a brand. The smaller audience makes it easier to target specific demographics.	Everyday people with a large following on social media platforms.
8	The importance of employee advocacy.	Employees should be stimulated to share information about their employer. As studies show that employee generated content is trusted more than any other source.	Sharing content on their LinkedIn profile.
9	The growth of visual content	Visuals can be used in many ways to promote products and services. In the likes of Augmented reality, virtual reality, or 3D graphics. In addition, it is important to adjust the images according to the platform preferences.	Graphs; Reels; TikTok; Facebook; Pinterest; YouTube
10	Increased cost pressures on the media consumer due to	With the increasing inflation, and the pressure of rising prices the consumer will most likely	Streaming services, such as Netflix, Disney +, Apple TV, Amazon prime video, etc.

	economic conditions.	spend less on media and entertainment.	
11	Continued consolidation within the streaming space, both intercompany and intra-company.	After years of strong consumer demand and numerous streaming launches, the market has become saturated. 2023 will mark a year of significant consolidation as streamers shift their focus to a different set of KPIs, including ARPU, churn and profitability.	Increasing the price for their services, improve their churn rate to have more long-term customers.
12	Advertising markets will be challenged, with predicted growth far less than last year's pace.	With less revenue from advertising a different business model is needed. As the growth in the ad market is expected to slow appreciably from '22 levels.	Different strategies to marketing.
13	Sports teams will continue to be a vibrant market, with an active M&A market combined with the emergence of direct-to-consumer sports offerings as well as niche sports proliferation	More premier franchises will change hands in 2023 compared to other branches. Additional leagues and teams will offer direct to the consumer, a trend that already started in 2022. Niche sports will continue to pop up on the mainstream radar.	Big firms will be up for sales; direct to consumer services; niche sports will grow in popularity.
14	Media companies refocus on profitability.	More companies shift their focus from an era of growth to a focus on profitability. They will look to streamline their current services.	Different strategies; target more specifically
15	Brands answer economic instability with marketing investments.	Financial uncertainty such as inflation, supply issues and a looming recession is the top-of-mind concern for brands globally. Rather than cost cutting, brands surveyed are planning to weather financial uncertainty with marketing investments.	Accelerating to new digital platforms/technologies.; expanding into new markets, segments, and geographies, implementing systems (such as AI) to create greater customer personalization.
16	Chief marketing officers drive growth through internal sustainability efforts.	Leading by example. Brands are concentrating their efforts on-shoring up the sustainability of their own internal practices. These efforts establish an authenticity to brands, marketing initiatives and leverages	Improving the sustainability of internal marketing practices; promoting more sustainable product and service offerings, establishing long-term sustainability commitments.

		heightened awareness of global uncertainties to help build a more secure, sustainable future.	
17	Creativity as a force for growth	High-growth brands surveyed are prioritizing creativity as a force for long-term growth over their low-growth counterparts. High-growth brands also place a higher priority on increased risk taking, cross functional collaboration, and looking to the marketing function for its most creative ideas.	Encouraging risk taking. Organization relying on creative ideas from the marketing department. The organization promotes cross functional collaboration to foster new ideas. The organization's long-term success depends upon its ability to foster creative ideas that can transform the business, the organization's long-term success depends upon its ability to integrate sophisticated analytical capabilities into its strategy.
18	Rising technologies for marketers to watch	Marketers have their eye on expanding their investment in blockchain and the metaverse. Although nascent, marketers are laying the groundwork for adoption of new technologies this year. To stay relevant, brands should consider laying out strategies that will benefit them in the long term.	Metaverse, implementing blockchain technologies, cryptocurrencies, such as Bitcoin.
19	Influencer culture continues to rise	Businesses can harness the power of social media to get an edge on their competitors. Using influencers with large followings to promote their products.	Promoting a product on their Instagram, Twitter, Tik Tok, etc.
20	A reel is worth a thousand words (Plummer, 2023)	The increasing popularity of Instagram, YouTube and Tik Tok shows that the best way to get consumers attention is to give them something to look at. Reels grew by 220 million users between July and October. Tik Toks 732 million users are expected to keep growing.	Short interactive videos, posted on YouTube, Instagram, and Tik Tok.
21	Take advantage of user-generated content. (Plummer, 2023)	People posting your product on their social media channel can carry more weight with customers as opposed to you blowing your own horn.	Pictures of the product on the social media profiles of people outside of your reach, reviews on Google, Yelp or Trustpilot

22	Email is still an efficient engagement method. (Plummer, 2023)	The average return on investment for email marketing is 36 dollars for every dollar spent. An email is a way to connect directly to current customers. By personalizing the email based on their purchases, you have a better chance of keeping them engaged.	Creating newsletter, personalized emails, offer discount via email.
23	Combine strategies for an omnichannel approach. (Plummer, 2023)	The marketing strategy needs to be reviewed regularly to make sure it is growing and changing along with your business. By staying abreast of the latest trends, you will best position your company to catch the attention of the consumers who may one day become your customers.	Ensure that the marketing strategy is consistent; communicate the specifics to your marketing team. They must understand exactly what you are trying to do.

Source: Trends 1-5 (Hall, 2022), 6-9 (Entrepreneur, 2023), 10-14 (KPMG, 2022), 15-18 (Deloitte, 2023), 19-23 (Plummer, 2023)

Companies that implement sustainable practices, primarily not by legal impositions but by the companies themselves, considerably increase their value chain and profitability. Building on earlier works of Philip Kotler, Mariusz Soltanifar defines **exodus marketing** as "a process that is used to regulate which products or services may be of interest to customers and describes a set of activities a company undertakes to gain new customers or retain existing ones in perfect harmony with the planet and most importantly the human heart".

As such, marketing is responsible for determining the strategy for sales, communications, business development, and, most importantly, for changing human life.

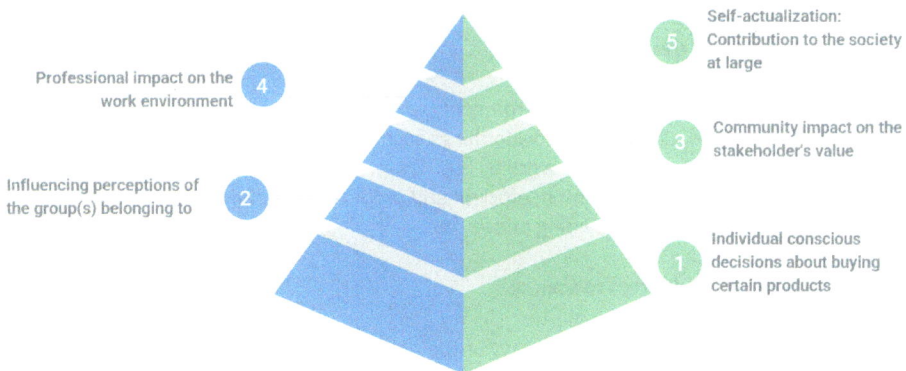

Figure 15.4: Purpose Marketing Pyramid ModelTM by Mariusz Soltanifar.

Below is a short interpretation of all the layers.

1. Individual conscious decisions about buying certain products.

People buy products that align with their beliefs and are socially justifiable—for instance, products labeled as sustainable. For instance, people value buying meat from suppliers who brand their animal-friendly products. Many products are labeled to attract their target group.

In addition, more and more customers value sustainability, LHBTQ, genders, etc. For instance, Starbucks takes a stance on a problem that is important for their target group and is used to improve their morale and to attract their target group optimally.

2. Influencing perceptions of the group belonging to.

Influencing the perceptions of the target group can be done in multiple ways. A company wants a specific target group that can be influenced differently. It can be done by taking a stance on a public matter or affecting their decisions through social media. Social media channels, such as Tik Tok and Instagram, are important platforms that can easily be used to influence the decisions of a target group.

Step-by-step, a target group can be influenced by showing content related to one topic. Suppose a person feels connected to the topic. In that case, it means that they could become a long-term follower of the company and be transformed into a long-term customer that is extremely valuable to the company.

3. Community impact on the stakeholder's value.

A company desires to target its (potential) customers to the best of its ability. The company makes a living from the customers that purchase its products. Therefore, reaching the target group based on their wishes and needs is important.

In the last couple of years, more and more companies have shifted their focus from maximizing their profits to giving something back to the community. This is the effect of a company seeing the needs of its customers. For instance, if the target group values sustainability, it will be something that can be seen on their product, website, social media, etc. Not only does this increase a chance of a potential sale, but it also creates a brand image. A company that gives back to the community can find employees more easily, increase their profit margin, and impact a person's life.

4. Professional impact on the work environment.

Companies want to improve their work environment, which could mean providing a work environment where employees can thrive. Companies provide things such as a ping pong table to improve productivity, flexible work locations, and bus passes to work by bus. Creating an environment that stimulates a healthy lifestyle, a carbon-neutral future, and a more efficient and productive employee but also a happy employee that can boost morale, improve future hiring efforts, etc.

5. Self-actualization: Contribution to society

More and more companies are becoming aware of their impact on society. For instance, sustainability is becoming an important topic for companies and creating equality and diversity within their companies to benefit less fortunate people. A company should also be aware of the needs of its direct environment and try to maximize its contribution to society. That means creating equality, diversity, sustainability, animal health, and employee happiness.

Concluding, making an impact through social activities is well presented globally; and The Türkiye is a great reflection of global trends. We have examples of companies involved in activities for society, the environment, and companies' communities, and they are largely well-planned and structured as a part of sequential and frequent marketing activities. Thus, the world is keen for The New Marketing Normal: Digitized, Disrupted, and Ready for Upskilling & Upscaling.

REFERENCES

Baker, W., and Sinkula, J.M. (2002), "Market orientation, learning orientation and product innovation: delving into the organization's black box", Journal of Market Focused Management, Vol. 5 No. 1, pp. 5-23.

Barczak, G. (2012). 'The future of NPD/innovation research', Journal of Product Innovation Management, 29, pp. 355–357.

Blackwell, S.S. (2006), "The influence of perception of organizational structure and culture on leadership role requirements: the moderating impact of locus of control and self-monitoring", Journal of Leadership & Organizational Studies, Vol. 12 No. 4, pp. 27-49.

Bogers, M., Afuah, A. and Bastian, B. (2010), "Users as innovators: a review, critique, and future research directions", Journal of Management, Vol. 36, pp. 857–875.

Damanpour, F. (1991), "Organizational innovation: a meta-analysis of effects of determinants and moderators", The Academy of Management Journal, Vol. 34 No. 3, pp. 555-90.

De Jong, J.P., Bruins, A., Dolfsma, W. and Meijaard, J. (2003), "Innovation in service firms explored: what, how and why", Business and Policy Research (EIM), Zoetermeer.

Eraydin, A., and Armatli-Köroğlu, B. (2005), "Innovation, networking and the new industrial clusters: the characteristics of networks and local innovation capabilities in the Turkish industrial clusters", Entrepreneurship & Regional Development, Vol. 17 No. 4, pp. 237–266.

Frow, P., Nenonen, S., Payne, A., and Storbacke, K. (2015), "Managing Co-creation Design: A strategic Approach to Innovation", British Journal of Management, Vol. 26, pp. 463–483.

Gopalakrishnan, S. and Damanpour, F. (1997), "A review of innovation research in economics, sociology and technology management", Omega, Vol. 25 No. 1, pp. 15-28.

Hult, G. T. M., Hurley, R. F. and Knight, G. A. (2004), "Innovativeness: its antecedents and impact on business performance", Industrial Marketing Management, Vol. 33 No. 5, pp. 429-38.

Kandampully, J. and Duddy, R. (1999), "Competitive advantage through anticipation, innovation and relationships", Management Decision, Vol. 37 No. 1, pp. 51-56.

Li, H. and Atuahene-Gima, K. (2001), "Product innovation strategy and the performance of new technology ventures in China", Academy of Management Journal, Vol. 44 No. 6, pp. 1123-34.

Mahmoud, M. A., Hinson, R. E., and Anim, P. A. (2018), "Service innovation and customer satisfaction: the role of customer value creation", European Journal of Innovation Management, Vol. 21 No. 3, 2018 pp. 402-422.

Mahmoud, M. A., Hinson, R. E., and Anim, P. A. (2018), "Service innovation and customer satisfaction: the role of customer value creation", European Journal of Innovation Management, Vol. 21 No. 3, 2018 pp. 402-422.

Michel, S., Brown, S. W. and Gallan, A. S. (2008), "Service-logic innovations: how to innovate customers, not products", California Management Review, Vol. 50 No. 3, pp. 49-65.

Mone, M. A., McKinley, W. and Barker, V. L. (1998), "Organizational decline and innovation: a contingency framework", Academy of Management Review, Vol. 23 No. 1, pp. 115-32.

Payne, A. and Frow, P. (2005), "A strategic framework for CRM", Journal of Marketing, Vol. 69, pp. 167–176.

Prahalad, C. K. and Ramaswamy, V. (2000), "Co-opting customer competence", Harvard Business Review, Vol. 78, pp. 79-87.

Prahalad, C. K. and Ramaswamy, V. (2004), "Co-creation experiences: the next practice in value creation", Journal of Interactive Marketing, Vol. 18 No. 3, pp. 5-14.

Price, R.M. (1996), "Technology and strategic advantage", California Management Review, Vol. 38 No. 3, pp. 38-56.

Sanchez-Gutierrez, J., Cabanelas, P., Lampon, J. F., Gonzalez-Alvarado, T. E. (2019). "The impact on competitiveness of customer value creation through relationship capabilities and marketing innovation", Journal of Business & Industrial Marketing, Vol. 34 No. 3, pp. 618–627.

Storper, M. (1995), "The resurgence of the regional economies ten years later: the region as a nexus of untraded interdependencies", European Urban and Regional Studies, Vol. 2 No. 3, pp. 191–215.

Troye, S. V. and Supphellen, M. (2012), "Consumer participation in coproduction: 'I made it myself' effects on consumers' sensory perceptions and evaluations of outcome and input product", Journal of Marketing, Vol. 76, pp. 33–46.

Ulaga, W. and Eggert, A. (2006), "Value-based differentiation in business relationships: gaining and sustaining key supplier status", Journal of Marketing, Vol. 70 No. 1, pp. 119-136.

Uzkurt, C., Kumar, R., Kimzan, H.S. and Eminoglu, G. (2013), "Role of innovation in the relationship between organizational culture and firm performance", European Journal of Innovation Management Vol. 16 No. 1, pp. 92-117.

Vargo, S. L. (2008), "Customer integration and value creation: paradigmatic traps and perspectives", Journal of Service Research, Vol. 11, pp. 211–215.

Vargo, S. L. and Lusch, R. F. (2004), "Evolving to a new dominant logic for marketing", Journal of Marketing, Vol. 68 No. 1, pp. 1-17.

All4Comms. (2021, December). The six (6) most interesting marketing campaigns in Poland in 2021. Retrieved from all4comms.com: https://all4comms.com/the-most-interesting-marketing-campaigns-in-poland-in-2021/

All4Comms. (2021, December). Trends in Polish social media marketing that will dominate 2022. Retrieved from all4comms.com: https://all4comms.com/trends-in-polish-social-media-marketing-that-will-dominate-2022/

Always. (n.d.). Always is Helping Keep Girls in School. https://www.always.com/en-us/about-us/keeping-girls-in-school.

Beeckestijn Business School. (2022, December 12). De vijf belangrijkste digital marketing trends voor 2023. Retrieved from www.marketingfacts.nl: https://www.marketingfacts.nl/berichten/de-vijf-belangrijkste-digital-marketing-trends-voor-2023/

Blayer, R. (2022, May 24). Best Practices For Brands Taking Activist Positions. Forbes. https://www.forbes.com/sites/forbesbusinesscouncil/2022/05/24/best-practices-for-brands-taking-activist-positions/?sh=29a3ae48425d

Bogliari, A. (2023, March 15). B2B Influencer Marketing: The Benefits Plus 5 Tips For Success. Forbes. https://www.forbes.com/sites/forbesagencycouncil/2023/03/15/b2b-influencer-marketing-the-benefits-plus-5-tips-for-success/?sh=6abc84e35db4

Brand24. (2022). Top 100 digital marketing influencers. Retrieved February 15, 2023, from https://brand24.com/top-marketing-influencers/

Cliqi. (n.d.). WAT IS TRADITIONELE MARKETING? Retrieved from cliqi.nl: https://cliqi.nl/kennisbank/traditionele-marketing/

Content Conference | 1 juni 2023 | Frankwatching. (2023, March 16). CoCo. https://www.frankwatching.com/contentconference/

Conversational Conference | 21 September 2023 | Frankwatching. (2023, March 15). CC. https://www.frankwatching.com/conversationalconference/

Countingup. (2022, January 14). What are social trends in business? Retrieved from countingup.com: https://countingup.com/resources/what-are-social-trends-in-business/#:~:text=Social%20trends%20are%20ideas%20and,and%20fairer%20society%20for%20everybody.

Crain, G. (2022, October 26). Why Influencer Marketing Is Important For Brands In 2022. Forbes.https://www.forbes.com/sites/forbesagencycouncil/2022/10/26/why-influencer-marketing-is-important-for-brands-in-2022/?sh=b2b8b1b431f2v

Degrowth: What's behind this economic theory and why it matters today. (2022, November World Economic Forum. https://www.weforum.org/agenda/2022/06/what-is-degrowth-economics-climate-change/#:~:text=What%20is%20degrowth%3F,planet%20by%20becoming%20more%20sustainable.

Deloitte. (2022). Global Marketing Trends in the Dutch Market - Seizing opportunities for growth. Retrieved from Deloitte.com: https://www2.deloitte.com/nl/nl/pages/customer-and-marketing/articles/global-marketing-trends.html

Deloitte. (2023). 2023 Global Marketing Trends. 2.Deloitte. Retrieved March 18, 2023, from https://www2.deloitte.com/content/dam/Deloitte/xe/Documents/consulting/2023_GMT_uae_full-report.pdf

Deloitte. (2023). Introducing the 2023 Global Marketing Trends . Retrieved from view.deloitte.nl: https://view.deloitte.nl/2023-global-marketing-trends-report.html

Disciple | 8 examples of outstanding brand communities. (2021, July 7). Disciple. https://www.disciplemedia.com/engaging-your-community/8-brand-communities-examples/

Dopper. (n.d.). Dopper. Retrieved March 23, 2023, from https://dopper.com/blogs/dopper-inspiration/dopper-wave

Dziewguc, M. (2021, May). How the Google Cloud region in Poland helps local businesses accelerate in the new digital economy. Retrieved from thinkwithgoogle.com: https://www.thinkwithgoogle.com/intl/en-cee/future-of-marketing/emerging-technology/how-the-google-cloud-region-in-poland-helps-local-businesses-accelerate-in-the-new-digital-economy/

Events | MarketingTribune meer over marketing. (n.d.). MarketingTribune. https://www.marketingtrib-une.nl/algemeen/events/index.xml#:~:text=Save%20the%20date%20voor%20h%C3%A9t,je%20altijd%20iets%20van%20opsteekt.

GoodUp. (2023, April 3). GoodUp - Let your employee drive change. https://goodup.com/

Growth Marketing Event | Frankwatching. (2023, March 6). Growth Marketing Event. https://www.frank-watching.com/growthmarketingevent/

Hall, J. (2022, September 11). 4 Marketing Trends On The Horizon This Year. Forbes. https://www.for-bes.com/sites/johnhall/2022/09/11/4-marketing-trends-on-the-horizon-this-year/?sh=6aa6c70d2eae

Hall, J. (2022, November 27). 3 Ways Influencers Can Boost Brand Awareness. Forbes. https://www.for-bes.com/sites/johnhall/2022/11/27/3-ways-influencers-can-boost-brand-awareness/?sh=133e2aa936b9

Hornbach's sustainability. Hornbach Holding. (n.d.). Retrieved March 23, 2023, from https://www.horn-bach-holding.de/en/responsibility/

How to help stop human trafficking - Airbnb Help Centre. (n.d.). Airbnb. https://www.airbnb.com.sg/help/article/3275?_set_bev_on_new_do-main=1681640847_NmQ3NGU5N2YxYmEy

IBM. (n.d.). Blockchain success starts here. Retrieved from ibm.com: https://www.ibm.com/topics/block-chain#:~:text=Blockchain%20defined%3A%20Blockchain%20is%20a,patents%2C%20copyrights%2C%20bra nding

Impact on the Beach | Change Inc. (n.d.). https://www.change.inc/evenementen/impact-on-the-beach

Influencer Marketing for Small Businesses. (2022, September 15). Neil Patel. Retrieved February 17, 2023, from https://neilpatel.com/blog/influencer-marketing-for-small-businesses/

Jack, A. (2019, October 21). Social purpose: how business schools around the world measure up. Financial Times. Retrieved April 18, 2023, from https://www.ft.com/content/b6bcfa02-ef37-11e9-ad1e-4367d8281195

Kemp, S. (2023, February 13). Digital 2023: Poland. Retrieved from datareportal.com: https://datare-portal.com/reports/digital-2023-poland

KPMG. (2022, December 21). 2023 Media trend predictions. https://advisory.kpmg.us/blog/2023/media-trend-prediction.html

Linkdex. (2016, November 4). 10 Exceptional Examples of Brand Communities. Retrieved April 3, 2023, from https://www.linkdex.com/en-us/inked/10-exceptional-examples-of-brand-communities/

McCormick, E. (2022b, September 15). Patagonia's billionaire owner gives away company to fight climate crisis. The Guardian. https://www.theguardian.com/us-news/2022/sep/14/patagonias-billionaire-owner-gives-away-company-to-fight-climate-crisis-yvon-chouinard

Microsoft. (2019). Environmental Sustainability – Microsoft CSR. Microsoft.com. https://www.micro-soft.com/en-us/corporate-responsibility/sustainability

Nethi, M. (2023, January 27). 5 Sales and Marketing Trends for 2023 You Must Know. Entrepreneur. https://www.entrepreneur.com/growing-a-business/5-sales-and-marketing-trends-for-2023-you-must-know/443051

Nielsen. (2018, June 28). Consumer Goods Brands That Demonstrate Commitment To Sustainability Outperform Those That Don't. Prnewswire. https://www.prnewswire.com/news-releases/consumer-goods-brands-that-demonstrate-commitment-to-sustainability-outperform-those-that-dont-300157905.html

NielsenIQ. (2022). Breakthrough Innovation Poland 2021: How innovations are changing the Polish retail market. Retrieved from nielseniq.com: https://nielseniq.com/wp-content/up-loads/sites/4/2022/06/NielsenIQ-Breakthrough-Innovation-Poland-Report_2021.pdf

Our Social Good Mission – HALF UNITED. (n.d.). HALF UNITED. https://www.halfunited.com/pages/our-so-cial-good-mission

Patagonia Outdoor Clothing & Gear. (n.d.). Www.patagonia.com. https://www.patagonia.com/sustainabil-ity/

Peckover, T. (2020, January 7). The 8 Best Brand Communities and Why They are Successful. The Smile.io Blog. https://blog.smile.io/8-best-brand-communities/

Pencils of Promise. (2023, January 13). Home - Pencils of Promise. https://pencilsofpromise.org/

Plummer, M. (2023, February 28). 2023 Marketing Trends You Should Pay Attention To. Forbes. https://www.forbes.com/sites/forbestechcouncil/2023/02/28/2023-marketing-trends-you-should-pay-at-tention-to/?sh=698d67804ba5

Poverty. (2022, November 30). World Bank. Retrieved April 18, 2023, from https://www.worldbank.org/en/topic/poverty/overview#3

Sailer, A., Wilfing, H., & Straus, E. (2022). Greenwashing and Bluewashing in Black Friday-Related Sustainable Fashion Marketing on Instagram. The University of Vienna. https://doi.org/10.3390/su14031494

Schwarz, R. (2019, June 24). Generate Marketing Impact, Not Only Impressions. Forbes. https://www.for-bes.com/sites/forbescommunicationscouncil/2019/06/24/generate-marketing-impact-not-only-impressions/?sh=79630336220b

SocialToday Event | 15 February 2024 | Frankwatching. (2023, March 14). STE. https://www.frankwatch-ing.com/socialtoday/

Statista. (2022, December). Digital versus traditional media use in Poland in 2014 and 2020. Retrieved from statista.com: https://www.statista.com/statistics/1035670/digital-traditional-media-use-poland/

Studio, Q. I. D. (n.d.). Home. B Lab Europe. Retrieved March 23, 2023, from https://bcorporation.eu/direc-tory/dopper-b-v

Swier, A. (2021, December 27). 9 trends en ontwikkelingen voor content marketing in 2022. Retrieved from marketingfacts.nl: https://www.marketingfacts.nl/berichten/9-trends-en-ontwikkelingen-voor-content-marketing-in-2022/

The Economist. (2022, December 1). Companies are expected to take a stand on more social issues. https://www.economist.com/the-world-ahead/2022/11/18/companies-are-expected-to-take-a-stand-on-more-social-issues

Tretyakova, E., Poletajevas, B., & Misiunaite, D. (2022, August 16). Top Five Consumer Trends in Poland. Retrieved from euromonitor.com: https://www.euromonitor.com/article/top-five-consumer-trends-in-poland

Tucci, L., & Needle, D. (2022, November 18). What is the Metaverse? An explanation and in-depth guide. Retrieved from techtarget.com: https://www.techtarget.com/whatis/feature/The-metaverse-explained-Everything-you-need-to-know#:~:text=The%20metaverse%20is%20a%20vision,not%20in%20the%20physical%20world

Unilever. (2018). Sustainable Living. Unilever Global Company Website. https://www.unilever.com/sustainable-living/

Van Der Weerd, J. (2023, January 13). De 10 belangrijkste online marketing trends van 2023. Onwise. https://onwise.nl/blog/online-marketing-trends/

WorldAtlas, & Mala, A. (2023, January 10). The world's 15 poorest countries. WorldAtlas. https://www.worldatlas.com/articles/the-poorest-countries-in-the-world.html

(N.d.). Businessinsider.com. Retrieved March 23, 2023, from https://www.businessinsider.com/how-walmart-conquered-retail-price-2019-9

Made in the USA
Las Vegas, NV
25 November 2024